HyperTalk 2.2
The Book

Second Edition

HyperTalk 2.2
The Book

Second Edition

Dan Winkler
Scot Kamins
Jeanne DeVoto

RANDOM HOUSE
ELECTRONIC PUBLISHING

HyperTalk 2.2: The Book, Second Edition

Page composition by Real Communications, Inc. and Page Graphics.

Published in the United States by Random House, Inc., New York, and simultaneously in Canada by Random House of Canada, Limited.

Manufactured in the United States of America

First Edition

0 9 8 7 6 5 4 3 2 1

ISBN 0-679-79171-X

New York   Toronto   London   Sydney   Auckland

The finer parts of this book are dedicated to
Bill Atkinson
Dan Winkler's friend and partner; and to
Ed Kammerer
Scot Kamins's friend and first computer mentor; and also to
Rhett Savage
Jeanne DeVoto's friend and partner in crime.

Foreword to the Second Edition

When the first edition of this book appeared, simultaneously with the introduction of HyperCard 2.0 by Apple Computer, Dan Winkler and Scot Kamins were justly proud of having produced the first complete reference to the HyperTalk language. But time, the authors, and HyperTalk have all moved on—the authors to new projects and enterprises, time in its usual direction, and HyperTalk to new development teams and new versions, with added depth, increased utility, and novel behaviors. With HyperCard 2.1, HyperTalk began to communicate with other applications, even across a network. With HyperCard 2.2, HyperTalk will begin to communicate with scripts written in other languages, including AppleScript. These major changes, along with a good number of other improvements and a new set of bugs, require the same in-depth treatment that HyperTalk 2.0 was given in the first edition. Keep all the great stuff from that book, correct it where it needs correcting, add the great stuff you need to know about what's new since then, and you've got this book.

While time, the authors, etc. have all been on the move, HyperCard, with HyperTalk as its native language, has formed the basis for an increasing number and range of computer programs that are now in use in schools, homes, and businesses, as well as hospitals, theaters, and museums, among other likely and unlikely places. These programs have helped to broaden the popular idea of where a computer is likely to be found and how it is likely to be used. At the same time, they have helped to overturn old notions of how useful and interesting programs are created and who is capable of creating them. In schools, they are now created by students and teachers and applied to the art of learning. In hospitals, they are created by doctors and nurses and applied to the practices of healing and patient care. Stage managers write programs. Stock brokers write programs. In short, HyperTalk has succeeded—almost to a degree that justifies the sweeping claims made by Apple Computer at its first introduction in 1987—in "liberating programming from the priesthood of nerds and making it accessible to the lay person."

vii

These are soberer times, but such words seemed appropriate back when Bill Atkinson and Dan Winkler made their triumphal entry into Boston and revealed HyperCard to the public for the first time at the MacWorld Exposition. They touched off a wave of excitement and inspired a group of followers who expected nothing less than the full and immediate delivery of the power of computing devices into their hands, especially the power to offer and to communicate information. The brain trust at Apple, knowing a good thing when they saw it but perhaps not knowing it well, suggested to an eager band of entrepreneurs that HyperCard could make the business of producing general-purpose commercial software less difficult and expensive than it persistently proves to be. There was a religious fervor then, and maybe a few folks got carried away. HyperCard wasn't designed to revolutionize the work of professional software developers; it was intended to enable an entirely different group of people to create their own particular-purpose software—the students, the stock brokers, and the stage managers. But the principals at Apple and elsewhere were looking at what HyperCard and HyperTalk might become rather than at what they were. The inevitable result was confusion about HyperCard, some disappointment, and a subsequent period of retrenchment.

Now, thanks to the many people who have given them a place among their valued tools, HyperCard and HyperTalk are moving past all that. We've heard the hailing of their untested glory and the keening of their presumed demise; in the meantime, with a lot less fanfare, a large number of folks have aptly and even lovingly applied them to their personal and professional pursuits. And finally, for the first time in more then two years, Apple is about to release an improved version of HyperCard with an enhanced version of HyperTalk. If my position allows me to do so, I'd like to dedicate this new version to the creative and industrious people who have given life to HyperCard — the students, the teachers, the doctors, the nurses, the stage managers, the stock brokers, et al. It's for you. Make of it what you will.

I expect that you have this book in your hands because you have a job, a task, or a labor of love that has involved you in HyperTalk programming. You've come to the right place. While upholding the high standards of clarity and reliability that were set by Dan and Scot in their original material, Jeanne DeVoto has mined the full depth of her considerable knowledge of HyperTalk in updating, revising, and expanding it. She has conferred with the HyperCard team during the development of HyperCard 2.2 and shaken us down for the kind of detail that you will prize. In sum, you have in this book the best source of information about HyperTalk that's available anywhere. It will serve you well.

Kevin Calhoun
HyperCard Technical Manager
Apple Computer, Inc.

Foreword to the First Edition

I have fond memories of the year that Dan Winkler spent six days a week, working very long hours over at my house to create the original HyperTalk language. In my mind I picture him hunched over and concentrating on the screen of a prototype Mac II, then known as a Reno, as our cat Sarah sat on his lap and drooled every time he pet her. Sometimes I picture him sitting in the big sofa chair in the corner, playing the guitar while he pondered a tough design problem, and sometimes I picture him discussing the syntax for a new command and how to present it in the simplest and clearest manner. I think of Dan with my daughter Laura and appreciate his warmth and playfulness. It was a fun and exciting time working together with Dan, and a privilege to share his company. I want to acknowledge Dan as a person with great sensitivity, passion, and determination.

I also want to acknowledge Dan for what he has accomplished with his work. Hundreds of thousands of people around the world who never used any other computer language before have found they can create useful scripts with HyperTalk, and customize their computers to do what they want them to do. What Dan has created with HyperTalk has liberated programming from the priesthood of nerds and made it accessible to the lay person.

HyperTalk: The Book is the most complete and correct source of information on HyperTalk available anywhere. It contains valuable insights and details that only the author of the language could know. It's like having Dan's home phone number, except it's even better because Dan isn't always home. This book tells the truth, even when that means revealing bugs. It tells you what you need to know to get the job done.

This book is accessible. It makes it easy to find the information you need when you have a question. It's heavily cross-referenced, so you can jump in anywhere and quickly find all the related details. And it's written in Scot's clear, direct prose, which anyone can understand.

This book offers unusually well-written sample scripts that provide clean solutions to many common tasks, and also teach good programming style by example. Dan's scripts work well and are a pleasure to read. This is the book that any serious HyperTalk scripter will want to have by his side when he's at work.

This book comes out of Dan's passion and commitment to make tools that empower people to accomplish what they're up to, and let them have fun in the process. He has succeeded in a big way by putting a piece of himself into every HyperCard stack and into this book. I hope you enjoy it.

Bill Atkinson
Menlo Park, California

Acknowledgments

Besides the people whose names appear on the cover, nearly four dozen people contributed their time, effort, and creativity to the development of the first and second editions of this book. Without their comments and suggestions, this book would have ended up in even worse shape. No kidding.

Elaine Ung, tester extraordinaire, answered scads of questions about the weird and wacky world of AppleEvents™.

Kevin Calhoun, chief bean of the HyperCard 2.2 development team, has generously posted a huge amount of useful information to various online locations over the past several years, including examples, advice, and arcane technical data about HyperCard. Much of that information ended up in this book.

Rhett Savage, HyperTalk art critic and seeker of Cosmic Programming Truth, gave encouragement, help, support, advice, and found a couple of really embarrassing errors. He is also the one to whom credit and/or blame is due for introducing Jeanne DeVoto to HyperCard.

Alan Spragens, senior writer at Apple and author of Apple's original *HyperTalk Script Language Guide*, was the real author of much of the appendix on "The Translator Interface"; we just edited his work a little. He also helped us straighten out the information about message passing.

Clay Nixon, Louisville's finest cinematographer, reviewed the manuscript from the point of view of the new scripter. He managed to find several hundred ways to say "What are you people talking about?" without repeating himself once. His help was absolutely invaluable.

Gary ("XCMDs-R-Us") Bond, an engineer on the HyperCard 2.0 test team and a fine writer to boot, wrote a bunch of creative examples for the book when we ran dry. In addition, he scrupulously read the manuscript from the point of view of the advanced scripter, someone who's already an expert on HyperTalk. While he found just one way to say "You call this quality work?", he repeated it enough times so that we finally started to listen to him. Anything in the text that's useful for advanced scripters was made more useful by his comments and suggestions.

Steven Smith, Real Live Developer and partner at San Francisco's CommuniTree Group, read the manuscript from the point of view of the developer. His suggestions for rearranging and adding material made the book three pounds heavier, and it's a far better work for it.

Bennet Marks, another member of the HyperCard 2.0 development team at Apple, read the manuscript from the point of view of a professional programmer who wants to learn HyperTalk. He insisted on better examples; we hope we came through for him.

Scott Bongiorno, HyperCard 2.0 testing engineer at Apple, made excellent suggestions for changing the way some of the material was phrased, and spotted many areas that needed clarification.

Robin Shank, yet another HyperCard 2.0 testing engineer and windoid washer at Apple, contributed a number of examples and gave us extremely valuable feedback on the major reference chapters.

Tim Pozar, resident C Programmer and source of the most technical data imaginable at San Francisco's Late Night Software, provided the information we needed to see how buggy the **dial** command really is.

James Francis Redfern, still another HyperCard 2.0 testing engineer at Apple, provided arcane information about the file system and about some amusing HyperTalk anomalies, tried to crash our externals, and participated in a number of brainstorming sessions that formed the basis of the more advanced material in the book.

Dr. Jerome Coonen of Apple Computer, a member of the original Macintosh development team, told us why midnight, January 1, 1904 was chosen as the Beginning of Time in the mind of the Macintosh.

Paul Finlayson, engineer with the SANE (Standard Apple Numeric Environment) Group at Apple Computer, showed us how **ln1** and **exp1** are used to calculate compound interest.

Ed Kammerer, cosmic hacker of the Great Northwest and the man most responsible for turning Scot Kamins into a computer nerd, reminded us to remember the art of Ralph Steadman.

Scott Knaster, whose name needs no comma-separated explanation, almost bought the pizza once.

Additional feedback, comments, encouragement, and suggestions also came from: Sedge Bekkala, Parry Forcier, Carol R. Freneier, Robert C. Frenier, Martin Gannholm, Dean Gengle, Amanda Goodenough, Chris Crawford, Sioux Lacy, David Leffler, Steve Maller, Michelle McCoskey, Ron Metzker, Doris Mitsch, Tim Oren, and Giovanni Paoletti.

Dan Winkler especially wants to thank the people who laid the foundation for HyperTalk before he even joined the HyperCard team. At Apple Computer, those folks include **Bill Atkinson**, **Ted Kaehler**, **Dan Ingalls**, and **Alan Kay**. And outside of Apple, the major influencers were **Eric Roberts** and **Greg Nelson**, who invented the recursive descent operator precedence expression parser that HyperTalk uses to parse expressions. (Dan learned of this algorithm in Computer Science 163, taught by Eric Roberts at Harvard in the spring of 1985.)

Finally, **The HyperCard Development Teams**, past and present, have over the years had to put up with more in the way of corporate politics than any sane human being should have to. That HyperCard exists at all is a tribute to their dedication; that it has continued to grow more powerful with every new release is a tribute to their skill; and that it has inspired and continues to inspire thousands of people all over the world to become creators of software is a tribute to the creativity and integrity of their vision.

Lastly, to borrow from Dan's advisor at Harvard, Harry R. Lewis, from his book *An Introduction to Computer Programming and Data Structures Using MACRO-11* (Boston Publishing Company, 1981): To the others, not mentioned here by name, we apologize for our ignorance of their contributions.

Book Overview

Contents

3   Style, Memory, and Performace   39

4   Using XCMDs, XCFNs, and Resources   55

5   AppleScript and AppleEvents   63

8   Sources of Value, Containers, and Chunk Expressions   105

The Elements of HyperTalk   143

Part IV   Appendixes

Appendix A: ASCII Chart

Appendix B: Boundaries and Limits

Appendix C: HyperTalk Error Messages

Appendix D: Formal Syntax Description

Appendix E: The Translator Interface

HyperTalk Elements by Category

*This listing divides HyperTalk's commands, functions, and properties into basic categories. A complete explanation of each word listed appears in Part III, "The Elements of HyperTalk." Not all native vocabulary words appear here. (For example, keywords like **if** and **repeat** are left out.)*

AppleEvents and Inter-Application Communication

address
answer program
close application
open application
print document
programs
reply
request
request appleEvent
run
send to program

Backgrounds

cantDelete
dontSearch
ID
name
number of object
showPict

Buttons

autoHilite
disable
enable
enabled
family
hilite
icon
ID
location
name
number of object
partNumber
rectangle
selectedButton
sharedHilite
showName
style
textAlign
textFont
textSize
textStyle
visible

Cards

cantDelete
ID
name
number of object
showPict

Fields

autoSelect
autoTab
dontSearch
dontWrap
fixedLineHeight
ID
location
lockText
multipleLines
name
number of object
partNumber
rectangle
scroll
sharedText
showLines
style
textAlign
textFont
textHeight
textSize
textStyle
visible
wideMargins

File Manipulation

answer file
ask file
close application
close file
create stack
export paint
import paint
open application
open file
print document

read
save stack as
write

HyperCard Environment

address
blindTyping
cantAbort
editBkgnd
environment
lockErrorDialogs
lockMessages
lockRecent
lockScreen
name
numberFormat
programs
screenRect
stacks
suspended
systemVersion
textArrows
tool
userLevel
userModify
version

Hypertext

autoSelect
clickChunk
clickLine
clickText
multipleLines
selectedLoc

Keyboard

arrowKey
commandKey
commandKeyDown
controlKey
enterInField
enterKey
functionKey

keyDown
optionKey
returnInField
returnKey
shiftKey
tabKey
type

Mathematics

abs
add
annuity
atan
average
compound
cos
divide
exp
exp1
exp2
ln
ln1
ln2
max
min
multiply
numberFormat
random
round
sin
sqrt
subtract
sum
tan
trunc

Memory and Disk

diskSpace
freeSize
heapSpace
stacksSpace

Menus

checkMark
commandChar

create menu
delete menu
disable
doMenu
enable
enabled
hide menubar
ID
markChar
menuMessage
menus
name of menu
put into menu
reset menubar
show menubar
textStyle

Messages

do
pass
send
stacksInUse
start using
stop using

Mouse

choose
click
clickH
clickLoc
clickV
doMenu
drag
dragSpeed
mouse
mouseClick
mouseH
mouseLoc
mouseV
select

Navigation

destination
go
help

pop
push

Painting

brush
centered
choose
drag
dragSpeed
export paint
filled
grid
lineSize
multiple
multiSpace
pattern
polySides
powerKeys
reset paint
textAlign
textFont
textHeight
textSize
textStyle

Printing

copy template
close printing
open printing
open report printing
print
print card
print document
printMargins
printTextAlign
printTextFont
printTextHeight
printTextSize
printTextStyle
reset printing
reportTemplates

Script Editing and Debugging

debug checkpoint

debugger
edit
hBarLoc
hideIdle
hideUnused
language
lock error dialogs
lockErrorDialogs
messageWatcher
nextLine
script
scriptEditor
scriptingLanguage
scriptTextFont
scriptTextSize
text
traceDelay
unlock error dialogs
variableWatcher
vBarLoc

Search

debug
dontSearch
find
foundChunk
foundField
foundLine
foundText
mark
marked
offset
sort
sort container
unmark

Sound

beep
play
sound

Stack

cantDelete
cantModify
freeSize

name
size
version

Text and Text Editing

charToNum
keyDown
length
number
numToChar
offset
selectedChunk
selectedField
selectedLine
selectedLoc
selectedText
selection
textAlign
textFont
textHeight
textSize
textStyle
type

Time and Date

convert
date
seconds
ticks
time

User Interaction and I/O

answer
answer file
answer program
ask
ask file
cantAbort
cantPeek
dial
dialingTime
dialingVolume
lock error dialogs
lockErrorDialogs
unlock error dialogs

Value Transfer

answer
ask
function
get
global
param
paramCount
params
pop
put
read
result
return
set
write

Visual Appearance

cursor
hide
lock screen
lockScreen
show
show cards
show picture
unlock screen
visual effect

Windows

close window
flash
height
hide
location height
longWindowTitles
moveWindow
palette
picture
rectangle
screenRect
scroll of window
show
sizeWindow
visible
width
windows
zoomed

0

Rationales, Histories, and Guides

This chapter provides a frame of reference for using this book. It tells why this book was written, gives some historical perspectives on the development of the HyperTalk language, tells what's where in the book, and makes suggestions about how to get the most out of your reading.

This book is the definitive reference guide to the HyperTalk programming language. It provides information unavailable anywhere else, even in the official HyperCard publications written and published by Apple Computer Inc.

We know the language better than anyone else because one of us (Dan Winkler) designed and wrote it, and another one of us (Scot Kamins) cajoled, tormented, praised, beat up, and manipulated his partner until he (Winkler) gave up all the secrets of the language—even the ones that hurt. And then the third one of us came along and squeezed out all remaining information from both of 'em.

So this book tells what HyperTalk does. It also tells what it's supposed to do, but it emphasizes what it *does*. And it reveals where the sore points are, the bugs and glitches in the language—the anomalies that bite you on the backside when you least expect it.

In short, it tells the truth.

How This Book Came to Be Written

We wrote this book because somebody had to. While books about HyperTalk abound, none contains the whole truth. Most have factual errors; some miss the point of how the language works; none gives a clear portrayal of where the holes are; and certainly, none is complete. Even Claris's and Apple's own documentation suffers from a lack of detail in some arcane areas, and a certain paucity of example.

Apple's original *HyperCard Script Language Guide* comes close to being complete for most early versions. Its unsung author, Alan Spragens, did a remarkable job of collecting information for that book while HyperCard was nearing release—a period of turmoil that was frenetic even by Apple's hurricane standards. But even Spragens's incredible integrity and dedication to excellence couldn't totally overcome the obstacles of unavailable engineers and the madness of impossible deadlines.

1

Then too, that book didn't have the advantage of time. HyperCard had been out for nearly three years at the time the first edition of this book was written—enough time for both the opulence and the poverty of HyperTalk to emerge.

A MONASTERY OF SCRIPTERS

Actually, in the early days preceding the release of HyperCard, few members of the HyperCard development team thought that extensive language documentation would be necessary. The primary purpose of HyperTalk was to allow stacks to contain intelligence in the form of scripts. The original idea was to allow nonprogrammers to move that intelligence around by cutting and pasting pre-scripted buttons. We (the members of the original HyperCard team) thought that most people who wanted to create their own stacks would copy the models we gave them—either they'd modify the stacks that came with HyperCard, or they'd make new creations by raiding those stacks for pre-scripted buttons. We also believed that, at most, 25 percent of the people who used HyperCard would also want to write scripts for it.

We seriously underestimated the numbers. Time and the experience of 20-20 hindsight have shown that the original thinking about who would want to learn scripting was pretty far off. It's hard to come up with real numbers, but it looks like at least 40 percent of HyperCardiacs— nearly twice the original estimate—are doing their own scripting; and a sizeable percentage of that group wants highly detailed information about every aspect of the language.

What happened to in-box HyperTalk documentation for version 1.0?

Several powerful members of the original HyperCard development team, back in 1987, estimated that 50 percent of nonprogrammers would use the stacks as they came from Apple or from other developers, making only minor modifications; another 25 or 30 percent would create their own stacks from scratch, doing just a little scripting; and the remaining 20 or 25 percent would venture shyly into scriptwriting.

(Other members of the team objected to these estimates, insisting that a far greater percentage of people would quickly move into scripting. These objections, however, were—umm—overcome.)

Because of these estimates, plus the rising cost of what was to be essentially a free product, little HyperTalk documentation was packaged with the very first version of HyperCard. The argument was that the small percentage of people who would want to learn scripting in detail could get the information they needed from the online documentation, from studying the scripts of included stacks, or from the purchase of outside documentation. Yeah, well…

Since then, of course, the light has been seen, and development versions of HyperCard from 1.2.1 (or so) on have included a full set of language documentation. Even the first version came with the excellent Help stack, from which a lot of people got their very first lessons in HyperTalk. Live and learn.

Whom This Book Is For

This book is aimed at scripters with a variety of expertise. The lowest level we wrote for are those folks who have been scripting for at least a couple of months or who have extensive experience in at least one other programming language (even BASIC). At the other end, we aim at hard-core programmers—those who know the art of programming in general, and this language in particular, inside and out, and who want to take HyperTalk far beyond its original limits.

We originally conceived of this book as a tool for advanced scripters who already knew both the HyperTalk language and the fundamentals of programming. But the paucity of good material for intermediate scripters, strong feedback from early reviewers, and the powerful urgings of newer scripters—especially Clay Nixon, a remarkable cinematographer from the wilds of Louisville —convinced us to change the book's focus to make it more useful to a broader audience.

Still, even though HyperTalk has been designed to be The Language For the Rest of Us, this book is not a tutorial. If you're new to HyperCard, we suggest you read Danny Goodman's *The Complete HyperCard Handbook* from Random House to get acquainted with how HyperCard works before you jump into scripting.

What's Where in This Book

This book is designed so that the further you read, the more sophisticated the material becomes. Information needed by newer scripters comes early on, with the most arcane facts left for the later chapters.

The book is broken into four major sections. Part I, "Scripting in HyperTalk," consists of background information about the language, along with useful information about programming style, extending HyperTalk with externals and AppleEvents, and designing scripts for use in special environments like standalone applications and CD-ROMs. Part II, "HyperTalk Reference," contains chapters on the gory details of HyperTalk syntax: how to refer to objects, how to construct expressions, and what user actions trigger which messages. Part III, "The Elements of HyperTalk," lists all HyperTalk keywords, commands, functions, properties, and messages alphabetically, with detailed information and examples. You'll refer to this material on a daily basis. Finally, the Appendixes contain a collection of reference information that you're likely to thumb through often.

Here are the details, chapter by chapter:

Chapter 0, "Rationales, Histories, and Guides," is the one you're reading now. It tells why this book was written, gives some historical perspective on the development of the language, and contains suggestions about how to get the most from your reading.

PART I: SCRIPTING IN HYPERTALK

Chapter 1, "The Basics of HyperTalk," deals with the three fundamental elements of the HyperTalk language: messages, handlers, and the message-passing path. These three elements are intricately interwoven; it's impossible to understand any one of them completely without understanding the other two. Even if you think you know how HyperTalk works, read this chapter anyway. You'll be surprised.

Chapter 2, "Writing and Debugging Scripts," describes the script editor and integrated debugger. It includes information on bringing a script into the script editor, breaking long lines into manageable segments, commenting your code, using automatic script formatting to check your code's syntactic correctness, and using the debugging tools.

Chapter 3, "Style, Memory, and Performance," gives you instructions and tips on designing stacks and writing your scripts so that they're orderly and easy to read and debug, and tells how you can get the most speed from a handler.

Chapter 4, "Using XCMDs, XFCNs, and Resources," explains what XCMDs and XFCNs are and what they can do, how to use them to extend HyperTalk with new capabilities, and when to use an external in your stacks. This chapter also discusses using sounds, color pictures, and other resources in your stacks.

Chapter 5, "AppleEvents and AppleScript," describes how to attach code written in AppleScript (or another Open Scripting Architecture-compatible language) to a HyperCard object, how to use AppleEvents to control other applications, and how to interpret incoming AppleEvents sent by other applications to your stack.

Chapter 6, "Coding for Special Environments," contains pointers, cautions, and recommendations for writing HyperTalk code that will run as part of a standalone application, in a stack that's on a CD-ROM, or in a multistack system communicating over a network.

PART II: HYPERTALK REFERENCE

Chapter 7, "Referring to Objects," explains in precise detail the often misunderstood but vital process of naming and referring to objects. (The amount of misinformation on this subject is staggering.)

Chapter 8, "Sources of Value," defines the sources of value common to most languages (functions, literals, constants, and variables) plus the ones that are either unique to HyperTalk or uniquely implemented (properties, fields, the message box, the selection, and chunks).

Chapter 9, "Expressions and Operators," shows how to construct arithmetic, geometric, logical, and textual expressions using operators and sources of value. It explains how to use (and override) operator precedence and discusses the important difference between factors and expressions.

Chapter 10, "Messages and the Message Order," describes special aspects of the message path and the order in which messages are sent. (We note when the message-sending order is less than intuitive.)

PART III: THE ELEMENTS OF HYPERTALK

This section lists each keyword, command, function, message, and property in the language in alphabetical order. Each element has detailed information, including a complete description of the syntax, return values (if any), technical notes and comments about oddities and version changes, and many examples. Where these elements are referred to elsewhere in the book, they appear in bold type.

APPENDIXES

Appendix A, "ASCII Chart," is a listing of all the available characters and their numeric equivalents. This chart is useful for encoding and decoding information for the **numToChar** and **charToNum** functions, but it's here mainly because there is a regulation requiring an ASCII chart in all programming manuals.

Appendix B, "Boundaries and Limits," lists the limiting numbers for HyperCard, such as the maximum number of characters in a field, the disk overhead for each new object, limits on variable and object name lengths, and so on.

Appendix C, "HyperTalk Error Messages," lists the script error messages, tells what conditions in your code might produce the error, and suggests ways of correcting the problem where such solutions aren't obvious.

Appendix D, "Formal Syntax Description," includes the complete syntax of HyperTalk versions 2.2 and 1.2.5.

Appendix E, "The Translator Interface" (the first half of which was essentially written by Alan Spragens), describes the poorly understood translator interface, the filter that sits between the disk and the script editor and performs translations on script editor text. While translators are most commonly used to translate scripts from English to non-English languages, you can also use them for other tasks. This chapter shows you how to do it.

Changes from the First Edition

We have added a great deal of new material to this book since the first edition.

First of all, many new commands, functions, and properties have been added to HyperTalk since version 2.0; we have included these new language elements in Part III, along with the elements that in the first edition appeared in Appendix I (Late-Breaking News). The reference section is now as complete as we can make it.

In addition to documenting new HyperTalk words added since version 2.0, we've included many new examples and newly discovered details. As HyperTalk has progressed, the syntax of many language elements has expanded and changed; we've added notes on these changes in the language.

We've also added chapters on new areas, such as using AppleScript and AppleEvents, and on writing code for special environments, such as the HyperCard Player and standalone applications.

This second edition of *HyperTalk: The Book* also has several organization changes.

The HyperTalk Reference (which is now Part III) has been reorganized, with all HyperTalk words appearing in alphabetical order instead of grouped by type. This means you can look up **the suspended**, for example, without having to rack your brains in order to remember whether it's a function or a property.

To make space for new information about HyperTalk itself, and because they covered only versions through 1.2.5, the chapters "Overview of Externals" and "Glue Routine Reference" have been removed from this edition. (A more complete treatment of this information, including the 2.0 XWindow interface, can be found in Apple's *HyperCard Script Language Guide*, Third Edition, Appendix A.) However, since the Translator interface is not documented anywhere else that we know of, the chapter covering it has been retained and can be found in Appendix E of this book.

Conventions and Assumptions

A reference to "version 1.x" means the information applies to all releases of HyperCard before 2.0.

The syntax descriptions in Part III use the following conventions:

- Square brackets ([ ]) enclose optional terms. You can either include or ignore them.
- Curly braces ({ }) enclose a group of terms from which you must pick one. Within a group, the choices are separated from each other by a vertical bar (|).
- *Italics* indicate a parameter. In the actual HyperTalk statement, you'll replace the italicized word with a specific instance of that term.
- Words that aren't italicized are literals. You should type them exactly as they appear.

Most of the directions in this book assume the **userLevel** property is set to 5.

From time to time throughout this book, two different kinds of boxes appear. The first is for bugs and anomalies that are likely to be fixed in future versions of HyperCard. Bug boxes look like this:

This command blows up computer

Take particular care when you use the **destroy machine** command. We've had several reports that it causes smoke to rise out of your monitor. Since we've chosen not to test this command with our own equipment, we can't be sure that these reports are unfounded.

The second box type is for special features, historical notes, or bonus examples. Feature boxes look like this:

Previously undocumented help feature

The following previously undocumented form for **dial with modem** dials the home of Dan Winkler:

```
dial home(winkler) with modem "ATWinkler"
```

Dan likes to write code far into the night when most people are asleep, and enjoys answering HyperTalk questions to break up the work.

Part I

Scripting in HyperTalk

1

The Basics of HyperTalk

This chapter deals with three fundamental elements of HyperTalk: messages, handlers, and the message-passing path. These three elements are intricately interwoven; it's impossible to understand any one of them completely without understanding the other two.

Even if you already know how HyperTalk works, please read this chapter anyway. If you're impatient to get on to the references sections of the book, at least read the first section, "A Frame of Reference"; it's a summary of the main points in the chapter and ties the fundamental concepts together.

For native speakers of other programming languages, the last section gives an overview of HyperTalk's similarities to and differences from other languages.

A Frame of Reference

In order to understand how HyperCard works, you must first understand three concepts: messages, handlers, and the message-passing path. The challenge is that it's difficult to understand any of these things without understanding all three. This section provides a quick overview of all three concepts for you to keep in mind as you read this chapter. Later in the chapter, each concept is discussed on its own in greater detail.

A BRIEF OVERVIEW OF HANDLERS AND MESSAGES

An *object* is any HyperCard unit capable of sending and receiving messages. Objects include buttons, fields, cards, backgrounds, stacks, and HyperCard itself.

A *script* is the collection of statements associated with a particular object. Within a script, statements are grouped into *handlers*. An object executes the statements within one of its handlers when it receives an instruction to do so. That instruction is called a message. (See Figure 1.1.)

Handlers and messages both have names. The handler executes when the object containing it receives a message of the same name. Figure 1.1 shows a handler from the script belonging to a button. Statements in the handler execute in response to the message **mouseUp**.

This object is a button named "Click Me".	▤☐▤ **Script of card button id 28 = "Click Me"** ▤
	Scripting language : ⸢ **HyperTalk** ▼ ⸥

The handler called "mouseUp" executes when this object receives a mouseUp message	`on mouseUp`
	`   go to next card`
	`end mouseUp`

Figure 1.1   Part of a script

A BRIEF OVERVIEW OF THE MESSAGE-PASSING PATH

The message-passing path is the set of rules that determines which objects, in which order, are given the opportunity to respond to a message.

Each message has a *target*—the object that the message goes to first. For example, if you click on the screen, HyperCard sends a **mouseUp** message to the object you clicked on. If that object has a handler for the message, HyperCard executes the statements in the handler, and the message stops at that object. However, if the target object doesn't have a handler for that message, the message goes to the next object on the message-passing path to see if that object has a handler for it, and so on.

The order of the message-passing path is determined by which objects contain others. For example, each button is contained by the card it's on, and each card is contained by its background. So a message that's sent to a button that doesn't have a handler for that message goes next to the script of the card that the button's on. If the card doesn't catch the message, it's sent to the card's background, and so on.

The last object in the message path is the HyperCard application itself. If no handler catches it along the way, the message ends up at HyperCard. What HyperCard does depends on what kind of message it is:

- If the message is a built-in command or function name, HyperCard executes that command or function.

- If the message isn't a built-in command name, HyperCard checks whether it's the name of another type of message that it knows about, called a *system message*. (System messages are the messages HyperCard sends automatically in response to actions. For example, **mouseUp** is a system message.) If it's a system message, HyperCard discards it. Once a message has reached HyperCard, it's already passed through the whole message path, so it has no further use.

- If the message isn't a built-in command or function and it's not a system message, HyperCard puts up an error dialog indicating that it doesn't know what to do with this message.

A BRIEF LOOK AT USING MESSAGE PASSING

HyperTalk provides ways for you to change the normal message-passing path. You can either let a message go through the normal path described above, or reroute it, depending on the situation.

For example, as explained above, messages caught by a same-named handler usually die when that handler finishes executing. But HyperTalk lets you breathe new life into a message with the keyword **pass**, which sends the message to the next stop on the message path (even though it's been caught by a handler).

Once you become more familiar with how message passing works, you can make a single handler do the work of many handlers. For example, instead of putting similar code into each button on a card, you can use a single **mouseUp** handler in the card's script, which handles the click action for all the card's buttons. There's an example in the section "Placing Handlers for Best Effect," later in this chapter.

For more details about overriding the usual message-passing path, see Chapter 10.

Messages

A *message* is an announcement of an event that's sent to an object in order to trigger an action. The sending and receiving of messages is fundamental to HyperCard. Without messages, nothing would ever happen.

Every statement in a HyperTalk script, except those that start with keywords, is a message. A message is made up of the message name—which is always a single word—and an optional set of one or more *parameters* (a parameter is any piece of data that the message uses):

```
doMenu "Compact Stack" -- message name "doMenu" with parameter "Compact Stack"
mouseUp -- system message, meant to execute handler named
"mouseUp" doMyHandler -- custom message, looking for handler "doMyHandler"
```

The double dashes (--) in each of the three lines above are used to indicate *comments*, which are notes for people reading scripts. HyperTalk ignores anything in a script that comes after a double dash. Since comments are not executed, you can (and should!) use them to explain your code.

One message or another is always moving through the message-passing path. When a message is finished, the next one takes its place. You make HyperCard generate messages whenever you click the mouse, move the pointer over an object, or press a key. You can also send any specific message by typing it into the message box and pressing Return (which, by the way, is why it's named the message box). Objects can also generate messages of their own in response to messages they receive. If nothing else is happening at any given time, HyperCard generates an **idle** message.

You can use the Message Watcher to see all the messages HyperCard is sending. Type mw into the message box and press Return to bring up the Message Watcher. Then try clicking, typing, and moving the mouse around to see what messages HyperCard sends. You can write handlers to execute the steps of your choice whenever any of these messages is sent.

HyperCard has three kinds of messages:

- HyperCard sends *system messages* when some event occurs in the HyperCard environment. For example, **mouseUp** is sent when the user releases the mouse button, and **newCard** is sent when a new card is created. When nothing else is happening, HyperCard sends the system message **idle**.

- Your handlers send *command messages* whenever they execute a command. If a command message moves all the way along the message path and gets to HyperCard, HyperCard responds by performing whatever action the command calls for. But since commands, like other messages, move along the message-passing path, you can trap them with a same-named handler if you want to override the command's normal behavior.

- Your handlers can also send *custom messages*, to be trapped by handlers farther along the message path. Those handlers, presumably, execute commands that ultimately go to HyperCard for execution. Such a message is called "custom" because you define exactly what it does by writing a handler for it.

If you send a custom message for which there is no handler in the message path, or if you misspell the name of a message, it eventually reaches HyperCard. When it gets there, HyperCard doesn't know what to do with it, and displays a dialog box saying so.

A MESSAGE'S AUDIENCE

You can think of a message as a general announcement to the HyperCard environment that something has happened or is about to happen. It's like a town crier, walking along town paths announcing the daily news: "The mouse button is down!" "A card is about to be deleted!" "Bring out your dead!"

All messages are sent to one specific recipient. For example, when you click a button, you're sending a message to that button: "I just clicked you." You assume that your action will make something happen: You want the button to know that you clicked it, and you hope that the button will do something appropriate in return. If you send a command message or custom message from inside a handler, that message is sent to the object the handler belongs to. If the object doesn't have a handler for it, the message continues along the message path in the usual way until it either finds a handler or reaches HyperCard.

Handlers

A handler is a group of HyperTalk statements, and is the basic structure of HyperTalk code. The script of an object is made up of one or more handlers. Each handler is designed to respond to a specific message. A message's name is the key that causes the statements in a handler to execute.

MESSAGE HANDLERS VERSUS FUNCTION HANDLERS

There are two kinds of handlers: *message handlers* and *function handlers*. Message handlers carry out a series of commands in order to get some larger job done. Function handlers compute a specific value, perhaps carrying out a series of commands to calculate that value.

The anatomies of message handlers and function handlers differ only slightly. Message handlers begin with the keyword **on**, while function handlers begin with the keyword **function**. The handler title (**on** or **function**) is followed by the name of the message it responds to, plus a list of any parameters. Message handlers sometimes have parameters; function handlers usually do. For more details on the structure of function handlers and message handlers, see **on** and **function** in Part III.

Figure 1.2 shows a typical message handler. Its statements execute when an object receives the message getTotals.

Figure 1.3 shows a typical function handler. It serves the message handler above by computing a sum in response to the function call `sum(field "Prices of Items")` in the third line of the message handler.

The example in Figure 1.3 shows a message handler and a function handler working together to produce a complete result—a sales report. The third line of the message handler `getTotals` calls the function handler sum to add up all the prices; `getTotals` uses the value returned by sum to do the rest of the calculations.

When one handler calls another handler, HyperTalk returns control to the calling handler when the statements in the called handler finish executing. So, in the example above, the first line of `getTotals` executes first. Then, when it calls `sum`, all the statements in `sum` execute. And finally, control returns to `getTotals` and the rest of its statements execute.

It's all the same to HyperCard

HyperCard uses the same internal code for function handlers and message handlers. The only real differences are the way you call them and the way they return values.

About Message Handlers

When a message triggers a handler, it sets off a series of events (the statements in the handler) that end up doing a job, such as going to another card, moving a graphic across the screen, locating the name and address of your dentist, and so on. You invoke a message handler by sending its name as a message, either through the message box or from within another handler:

```
on placeOrder
   getTheOrder
   getTotals -- this runs the message handler in Figure 1.2
   askForMore
   showThankYou
   printReceipt
end  placeOrder
```

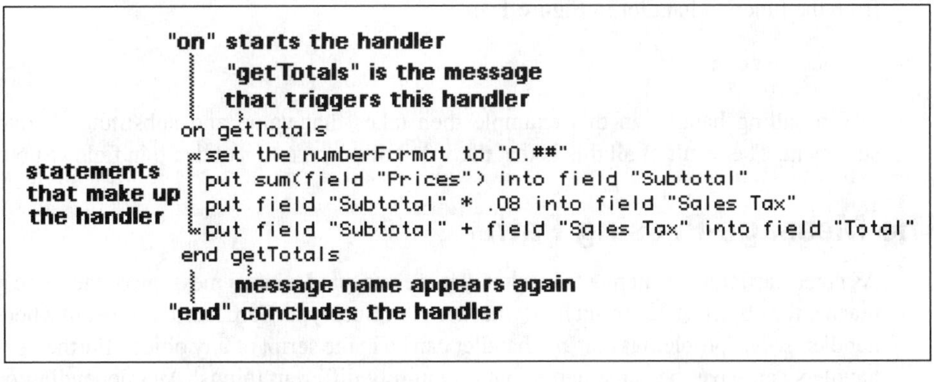

```
"on" starts the handler
   "getTotals" is the message
   that triggers this handler
on getTotals
   set the numberFormat to "0.##"
   put sum(field "Prices") into field "Subtotal"
   put field "Subtotal" * .08 into field "Sales Tax"
   put field "Subtotal" + field "Sales Tax" into field "Total"
end getTotals
   message name appears again
"end" concludes the handler
```

statements that make up the handler

Figure 1.2   A typical message handler

```
                "function" starts the handler
                    |  "sum" is the function message
                    |     that triggers this handler
                    |
        function sum listOfItems ———— a parameter
                  put 0 into totalSum
statements        repeat with x = 1 to the number of lines in listOfItems
that make up        add line x of listOfItems to totalSums
the handler       end repeat
                  return totalSum
        end sum
                 |    message name appears again
        "end" concludes the handler
```

Figure 1.3   A typical function handler

When you call a message handler, you put its parameters after the message name, separated by commas:

```
myMessage firstParameter,secondParameter
    -- runs a handler called myMessage
```

Message handlers are discussed in detail in the section about the **on** keyword in Part III.

About Function Handlers

Function handlers (which are discussed in detail under the **function** keyword in Part III) exist to get back a value—like you'd get an answer to a question. Function-handler calls appear as expressions within a line, with their parameters inside parentheses. This example is from the handler in Figure 1.2:

```
put sum(field "Prices of Items") into field "Subtotal"
```

The sum function has one parameter: whatever is in the field named "Prices of Items". The expression sum(field "Prices of Items") is the function call. Function handlers use the **return** keyword to send the final value back to the calling handler. This example is from the function handler in Figure 1.3:

```
return totalSum
```

The calling handler in this example then takes that value and substitutes it into the statement. The result of all this is that the value of totalSum ends up in field "Subtotal".

The Message-Passing Path

As noted earlier, the statements in a handler are executed when a message of the same name reaches the object whose script holds that handler. But HyperCard has to figure out where that handler is. The problem is that any handler can be in the script of any object. Further, several handlers can have the same name, but do entirely different things. And depending on the object that receives a message, the same message can trigger several different handlers with totally different results.

So when HyperCard is trying to find a handler for a particular message, it needs a mechanism to decide (1) which object to look at first; (2) how to proceed if it can't find a handler in the first place it looks; and (3) what to do if more than one handler of the same name exists. That mechanism is the message-passing path.

GETTING THE MESSAGE

Every message has a *target*, which is the object that gets the first chance to respond to that message. The target object is a message's first, and perhaps only, stop on the message-passing path.

For example, when you press the mouse with the pointer over a button, HyperCard sends the system message **mouseDown** to that button. The button is the target of the system message. Similarly, immediately after you create a new card, HyperCard sends the system message **newCard** to the newly created card—the new card is the target of the **newCard** message.

Both the examples in the previous paragraph are system messages—messages sent by HyperCard to announce that something has just happened. Messages generated by a handler (custom messages or command messages) also have a target; such a message is sent first to the object whose script contains the handler. In either case, if the target object doesn't have a handler for that particular message, the message proceeds along the message-passing path.

You can also use the **send** keyword to send a message directly to any object you want. For more information about **send**, see Part III.

PASSING ALONG THE MESSAGE

The message-passing path determines what happens when an object doesn't have a handler for a message it receives. All messages travel from the target object through the message path, looking for a handler to execute.

The message-passing path of any object is made up of the object itself plus the objects that contain it. A card contains fields and buttons, a background contains cards, a stack contains backgrounds, and HyperCard contains stacks. The path goes in increasing order of containing unit (for example button to card, card to background, etc.) from the starting point through HyperCard. The Home stack is added between the current stack and HyperCard.

For example, suppose you click a button. HyperCard sends **mouseDown** to the button in response to the click. The message-passing path for that **mouseDown** consists of:

1. The button itself
2. The card the button is on
3. The background the card belongs to
4. The stack the background is in
5. The Home stack
6. HyperCard itself

This doesn't mean that a message would have to go to all of these objects. If the message finds a corresponding handler in any of the scripts it checks, the message stops at that level and goes no further. Rather, these are all the stops that a message might make looking for a matching handler. As soon as it finds a matching handler the message stops its trip along the message passing path. A message that starts out further along the path—say, at the card level—wouldn't go back to a previous level; it would just go further along, to the background, then the stack, and so on.

You can alter the usual message path by adding stacks to it (see the **start using** command in Part III). Under some circumstances, HyperCard itself adds objects to the path. See Chapter 10 for a more complete description of the subtleties of the message path.

USING THE MESSAGE PASSING PATH

The basic premise of all HyperTalk programming is this: When a message is sent, a handler that you've written can catch it.

That goes for all kinds of messages—system, custom, or command. All messages are equal when they start out. You can intercept a command message just as easily as a custom message. You can redefine any HyperTalk command or function by writing a custom handler for it.

For example, here's one of the most common handlers in HyperTalk:

```
on mouseUp
    go to next card
end mouseUp
```

This handler traps the message **mouseUp**, which HyperCard sends when the mouse button is released. When this handler is activated, it sends the command message **go**. If the **go** message gets to HyperCard, it activates the **go** command. But if any object in the message-passing path has a handler for the **go** message, the message never gets to HyperCard. This handler redefines the **go** command:

```
on go
    global goTries
    add 1 to goTries
    if goTries = 1 then
      answer "I'm sorry — you can't do that."
    else if goTries = 2 then
      answer "I'm tired of talking to you about this."
    else
      answer "I warned you..."
      doMenu "Quit HyperCard"
    end if
end go
```

What's Catchable?

You can never catch a keyword. Keywords are interpreted directly by HyperCard and don't go through the message-passing path. You cannot catch properties either, although you can

> ### What happens to uncaught (or passed) messages?
>
> Messages that get all the way to HyperCard without being intercepted by a handler receive different treatment, depending on their type:
>
> **System messages**: Once they've had a chance to do their work, they serve no further use. So HyperCard casts system messages aside. (Who wants yesterday's news?)
>
> **Command messages:** HyperCard has the equivalent of built-in handlers for commands, so it carries them out as specified in Part III.
>
> **Custom messages:** HyperCard itself has no way of understanding custom messages. (That's the job of handlers.) If one of these gets all the way through the message-passing path, either you forgot to write a handler for it, the handler is in the wrong part of the message path to catch the message, or there's some other problem (such as the message being misspelled). HyperCard puts up a "Can't understand..." dialog box to indicate that it doesn't know what to do with this message.

catch the **set** command message, thus changing a property before it gets to HyperCard. You can catch commands, and you can catch built-in functions that use the parenthetical form (as in `sin (numExpr)`. But you can't catch functions called with `the`. (For more information about functions and their forms, see the **function** keyword in Part III.)

Overriding Built-In Commands Is Tricky

You can catch a command and easily do something other than what that command usually does. But changing how a command operates is tricky at best. The syntax of parameters for handlers is difficult, and intercepting some commands (such as **doMenu**) can be downright dangerous. (What happens when your handler prevents HyperCard from acting on menu items, and you try to choose Quit? Oops.) We leave it as an exercise to the highly expert scriptwriter.

PLACING HANDLERS FOR BEST EFFECT

Knowing how to use the message-passing path can save lots of code. A card, background, or stack script can have code that defines the behavior for all the buttons, fields, cards, and/or backgrounds in that domain.

For example, suppose you've created a card with a bunch of buttons. Each button goes to a different card in a stack when you click it. You can tell the buttons apart because each button has the same name as the card that is its destination. One way to handle the code for this is to write a separate script for each button, as shown in Figure 1.4:

This will work fine. But what if you want to make a change to each button (for instance, to add a visual effect)? You'd have to make the same change half a dozen times. It's better to write a single handler, placed in the script of the current card, as shown in Figure 1.5.

When you use the method shown in Figure 1.5, clicking on one of these buttons goes to the intended card, even though the button you click has no script. Here's how it works.

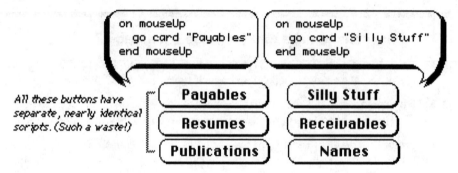

Figure 1.4   Separate scripts

Because the button you click has no **mouseUp** handler to catch the **mouseUp** message, the message proceeds along the message-passing path. The next object in the path is the card, and it *does* have a **mouseUp** handler that catches the message. That handler, which you can see in Figure 1.5, takes you to the card whose name is the same as the button you pressed.

The **if** construct makes sure that what you clicked was a button. If you clicked something else, the handler uses the **pass** keyword to put the **mouseUp** message back on the message-passing path.

The Rule for the Proper Placement of a Handler

Put a handler in the script of the object as far along the message-passing path as it needs to be in order to be shared by every object that uses the handler, but no farther. In the above example, the **mouseUp** handler is in the card script because the buttons are all on the same

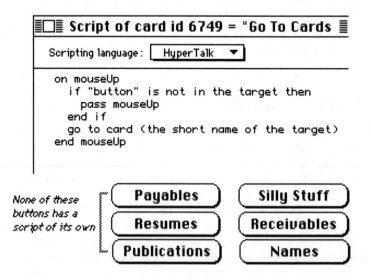

Figure 1.5   All handled at once

card, so the card is in each of their message paths. Putting the handler in the background script might not be appropriate. For example, you might want a set of buttons on another card of that background to react differently than the buttons on this card.

If you put a handler in the Home stack script, it affects objects throughout HyperCard. For example, HyperCard comes with the handler searchScript in the script of the Home stack. This handler makes HyperCard show you the scripts of all objects in the current stack that contain a particular string. No matter what stack you're in, you can type searchScript *string* into the message box and press Return to execute this handler. For example, typing searchScript "pass mouseUp" would open the script of the card in the example above.

At the other end of the message path, a script in a button or field affects only that button or field. If there's more than one handler with the same name in a script, HyperTalk executes the first handler with the message name, and ignores the rest. This feature lets you write and test several variations of the same handler: Just put the version you want to test at the top of the script.

A HyperTechnicality: the message box and message passing

You can always use the message box to get a message into the message-passing path quickly and easily. Here's how it works. If there's no text selection or blinking insertion point in any field, pressing the Return or Enter key sends the **returnKey** or **enterKey** message to the current card. If no object in the card's message path catches the message before it gets to HyperCard, HyperCard executes the **returnKey** or **enterKey** command. Both these commands do the same thing: evaluate or execute whatever is in the message box.

First, HyperCard tries to evaluate the contents of the message box as an expression. If that works, HyperCard puts the value of the expression into the message box, replacing the original contents. This means you can type any expression directly into the message box— sqrt(65536), pi * 75 ^2, the time && the date —without having to preface it with the word **put**.

If HyperCard can't evaluate the contents of the message box as an expression, it sends the contents as a message to the current card.

HyperTalk for Native Speakers of Other (Programming) Languages: A Brief Guide for the Perplexed

If you're new to HyperTalk, but already know another programming language such as C, Pascal, or SmallTalk, many of the basic features of the language will be familiar to you, but some will differ. This section gives a brief explanation of some of the most important facts about HyperTalk in relation to other languages.

STANDARD PROGRAMMING CONSTRUCTS

You'll find most of the standard components of a procedural language in HyperTalk: loops, variables, conditionals, and so forth.

Overall Structure of a Program

HyperTalk is inherently event-driven. As explained in previous sections of this chapter, all HyperTalk code is contained in handlers, each of which responds to a specific message. There is no explicit event loop or main() function. HyperCard sends an **openStack** message when a stack is opened, and you can write a handler for this message to initialize the stack's environment as appropriate. (Also see the **startup** and **closeStack** messages, which are described in detail in Part III.)

Variables

HyperTalk is a typeless language: All variables are treated as strings. (HyperTalk converts variables internally to other data types when necessary for evaluation.) This means you don't have to worry about whether the data type of your variable is compatible with an operation you want to perform on it. For example, you can execute the following code to let the user enter a number to be added without needing to do any conversions; HyperTalk handles any necessary typecasting for you.

```
ask "What number do you want to add?" -- puts up dialog for response
add it to originalNumber
```

Local variables are scoped to the current handler, and are implicitly declared when you initialize them. This means that you don't need a separate declaration statement for a variable; HyperTalk creates it automatically when you start using it. A local variable is initialized by setting it to a value. This is done with the **put** command:

```
put "123" into myVariable
put empty into anotherVar -- null value
```

Global variables can be used throughout all handlers in HyperTalk. Global variables, unlike local variables, must be declared in each handler you want to access them in. Globals are declared with the **global** keyword (see Part III).

Being typeless, HyperTalk does not explicitly support arrays and data structures. However, it has a very flexible syntax, called *chunking*, for addressing parts of a string, and this capability can easily be exploited to create various structures for variable data. For more information about chunking and chunk expressions, see Chapter 8.

Other Sources of Value

In addition to variables, HyperTalk can take sources of value from built-in functions, parameters, the contents of fields, properties of objects in the HyperCard environment, and parts of other sources expressed as chunks. For more information about sources of value, see Chapter 8.

Subroutines

Any HyperTalk handler can call any other message or function handler, subject to the constraints of the message-passing path (see previous sections in this chapter). HyperTalk always passes parameters by value.

Control Structures

HyperTalk includes structures for conditionals and loops. For more information, see the sections about **if...then...else** and **repeat** in Part III.

Extensibility

If you need to use the facilities of another language, or if you need direct access to the Macintosh toolbox routines in addition to HyperCard's own toolbox of objects, you can add standalone code segments called XCMDs (which are equivalent to message handlers) and XFCNs (function handlers) to the resource fork of any stack in the message path. For more information about installing and using externals (XCMDs or XFCNs), see Chapter 4.

HYPERTALK AND OBJECT-ORIENTED LANGUAGES

HyperTalk is essentially object-oriented. That is, it consists of objects which respond to messages, and those messages are passed to objects in an order determined by an object hierarchy; objects inherit the behavior of other objects higher in the hierarchy. However, the language has some differences and limitations relative to other such languages:

Is-Part-Of Object Hierarchy

The hierarchy of objects, which determines the message-passing path, is based on an "is-part-of" criterion, rather than "is-a". For example, buttons inherit the scripts of the cards they belong to—but a button is part of a card, rather than being a kind of card.

Classes Are Predetermined

HyperTalk's object classes are determined by the HyperCard environment in which it's embedded. These classes consist of stacks, backgrounds, cards, buttons, and fields. (For more information about these objects, see your HyperCard documentation.)

Overriding the Hierarchy

You can use the **send** and **pass** keywords to temporarily change the normal message-passing path. These keywords are explained in detail in Part III.

HYPERTALK AND APPLICATION MACRO LANGUAGES

Like a macro language, HyperTalk is embedded in a particular application environment—HyperCard—and has many special features that integrate it with its environment. However, most macro processors allow only limited actions and are not true programming languages. Unlike most macro languages, HyperTalk is a full-fledged programming language, with variables, loops, conditionals, and subroutines. If you're used to controlling applications with built-in macro processors, you'll find that HyperTalk lets you do much, much more.

ADVANTAGES OF HYPERTALK

Integration with the HyperCard Environment

The HyperCard application gives you a full array of user-interface tools, including windows, clickable buttons, styled text fields, bitmapped graphics, and a menu bar. You can completely control all these application aspects from HyperTalk, making it a superior tool for prototyping.

Readability

HyperTalk is verbose, with an English-like syntax. The following statements are all legal:

```
put the date into field "Current Date"
wait until the sound is done
go to the next card in this stack
```

HyperTalk's syntax is flexible and forgiving, with a number of optional words you can use to improve readability. The following statements are all equivalent:

```
go next
go next card
go to next
go to next card
go to the next card
go to the next card in this stack
```

(Appendix D contains HyperTalk's full syntax in BNR form.)

All this makes well-written HyperTalk easier to read and maintain than code written in most other languages. It's easy to use HyperTalk as a working pseudocode: A procedure can be prototyped and tested for algorithmic suitability in HyperTalk, then, if necessary, converted to another programming language.

Text-Manipulation Capabilities

HyperTalk's chunk syntax lets you directly address any part of a string. You can access or change individual characters, words, and lines in any variable or HyperCard field:

```
get line 7 of myVariable
put word 3 to 5 of card field "Text" into theText
delete last char of thatGlobal
```

You can also use the **itemDelimiter** property to directly address text delimited by any character. In combination with the **read** and **write** commands, chunk expressions give you an easy way to filter and transform any text file.

2

![banner]

Writing and Debugging Scripts

This chapter describes the structure of a script as it appears in the script editor. It includes information on how to bring a script into the script editor, what you can do to a script once the editor is operating, and how to use HyperCard's debugging tools to find problems in your handlers.

This chapter also covers the mechanics of breaking a long line into more manageable parts, adding comments, and using automatic script formatting to get an indication of whether or not your scripts are syntactically correct.

For suggestions on how to organize your scripts, see Chapter 3. For information about where you should place a handler for best effectiveness, see Chapter 1.

Every object except HyperCard itself—buttons, fields, cards, backgrounds, and stacks—has a script you can look at. You look at a script with the *script editor*. The script appears as a collection of comments and handlers (see Figure 2.1).

Script limits and TextEdit: A script is limited to 30,000 characters, or about 2,000 characters less than the limit of TextEdit. TextEdit is the simple (some would call it simpleminded) word processor built into the Macintosh operating system. It's the standard editing medium that lets programmers easily localize Macintosh applications so that they'll run in any country. HyperCard builds upon TextEdit to display text in fields and to edit scripts, so the script editor inherits TextEdit's limits.

Summoning the Script Editor

You can use several methods to bring up the script of an object:

- Click the Script button in the object's Info dialog box.
- Click the Script button in a script error dialog.
- Use one of the keyboard shortcuts (see Table 2.1 below).
- Execute the command **edit script.**

The **userLevel** must be set to 5 (Scripting) before you can edit a script.

23

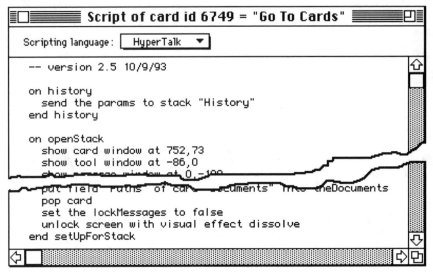

Figure 2.1   The script editor with a script

THE SCRIPT BUTTON

Every HyperCard object except for HyperCard itself has an Info dialog box, which you can access with the items in the Objects menu. (See Figure 2.2.) This dialog has a script button. If the user level is set to 5, clicking that button brings up the script editor and shows the script of the object you've chosen.

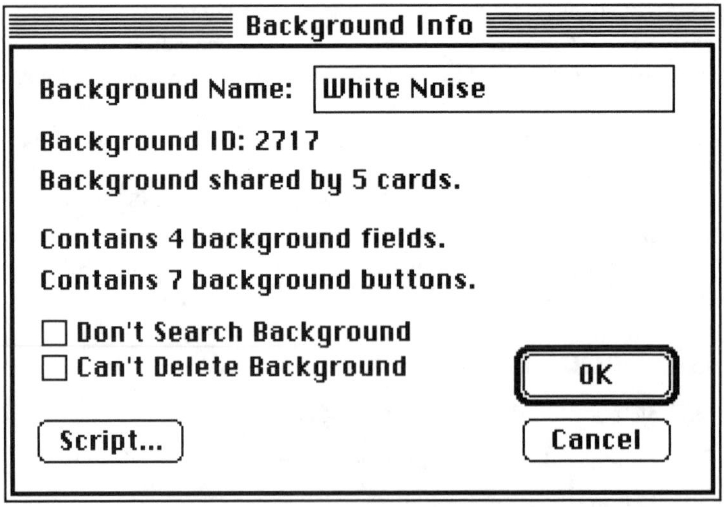

Background Info

Background Name: |White Noise

Background ID: 2717
Background shared by 5 cards.

Contains 4 background fields.
Contains 7 background buttons.

☐ Don't Search Background
☐ Can't Delete Background

OK

Script...   Cancel

Figure 2.2   A background's Info dialog with Script button

KEYBOARD SHORTCUTS

HyperCard provides several keyboard shortcuts you can use to bring up scripts. What a shortcut does depends on the currently active tool (see Table 2.1).

You can't use keyboard shortcuts to see the script of a hidden button or hidden field. The shortcuts aren't available if the **cantPeek** property is true.

Table 2.1   Keyboard Shortcuts

Tool	Keypress	Action
Browse	Command-Option	Displays an outline around all visible buttons; click one to see its script.
	Shift-Command-Option	Displays an outline around all visible buttons and fields; click one to see its script.
Field	Command-Option	Displays an outline around all visible and invisible fields; click a visible field to see its script.
Button	Command-Option	Displays an outline around all visible and invisible buttons; click a visible button to see its script.
Any tool	Command-Option-C	Displays the script of the current card.
	Command-Option-B	Displays the script of the current background.
	Command-Option-S	Displays the script of the current stack.

THE EDIT COMMAND

You can use the **edit** command to edit the script of any button or field on the current card, any background or card in the current stack, or any stack:

```
edit the script of button 3
edit the script of background field "CD Titles"
edit the script of card 1
edit the script of background "Compact Disks"
edit the script of stack "Accounts Receivable"
```

You'll usually use **edit** in the message box, but you can also use the command in a handler. When **edit** is used in a handler, the handler pauses while you edit the script, and continues once the script window is closed. The **edit** command is described in detail in Part III.

The Script Editor

When you call for the script of any object, HyperCard opens the *script editor*. This section describes the built-in script editor. (For advanced information about how to use a custom script editor in place of the built-in one, see the description of the **scriptEditor** property in Part III.)

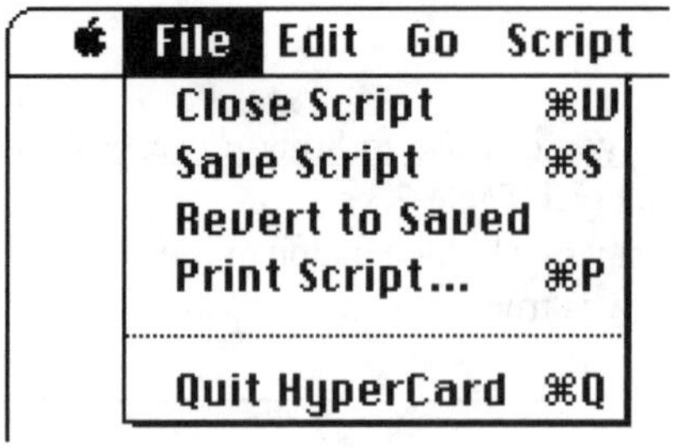

Figure 2.3   Script editor's File menu

You can have several scripts open at one time, each in its own window. While in the script editor, you have full access to all the normal text-editing functions: You can type, select, cut, copy, paste, and use the arrow keys to move the insertion point.

The script editor also has its own set of menus, which replace the standard HyperCard menus as long as the script window is frontmost. The sections below describe the script editor's menus.

THE FILE MENU

Close Script puts the script away. If you've made any changes to the script since the last save, HyperCard puts up a dialog asking you whether to save the changes.

Save Script saves any changes you've made to the script.

Revert to Saved discards any changes you've made since the last time the script was saved.

Print Script prints the script in the frontmost window. The wording of this item changes to **Print Selection** if any text in the script is selected, and prints only the current selection. A header containing the date, time, script name, and page number appears at the top of every printed page.

Quit HyperCard closes the script window and quits HyperCard. If you've made any changes to any open script, HyperCard asks whether you want to save the changes.

THE EDIT MENU

The commands in the Edit menu provide the basic Macintosh editing capabilities, as described in your owner's manual and countless other Mac books. As this book is already massive enough to flatten a Texas cockroach, we'll move right along.

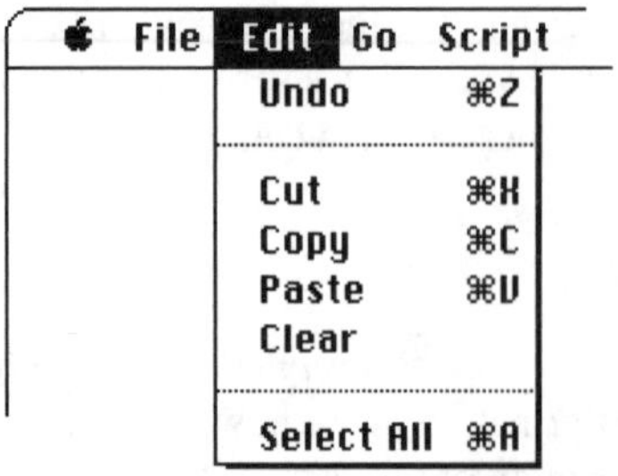

Figure 2.4   Script editor's Edit menu

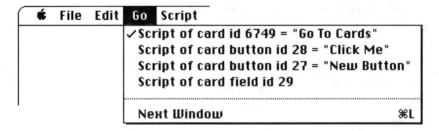

Figure 2.5   Script editor's Go menu

THE GO MENU

The Go menu lists all the open script windows. Choose any script's name to bring it to the front. The frontmost script window is checkmarked.

Next Window lets you cycle through all the open windows, including stack and picture windows. To bring the rearmost window to the front (thus cycling backward through the open windows), hold down the Shift key while choosing Next Window.

THE SCRIPT MENU

Find brings up the Find dialog (Figure 2.7). If the script editor locates the string you type in, it selects it; otherwise, it beeps. The Find dialog lets you either find the requested string anywhere or limit the search to finding the entire word or words you specified. You can make the search case sensitive by clicking the Case Sensitive checkbox. (A case sensitive search treats uppercase and lowercase as different characters.) By default, the search starts from the insertion point and stops at the end of the script. If you want the search to go back to the top of the script and start again from there, turn on Wraparound Search.

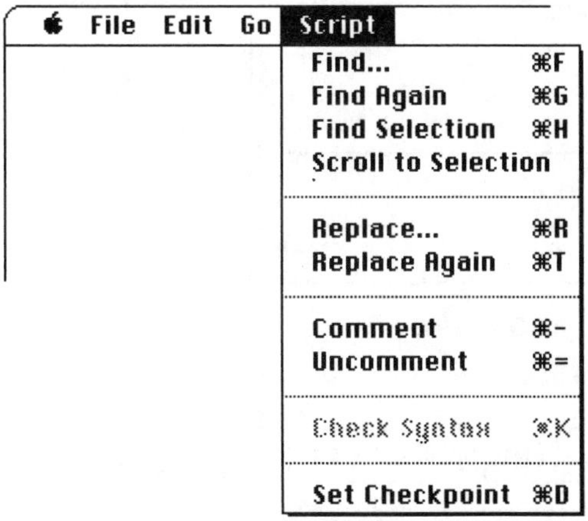

Figure 2.6   Script editor's Script menu

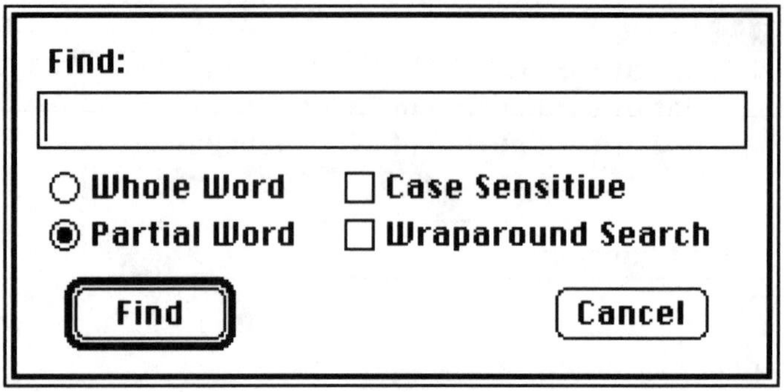

Figure 2.7   Script editor's Find dialog

Find Again searches for the next occurrence of the string in the Find dialog. This command respects the options set in the Find dialog.

Find Selection uses whatever text is currently selected as the search string, placing it in the Find dialog.

Scroll to Selection moves the vertical scrollbar to bring the line with the selection into view. However, it doesn't scroll the script window horizontally. (The script editor doesn't autoscroll horizontally, either. Bummer.)

Replace brings up the script editor's Replace dialog (Figure 2.8). The options are the same as those in the Find dialog. You can delete all occurrences of the string in the Find field by leaving the Replace With field empty and clicking Replace All. (Be careful, because you can't undo Replace All.)

Replace Again replaces the next occurrence of the string specified in the Replace dialog, respecting all the current settings in that dialog.

Comment comments out all currently selected lines by placing a comment delimiter, the double dash (--), in front of them. (HyperTalk doesn't execute commented statements.) If a

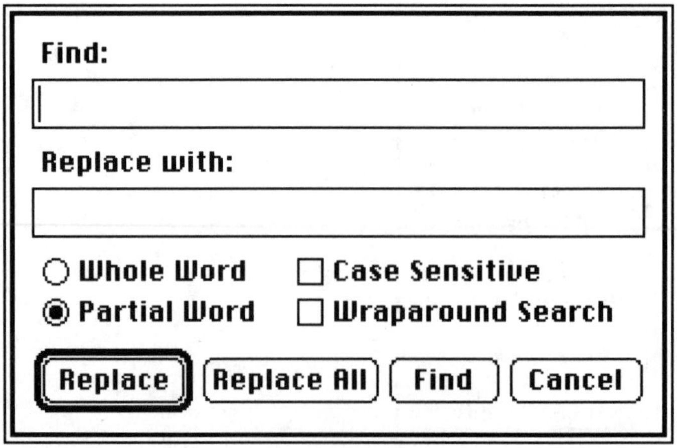

Figure 2.8   Script editor's Replace dialog

partial line is selected, or if there is no selection, this command comments out all the text after the insertion point or the start of the selection.

Uncomment removes the comment delimiter from all selected lines, making them an active part of the script again. If there's no selection, the script editor removes the double dash immediately before the insertion point. If there is no double dash there, the double dash immediately after the insertion point is removed. If the insertion point is not next to a double dash, this command doesn't do anything.

Check Syntax performs a syntax check on the current script. If the current script's Scripting Language popup menu is set to "HyperTalk", this menu item is disabled. (See "Using the Script Editor with Other Script Languages," below.)

Set Checkpoint/Clear Checkpoint toggles a *checkpoint* at the start of the line containing the selection or insertion point. A checkpoint is an instruction to HyperCard to pause at that line and bring up the debugger whenever that handler is executed. You can also set a checkpoint by Option-clicking a line in the script.

USING THE SCRIPT EDITOR WITH OTHER SCRIPT LANGUAGES

In HyperCard version 2.2, you can write scripts in any OSA-compliant script language, such as AppleScript and UserTalk, not just HyperTalk. Each script window has a Scripting Language popup menu, which lists HyperTalk along with all the scripting languages available on your system. To change the script language of an object, just choose the language you want from the popup menu at the top of its script window. (See also the **scriptingLanguage** property, described in Part III.)

Unlike HyperTalk scripts, scripts in other languages are compiled and checked for syntax errors when you close the script editor. (HyperTalk scripts aren't compiled until it's time to run a handler.) This means, among other things, that you may notice a delay when you close an OSA script, while the script is compiled. If you want to check the script's syntax before you close it, use the Check Syntax menu item in the Script menu.

CLOSING THE SCRIPT EDITOR

If you close a script window by clicking its close box, Command-Option-clicking in the window, or choosing Close Script from the File menu, HyperCard asks you whether you want to save changes. To close the editor and automatically save changes, press Enter. To close the editor and automatically discard any changes, press Command-period.

Change to the Script Editor: In 2.0 and later versions of HyperCard, if you've edited a script in another stack, when you close the script editor you're returned to the card you came from. However, in version 1.x, you end up on the first card of the stack. This was considered a "bug."

SCRIPT EDITOR SHORTCUTS

Table 2.2 summarizes the keyboard shortcuts you can use from within the script editor.

Table 2.2   Script Editor Shortcuts

Keypress	Operation
Option-Return	Break line with continuation character (¬)
Triple-click	Select line
Tab	Reformat script
Command-Z	Undo last change
Command-X	Cut selected text
Command-C	Copy selected text
Command-V	Paste selected text
Command-A	Select entire script
Command-P	Print selection or entire script
Command-F	Bring up Find dialog
Command-H	Find selected text
Command-G	Repeat last Find
Command-R	Bring up Replace dialog
Command-T	Repeat last Replace
Command-minus	Comment out selected lines
Command-plus	Uncomment selected lines
Command-D or Option-click	Toggle checkpoint
Enter	Close script and save changes
Command-period	Close script and discard changes
Option-close	Close all open scripts

SCRIPT EDITOR GLOBALS

The script editor maintains a number of global variables, which it uses to hold various script editor settings. The editor creates these globals when you set a script property to something other than the default, and it retains the settings for the rest of the session (or until you change the setting again). The globals are as follows:

- `scriptCaseSens`—True when the Case Sensitive checkbox in the Find dialog is checked.

- `scriptDebugging`—The script editor uses this global internally. Don't, for God's sake, change it.

- `scriptFindString`—The current search string.

- `scriptReplaceString`—The current replace string.

- `scriptWholeWord`—True when the Whole Word radio button in the Find dialog is selected.

- `scriptWrapAround`—True when the Wraparound Search checkbox in the Find dialog is checked.

- `scriptWindowRects`—Four comma-separated integers giving the left, top, right, and bottom edges of a script window when it first comes up.

HyperCard also lets you set the font and size of the text in the script editor with the **scriptTextFont** and **scriptTextSize** properties. The following set of handlers stores the script editor settings when you quit HyperCard and restores them the next time you start up:

```
on restoreScriptSettings
    -- call this handler from your Home stack's startup handler
    -- this handler assumes there's a field called "Script Prefs"
    -- on the first card of your Home stack
    global scriptCaseSens,scriptWholeWord,¬
    scriptWrapAround, scriptWindowRects
    --
    lock screen
    lock messages
    go card 1 of Home
    get field "Script Prefs"
    go recent card
    unlock screen
    unlock messages
    --
    put line 1 of it into scriptCaseSens
    put line 2 of it into scriptWholeWord
    put line 3 of it into scriptWrapAround
    put line 4 of it into scriptWindowRects
    set the scriptTextFont to line 5 of it
    set the scriptTextSize to line 6 of it
end  restoreScriptSettings

on  saveScriptSettings
    -- call this handler from your Home stack's quit handler
    -- this handler assumes there's a field called "Script Prefs"
    -- on the first card of your Home stack
    global scriptCaseSens,scriptWholeWord,¬
    scriptWrapAround, scriptWindowRects
    --
    put scriptCaseSens into line 1 of it
    put scriptWholeWord into line 2 of it
    put scriptWrapAround into line 3 of it
    put scriptWindowRects into line 4 of it
    put the scriptTextFont into line 5 of it
    put the scriptTextSize into line 6 of it
```

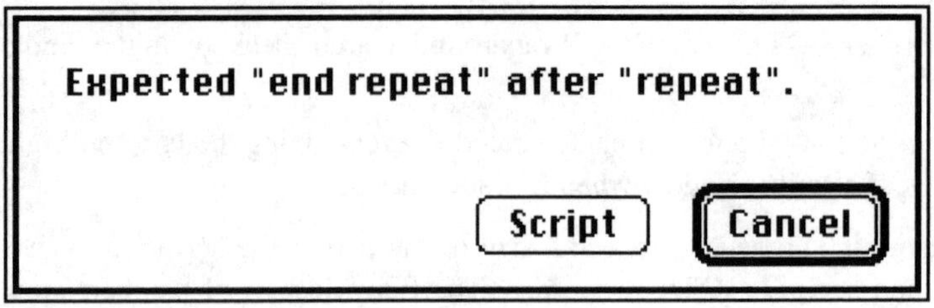

Expected "end repeat" after "repeat".

Script   Cancel

Figure 2.9   Compile-time error dialog

```
      --
    lock  screen
    lock  messages
    go card 1 of Home
    put it into field "Script Prefs"
    go recent card
    unlock screen
    unlock messages
end saveScriptSettings
```

The Debugger

The Debugger is a set of tools that let you follow the progress of your code step by step, while examining the values of variables and the messages being sent at any point in the code.

SCRIPT ERRORS

HyperTalk distinguishes between two kinds of script errors—compile-time and runtime errors.

A compile-time error is a problem that prevents HyperCard from compiling the script— for example, a **repeat** statement with no matching **end repeat**. Compile-time errors prevent the script from running at all. Compilation error dialogs have two buttons: one that lets you bring up the offending script with the insertion point on the problem line, and one to simply cancel the handler (see Figure 2.9).

A runtime error is a script problem that doesn't prevent HyperCard from compiling the script, but causes a problem while it's running—for example, a reference to a nonexistent object. Runtime error dialogs have an additional Debug button that lets you enter the debugger at the error point (see Figure 2.10).

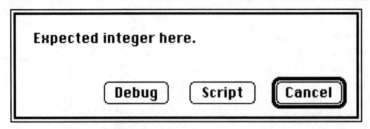

Figure 2.10   Runtime error dialog

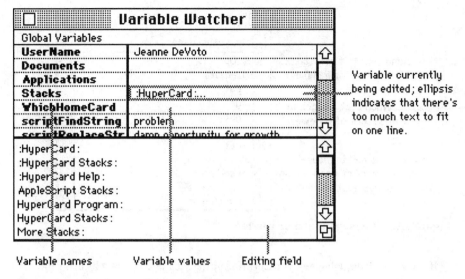

Figure 2.11   Variable Watcher window

THE VARIABLE WATCHER

The Variable Watcher is a window that lets you see and edit the values of variables (see Figure 2.11). If you're looking at a script in the debugger, the Variable Watcher shows all variables in the current handler; otherwise, it shows all global variables (plus the **result** function).

If you're not in the debugger, you can bring up the Variable Watcher by using the command

```
show variable watcher
```

in the message box or a handler. The Home stack script contains a handler that provides a shortcut:

```
vw -- equivalent to "show variable watcher"
```

Clicking on a variable puts its value into the editing field at the bottom of the window. (If the value takes up more than one line, you can change the size of the window or drag the horizontal divider to see all of it.) You can change the value of the variable in the editing field. To update the variable with the new value, press Enter. This "live editing" of variables is particularly useful when you're in the debugger, looking at the current values of variables. It lets you play out all sorts of "What if" scenarios that might be difficult to implement any other way.

THE MESSAGE WATCHER

The Message Watcher (see Figure 2.12) is a window that shows the last 150 messages that passed through the message path. Indentation shows which handlers sent which messages. Messages that were not handled by any handler are shown in parentheses. Messages sent to objects whose scripting language is not HyperTalk are shown in brackets.

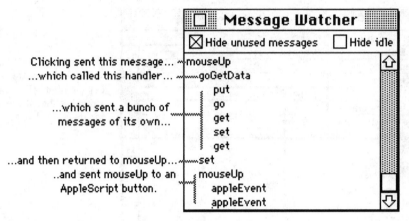

Figure 2.12   Message Watcher window

If you're not in the debugger, you can bring up the Message Watcher by using the command

```
show message watcher
```

in the message box or a handler. The Home stack script contains a handler that provides a shortcut:

```
mw -- equivalent to "show message watcher"
```

To avoid having irrelevant messages scroll by, you can set the checkboxes at the top of the window to hide unused messages—that is, messages that won't be caught by any handler in the message-passing path—or hide **idle** messages, which HyperCard sends continuously as long as no other message is being handled. If you want to see *all* messages passing through the message path, turn both checkboxes off.

ENTERING THE DEBUGGER

You can only use the debugger while a handler is actually running. There are several ways to bring up the debugger during handler execution:

- HyperCard puts up a script error dialog, and you click the Debug button.
- A handler executes a **debug checkpoint** command.
- HyperCard is about to execute a line of code with a checkpoint set in the script editor.
- You press Command-Option-period while a handler is running.

When the debugger comes up, it displays the script containing the current handler in a window, with the current line of code outlined. The handler pauses at that point, but is not aborted. The debugger also adds a menu to the menu bar (see below). While you are in the debugger, you can move windows, check menu items, and bring other script windows to the front, but you can't edit in any script window until you leave the debugger.

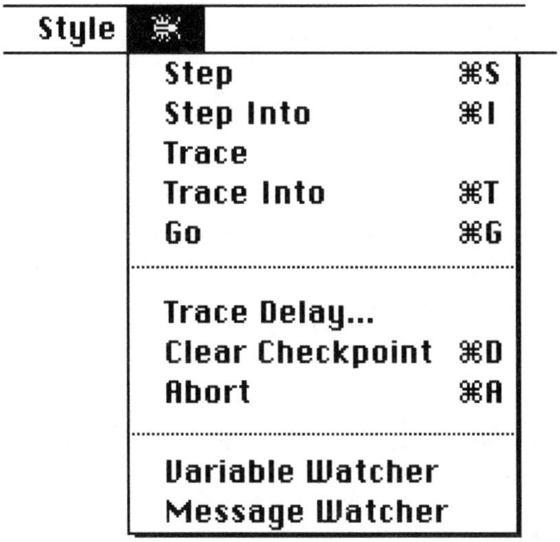

```
Style  🐛
            Step            ⌘S
            Step Into       ⌘I
            Trace
            Trace Into      ⌘T
            Go              ⌘G
            ·····························
            Trace Delay...
            Clear Checkpoint  ⌘D
            Abort           ⌘A
            ·····························
            Variable Watcher
            Message Watcher
```

Figure 2.13   The Debug menu

THE DEBUG MENU

Step lets you continue executing the current handler one line at a time. Each time you choose Step, another line executes. The debugger outlines the line that's about to execute, and brings the window of the script that contains the handler to the front (if it wasn't already frontmost).

Step Into acts like Step, except that when you reach a call to another handler, or when you complete the current handler and return to another, you continue stepping into that handler instead of executing it as a single step. Step Into is most useful when you're tracing the interaction of several handlers.

Trace executes the current handler, one line at a time, and keeps doing so until you choose Step or Step Into, or until the handler completes.

Trace Into acts like Trace, except that, like Step Into, it continues into other handlers; its operation isn't limited to the current handler.

Go exits the debugger and resumes normal execution of the handler.

Trace Delay lets you set a pause between steps when Trace or Trace Into is active. The delay is specified in ticks (a tick is 1/60th of a second). By default, the trace delay is 0, and tracing executes each step one after the other without pausing.

Set Checkpoint/Clear Checkpoint toggles a checkpoint at the start of the currently executing line. (The debugger outlines the current line.)

Abort halts the current handler (and all pending handlers) and exits the debugger, while leaving the script window open.

Variable Watcher brings up the Variable Watcher window, described above.

Message Watcher brings up the Message Watcher window, described above.

EXITING THE DEBUGGER

HyperCard exits the debugger automatically if you finish stepping or tracing through all pending handlers. To exit the debugger and continue executing the handler, choose Go from the Debug menu. To halt the pending handlers and exit the debugger, choose Abort from the Debug menu, or press Command-period.

Formatting

HyperCard's script editor indents your handlers automatically to show their structure. The script editor handles formatting automatically whenever you open a script. You can force the script editor to format an open script by pressing Tab. Pressing Return to add a new line also formats the script.

FORMATTING DETAILS

The opening and closing lines of each handler start at the left margin of the editor. All lines within the handler are indented two spaces:

```
on  makeNewPicture  thePoint
  set  the  editBkgnd  to  true
  doMenu  "Paste  Picture"  with  shiftKey
  drag  from  256,170  to  thePoint
  set  the  editBkgnd  to  false
end  makeNewPicture
```

Any lines contained within an **if...then...else** or **repeat** structure are indented an additional two spaces. Nested structures are indented again as appropriate:

```
on mouseUp
  -- compress multiple spaces in field 1
  put 1 into charNumber
  repeat while char charNumber of field 1 is not empty
    if char charNumber of field 1 is space then
      repeat while char (charNumber + 1) of field 1 is space
        delete char charNumber + 1 of field 1
      end repeat
    end if
    add 1 to charNumber
  end repeat
end mouseUp
```

The script's formatting strips any extra leading spaces from each line.

You can use the automatic script formatting to check whether your structures are valid. For example, if you've created a **repeat** statement without a matching **end repeat**, pressing the Tab key will let you see that there's something wrong with the formatting, and therefore with the syntax of your handler:

```
on mouseDown
  if word 2 of the name of the target is "button" then
    repeat for 3 times
```

```
beep
set the hilite of the target to true
set the hilite of the target to false
end if        -- missing "end repeat" causes the script
end mouseDown -- editor to fail to indent properly here
```

Formatting isn't always right

Usually, code that indents incorrectly has a syntax error and won't run. However, there are a few situations in which the script editor won't format correct code properly. For example, the script editor sometimes thinks comments are part of the code:

```
on checkNumber theNumber
   if theNumber is 3 then flash theNumber
   -- this is a comment about the upcoming else
   else beep it
   end checkNumber
```

The above handler is correct code and will run, but the formatter is thrown off by the keyword **else** in the comment.

Formatting is an aid to writing code, but in the end, running it is the only way to tell whether the code is correct.

BREAKING A LINE INTO VIEWABLE SEGMENTS

A line of code can be up to 254 characters long. However, this is too long to be seen in its entirety on most screens. Although the script editor lets you scroll horizontally, it's easier to read code if you can see all of it at once.

The line continuation character (¬) lets you break up a long line into several lines, while telling HyperTalk to treat the whole thing as a single line of code. You produce a line-continuation character by pressing Option-L. When this character appears at the end of a line, it tells HyperTalk to join the next line onto this one:

```
on mouseUp
   if the top of field 1 is the top of field 10 ¬
   and the hilite of card button 12 is true then
      put "It works great!" into field 7
   end if
end mouseUp
```

The first two lines in the above handler appear as separate lines in the script editor, but when running the handler, HyperTalk treats them as a single line.

To enter a line-continuation character and go to the next line in one keystroke, use the shortcut Option-Return. You can put as many line-continuation characters as you want in a line of code, as long as the total length of the line is less than 255 characters.

You can't use a line-continuation character within quotation marks, since HyperCard interprets anything in quotation marks as part of a literal string. If you need to break up a quoted string, break it into multiple strings and connect them with the ampersand operator:

```
on fillTheField
   put "When I was a boy in Boston, I'd sometimes go to" & ¬
   " Boston Commons on weekends to watch Mrs. McGinty" & ¬
   " poisoning the pigeons, chipmunks, children, and other" & ¬
   " small undesirable wildlife." ¬
   into field "Charming Characters I Have Known"
end fillTheField
```

COMMENTS

A comment is an explanation or note within a script, intended for people reading the script. Comments are not part of the code, and HyperTalk ignores all comments when executing handlers. To enter a comment, precede it with a double dash (--):

```
on closeField
   -- update the last modified field for this card
   put the date into field "Last Modified"
   pass closeField
end closeField
```

HyperTalk ignores everything between the double dash and the end of that line, so you can also put comments next to a line of code:

```
put 3 into myVar -- myVar holds the flash count
```

If you write a comment that's not in any handler, you don't need to precede it with a double dash. However, it's a good idea to do so anyway, for two reasons. First, some people find it confusing when comments don't start with the double dash. Second, if you happen to start an uncommented line with the word "on" or "function", you'll find that it messes up script formatting (because HyperTalk thinks these words are the start of handlers).

3

Style, Memory, and Performace

Too often in computer languages, you face an unhappy choice: Your code can have speed or it can have good style, but not both. In HyperTalk, however, the most readable code is also often the fastest and most efficient.

This chapter is divided into three sections. The first section, "Writing the Fastest Code Possible," concentrates on how to get the most speed from a script without compiling it. The second section, "Style Issues," shows how to write orderly and easy-to-read scripts without sacrificing speed. The third section, "Organizing a Script," deals with the placement of handlers in the message-passing path and the order of handlers within a script. The last section, "Memory," describes how to avoid having your stack run out of memory.

Writing the Fastest Code Possible

Many of the operations HyperCard does are slow by nature. This is particularly true for operations that access the disk—and HyperCard is disk-intensive. By avoiding or limiting slow operations, you can make your handlers up to an order of magnitude faster.

Time savings are relative

This section quotes different time savings for different techniques. The actual performance you get will vary from machine to machine and from situation to situation. But if you follow all the recommendations in this chapter, your code will run as fast as possible.

Here's a quick summary of principles to make your stacks run as fast as possible. They're listed in order of importance. You'll find details and examples for them later in the chapter:

- Change stacks as seldom as possible.

- Use variables instead of fields whenever you can.
- Use externals for repetitive tasks.
- Refer to a remote card rather than going there.
- Take unnecessary code out of loops.
- Don't check properties before setting them.
- Use quoted instead of unquoted literals.
- Lock the screen to avoid needless redrawing.
- Lock messages during card-to-card data collection.
- Send as few messages as possible.
- Use in-line statements rather than handler calls.
- Do complex calculations once.
- Refer to variables as infrequently as possible.
- Do visible work first.

CHANGE STACKS AS SELDOM AS POSSIBLE

Changing stacks requires HyperCard to read from a storage device like a disk or CD-ROM. And getting information to or from storage takes more time than any other Macintosh operation. Therefore, it makes sense to keep all related data in the same stack, so you don't have to go to another stack very often. If you have substantially different interfaces (for example, one interface to take phone orders, another interface to do inventory, etc.) and you need to cross boundaries frequently, use multiple backgrounds in the same stack rather than separate stacks. When you need to get data from another stack, go to that stack only once. Get (or put) everything you need at the same time.

The following handler does everything in one trip. It scans a stack of phone company customer records and creates a new stack with the names, addresses, and phone numbers of those that have the highest phone bills:

```
on windBags
  lock screen
  repeat with i = 1 to the number of cards
    go to card i
    if field "Phone Bill" > 100 then -- found a big spender
      put field "Name" into name
        put field "Address" into address
        put field "Phone Number" into phoneNum
        -- got everything we need
        -- now go put it in the other stack
        push card
        go to last card of stack "WindBags"
        doMenu "New Card"
        put name & return & address into field "Address"
```

```
       put phoneNum into field "Phone"
       pop card -- return to other stack
     end if
     end repeat
  end windBags
```

There Are Always Exceptions

There are a few good reasons to use more than one stack for closely-related data. The main one is stack size—you might need to make sure that each stack fits on a single floppy to make transport or backup easier.

> **Warning to giant stack makers**
>
> A bug in versions before 1.2.5 corrupts stacks larger than 8 megabytes.

USE VARIABLES INSTEAD OF FIELDS WHENEVER YOU CAN

As much as possible, do all operations—sorting, data collecting, calculations—in variables rather than in fields. Operations happen much faster in variables than they do in fields. Use fields to display data and for long-term storage. You can put the contents of a field into a variable, perform an operation on the variable, and then put the contents back into the field. This is much faster than operating directly on the field.

HyperCard keeps field information stored on disk and draws that information onto the screen. Variables, on the other hand, live in RAM. And (as you probably know) information stored in RAM is available quickest.

Collecting data on different cards into a variable is at least 50% faster than collecting it into a field. For example, suppose you want to collect the names from the "Name and Address" field of your Address stack:

```
on mouseUp
  lock screen
  push card
  set cursor to watch
  repeat with i = 2 to the number of cards
    go to card i
    put line 1 of field "Name and Address" & return after ¬
    card field "collector" of card 1
  end repeat
  pop card
  unlock screen
end mouseUp
```

The following code takes about half the time. It collects the data into a variable and, after the collecting is done, puts all the data into a field at once:

```
on mouseUp
  set the cursor to watch
  put empty into allNames
  repeat with i = 2 to the number of cards
    put line 1 of (field "Name and Address" of card i) & return ¬
    after allNames
  end repeat
  put allNames into card field "collector"
end mouseUp
```

You get even more of a speed difference using variables when you're doing calculations (for example, adding the contents of a series of fields from different cards). Everything that goes into a field is converted to a string, no matter what its original format was. The numeric content of variables, on the other hand, is nearly always stored in binary format, which makes calculations more efficient and more precise.

The same considerations apply when you're reading and writing text files using the **read** and **write** commands. Text files are on the disk (obviously), so when HyperCard uses them it takes the same disk-related speed hit as with fields. To work with text files as fast as possible, read all your data into a variable, then write it to the file all at once:

```
repeat with x = 1 to the number of cards -- very slow
  write field "Text" of card x & return to file myFile
end repeat

repeat with x = 1 to the number of cards -- much faster
  put field "Text" of card x & return after myVariable
end repeat
write myVariable to file myFile
```

Similarly, if you're importing text from a file, read it all at once into a variable, then process it into individual fields. Don't do a separate **read** for each bit of data.

MIGRATE TO EXTERNALS FOR REPETITIVE TASKS

For repetitive time-intensive tasks, use externals. They have the same calling interface as other commands (that is, you use them the same as any HyperTalk command), so they're no harder to use than handlers. (This one might have a greater effect on speed than anything else on the list, depending on the number of iterations in the task.)

If you don't know how to write XCMDs and XFCNs, you can still find externals to use for your stacks. The online services (CompuServe, America Online, and so on) and nationwide user groups such as BMUG and BCS all have HyperCard libraries packed with public domain or shareware externals. For more information on using externals, see Chapter 4.

REFER TO A REMOTE CARD RATHER THAN GOING THERE

If you're going to collect data from fewer than 10 fields in another card, it's faster to refer to the card than to go there to collect the information. To collect data from 10 or more fields, it's faster to go to that card and then collect the data.

The following three examples illustrate collecting data in a field, collecting data in a variable, and collecting data in a variable by referring to a remote field. Each one has timing code included so you can compare their speed. If there are fewer than 10 fields, these examples are in order of increasing speed:

```
on mouseUp
   -- collect one data item in a field
   put empty into card field "Collector"
   get the ticks
   lock screen
   push card
   set the cursor to watch
   repeat with i = 2 to the number of cards
      go card i
      put line 1 of field "Address" & return after ¬
      card field "Collector" of card 1
   end repeat
   pop card
   unlock screen
   put (the ticks - it)/ 60 && "seconds."
end mouseUp


on  mouseUp
   -- collect one data item in a variable
   put empty into card field "Collector"
   get the ticks
   lock screen
   push card
   set the cursor to watch
   put empty into allNames
   repeat with i = 2 to the number of cards
      go card i
      put line 1 of field "Address" & return after allNames
   end repeat
   pop card
   put allNames into card field "Collector"
   unlock screen
   put (the ticks - it)/60 && "seconds."
end  mouseUp


on  mouseUp
   -- collect data items in a variable by referring to
   -- remote field; this version runs in about half the
   -- time of the first example
   put empty into card field "Collector"
   get the ticks
   set  the  cursor  to  watch
```

```
      repeat with i = 2 to the number of cards
        put line 1 of (field "NameAddress" of card i) & return ¬
        after allNames
      end repeat
      put allNames into card field "Collector"
      put (the ticks - it)/ 60 & "seconds."
    end mouseUp
```

PUT CODE OUTSIDE OF LOOPS WHENEVER POSSIBLE

Short handlers take less time to run than longer ones. Repeat loops magnify this effect. You can think of a loop that's six lines long and that runs six times as being roughly the equivalent of 25 lines of code (roughly, because loops have two extra lines—the **repeat** and **end repeat** statements—that wouldn't be there if you "unwrapped" the code, plus a certain amount of overhead). So every extra line in that six-iteration loop counts as six lines. Now consider what happens in a loop that runs for 1000 times.

The **lock screen** in the following code should precede the loop. If it were placed before the loop starts, the effect would be exactly the same. In its present position, it wastes a great deal of time:

```
on  collectNames
  -- this is where "lock screen" should be
  repeat with i = 1 to 300
    lock screen -- No! Get out of the loop! Bad line!!! Bad!!!
    put line 1 of field 1 & return after dataCollector
  end repeat
end collectNames
```

DON'T CHECK PROPERTIES BEFORE SETTING THEM

Unless the new setting depends on the old one, don't check property settings before you change them. For example, even if the message box is already at 10, 364, it takes much longer to execute the lines

```
if the loc of message box is not "10,364" then
  set the loc of message box to 10,364
end if
```

than it does to just set it to what you want:

```
set the loc of msg to 10,364
```

And if you're checking in a loop, the time difference really adds up.

USE QUOTED LITERALS INSTEAD OF UNQUOTED LITERALS

When HyperTalk comes across an ambiguous word—one that might be a literal, function call, variable, or whatever—it must check all the possibilities to discover what the word really is. The first possibility that HyperTalk considers is that the word is a quoted literal; the last thing it considers is that the word is an unquoted literal. Enclosing literals in quotation marks can result in considerable time savings—up to 20% for loops with several hundred or thousand repetitions.

LOCK THE SCREEN TO AVOID REDRAWING

Redrawing the screen takes time. It makes no sense to let the screen change when all you're doing is collecting data (unless you want to wow the user and you think that's worth spending the time that redrawing takes). This is especially true when going from card to card to collect data.

LOCK MESSAGES DURING DATA COLLECTION

The **lock messages** command prevents HyperCard from sending the open and close messages associated with cards, backgrounds, and stacks. If you're moving from card to card or from stack to stack, **lock messages** prevents any handlers associated with opening and closing cards, backgrounds, and stacks from running. This saves considerable time. If you have no such handlers, **lock messages** still saves the time that it takes for these messages to traverse the message-passing path. (And remember that the path is a third longer if you're collecting data from a remote stack, since in that case the dynamic path comes into play—see Chapter 10).

COMBINE MULTIPLE MESSAGES

Message-sending is relatively expensive because each message traverses the entire message-passing path. So here are a bunch of techniques that, when taken together, can save lots of time:

Use Operators instead of Functions

Operators are interpreted directly and don't incur the cost of message sending. They're quite fast compared to everything else. So lines like

```
myContainer contains theString
theString is in myContainer
```

are both faster than

```
offset(theString,myContainer) is 0
```

because the operators are interpreted directly, not sent as messages. The same thing goes for use of the **add**, **subtract**, **multiply**, and **divide** commands, as opposed to their operator counterparts.

Use "the" for Functions

Calling a built-in function with its "the" form (if it has one) is faster than calling it with parentheses, because "( )" functions traverse the message path. So using date( ) is slower than the date.

Assign Values Directly

Getting a value and putting it somewhere is slower than putting it directly, because two statements take longer to execute than does one. So

```
add 1 to x
divide x by 4
```

is slower than

```
put (x+1)/4 into x
```

A highly technical point: sometimes avoiding the journey is the reward

Because an entire handler is converted to executable code before it starts running, normal in-line message sending doesn't require HyperTalk to do any lexical analysis. But when you use the **send** keyword, the message being sent must be analyzed before the **send** keyword can execute. So

```
foo
```
is faster than
```
send "foo"
```

USE IN-LINE STATEMENTS RATHER THAN HANDLER CALLS

It always takes time to get from here to there and back again. When you call code that's in another handler, you're adding travel time. And every time you pass a parameter, you not only do some traveling, but you have to load up your backpack before you leave and unpack it again when you arrive. (Don't you love these outdoorsy California metaphors?)

Putting all your code in-line instead of breaking it into separate handlers saves execution time. The problem is that it can make your code harder to read. (This is one of the few areas in which good HyperTalk style actually makes your code slower.) Consider this easy-to-read handler, which calls several other handlers to do its work:

```
on checkSchedule
   getTheDayAndTime
   getNewAppointment day, time
   checkForConflicts
   addToSchedule
   askForOtherAppointments
end checkSChedule
```

Written this way, the handler and all its subhandlers take more time to execute than if all the code were dumped into a single handler. But they're very easy to read and make sense of. The speed increase might not be worth it. You'll need to decide this on a case-by-case basis, but the best solution is usually to write most of your handlers like the one above, and put all your code in-line only for repetitive, time-intensive stuff that you haven't relegated to externals.

Another good compromise is to call handlers only when you have to. That is, check whether you need to execute a handler before you call it. For an example of this, see "Use Structures Judiciously" in the Style section.

DO COMPLEX CALCULATIONS ONCE

If you know a value isn't going to change, check it only once, and store the result in a variable for later use. (This includes getting properties or the contents of fields.) Referring to a variable is a great deal faster than checking a property or computing a function, so if you need to refer to the value more than once, this method is faster. Again, the time you save by doing this is magnified if you're using a **repeat** loop.

This first handler is pretty slow because it continually recomputes the value of a user-defined function, `sortLines(values)`:

```
on findADuplicate values
   repeat with i = 2 to the number of lines in sortLines(values)
      if line i of sortLines(values) ¬
      is line i - 1 of sortLines(values) then
         put line i of sortLines(values) && "is a duplicate."
         exit findDuplicates
      end if
   end repeat
   put "No duplicates."
end findADuplicate
```

The next handler does the same thing, but it's much faster, because it computes `sortLine(values)` only once:

```
on findADuplicate values
   get sortLines(values)
   repeat with i = 2 to the number of lines in it
      if line i of it is line i - 1 of it then
         put line i of it && "is a duplicate."
         exit findDuplicates
      end if
   end repeat
   put "No duplicates."
end findADuplicate
```

REFER TO VARIABLES AS INFREQUENTLY AS POSSIBLE

Although variables are the fastest way to access data, the statement `add x to y` is slightly faster than `put x + y into y` because the second has three variable references while the first has only two.

DO ALL VISIBLE WORK FIRST

If you're going to be doing a number of operations in one handler, do any that are visible to the user first. Put data into fields, hide and show objects, create menus before adding menu items or doing other things that the user can't immediately see. You can also give the user something to look at or some music to hear while you do some heavy-duty, time-consuming work. This technique is strictly sleight-of-hand Houdini stuff. It doesn't make your code any faster, but it distracts the user from noticing the time so much. This technique doesn't speed up the actual time it takes for the code to run, but it makes it seem faster.

Here's a handler from a script that shuffles a deck of cards before dealing:

```
on mouseUp
   global theDeck
   put empty into field "Your Hand" -- user thinks we're done now
   repeat with i = 1 to 100 -- but we keep shuffling
      put random(52) into cardA
      put random(52) into cardB
      get line cardA of theDeck
      put line cardB of theDeck into line cardA of theDeck
      put it into line cardB of theDeck
   end repeat
end mouseUp
```

SOME MYTHS ABOUT SPEED

There are a lot of strange concepts going around about how to make HyperTalk code run faster. These are our top four all-time favorites:

Myth #1: Fewer Comments Means Faster Speed

Comments, blank lines, and embedded spaces are all stripped out before the handler runs, when all handler text is converted to executable tokens. So the number and length of comments makes absolutely no difference in a handler's speed.

Myth #2: Card Changes Are Slow, So Always Pre-Warm a Stack

Initial card changes are sort of slow, because the card elements need to be read from disk. But after a card appears, HyperCard caches it in memory. (It also automatically caches the next card in the stack, figuring you'll want to go there soon.) And if you lock the screen when you're going through a stack to collect data programmatically, the amount of time it takes to go from card to card even the first time through isn't that great. You can use the following code to pre-warm a stack for bursts of speed (which is effective if you're doing animation), but in most cases it isn't necessary:

```
on  openStack
   go card "Show me first" -- Give user something to look at
```

```
      lock screen
      set lockMessages to true
      show all cards
      ...-- other openStack stuff goes here
      pass openStack
   end openStack
```

Myth #3: Short Variable Names Make Handlers Run Faster

Pah! The variable name `This_Is_My_Fave_Variable_Name` has the same impact on speed as does the `name T7` —practically none.

Myth #4: Placement of a Handler Impacts Speed

Wrong again! The position of a handler in a script or in the message-passing has no noticeable impact on how quickly that handler reacts to a message or how quickly the statements in that handler execute.

Style Issues

Robustness in programming means that code works right in all possible cases now, and can stand changes to its environment in the future. This section makes suggestions for a style that produces robust, elegant, and efficient scripts that are easy to debug and maintain through all versions of HyperCard.

COMMENT PLENTIFULLY

Use comments wherever they might improve a script's readability. It's a good idea to put a general comment at the top of each handler that briefly explains what the handler does. If you use an unusual or convoluted technique, explain it in a comment.

USE DESCRIPTIVE NAMES

When naming handlers, objects, and variables, choose names that describe what they do, rather than cryptic labels such as "a" or "b72". Long names will help you immensely during debugging. Using abbreviations saves a few bytes of space, but it also makes it harder to make sense of what you've written.

QUOTE ALL LITERALS

HyperTalk lets you use unquoted literals in many situations. But if you use variable names that are the same as unquoted literals, you can get in trouble. For example, assume you have a field called "Names" as well as a variable called `names`:

```
put "John Scribblemonger" into names
put names into field Names
```

HyperCard tries to evaluate a word as a variable before it tries to evaluate it as an unquoted literal. So, because the variable names has a value (defined in the first line of code), HyperTalk assumes that the unquoted word "Names" (at the end of the second line of code) is the same variable, and treats it as such. Unless you have a field called "John Scribblemonger", this code causes an error dialog.

COMPARE **THE RESULT** TO EMPTY

Some commands, such as **find** and **go**, set the **result** function to a string. If the command is successful, it sets **the result** to empty. If the command fails, it generally sets the result function to a useful error message (like "No such card"). But the string that each command sets the result to may change from version to version of HyperCard, so you can't rely on it. Therefore, it makes sense to check whether **the result** is empty or not empty, rather than checking its exact contents.

For example, if you're checking to see whether a **go** command worked, use:

```
if the result is not empty -- This will always be reliable
then answer "Sorry -" && the result
```

This will always work. But the following code may fail in a future version of HyperCard:

```
if the result is "no such card" -- Might change in later versions!
then answer "Sorry - No such card!"
```

You have been warned.

USE STRUCTURES JUDICIOUSLY

Test for success (or failure) as early in a **repeat** structure as you can. This makes constructing the rest of the code cleaner and easier to deal with, because you'll have the "no-go" cases taken care of first and you won't have to think about them any more:

```
repeat
   if myVar = 100 then exit repeat -- get out now, if you can
   add 1 to myVar
   doSomeRoutine
end repeat
```

The same principle applies to other handler structures— get out if the code doesn't apply:

```
on mouseUp
   if "field" is not word 2 of the target then pass mouseUp
   put me after field 2
   beep
   answer the target && "appended."
end mouseUp
```

KEEP A HANDLER'S INTERFACE AND IMPLEMENTATION SEPARATE

The parameters to a handler should be as simple as possible; the handler itself should do the work. As you find better ways of doing things, you have to change only the handler itself, rather than changing every place that you call it.

For example, if you have a stack that does a lot of telephone dialing, the interface should get the number to be dialed, and then pass it to the implementing handler. The dialing handler should supply all the other information (outside dialing codes, necessary pauses, credit card number, and so on). For an example, see the Address stack that came with HyperCard.

KEEP HANDLERS GENERAL AND REUSABLE

This suggestion follows naturally from the last one. Handlers need to be flexible so that they can handle as many situations as possible. So a sort routine, for example, shouldn't refer to specific containers, and shouldn't expect the names of containers to be passed to it. Rather, it should expect to get, and to pass back, values in a simple parameter:

```
function sortExpr data, direction
   -- sort code goes here
   return data -- returns the data all sorted to the caller
end sortExpr
```

A handler that operates on any kind of expression can take parameters from and return results to anywhere.

SETTLE ON A NAMING CONVENTION

This makes your code easy to read, and therefore easy to debug and change. It doesn't matter what forms you ultimately decide on, as long as you're consistent. Here are a few suggestions (none of which have any intrinsic value, beyond the fact that together they consitute a consistent system).

- Start all variables and handler names with lowercase letters, but capitalize embedded words: `myVarName`, `mouseLocation`, `lastName`, `newData`.

- Use the underscore symbol in names that are long or where capitalization doesn't seem to work well: `my_Very_Longest_Name`, `a_Lot_Of_Info`.

- Start global variables with the word "the" to indicate that they're unique throughout HyperCard: `theUserName`, `thePayrollList`, `theBook`.

- Avoid using negative forms in names; they're bound to be confusing. For example, when you need to know whether the Mac running your stack is a fast model, use forms like `if fastMac then callA` or `if slowMac then callB`. Don't use negative forms like `if not slowmac then...` or (by far, the worst case) `if not nonFastMac then...`.

USE GLOBALS SPARINGLY

The great thing about globals is that they stay alive throughout all of HyperCard until you quit. And that's also the problem with globals. Because they're always around, they're easy both to clobber and to forget to clobber. This is especially true if you have some favorite global names: You're liable to use the same ones in several stacks, perhaps forgetting to reset them to empty when you close the stack. Where you can, write code that passes parameters from handler to handler, instead of using global variables to pass data.

Organizing a Script

You organize a stack to make editing and reading code more efficient. Most people find that a top-down organization works best. The brief suggestions in this section use a top-down approach.

HANDLERS THAT BELONG IN A PARTICULAR SCRIPT

The handlers in a script should be called from that script's object, or from objects earlier on the message-passing path. A card script, for example, should contain only handlers that respond to card messages (such as **openCard** and **closeCard**), custom handlers that you call from another handler, and handlers that respond to messages sent to a button or field that's earlier in the message-passing path.

THE ORDER OF HANDLERS WITHIN A SCRIPT

The first handler in a script should be the primary handler for that object, followed by any handlers the primary one uses. Most of the time, the primary handler is one that responds to a system message, such as **openCard** for a card script or **mouseUp** for a button script.

List additional handlers in the order they appear in the primary handler. In the case of nested utility handlers, follow the order of the nesting. So if the order of calls looks like this:

```
on mainHandler
   subHandler1
   subHandler2
   -- subHandler1 calls subUnderHandler1, subUnderHandler2,
   -- and subUnderHandler3, in that order
   subHandler3
end mainHandler
```

then list the handlers in the script like this:

```
mainHandler
subHandler1
subHandler2
subUnderHandler1
subUnderHandler2
subUnderHandler3
subHandler3
```

Some people prefer to put all handlers after the primary one in alphabetical order. This can make handlers easier to find in very long scripts.

Performance effects of organization

Organization is a matter of personal convenience. HyperTalk doesn't care about the order of handlers in a script, unless there are two handlers with the same name in the same script. In this case, the first handler responds to the message.

The only measurable effect on performance is when you use **send** to call a handler in another stack. Since moving between stacks takes a lot of time, using **send** under these circumstances is slow.

IF YOUR SCRIPT IS TOO LONG

HyperCard limits the length of a script to 29,996 characters. Occasionally, you may write a script so long that it runs into this limit. This is most likely in stack scripts, which may hold utility handlers used by other objects throughout the stack.

First of all, avoid the temptation to save space by replacing all your descriptive names for variables and handlers with single-character names, and removing all comments and blank lines. This will indeed make your script shorter, and it's usually the first impulse of an inexperienced programmer who encounters this situation. But it's a poor choice of strategies, since it makes your code almost impossible to read, debug, and maintain.

If you do run into this limit, there are a number of ways to deal with it:

- Place another stack in the message-passing path with the **start using** command. This approach is particularly appropriate if you're developing a multiple-stack application. A **start using** stack can act like a library of handlers, eliminating the need to put a copy of each one in each stack.

- Move handlers to an earlier level in the message-passing path, if possible. If your stack script contains a handler that's used only by objects on one particular card, move that handler to the card's script to free some space in the stack script.

- Create a library object (perhaps a hidden button) and move handlers there. This can help you organize the overflowing script. For instance, if you have a number of handlers that all deal with some aspect of maintaining the menu bar, you might put all of them into a single button and use statements such as `send "updateMenuForGraphics" to background button "Menu Handlers"`.

Memory

Normally, HyperCard's application memory provides plenty of room for stack operations. If you need to use more, you can boost HyperCard's memory allocation from its Get Info box in the Finder.

However, there are situations in which you can't increase the memory allocated to HyperCard. Your stack's use of memory is affected by a number of things, some of which you can change to make it less likely that users will run out of memory while using your stack.

TRADE OFF VARIABLE SIZE FOR SPEED

As mentioned earlier in this chapter, it's faster to access information when it's stored in a variable than when it's contained in a field or a text file on disk. However, if you need to manipulate a vast store of data, you may run out of memory if you try to read all of it into a variable at once.

To avoid this problem, you might want to read in data a piece at a time. For example, this handler reads from a file and places the resulting data into fields, but it reads only 30K at a time. This ensures that the handler won't run out of memory, even if you use it to read a multimegabyte text file:

```
on getFile theFile
   open file theFile
   read from file theFile for 30000 -- maximum memory use
   repeat until it is empty
      repeat with x = 1 to the number of lines in it - 1
         doMenu "New Card"
         put line x of it into field "Text"
      end repeat
      put last line of it into partialLine
      read from file theFile for 30000
      put partialLine before it
   end repeat
   close file theFile
end getFile
```

This handler is slightly slower than one that reads the data all at one time, but it's still a great deal faster than one that reads only a line at a time.

EMPTY OUT GLOBALS YOU NO LONGER NEED

As has been mentioned elsewhere, global variables stay around until you quit HyperCard. If you place data in a global, the data keeps taking up memory until you quit. So once you're finished with a global's data, put empty into the global to free up the memory it uses.

CHECK THE HEAPSPACE BEFORE DOING MEMORY-INTENSIVE TASKS

Certain tasks, such as displaying large color pictures or using the paint tools, take more memory. If there is any question about whether enough memory will be available, use the **heapSpace** function first to check whether there's enough to do what you want to do.

4

Using XCMDs, XCFNs, and Resources

This chapter tells you where to find XCMDs, XFCNs, digitized sound files, and other resources, and explains how to install and use them in your stacks. To find out how to write your own XCMDs and XFCNs, see Apple's Script Language Guide.

How Resources Work

Each Macintosh file consists of two parts, a *data fork* and a *resource fork*. The data fork of a stack contains all the information about the stack's objects, its scripts, text, and so on. The resource fork of a stack can either be empty or contain ancillary data in special formats, such as icons and externals. Each piece of data in the resource fork is a separate resource.

Each kind of resource has a four-character type signature associated with it. Table 4.1 lists some kinds of resources that can be used in stacks, along with their resource type signatures.

Table 4.1 Resource Types

Type	Kind of Resource
CURS	A custom cursor
FOND	A font family resource
FONT	A bitmapped font
ICON	A black-and-white icon
PICT	A color or black-and-white picture (see the **picture** command in Part III)
PLTE	A floating palette (see the **palette** command in Part III)
snd	A digitized sound (Note: The last character of this type is a space.)
XCMD	An external command
XFCN	An external function

Each resource of a particular type has a resource ID number that's unique within that type. Resources can also have names.

HyperCard can use resources stored in the resource fork of the current stack, any stack in use, the Home stack, HyperCard itself, or the System file. For more information about how HyperCard uses resources, see Chapter 10.

EXTERNALS

HyperCard external commands and functions (or, more simply, externals) are resources that contain compiled code, which can be written in almost any Macintosh programming language. Because they're resources, externals can reside in the resource fork of any stack, HyperCard itself, or the System file.

From the viewpoint of a scripter, an XCMD is a command added to HyperTalk's vocabulary, just like a custom message handler (see the **on** keyword in Part III), and an XFCN is a function added to HyperTalk's vocabulary, just like a custom function handler (see the **function** keyword in Part III). Externals are called in the same way as custom handlers.

You can use externals to do things that HyperTalk doesn't let you do (such as gaining access to some aspects of the hardware or operating system, or controlling an external device) and things that a general-purpose language like HyperTalk isn't well-suited for (like complex numeric calculations). Thousands of externals have been written to do all sorts of things. A few examples are:

- Fast computation and number-crunching
- Changing the current printer
- Displaying a floating palette with scrolling text
- Resetting the system clock
- Controlling a videodisk player
- Printing a PICT file

HyperCard itself has several externals built in: The script editor and debugger, the Variable Watcher, the Message Watcher, and the **flash**, **palette**, and **picture** commands are all XCMD resources located in HyperCard's resource fork.

SOUNDS, PICTURES, CURSORS, AND ICONS

HyperCard lets you place digitized sounds, pictures, cursors, and icons in the resource fork of any stack:

- To play digitized sounds through the Macintosh speaker, use the **play** command.
- To display a picture resource, use the **picture** command.
- To use a custom cursor, set the **cursor** property.
- To have a button display a custom icon, set the button's **icon** property.

Embedding fonts in a stack

Apple Developer Technical Services states the following, in the technical note on Fonts: "Fonts should never be stored in a document's resource fork. If you close a font-laden document, the system will retain references to memory which was deallocated when the document closed; the system could then alter memory at those locations and corrupt the heap. In addition, System 7 does not support the storing of fonts in document resources. Note that HyperCard stacks are documents. If you feel that your stack loses all its artistic merit without a certain font, you should license it for distribution in a suitcase file and let the users install it in their systems."

On the other hand, many, many developers—including groups within Apple—have released stacks with embedded fonts, and we aren't aware of any problem that the practice has caused in actual use. The memory problem described appears to be unlikely to crop up unless the user closes stacks and opens new ones several times within a single session. And the suggested solution of requiring users to install a font in their system files is unsatisfactory, particularly for commercial and freeware stacks. However, it is unlikely that DTS would have released this warning for no reason. The best solution is probably to avoid embedding fonts unless necessary, and to be watchful for signs of trouble—particularly out-of-memory problems—when developing and testing stacks with embedded fonts.

BITMAPPED FONTS

If you use particular fonts in your stack's fields, and you don't know whether your users will have those fonts, you'll need to do something about providing them. Users who don't have the fonts will still be able to open and use your stack, but HyperCard will attempt to substitute other fonts, and the results may be ugly. Some of your text may not be readable if font substitution takes place.

Assuming the menu bar is in its default state, you can use the following function from within a handler to tell whether a particular font is available:

```
function isInstalled theFonts
   if there is no menu "Font" then return "Error: no font menu"
   repeat with x = 1 to the number of items of theFonts
     get item x of theFonts
     if there is no menuItem it in menu "Font"
     then return false
   end repeat
   return true
end isInstalled
```

You might use the function like this:

```
on  openStack
   if not  isInstalled("Avant Garde")  then
     beep
     answer "This stack uses the Avant Garde font, which is" ¬
     && "not installed. If you don't install Avant Garde," ¬
     && "you can still use the stack, but you may notice" ¬
     && "some cosmetic problems."
   end if
end openStack
```

By the way, if you do decide to put a font in your stack's resource fork, do *not* use ResEdit or another resource mover to install it. Instead, use Font/DA Mover. (Font/DA Mover lets you open stack files if you hold down the Option key while clicking Open.) Font/DA Mover, unlike ResEdit, installs the important FOND resource along with the font.

If you install a font into a stack, compact it afterwards while holding down the Option and Command keys. This rebuilds the stack's internal font table and helps to avoid problems with font conflicts.

WHERE TO GET EXTERNALS AND RESOURCES

Of course, you can always learn to write your own externals, use sound-recording software and hardware to digitize your own sound resources, and so on. However, there are literally thousands of XCMDs and XFCNs available free or for a small fee. (If you're planning to use someone else's XCMD in a commercial stack, check with the XCMD author to see whether he or she allows such distribution. Most authors will; some ask an additional fee if you're going to sell a stack that uses their XCMD.) There are also plenty of short sound clips and clip art in the public domain, and some packages are available commercially.

The resource utility ResEdit is owned by Apple, but you can get it from licensed distributors such as APDA (the Apple Programmers' and Developers' Association). You can contact APDA at 800/282-2732 or 716/871-6555. Many user groups and online services are also licensed by Apple to distribute ResEdit. Many user groups also offer public-domain software for a small charge per disk, including clip art, sounds, stacks, and externals.

USER GROUPS

If you have no local user group, you can obtain a wide variety of software from these two national user groups:

BMUG (Berkeley Macintosh User Group)
1442 A Walnut St. # 62
Berkeley, CA 94709
510/849-2684
bmug@aol.com

BCS (Boston Computer Society)
48 Grove St.
Somerville, MA 02144
617/252-0600

ONLINE SOURCES

If you have a modem, you can access a number of software collections available for downloading.

CompuServe

ResEdit can be found in the Mac Developer's forum (GO MACDEV); a large collection of externals and stacks is available in the HyperCard forum (GO HYPER).

AppleLink

ResEdit is available for downloading in the Developer Services folder. The Code Exchange folder also offers a number of wide-ranging XCMD collections.

Internet

The site ftp.apple.com offers ResEdit for anonymous ftp. There are also a number of ftp archive sites offering collections of stacks, externals, sounds, pictures, and other software.

ROLLING YOUR OWN

If you're an experienced programmer using another development system in a compiled language like C or Pascal, you can write your own externals if your compiler can create standalone code resources.

If you prefer to write your externals in HyperTalk, CompileIt! from Heizer Software lets you do just that. CompileIt! gives you full access to the Macintosh operating system's Toolbox routines from within a HyperTalk handler that you compile into an XCMD or XFCN. You can reach Heizer Software at:

Heizer Software
1941 Oak Park Blvd., Suite 30
P.O. Box 232019
Pleasant Hill, CA 94523
800/888-7667
510/943-7667

To create icons, you can use HyperCard's own icon editor. Choose Icon from the Edit menu to bring up the icon editor. The icons you create in the icon editor are stored in the current stack.

Here's a handler that asks a user to create a new icon for a button:

```
on makeIconFor theButton
   answer "Please create a new icon for this button."
   select button theButton
   doMenu "Icon..."
   -- set up button properties
```

```
set the height of button theButton to 60
set the width of button theButton to 60
set the showName of button theButton to false
set the style of button theButton to transparent
choose browse tool
end makeIconFor
```

Installing Resources

The most widely used tool for resource copying is ResEdit, which is a utility program published by Apple Computer. ResEdit's operation is simple. Each open file appears as a window with a list of resource types. Select and open a resource type to display all the resources of that type in the file. You can use the usual Cut, Copy, and Paste menu items to move resources from one file to another.

Another useful tool for resource management is the ResCopy card in the Power Tools stack that comes with HyperCard. (This card is based on a more flexible external written by Steve Maller for HyperCard 1.x. Unfortunately, this original ResCopy long since vanished into the bowels of Apple and was never seen again.) The ResCopy card works like Font/DA Mover. You can open two files at once, and the resources in each file will appear in a scrolling field. You can select, copy, and remove resources using the ResCopy card.

Caution: Moving resources is one of those things that can be dangerous. If there's a crash while you're in the midst of moving a resource into a stack, the stack may be rendered unusable. So when you're playing with resources, always make sure you have a current backup of the stacks you're working on.

Using Externals in Handlers

As noted above, XCMDs and XFCNs act like message handlers and function handlers, respectively, and you call them the same way from a handler. The function or command call sends a message through the message-passing path, and the XCMD or XFCN of the same name traps that message. (For more about the role of resources in the message-passing path, see Chapter 10.)

For example, suppose you want to use an XCMD named setSoundVolume, which sets the volume of the speaker to some number that you pass:

```
on speakerVolume
   repeat -- loop until you get a valid volume
     ask "What volume (between 1 and 7)?" with 5
     put it into newVolume
     if newVolume ≥1 and newVolume ≤7 then exit repeat
     else beep 2 -- get user's attention if invalid value
   end repeat
   setSoundVolume newVolume -- call the setSoundVolume XCMD
end speakerVolume
```

To invoke an XFCN in HyperTalk, you use it as if it were a function. For example, suppose the XFCN `currentPrinter` returns the name of the currently selected printer:

```
on printStatusReport
  global colorPrinterName
  if currentPrinter() is not colorPrinterName then
    doMenu "Chooser"
    put "Click when ready..."
    wait until the mouseClick
  end if
  open report printing with template "Status"
  print 5 cards
  close printing
end printStatusReport
```

Since XCMDs and XFCNs respond to messages, they can trap messages. For example, you can override any HyperTalk command or function called from within the current stack by placing an XCMD or XFCN with the same name in the resource fork of the current stack.

Freedom and responsibility department

When an external starts running, HyperCard relinquishes control of the computer to it. This means, among other things, that you can't stop a runaway external by pressing Command-period. An external that doesn't follow the rules of Macintosh programming can destroy the current stack. (As James Redfern, HyperCard tester and one of the original members of the HyperCard Development team, once said, "We've got to stop these people before they kill again!")

If you've just gotten a new external, test it in a backup of your stack. Do not subject the only copy of your precious data to the uncertain mercies of an XCMD whose stability you are unsure of.

USING EXTERNALS WITH OTHER SCRIPT LANGUAGES

XCMDs and XFCNs are fully accessible to AppleScript and other OSA script languages. You use the same calling sequence that's used for commands and functions in that language.

There's one small difference between the way externals are treated in HyperTalk and the way they behave with other script languages. When an OSA call that's moving through the message-passing path reaches the resource fork, HyperCard looks first for an XCMD with the same name, then (if there's no XCMD) for an XFCN. This is the opposite of the precedence in HyperTalk.

5

AppleScript and AppleEvents

HyperTalk not only lets you control all elements of the HyperCard application, it gives you the means to communicate with other applications running on your Mac, or even with other Macs on the same network. You do this by using messages called AppleEvents.

The first three sections of this chapter describe AppleEvents, the Mac operating system's method for communicating between applications, and tells you how to control them with HyperTalk. The last four sections concentrate on AppleScript, Apple's systemwide scripting language, and how to use it in your HyperCard stacks.

Important: *To use the features described in this chapter, you must be using System 7.*

What Are AppleEvents?

An AppleEvent is a message that one program (the sender) sends to another program (the target). Typically, an AppleEvent asks the target to perform some action, like printing a document or closing a window, or to send back information.

In order to send and receive AppleEvents, a program must be "AppleEvent-aware." That is, it must support the programming calls that the operating system provides to access AppleEvents. A sender can send AppleEvents to any other AppleEvent-aware program running on the same Macintosh. If your Mac is connected to a network, its applications can send and receive AppleEvents from any other AppleEvent-aware program running on any Mac on the network.

THE PARTS OF AN APPLEEVENT

Each AppleEvent contains several distinct parts. The most important parts for HyperTalk scripters are as follows:

Event Class

The event class is a four-character code that designates the general group the AppleEvent is in. Typical event classes include:

- `aevt`: the set of AppleEvents required for System 7
- `core`: AppleEvents sent by many AppleScript commands
- `WILD`: AppleEvents sent by many HyperCard-specific commands used in AppleScript
- `misc`: miscellaneous useful AppleEvents

In order to be System 7-friendly, an application must accept the four events of the `aevt` class. These are the events that launch the application, open or print a document, and quit the application.

Event ID

The event ID is a four-character code that designates exactly what event is being sent. Here are some commonly used event IDs:

- `clos` (close document): close a document
- `dosc` (do script): execute a set of statements using the target's script language
- `eval` (evaluate): compute the value of an expression
- `oapp` (open application): open the application
- `odoc` (open document): open one or more documents
- `pdoc` (print document): print one or more documents
- `quit` (quit): quit the application

AppleEvent Data

The data contains the meat of the AppleEvent. For example, the data portion of an `odoc` event is a list of the documents to be opened.

You can use the **request** command to examine the various parts of an AppleEvent that's been sent to HyperCard.

For more information about AppleEvents and the AppleEvent data structure, see *Inside Macintosh: Interapplication Communication.*

Sending AppleEvents from a Handler

A number of HyperCard commands work by sending AppleEvents to other programs:

- The **open application** command has the effect of sending the `odoc` AppleEvent to the application if you specify a document to open. If you specify only the application, with no document, it has the effect of sending the `oapp` AppleEvent instead. All System 7-friendly applications accept these AppleEvents.

- The **print document** command has the effect of sending a `pdoc` AppleEvent to the application. All System 7-friendly applications accept this AppleEvent.

- The **close application** command sends the `clos` AppleEvent if you specify a document to close. If you specify only the application, with no document, it sends the `quit`

AppleEvent instead. All System 7-friendly applications accept the `quit` AppleEvent, but those with minimal AppleEvent support may not accept `clos`.

- The **send to program** command sends the `dosc` AppleEvent. This AppleEvent is supported by many applications that have their own scripting systems, such as MPW, HyperCard, and FileMaker Pro.

- The **request** command sends the `eval` AppleEvent. This AppleEvent is supported only by applications that can evaluate expressions.

Handling AppleEvents

You write a handler to intercept AppleEvents that other programs send to HyperCard. From within the handler, you can check which program or Mac sent the event, what kind of event it is, and other information about it, and filter the AppleEvents, depending on your own criteria. Some AppleEvents cause HyperCard to perform some action, and you can also use handlers to override HyperCard's usual behavior for these AppleEvents.

THE APPLEEVENT MESSAGE

Whenever another application sends HyperCard an AppleEvent, HyperCard sends an **appleEvent** message to the current card. The following example posts an alert each time HyperCard receives an AppleEvent, and lets you either accept or reject it:

```
on appleEvent
   answer "The following AppleEvent was received:" ¬
   & return & the params & return & return ¬
   & "Do you wish to accept it?" with "Reject" or "Accept"
   if it is "Accept" then pass appleEvent
end appleEvent
```

To use the above handler to check all AppleEvents, add the handler to the script of the Home stack.

AppleEvents and AppleScript Commands

HyperCard lets you use many of its commands in AppleScript scripts. When another application sends an AppleScript command to HyperCard, HyperCard sends the **appleEvent** message to the current card. However, if you use an AppleScript command from within HyperCard, no **appleEvent** message is sent. HyperCard only sends the **appleEvent** message in response to commands from other programs.

THE REPLY AND REQUEST APPLEEVENT COMMANDS

You can use the **reply** command within an **appleEvent** handler to send back a response to the program that sent the AppleEvent. You might want to do this to return an error message if the AppleEvent is rejected:

```
on appleEvent
   answer "The following AppleEvent was received:" ¬
   & return & the params & return & return ¬
   & "Do you wish to accept it?" with "Reject" or "Accept"
   if it is "Reject" then reply "Event was rejected by user."
   else pass appleEvent
end appleEvent
```

The **request appleEvent** command lets you examine portions of the AppleEvent's data structure. For more information, see the **request appleEvent** command.

SETTING UP YOUR MAC FOR NETWORK APPLEEVENTS

You don't need to do anything special before sending AppleEvents between programs on your own Mac. However, before other Macs on the network can send AppleEvents to your Mac, you need to set up the Mac for program linking. To turn on program linking, open the Sharing Setup control panel and click Start in the Program Linking section (see Figure 5.1).

This setting allows registered users to send AppleEvents to programs running on your Mac. The next step is to create registered users and give them individual permission to link to programs on your Mac. Open the Users & Groups control panel (Figure 5.2) to specify which users may send you AppleEvents.

To let a specific user send AppleEvents to your programs, open the user's icon and check the Allow User To Link checkbox. If you want to let any user on the network send AppleEvents to your programs, open the Guest icon and check the Allow Guests To Link checkbox.

Finally, to let other Macs send AppleEvents to your copy of HyperCard, select the HyperCard application in the Finder, choose Sharing from the File menu, and check the Allow Remote Program Linking checkbox.

Important: AppleEvents can be used to control many aspects of applications on your Mac. If you give Program Linking privileges to guests, anyone on the network with the proper

Figure 5.1   Sharing Setup control panel

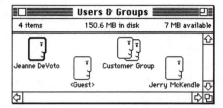

Figure 5.2   Users & Groups control panel

software can potentially interfere with programs running on your Mac. Consider carefully which users you want to allow to link to your Mac's programs.

For more information about users, groups, and program linking, see Apple's *Macintosh Networking Reference* or other documentation that came with your Macintosh.

HyperCard and AppleScript

AppleScript is a general, system-wide script language. You can write AppleScript code within HyperCard as well as within other applications such as Apple's Script Editor. Most AppleScript code is written either to control other applications or to get information from them. The ability to write AppleScript scripts in an application, tying them to objects in that application, is referred to as *attachability*.

AppleScript works by sending AppleEvents to the target program. The AppleScript language itself contains only the most general commands and functions, but target programs can implement their own AppleScript commands to control that application's elements. Applications which can be controlled by AppleScript and provide additional AppleScript commands of their own are called *scriptable* applications.

HyperCard version 2.2 is both attachable and scriptable.

ATTACHABILITY

In HyperCard, you write scripts in AppleScript the same way you write them in HyperTalk. Any HyperCard object can have a script, and you can specify HyperTalk or AppleScript as the script language for that object. (But you can't write part of a script in HyperTalk and part in AppleScript.) If you want to, you can write all the scripts in your stack in AppleScript.

AppleScript scripts can contain handlers, just like HyperTalk scripts. AppleScript responds to all HyperCard's system messages (although the names differ in a few cases), so you can write a button script that looks like the one below and the handler will run when you click the button:

```
on mouseUp -- this is AppleScript code
   copy (seconds) to theSeconds
   tell application "Super Spreadsheet"
      copy theSeconds to cell 10 of row 1 -- centered
   end tell
end mouseUp
```

As you can see, AppleScript looks very much like HyperTalk (although there are a number of areas of difference, which are outlined briefly in the section "The HyperTalk Language and AppleScript" in this chapter).

AppleScript scripts, unlike HyperTalk scripts, can contain statements that are outside any handler. To execute such scripts, send the **run** message to the object. This message executes all statements in the object's script that aren't contained in a handler.

Most of the time, you'll use AppleScript in HyperCard objects to control other AppleScript-savvy applications, and to do things (like access the contents of the Clipboard) that HyperTalk doesn't easily support.

You enter and edit AppleScript scripts just like HyperTalk scripts. Open the script editor using any of the methods described in Chapter 2. The HyperCard 2.2 script editor has a Scripting Language popup menu at the top of the script window. To change an object's script language, just select the language you want from the popup menu. Changing the scripting language does not affect the contents of the script window, so if you change an object's script language, you'll also need to rewrite any existing statements to run in the new language.

You can also use the **scriptingLanguage** property to change the script language an object uses. The following statement changes the script language accepted by the message box:

```
set the scriptingLanguage to AppleScript
```

AppleScript, unlike HyperTalk, compiles scripts when you close and save the script. Because of this, you may notice a delay when you close a script written in AppleScript. The script editor will also warn you about any syntax errors when you save the script, instead of waiting until you try to run it.

Don't compact with earlier versions of HyperCard

You can open stacks created with HyperCard 2.2 in earlier 2.0 versions (although 2.2-specific features won't work properly). But if the stack contains AppleScript scripts (or scripts written in any language other than HyperTalk), compacting it under earlier versions will truncate those scripts, and may corrupt the stack.

SCRIPTABILITY

The AppleScript language itself contains only basic commands. However, an individual application can extend AppleScript by making application-specific commands, functions, and objects available to all AppleScript scripts. AppleScript scripts written to control that application can then use these application-specific elements.

HyperCard 2.2 uses this mechanism to make much of the body of HyperTalk language elements available to AppleScript scripters, letting them control specific elements of the HyperCard interface (windows, buttons, fields, and so on) from AppleScript scripts.

These language elements are defined in the `aete` resource in the HyperCard application. You can view the contents of this resource by opening the AppleScript Script Editor application (which is copied to your disk when you install AppleScript) and choosing the

Open Dictionary command from the File menu. The dictionary displays the `aete` resource of any application, letting you check the syntax of each command that HyperCard makes available to AppleScript (see Figure 5.3).

For more information about the HyperTalk commands you can use in AppleScript scripts, see the *HyperCard AppleScript Reference* stack.

The HyperTalk Language and AppleScript

This section describes some elements of AppleScript from the viewpoint of an experienced HyperTalk programmer. However, a complete description of the AppleScript language is beyond the scope of this chapter. For more information about programming in AppleScript, see Apple's *AppleScript Language Guide*.

SIMILARITIES AND DIFFERENCES

As programming languages, HyperTalk and AppleScript are closely related. Both use an English-like syntax, and both communicate using events and message-passing. Some of the vocabulary is different, sometimes in subtle ways, but if you are comfortable with HyperTalk, you'll be able to write AppleScript code after only a little study. Mechanics like the comment delimiter (--) and the line-continuation character (¬) are the same in both languages.

Many of the differences result from the fact that HyperTalk is specialized to control all aspects of the HyperCard application, while AppleScript is a system-wide scripting language that can be used with any application capable of supporting AppleEvents. The AppleScript language itself contains only basic commands; it is a sparser language with fewer elements than HyperTalk. HyperCard extends AppleScript by making application-specific commands, functions, and objects available, so AppleScript scripts written to control HyperCard can use any of these elements.

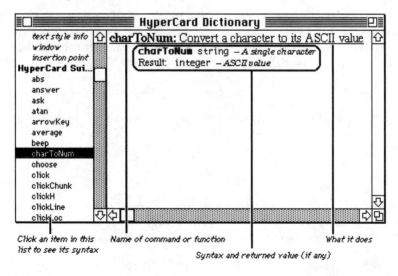

Figure 5.3   Viewing the HyperCard dictionary in the Script Editor application

COMMON GOTCHAS FOR NATIVE HYPERTALK SPEAKERS

As mentioned above, HyperTalk and AppleScript have many similarities. This section mentions some of the subtle differences that can trip up a programmer who's used to HyperTalk.

You Can Refer to an Object Directly or within a "tell" Structure

For example, the following structure sets a field property:

```
tell application "HyperCard 2.2"
   tell stack "Home"
     set the fixedLineHeight of card field 12 ¬
     of first card to true
   end tell
end tell
```

And this structure does the same thing:

```
tell application "HyperCard 2.2"
   tell stack "Home"
     tell card 1
        set the fixedLineHeight of card field 12 to true
     end tell
   end tell
end tell
```

AppleScript Variables Are Typed

HyperTalk is a typeless language, meaning that all variables and containers are of the same type. However, AppleScript has various variable types; certain operations will accept only certain variable types, and you have to make certain the types match. In some cases, you'll need to temporarily convert a variable's type during the operation, using the as *type* option:

```
copy the clipboard as text to line 1 of card field 1
```

The necessity of using file references rather than pathnames is related. In HyperTalk, you can simply use a file's pathname to refer to it:

```
put "My Disk:Test" into myFile
open file myFile
```

However, AppleScript does not recognize a text string as a reference to a file; you have to specify that the pathname is a file reference, or AppleScript will be unable to work with it. This is the AppleScript equivalent of the above two HyperTalk lines:

```
copy (a reference to the file "My Disk:Test") to myFile
open  myFile
```

AppleScript's "result" Variable Is Not the Same as HyperTalk's "result" Function

Although they have the same name, AppleScript's "result" and HyperTalk's "result" are not at all the same thing. After every AppleScript evaluation, the resulting value is placed in the result variable. AppleScript's result variable is used somewhat like the **it** variable in HyperTalk.

AppleScript's "it" Variable Is Not the Same as HyperTalk's "it" Variable.

Naturally, AppleScript has a variable named "it". And naturally, it doesn't mean the same thing that **it** does in HyperTalk, so you also need to watch out for statements that use "it". In AppleScript, the **it** variable refers to the object currently being controlled in a **tell** structure:

```
tell application "FileMaker Pro"
   get word 2 of it -- yields "Pro"
end tell
```

AppleScript Scripts Can Have Statements that Are Outside Any Handler.

In HyperTalk, all statements are executed as the result of a message, and must be enclosed in a message handler. You can type statements into a script and leave them outside any of the script's message handlers, but they're never executed and HyperCard treats them like comments.

In AppleScript, an object's script can contain lines outside any handler. This code runs when you send a **run** message to the object. However, most of the time you'll probably prefer to enclose your statements in handlers for convenience.

Using Other Scripting Languages

Apple's Open Scripting Architecture (OSA) provides system-level support for a variety of script languages. You can write HyperTalk scripts in any OSA language, not just AppleScript, using the methods discussed earlier in this chapter. Any OSA languages you have installed on your system appear in the Scripting Language pop-up menu in the script editor, and you can set the **scriptingLanguage** property to any installed language. However, there are a few differences between the way HyperCard handles AppleScript and the way it handles other OSA languages.

The Message Watcher shows all messages, even those that are being sent to objects whose scripting language is not HyperTalk. However, if the target object's scripting language is something other than HyperTalk or AppleScript, the Message Watcher can't tell whether the object will handle the message, so it encloses in brackets messages heading for such objects.

The AppleScript language understands the concept of messages sent to an object. This means that, just like in HyperTalk, you can enclose code in a message handler, and when the object receives that message, it executes the statements in the handler. However, some OSA languages don't incorporate the concept of messages. A script in such a language has no handlers and can't be triggered by an ordinary message. HyperCard provides the **run** message to let you execute scripts in such languages:

```
send "run" to card button "QuicKeys Script"
```

6

Coding for Special Environments

When you develop a stack, you use the full scripting-capable version of HyperCard, and normally the stack resides on a hard disk. However, some stacks you develop may need to run under conditions that are different from this typical development setup. This chapter shows you how to adapt your HyperTalk code for best performance in three such situations, and describes the special considerations you need to be aware of.

The first section tells you how to write stacks to be used with the HyperCard Player. It also reveals the special problems and pitfalls of constructing standalone applications. The second section discusses some of the special considerations you need to be aware of when writing code for a stack to be distributed on CD-ROM. And the third section shows you how to use HyperTalk to improve users' ability to access your stack over a network.

The Player and Standalone Applications

Apple has included a copy of the HyperCard Player with each Macintosh sold since sometime in 1992. The Player is essentially a version of HyperCard from which all authoring and scripting features have been removed. The Player lets people use stacks developed by others, but doesn't let them create their own stacks.

HyperCard version 2.2 lets you make any stack into a standalone application. These applications behave like any other Macintosh application. You launch them by double-clicking them, and they don't require HyperCard to work. However, both the Player and standalones have certain limitations and special considerations you should be aware of when programming for these environments.

LIMITATIONS OF THE PLAYER

For the most part, the Player works the same way as the HyperCard development environment. However, there are a few differences, which are listed in this section. When you're writing scripts for a stack that will be used with the Player, you'll need to keep the following limitations in mind. (You can check the **environment** property from within a handler to see whether your stack is running under HyperCard itself, or under the Player or a standalone.)

User Level

In the Player, the **userLevel** is limited to 4 (Authoring). The command `set the userLevel to 5` sets the user level to 4. A handler can execute all the commands available from this user level.

However, users are effectively limited to a user level of 3. Users cannot choose the button or field tool manually, and the Objects menu does not appear when in the Player regardless of the user level setting. A handler can choose the button or field tool; however, if one of these tools is chosen, the Player reverts to the browse tool when all the running handlers finish.

Printing

When you launch the Player, all the menu items relating to printing, except Print Card and Page Setup, are disabled. You can enable these items in a handler, but the Player does not include the dialogs for Print Stack, Print Field, and Print Report. So choosing these menu items does nothing unless your stack has a **doMenu** handler to intercept these menu choices.

Since the printing dialogs aren't included in the Player, commands that depend on those dialog boxes will fail. Nothing happens when these commands are executed by the Player:

```
open printing with dialog -- does nothing in the Player
open report printing with dialog -- ditto
```

However, the Player will execute these commands in any form that doesn't present a dialog:

```
open printing -- these commands work fine in the Player
open report printing
open report printing with template templateName
```

Menu Items and Dialogs

The Objects menu does not appear in the Player, even if the **userLevel** is set to 4. The Info dialogs for various objects are not included in the Player. However, you can choose other items from the Objects menu (New Button, New Field, New Background, Bring Closer, Send Farther) using a **doMenu** command.

The Icon menu item in the Edit menu is disabled when the Player starts up, and the icon editor is not included in the Player. You can enable the menu item in a script, but, as with the printing menu items, choosing it does nothing.

When the Player starts up, the New Stack menu item is disabled. But a handler can use the **enable** command to make this menu item available to users.

No Peeking Allowed

The **cantPeek** property is set to false. The "Can't Peek" checkbox in the Protect Stack dialog is disabled, and trying to change the property from a handler has no effect.

Message Box Limitations

In the development version of HyperCard, you can execute any HyperTalk command, or evaluate any expression, by typing it into the message box and pressing Return or Enter. However, the Player does not let users evaluate expressions in the message box, and the only command it executes is **find**. You can use any form of the **find** command in the Player's message box, but if you type in any other command or expression and press Return or Enter, the Player only beeps.

You can use the **put** command to put anything you want into the message box, so it is still useful for displaying information to the user.

If you put the following handlers into your stack scripts, users with the Player can execute HyperTalk commands and evaluate expressions in the message box when using your stack. This can be invaluable when you're testing your stack with the Player and need to make changes or check properties on the fly:

```
on returnKey -- to send a message
   do message box
   select empty
end returnKey


on enterKey -- to evaluate an expression
   put value(message) into message box
   select empty
end enterKey
```

Scripting and Script Errors

All scripting tools, including the script editor and debugger, the Message Watcher, and the Variable Watcher, have been removed from the Player. You cannot use any of the methods described in Chapter 2 to edit scripts. However, you can still use the **get** and **set** commands to view and change scripts from within a handler.

If a handler causes a runtime error, the dialog in Figure 6.1 appears. The text that appears in the dialog is in the following form: "This operation can't continue because an error has occurred: *errorText* in *handlerName*. Please contact the author of this stack for assistance." The *errorText* is what would appear in the script error dialog if you got this error in HyperCard (see Figure 6.2).

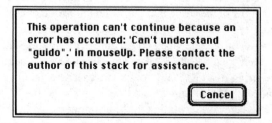

Figure 6.1   Player's script error dialog

**Figure 6.2   Same script error, but in the development
version of HyperCard**

You can set the **lockErrorDialogs** property to let you intercept script errors. If **lockErrorDialogs** is set to true, a script error sends an **errorDialog** message instead of putting up a dialog; you can then write a corresponding handler to do whatever you want with the message. The parameter to the **errorDialog** message is the *errorText* from the dialog: In this example, that text is

```
Can't understand "Guido".
```

Player 2.1 handles errors differently

Version 2.1 of the Player handles script errors differently from version 2.2. In 2.1, both compile-time and runtime errors produce an error code, rather than the usual error text (Figure 6.3).

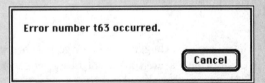

Figure 6.3   Player 2.1 error dialog

If the **lockErrorDialogs** property is true, the contents of this dialog is sent as the parameter to the **errorDialog** message, rather than being displayed in a dialog box.

The error code is actually a reference to a string resource within HyperCard. The first character of the error number, "t", indicates that the dialog corresponds to the STR# resource which contains HyperTalk error messages. This is STR# 132. The remainder of the error code corresponds to the number of the string that makes up the error message.

You can use ResEdit or another resource-editing utility to read the error string resources. To check the meaning of an error code, open HyperCard 2.1 with ResEdit, open the STR# resource window, then open STR# 132. The number in the error code corresponds to the number of the string in STR# 132. For example, if you get error number t63, look up string number 63 ("Can't understand ^0.") in the STR# 132 resource. This string is the error message corresponding to the error code t63.

You can create a table of error numbers and their corresponding strings, and use the table in an **errorDialog** handler to translate these strings into human-readable form.

STANDALONE APPLICATIONS

When you create a standalone application from a stack, the stack—its objects, scripts, card and background pictures, and so on—is placed in the data fork of the standalone, and all the resources belonging to the Player are put in the resource fork. A standalone application is essentially made of the Player plus your stack. This means, among other things, that standalones have the same limitations as stacks run with the Player: The **userLevel** is limited to 4, some menu items are disabled, and so on.

When to Make a Standalone

Since all Macs for the past several years have been bundled with either HyperCard or the Player, most Mac owners will have the program they need to run your stack. However, despite this, there are several reasons you might want to make your stack into a standalone application.

First, while almost all Mac owners have either HyperCard or the Player, some people might not have it installed on their systems. Such users can run a standalone application without having to locate and install HyperCard first.

Second, your users may have a version of HyperCard that's not recent enough to run your stack. If the stack uses capabilities that are available only in recent versions of HyperCard, distributing it in standalone form ensures that users won't have compatibility problems.

Third, standalone applications are ideal when you're developing a multistack application. Many multistack applications make changes to the environment—such as adding custom menus and menu items. Such changes must be removed whenever the user switches to a stack that's not part of the application, and restored when the user returns. This can cause a significant slowdown, particularly when switching from one stack to another. Since the standalone is intended to run only the stacks in a single application, and not other stacks, this overhead is not necessary in the standalone environment.

If you're designing such an application, choose one stack to be the standalone. This should be the stack you want the user to see first when starting up your application. Since a standalone has all the capabilities of the Player, it can open any other stack in your application. (Don't make each stack into a standalone. If you do, each one will run as a separate application, and they won't be able to communicate with each other.)

A fourth reason to make your stack into a standalone is so it can use documents other than stacks. Only stacks can belong to HyperCard, but a standalone application can use documents of any type (see "Creating a Standalone," below, for more information about specifying a document type). When you save a standalone, you can specify a document type for that standalone to open. Under System 7, dropping a file of that type onto the standalone's icon launches the standalone.

For example, suppose you've written a standalone to work with text files. If you've specified TEXT as the document type for your standalone, you can drop any text files onto the standalone's icon. The standalone then processes those files in whatever way you specify, by intercepting the **appleEvent** message that HyperCard (or, in this case, the standalone) sends when it opens a file. The following example prints the incoming text files and quits when it's finished:

```
on appleEvent theClass,theID,theSender -- collect text files
   -- hold down command-option-shift to open the standalone
   if the optionKey is down and the commandKey is down ¬
   and the shiftKey is down then pass appleEvent
   -- get just the name of the sending program
   get the itemDelimiter
   set the itemDelimiter to colon
   put last item of theSender into sendingProgram
   set the itemDelimiter to it
   -- did the event result from dropping a file on me?
   if theClass is "aevt" and theID is "odoc" ¬
   and sendingProgram is "Finder" then
      -- set up printing properties, which are stored in the stack
      set the printTextFont to card field "Font"
      set the printTextSize to card field "Size"
      -- read and print each file
      lock screen
      lock messages
      set the cursor to watch
      put "Reading text files..."
      request appleEvent data -- this is the file pathnames
      put it into filenameList
      repeat with x = 1 to the number of lines of filenameList
        open file (line x of filenameList)
        read from file (line x of filenameList) until end
        close file (line x of filenameList)
        print it
      end repeat
      doMenu "Quit HyperCard"
   else pass appleEvent
end appleEvent
```

The standalone described above takes and prints whatever files you drop onto its icon, quitting when it's finished. Such an application is called a *droplet*. You can use an AppleEvent handler like the one above to make droplet applications for almost any purpose. A droplet standalone can do any of the following tasks, and many more:

- Display a PICT file dropped onto it, using the **picture** command

- Filter all control characters out of a text file and write the file back to disk

- Concatenate the text files that are dropped onto it into a single file

- Convert a comma-delimited database file to a tab-delimited file

Limitation on 2.1 standalones

If you're using a standalone created by HyperCard 2.1 Player Tools, you can drop non-stack files onto it only if the standalone is already open. The reason has to do with the way HyperCard handles the first odoc (open document) AppleEvent it receives when starting up.

A user can launch an application by double-clicking the application, by selecting and double-clicking one or more files belonging to the application, or (with System 7) by dropping one or more files onto the application's icon. When the Finder first launches an application, it sends the application an open document AppleEvent, with a list of all the files the user double-clicked or dropped. When HyperCard receives this AppleEvent, it opens the first stack on the list. Then, if there's more than one stack, it removes that first stack from the list and sends an **appleEvent** message to the current card. This means that the stack doesn't get a chance to handle the first stack.

Unfortunately, 2.1 standalones do the same thing when they're launched: They assume the first file on the list is a stack, and try to open it. If the file isn't a stack—for example, if it's a text file—the standalone puts up an error dialog.

CREATING A STANDALONE

The procedure for creating a standalone application is simple. After you've completed your stack, choose Save a Copy from the File menu, and choose Application from the popup menu. If you want to set a version number, or if your standalone will use files other than stacks, click More Choices in the resulting dialog. The full dialog for saving standalones is in Figure 6.4. This dialog box lets you set a number of choices that will determine your application's behavior:

- The Creator box holds a four-character code that the Finder uses to determine which files

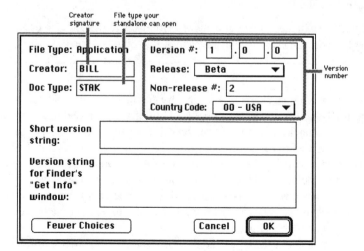

Figure 6.4   Standalone "More Choices" dialog

belong to which application. Each application has a unique creator signature, and the files that belong to it share that creator signature. When you double-click a document, the Finder looks at its creator to figure out which application to launch.

Multistack Applications

If your standalone is part of a multistack application, save the other stacks using the Custom File Type option from the popup menu in the Save a Copy dialog. This choice brings up a dialog similar to the one shown in Figure 6.4. Make sure the creator of the other stacks matches the creator you chose for the standalone. Doing this will let users launch the standalone by double-clicking any of the stacks that belong to it.

The mystery of creation

Because the Finder uses the creator signature to figure out which documents belong to which applications, you can get conflicts and strange results if more than one application on your system has the same creator, or if a non-application, such as an extension, has the same creator as one of your applications.

To prevent users from experiencing this problem with conflicting creator signatures, Apple's Developer Support Center maintains a registry of creator types, so developers can avoid reusing a creator type that's already in use. If you're planning to distribute your standalone, you should contact DTS to register your signature and confirm that no one else is already using it. You can contact the registry at this address:

Developer Support Center
Attn: C/F Type Administrator
20525 Mariani Avenue, M/S 303-2T
Cupertino, CA 95014
AppleLink: DEVSUPPORT

If you have online access, there is a document describing the registration procedure in the Developer Support folder on AppleLink, and at ftp.apple.com on the Internet.

- The Doc Type box holds a four-character file type. By default, this type is STAK, which is the file type for HyperCard stacks. Dropping a file of the specified type onto the standalone's icon will launch the standalone and send it an "open document" AppleEvent. The Player, and therefore all standalones, knows how to open stacks. But it does not know how to open other kinds of documents. If you substitute another file type code in this box, your standalone must contain code that opens the file (or does whatever you want to do with it.) To see how to do this with a text file (file type TEXT), see the example in "Standalone Applications," above. You are responsible for writing the handlers to deal with any non-stack files your standalone uses!

  For more information about file types and creator signatures, see *Inside Macintosh*.

- The items in the top right corner let you set the version number of your standalone. The top line sets the major rev, minor rev, and bugfix rev. The popup menu sets the development stage. For products that are not in the final development stage, the Non-release # specifies the number of this version within the current development stage.

    All these items correspond to the items reported by the **version** property. The statement `get the long version`, when executed from within the standalone, returns a value determined by what you type into these fields. The statement `get the version` returns the number of the HyperCard version that created the standalone.

STANDALONE LIMITATIONS

Since a standalone application includes what is essentially an embedded copy of the Player, it shares all the limitations detailed in "Limitations of the Player," earlier in this chapter. Furthermore, a standalone application, unlike HyperCard or the Player, does not have a Home stack. More precisely, a standalone *is* its own Home stack. It works like this. Whenever the Player starts up, it looks inside its data fork for a stack. If there is a stack there—that is, if this is a standalone rather than the Player application itself—that stack is treated as the Home stack. Otherwise, the Player looks for a stack named Home to use.

This has several consequences that you need to be aware of when writing the code for a stack that's destined to be made into a standalone application:

- The standalone's stack script must perform all the tasks the Home stack normally takes care of. For example, the Home stack's getHomeInfo handler sets the **userLevel** to the user's preferred level when HyperCard starts up. If your standalone does not set the user level, it starts up in user level 2 by default. If you need a higher user level, you'll need to set it yourself.

    The Home stack also stores a set of locations where HyperCard looks for stacks, documents, and applications. If your standalone goes to other stacks, or opens other applications or documents, you'll need to store these paths and maintain the globals that go with them. Otherwise, every time your standalone tries to access another file, it will ask the user to locate the file. To see how you need to maintain these globals, look at the `getHomeInfo` handler in the Home stack script.

- If your standalone opens other stacks, the statements `go home` and `doMenu "Home"` go to your standalone, since it's acting as the Home stack.

- The standalone's stack script appears just before HyperCard in the message-passing path, where the Home stack script would appear if you were running HyperCard itself.

One way to test your standalone-to-be is to move your Home stack temporarily out of HyperCard's folder. When you launch HyperCard, it will ask where your Home stack is. Tell it your stack is Home. Does everything work properly? If not, your stack may be missing some of the functionality that the Home stack provides.

A FINISHING TOUCH

In most applications, the first item in the Apple menu brings up an About dialog describing the application. HyperCard is no exception. However, if you're making a standalone application, it's appropriate to change the About HyperCard menu item to one that refers to your program.

Suppose your standalone is called "SuperText". You can change the About menu item's name and operation by adding the following two lines to your startup handler:

```
set the name of menuItem 1 of menu "Apple" to "About SuperText"
set the menuMessage of menuItem 1 of menu "Apple" to showAbout
```

This next handler responds to the **menuMessage** you set in the previous line, displaying a PICT resource when the user chooses About SuperStack:

```
on showAbout -- displays a credits PICT
   picture "Credits",resource,dialog
   if the result is not empty then -- didn't get displayed
      beep
   else
      wait until the mouseClick
      close window "Credits"
   end if
end showAbout
```

CD-ROM and Locked Media

CD-ROM publishers often use HyperCard stacks as a front end to their collections of information. HyperCard's user-interface capabilities make it particularly suitable for giving users easy ways of accessing large amounts of data. And CD-ROMs let you use a lot of space for color pictures, animated clips, digitized sounds, and so on.

Some special considerations apply when you're programming a stack to be used on a CD-ROM, though. Some of these same considerations also apply to programming other read-only stacks, such as locked stacks accessed from a file server. This section describes a few rules you should keep in mind when writing handlers in such stacks.

REMEMBER THAT YOUR STACK WON'T CHANGE

To properly design a stack that's going to be used on a CD-ROM, bear in mind that the stack will be frozen when the CD-ROM is made, and won't change from then on. That means that changes to the **hilite** states of buttons, the text in fields, the selection, and every other change that a user or a handler might make will be lost as soon as you leave the current card.

Make Sure Your Stack Can Locate Other Stacks and Files

If the HyperCard application (and the Home stack) is run from the CD-ROM, or if your stack is a standalone application, HyperCard won't be able to update the list of paths for stacks, applications, and documents. (HyperCard checks these locations when HyperCard goes to a stack or opens an application or document. They are stored in the global variables Stacks, Applications, and Documents.) When you go to a stack or open an application or document that's not in any of these locations, HyperCard puts up a "Where is this file?" dialog. When you locate the file, HyperCard adds the path to the list of locations it will check in the future. The Home stack stores these global variables in fields when you quit HyperCard.

If your Home stack or standalone is on the CD-ROM, it cannot add any new locations, since a stack can't change the contents of its fields once it's on CD-ROM. So you need to make certain that before your stack is put on CD-ROM, you store all the locations it might use on the appropriate card of the Home stack, or, if your stack is a standalone, somewhere in a script or field where they can be accessed.

Letting Users Make Temporary Changes

If you set the **userModify** property to true, users will be able to make changes to the stack, such as typing text into fields and highlighting checkboxes. Since the stack is locked, these changes will be lost as soon as the user leaves the current card.

However, you can store such changes in a global variable, and restore them when the user returns to the card:

```
on closeCard
   global userNotes
   put card field "Notes" into userNotes
end closeCard

on openCard
   global userNotes
   put userNotes into card field "Notes"
end openCard
```

Creating a Preferences File

You can provide more permanent storage for such changes by creating a preferences file on the user's startup disk (which presumably is not locked). The following example, which assumes you have an XFCN that gets the name of the System Folder and an XCMD that will create a folder, shows how you might use such a file:

```
on getPrefs
   global stackPrefs, prefsLocation
   -- figure out where the prefs file is
   put systemFolder() into prefsLocation   -- an XFCN
   put "Preferences:" after prefsLocation
   if there is no folder prefsLocation
   then createFolder prefsLocation          -- an XCMD
   put "Super CD Prefs" after prefsLocation
   -- if the prefs file already exists, get the existing
   -- preferences and read them into the global variable
   if there is a file prefsLocation then
      open file prefsLocation
```

```
      read from file prefsLocation until end
      close file prefsLocation
      put it into stackPrefs
   else
      open file prefsLocation
      if the result is not empty then
         answer "There was a problem creating the preferences" && ¬
         file:" & return & the result & return & ¬
         "Your preferences for this session won't be saved."
         put empty into prefsLocation
      else
         close file prefsLocation -- empty file created
      end if
   end if
end getPrefs
```

Of course, you'll also write a **closeStack** handler that stores the contents of the global stackPrefs to the preferences file.

OPTIMIZING YOUR STACKS FOR CD-ROM

The CD-ROM medium is inherently slow. Any operation that requires the system to access the disk is sluggish. If your stack is destined for CD-ROM, it's vital to make it as fast as possible to offset this slowness of the medium. Several tactics are useful to ensure that your stack's performance is acceptable.

Avoid Reading Information from the Disk

Whenever you go to another card or stack, or read information from a text file, HyperCard must read from the disk. Since disk access on a CD-ROM is even slower than on a hard drive, unnecessary navigation slows things down enormously. When possible, get information from other cards remotely, instead of going to the card.

Since the stack isn't going to change once it's placed on the CD-ROM, and since a CD-ROM is so large that you can usually afford to take up extra space, you might also consider duplicating data. For example, if the contents of a field is used on several cards, you may want to place a copy of the field on each card that uses its information. This lets handlers on all the cards use this information, without imposing the slowdown caused by getting it from another card.

Hard-Code Values to Speed Up Operations

Normally, the practice of hard-coding values (such as the number of buttons on a card or the text in a field) is a style no-no, since if the value changes—for example, if a button is added—your code will no longer work properly.

However, if you're writing for CD-ROM, this consideration becomes less important, because CD-ROMs don't change. Hard-coding still has its disadvantages, because it makes the stack harder to maintain and update for future versions. However, sometimes it's a reasonable tradeoff for increased speed.

Make sure to explain any hard-coded values you use in a comment, so you (or someone else) can understand the code later.

Use Legerdermain to Disguise Slow Activities

If you're performing several operations, do the ones that the user can see first. For example, if you're writing a handler that goes to several cards, go to the last one first and then lock the screen while visiting the rest. This makes the handler seem to run faster, since the final screen image appears almost as soon as the handler starts. Sleight-of-hand techniques like this are useful for any stack, but they're particularly important for CD-ROMs.

Other ways to keep users from getting annoyed by slow operations include changing the cursor and displaying a progress message while the operation is going on. When the stack is on a hard disk, an operation may finish quickly enough so that it's not necessary to provide any user notification. But moving the same stack to a CD-ROM may slow down the operation enough to irritate the user if no notification is provided. When you're deciding whether to provide this sort of user notification, remember that disk activities are slower on CD-ROM, and take that additional time into account.

Multiuser Environments

HyperCard was not designed as a multiuser database. In general, only one person can open a stack at any particular time. If a second user tries to open it, HyperCard puts up an error dialog. However, there are a number of ways you can write your handlers to make it easier to share stack data among several people.

SHARING A STACK ON A FILE SERVER

One way to share stack data is to put the stack on a file server so that all the users can access the same copy of the stack.

Read-Only Stacks

If many users need to have access to the stack's data, but they don't need to make changes or additions, sharing the data is simple. All you have to do is lock the stack in the Finder's Get Info dialog. Now any number of people can open the stack, although they can't make changes to it. This arrangement is best for electronic reference books and other collections of information that don't need to be changed every day.

If you want users to be able to make temporary changes—for example, if the stack has a Find card where the users need to type a search string into a field—set the **userModify** property to true. For more information about the way locked stacks work, see the **userModify** and **cantModify** properties, and see the section, "CD-ROM and Locked Media," earlier in this chapter.

Stacks with User-Specific Information

If the main data in the stack doesn't change, but you want each user to be able to add ancillary data, such as notes and personal preferences, use a variation of the setup for sharing read-only stacks. Share the main stack as above, and give each user an additional stack in which preferences, notes, and so on can be stored.

The preferences stack resides on the user's own hard drive. Since each preferences stack is used by only one person, there's no problem making changes to it. So you can store any preferences or other information in the preferences stack, reading from it when necessary. You can even make it look as if the user is making changes in the main stack.

For example, suppose the read-only stack has a Notes button that brings up a Notes field. Since the stack is locked, the user can't make permanent changes to this field. However, you can make clever use of the **userModify** property to let each user edit individual notes from within the read-only stack's Notes field. Here's how to set it up:

```
on mouseUp -- in Notes button of read-only stack
   set the userModify to true
   lock screen
   lock messages
   push this card
   if the visible of field "Notes" then
      -- store new notes in Prefs stack
      go to card "Stored Notes" of stack "Preferences"
      get field "Stored Notes"
      pop card
      show field "Notes"
      put it into field "Notes"
      unlock screen with visual effect dissolve
   else
      -- get old notes from Prefs stack
      get field "Notes"
      go to card "Stored Notes" of stack "Preferences"
      put it into field "Stored Notes"
      pop card
      hide field "Notes"
      unlock screen with visual effect dissolve
   end if
end mouseUp
```

Stacks That Must Be Updated by Multiple Users

Some shared stacks need to be updated frequently by several users. To accomplish this, you need to keep the stack unlocked so that users can make changes to it. But only one person at a time can use an unlocked stack, so if one person already has the stack open, all other users are locked out until the first user leaves the stack.

One solution to this problem is to let the user enter the update information into a stack on the local hard drive, like the preferences stack described above. Then, when the new information is complete and ready, the user clicks a button to move the new information into the server stack. This means the server stack is in use for only a minimal amount of time, so there's less chance that someone else will want to access the stack while it's being updated.

The following handler shows how to open an unlocked server stack. If the stack's already being used by someone else, the handler asks the user whether to wait for the stack to become available or to cancel the operation.

```
on goServerStack -- in local stack
   put the seconds into startTime
   put 0 into timeWaiting
   repeat
      go to stack "Customer Tracking" without dialog
      -- if result is "No such stack", HC couldn't find
      -- the stack, so present the Where Is dialog to user
      if the result contains "No such stack"
      then go to stack "Customer Tracking"
      -- if the result is empty then we got in
      if the result is empty then exit repeat
      -- otherwise, we wait for the stack to be free
      else
         answer "You've been waiting for the stack for" && timeWaiting ¬
         && "minutes. Keep waiting?" with "Cancel" or "Wait"
         if it is "Cancel" then return "Canceled"
         put "Waiting for Customer Tracking..."
         wait for 60 seconds
         put (the seconds - startTime) div 60 into timeWaiting
      end if
   end repeat
   put empty
   hide message box
end goServerStack
```

SENDING INFORMATION ACROSS THE NETWORK

If your users are running System 7, you can use AppleEvents to share data in a distributed application. Instead of keeping all the information in a central stack on a server, you divide the data among several stacks. Each stack is located on a different user's hard drive; none of the stacks are on a file server. The stacks use AppleEvents to communicate with one another, sending data and requests for data back and forth over the network. (For more information about AppleEvents, see Chapter 5.)

The example below uses the **send to program** command to exchange electronic mail messages between two users on the same network. Both users must be running HyperCard, and the e-mail stack must either be frontmost or have been placed in the message-passing path with the **start using** command:

```
on  sendEmailTo  theAddress,theMessage
   -- on the sender's stack
   send "receiveEmail" && quote & the address & quote ¬
   & comma & quote & theMessage & quote ¬
   to program theAddress with reply
   if the result is "Timeout." then
      answer "Couldn't deliver the mail."
   else answer the result
end sendEmailTo


on receiveEmail theSender,theMessage
   -- in a stack in use, or the frontmost stack, on the
   -- recipient's Mac
   reply "Mail was received by" && the address
   answer "You have new mail from" && theSender ¬
   & ". Read it now?" with "Read Later" or "Read Now"
   put it into whatToDo
   appendToFile theSender,theMessage -- another handler
   if whatToDo is "Read Now" then
      go to card "Incoming" of stack "Email" in a new window
      put theMessage into field "Message"
   end if
end receiveEmail
```

You can use the same technique to alert other stacks on the network that a change has been made to a card on your stack. If you send the changed information as a parameter to the update message, the other stacks can update their own information to match. You can write handlers like this to keep all the copies of the stack synchronized.

Part II

HyperTalk Reference

7

Referring to Objects

The HyperCard environment is composed mainly of objects. Nearly all scripting deals with one object or another. This chapter describes in precise detail the process of referring to objects.

Specifying Objects

You can specify any object by giving its name. You can specify any object other than a stack or HyperCard by its ID or by positional number.

Objects include stacks, backgrounds, cards, buttons, fields, and HyperCard itself. Windows, menus, and menu items are not objects, since they aren't in the message-passing path. However, you refer to these elements the same way as you refer to objects: by their names, IDs, or numbers.

NAMES

Every stack must have a name. All objects other than stacks can, but don't have to, have names. You can change the name of any object (except HyperCard) by setting its **name** property:

```
set the name of stack "My favorite stack" to "Fave Rave"
```

A stack's name can have up to 31 characters. It can include letters, numbers, and special characters like $,#,•, and so on, but the name of a stack, like all Macintosh files, can't include a colon (:). Both of these limitations are imposed by the Macintosh operating system and apply to any file, not just stacks. All filenames are limited to 31 characters, and the colon is the Macintosh separator for file paths, so file, folder, and disk names may not contain colons. HyperCard 2.2 won't let you give a stack a name starting with a period (.); this is to avoid triggering an obscure operating-system problem with such filenames.

File Pathnames

A file pathname specifies the location of a file. A file's full pathname consists of the name of the disk it's on, the folder hierarchy that describes its location, and the file's name. The elements of the pathname are separated with colons (:). For example, suppose you have a stack named "My Stack", located on a disk named "Hard Disk", inside a folder named "Project", which in turn is in a folder named "Stacks". The full pathname of "My Stack" is

```
Hard Disk:Stacks:Project:My Stack
```

You can also specify a partial pathname. The partial pathname begins with a colon, which stands for "the current folder". (In almost all cases, this is the same as the folder the current stack is in.) So if you want to specify a file called "My File" that's in a folder called "Text Files", and "Text Files" is in the same folder as the current stack, you can refer to the file like this:

```
:Text Files:My File
```

The names of objects other than stacks can be up to 255 characters long, and can contain any characters, including letters, numbers, special characters, and even the colon and period.

A name can have any number of spaces within it. In general, you must enclose names containing spaces in quotation marks. In fact, it's good practice to enclose all names in quotes, even if they have no spaces.

You can put the name of any object into a variable and refer to the object by referring to the variable:

```
put "Fave Rave" into myFavoriteStack
go to stack myFavoriteStack
```

Name Forms

You can get the name of an object using one of three forms of the object's **name** property: the `short name`, `the name`, or `the long name`.

The form `the short name` is just the name of the object:

```
My Button
My Field
My Background
```

If the object doesn't have a name, `the short name` is the object's type and ID:

```
card button id 4
card id 3745
bkgnd id 5170
```

The form `the name` is the object's type plus its `short name`:

```
card button "My Button"
bkgnd field "My Field"
stack "My S3tack"
```

The form `the long name` is the object's `name` preceded by its full path:

```
stack "Hard Disk:Folder:My Stack"
bkgnd "My Ba2ckground" of stack "Hard Disk:Folder:My Stack"
card "My Card" of stack "Hard Disk:Folder:My Stack"
```

Windows, menus, and menu items are referred to by their `name`, with no modifiers:

```
"My Picture Window"
"Cut Text"
"File"
```

Also see the **name** and **name of menu** properties in Part III.

IDS

All objects within a stack (but not the stack itself) have IDs. When a background, card, field, or button is created, HyperCard assigns it a permanent ID. While several objects of the same type might have the same name, they'll never have the same ID in places where such a similarity might cause confusion. For example, no two buttons on the same card can have the same ID, although all the buttons might have the same name.

Windows and menus (but not menu items) also have IDs.

You can change the name of an object, but you can't change its ID.

The ID is a property of an object. For more information on IDs, including how to use them, see the **ID** property in Part III.

NUMBERS

An object's number is that object's position in its domain. All objects within a stack (but not the stack itself) have numbers:

- A button's number is its layer from back to front among all buttons in its background or on its card (higher numbers closer to the front).

- A field's number is its layer from back to front among all fields in its background or on its card (higher numbers closer to the front).

- A card's number is the card's position in its stack.

- A background's number reflects the order in which it was created in the family of backgrounds for that stack.

The positional number is a property of an object. For more information on numbers, see the **number of object** function in Part III.

How to Refer to Objects

This section shows the complete and exact syntax for referring to all HyperCard objects. All exceptions and anomalies are noted. The reference description for each object starts with a list of all allowable forms for referring to that object. After that come a series of one-line examples showing how to apply the syntactic forms. Finally, there's a list of notes, as applicable.

REFERRING TO HYPERCARD

```
HyperCard
```

There is no other syntax for HyperCard. The word has few uses, except to bypass the usual message path:

```
send "Find" && thisString to HyperCard
```

REFERRING TO STACKS

```
this stack|stack <endLine>|stack <expr>
```

A stack always has a name, which you assign when the stack is created and can change at any time:

```
the freeSize of stack           -- current stack
the short name of this stack -- current stack
set the name of this stack to "My Stack"
go stack Some Other One     -- likely to be some other stack
go stack "Some Other One"  -- quotation marks always allowed with literals
go stack notThisStack -- a variable
```

The word "stack" used by itself (meaning the current stack) can appear only at the end of a line:

```
put name of stack
```

But you can use the form "this stack" anywhere in a line:

```
put name of this stack into oldStack
```

Unknown Stack

If you refer to a stack that HyperCard doesn't know about, HyperCard puts up a dialog called the standard file dialog box (see Figure 7.1) listing all the folders and stacks, and asks you where the stack is. HyperTalk assumes that whatever stack name you click is the stack you want, whether or not that stack has the same name as the one the code asks for.

HyperCard adds this location to the Stack Search Paths card in the Home stack, if it's not there already. But if the stack is misnamed, its name isn't added; each time you ask for that stack, you'll have to tell HyperTalk where to find it.

The Stack Name Is the File Name

The name of a stack is the name of that file as it appears in the Finder. So no two stacks in the same folder can have the same name.

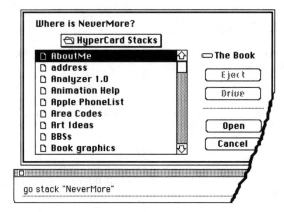

Figure 7.1 "Stack? What stack?"

REFERRING TO BACKGROUNDS

```
background {id <unsigned>|<endLine>|<expr>}
```

or

```
<ordinal> background
```

or

```
{this|next|previous} background
```

Legal synonyms for the word background are bkgnd and bg.

```
bkgnd id 5
the number of cards in background -- the current background
bg 3
fifth background -- of this stack
background "The Background" -- name is "The Background"
this bg
next bg
background theBackground -- could be either variable or literal
```

In the last example, HyperTalk tries to interpret theBackground as a variable name first. If no variable by that name exists, then it assumes that theBackground is an unquoted literal.

The word "background" used by itself (meaning the current background) can appear only at the end of a line:

```
put the name of background
```

But you can use the form "this background" anywhere in a line:

```
put the name of this background into oldStack
```

Background References with Go Command

When you use a background reference in a **go** statement, you can add the syntax [of *<stack>*] to the end of both of the syntax definition lines:

```
go bg 3 of "My Stack"
go third bg of stack myStack
```

Unknown Background

When your code specifies a background that doesn't exist, HyperTalk puts up the error dialog "No such card", shown in Figure 7.2.

REFERRING TO CARDS

```
card {id <unsigned>|<endLine>|<expr>} [of <bkgnd>]
```

or

```
<ordinal> card {of <bkgnd>}
```

or

```
{this|next|previous} [marked] card
```

or

```
<ordinal> marked card
```

or

```
recent card
```

or

```
back
```

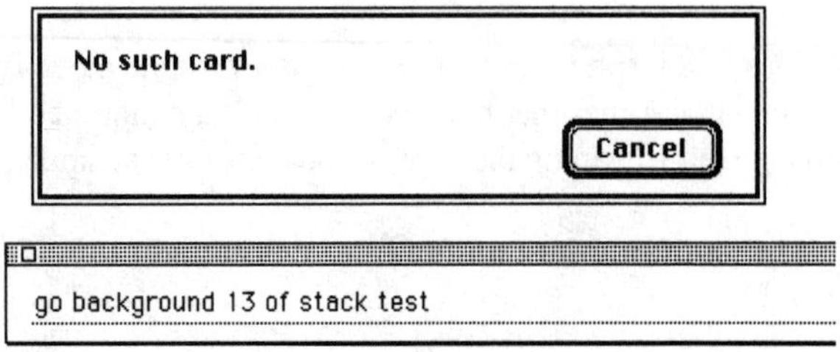

Figure 7.2   No background 13 in this stack.

or

```
forth
```

The word cd is a legal synonym of card.

```
card id 2
the ID of card
the id of cd 3 of bg 4
card thisNumber - thatNumber
fifth cd
the name of this card is not "foo"
recent card
button 3 of back
```

Note that the syntax calls for an expression, not a factor. (See the discussion of expressions and factors in Chapter 9). So the expresssion

```
get field 1 of card 2 + 1
```

gets field 1 of card 3, instead of 1 added to the contents of the first field on card 2. To get the latter, use this form:

```
get (field 1 of card 2) + 1
```

Here are a few more examples:

```
card <endLine> -- means this card
card 3 + 4 -- means card 7
field 1 of card 3 + 4 -- means first field of 7th card
(field 1 of card 3) + 4 -- 4 + numeric value of first field of third card
```

Card References with the Go Command

When you use a card reference in a **go** statement, you can add the syntax [of <*stack*>] to the end of the first four syntax definition lines:

```
go cd 3 of stack myStack
go third card of stack myStack
```

Unknown Card

When you ask for a card that doesn't exist from the message box, HyperTalk puts up the error dialog "No such card". When you ask for a nonexistent card from a script, HyperTalk sets the value of the **result** function, but doesn't put up a dialog.

For the causes and cures of some common errors with cards, see "Object References and the Parsing of Expressions" at the end of this chapter.

REFERRING TO FIELDS

```
[card|bkgnd] field [id <numericFactor>|<factor>] [of <card>]
```

or

```
<ordinal> [card|bkgnd] field [of <card>]
```

Instead of the word field, you can substitute its legal synonym fld.

```
fld ID thisNumber
card field 12 of card 18
field "Counties"
field "data" of card 1
any card field
fifth field of card 325
field fred
```

Note that the syntax calls for a factor, not an expression. So the statement put field 1 + 7 adds 7 to the contents of field 1 and puts the total into the message box; it does not put the contents of field 8 into the message box.

A field reference must always be to a field in the current stack. If you don't specify whether you're referring to a card or to a background field, HyperCard assumes you're referring to a background field. If you don't say what card or background the field is on, HyperTalk assumes that it's on the current card or background.

Unknown Field

When your code specifies a field that doesn't exist, HyperTalk puts up an error dialog saying that it never heard of the field you referenced. (See Figure 7.3).

For the causes and cures of some common errors with fields, see "Object References and the Parsing of Expressions" at the end of this chapter.

REFERRING TO BUTTONS

```
[card|bkgnd] button {id <numericFactor>|<factor>} [of <card>]
```

or

```
<ordinal> [card|bkgnd] button [of <card>]
```

Instead of the word button, you can substitute its legal synonym btn.

```
btn ID thisNumber
bg btn 12 of card 18
button myButton
button "Additional Info" of card 1
any background button
fifth button of card 325
```

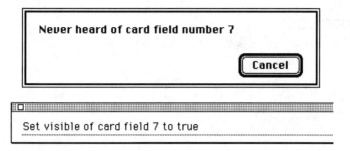

Figure 7.3 Non-existent field reference

You can refer only to buttons in the current stack. If you don't specify whether you're referring to a card or to a background button, HyperCard assumes you're referring to a card button. If you don't say what card or background the button is on, HyperTalk assumes that it's on the current card or background.

Unknown Button

When your code specifies a button that doesn't exist, HyperTalk puts up an error dialog saying that it never heard of the button you referenced.

REFERRING TO PARTS

```
[card|bkgnd] part {id <numericFactor>|<factor>} [of <card>]
```

or

```
<ordinal> [card|bkgnd] part [of <card>]
```

```
card part ID 17
bg part "Next Button"
part myField
any card part
```

Parts are either buttons or fields. You can refer only to parts in the current stack. If you don't specify whether you're referring to a card or to a background part, HyperCard assumes you're referring to a card part.

Unknown Part

When your code specifies a part that doesn't exist, HyperTalk puts up an error dialog saying that it never heard of the part you referenced.

REFERRING TO WINDOWS

```
window {id <unsigned>|<factor>}
```

or

```
<ordinal> window
```

or

```
card window
cd window
window ID 23876
message window
window "My New Picture"
window (the number of windows)
fifth window
```

You can refer to any open window. (HyperCard keeps some of its built-in windows, such as the message box, open at all times. Clicking the close box of such a window only hides it.)

HyperTalk lets you use the following synonyms for built-in windows:

```
window  "Message"              {message|msg}  {box|window}
window  "Tools"                tools  window
window  "Patterns"             pattern  window
window  "Scroll"               scroll  window
window  "FatBits"              fatBits  window
window  "Message  Watcher"     message  watcher
window  "Variable  Watcher"    variable  watcher
```

REFERRING TO MENUS

```
menu {id <unsigned>|<expr>}
```

or

```
<ordinal> menu
```

```
menu ID 3456
menu 3
menu "Edit"
last menu
```

You can refer to any menu in the menu bar. Referring to a nonexistent menu causes a "no such menu" error message.

Like fields and buttons, menus are containers; they contain a return-separated list of all the menu items in the menu.

REFERRING TO MENU ITEMS

```
menuItem <expr> of <menu>
```

or

```
<ordinal> menuItem of <menu>
```

```
last menuItem of menu "Apple"
menuItem "Recent" of menu "Go"
menuItem 6 of menu ID 32
```

Me and the Target

Me and the target are special synonyms for objects. Me is the object containing the currently running script; the target is a function that returns the name of the object that the current message was first sent to.

ME

When you use the script editor to look at a script that has the word me in it, you can immediately tell who me is—it's the object whose name is the title of the script editor window.

In Figure 7.4, me refers to the card button named "Book graphics". This button might have a handler that alternately changes its name to reflect a current condition:

```
on setName
   if the visible of field "Extra Information" is true
   then set the name of me to "Hide Info"
   else set the name of me to "Show Info"
end setName
```

The following statements all work as you'd expect if you'd specified the object by name:

```
put the short name of me
put the name of me
put the long name of me
```

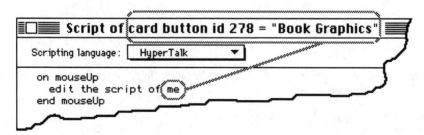

Figure 7.4   Who's me?

When "me" is a field or button

Fields and buttons (in HyperCard 2.2) are the only objects that are also containers. So HyperTalk gives me special consideration when me refers to a field or button. The statement put me into thisVar copies the contents of me into thisVar. Similarly, the statement put thisVar into me copies the contents of the variable thisVar into whatever field me represents. But statements like put the name of me work for fields and buttons as they do for any other object.

THE TARGET

The target is the object that gets the first chance to respond to a message. The target never changes while a handler is running, and there's no way you can change the target from within a handler: The target was set up before the handler started running.

For example, suppose a card script has the following handler in it:

```
on mouseUp
   if "card button" is not in the target then pass mouseUp
   beep
   put the target
end mouseUp
```

(The terms the target and the name of the target are synonymous in the above construction.) In this example, whenever you click on a button on the card, if that button has a script with no **mouseUp** handler, HyperCard beeps and puts the name of that button into the Message box. The button you clicked was the first recipient of the **mouseUp** message— that is, it was the target of the message. If the third line of that handler were changed to:

```
   put the target && "of" && the the name of me
```

you'd get the name of the button and the name of the card that holds the handler. For example, you might get card button "New Button" of card "Home".

"Target" versus "the target"

Fields and buttons get special treatment with **the target**, as with me. When a field is the target, you can use the term target, without the, to refer to the contents of the field or button in question. For example, suppose card field ID 3 has this script in it:

```
on  differences
   answer the target & return & target
end differences
```

If card field 3 contains the text "The contents of the target field", you can enter this into the message box and press Return:

```
send "differences" to card field id 3
```

Figure 7.5 shows what happens. This is the only case where using the word the changes the meaning of a statement.

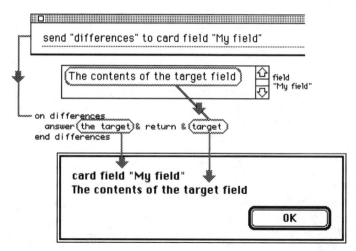

Figure 7.5 **"Target" versus "the target"**

Object References and the Parsing of Expressions

Be sure to religiously follow the rules outlined in this chapter when you refer to objects. Some constructions can look tricky at first, but are all explainable (they said, with a wise expression) in terms of these rules.

For example, the syntax for referring to cards says that HyperTalk looks for a factor after the word "field" and for an expression after the word "card". Here's the tricky part: When HyperTalk evaluates an expression, it goes as far as it can. And an expression often includes an operand, an operator, and another operand:

```
if the short name of card 3 is "foo" then beep 3 -- fails
if (the short name of card 3) is "foo" then beep 3 -- succeeds
```

In the first line, HyperTalk thinks the name of the card is the expression `3 is "foo"`. That expression evaluates to false, which gives you `the short name of card false`—and `card false` doesn't exist. The next example is similar:

```
if field 1 of cd i contains "bozo" then go stack "Bus" -- fails
if (field 1 of cd i) contains "bozo" then go stack "Bus" -- succeeds
```

Here, HyperTalk thinks the name of the card is supposed to be the result of the expression `i contains "bozo"`, which is false, and so you get the same sort of result as in the card example above.

A third example adds a new twist: HyperTalk thinks that the name of the card is the concatenation of `i` and a return character.

```
put fld 1 of cd i & return after cd fld "Contents" of cd 1 -- fails
put (fld 1 of cd i) & return after cd fld "Contents" of cd 1 -- succeeds
```

If you're getting strange error dialogs (such as "no such card"), check the phrasing of your references and add parentheses as appropriate.

8

Sources of Value, Containers, and Chunk Expressions

This chapter defines the basic elements from which all HyperTalk expressions are constructed. It holds a description of sources of value common to most languages (functions, literals, constants, parameters, and variables), plus the ones that are either unique to HyperCard or uniquely implemented (properties, fields, buttons, menus, the message box, the Selection, and chunk expressions). All of these sources of values can be used interchangeably to construct expressions, the details of which appear in Chapter 8.

HyperTalk has six basic categories for sources of value: functions, properties, literals, constants, and containers. This chapter describes each of these in turn, with special emphasis on containers.

Functions and Properties

These sources of value are each described in detail in Part III, "The Elements of HyperTalk." A brief description is included here for completeness.

FUNCTIONS

A function returns a value, usually based on one or more *arguments*. An argument is a value passed to the function and upon which the function operates. Certain system functions such as **the date** and **the time** require no argument; these functions return a value reflecting the current state of the system. In either case, the value of a function is changeable, and is calculated at the time that it's called:

```
put the long date
put random(500) into field 12
put average(field 3, field 4, field 5) into averageAge
```

PROPERTIES

A property is an attribute of an object, window, menu, menu item, or chunk of text. Properties return a logical, numeric, geometric, or string value, depending on the specific attribute. You can set most properties with the **set** command, although a few are read-only:

```
put the hilite of button "Click Me" into onOff
put the freeSize of stack "Home"
put the multiSpace after line 3 of field "System State"
```

Literals

A literal is a string whose value is the string itself. HyperTalk has three types of literals: quoted, unquoted, and numeric.

QUOTED

A quoted literal is a string that appears within double quotation marks ("):

```
put "What — me worry?" into field "Quotations" -- two quoted literals
```

You can include any character except return, ¬(option-Return), and the double quotation mark itself in a quoted literal.

UNQUOTED

An unquoted literal is one that doesn't have quotation marks around it:

```
put the freeSize of stack Home -- "Home" is an unquoted literal
```

Unquoted literals and objects

You can use a single-word unquoted literal when you refer to any object name:

```
put 0 into field Payment -- Payment is an unquoted literal
```

Only a stack name at the end of a line can be a multiple-word unquoted literal:

```
go to stack All The World's a Stage
```

You're guaranteed to get an error if you use multiple-word unquoted literals for any object other than a stack:

```
put field All My Wives into field Soaps -- looks for field "All"
```

See Chapter 7 for details about how to refer to objects.

Unquoted Literals Are Not Recommended

While HyperTalk lets you use unquoted literals in some situations, you should avoid doing so. You reduce your chances for error substantially if you enclose all literals within quotation marks. For example, you might use an unquoted literal early in the development process, and later decide to use that same word as the name of a variable. When HyperCard comes across an ambiguous situation where that literal/variable pops up, you're likely to get unwanted results.

NUMERIC

A numeric literal is a digit (0,1,2,3,4,5,6,7,8,9) or a combination of digits (42, 65536, 98.6, 3.14159, etc.). Numbers require no quotation marks:

```
add 3 to totals
```

Because HyperTalk is a typeless language, even numbers are treated as strings. Thus you can have a form such as

```
answer "What number?" with char 2 of 45673 -- yields 5
```

Constants

A constant is a source whose value never changes. Because you refer to constants by name, you can think of them as variables with permanent values. Table 8.1 lists all the constants in the language with their values. Notes appear after the table for items followed by a dagger (†).

About Up and Down

While up and down are constants, in versions before 2.0, "left" and "right" are not.

About ASCII

ASCII is an acronym for American Standard Code for Information Interchange, a system whereby a specific integer represents a text character or special code. See Appendix A for a list of these codes.

About the Empty Constant and Nulls

All HyperTalk strings are stored internally in a format that ends in the null character (ASCII zero). This means that you cannot work directly with the null character in HyperTalk, since the language interprets it as simply an empty string. If you're using HyperCard for certain telecommunications protocols or other specialized tasks that require use of the null character, you'll need to use an XCMD.

Table 8.1   Constants and Their Values

Constant	Value/Comment
up†	"up"—The name is the value, as in if the shiftKey is up
down†	"down"—The name is the value
true	"true"—The logical value
false	"false"—The opposite of true
empty†	"" (ASCII 0)—The empty string
space	" " (ASCII 32)
colon	":" —The colon character
comma	"," —The comma
pi†	3.14159265358979323846
zero	0
one	1
two	2
three	3
four	4
five	5
six	6
seven	7
eight	8
nine	9
ten	10
tab†	ASCII 9
formfeed†	ASCII 12
linefeed†	ASCII 10
quote†	", ASCII 34
return†	ASCII 13

About Pi

Pi is a string constant. Doing math on it forces its conversion to a binary number. Putting the result of that math into a field converts the result back to a string. That string is displayed using the current setting of **numberFormat**. For example, the default value for numberFormat is 0.######—which means that pi + 0 would yield the string 3.141593, and not 3.14159265358979323846. See the **numberFormat** property in Part III for details.

About Tab, Formfeed, etc.

These constants exist because you can't type the characters they represent in a script:

```
set the script of button 2 to ¬
"on upDate" & return & ¬ -- return character isn't typeable
 --embed quotations
"set the visible of button" && quote & "Text Arrows" & quote && ¬
"to the userLevel >= 2" & return & ¬
"end upDate"
```

Containers

A container holds information that you supply. HyperTalk has seven kinds of containers: fields, buttons, menus, variables, parameters, the selection, and the message box. Additionally, HyperTalk lets you specify a *chunk*, which is a portion of a container and is also itself a container.

You have complete control over the contents of any container. So you can create, edit, or delete the text in any container at any time, and you can copy all or some of the contents of any container into any part of any other container.

FIELDS

A field (see Figure 8.1) has the following characteristics:

- It's also an object: You can send a message to it.

- You can delete it.

- It can contain up to 29,996 characters.

- HyperCard stores its contents on disk (and thus its contents are not lost when you quit HyperCard).

To create a field from within a handler, do any of the following:

- Copy an existing field by dragging off a copy:

```
on copy_Field choice, hor, vert
   choose field tool
   drag from the loc of card field choice to hor,vert with optionKey
   choose browse tool
end copy_Field
```

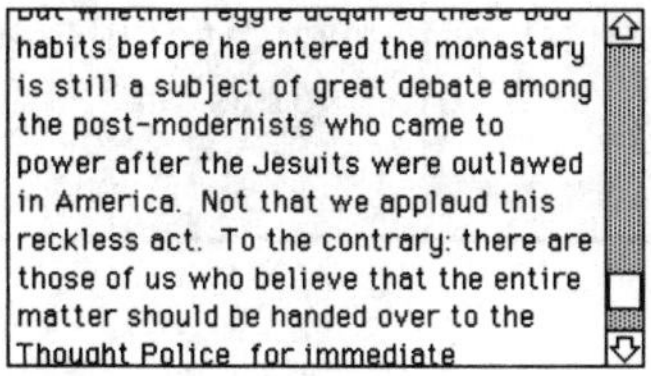

Figure 8.1   A field

- Drag out a field from scratch:

```
on drag_Field left,top,right,bottom -- you set these values
  choose field tool
  drag from left,top to right,bottom with commandKey
  choose browse tool
end drag_Field
```

- Use the menu command "New Field":

```
on menu_Field left,top,right,bottom
  doMenu "New Field"
  set the rect of last card field to left,top,right,bottom
  choose browse tool -- "New Field" chooses Field tool
end menu_Field
```

HyperCard writes the contents of a field to disk at **idle** time (that is, when no handler is running) if it has changed.

BUTTONS

Beginning with HyperCard 2.2, any button can be used as a container. A button has the following characteristics:

- It's also an object: You can send a message to it.
- You can delete it.
- It can contain up to 29,996 characters.
- HyperCard stores its contents on disk (and thus its contents are not lost when you quit HyperCard).

If the button is a popup menu (that is, if its **style** property is set to "popup"), its contents is a return-separated list of the menu items in the popup. Otherwise, HyperCard does not use or display the button's contents; you can use such buttons in any way you want.

HyperCard writes the contents of a button to disk at **idle** time (that is, when no handler is running) if it has changed.

Compact stack after field or button deletions

When you delete a field or button, you're actually just resetting pointers. The disk space that the part and its text take up in the stack is still allocated. To free up this trapped disk space, use the Compact Stack menu item.

MENUS

A menu is a special-purpose container. It contains a list of the menu items in the menu:

```
menu "Font" -- yields a return-separated list of fonts
line 1 of first menu -- yields "About HyperCard..."
```

VARIABLES

A variable is a container that you create. You can create a variable any time you need one, and there's no limit (other than available memory) to the number of variables you can create or to their size. You can put anything at all into a variable.

HyperTalk has two types of variables: global and local. Both types reside in memory and are never stored on disk. The difference between the two types is in how long their value lasts and where you can access them. Once you create a global variable, you can access and change its value throughout HyperCard for the current session (that is, until you quit HyperCard). However, a local variable lasts only as long as the handler that created it is running, and you can access the value of a local variable only in this handler.

Global Variables

You create a global variable (or gain access to one that's already been created) by using the **global** keyword within a handler. The following handler creates a global variable called theRealName:

```
on create_Global
   global theRealName -- theRealName created here as global
   ask "What's your name?" with "John Scribblemonger"
   put it into theRealName -- store value in the new global
end create_Global
```

Once the global is created, its value is available throughout HyperCard to any handler that asks for it. Assuming that the above handler has already run, the following handler can access the value of the global variable theRealName defined above:

```
on use_Global
   global theRealName -- theRealName has a value already
   put "Have a great day," && theRealName into the Message box
end use_Global
```

Global Variables and the Message Box

You can also access the global's value from the message box, since HyperCard assumes all variable names used in the message box are globals. You don't need to type the line

```
global theRealName
```

into the message box to access a global.

Local Variables

You create a local variable by putting a value into it:

```
put the time into currentTime
pop card into top_Of_Stack
put empty into myVariable
```

Local variables go out of existence as soon as the handler in which they're created finishes running. In the next handler, the variables named "hours" and "minutes" have life spans limited to that of the running handler:

```
on local_Vars
   put round(the ticks/60/60) div 60 into hours
   put round(the ticks/60/60) mod 60 into minutes
   put "System on for" && hours && "hours," && minutes && "minutes"
end local_Vars -- "hours" and "minutes" now gone
```

When one handler invokes another, and they both use local variables with the same name, the values of the variables aren't shared between the handlers:

```
on firstHandler
   put 10 into localVar
   put localVar -- puts 10 into message box
   secondHandler -- calls other handler
   put space & localVar after msg -- localVar till has value 10
end firstHandler

on secondHandler
   put 5 into localVar
   put space & localVar after msg -- puts "5" at end of message box
end secondHandler
```

The special variable "it"

The variable named "it" is special in that the commands **ask, answer, read**, and **get** automatically put their values into **it** (and only into **it**), automatically creating **it** as a local variable. The **convert** command also uses **it** to hold conversion results if you don't specify another container. This practice dates back to a time before the first release, when **it** was the only variable allowed in HyperTalk.

Rules for Variables

Here are all the restrictions on variables:

- You can't use global and local variables with the same name in the same handler.

- A variable must already exist before you can operate on its contents. That is, you can't say add 3 to adder if adder hasn't already been created.

- A variable name can be up to 31 characters long.

- A variable name must start with a letter or underscore (_), and can contain letters, digits, and underscores.

- You can't use any punctuation or other special characters in a variable name (for example: $,%, ?, ¥).

- A variable name cannot be a keyword or either of the special words **target** or **me**. Here's a complete list:

```
do     end    exit   function   global   if       then   else
me     next   on     pass       repeat   return   send   target
```

In fact, to avoid any possible confusion (yours or HyperTalk's), it's best to avoid giving a variable the same name as any word that has a special meaning in HyperTalk.

Variables always in memory

All variables are always in memory and never put on disk. The implications of this are as follows:

- Variables are far faster than fields for storing and retrieving values.

- You can create as many variables as you want.

- Global variables take up memory. To free up this memory, clear the value of unneeded globals by putting empty into them.

- If you want to keep the value of a variable between sessions, store its value in a field or button.

Parameters and Parameter Passing

Parameters are values that can be passed from handler to handler. The following statement sends the message updatePhoneNumber and passes two parameter values along with it:

```
updatePhoneNumber "(617) 555-1212", "(503) 555-1212"
```

The updatePhoneNumber handler accepts the values into parameter variables (also called *formal parameters*) in the order that they were passed:

```
on updatePhoneNumber oldPhone,newPhone -- parameters captured here
    -- Using the above example, the first value passed
    -- ("(617) 555-1212") is placed in the parameter "oldPhone".
    -- Likewise, the second value from the above example is
    -- placed in "newPhone".
    find oldPhone in field "telephone number"
```

```
     do "put newPhone into" && the foundLine
  end updatePhoneNumber
```

Parameters are local variables, so they are only accessible from within their own handler, and they go out of existence as soon as the handler stops running.

A receiving handler can have more or fewer formal parameters than the number of parameter values that were passed to it. If there are more formal parameters than values to put in them, HyperTalk puts empty into the extra parameter variables:

```
-- update just two fields
updateAddress "John  Scribblemonger",  "123  Alcott  Lane"

on  updateAddress  name,street,city,state,zip
  -- update only fields that have been changed
  if name is not empty then put name into field "name"
  if street is not empty then put street into field "street"
  if city is not empty then put city into field "city"
  if state is not empty then put state into field "state"
  if zip is not empty then put zip into field "zip"
end updateAddress
```

If there are more values passes than there are parameters to receive them, you can still access the extra values with the **param** function:

```
put  product(12,  24,  36,  48)

function  product  firstFactor,secondFactor
  put firstFactor * secondFactor into total
  repeat with i = 3 to the paramCount -- use all parameters
    multiply total by param(i)
  end repeat
  return total
end product
```

For more information about parameters, see the keywords **on** and **function** in Part III.

How Many Parameters?

When you call a function or handler, you separate the values you want to pass with commas. If you want to pass a parameter that contains commas, enclose it in quotation marks. This makes HyperTalk treat it as a single parameter:

```
product(12, 24, 36)      -- 3 parameters
product("12", "24", "36") -- 3 parameters
product("12, 24, 36")    -- 1 parameter
product(field 1) -- 1 parameter, even if it contains commas
```

When you refer to a container, the entire content of the container is passed as a single parameter. If you want to pass each item in a container as a separate parameter, use the **value** function or the **do** keyword:

```
the value of "product(" & field 1 & ")"
do "get product(" & field 1 & ")"
-- each item in field 1 is a separate parameter
```

The Selection

The Selection is a reference to the currently selected text, which may be in a field (see Figure 8.2) or in the message box. When no text is selected but the blinking insertion point is present, the selection is the insertion point. The selection is always associated with text: Graphics or objects can be selected, but they cannot be `the selection`.

When you say `put the selection into field 1`, a copy of the selected text goes into field 1, replacing the old contents of field 1. When you say `put field 1 into the selection`, a copy of the text in field 1 replaces the currently selected text. If no text is selected but an insertion point is present, then a copy of the text in field 1 appears at the insertion point.

You can use the **select** command to select any text or to put the insertion point wherever you want it:

```
select text of field "Content"
select after word 3 of field "Content"
```

You Can't Always Count on the Selection

The selection is quite fragile; lots of actions can deselect it, including (but not limited to) the following:

- A **find**, **enterInField**, **enterKey**, **returnInField**, **returnKey**, **tabKey**, or **sort** command executes.
- The **hilite** of any button, or the **cantModify** property, changes.
- A new tool is chosen.

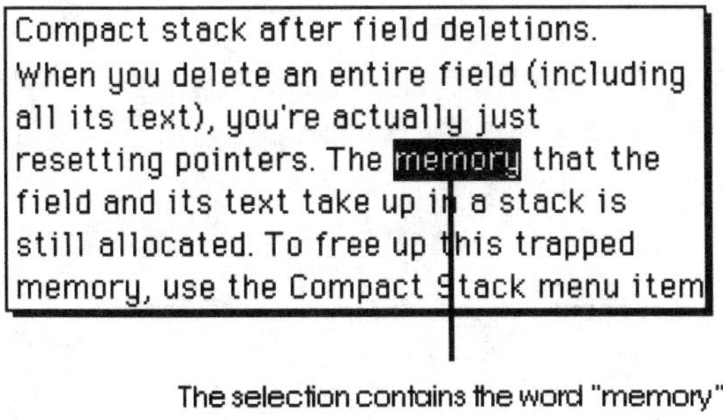

```
Compact stack after field deletions.
When you delete an entire field (including
all its text), you're actually just
resetting pointers. The memory that the
field and its text take up in a stack is
still allocated. To free up this trapped
memory, use the Compact Stack menu item
```

The selection contains the word "memory"

Figure 8.2   A Selection

```
How much wood would a woodchuck chuck if a woodchuck could chuck...
```

Figure 8.3   Message box

- HyperCard moves from one card to another.
- Any key is pressed.
- The mouse is clicked.

The wise scripter acts upon the selection as soon as is practicable after the selection appears.

For more ways to use the selection, see the **selectedChunk**, **selectedLine**, and **selectedText** functions.

THE MESSAGE BOX

The message box is a one-line container. Only the first line of what you put into the message box is used; any lines beyond the first are discarded. (All other containers can hold multiple lines.) The line can be of any length, and so it can extend off the display.

You can refer to the message box in a number of ways. Here's the syntax:

```
[the]  {msg|message}  [box|window]
```

```
put line 3 of field "My favorite candidates" into msg
put total_Taxes after the message window
```

Chunk Expressions

A *chunk* is a portion of the text of any source of value. A chunk can be a character, word, item, or line, or a range of any one of these.

You can put text into any chunk of any container:

```
put char 85 of field 1 into word 5 to 12 of the Selection
put field 3 into word 6 of field "Running Text"
pop card before line nextLine of field "My favorite cards"
```

You refer to a chunk using one of these forms:

```
{char[acter]|word|item|line}  <integer>  [to  <integer>]  of  <factor>
```

or

```
<ordinal> {char[acter]|word|item|line} of <factor>
```

For example, the following are all valid chunk expressions:

```
char 4 of message box
word 17 to 21 of field "Text"
second item of myVariable
last char of line 1 of theText
```

A chunk specification always moves from the smallest unit to the largest containing unit. The last designation in a chunk specification is the source itself.

CHARACTER

Character (or *char*) designates a single character, the smallest possible unit of any source:

```
character 3 of "wonderful" -- yields n
character 3 of pi -- yields 1 (1 is 3rd char of 3.1415...)
char 12 of line 6 of field myField
fifth char of line 6 of the Selection
```

Spaces and return characters are considered characters.

WORD

Word designates any text separated by any number of space characters (ASCII 32) or return characters (ASCII 13). Any text within quotation marks makes up a single word. For example, each of the following phrases contains three words:

```
a test phrase
this "brief example contains three" words
```

The first word of a container includes all text up to the first space. (Leading spaces are ignored.) The last word of a container includes all text between a final space and the end of the container. (Trailing spaces are also ignored.)

A word can contain any other characters, including punctuation marks, hyphens, and option-spaces (ASCII 202):

```
word 4 of "this petty-paced day"-- yields day
```

ITEM

Item designates text separated by commas:

```
item 3 of "bell, book, and candle" -- yields " and candle"
item 2 of "Sorry, this" & return & "is a test"
-- yields " this
          is a test"
```

To find out how to temporarily change the character HyperCard uses to separate items, see the **itemDelimiter** property in Part III.

The first item of a container includes all text up to the first comma. The last item in a container includes all text from the last comma to the end of the container, including return characters.

Items penetrate quotation marks:

```
-- myField contains "a,b",c
get item 2 of myField -- yields b"
```

Empty items don't always work correctly

Commas are meant to separate items. So it is the intent of the language that a source with a single comma has two items in it, even though there might be nothing either before or after the comma. However, if the last non-space character of a source is a comma, that comma is not considered to be an item delimiter. So the source contains one item fewer than you'd expect. To work around this bug, put a space after any final comma that comes at the end of a container.

LINE

Line designates text separated by return characters:

```
line 6 of field whatEver
last line of my_Most_Favorite_Variable
```

The first line of a container includes all text up to, but not including, the first return character. The last line of a container includes all text from, but not including, the last return character to the end of the container. If the expression contains no return characters, it's composed of a single line.

Lines penetrate quotation marks:

```
put quote & "Hello" & return & "there" & quote into myVar
get line 1 of myField -- yields "Hello"
```

A blank line at the end of a container counts as a line only if there is more than one. (See Figure 8.4.)

An empty field has zero lines. A field containing any single character, even if that character is a return, has one line.

RANGE OF A CHUNK

You can specify a range using the following form:

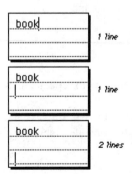

Figure 8.4   Counting lines

```
<chunkName> <start> to <end> of <factor>
```

These are examples of range chunk expressions:

```
character 12 to 15 of Msg
word 5 to 12 of the Selection
item 3 to 6 of line 15 of myVariable
char start to finish of item this to that of line 6 to 10 of theSource
char 2 of (9 * field 1) -- if field 1 contains 3, this yields 7
```

If you ask for an item that's out of range or that doesn't exist, you get nothing. If you ask for a range that is partially out of range, you get as much as is within range:

```
put char 5 to 7 of "word" -- yields empty
put char 3 to 5 of "word" -- yields rd
```

Chunk Range within Chunk Range within...

When you specify a chunk range within a chunk range, evaluation happens from largest to smallest. Figure 8.5 shows what happens to the following example:

```
char 13 to 18 of word 3 to 5 of item 8 to 10 of line 2 to 5 of theSource
```

HyperTalk first gets lines 2 through 5 from the rest of the variable theSource. Next, it gets items 7 through 8 from this new, four-line string. Then it gets words 3 through 5 of the still shorter two-item string composed of items 7 and 8. Finally, it ends up with the thirteenth through the eighteenth characters of the resulting three-word string:

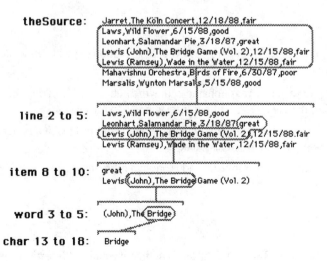

Figure 8.5   Specifying a range within a range

How HyperCard counts chunk characters

Consider a variable called `source` whose contents looks like this:

```
first     last
```

Assume there are five spaces between the words first and last:

```
put length of word 1 of source -- yields 5
```

```
put length of word 2 of source -- yields 4
```

But:

```
put length of word 1 to 2 of source -- yields 14
```

Word 1, word 2, and word 1 to 2 are three different strings. The range word 1 to 2 designates a string that starts at the beginning of word 1 and goes through the end of word 2, and thus includes the intervening spaces. What applies to words also applies to lines: Unless a line has only one word in it, *the length of a line is greater than the length of the sum of the lengths of its words* (because a word doesn't include its spaces) *or of its items* (because an item doesn't include its commas).

Assigning Out-of-Range Chunks

Sometimes you put text into a chunk that doesn't exist in the named container. For example, your code says

```
pop card into line 5 of field 8
```

when field 8 only has 3 lines in it. What happens in such a situation depends on what kind of chunk you've specified:

- Putting something into an out-of-range character or word puts the value of that character or word at the end of the container, without inserting any extra spaces.

- Putting something into an out-of-range item adds enough commas (each one defining an empty item) to bring that item into existence.

- Putting something into an out-of-range line adds enough return characters to bring that line into existence.

Expanded Text

Suppose you have a field named "Running Text" and another one named "Insertion", which contains the text John Q. Public. If you issue the statement

```
put field "Insertion" into word 6 of field "Running Text"
```

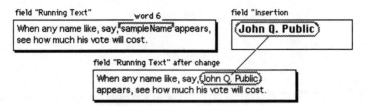

Figure 8.6   Inserting text by using chunk expressions

word 6 of field "Running Text" is replaced and expanded to accommodate all the text from field "Insertion". Any text after word 6 of field "Running Text" is pushed ahead to accommodate the inserted text (see Figure 8.6).

Using Structured Variables

As mentioned above, HyperTalk is a typeless language. This means that all variables are stored and treated the same way, so you can do any operation on a variable without worrying about whether it contains a number, a boolean value, a string, or information in some other format.

One consequence of typelessness is that HyperTalk does not provide explicit variable types for arrays and data structures, at least not the way they're implemented in other programming languages. (Data structures let you put several kinds of information into a single variable but access each item separately. For example, you might have a data structure to hold a mailing address, with separate items for the city, state, zip code, and so forth. An array is simply a list of values you can access by number.)

In HyperTalk, you can set up data structures by using chunk expressions. For example, you can create an array by using the lines of a container:

```
put it into line 6 of myArray
get line nextLine of field "Index Array"
```

You can set up a two-dimensional array using items or words to subdivide each line:

```
put 3 into item x of line y of my2DArray
```

If your data contains commas, use the **itemDelimiter** property to change the character that separates items to one that isn't found in your data.

9

Expressions and Operators

This chapter explains how to construct arithmetic, geometric, logical, and textual expressions using operators and sources of value. It describes how to use (and override) operator precedence and discusses the important difference between factors and expressions.

For information on the sources of values that constitute expression operands, see "Sources of Value," Chapter 8. For examples that show expressions in relation to objects, see "Referring to Objects," Chapter 7.

Some Basic Definitions

An *expression* is any source of value, or combination of sources of value. The sources discussed in the previous chapter are the simplest types of expressions. You can use operators to combine these sources to produce more complex expressions.

A *factor* is the first fully resolvable portion of an expression. All factors are expressions, but not all expressions are factors. Enclosing an expression in parentheses turns it into a factor.

The following lists illustrate the differences:

Expression	Its First Factor
3 + 4	3
(3 + 4)	(3 + 4)
(3 + 4)/field 4	(3 + 4)
field 6 * pi	field 6
sin of pi / 4	sin of pi
sin(pi/4)	sin(pi/4)
sin(pi/4) * exp2(12)	sin(pi/4)
whole world	whole
"whole world"	"whole world"

123

Who Cares?

The difference between expressions and factors makes a difference when you're using certain HyperTalk vocabulary words. For example, when you call a function using the form `the functionName of param`, *param* must be a factor. So if you ask for `the round of pi/4`, HyperTalk first finds `the round of pi` (which is 3) and divides the results by 4, ending up with `.75`. If you really want to round off π/4, you need to enclose the expression `pi/4` in parentheses, turning it into a factor.

The syntaxes of objects also differ. References to a field, for example, are always factors. If you refer to `field 7 + 1`, you don't get field 8; rather, the syntax takes the value of field 7 and adds 1 to it. But references to cards are expressions: If you refer to `card 2 + 3`, you get card 5, and `field 1 of card 2 + 3` gets you field 1 of card 5.

Types of Values

All values in HyperTalk are strings. But HyperTalk converts strings to logical or numeric values as such values are needed. For example, the functions **sin** and **cos** take numeric arguments, **charToNum** and **length** take string arguments, and comparisons return logical results. See the **is a** operator in Part III for more information about the types of data you can use.

LOGICAL

Logical values are always represented by the words true or false, and represent the outcome of some comparison:

```
10 > 7 -- true, because 10 is greater than 7
A = 12 -- true if the value of variable A is 12,
       -- false in all other cases
field 2 is empty -- true if field 2 is empty, false if not empty
7 < 3 = field 7  -- true if field 7 holds the string value "false"
```

STRINGS

String values are groups of ASCII characters meant to be taken literally:

```
put charToNum("Q")
put "Nuclear war is unthinkable" into field 12
```

NUMERIC

Numeric values are groups of characters that represent numbers. Such values consist of the digits 0 through 9, with the period(.) representing the decimal point.

International Hyperdecimals

Even though many countries use the comma (,) to represent the decimal point, all versions of HyperTalk use the period. When you localize your stack, you might want to use commas as decimal points in order to be sensitive to local custom. The following handler does it for you:

```
function localize numToChange
   if numToChange contains "." then
      put comma into char offset(".", numToChange) of numToChange
   end if
   return numToChange
end localize
```

Operators

Operators act upon the value of expressions. HyperTalk has a variety of operators, all of which are defined in this section.

RELATIONAL OPERATORS

A relational operator compares the relationship between two sources and produces a logical (true or false) result. (See Table 9.1.)

Table 9.1   Relational Operators

Operator	Relationship
is, =	Equal to
is not, <>, ≠	Not equal to
>	Greater than
<	Less than
>=, ≥	Greater than or equal to
<=, ≤	Less than or equal to
contains	Presence of
is in	Presence of
is not in	Absence of

Here are some examples:

```
x = y        -- x and y evaluate to the same value
x is not y   -- x and y do not evaluate to the same value
```

```
x > y        -- value of x is greater than the value of y
x < y        -- value of x is less than the value of y
"rats" contains "at" -- true because the string "at" is in "rats"
"at" is in "rats"  -- true because the string "at" is in "rats"
foo is in field 3   -- true if the contents of foo is in field 3
joy is not in wealth -- true if the contents of joy is not
                     -- an exact match for a pattern of characters
                     -- in the contents of wealth
```

Most relational comparisons are used within **if...then...else** constructs. But you can test relationships within the message box, since entering any expression into the message box gets its value:

```
userName = "John Scribblemonger"  -- returns true or false
field 12 = 17              -- ditto
```

Techie Alert

When you compare two floating point numbers for equality, in order to compensate for low bit error HyperTalk checks whether the numbers are really close rather than exactly equal. Here's what the code looks like internally:

```
floatThresh = 0.00000000001;
EQ := ABS(num1 - num2) < floatThresh;
NE := ABS(num1 - num2) > floatThresh;
```

CONCATENATION OPERATORS

Concatenation operators tie separate strings together.

Table 9.2   Concatenation Operators

Operator	Effect
&	Concatenates operands
&&	Concatenates operands, adding a space between them

Here are some examples using string operators:

```
"a" & "b"   -- yields "ab"
"a" && "b"  -- yields "a b"
foo & bar -- yields contents of foo combined with contents of bar
```

ARITHMETIC OPERATORS

Arithmetic operators combine two numerical values to produce an arithmetic result.

Table 9.3   Arithmetic Operators

Operator	Operation	Example	Yields
^	Exponentiation	`13^3`	2197
*	Multiplication	`13 * 3`	39
/	Floating point division	`13/3`	4.333333
div	Integer division	`13 div 3`	4
		`-13 div 3`	-4
mod	Modulus division	`13 mod 3`	1
		`-13 mod 3`	-1
+	Addition	`13 + 3`	16
-	Subtraction	`13 - 3`	10

About div, /, and mod

The **/** operator divides the second number by the first and returns the dividend. The **div** operator divides the second number by the first and returns the integer part of the dividend. The **mod** operator divides the second number by the first and returns the remainder.

If the second operand for the **/** operator is 0, you'll get the value `INF`, meaning "an infinite number." If you use 0 as the second operand of either **mod** or **div**, you get an error message.

LOGICAL OPERATORS

Logical operators combine logical (true or false) values and produce a logical result:

```
if Val > Cost and this = that then doSomeHandler
```

HyperTalk has three logical operators: **not**, **and**, and **or**. When you combine two values using **and**, both operands must be true to get a true result. When you combine two values using **or**, if either value or both values is true, the result is true.

For the above example, HyperTalk performs the following steps:

1. The contents of `Val` is compared to the contents of `Cost`. The comparison is numeric if both variables contain numbers, alphabetic if not. If `Val` is greater than `Cost`, then the result is true. Otherwise the result is false.

2. The contents of `this` is compared to the contents of `that`. The comparison is numeric if both variables contain numbers, alphabetic if not. If the values are the same, then the result is true. Otherwise the result is false.

3. The result of comparison 1 is logically combined (that is, ANDed) with the result of comparison 2. If both results are true, then the value of the whole expression `Val > Cost and this = that` is true, and the handler `doSomeHandler` is called.

Table 9.4 shows how HyperTalk combines the results of relational operations using the **and** and **or** logical operators.

Table 9.4   Logical Operators

Operator	1st Operand	2nd Operand	Result
and	true	true	true
	true	false	false
	false	false	false
	false	true	false
or	true	true	true
	true	false	true
	false	false	false
	true	false	true
not	true		false
	false		true

Assume that the expression "a = b" is true, and that the expression "c = d" is also true:

```
a = b and c = d   -- yields true
a = b or c = d    -- yields true
a = b and c ≠ d   -- yields false
a = b or c ≠ d    -- yields true
a ≠ b and c ≠ d   -- yields false
a ≠ b or c ≠ d    -- yields false
a ≠ b and c = d   -- yields false
a ≠ b or c = d    -- yields true
```

Not

The **not** operator (called a *unary* or *prefix* logical operator, because it takes only one operand) negates the value of the factor immediately following it:

```
not (a = b) and c = d   -- yields false
not (a = b or c = d)    -- yields false
a = b and not (c ≠ d)   -- yields true
not (a = b) or c ≠ d    -- yields false
not (a ≠ b and c ≠ d)   -- yields true
not (a ≠ b) or c ≠ d    -- yields true
not (a ≠ b) and c = d   -- yields true
a ≠ b or not (c = d)    -- yields false
```

The expression `not (a = b)` is the same as `a ≠ b`.

Not takes a factor, so if a and b both contain false, then `not a and b` yields false, but `not (a and b)` yields true.

Combining Logical Operations

You can chain logical operations to any length. The order of precedence in logical operations from highest to lowest is parentheses, **not**, **and**, **or**:

```
not (a = b) and c = d or not (a = b or c = d) -- yields false
a = b and c = d or not (a = b or c = d)        -- yields true
```

EXISTENCE AND TYPE OPERATORS

The existence operators **there is a** and **there is no** are unary (that is, they take a single operand) and report whether the specified element exists. The type operators **is a** and **is not a** report whether the specified element or container is a particular kind of thing or not.

For more information about the details of these operators, see **there is a** and **is a** in Part III, "The Elements of HyperTalk." Because of their complexity, these operators are fully documented in that section.

GEOMETRIC OPERATORS

HyperTalk's geometric operators **is within** and **is not within** report whether a point is within a rectangle (true or false). A point is two integer items; a rectangle is four integer items. (An integer is any whole number.)

```
the mouseLoc is within "10,10,100,100"
the location of field 2 is within the rect of field 1
this is within that
"20,30" is within "10,10,100,100"
the topLeft of field 6 is not within field 7
the bottomRight of button 7 is not within "20,30,50,100"
```

If you are specifying a literal value for the operands, you must enclose it in quotation marks. Otherwise, HyperTalk interprets the separate items as different parameters, causing an error message to appear.

Operator Precedence

Precedence determines the order in which HyperTalk carries out calculations on expressions. If an expression contains more than one operator, the operators with higher precedence are calculated before items with lower precedence.

Table 9.5 shows all operators from highest precedence to lowest precedence. If two or more operators with the same precedence appear within an expression, HyperTalk evaluates the expression from left to right (except for exponentiation, which is evaluated right to left).

Table 9.5   Operator Precedence

Precedence	Operators
1	unary -, not, there is a, there is no
2	^
3	*, /, mod, div
4	+, -
5	&, &&
6	>=, ≥, >, <=, ≤, <
	contains, is in, is not in,
	is within, is not within,
	there is a, there is no
7	=, is, <>, ≠, is not
8	and
9	or

You can use parentheses to override the normal order of calculations. Anything inside parentheses is computed first, regardless of the precedence of the operators inside the parentheses.

Here are some examples of precedence in the evaluation of numeric expressions. Each example shows the intermediate steps that Hypertalk takes to evaluate the expression. The portion of the expression currently being evaluated is underlined. Expressions on the same line begin with similar operators and values, but the ones on the right demonstrate how parentheses change evaluation:

```
5 * 3 + 20 div 3^2        5 * ( (3 + 20) div 3)^2
5 * 3 + 20 div 9          5 * (23 div 3) ^ 2
15 + 2                    5 * 7 ^ 2
17                        5 * 49
                          245
```

```
2^3^.5                   (2^3)^.5
2^1.732051               8^.5
3.321997                 2.828427
```

```
12.5 mod 5 * 4 div 3     12.5 mod 5 * (4 div 3)
2.5 * 4 div 3            12.5 mod 5 * 1
10 div 3                 2.5 * 1
3                        2.5
```

String Comparisons, ASCII, and Non-English Alphabets

HyperTalk uses simple dictionary ordering, without regard to capitalization, when you ask whether two strings are equal or whether one string contains or is in another string:

```
"A" is "a"          -- yields true
"Peace" = "peace"   -- yields true
"P" is in "peace"   -- yields true
```

But it uses ASCII ordering for other comparisons:

```
"Peace" < "peace"   -- yields true (uppercase letters precede
                    -- lowercase ones in ASCII ordering)
```

Characters from non-English alphabets (for example å, ë, œ, æ) also follow this approach to ordering in greater-than and less-than comparisons:

```
"a" = "å"      -- yields true (the base character "a" is the same)
"åø" = "ao"    -- ditto
"a" < "å"      -- yields true, because < uses ASCII ordering
```

If you intend to write stacks that need to compare non-English characters, see the chapter on international utilities in *Inside Macintosh* (Volume 1).

10

Messages and the Message Order

This chapter describes the message-sending path in detail. Before you can understand this chapter, you need to read the sections in Chapter 1, "The Basics of HyperTalk," that describe messages and the message path.

HyperCard's internal "send message" primitive

HyperCard has at its core a "send message" primitive. This primitive takes as its parameters a message and a starting object. In effect, it asks "What's the message, and where do I start looking for a handler to act on it?" For example, the primitive might be `send mouseUp to button 1`. Every message has an implied "send" before it and a "to object" after it. The destination is the target. If the target doesn't want it (that is, if the target's script doesn't have a handler whose name matches the message name) the message goes to the next object in the message-passing path to see if it wants the message; and so it goes through the message-passing path.

HyperTalk System Messages

HyperCard sends a system message whenever some event of significance, such as a mouse click, has happened while the browse tool is active. These are the system messages, listed by the object HyperCard first sends them to:

Buttons

deleteButton	mouseEnter	mouseUp
mouseDoubleClick	mouseLeave	mouseWithin
mouseDown	mouseStillDown	newButton

133

Fields

closeField	mouseDown	mouseWithin
deleteField	mouseEnter	newField
enterInField	mouseLeave	openField
exitField	mouseStillDown	returnInField
keyDown	mouseUp	tabKey
mouseDoubleClick		

Cards

appleEvent	functionKey	newCard
arrowKey	help	newStack
choose	hide	openBackground
close window	idle	openCard
closeBackground	keyDown	openStack
closeCard	mouseDoubleClick	quit
closeStack	mouseDown	resume
commandKeyDown	mouseEnter	resumeStack
controlKey	mouseLeave	returnKey
deleteBackground	mouseStillDown	sizeWindow
deleteCard	mouseUp	startup
deleteStack	mouseWithin	suspend
doMenu	moveWindow	suspendStack
enterKey	newBackground	tabKey
errorDialog		

HyperCard sends messages pertaining to a background or stack, such as **openBackground**, to the current card first. The background and stack objects see such messages only after they've passed through the message-passing path and reached that level. (This applies only when HyperCard automatically sends such messages. You can always send the message explicitly to a background or stack.) Messages you type into the message box are sent first to the current card.

The exact path a message traverses depends on whether the current handler has gone to a different card.

The Static Path

The static message-passing path of any object is made up of the object itself plus the objects that contain it. A card contains fields and buttons; a background contains cards; a stack contains backgrounds; HyperCard contains stacks. The message moves from the starting object through levels of increasing scope to HyperCard.

For example, if you click a button, the resulting **mouseDown** message first checks the button's script to see whether there's a handler for it. If not, it checks the current card's script; if there's no **mouseDown** handler there, it goes to the background's script; and so on, until it reaches HyperCard itself. If a message is first sent to a card, it starts at the card level, then goes on to the background the card belongs to, and so on. The message stops as soon as it finds a matching handler.

Functions and custom messages work the same way. If you call a function from a card's script, HyperCard first checks the card script to see whether it contains a handler for that function. If not, it checks the background script. Then it checks the stack script. Then it checks whether the stack contains an XFCN that can handle the function, and the call proceeds through the entire message path until either it finds a corresponding handler or it reaches HyperCard, the last point in the message-passing path.

This is the complete message path:

1. Button or field script
2. The script of the card that the button or field is on
3. The script of the background that card belongs to
4. The script of the stack that background is in
5. The XCMDs and XFCNs in that stack's resource fork
6. The script of the first stack (if any) in the **stacksInUse**, followed by its XCMDs and XFCNs, followed by any other stacks in use and their XCMDs and XFCNs
7. The home stack script
8. The XCMDs and XFCNs in the home stack
9. Any XCMDs and XFCNs in the HyperCard application
10. Any XCMDs and XFCNs in the System file
11. HyperCard itself

What happens if the message reaches HyperCard without being caught depends on whether it's a system message, a command message, or a custom message. If the message or function call corresponds to a built-in command or function, HyperCard executes that command or function. If HyperCard doesn't recognize the message at all—as in the case of misspellings, user-defined messages that aren't caught by handlers, and other mistakes— HyperCard puts up an error dialog.

The Dynamic Path

The dynamic path is an extended message path. If one of the executing handlers has gone to a card other than the original card, HyperCard inserts the current card, stack, and background into the message path for as long as the handler is executing, until it returns to the starting card. Here's an example:

```
on mouseUp
   push this card           -- using the static path
   go to stack "Addresses"  -- start using dynamic path
   get field 3
   pop card                 -- resume using static path
   put it into card field "New Address"
end mouseUp
```

This is the dynamic message path (steps that aren't in the static path are marked with *):

1. Button or field script

2. The script of the card that the button or field is on

3. The script of the background that card belongs to

4. The script of the stack that background is in

5. The XCMDs and XFCNs in that stack's resource fork

* 6. The script of the current card

* 7. The script of the current card's background

* 8. The script of the current card's stack

* 9. The XCMDs and XFCNs in the current stack's resource fork

10. The script of the first stack (if any) in the **stacksInUse**, followed by its XCMDs and XFCNs, followed by any other stacks in use and their XCMDs and XFCNs

11. The home stack script

12. The XCMDs and XFCNs in the home stack

13. Any XCMDs and XFCNs in the HyperCard application

14. Any XCMDs and XFCNs in the System file

15. HyperCard itself

Overriding the Message Path

Once a message is caught by a handler and the handler runs, the message ordinarily is discarded and doesn't proceed any farther along the message path. However, you can use the keywords **pass** and **send** from inside a handler to either put the current message back on the message-passing path (**pass**) or send any message directly to another object (**send**).

The statement pass *messageName* immediately transfers control out of the current handler and passes *messageName*, along with any parameters it has, to the next step on the message-passing path.

The statement send *message* to *object* sends *message* directly to the *object* without traversing HyperCard's normal message path to get to that object. You can send a message to a point farther along the message-passing path, earlier in the path, or to another object at the same level. For example, a card handler can send a message to a stack, to another card in the same stack, to a button or a field, to HyperCard, or to any other object that's either in the message path or in the current stack.

Once a message gets to its intended object, it moves through the normal message path starting from that object. For instance, if you send a message to a card, if that card has a handler for that message, the handler is executed; otherwise, the message goes next to that card's background, then to the stack, and so forth.

The Resource Path

When you call for a resource—for example, when you ask the **picture** command to display a PICT resource—HyperCard looks for it in the resource forks of the following files, in order:

1. The current stack

2. Any stacks in use, in order

3. The Home stack

4. The HyperCard application

5. The System file

As with the message-passing path, once HyperCard finds a resource with the specified name or ID, it uses that resource and looks no further.

One implication of the resource path is that resources in your stack can override HyperCard's own resources. You should therefore be careful not to give your own icons, pictures, sounds, palettes, and other resources IDs that will conflict with the IDs HyperCard uses for its own resources. If there is a conflict—for example, if HyperCard tries to display a dialog that contains a PICT of its own, but your stack contains another PICT with the same ID—your resource will be used in place of the standard one, and this may lead to unexpected results.

Message Sending Order

Many events make HyperCard send multiple messages. Table 10.1 lists multiple message events, and shows the order in which the messages are sent. All the messages listed in Table 10.1 are first sent to the current card. (Messages that are marked with an asterisk (*) are sent only when MultiFinder is not running.) Message names are enclosed in parentheses if they're sent only under certain circumstances. For example, the action of deleting a card sends a **deleteBackground** message only if the card that's being deleted is the only one of its background. In this case, deleting the card also removes all traces of the background, so HyperCard sends **deleteBackground** as sell as **deleteCard.**

Table 10.1   Multiple Message Events

Event	Message Order

Start HyperCard	`startup`
	`openStack`
	`openBackground`
	`openCard`

Suspend for launch*	`closeCard`
	`closeBackground`
	`closeStack`
	`suspend`

Resume from launch*	`resume`
	`openStack`
	`openBackground`
	`openCard`

(Continued)

Table 10.1   Multiple Message Events *(Continued)*

Event	Message Order

Quit HyperCard	`closeCard`
	`closeBackground`
	`closeStack`
	`quit`

Stack change	`closeCard`
	`closeBackground`
	`closeStack`
	`openStack`
	`openBackground`
	`openCard`

Background change	`closeCard`
	`closeBackground`
	`openBackground`
	`openCard`

Card change	`closeCard` `openCard`

New stack	`closeCard`
	`closeBackground`
	`newStack`
	`newBackground`
	`newCard`
	`openStack`
	`openBackground`
	`openCard`

New stack in new window	`suspendStack`
	`newStack`
	`newBackground`
	`newCard`
	`openStack`
	`openBackground`
	`openCard`

New background	`closeCard`
	`closeBackground`
	`newBackground`
	`newCard`
	`openBackground`
	`openCard`

(Continued)

Table 10.1   Multiple Message Events   *(Continued)*

Event	Message Order

New card	`closeCard`
	`newCard`
	`openCard`

Delete stack	`closeCard`
	`closeBackground`
	`closeStack`
	`deleteStack`

Delete background	`closeCard`
	`closeBackground`
	`deleteCard`
	`deleteBackground`

Delete card	`closeCard`
	`(closeBackground)`
	`deleteCard`
	`(deleteBackground)`
	`(openBackground)`
	`openCard`

Paste card	`(newBackground)`
	`newCard`
	`(openBackground)`
	`openCard`

Cut card	`closeCard`
	`(closeBackground)`
	`deleteCard`
	`(deleteBackground)`
	`(openBackground)`
	`openCard`

Message Anomalies

The act of opening and closing a script doesn't send any messages, even if the script you're opening is the script of a remote card or stack.

In versions of HyperCard from 2.0 through 2.1, under certain circumstances, HyperCard uses the dynamic message path when it shouldn't. Specifically, on any card except the first one in the stack (or the first one you went to with the statement `go to card of stack stackName`), HyperCard uses the dynamic path instead of the static path. So, for example, if the stack script sends a message, that message goes first to the stack, then to the current card, and so on through the message path. This bug is fixed in version 2.2.

Part III

The Elements of HyperTalk

The Elements of HyperTalk

Part III lists all the keywords, commands, functions, properties, and system messages of the HyperTalk language, in alphabetical order.

Commands

Commands are statements that tell HyperCard to perform some action. Each command is sent as a message through the message-passing path. If the message travels all the way to HyperCard without being intercepted by a handler, HyperCard performs the action. You can think of commands as messages for which HyperCard has built-in handlers.

Some commands are also system messages. If a command can be triggered by a user action (such as pressing a key) as well as by explicitly issuing it in a handler, it is classified as a command/message.

Functions

Functions are questions you ask of HyperCard. A function returns a value, which may be based on one or more arguments passed to it. Some functions, such as **the date** and **the time**, return a value reflecting the current state of the system. The value of a function can change over time; HyperCard calculates a function's current value when it's called.

Most functions have two forms: one in which the arguments are enclosed in parentheses and one with no parentheses. When you use a form that contains parentheses, the function is sent as a message through the usual message-passing path, and it can be intercepted and redefined by a handler somewhere in the path. Function forms that don't contain parentheses send the function directly to HyperCard; such function calls don't go through the message path, so you can't override them with a handler.

When you're using a form that doesn't include parentheses, any arguments must be factors (see the discussion of factors and expressions in Chapter 9). When you're using a form with parentheses, the arguments can be either factors or expressions. (You can make an expression into a factor by enclosing it in parentheses.)

Keywords

Keywords form the skeleton that all handlers are built around.

Statements containing keywords aren't sent as messages. This means they don't go through the message-passing path. Instead, HyperCard executes them directly. So you can't catch and redefine keywords the way you can redefine commands and functions.

Messages

Messages (also called system messages) are sent by HyperCard to particular objects in response to some event. The event may be a user action such as clicking the mouse or typing a key, or it may be caused by HyperCard itself (such as the **idle** message that's sent repeatedly when nothing else it happening).

Some system messages are also commands. If a message causes HyperCard to perform some action when it finishes traversing the message-passing path and gets to HyperCard, it is classified as a command/message.

Operators

Operators act on one or more values to produce a result. Most operators are listed earlier in the book, in the chapter on "Expressions and Operators." However, because of their complexity, two operators are listed and fully explained in this section: **there is a** and **is a**.

Properties

Properties reflect the current state of some attribute of an object, window, or menu. You can set most properties with the **set** command, although a few are read-only.

Throughout Part III, the following conventions are used when describing syntax:

- *Italics* indicate a parameter. In the actual HyperTalk statement, you'll replace parameters with a specific instance of that term.

- Square brackets ([]) enclose optional terms. You can either include or ignore them.

- Curly braces ({}) enclose a group of terms from which you must pick one. Within a group, the choices are separated from each other by a vertical bar (|).

abs function

FORMS

the abs of *number*
abs(*number* **)**
```
abs(-3) -- yields 3
abs(3)  -- yields 3
the abs of sin(myAngle)
abs(it - 17)
```

ACTION

The **abs** function returns the *absolute value* of its argument. The absolute value of a number is its numerical value without regard to sign. For instance, the absolute value of 22.73 is the same as the absolute value of –22.73. More generally, the absolute value of a positive number is simply the number; the absolute value of a negative number is the negative of that number.

COMMENTS

You can use the **abs** function to determine the difference between two values. It's particularly useful when you do not know in advance which value is larger. The following handler reports the difference in temperature between two locations:

```
on weather
   ask "What's the temperature in San Francisco?"
   put it into sfTemp
   ask "What's the temperature in Boston?"
   put it into bostonTemp
   put the abs of (sfTemp - bostonTemp) into tempDifference
   answer "That's a difference of" && tempDifference && "degrees!"
end weather
```

The following useful handler computes the horizontal and vertical distance between any two points. It's especially handy for computing the offset of one object from another:

```
on measure
   put "Click at first point..." into message
   wait until the mouseClick
   put the clickLoc into firstPoint
   put "Click at second point..." into message
   wait until the mouseClick
   put the clickLoc into secondPoint
   -- compute difference
   put abs(item 1 of firstPoint - item 1 of secondPoint) ¬
   into horizDistance
   put abs(item 2 of firstPoint - item 2 of secondPoint) ¬
   into vertDistance
```

```
   -- report difference
   put "That's" && horizDistance && "pixels horizontally and " ¬
   && vertDistance && "pixels vertically." into message
end measure
```

Techie Alert: The **abs** function does its computations using integer math if the expression is already in integer form: for instance, `abs(1 - 3 + 2)` or `abs(the number of this card - the number of card "Fred")`. Otherwise, **abs** is computed using floating-point math.

add command   Introduced in version 1.0

FORMS

```
add number to [chunk of] container
add 5 to it
add insult to field "Injury"
add subtotal to runningTotal
add field "State Taxes" to last line of addItAll
add (message div 5) to message
```

ACTION

The **add** command adds a numeric value to the value in a container, and places the resulting sum in the container.

The original number in the container is lost, since the container is overwritten by the final sum. However, the value of the expression being added to the container is unchanged.

COMMENTS

In the following example, the global variable `subtotalHolder` holds a previously calculated subtotal in each of its lines. The example handler adds those subtotals together to compute the grand total:

```
on addEmUp
   global subtotalHolder
   put 0 into grandTotal
   repeat with subtotal = 1 to the number of lines in subtotalHolder
      -- here's the action
      add line subTotal of subTotalHolder to grandTotal
   end repeat
   put grandTotal into field "Total"
end addEmUp
```

The **add** command always puts its result into a container. You cannot add one number directly to another using **add**. If you want the sum of two numbers, use the **+** operator instead.

The container must contain a number. If you try to add a number to a container that contains something other than a number, you will get an error dialog. (You can check a container before adding something to it with the **is a number** operator.)

You can add a number to an empty container; **add** acts as though it contained the number 0. Remember, though, that you have to put something into local variables before you can use them. If you have not yet put something—even "empty"—into the local variable `foo`, the statement `add 22 to foo` will produce an error message, since you have not initialized `foo`.

If the *container* is a field or the message box, the **numberFormat** property determines the format of the resulting sum.

You can add a container to itself.

Techie alert: If both values to be added are integers, and if both have absolute values less than 1,073,741,823 (the greatest value possible for a 30-bit number), HyperCard uses integer math to compute the sum. Otherwise, the sum is computed using floating-point math.

The **add** command uses the same code as the + operator.

ALSO SEE

divide command; **is a** operator; **multiply** command; **numberFormat** property; **subtract** command

---

address property
Introduced in version 2.1

FORMS

```
the address [of HyperCard]
get the address
put the address of HyperCard into whereAmI
```

ACTION

The **address** global property describes the full AppleTalk address of the currently running copy of HyperCard. It is read-only and cannot be set by a handler.

This property only works when you're using System 7.

COMMENTS

The **address** reports the name of the zone your Mac is in, the name of the Macintosh (which is set in the Sharing Setup control panel), and the name of the HyperCard program or standalone application that's currently running. This function returns the name of the Macintosh:

```
function macName
  get the address
  set the itemDelimiter to colon
  return item 2 of it
end macName
```

The full AppleTalk address consists of three parts, separated by colons (:):

- The zone your Macintosh is in
- The name of your Macintosh
- The name of HyperCard

For example, if a Mac is named "North America" and resides in the zone "World Zone", the AppleTalk address of a copy of HyperCard running on that Mac is written as follows:

```
"World Zone:North America:HyperCard"
```

If the Mac is not on a network, or the network consists of only one zone, an asterisk is substituted for the zone name:

```
"*:North America:HyperCard"
```

The following handler lets you send a message to an application running anywhere on the network, but does not allow the send if the selected Mac is in a different zone:

```
on mouseUp
   answer program "Please select an application:"
   if it is empty then exit mouseUp -- user cancelled
   put it into destinationAddress
   set the itemDelimiter to colon
   if item 1 of destinationAddress is item 1 of the address then
      set the itemDelimiter to comma
      sendAppMessage
   else answer "You cannot send a message outside this zone."
end mouseUp
```

Error message under System 6:   The **address** property requires System 7 to work. If you use it with an earlier system version, it reports the message "Not supported by this version of the system."

ALSO SEE
answer program command; **send to program** keyword; **systemVersion** function

---

annuity function   Introduced in version 1.0

FORMS
annuity(*interestRate, numberOfPeriods***)**
annuity(.015,12)
annuity(field "Current Rate",monthsPerLoan)

ACTION
The **annuity** function returns the value of an ordinary annuity with payments of one unit, at the specified rate of interest per period and number of periods.

The formula for **annuity** is $(1 - (1 + interestRate)^{(- numberOfPeriods)})/interestRate$.

COMMENTS

The *interestRate* is expressed as a fraction of 1 rather than as a percentage of 100, so you must convert percentages (for example, 8.5%) to their floating-point equivalent (0.85) by dividing by 100.

You can use the **annuity** function to compute the amount of a loan payment. For example, the following handler calculates the amortized monthly payment for any loan amount:

```
on mortgagePayments currentRate
  ask "What's the loan amount?" with "15000"
  if it is empty then exit mortgagePayments
  if it is not a number then
    answer it && "is not a valid number!"
    exit mortgagePayments
  end if
  put it into loanAmount
  ask "How many years?" with "30"
  if it is empty then exit mortgagePayments
  put it * 12 into termInMonths
  put loanAmount/annuity(currentRate/12,termInMonths) into payment
  set the numberFormat to "0.00"
  answer "Your monthly loan payment is $" & payment with "Yikes!"
end mortgagePayments
```

The built-in **annuity** function is slightly more accurate than the computed formula above for very small values of *interestRate* (below 0.00001%).

Who ordered this?   Many people have wondered why HyperTalk has this somewhat obscure function in its built-in arsenal, since the formula (given above) can be readily implemented in a script if needed. What was the language designer thinking? Well, it turns out that the Standard Apple Numerics Package (SANE), the set of mathematics routines built into the Macintosh system software, includes the function that computes an annuity, so any application (like HyperCard) that uses the SANE routines gets access to SANE's annuity function more or less for free. (The reason the SANE engineers chose to include this function as a primitive must await future researchers.)

ALSO SEE

compound function; **numberFormat** property

answer command

FORMS

```
answer [normal] prompt [with button1[ or button2[ or button3]]]
answer "I'm sorry; that's not an option."
answer "OK — what'll it be?" with "Door #1" or "Door #2" or "Door #3"
answer field "Question" with field "Answer" or line 3 of field "Guess"
answer "Today is" && the long date & "."
answer the windows
```

ACTION

The **answer** command displays a modal dialog box (Figure III.1) containing a question or statement and one, two, or three buttons. The last button named is the default button. If you don't specify any button names, the dialog displays a single OK button.

The user clicks one of the buttons to dismiss the dialog. The name of the clicked button is returned to the handler in the **it** variable.

COMMENTS

This handler produces a dialog to ask the user whether to print certain cards before quitting:

```
on doMenu theItem
   if theItem is "Quit HyperCard" then
      -- display dialog of Figure III.1
      answer "Print marked cards before quitting?" with "No" or "Yes"
      if it is "Yes" then print marked cards
   end if
   pass doMenu
end doMenu
```

While the dialog is on the screen, the handler that displayed it is suspended until the user dismisses it. There is no way to click one of the buttons from a script.

The dialog box stays on the screen until the user clicks a button to reply, or presses Return, Enter, or Command-Period. Pressing Return or Enter is equivalent to clicking the default button (the one with a bold outline); in a dialog box produced by **answer**, the default button is always the one at the far right. Pressing Command-Period dismisses the dialog and aborts the rest of the running handler or handlers.

While the answer dialog is displayed, the cursor is changed to an arrow. If you have set the **cursor** property to use a custom cursor, you must set it back after the **answer** statement.

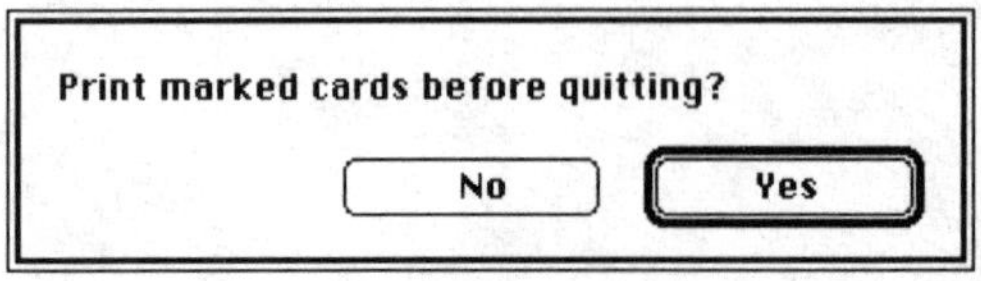

Figure III.1   Answer dialog box with alternative answers

Get Your Priorities Straight

This three-handler example helps you select the top priority from a range of choices. If you want to extend the list, just modify the `initProblems` handler.

```
on changeTheWorld
  global problemList
  if problemList is empty then initProblems
  -- start with the first problem....
  put line 1 of problemList into worstProblem
  -- ...and check each problem
  repeat with problemLine = 2 to the number of lines in problemList
    put line problemLine of problemList into newProblem
    repeat -- until the user either chooses or decides to quit
      answer "Which is worse?" with item 1 of worstProblem ¬
      or item 1 of newProblem or "Give Up"
      if it is "Give Up" then
        play harpsichord
        answer "You really can make a difference!" with "I Quit" ¬
        or "Press On"
        if it is "I Quit" then
          exit changeTheWorld
        end if
      else -- made a choice other than "Give Up"
        exit repeat
      end if
    end repeat
    if it is item 1 of newProblem then put newProblem into worstProblem
  end repeat
  answer "Call" && item 2 of worstProblem && "at" ¬
  && item 3 of worstProblem & "."
end changeTheWorld


on initProblems
  global problemList
  put empty into problemList
  addProblem("Homelessness,Habitat for Humanity,912-924-6935")
  addProblem("Injustice,Amnesty International,800-AMNESTY")
  addProblem("Ignorance,Project Literacy U.S.(PLUS),212-555-1212")
  addProblem("Disease,The Names Project,415-863-5511")
  addProblem("Pollution,The Nature Conservatory,703-841-5300")
end initProblems


on addProblem theProblem
  global problemList
  put the number of lines of problemList into numberLines
  put theProblem into line (numberLines + 1) of problemList
end addProblem
```

The **answer** command displays the prompt and the button names in 12-point Chicago type. The prompt is left-aligned and the button names are centered.

The prompt can be up to 255 characters long and up to 14 lines. The buttons are wide enough to show about 12 characters each, depending on the width of the actual characters. Button names should be one line. If a button name has more than one line, the dialog tries to vertically center the name, so if the name has an odd number of lines the middle line will be displayed, and if the name has an even number of lines you will see the bottom of one line and the top of the next.

Changes to HyperTalk: In versions earlier than 2.0, the **answer** dialog has room to display only about 38 characters for the prompt, and the prompt is limited to one line. If the prompt parameter contains more than one line, 1.x only shows the first line (or as much of it as will fit). If a button name has more than one line, 1.x uses only the *last* line.

If you want to ask a longer question or offer more than three options to the user, consider constructing a questionnaire on a card, using buttons and fields to simulate a complex dialog box.

ALSO SEE
ask command; **answer file** command; **it** variable (Chapter 8)

---

answer file command   Introduced in version 2.0

FORMS

```
answer file prompt [of type fileType1[ or fileType2[ or fileType3]]]
answer file "What application do you want to launch?" of type "application"
answer file field picturePrompt of type "TIFF" or "PICT" or "PNTG"
answer file empty of type "text"   -- no prompt appears
```

ACTION

The **answer file** command brings up a standard file selection dialog (the same one most applications display in response to the Open command), so the user can select a file. If you specify one or more file types, the dialog shows only files of that type or types, and filters out all others. If no file type is specified, the dialog lists all files, including invisible files.

The full pathname of the selected file is returned in the **it** variable. If the user clicks the Cancel button instead of choosing a file, **it** is set to empty and the **result** function is set to "Cancel".

COMMENTS

The **answer file** command does not open the file; it only returns the name of the selected file. If you want the file opened or otherwise operated on, you must do so explicitly in your handler.

This handler lets the user select a text file to be edited with a favorite editor:

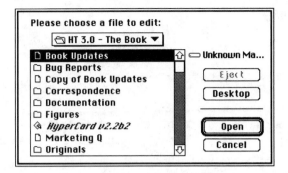

Figure III.2 Answer File dialog box

```
on editFile textEditor,fileType
   -- displays the standard file dialog - see Figure III.2
   answer file "Please choose a file to edit:" ¬
   of type fileType or "TEXT"
   if it is empty then exit to HyperCard
   open it with textEditor
end editFile
```

You might call the handler like this:

```
editFile "MacWrite II","MWII"
```

While the dialog is on the screen, the handler that displayed it is suspended until the user dismisses it. There is no way to click one of the buttons from a script.

The dialog box stays on the screen until the user double-clicks a filename, clicks the Open or Cancel button, or presses Return, Enter, or Command-Period. Pressing Return or Enter is equivalent to clicking Open. Pressing Command-Period dismisses the dialog. To dismiss the dialog and abort any running handlers, press Command-Shift-Period; to enter the debugger, press Command-Option-Period.

While the dialog is displayed, the cursor is changed to an arrow. If you have set the **cursor** property to use a custom cursor, you must set it back after the **answer file** statement.

The prompt string appears in 12-point Chicago type. It can be up to 254 characters and up to six lines. If the prompt string is more than one line, the dialog box grows to accommodate it.

The next handler lets the user select a text file, imports the contents, strips out any superfluous return characters, and puts the text into a field named "Imported Text":

```
on mouseUp
   -- prompt user for a file
   answer file "Import text from:" of type "text"
   if it is empty then exit mouseUp -- user cancelled
   -- import text
   put it into fileToImport
   set the cursor to watch
   open file fileToImport
```

```
      read from file fileToImport until end
      put it after fileText
      close file fileToImport
      -- strip extra returns
      put the length of fileText into lastCharPosition
      put 1 into startChar
      repeat until startChar ≥ lastCharPosition
        get offset(return,char startChar to lastCharPosition of fileText)
        if it is 0 then exit repeat  -- no returns remaining, so we're done
        if char (it + 1) of fileText is not return
        then put space into char it of fileText
        put it + 2 into startChar
      end repeat
      -- put finished product into a field
      put fileText into card field "Imported Text"
    end mouseUp
```

Parameters: The prompt can be any expression. However, the file type parameters must be factors. In practice, if you are using a complicated expression to indicate a file type, be sure to enclose it in parentheses to make certain it is evaluated correctly. (See the discussion of factors and expressions in Chapter 9 for some examples.)

If you forget to include a prompt parameter, HyperCard interprets the word "file" as the prompt and displays an **answer** dialog box instead, as shown in Figure III.3.

File types: All Macintosh files have a four-character file type and a four-character creator signature. The file type indicates the kind of file. For example, all applications have type APPL, all plain text files are type TEXT, and all HyperCard stacks are type STAK. Utilities such as ResEdit let you learn a file's type.

HyperTalk recognizes synonyms for some common file types. You can use the synonyms in Table III.1 in place of the four-character type to make your code a little more readable.

Table III.1   File Type Synonyms

Type	Synonym	Meaning
APPL	application	Application
PICT	picture	PICT format document
PNTG	paint, painting	MacPaint document
STAK	stack	HyperCard stack
TEXT	text	Plain text document

Figure III.3   Probably not what you had in mind

ALSO SEE

answer command; **ask file** command; **it** variable (Chapter 8); **open application** command; **open file** command; **read** command

---

answer program command   Introduced in version 2.1

FORMS

```
answer program prompt [of type programType]
answer program "Which copy of Excel do you want to use?"
answer program linkToPrompt
answer program empty of type "spreadsheet"
answer program field "Where is" of type "WILD"
```

ACTION

The **answer program** command displays a Process-to-Process Communication (PPC) dialog box that lists all linkable processes running on all Macs on the network.

The full AppleTalk address (zone, Mac name, and program name) of the process the user selects is placed in the **it** variable. If the user clicks Cancel instead of choosing a process, **it** is empty and **the result** is set to "Cancel".

This command requires System 7.

COMMENTS

The **answer program** command does not establish a link to another program; it only lets you choose among the programs available for linking. If you want to link to that program, you must take care of it explicitly in your handler, using **send to program** or **request**.

This example displays the dialog shown in Figure III.4 to let the user select a process on a target Mac, then attempts to quit that process:

```
on mouseUp
  answer program "Where do you want to send the message?"
  if it is empty then exit mouseUp -- user cancelled
  send "myMessage" to program it
end mouseUp
```

The *prompt* appears centered at the top of the dialog. Only the first line of the *prompt* appears in the dialog. If you specify an empty *prompt*, the dialog appears with the default prompt "Choose a program to link to:". (If you are not on an AppleTalk network, or if your network is divided into zones, the dialog you see will look a little different.)

Figure III.4   The answer program dialog

If you forget to include any *prompt* parameter at all, however, HyperCard will interpret the word "program" as the *prompt* and give you an **answer** dialog box instead (Figure III.5).

The dialog shows only linkable processes that are running on Macs whose Sharing Setup control panel has the Program Linking checkbox turned on. If a Mac on the network does not have program linking enabled, it will not appear in the list of Macintoshes. If an application is not System 7-friendly, it will not appear in the list of programs, even if the Mac it's running on has Program Linking enabled.

The **answer program** command returns the full AppleTalk address of the process chosen, in the **it** variable. An AppleTalk address consists of three parts, separated by colons (:):

- The zone the Macintosh is in

- The name of the Macintosh

- The name of the program

For example, if a Mac is named "Bug Central" and resides in the zone "Software QA Zone", the AppleTalk address of a copy of HyperCard running on that Mac is written as follows:

```
"Software QA Zone:Bug Central:HyperCard"
```

The AppleTalk address is similar to a file pathname, as you can see. Each successive part of the address is nested one level deeper, down to the application itself.

If the network consists of only one zone, an asterisk is substituted for the zone name:

```
"*:Bug Central:HyperCard"
```

If you want to restrict the dialog to show only certain kinds of programs, use the *programType* parameter. A *programType* consists of the application's four-character creator signature. For example, the HyperCard application's signature is WILD, so to put up a dialog

Figure III.5   Probably not what you had in mind

box that shows all copies of HyperCard that are running on the network (but no other applications), use the following statement:

```
answer program "Where is the HyperCard you want to link to?" ¬
of type "WILD"
```

File types: All Macintosh files have a four-character file type and a four-character creator signature. All applications have the file type APPL. Utilities such as ResEdit let you learn an application's creator signature.

Techie alert: For more information about the *programType*, and ways in which an application can list itself with a type other than XXXX, see *Inside Macintosh*, Vol. VI (The PPC Toolbox).

ALSO SEE

address function; **it** variable (Chapter 8); **request** command; **send to program** keyword; **systemVersion** function

appleEvent message

Introduced in version 2.1

FORMS

```
appleEvent class,id,sender
appleEvent "aevt","odoc","*:Unknown Magnanimity:Finder"
appleEvent "misc","dosc","Corporate:Server:HyperCard 2.1"
```

ACTION

The **appleEvent** message is sent to the current card whenever HyperCard (or a standalone application) receives an AppleEvent.

To use AppleEvents, you must be using System 7.

COMMENTS

You should handle the **appleEvent** message if you want to block certain standard AppleEvents, or if you want to implement custom AppleEvents in your stack that HyperCard does not normally handle.

The following example shows how to trap for a specific AppleEvent:

```
on appleEvent theClass,theEvent,theSender
  if theEvent is "t234" then -- the name of your custom event
    request AppleEvent data -- get contents of AppleEvent
    send "handleCustomEvent" && it to this card -- custom handler
  else
    pass appleEvent -- let HyperCard handle event
  end if
end appleEvent
```

The *class* parameter is the AppleEvent's class designation. Typical class designations include `aevt` (required AppleEvents such as "open document") and `misc` (miscellaneous AppleEvents such as "do script").

The AppleEvent data component contains the meat of the AppleEvent. The data for the "open document" event is a return-separated list of the documents to be opened, the data for "do script" is the list of statements to be executed, and so on.

The *id* parameter is the name of the event that's been received. HyperCard recognizes seven standard AppleEvents:

- `clos` (close): closes the stack whose name is in the AppleEvent data.

- `dosc` (do script): executes the HyperTalk statements in the AppleEvent data.

- `eval` (evaluate): evaluates the AppleEvent data as a HyperTalk expression.

- `oapp` (open application): opens the application whose name appears in the AppleEvent data as if it had been launched by the Finder.

- `odoc` (open document): opens the stacks whose names appear in the AppleEvent data as if they had been double-clicked in the Finder.

- `pdoc` (print document): prints the stacks whose names appear in the AppleEvent data as if the user had selected them in the Finder and chosen Print from the File menu.

- `quit` (quit): quits HyperCard as though the user had chosen Quit HyperCard from the File menu.

The `dosc` and `eval` AppleEvents are of class `misc`; the rest are of class `aevt`. You can also trap for other events and handle them yourself, as shown in the example above.

The *sender* is the full AppleTalk address of the program that sent the AppleEvent. The address consists of three parts separated by colons:

- The zone the sending Macintosh is in

- The name of the sending Macintosh

- The name of the program that sent the AppleEvent

If your network doesn't have separate zones, the zone part of the address is "*".

The following handler (written by Kevin Calhoun) lets a "do script" AppleEvent execute the contents of a file, whose name is sent as the AppleEvent data:

```
on appleEvent class,ID
   if class is "misc" and id is "dosc" then
     request appleEvent data -- get the content of the AppleEvent
     put it into fileName
     if there is a file fileName then   -- if it's a filename
       open file fileName              -- do the script contained therein
       read from file fileName until end
       close file fileName
       do it
       exit appleEvent
     end if
```

```
      end if
      pass appleEvent
   end appleEvent
```

With HyperCard version 2.1 and later, if you double-click a stack in the Finder while HyperCard is running, the stack opens in a new window. This is a change from the behavior of older versions, in which the newly opened stack replaced the frontmost stack. The following handler, placed in your Home stack script, restores the old behavior:

```
   on appleEvent eventClass,eventID
      if eventID is "odoc" then
         request appleEvent data
         put line 1 of it into stackToOpen
         go to stack stackToOpen
      else pass appleEvent
   end appleEvent
```

Techie alert: For more information about the internal workings of AppleEvents, check *Inside Macintosh*, vol. VI.

Changes to HyperTalk: In versions of HyperCard before 2.2, HyperCard eats the initial odoc or pdoc AppleEvent if it is sent at launch time. Version 2.2 changes this behavior slightly. The first stack file is opened by HyperCard (and its name is removed from the AppleEvent data list), and then the odoc or pdoc AppleEvent message, with the remaining filenames, is sent to the current card. What this means is that in versions before 2.2, you cannot intercept the AppleEvent corresponding to the launch of HyperCard. But in version 2.2, you can handle the opening of all files except the first stack to be opened.

ALSO SEE

address property; **programs** function; **request** command; **request appleEvent** command; **send to program** keyword

---

arrowKey command/message   Introduced in version 1.0

FORMS

arrowKey {up|down|left|right}
arrowKey left
arrowKey myKey

ACTION

The **arrowKey** message is sent to the current card when the user presses any of the arrow keys. As with all messages, it can also be sent explicitly from a handler. You can write an **arrowKey** handler to trap this message if you want to override its behavior.

If there is no **arrowKey** handler in the message path, the action of **arrowKey** depends upon the setting of the **textArrows** property:

If **textArrows** is true and there is a selection in a field or the message box (a blinking insertion point is a selection, of zero length), pressing the arrow keys moves the insertion point one line or character in the indicated direction:

Up	Moves up one line
Down	Moves down one line
Left	Moves back one character
Right	Moves forward one character

If **textArrows** is false, or if it's true but there's no selection, pressing the arrow keys moves you to another card:

Up	Card viewed immediately after this one (can only be used after a "down")
Down	Card viewed immediately before this one (same as menu item Back)
Left	Previous card in the stack (same as menu item Prev)
Right	Next card in the stack (same as menu item Next)

COMMENTS

The most common use of **arrowKey** is to write a handler that overrides the arrow keys' normal behavior. For example, if your stack requires users to visit cards in a certain order, you may want to lock out use of the arrow keys entirely:

```
on arrowKey theKey
   -- no code-this handler just prevents arrowKey from being passed on
end arrowKey
```

You can also write a handler to let the user make some other, appropriate use of the arrow keys. The following example assumes that you have three fields side by side, and that the user may select any line of any of the fields as a separate cell (Figure III.6). It operates like a mini-spreadsheet, and the arrow keys move from cell to cell:

```
on arrowKey direction
   get the selectedLine
   -- the selectedLine is in the form "line x of card field y", so we
   -- will be concerned with word 2 (the line or row number) and the
   -- last word (the field or column number).
   if it is empty then pass arrowKey
   -- figure out which "cell" to move to
   if direction is "up" then add 1 to word 2 of it
   else if direction is "down" then subtract 1 from word 2 of it
   else if direction is "right" then add 1 to last word of it
   else if direction is "left" then subtract 1 from last word of it
   -- if we've gone off the spreadsheet borders, wrap around
   -- 1 is the first row, lastLine is the last row:
```

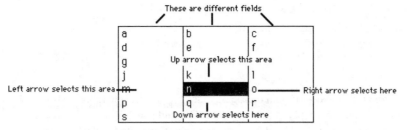

Figure III.6   Arrow keys in a spreadsheet

```
      put the number of lines in card field 1 into lastLine
      if word 2 of it < 1 then put lastLine into word 2 of it
      else if word 2 of it > lastLine then put 1 into word 2 of it
      -- 1 is the first column, 3 is the last column:
      if last word of it < 1 then put 3 into last word of it
      else if last word of it > 3 then put 1 into last word of it
      -- select the new "cell"
      select it
  end arrowKey
```

Pressing the down arrow can bring you through the last 100 cards viewed. However, revisiting one of the last 100 cards doesn't add that card to the list again.

Pressing the up arrow has no effect until you have backed up through one or more recent cards by using the down arrow, the Back item from the Go menu, or pressing the Escape or ~ keys.

ArrowKey interacts with keyDown: If there is a **keyDown** handler in the message-passing path, and it does not pass **keyDown**, it also traps the **arrowKey** message. If you want to use arrow keys, make certain that any **keyDown** handler contains the line

```
  pass keyDown
```

Changes to HyperTalk: In HyperCard versions before 1.1, the **textArrows** property does not exist, and pressing the arrow keys always moves the user to another card.

ALSO SEE
doMenu message; **textArrows** property

---

ask command Introduced in version 1.0
Last changed in version 2.0

FORMS
```
  ask [password [clear]] question [with defaultReply]
  ask "Please type your name:"
  ask "Who discovered water?" with "Somebody who wasn't a fish."
  ask card field "Question" with myPossibleAnswer
```

```
ask "Please enter the start time:" with the time
ask password "What's the password?"
ask password clear "Please set a new password:"
```

ACTION

The **ask** command displays a modal dialog box (see Figure III.7) with a question, a text field where the user can type a reply, and buttons for OK and Cancel.

If the user clicks OK to dismiss the dialog, the contents of the text field is placed in the **it** variable. If the user clicks Cancel, the **it** variable is empty (and the **result** function returns "Cancel".

The **ask password** variation, instead of returning the text of the user's reply, encrypts the text into a number and places the number into the **it** variable. Each character the user types appears in the dialog box as a bullet (•), so that others looking at the screen cannot see what the user has typed. This helps protect the privacy of passwords.

The **ask password clear** variation also uses bullets, but does not encrypt the reply.

COMMENTS

This handler asks for the name of the user. It presents, as the default answer, the contents of the userName variable, which is set up automatically by the Home stack from the User Preferences card:

```
on getTheName
   global userName
   -- displays the dialog box seen in Figure III.7
   ask "Please type your name:" with userName
   if it is not empty then put it into userName
end getTheName
```

If you provide a *defaultReply*, it's selected when the dialog appears, so whatever the user types replaces it automatically. The dialog box stays on the screen until the user clicks a button or presses Return, Enter, or Command-Period. Pressing Return or Enter is equivalent to clicking the OK button (the one with a bold outline). Pressing Command-Period is equivalent to clicking Cancel. Pressing Command-Shift-Period dismisses the dialog and halts all running handlers (it's the equivalent of an **exit to HyperCard** statement).

While the dialog is on the screen, the handler that displayed it is suspended until the user dismisses the dialog. There is no way to click one of the buttons from a script.

When the ask dialog is displayed, the cursor is changed to an arrow. If you have set the **cursor** property to use a custom cursor, you must set it back after the **ask** statement.

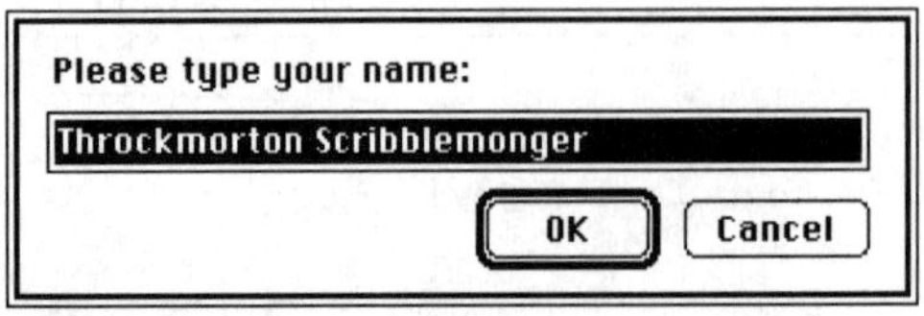

Figure III.7　Ask dialog box

Dialog format details: The *question* can be up to 254 characters long. The reply field can hold up to 254 characters.

Normally, the reply field is one line, and there is room for up to about 38 characters to be shown. (You can drag left or right to display more characters.) However, if the *defaultReply* parameter is more than one line, the text box will be expanded to the number of lines in the default reply. For example, the following statement will display an ask dialog with multiple lines (Figure III.8):

```
ask "Please type in a long phrase." with "What phrase?" & return & return
```

However, the user cannot type return characters into the reply field, even if the field is more than one line deep, since pressing Return is equivalent to clicking OK.

The maximum total number of lines for the *question* plus the *defaultReply* is 14.

About passwords: A password you set with **ask password** is different from the password you can set with the Protect Stack menu item. The Protect Stack password, if you set one, is required every time you enter the stack. With **ask password**, on the other hand, you can separately password-protect any part of a stack.

For example, you might require the user to enter a password before performing a certain function in a stack, such as adding new names to a list. This handler creates a password and stores the result (the encrypted number) in a hidden field called "Key":

```
on createPassword
   ask password "What's the password gonna be?"
   put it into card field "Key"
end createPassword
```

Once the password has been created, the button that adds new names to the list will ask for the password before performing its action. The button might contain two handlers:

```
on mouseUp
   checkPassword -- call the handler below
   if the result is not empty then -- didn't have the right password
     play "Dragnet Theme"
     answer "Sorry. Please make yourself comfy...." with "Rats!"
     go to card "Alert Security"
   else -- password checked out
     ask "What's the new student's name?"
     if it is not empty then put return & it after field "Student List"
```

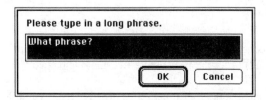

Figure III.8   Long answer in ask dialog box

```
    end if
end mouseUp

on checkPassword
    ask password "Please enter your password:"
    if the result is "Cancel" then exit to HyperCard -- user cancelled
    else if it is not card field "Key" then return "Wrong password"
    -- note: using "return" in a message handler sets the result
    -- function. The result is checked in the mouseUp handler above.
end checkPassword
```

As you can see, since the encrypted password needs to be stored somewhere, and the code has to say where it is, this password protection is not difficult for a determined person to defeat. The protection offered by **ask password** is useful mostly for protecting against casual, non-malicious snoopers. It will also slow down rank amateurs, preschool children, and politicians.

The encryption used by **ask password** is not case-sensitive, and accented characters are considered the same as their unaccented counterparts.

Changes to HyperTalk: In versions of HyperCard before 2.0, the **ask** dialog has room to display only about 38 characters for the question, and the question is limited to one line. If the question parameter contains more than one line, 1.x only shows the first line (or as much of it as will fit). The reply field is likewise limited to one line.

Furthermore, characters the user types into an **ask password** dialog are not changed to bullets when displayed on the screen, and you can't use the editing functions (Cut, Copy and Paste) while in a dialog.

ALSO SEE

answer command; **ask file** command; **it** variable (Chapter 8)

---

ask file command   Introduced in version 2.0

FORMS

```
ask file prompt [with defaultFileName]
ask file "Please name the text file:"
ask file card field "Save Prompt" with "Saved File"
ask file "Export text to:" with "Text From" && the short name of this stack
```

ACTION

The **ask file** command presents a standard file dialog (which is displayed by most applications in response to the Save command) to let the user type a file name and specify a file location. (See Figure III.9.)

The full pathname, including the filename the user typed, is returned in the **it** variable. If the user clicks Cancel, **it** is set to empty and the **result** function is set to "Cancel".

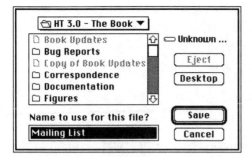

Figure III.9   Ask File dialog

COMMENTS

You can use the **ask file** command to let the user specify the name and location of a text file that your handler will create with the **open file** and **write** commands. This handler is an example:

```
on storeFile
  -- the following line displays the dialog box of Figure III.9
  ask file "Name to use for this file?" with "Mailing List"
  if it is empty then exit to HyperCard
  open file it   -- creates the file, if it doesn't already exist
  repeat with cardNumber = 1 to the number of cards
    write field "Names & Addresses" of card cardNumber to file it
  end repeat
  close file it
end storeFile
```

The **ask file** command does not create or save the file; it only lets the user specify the name and location. You must create the file yourself in your handler, as seen above.

While the dialog is on the screen, the handler that displayed it is suspended until the user dismisses it. There is no way to click one of the buttons from a script.

The dialog box stays on the screen until the user clicks Save or Cancel, or presses Return, Enter, or Command-Period. Pressing Return or Enter is equivalent to clicking Save. Pressing Command-Period dismisses the dialog. (To dismiss the dialog and abort any running handlers, press Command-Shift-Period; to enter the debugger, press Command-Option-Period.) In this dialog, Save is disabled if the text field is empty; there is no way to enter an empty file name.

While the dialog is displayed, the cursor shape is an arrow. If you have set the **cursor** property to use a custom cursor, you must set it back after the **ask file** statement.

The prompt appears in 12-point Chicago type. It can be up to 254 characters and up to seven lines long. If the prompt string is more than one line, the dialog box grows to accommodate it.

If you forget to include a prompt parameter, HyperCard will interpret the word "file" as the prompt and give you an **ask** dialog box instead, as shown in Figure III.10.

The following example creates a Save As menu item in the File menu. This extremely useful menu item (unaccountably missing from HyperCard) saves a copy of the current stack

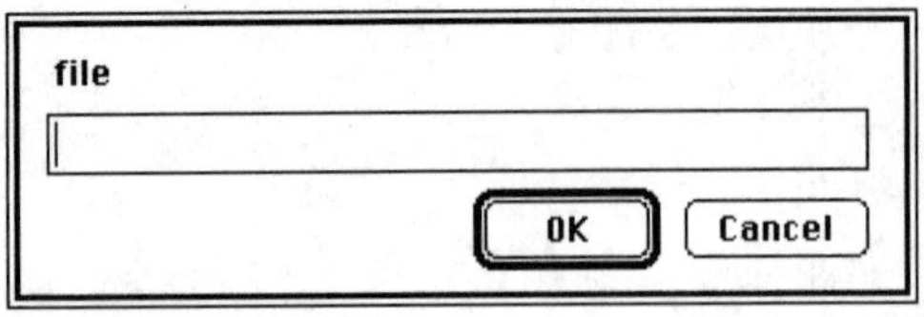

Figure III.10   Oops

under a new name, leaving you in the new stack. The following two lines of code should be placed in the Home stack's **startup** handler, so that the menu item is available in every stack:

```
put "Save As..." after menuItem "Save a Copy..." of menu "File" ¬
with menuMessage "userSaveAs"
```

When a user chooses Save As, the following handler is executed:

```
on userSaveAs -- should be in Home stack script
   ask file "Save stack as:" with the short name of this stack
   if it is not empty then
     save this stack as it
     go to it
   end if
end userSaveAs
```

ALSO SEE

answer file command; **ask** command; **it** variable (Chapter 8); **open file** command; **write** command

---

atan function   Introduced in version 1.0

FORMS

[the] atan of *number*
atan(*number* **)**
```
-(the atan of -1) * 4 -- yields π
atan(tan(1))          -- yields 1
atan(sqrt(3)) * 3     -- ditto
the atan of myResult
```

ACTION

The **atan** function returns the arc tangent of a number, in radians. (The arc tangent of a number is the angle whose tangent equals that number.)

COMMENTS

HyperTalk doesn't have arc sine or arc cosine functions, but, using the algorithms presented in the Apple Numerics Manual, you can write them like this:

```
function asin x
  put the abs of x into y
  if y ≤ 2^-33 then return x
  if y ≤ 0.5 then
    put 1 - y*y into y
  else
    put 1 - y into y
    put 2*y - y*y into y
  end if
  return atan(x/the sqrt of y)
end asin

function acos x
  return 2 * the atan of the sqrt of ((1 - x)/(1 + x))
end acos
```

Convert radians to degrees: One radian is $180/\pi$ degrees. To convert an angle in radians to one in degrees or vice versa, use the following handlers:

```
function toRadians theDegrees
  return pi * theDegrees/180
end toRadians

function toDegrees theRadians
  return 180 * theDegrees/pi
end toDegrees
```

ALSO SEE

cos function; **sin** function; **tan** function

autoHilite property

Introduced in version 1.0

FORMS

```
set [the] autoHilite of button to {true|false}
set the autoHilite of button "New Button" to true
```

ACTION

The **autoHilite** property determines whether a button highlights automatically when you click it.

Setting a button's **autoHilite** property is equivalent to setting the Auto Hilite checkbox in the Button Info dialog. By default, buttons created with the New Button command have their **autoHilite** set to false; buttons created by Command-dragging with the button tool have it set to true.

COMMENTS

If a button's **autoHilite** property is true, clicking the button causes it to reverse-highlight (for all button styles except popup, radioButton, and checkbox). This provides visual feedback to the user for the click, and it's a standard part of the Macintosh user interface. The button is highlighted while the mouse is pressed over it; when you move the mouse off the button, or release the mouse, the button is unhighlighted. (See Figure III.11.)

From a programming point of view, clicking an autohiliting button sets its **hilite** property to true momentarily, just before HyperCard sends the **mouseDown** message associated with the click.

If the button is a radio button, highlighting it puts a dot in its center. If the button is a checkbox, highlighting it puts an X in the box, and clicking it again removes the X. From a programming standpoint, clicking such a button sets its **hilite** property to true, and clicking it again sets its **hilite** to false.

The following example creates, vertically aligns, and names a row of check boxes:

```
on newCheckboxes topEdge,leftEdge
   repeat with x = 3 to the paramCount
      if x is not 3 -- not the first button
      then add the height of last button to topEdge
      doMenu "New Button"
      set the style of last button to checkbox
      set the autoHilite of last button to true
```

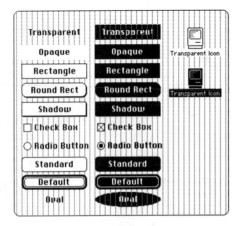

Figure III.11   Unhilited and hilited buttons

```
        set the name of last button to param(x)
        set the left of last button to leftEdge
        set the top of last button to topEdge
    end repeat
    choose browse tool
end newCheckboxes
```

Here's how to call the handler:

```
newCheckboxes 40,200,"Checked-Scot","Checked-Jeanne","Checked-Dan"
```

Autohiliting buttons and the text selection: Clicking an autohiliting button deselects the selected text. In fact, you lose the selection whenever a button's highlight changes. Instead of setting a button's **autoHilite** property to true, you can use the following handler, which doesn't interfere with the text selection:

```
on mouseDown
    put the selectedChunk into theSelection -- preserve selection
    set the hilite of the target to true
    repeat until the mouse is up
      if the mouseLoc is within the rect of the target
      then set the hilite of the target to true
      else set the hilite of the target to false
    end repeat
    if the mouseLoc is within the rect of the target
    then send mouseUp to the target
    set the hilite of the target to false
    select theSelection -- restore original selection
    exit to HyperCard    -- prevent mouseUp from being sent
end mouseDown
```

Autohiliting and button families: Buttons that belong to a family automatically have their **autoHilite** property set to true. Clicking a button that belongs to a family sets that button's **hilite** property to true, regardless of the button style.

Autohilite and disabled buttons: If a button's **enabled** property is set to false—that is, if the button is disabled—the setting of **autoHilite** has no effect.

Changes to HyperTalk: In versions of HyperCard before 2.2, the behavior of autohiliting radio and checkbox buttons is slightly different: the button changes to its hilited state as soon as you press the mouse. In version 2.2, the autohiliting is indicated instead by a border drawn inside the checkbox or radio dot, and the button only changes to its hilited state when you release the mouse. This is closer to the standard behavior for Macintosh applications.

ALSO SEE
family property; **hilite** property; **mouseDown** message

autoSelect property

FORMS

```
set [the] autoSelect of field to {true|false}
set the autoSelect of last card field to true
set the autoSelect of card field "List" to false
```

ACTION

The **autoSelect** property determines whether a field behaves as a clickable list. Setting the **autoSelect** property is equivalent to setting the Auto Select checkbox in the field's Info dialog. By default, the **autoSelect** of newly created fields is false.

COMMENTS

To make a field into a clickable list, set its **autoSelect** property to true. List fields respond to a mouse click by highlighting the line that was clicked, from the left edge to the right edge of the field (see Figure III.12).

A handler can determine which line was clicked and the text of the clicked line using the **selectedLine** and **selectedText** functions. The following example, which executes when a user clicks in a list field to select a line, shows first the old line's attributes, then the new line's:

```
on mouseDown
    -- selection of new line takes place after mouseDown, so
    -- this handler shows the old selected line:
    answer the selectedText of me & return & the selectedLine of me
end mouseDown

on mouseUp
    -- selection of new line takes place before mouseUp, so
    -- this handler shows the new selected line:
    answer the selectedText of me & return & the selectedLine of me
end mouseUp
```

Lists are usually scrolling fields, but a list field can have any style.

This property is usually set from a script only when creating the field:

```
on makeListField
    doMenu "New Field"
    set the name of last card field to "New List"
```

Figure III.12   Clickable list field

```
        set the dontWrap of card field "New List" to true
        set the autoSelect of card field "New List" to true
        set the style of card field "New List" to scrolling
        set the textFont of card field "New List" to Chicago
    end makeListField
```

The autoSelect and other field properties: The **multipleLines** property determines whether the user can select multiple lines from the field by dragging or by Shift-clicking. The setting of this property has no effect unless **autoSelect** is true.

Setting the **dontWrap** of a field to false automatically sets its **autoSelect** to false.

If the **lockText** of a field is false, it behaves as an editable text field, regardless of the current setting of its **autoSelect** property. To behave as a list field, a field must be locked.

Background fields and autoSelect: If a background field's **autoSelect** property is set to true, its selected line is the same across all cards of that background. This can cause serious confusion if the field's text is different for each card. Because of this, if you're using a background field as a list, it's usually best to set its **sharedText** property to true so the field has the same text on each card.

ALSO SEE

lockText property; **multipleLines** property; **select** command

---

autoTab property

Introduced in version 1.2

FORMS

```
set [the] autoTab of field to {true|false}
set the autoTab of last field to true
set the autoTab of field "New Entry Notes" to false
```

ACTION

The **autoTab** property determines what happens when the user presses Return on the last visible line of a nonscrolling field. If **autoTab** is true, pressing Return moves to the next field (as though the user had pressed Tab); if **autoTab** is false, pressing Return simply moves to the next line of the field.

Setting a field's **autoTab** property is equivalent to setting the Auto Tab checkbox in the Field Info dialog.

COMMENTS

The **autoTab** property is particularly useful when designing onscreen forms, since it lets the user simply press either Tab or Return to go to the next field, and avoids the problem of losing the blinking insertion point because it's outside the field's visible rectangle.

The following handler sets the **autoTab** of all nonscrolling fields in the current background to true:

```
on setUpForm
   repeat with i = 1 to the number of fields
      if the style of field i is not scrolling
      then set the autoTab of field i to true
   end repeat
end setUpForm
```

The tabbing order is as follows:

- If there is no selection, pressing Tab selects the text of the first visible, unlocked background field.

- If the insertion point or selection is already in a background field, pressing Tab (or Return, if the current field's **autoTab** property is true) selects the text of the next unlocked background field. If you're already in the last background field, tabbing moves to the first card field.

- If the insertion point or selection is in a card field, tabbing moves to the next card field. If you're in the last card field, tabbing moves to the first background field.

You can change the tabbing order by changing the ordering of the fields. This is done either by selecting the field and choosing Bring Closer or Send Farther from the Objects menu or by changing the field's **partNumber** property.

The setting of **autoTab** has no effect on scrolling fields.

Changing the default value: The default value of **autoTab** for newly created fields is false. If you want all new fields created on a particular card to have **autoTab** set to true, put the following handler in the card script:

```
on newField
   set the autoTab of the target to true
end newField
```

Beware the automatic selection: Tabbing, whether with the Tab key or **autoTab** and the Return key, selects all the text in the destination field, so pressing any key replaces that text. To avoid this danger, use the following handler, which deselects the text and places the insertion point at the end:

```
on openField
   select after text of the target
   -- if you want to put the insertion point at the text start
   -- instead of the end, substitute "before" for "after"
end openField
```

ALSO SEE

select command; **tabKey** message

average function Introduced in version 1.0

FORMS

```
average(numberList)
average(100,85,97,90) -- yields 93
average(var1,var2,var3)  -- yields average of values of variables
average(line 2 of field "Grades) -- average of items in line 2
```

ACTION

The **average** function returns the average of its arguments.

COMMENTS

The **average** is computed by dividing the sum of the items in *numberList* by the number of items. The formula for **average** can be expressed as follows:

```
sum(theList)/the number of items of theList
```

The *numberList* is a comma-separated list of up to 64 numbers. If any of the items in *numberList* isn't a number, HyperCard puts up a script error dialog.

The following handler, when you pass it a comma-separated list of numbers, draws a bar chart of the data, with a line across the chart marking the average (Figure III.13):

```
on makeBarChart theData
    put 10 into topEdge
    put 10 into leftEdge
    put the height of this card - 10 into bottomEdge
    put the width of this card - 10 into rightEdge
    -- clear screen and set up tools
    reset paint
    choose select tool
```

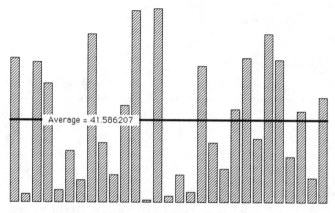

Figure III.13   Using average with a bar chart

```
        doMenu "Select All"
        doMenu "Clear Picture"
        choose rectangle tool
        set the pattern to 14
        set the filled to true
        -- draw the chart
        put leftEdge into currentBar
        put max(theData) into maxValue
        put the number of items in theData into dataCount
        put round((rightEdge - leftEdge)/dataCount) into horizStep
        put round(horizStep * 3/4) into barWidth
        repeat with nextBar = 1 to dataCount
          put round((bottomEdge - topEdge) ¬
          * item nextBar of theData / maxValue) into barHeight
          drag from currentBar,(bottomEdge - barHeight) ¬
          to (currentBar + barWidth),bottomEdge
          add horizStep to currentBar
        end repeat
        -- draw average line across chart
        choose line tool
        set the lineSize to 3
        put bottomEdge ¬
        - round((bottomEdge - topEdge) * average(theData) / maxValue) ¬
        into lineHeight
        drag from leftEdge,lineHeight to rightEdge,lineHeight
        choose text tool
        click at leftEdge + 50, lineHeight + 5
        type " Average =" && average(theData) & space & space
        choose browse tool
      end makeBarChart
```

ALSO SEE

max function; **min** function; **sum** function

---

beep command

Introduced in version 1.0

FORMS

beep [*numberOfBeeps*]
```
beep
beep 7
beep card field "Beep Count"
```

ACTION

The **beep** command sounds the system beep. If you specify an integer as a parameter to **beep**, the Macintosh beeps the number of times you specify.

The beep volume (and, in System 7.0, the sound used for the beep) is set in the Sound control panel. If the beep volume is set to 0, the system flashes the menu bar instead of sounding a beep.

COMMENTS

You'll usually use the **beep** command to alert the user to a condition that needs attention, or to signal the completion of a lengthy process. For instance, the following handler makes the speaker beep twice to let the user know that a dialog needs an answer:

```
on panic
  beep 2
  answer "Commies! What should we do?" with "Run away" or "Bomb 'em!"
  if it is "Run away" then evacuateSystem
  else launchCounterattack
end panic
```

Watch the beep count. Multiple beeps can be a terrible annoyance, particularly if the user has set the beep to a lengthy sound. For the sake of your users, in most situations keep the number of beeps low.

For a refreshing alternative, consider using `play harpsichord` or `play boing` instead of beeping. Both of these sounds are built into every version of HyperCard. You can even override the normal behavior of **beep** by placing the following handler in your Home stack script:

```
on beep
  -- whenever beep is used, play a sound instead:
  play harpsichord
end beep
```

The **beep** command, unlike **play**, is synchronous: that is, processing of the current handler waits until the beep sound is done before continuing. The sound channel cannot be used for beeps and played sounds at the same time, so **beep** cancels the playing of any sounds that have been queued up by **play**.

Techie alert: The **beep** command calls the system routine `Sysbeep(1)` *numberOfBeeps* times.

ALSO SEE

play command

blindTyping property

FORMS

```
set [the] blindTyping [of HyperCard] to {true|false}
set the blindTyping to true
set the blindTyping to not the visible of message box
```

ACTION

The **blindTyping** global property controls whether you can type into the message box while it's hidden. The "Blind Typing" checkbox on the User Preferences card of the Home stack sets the default value for the **blindTyping** property.

COMMENTS

If the message box is visible and there is no text selection or insertion point, anything you type goes into the message box. When you press Return or Enter, whatever's in the message box is executed. If the **blindTyping** property is false, trying to type while there is no selection and the message box is hidden causes HyperCard to beep; if **blindTyping** is true, the typed text is placed in the message box.

Blind typing does not show the message box; however, using the **put** command to put text into the message box shows the box.

Because pressing Return or Enter executes the contents of the message box, you can use the **blindTyping** to set up a repeated command that is executed again when the user presses one of these keys. This example sets up a custom Find command:

```
on startFinding
   ask "What do you want to find?"
   put it into myString
   set the blindTyping to true
   type "find string" && quote & myString & quote & return
end startFinding
```

The above handler places the string

```
find string "stringToFind"
```

in the message box. When the user presses Return, the above command is executed and the next occurrence is found. If the **blindTyping** is false, the message box appears every time the user presses Return, and the command can be seen; however, with the **blindTyping** set to true, the message box does not appear. You can also use this trick for more complicated commands.

ALSO SEE

hide command; **show** command

bottom property

Introduced in version 1.2
Last changed in version 2.2

FORMS

```
set [the] bottom of {part|button|field|window} to integer
the bottom of {menubar|card}
set the bottom of message window to the top of card window
set the bottom of field x to 127
```

ACTION

The **bottom** property describes where the bottom edge of an element is.

COMMENTS

The following handler lines up the bottom edges of all the fields in the current background:

```
on verticalAlign
   repeat with i = 2 to the number of fields
      show field i
      set the bottom of field i to the bottom of field 1
   end repeat
end verticalAlign
```

The *button*, *field*, or *card* is a descriptor of any button, field, or card in the current stack. A *window* can be a descriptor of any open stack window, HyperCard window, or external window.

The **bottom** of a stack window and the **bottom** of a card in that stack may be different if the window has been sized smaller than the card size (for example, using the Scroll command in the Go menu).

The *integer* is the vertical distance in pixels from the top edge—of the screen for stack windows, or of the current stack window for cards, buttons, fields, and other windows—to the element's bottom edge. If the *integer* is negative, the element's bottom edge is *integer* pixels *above* the top edge of the screen or stack window.

The bottom and other location properties: The **bottom** of an element is the same as item 2 of its **bottomRight** property, and also the same as the last item of the element's **rectangle** property.

However, changing the **bottom** of an element moves the element without changing its size, while changing item 4 of the element's **rectangle** changes its size without moving its other three edges.

Changing the bottom property: Anything that moves or resizes an element may change its **bottom** property: for example, dragging the element manually or from a script, or changing its **location** or **rectangle** property, or using the **show** command with a new location.

Changes to HyperTalk: In versions of HyperCard before 2.2, you cannot describe a button or field with a part descriptor, and you cannot get the **bottom** of the menu bar.

ALSO SEE

bottomRight property; **location** property; **rectangle** property; **right** property; **show** command; **top** property

---

bottomRight property

Introduced in version 1.2
Last changed in version 2.2

FORMS

```
set [the] bot[tom]Right of {part|button|field|window} to location
the bottomRight of {menubar|card}
set the bottomRight of field "Listings" to 100,120
set the botRight of card button nextButton to the loc of field 2
```

ACTION

The **bottomRight** property describes the location of an element's lower right corner.

COMMENTS

The following handler lines up all the buttons on the current card on a diagonal:

```
on alignButtons
   repeat with i = 1 to the number of buttons
      show button i
      set the topLeft of button i to the bottomRight of button (i - 1)
   end repeat
end alignButtons
```

The *button*, *field*, or *card* is a descriptor of any button, field, or card in the current stack. A *window* can be a descriptor of any open stack window, HyperCard window, or external window.

The **bottomRight** of a stack window and the **bottomRight** of a card in that stack may be different if the window has been sized smaller than the card size (for instance, by using the Scroll command in the Go menu).

The *location* is a point on the screen, consisting of two integers separated by a comma: the first item is the horizontal distance in pixels from the left edge of the frontmost card window to the point, and the second item is the vertical distance from the top edge to the point. (For stack windows, the *location* is measured from the edges of the screen rather than the card window.) The top edge of the card window is at the bottom (not the top) of its title bar.

The name of this property is backward: Although the name is **bottomRight**, the coordinates appear in the order *right, bottom*.

The following button handler lets you drag a button around without having to choose the button tool first:

```
on mouseDown
  repeat while the mouse is down
    set the bottomRight of me to the mouseLoc
  end repeat
end mouseDown
```

The bottomRight and other location properties: Since the two coordinates of **bottomRight** are separated by a comma, you can refer to them independently as two separate items:

```
put item 1 of the bottomRight of field 6 into theHorizontal
```

In fact, item 1 of the **bottomRight** is the **right** of the element, and item 2 is the **bottom** property. The value of the **bottomRight** is the same as the last two items of the element's **rectangle** property.

Changing the bottomRight property: Anything that moves or resizes an element changes its **bottomRight** property: for example, dragging the element manually or from a script, or changing its **location** or **rectangle** property, or using the **show** command with a new location.

Changes to HyperTalk: In versions of HyperCard before 2.2, you cannot describe a button or field with a part descriptor, and you cannot get the **bottomRight** of the menu bar.

ALSO SEE

bottom property; **location** property; **rectangle** property; **right** property; **show** command; **topLeft** property

---

brush property

Introduced in version 1.0

FORMS

```
set [the] brush [of HyperCard] to brushNumber
set the brush to 7
set the brush to nextBrush
```

ACTION

The **brush** property reflects which of HyperCard's paintbrush shapes will be used when painting with the brush tool. (See Figure III.14.) Changing the **brush** property is equivalent to selecting a new shape in the Brush Shape dialog.

COMMENTS

The following handler lets you paint with randomly changing brushes, which makes it easy to produce clever forgeries of Ralph Steadman works:

```
on mouseDown
   choose brush tool
   repeat until the mouse is up
      set the brush to random(32)
      click at the mouseLoc
   end repeat
   choose browse tool
end mouseDown
```

The *brushNumber* is an integer between 1 and 32 (see Figure III.14). The default brush shape is 8, a medium dot shape. If you try to set the brush to a *brushNumber* less than 1 or greater than 32767, the brush is set to 1. If you use a *brushNumber* between 33 and 32767, the brush is set to 32.

The following handler draws a staccatto line:

```
on drawStaccatto
   choose brush tool
   set the brush to 32
   put "20,200" into startPoint
   put startPoint into endPoint
   repeat until item 1 of endPoint > 400
      add random(10) to item 1 of endPoint
      add random(21) - 11 to item 2 of endPoint
      drag from startPoint to endPoint
      put endPoint into startPoint
   end repeat
   choose browse tool
end drawStaccatto
```

ALSO SEE
   reset paint command

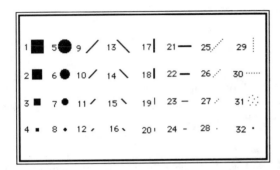

Figure III.14   Brush shapes

buttonCount property

FORMS

```
the buttonCount of window paletteWindow
put the buttonCount of window "Navigator" into theCount
if the buttonCount of window myNewPalette > 6 then beep
```

ACTION

The **buttonCount** is a property of floating palette windows created by the **palette** command. It reports the number of buttons on the palette.

This property is read-only and cannot be set by a handler.

COMMENTS

The following handler highlights each of a palette's buttons in turn:

```
on hilitePaletteButtons thePalette
  put the buttonCount of window thePalette into numberOfButtons
  repeat with thisButton = 1 to numberOfButtons
    set the hilitedButton of window thePalette to thisButton
  end repeat
  set the hilitedButton of window thePalette to 0 -- unhilite all
end hilitePaletteButtons
```

ALSO SEE

palette command

cantAbort property

FORMS

```
set [the] cantAbort of stack to {true|false}
set the cantAbort of this stack to false
set the cantAbort of stack "No Exit" to true
```

ACTION

The **cantAbort** property determines whether the user can press Command-Period to stop a running handler that's located in the *stack*. Setting this property is equivalent to setting the Can't Abort checkbox in the Protect Stack dialog.

COMMENTS

Use the **cantAbort** property when halting the script would cause problems: for example, to bracket critical sections of code. The following example shows how to use **cantAbort** to lock out interruptions where they could leave the stack in an inconsistent state:

```
on moveCardToEnd
  -- This handler sets the cantAbort to true so that the user can't
  -- halt the handler after the card is cut but before it's pasted.
  -- This prevents the stack from accidentally losing the card.
  set the cantAbort of this stack to true
  doMenu "Cut Card"
  go to last card
  doMenu "Paste Card"
  set the cantAbort of this stack to false
end moveCardToEnd
```

Danger, Will Robinson!   Be very careful when using **cantAbort**. If a script runs away while the property is set to true—for instance, if you've accidentally coded an infinite loop—the only way to stop may be to reboot the machine. This can be particularly unnerving if you're running HyperCard under MultiFinder and have unsaved work in other applications. (This is the Voice of Bitter Experience talking.)

To be safe, only install a `set the cantAbort to true` statement after your handler is thoroughly debugged, and always set the property back to false when you're done with the critical section of code.

ALSO SEE

lockErrorDialogs property; **Reset Switch**, *Macintosh Owner's Guide*

cantDelete property   Introduced in version 1.2

FORMS

```
set [the] cantDelete of {stack|background|card} to [true|false]
set the cantDelete of this stack to true
set the cantDelete of card "Summary" to false
```

ACTION

The setting of the **cantDelete** property determines whether the specified object can or cannot be deleted by the user or by a handler. Setting the **cantDelete** property of a card, background, or stack is equivalent to setting the Can't Delete checkbox in the Card Info, Background Info, or Protect Stack dialog, respectively.

COMMENTS

The following handler, which should be in the background or stack script, prevents a card from being deleted once text has been entered into any of its fields:

```
on closeField
  set the cantDelete of this card to true
end closeField
```

The *card* or *background* is any valid descriptor of a card or background in the current stack. The *stack* is any stack, open or closed.

If the **cantModify** property of a stack is true, the stack's **cantDelete** property is also automatically set to true.

Setting of cantDelete doesn't affect operations outside HyperCard: If the **cantDelete** of a stack is set to true, the Delete Stack item in the File menu is disabled. However, you can use another program to delete a stack (for instance, by dragging it to the Trash in the Finder), and the setting of **cantModify** will not prevent this.

Handler aborted if you try to delete a protected object: If a handler tries to delete a card, background, or stack whose **cantDelete** property is true, HyperCard puts up an error dialog, aborting the rest of the handler. To avoid this problem, make sure the object's **cantDelete** is set to false before trying to remove it:

```
set the cantDelete of card "Doomed" to false
doMenu "Delete Card"
```

The following handler sets the **cantDelete** of all cards that have scripts to true:

```
on mouseUp
   repeat with x = 1 to the number of cards
     if the script of card x is not empty
     then set the cantDelete of card x to true
   end repeat
end mouseUp
```

This next handler, which like the first example belongs in the stack or background script, prevents users who aren't scripters from deleting the current card:

```
on openCard
  set the cantDelete of this card to (the userLevel is not 5)
end openCard


on closeCard
  set the cantDelete of this card to false
end closeCard
```

Old HyperCard versions: In versions of HyperCard before 1.2, the **cantDelete** property doesn't exist. However, you can still prevent users from deleting a card or background by catching the **deleteCard** or **deleteBackground** message, copying the current card, and re-pasting it:

```
on deleteCard -- or deleteBackground
   answer "You'll never get rid of this card!" with "Moo-hah-ha"
   doMenu "Copy Card"
   doMenu "Paste Card"
end deleteCard
```

This method preserves the name, script, and other attributes of the card and background, but the newly pasted card may have a different ID from the one that was deleted.

ALSO SEE

cantModify property; **deleteBackground** message; **deleteCard** message; **deleteStack** message

---

cantModify property   Introduced in version 1.2

FORMS

```
set [the] cantModify of stack to {true|false}
set the cantModify of this stack to true
set the cantModify of stack "Archives" to the hilite of button "Lock"
```

ACTION

The **cantModify** property determines whether the contents of a stack can be changed. Setting this property is equivalent to setting the Can't Modify Stack checkbox in the Protect Stack dialog.

When the **cantModify** of the frontmost stack is true, HyperCard puts the cutest little padlock in the menu bar.

COMMENTS

This property is particularly useful in conjunction with **userModify**. This example shows a way to let the user scribble on a card and make other temporary changes without allowing any permanent change to the card:

```
on openCard
   set the cantModify of this stack to true
   set the userModify to true -- let user make temporary changes
end openCard

on closeCard
   set the cantModify of this stack to false
end closeCard
```

Making temporary changes while cantModify is true: With the **cantModify** of a stack set to true, the user can still click in unlocked fields, select and copy text and objects, and print; but the user cannot make changes to the stack. However, a handler can make changes to the current card (such as changing button or field properties) even while the **cantModify** is set to true. These changes are lost and the stack reverts to its former state when HyperCard changes cards or when the **cantModify** is set to false.

If **cantModify** is set to true and a handler tries to make a change that's not permitted (such as creating a new card), HyperCard puts up a script error dialog and aborts the handler.

The cantModify of a card or background

In versions of HyperCard since 1.2.5, you can set and get the **cantModify** property of a card or background, but the setting of this property has no effect on whether the card or background can be changed; only the **cantModify** of a stack has any effect. Isn't that special?

Write-protected stacks and the cantModify: If a stack is on a write-protected volume, if its Locked checkbox in Get Info is checked, or if it's a 1.x-format stack running under a later HyperCard version, the stack cannot be altered regardless of the setting of **cantModify**.

When **cantModify** is true, **cantDelete** is also set to true, regardless of its former setting. A stack with **cantModify** set to true cannot be compacted.

When you change the setting of **cantModify**, either from a script or using the Protect Stack dialog, the currently selected object or text is deselected.

Techie alert: When the **cantModify** setting changes, HyperCard purges all objects from its virtual memory.

ALSO SEE

cantDelete property; **userModify** property

---

cantPeek property   Introduced in version 2.0

FORMS

```
set [the] cantPeek of stack to {true|false}
set the cantPeek of stack "Somewhat Protected" to true
set the cantPeek of this stack to not the hilite of button "Peekable"
```

ACTION

The **cantPeek** property of a stack determines whether you can see the outlines of buttons (by holding down Command-Option) and fields (by holding down Command-Shift-Option), and whether you can use the Command-Option-click shortcuts for accessing scripts.

The setting of this property corresponds to the setting of the Can't Peek checkbox in the Protect Stack dialog.

COMMENTS

This property is especially useful for screen games, in which part of the fun is making the user guess where to click—it eliminates cheating by "peeking" at where the buttons are. Setting the **cantPeek** to true also offers some slight protection against users looking at or modifying the stack's scripts. However, you can still edit the script of any object with the command edit script of *object*, regardless of the setting of **cantPeek**.

This example turns **cantPeek** on when you enter a particular card, and turns it back off when you leave that card:

```
on openCard
   set the cantPeek of this stack to true
end openCard

on closeCard
   set the cantPeek of this stack to false
end closeCard
```

centered property

Introduced in version 1.0

FORMS

set [the] centered [of HyperCard] to {true|false}

```
set the centered to true
```

ACTION

The **centered** global property determines whether the shape paint tools (line, rectangle, round rectangle, oval, and regular polygon) will draw shapes from the center. If the **centered** property is false, shapes are drawn from the corner.

This property corresponds to the Draw Centered item in the Options menu, which is checked when the **centered** is true and unchecked when it is false. By default, the **centered** is false.

COMMENTS

Drawing from the center is particularly useful when you want a shape to center around a known point. The following example draws a thick rectangle around the button that holds this handler:

```
on mouseUp
   choose rect tool
   set the centered to true
   set the lineSize to 3
   drag from the loc of me to the right of me + 10, the bottom of me + 10
   choose browse tool
end mouseUp
```

The following handler draws a bullseye:

```
on bullsEye
   choose oval tool
   set the centered to true
   set the lineSize to 2
```

```
        put "100,100" into theCenter
        put theCenter into theEdge
        repeat 10 times
           add 5 to item 1 of theEdge
           add 5 to item 2 of theEdge
           drag from theCenter to theEdge
        end repeat
     end bullsEye
```

ALSO SEE

reset paint command

charToNum function

Introduced in version 1.0

FORMS

```
[the] charToNum of character
charToNum(character)
charToNum(5)          -- returns 53
charToNum("A")        -- returns 65
the charToNum of a    -- returns 97
charToNum("abc")      -- returns 97
the charToNum of fred -- returns ASCII of the value of variable fred
```

ACTION

The **charToNum** function returns the ASCII value of a specified character.

COMMENTS

The **charToNum** function is the inverse of **numToChar**. It's useful when you want to check the ordering of a character, or for any other reason convert it to a number.

The following function returns true if its argument is an uppercase letter and false otherwise:

```
function isUppercase theLetter
   get the charToNum of theLetter
   if (it ≥ charToNum(A)) and (it ≤ charToNum(Z)) then
      return true -- in uppercase range
   else
      return false
   end if
end isUppercase
```

The *character* can evaluate to any string. If the argument to **charToNum** is more than one character, **charToNum** returns the ASCII equivalent of the first character and ignores the rest.

You can also use the **charToNum** function to give your users some privacy. The encryption scheme described in the following example is one of the simplest known. It's called a Caesar cipher (because Julius Caesar used this scheme to encrypt his letters when on campaign in Gaul). It is a simple scheme and won't keep out a determined code-cracker for long, but it does give some privacy:

```
function caesar theText,theKey
   -- encrypts text with the specified key
   if theKey is empty then put 13 into theKey
   repeat with x = 1 to the number of characters in theText
      get numToChar((charToNum(char x of theText) + theKey) mod 255)
      if it is zero then add 255 to it
      put it into char x of theText
   end repeat
   return theText
end caesar


function brutus theText,theKey
   -- undoes caesar
   if theKey is empty then put 13 into theKey
   repeat with x = 1 to the number of characters in theText
      get charToNum(char x of theText) - theKey
      if it ≤ 0 then add 255 to it
      put numToChar(it) into char x of theText
   end repeat
   return theText
end brutus
```

You might use the above handlers like this to protect important information:

```
on openCard
   ask password clear "What is the cipher key?"
   if it is not an integer or it < 1 or it > 255 then
      beep
      answer "That is not a valid key!"
      go recent card
   end if
   put brutus(field "Confidential",it) into field "Confidential"
end openCard


on closeCard
   ask "Please give me a cipher key (an integer between 1 and 255):"
   if it is not an integer or it < 1 or it > 255 then
      beep
      answer "That is not a valid key!" ¬
```

```
        with "Try Again" or "Don't Encrypt"
        if it is "Try Again" then go recent card
    else
        put caesar(field "Confidential",it) into field "Confidential"
    end if
end closeCard
```

You won't believe this, but...

U.S. citizens who are developing privacy software like the handler shown above should be aware that the U.S. State Department's Office of Defense Technology Control considers such software to fall into the category of "munitions" under the regulatory interpretation of the International Trade in Arms Regulations (ITAR), and has recently informed one publisher of such software of the requirement to register as a "Producer of Defense Articles" and pay the $250 annual fee required of international arms dealers.

No, we're not joking. As U.S. citizens ourselves, we wish we were. However, this is quite serious: as this book goes to press, legal action is being contemplated against at least one software developer under the provisions of ITAR. Not for providing software to foreign nationals or otherwise exporting it, mind you, but simply for developing it and distributing it within this country.

The DoD may or may not be interested in suppressing simple, easily-broken encryption algorithms like the multi-key Caesar cipher in the above example...but their interpretation of the regulations, if read literally, includes it as an item of technology with serious national-security implications. So just to be sure, if you're planning to include *any* features to guarantee privacy in your published stacks, no matter how simple, you may want to give the State Department a call at 703/875-6650 and ask whether you should order their Munitions Manufacturer registration package. (The package is free, although registration is not.)

While you have the telephone handy, you may also want to give your Congresscritter a call, and ask what his or her position is on whether software used by U.S. citizens to guarantee their privacy should be regulated as munitions.

Changes to HyperTalk: In versions of HyperCard before 2.0, the *character* must be enclosed in quotation marks.

ALSO SEE

ASCII Chart (Appendix A); **numToChar** function

checkMark property

FORMS

```
set [the] checkMark of menuItem of menu to {true|false}
set the checkMark of menuItem 3 of menu "Additions" to true
set the checkMark of menuItem "Clipboard" of menu "Edit" to false
```

ACTION

The **checkMark** property of menu items determines whether a menu item is checked (or marked with another character) or not.

COMMENTS

Use the **checkMark** property, in accordance with the Apple User Interface Guidelines, to show that some option is currently operating. For an example, look at how the Style menu items work.

The following handler decides whether a beep should signal an error, depending on whether a menu item has been checked or not:

```
on oops -- user made an error
   if the checkMark of menuItem "Beep on errors" of menu "Prefs"
   then beep
   put "That's not correct!" into field "User Answer"
end oops
```

The *menuItem* is a descriptor of a specific menu item in the specified *menu*.

The following example creates a UserLevel menu and places a check next to the current level:

```
on openStack
   -- set up the UserLevel menu
   create menu "UserLevel"
   put "set the userLevel to" into theMessage
   put "Browsing,Typing,Painting,Authoring,Scripting" into levels
   repeat with itemNumber = 1 to the number of items in levels
      put item itemNumber of levels after menu "UserLevel" ¬
      with menuMessage theMessage && itemNumber
   end repeat
   set the userLevel to value(the userLevel)
   pass openStack
end openStack

on set
   -- check the appropriate menu item when the user level is set
   if param(1) is "userLevel" and there is a menu "UserLevel" then
      -- we are indeed setting the user level
```

```
      set the checkMark of menuItem value(the userLevel) ¬
      of menu "UserLevel" to false -- uncheck old user level
      send the params to HyperCard -- let HyperCard set new level
      set the checkMark of menuItem value(the userLevel) ¬
      of menu "UserLevel" to true  -- check new level
   else pass set
end set


on closeStack
   if there is a menu "UserLevel" then delete menu "UserLevel"
   pass closeStack
end closeStack
```

The checkMark and the markChar: The **checkMark** property is a special case of the **markChar** property: the statement set the checkMark of *menuItem* to true is equivalent to set the markChar of *menuItem* to numToChar(18). To place a character other than the check mark to the left of a menu item, set its **markChar**.

Setting the **markChar** of a menu item to something other than empty also sets its **checkMark** property to true.

Limitations of checkMark: The **checkMark** of all menu items reverts to false when the menu bar is reset. You can't set the **checkMark** property of items in the Apple, Tools, Font, Style, or Patterns menu.

ALSO SEE

> **markChar** property; **reset menubar** command

---

choose command/message

Introduced in version 1.0

FORMS

```
choose toolName tool
choose tool toolNumber
choose lasso tool
choose tool 7
choose myTool tool
```

ACTION

The **choose** command selects a tool from the Tools menu, as though the user had chosen it from the menu or palette. The tool names and corresponding numbers are shown in Figure III.15.

To choose a paint tool, the **userLevel** property must be set to 3 (Painting) or above. To choose the field or button tool, the **userLevel** must be at 4 (Authoring) or above. If the **userLevel** is set too low when the **choose** command is issued, an error dialog appears and the handler is aborted.

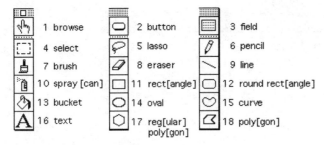

Figure III.15   Tool numbers and names

COMMENTS

You'll usually use the **choose** command when you want to use the paint tools to draw on the card from a script. This example chooses the pencil tool and calls another handler (not included here—you'll have to write your own) to draw a signature on the card:

```
on signTheCheck
    put the userLevel into oldLevel -- save original user level
    if the userLevel < 3 then set the userLevel to 3
    put the tool into oldTool
    choose pencil tool
    drawSignature -- a routine that hand-writes a name
    choose oldTool
    set the userLevel to oldLevel
end signTheCheck
```

Choosing a tool, whether you do it manually or from a handler, sends a **choose** message to the current card. The message has two parameters: the word "tool" and the number of the tool you chose. As with any command/message, you can write a custom handler to override the normal behavior of the action.

Power keys, which can be used when a paint tool is active, have no effect when the message box is visible, because in that case all typed characters go into the message box. The following handler by Robin Shank hides the message box whenever a paint tool is chosen:

```
on choose tool,toolNumber
    if toolNumber > 3 then hide message box
    pass choose
end choose
```

Other effects of changing tools: Choosing a new tool, manually or using the **choose** command, puts empty into the various **found** functions and removes the selection.

Some manual shortcuts: Pressing Command-Tab chooses the browse tool. Press it twice quickly to choose the button tool; press it three times to choose the field tool. These shortcuts let you move quickly among the three nonpainting tools.

Can't draw irregular polygons from a script: You can choose the polygon tool using **choose**, but you can't draw with it using the **drag** command; you can only use the polygon tool manually. You can work around this limitation by using **drag** with the line tool to draw the sides of the desired shape, then filling it in with the bucket tool.

Changes to HyperTalk: In versions of HyperCard before 2.0, choosing the browse tool manually or from a script turns off background mode if it was on.

In versions before 1.2.2, clicking on a tool in the tool windoid doesn't send the **choose** message. However, choosing the tool from the Tools menu does send the message.

The Command-Tab shortcuts for choosing the button and field tools do not work in versions before 1.2.

ALSO SEE

drag command; **tool** function; **userLevel** property

---

click command

Introduced in version 1.0

FORMS

```
click at location [with modifierKey1[,modifierKey2[,modifierKey3]]]
click at 250,300
click at the clickLoc
click at myClickPoint with optionKey,commandKey
```

ACTION

The **click** command simulates a click at the specified point on the current stack window, optionally "holding down" some combination of the Shift, Command, and Option keys.

The **click** command is not an exact substitute for clicking, since some of HyperCard's manual shortcuts require that the physical keys be down. For instance,

```
click at the loc of button "foo" with commandKey,optionKey
```

does not bring up the script of the button, even though the same action performed manually would do so.

COMMENTS

The following handler clicks each button on the current card:

```
on testButtons
  repeat with toTest = 1 to the number of card buttons
    put "Testing card button" && toTest
    click at the loc of card button toTest
  end repeat
end testButtons
```

The *location* is a point on the card, consisting of two integers separated by a comma. The first item is the horizontal distance in pixels from the left edge of the card window to the point; the second item is the vertical distance from the top edge to the point.

The *modifierKeys* can be `shiftKey`, `optionKey`, or `commandKey` (or a synonym, `cmdKey`). If you click in a field with `shiftKey`, the text from the beginning of the field to the clicked point is selected.

When the **click** command is issued, HyperCard sends the following messages to the clicked object (if no button or locked field is at the click point, the messages are sent to the current card):

mouseDown
mouseStillDown (10 times)
mouseUp
mouseLeave

However, **mouseEnter** and **mouseWithin** messages are not sent.

If *location* is within an unlocked field, an insertion point is placed in the field instead, and no messages are sent to the field.

Clicking in a field can add blank lines: When you click below the last line of text in an unlocked field, HyperCard adds empty lines to the end of the field to allow the insertion point to be placed where you clicked. To avoid this, use the **select** command to place an insertion point where you want it in a field, instead of using **click**.

Clicking and recursion: As mentioned above, clicking in a locked field sends messages to the field. One common mistake is to try to **click** in a field from within the field's **mouseDown** or **mouseUp** handler, without unlocking it first. For example, the following handler attempts to implement a hypertext feature:

```
on mouseDown    -- in the script of a locked field
   -- "set the lockText of me to false" should be here
   click at the clickLoc -- double-click would select the clicked
   click at the clickLoc -- word, if the field were unlocked
   find the selection
end mouseDown
```

However, since the field is still locked, the **click** statements each send a **mouseDown** message to the field. This **mouseDown** in turn triggers two more **click** statements, which send

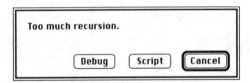

Figure III.16   Too much recursion

additional **mouseDown** messages, and so on. This infinite sequence goes on until HyperCard runs out of memory, at which point it displays the dialog shown in Figure III.16.

If the `set the lockText of me to false` line were in the handler, the clicks would take place on an unlocked field, so the additional **mouseDown** messages would never be sent and the recursion problem would be avoided. The moral? When using **click**, or other commands that can result in sending a message to an object, be certain they don't send the message corresponding to the handler they're in, or you'll end up in an infinite regress.

Selecting a Clicked Line

Many stacks and other applications present a list of choices in a scrolling field; the user is supposed to click one, and the clicked line is then highlighted. HyperCard lets you highlight a clicked line with the **clickLine** function. However, a line highlighted by selecting the **clickLine** is not highlighted all the way across; only the text in the line is highlighted, not the blank space at the end of the line.

The following handler shows you how to highlight the clicked line all the way across. This handler is a little complicated, so we've included comments to explain what each line does. Despite its complicated appearance, it is fast, and it lets you add one more little touch of polish to your stacks.

```
on mouseDown
    -- the clickLine is of the form "line X of field Y", so word 2 of the
    -- clickLine is the line number the user clicked
    put word 2 of the clickLine into lineNumber
    -- if user clicked first line, the hiliting starts at the first
    -- character
    if lineNumber is 1 then put 1 into startChar
    -- otherwise, we figure out where the first character of the clicked
    -- line is: get the number of characters in the text up to the end of
    -- the previous line, and then add two (one for the return after the
    -- previous line, and one more to point to the first character on
    -- the clicked line.
    else put the number of chars of (line 1 to (lineNumber - 1) of target) ¬
    + 2 into startChar
    -- get the last character on the line, and add 1 to include the return
    -- at the end of the line
    put the number of chars of (line 1 to lineNumber of target) + 1 ¬
    into endChar
    -- select the line
    select char startChar to endChar of the target
end mouseDown
```

Using click with the paint tools: You can duplicate most things that **click** can do using other commands—for example, by sending **mouseUp** to an object instead of clicking at its location. Here's an example of something only **click** can do: the following handler draws two overlapping shapes, then clicks with the bucket tool to fill their intersection.

```
on drawPicture
   reset paint -- restores paint properties to their defaults
   set the lineSize to 4                    -- for a bold border
   choose rectangle tool
   drag from 100,120 to 200,200 with shiftKey -- make a square
   drag from 150,150 to 250,300
   choose bucket tool
   set the pattern to 13                    -- light gray
   click at 175,165                         -- fill the intersection
   choose browse tool
end drawPicture
```

Techie alert: The **click** command is implemented internally as dragging from a point to the same point.

ALSO SEE

autoSelect property; **clickH** function; **clickLine** function; **clickLoc** function; **clickText** function; **clickV** function; **mouseLoc** function; **select** command

---

clickChunk function   Introduced in version 2.0

FORMS

```
the clickChunk
clickChunk()
put replacementWord into the clickChunk
```

ACTION

The **clickChunk** function returns the character position of the word or group most recently clicked in a locked field.

COMMENTS

Use the **clickChunk** function when you need to find out some attribute of the word the user clicked, other than the text itself. The **clickChunk** is particularly useful for hypertext applications. The following example checks the **textStyle** of the **clickChunk** to determine whether the clicked word is a cross-reference or not:

```
on mouseDown -- goes in the stack or background script
   if word 2 of the name of the target is "field" then
      get the textStyle of the clickChunk
      if it contains italic then
         show card field the clickText   -- annotation
      else if it contains bold then
         find the clickText              -- cross-reference
      else
```

```
      answer "No more information on" && the clickText
    end if
  end if
end mouseDown
```

The **clickChunk** returns the character position in the form:

```
char startChar to endChar of {card|bkgnd} field fieldNumber
```

(The field is assumed to be on the current card.) If the character you clicked has the text style "group", **the clickChunk** returns the position of entire group—that is, the largest continuous run of text with the "group" style. If the clicked text is not grouped, the function returns the beginning and end of the word that was clicked on. If you clicked on something other than a word, **the clickChunk** returns a *startChar* and *endChar* that are both equal to the clicked character's position.

To get the actual text of the clicked line, use the **clickText** function.

Clicking in an unlocked field does not update the **clickLine**, unless you clicked with the Command key held down.

Old HyperCard versions: In versions of HyperCard before 2.0, the **clickChunk** function is not available. However, you can get a descriptor of the chunk the user clicked in a locked field using the following trick:

```
on mouseDown -- in a field's script
  set the lockText of me to false
  click at the clickLoc
  click at the clickLoc
  get the selectedChunk
  set the lockText of me to true
  -- the clicked chunk is in "it" and you can do whatever you want
  -- with it.
end mouseDown
```

ALSO SEE

click command; **clickLine** function; **clickText** function

---

clickH function

Introduced in version 1.2

FORMS

the clickH
clickH()
put the clickH into horizontalDistance

ACTION

The **clickH** function returns the distance between the left edge of the card window and the last point clicked.

COMMENTS

The **clickH** is equal to item 1 of **the clickLoc**.

The following button script tells you whether you clicked in the right or left edge of the button (a useful technique for dividing a button into parts that act differently):

```
on mouseUp
   if the clickH < item 1 of the loc of me -- loc is center point
   then put "You clicked on the left side."
   else put "You clicked on the right side."
end mouseUp
```

The clickH is not necessarily equal to the mouseH: The horizontal location of the last mouse click is not necessarily the current horizontal position of the mouse, because the user might have moved the mouse since the last click. To get the current horizontal position of the mouse, use the **mouseH** function.

The following handler displays the **clickH** and **mouseH** continuously as you move the mouse around:

```
on mouseUp
   repeat until the shiftKey is down
      get the mouseClick -- resets the clickV
      put "The clickH is" && the clickH ¬
      && "and the mouseH is" && the mouseH
   end repeat
end mouseUp
```

For another example of breaking a button up into multiple areas, see the **height** property. The following handler measures the horizontal distance between two points:

```
on measure
   put "Click at the left edge..."
   wait until the mouseClick
   put the clickH into leftEdge
   put "Click at the right edge..."
   wait until the mouseClick
   put the clickH into rightEdge
   put "measure -- the horizontal distance is" ¬
   && abs(rightEdge - leftEdge) && "pixels."
end measure
```

This handler uses a neat trick: the first word placed in the message box is the handler name, and the rest of the message box content is preceded by the comment symbol "--", so the user can simply press Enter to measure something else.

ALSO SEE

click command; **clickH** function; **clickLoc** function; **mouseV** function

---

clickLine function

Introduced in version 2.0

FORMS

```
the clickLine
clickLine()
select the clickLine
set the name of this card to the value of the clickLine
```

ACTION

The **clickLine** function returns a descriptor of the line the user last clicked on.

COMMENTS

The following example lets you click an item to remove it from a "To Do" list and move it to a "Done" list:

```
on mouseDown
   get the value of the clickLine
   if it is empty then exit mouseDown
   delete the clickLine
   put it into line (the number of lines of field "Done" + 1) ¬
   of field "Done" -- puts it after last line with no extra returns
end mouseDown
```

The **clickLine** returns the line descriptor in this form:

```
line lineNumber of {card|bkgnd} field fieldNumber
```

(The field is assumed to be on the current card.) You can use expressions such as `word 2 of the clickLine` to get the number of the clicked line. If the character the user clicked on has the text style "group", and if the group contains more than one line, **the clickLine** always returns a descriptor of the first line of the group, no matter which line was actually clicked.

To get the actual text of the clicked line, use the **value** function:

```
get the value of the clickLine -- gets actual text
```

Clicking in an unlocked field does not update the **clickLine** unless you click with the Command key held down.

A *line* in HyperTalk is defined as being delimited by return characters. A line in a narrow field may wrap around several times, and look like more than one line on screen, but it is still considered a single line. The following example shows how to get the number of the screen line instead of the logical line:

```
function screenLine -- in a field script
  set the lockText of me to false
  click at the clickLoc
  if the style of me is scrolling
  then put the scroll of me into pixelsScrolled
  else put 0 into pixelsScrolled
  put item 2 of the selectedLoc - the top of me into totalPixels
  set the lockText of me to true
  return totalPixels div the textHeight of me
end screenLine
```

Old HyperCard versions: In versions of HyperCard before 2.0, the **clickLine** function is not available. However, you can get the line the user clicked in a locked field using the following trick:

```
on mouseDown
  set the lockText of me to false
  click at the clickLoc
  get the selectedLine
  set the lockText of me to true
  -- the clicked line is in "it" and you can do whatever you want
  -- with it.
end mouseDown
```

ALSO SEE
autoSelect property; **clickChunk** function; **click** command; **clickText** function

---

clickLoc function   Introduced in version 1.0

FORMS
```
the clickLoc
clickLoc()
click at the clickLoc
if the clickLoc is within the rect of me then beep
```

ACTION
The **clickLoc** function returns the location of the most recent mouse click.

COMMENTS
Use the **clickLoc** function when you want the user to point to something with the mouse during a handler, or when you want to find out exactly where the user clicked to trigger a **mouseDown**, **mouseUp**, or **mouseDoubleClick** message.

If the user dragged before releasing the mouse button, the **clickLoc** is the location where the mouse was first clicked, not where it was released.

The following handler draws a circle whose diameter the user specifies by clicking its two ends:

```
on drawCircle
   -- get points
   set the cursor to cross
   put "Please click at the first point..." into field "Instructions"
   wait until the mouseClick
   put the clickLoc into firstPoint
   put "...and at the second point." into field "Instructions"
   wait until the mouseClick
   put the clickLoc into secondPoint
   -- compute where the center and edge are
   put (item 1 of firstPoint + item 1 of secondPoint) div 2 into centerH
   put (item 2 of firstPoint + item 2 of secondPoint) div 2 into centerV
   put abs(item 1 of firstPoint - item 1 of centerPoint) into deltaH
   put abs(item 2 of firstPoint - item 2 of centerPoint) into deltaV
   put round(sqrt(deltaH^2 + deltaV^2)) into radius
   put centerH + radius into edgeH
   put centerV + radius into edgeV
   -- draw circle
   choose oval tool
   set the lineSize to 2
   set the centered to true
   drag from centerPoint to edgePoint
   choose browse tool
end drawCircle
```

The **clickLoc** returns a point: two integers separated by a comma, where the first number is the horizontal distance in pixels from the left edge of the card window, and the second is the vertical distance from the top edge. The two items of this point are equal to the **clickH** and **clickV** functions, respectively.

The following handler lets you click repeatedly, telling you where you clicked each time. You end it by pressing the Shift key.

```
on showClickLoc
   repeat forever
      wait until the mouseClick
      put (the shiftKey is down) into done
      put "You clicked at" && the clickLoc
      if done then exit showClickLoc
   end repeat
end showClickLoc
```

The clickLoc is not necessarily the mouseLoc: The location of the last mouse click is not necessarily the current mouse position, because the user might have moved the mouse since the last click. To get the current position of the mouse, use the **mouseLoc** function.

ALSO SEE

click command; **clickH** function; **clickV** function; **mouseDown** message; **mouseDoubleClick** message; **mouseLoc** function; **mouseUp** message

clickText function   Introduced in version 2.0

FORMS

```
the clickText
clickText()
find the clickText in field "Links"
put the clickText & return after wordsClickedThisSession
```

ACTION

The **clickText** function returns the word or group of characters the user last clicked on in a locked field.

COMMENTS

The **clickText** function is particularly useful when you want to attach actions to words, letting the user click on a word in order to do something. The following handler looks up the clicked word in a glossary stack:

```
on mouseDown -- goes in stack script
   if word 2 of the name of the target is not "field" then exit mouseDown
   get the clickText
   lock screen
   go to stack "Glossary"
   find it in field "Words"
   if the result is not empty then
     go back
     answer "Sorry, there is no further information on" && it
   end if
   unlock screen with visual effect zoom open
end mouseDown
```

If the character you clicked has the text style "group", **the clickText** returns the entire group—that is, the largest continuous run of text with the "group" style. If the clicked text is not grouped, the function returns the word that was clicked on. If you clicked on white space, **the clickText** returns empty.

Clicking in an unlocked field does not update **the clickText** unless you clicked with the Command key held down.

Old HyperCard versions: In versions of HyperCard before 2.0, the **clickText** function is not available. However, you can get the word the user clicked in a locked field using the following trick:

```
on mouseDown
  set the lockText of me to false
  click at the clickLoc -- double-click to select the word
  click at the clickLoc
  get the selectedText
  set the lockText of me to true
  -- the clicked word is in "it" and you can do whatever you want
  -- with it.
end mouseDown
```

ALSO SEE

click command; **clickChunk** function; **clickLine** function; **textStyle** property

---

clickV function   Introduced in version 1.2

FORMS

the clickV
clickV()
put the clickV into verticalDistance
if the clickV > the bottom of card window then beep

ACTION

The **clickV** function returns the vertical distance from the top of the card window (the lower edge of the title bar) to the last point clicked.

COMMENTS

The **clickV** is equal to item 2 of **the clickLoc**.

The clickV is not necessarily equal to the mouseV: The vertical location of the last mouse click is not necessarily the current vertical position of the mouse, because the user might have moved the mouse since the last click. To get the current vertical position of the mouse, use the **mouseV** function.

The following handler continuously displays the **clickV** and **mouseV** as you move the mouse around:

```
on mouseUp
  repeat until the shiftKey is down
    get the mouseClick -- resets the clickV
    put "The clickV is" && the clickV && "and the mouseV is" && the mouseV
  end repeat
end mouseUp
```

ALSO SEE

click command; **clickH** function; **clockLoc** function; **mouseV** function

---

close application command

Introduced in version 2.1
Last changed in version 2.2

FORMS

```
close [document {in|with}] application
close "Microsoft Word"
close "My Disk:Biz:Call Tracking Database" in "FileMaker Pro"
close theSpreadsheet with theAppPath
close "Chooser"
```

ACTION

The **close application** command closes a desk accessory or document, or quits a program that's running on the same machine as HyperCard.

The **close application** command is available only under System 7, and the *application* must be System 7-friendly and support AppleEvents.

COMMENTS

The **close application** command can be used in a variety of ways to control the Macintosh environment. This example forces all running programs except HyperCard and the Finder to quit:

```
on mouseUp -- quit all open programs except HyperCard
  put the programs into programList
  repeat with thisProgram = 1 to the number of lines of programList
    get line thisProgram of programList
    if it is not "Finder" and "HyperCard" is not in it
    then close thisProgram
  end repeat
end mouseUp
```

About quitting the Finder: You can use the **close application** command to quit the Finder, just like any other application. However, if the Finder is not running, desk accessories are not available. The Finder is automatically relaunched when you quit all open applications.

Since you can only send AppleEvents to a program that's running, the **close application** command is also useful in handlers that open a document in order to send an AppleEvent to its application:

```
on editMyDoc theDocument
  open theDocument with "FileMaker Pro"
  updateRecord theDocument -- updateRecord communicates with FM Pro
  close document theDocument in "FileMaker Pro"
end editMyDoc
```

If you try to close an application that's not running, **the result** is set to "No such application."

Changes to HyperTalk: In version 2.1, the **close application** command can't close desk accessories.

Techie alert: The form **close** *application* sends the `quit` AppleEvent. The **close** *document* form sends a `clos` AppleEvent.

ALSO SEE

appleEvent message; **open application** command; **programs** function; **systemVersion** function

---

close file command

Introduced in version 1.0
Last changed in version 2.2

FORMS

```
close file fileName
close file "Mailing List"
close file "FileNumber" && thisFileNumber
close file "Large Disk:Super Folder:Economy Size File"
```

ACTION

The **close file** command closes a text file you've previously opened with the **open file** command.

COMMENTS

Files that are opened with **open file** remain open (which means they cannot be accessed from any other program) until you close them. Since HyperCard can have only three files open at one time, you should use this command to close each file as soon as your script is finished with it.

HyperCard automatically closes any open files when you press Command-Period, when an **exit to HyperCard** statement is issued, when HyperCard puts up an error dialog, or when you quit HyperCard.

If *fileName* is not in the same folder as HyperCard, you must provide the full pathname of the file each time you refer to it. So it makes sense to put the full path into a variable for easy reference.

The following example reads from a file of student records. (It assumes the existence of two handlers.)

```
on distributeScholarships
   put "University:Main Campus:Student Records" into students
   open file students
```

```
      repeat
        read from file students until return  -- get next line
        if it is empty then exit repeat     -- no more records - we're done
        put item 1 of it into studentName
        put item 2 of it into gradePointAverage
        put item 3 of it into nameAndAddress
        put item 4 of it into studentActivities
        if gradePointAverage ≥ 3.8 then
          sendScholarshipOffer nameAndAddress    -- another handler
        else if gradePointAverage < 2.0 then
          if studentActivities contains "Varsity Football" then
            sendScholarshipOffer nameAndAddress
          else
            alertDraftBoard nameAndAddress       -- another handler
          end if
        end if
      end repeat
      close file students
  end distributeScholarships
```

Match close and open commands: In general, **close file** should always be paired with **open file**. If you try to close a file that is not open, **the result** is set to "File not open."

Changes to HyperTalk: HyperCard versions before 2.2 put up an error dialog instead of setting **the result** if you try to close a file that's not open.

ALSO SEE
exit to HyperCard keyword; **open application** command; **open file** command

---

close printing command   Introduced in version 1.0

FORMS
```
close printing
close printing
```

ACTION
The **close printing** command sends the contents of the current print job to the printer.

COMMENTS
Always use **close printing** to complete a print job started using **open printing** or **open report printing**. If you do not include **close printing**, your pages won't be printed until you either print something else or quit HyperCard.

This handler demonstrates how to search for and print selected cards:

```
on printBestSellers
  open printing
  repeat for the number of cards
    if field "Total Sales" > 500000 then print this card
    else go to next card
  end repeat
  close printing
end printBestSellers
```

ALSO SEE

open printing command; **open report printing** command; **print** command; **print card** command

---

close window command/message   Introduced in version 2.0

FORMS

```
close windowDescriptor
close card window
close window "Picture of Fruit"
close window thisPaletteName
close window line 11 of the windows
```

ACTION

The **close window** command closes either the current stack window or the specified external window.

COMMENTS

One of the uses for the **close window** command is to close external windows that don't have a close box. The following handler closes a picture window (displayed by the **picture** command) when the user clicks it:

```
on mouseDownInPicture thePicture
  close window thePicture
end mouseDown
```

Closing a window, either manually or from a script, sends a **close** message to the current card. The **close** message has one parameter, which is a descriptor of the window being closed. As with any message, you can write a custom handler to override the normal behavior of the action.

The **close window** command cannot be used to close a stack window other than the currently frontmost stack. Attempting to do so will generate an error dialog. To close a stack other than the frontmost stack, use the **show** command to bring that window to the front, then issue the statement `close card window`.

Attempting to close the card window when only one stack is open has no effect, since at least one stack must be open at all times in HyperCard.

ALSO SEE
hide command; **go** command; **windows** function

---

closeBackground message

FORMS
```
closeBackground
```

ACTION
The **closeBackground** message is sent to the current card when the user is moving to a card of a different background.

COMMENTS
You can write a **closeBackground** handler to perform any necessary cleanup tasks before the user leaves a particular background. However, since **closeBackground** is only sent after the close process has started, you can't prevent the user from leaving a background by intercepting this message.

When the user is about to leave the current background, the following messages are sent, in order, to the current card:

```
closeCard
closeBackground
openBackground
openCard
```

ALSO SEE
closeCard message; **closeStack** message; **openBackground** message

---

closeCard message

FORMS
```
closeCard
```

ACTION
The **closeCard** message is sent to the current card when the user is moving to another card.

COMMENTS
You can use a **closeCard** handler to perform any necessary cleanup tasks before the user

leaves a particular card. The following example uses **closeCard** and **openCard** handlers in conjunction to keep the user from seeing card cleanup. They belong in the background script:

```
on closeCard -- so screen is locked while switching cards
   lock screen
end closeCard


on openCard -- screen is locked, so this doesn't show:
   if field "Notes" is empty
   then set the icon of background button "Notes" to "No Notes"
   else set the icon of background button "Notes" to "Notes"
   unlock screen
end openCard
```

However, since **closeCard** is only sent once the close process has started, you cannot prevent the user from leaving a card by intercepting this message.

When the user is about to leave the current card, the following messages are sent to the card, in order:

```
closeCard
openCard
```

ALSO SEE
closeBackground message; **closeStack** message; **openCard** message

---

closeField message

Introduced in version 1.0

FORMS
```
closeField
```

ACTION
The **closeField** message is sent to a field when the selection (or insertion point) is being removed from that field, and text has been changed since the last time the field was opened.

COMMENTS
The selection can be removed from the current field by:

- Clicking outside the field
- Tabbing to another field
- Showing or hiding the message box
- Pressing the Enter key
- Switching into background mode

- Going to another card
- Pressing Command-Shift-Z to undo all changes to the field
- Quitting HyperCard

Changing a field's contents with the **put** command does not send a **closeField**.

This example shows how to make sure a field's content is the correct format after the user has made a change:

```
on closeField
   if me is not a number then
     beep
     answer "The Zip Code must be a number!"
     select text of me -- let the user change the field
   end if
end closeField
```

If the selection is being removed from a field but the text has not changed, the **exitField** message is sent instead.

ALSO SEE
exitField message; **openField** message

---

closePalette message

Introduced in version 2.0
Last changed in version 2.1

FORMS
```
closePalette paletteName,windowID
closePalette Contents,893467
```

ACTION
The **closePalette** message is sent to the current card when you close a floating window that was created by the **palette** command.

COMMENTS
The *paletteName* parameter is the same as the name passed to the **palette** command.

You can store the *windowID* reported in this message for later use. There may be more than one window with the same name, but the window ID is always unique, so you can use it as an unambiguous way to identify a window.

Changes to HyperTalk: In version 2.0, the **openPalette** and **closePalette** messages have the *name* parameter, but not the *windowID* parameter.

ALSO SEE
closeStack message; **close window** command; **openPalette** message; **palette** command

closePicture message

Introduced in version 2.0
Last changed in version 2.1

FORMS

```
closePicture windowName,windowID
closePicture Figure,987620
```

ACTION

The **closePicture** message is sent to the current card when you close a picture window that was created by the **picture** command.

COMMENTS

The *windowName* parameter is the same as the name passed to the **picture** command.

You can store the *windowID* reported in this message for later use. There may be more than one window with the same name, but the window ID is always unique, so you can use it as an unambiguous way to identify a window.

If the picture's window style is one that has a close box, this message is sent when the user clicks the close box. The message is also sent when a handler issues the **close window** command.

Changes to HyperTalk: In version 2.0, the **openPicture** and **closePicture** messages have the *name* parameter, but not the *windowID* parameter.

ALSO SEE

openPicture message; **openStack** message; **picture** command

---

closeStack message

Introduced in version 1.0

FORMS

```
closeStack
```

ACTION

The **closeStack** message is sent to the current card when a stack is about to be closed.

COMMENTS

Intercepting the **closeStack** message lets you perform any necessary cleanup tasks before the user leaves your stack. The following handler cleans out your changes to the menu bar when the stack is closed:

```
on closeStack
   reset menubar
end closeStack
```

However, since **closeStack** is only sent once the close process has started, you cannot prevent the user from leaving your stack by intercepting this message.

The following actions trigger the **closeStack** message:

- Executing a **go** command that moves to another stack

- Deleting the stack

- Closing the stack's window

- Quitting HyperCard

When the user is about to close the current stack, the following messages are sent, in order, to the current card:

```
closeCard
closeBackground
closeStack
openStack
openBackground
openCard
```

ALSO SEE

close command; **closeBackground** message; **closeCard** message; **openStack** message; **suspendStack** message

---

commandChar property   Introduced in version 2.0

FORMS

```
set [the] {commandChar|cmdChar} of menuItem to [character|empty]
```
```
set the commandChar of first menuItem of menu "Edit" to "U"
```
```
set the commandChar of menuItem "User Level" of menu "Utilities" to empty
```

ACTION

The **commandChar** property determines what Command-key combination, if any, corresponds to the specified menu item. The command character appears to the right of its menu item, along with the ⌘ symbol.

COMMENTS

The Command-key combinations serve as shortcuts, particularly for frequently-used menu items, so it's particularly appropriate to add them to custom menu items you use a lot. The following handler creates a menu for a role-playing game and sets Command keys for each direction you might move in:

```
on makeDirectionsMenu
   create menu "Directions"
```

```
    put "Left,Right,Up,Down,Forward,Back" into menu "Directions"
    repeat with thisItem = 1 to the number of menuItems in menu "Directions"
       set the commandChar of menuItem thisItem of menu "Directions" ¬
       to first char of the name of menuItem thisItem of menu "Directions"
    end repeat
  end makeDirectionsMenu
```

The *menuItem* is a descriptor of any menu item. You cannot set the **commandChar** of items in the Apple, Tools, Font, or Patterns menu. If you try, HyperCard puts up a script error dialog and aborts the rest of the handler.

The *character* can be any character. Case and the state of the Option key are not significant when the user presses the combination; however, if you specify a lowercase or option-key *character*, it will appear in the menu as typed. Customarily, uppercase characters are used for Command-key combinations. To eliminate an existing Command-key combination, set the menu item's **commandChar** to empty.

HyperCard uses most of the letters of the alphabet for its standard menus. Letters not used are **D**, **G**, **J**, **X**, and **Y**; **A** and **S** are used only when a paint tool has been chosen. HyperCard also uses the special characters **~ . ? + -**. You can use any other punctuation characters without conflicting with HyperCard's standard Command-key assignments.

Command key order: HyperCard checks for Command-key assignments from right to left across the menu bar, and within each menu from top to bottom. This means that Command-key assignments for custom menus on the right end of the menu bar have higher priority than those for HyperCard's standard menus.

For example, if you assign a **commandChar** of "C" to a custom menu item that appears in a menu to the right of the Edit menu, pressing ⌘C triggers the custom menu item, but ⌘C will no longer work for the Copy item in the Edit menu. To avoid confusing users by displaying Command-key combinations that don't work, be sure to remove the one that no longer works:

```
  set the commandChar of menuItem 4 of menu "Edit" to empty
```

(We used menuItem 4 rather than the name of the item because the name of the Copy item changes depending on what's selected. The dotted line after Undo counts as a menu item, so Copy is menu item 4.)

All command keys revert to their default assignments when you use the **reset menubar** command or when you quit HyperCard.

ALSO SEE

reset menubar command

commandKey function   Introduced in version 1.0

FORMS

```
the commandKey
the cmdKey
commandKey()
cmdKey()
if the commandKey is down then edit script of me
```

ACTION

The **commandKey** function returns the state of the Command key (up if the key is being pressed, or down if it's not).

COMMENTS

The **commandKey** function is often used to add an option to the behavior of a button press, menu choice, or other user action. The following example adds a level of safety to all the menu items that remove an object by first presenting a confirmation dialog. If the user holds down the Command key, the dialog is skipped:

```
on doMenu theItem
   if (theItem contains "Clear" or theItem contains "Delete") ¬
   and the commandKey is not down then    -- put up dialog
      answer "Do you really want to delete?" with "OK" or "Cancel"
      if it is "Cancel" then exit doMenu   -- never mind
   end if
   pass doMenu                            -- go ahead
end doMenu
```

ALSO SEE

commandKeyDown message; **optionKey** function; **shiftKey** function

---

commandKeyDown command/message   Introduced in version 2.0

FORMS

```
commandKeyDown theKey
commandKeyDown "e"
commandKeyDown char 1 of field "Keys"
```

ACTION

The **commandKeyDown** command simulates typing a character while the Command key is held down.

COMMENTS

Pressing a Command-key combination manually sends a **commandKey** message to the current card (or, if the insertion point is in a field, to that field). The message has one parameter, which is the character pressed with the Command key. As with any command/message, you can write a custom handler to override the normal behavior of the action.

This handler demonstrates a method of giving buttons Command-key equivalents:

```
on commandKeyDown theKey
   if theKey is "T" then
      send mouseUp to background button "Find Title"
   else if theKey is "A" then
      send mouseUp to background button "Find Author"
   else if theKey is "S" then
      send mouseUp to background button "Find Subject"
   else
      pass commandKeyDown
   end if
end commandKeyDown
```

The **commandKeyDown** message is not sent when you issue a **type** command to type a Command-key combination. It also is not sent when you type certain HyperCard shortcuts such as Command-Option-C (to open the current card's script).

The *theKey* parameter is not case-sensitive, and accented characters are treated as their unaccented counterparts.

ALSO SEE

type command

---

commands property

Introduced in version 2.0

FORMS

the commands of window *paletteWindow*
```
get the commands of window "Navigator"
put line nextButton of the commands of window myPalette into myCommand
answer the commands of window ID 8934534
```

ACTION

The **commands** property applies to the floating palette windows created by the **palette** command. It reports a list of the commands belonging to each button in the palette, separated by return characters.

This property is read-only and cannot be set by a handler.

COMMENTS

When you create a palette with the Palette Maker card in the Power Tools stack, you can specify one line of HyperTalk code for each button on the palette. This line is usually a custom message that triggers a handler in the stack where you're using the palette.

When you click one of the buttons in a palette, HyperCard sends the button's statement to the current card. If you checked Remain Hilited when creating the palette, the statement is sent when the user presses the mouse. If not, it's sent when the mouse button is released.

The following handler highlights each of a palette's buttons and displays the corresponding command in the message box:

```
on hilitePaletteButtons thePalette
   put the buttonCount of window thePalette into numberOfButtons
   repeat with thisButton = 1 to numberOfButtons
      set the hilitedButton of window thePalette to thisButton
      put line thisButton of the commands of window thePalette
      wait until the mouseClick --click to continue to next button
   end repeat
   set the hilitedButton of window thePalette to 0 -- unhilite all
end hilitePaletteButtons
```

ALSO SEE

palette command

---

compound function

Introduced in version 1.0

FORMS

compound(*interestRate*, *numberOfPeriods*)

```
compound(0.05,4) * 10000 -- 5% yearly interest over 4 years
put compound(percentRate/100,1) * principal into newValue
```

ACTION

The **compound** function returns the principal plus accrued interest on an investment of one unit, at the specified rate of interest per period and number of periods.

The formula for **compound** is $(1 + interestRate)^{(numberOfPeriods)}$. The built-in **compound** function is slightly more accurate than this computed formula for very small values of *interestRate*).

COMMENTS

The *interestRate* is expressed as a fraction of 1 rather than as a percentage of 100, so you must convert percentages (for example, 8.5%) to their floating-point equivalent (0.85) by dividing by 100.

You must give the *numberOfPeriods* in the same units of time as the *interestRate*. For example, if the interest is expressed as a monthly rate, the *numberOfPeriods* is the number of months.

You can use the following handler to compute the value of an investment after some period of time:

```
on futureValue
    ask "What's the investment amount?" with "1000"
    if it is empty then exit futureValue
    put it into theInvestment
    ask "What's the yearly interest rate?" with "5.5"
    if it is empty then exit futureValue
    put it/100 into interestRate
    ask "How many years?" with "3"
    if it is empty then exit futureValue
    put theInvestment * compound(interestRate,it) into endValue
    set the numberFormat to "0.00"
    answer "The compounded value is $" & endValue with "Wow!"
end futureValue
```

ALSO SEE
annuity function; **numberFormat** property

---

controlKey message   Introduced in version 2.0

FORMS
```
controlKey asciiValue
controlKey 7   -- control-G
controlKey 28  -- left arrow
```

ACTION
The **controlKey** message is sent to the current card (or, if a field is open for editing, to that field) when the user types a Control-key combination.

COMMENTS
The *asciiValue* parameter can be any value in Table III–2. If the *asciiValue* is not one of these valid numbers, the **controlKey** message will be ignored. The chart gives the key which, when pressed along with the Control key, produces the specified ASCII value. Certain special keys (most of them appear only on the extended keyboard) also send control characters.

Pressing a Control-key combination, manually or from a script, sends a **controlKey** message to the current card. The single parameter is the ASCII value of the Control-key combination typed.

One use for the **controlKey** message is to give users a variety of keyboard shortcuts without interfering with menu command keys. The following handler lets the user perform a variety of utility tasks via the keyboard:

```
on controlKey theNumber
    if theNumber is 3 then edit script of this card -- ^C
    else if theNumber is 2 then edit script of this background -- ^B
    else if theNumber is 19 then edit script of this stack -- ^S
end controlKey
```

Table III.2   ControlKey Parameter Values

Key Pressed	Value	Key Pressed	Value
A, home	1	], right arrow	29
B	2	up arrow	30
C, enter	3	- (dash), down arrow	31
D, end	4	' (single quote)	39
E, help	5		
F	6	*	42
G	7	+	43
H, delete	8	,	44
I, tab	9	- (keypad minus)	45
J	10	. (period)	46
K, page up	11	/	47
L, page down	12	0	48
M, return	13	1	49
N	14	2	50
O	15	3	51
P, function keys	16	4	52
Q	17	5	53
R	18	6	54
S	19	7	55
T	20	8	56
U	21	9	57
V	22		
W	23	;	59
X	24		
Y	25	=	61
Z	26		
[, esc, clear	27	~	96
\, left arrow	28	del (forward delete)	127

ControlKey interacts with keyDown: If there is a **keyDown** handler in the message-passing path, and it does not pass **keyDown**, it also traps the **controlKey** message. If you want to use control keys, make certain that any **keyDown** handler that's in the message path contains the line

```
pass keyDown
```

Techie alert: The **controlKey** message is implemented internally as a command.

ALSO SEE
commandKeyDown command/message

---

convert command

Introduced in version 1.0
Last changed in version 2.2

FORMS
```
convert inputDateTime [from dateFormat [and timeFormat]] to dateFormat [and timeFormat]
convert "7/1/93" to long date
convert line 1 of field "Time" to seconds
convert 2667139260 from seconds to short date and short time
convert last item of the version of this stack to date and time
convert the date && the long time to dateItems
```

ACTION
The **convert** command converts a given date and/or time to a specified format. If the *inputDateTime* is a container, HyperTalk puts the converted date/time in that container; otherwise, it is placed in the **it** variable.

COMMENTS
Calculations based on dates are often cumbersome because of the need to account for month lengths, leap years, and so on. The **convert** command lets you do calculations on dates without having to worry about these problems. For example, this function handler computes tomorrow's date in long format:

```
function tomorrow
   put 60 * 60 * 24 into secondsPerDay
   convert (the seconds + secondsPerDay) to long date
   return it
end tomorrow
```

The following chart shows the valid specifications for *dateFormat* and *timeFormat*:

U.S. Formats for the *convert* Command

`long date`	Thursday, July 7, 1988

The fully expanded date, including day of the week, month name, day number, and year.

`English date`	Thursday, July 7, 1988

Same as the long date (see below).

`abbr[rev[iated]] date`	Thu, Jul 7, 1988

An abbreviated version of the long date. Abbreviated day names are: `Mon, Tue, Wed, Thu, Fri, Sat`. Abbreviated month names are: `Jan, Feb, Mar, Apr, May, Jun, Jul, Aug, Sep, Oct, Nov, Dec.`

`[short] date`	7/7/88

The month number, day number, and last two digits of the year.

`long time`	4:01:11 PM (or 16:01:11)

The time in colon-separated form with seconds. Whether 12-hour or 24-hour clock format is used depends on what is set in the Control Panel.

`abbr[rev[iated]] time`	4:01 PM (or 16:01)

The time in colon-separated form without seconds.

`[short] time`	4:01 PM (or 16:01)

The time in colon-separated form without seconds (same as the abbreviated time).

`dateItems`	1988,7,7,16,1,11,5

A comma-separated list of items representing (in order) the year, month, day number, hour, minute, second, and day of week.

`seconds`	2667139260

The number of seconds since midnight, January 1, 1904 (don't ask...).

(25 bonus points if you can guess when this command's explanation was originally written.)

These formats might be localized to slightly different formats outside the U.S. (or if you have changed the date and time formats in the Control Panel). However, the `seconds` and `dateItems` formats are the same in every country. And the English date is guaranteed to always be the form shown above, regardless of the current system settings.

The **convert** command always returns its output in one of the above formats. However, HyperTalk is fairly forgiving when it comes to input format, and will accept dates that vary slightly from the format above. For example, `1/17/1993` is a valid date, even though it has a four-number year instead of just the last two numbers.

The `dateItems` format accepts even some invalid dates (and converts them to valid ones). This can come in very handy when doing calculations. For example, if you execute the following statements:

```
put "1988,7,7,16,1,11,5" into myDate
add 97 to item 3 of myDate -- add 97 days
-- but myDate is now July 104, 1988, not a valid date
convert myDate to long date
```

the resulting value will be "Wednesday, October 12, 1988"—which is 97 days after July 7.

If you convert a date to a format that includes the time, the **convert** command assumes a time of 12 midnight. If you convert a time to a format that includes the date, **convert** uses today's date. For example:

```
convert "4:01 PM" to date and time -- yields <today's date> 4:01 PM
convert "7/7/88" to date and time -- yields 7/7/88 12:00 AM
```

Put dates in quotes to avoid ambiguity: If the *inputDateTime* is a literal short date and you forget to enclose it in quotation marks, HyperCard will try to carry out meaningless calculations on what it thinks is an expression, yielding unexpected results. For instance, if HyperCard encounters the statement

```
convert 5/12/44 to seconds
```

it will divide 5 by 12, divide the result by 44, and try to convert the resulting number to seconds, yielding 0. To make sure this statement is evaluated the way you want, write it like this:

```
convert "5/12/44" to seconds
```

This gives the desired result.

Coping with international dates: If the time separator on your system is a decimal point (.), passing the short time to **convert** may confuse it. Since the short time in 24-hour mode is of the form *hour.minute*, the command interprets it as a number, and assumes it is in seconds format. To avoid this problem, use the **convert from** option:

```
convert "13.33" from short time to long time -- 1:33:00 PM
```

The convert command sets the result: If you supply something that's not a valid date to **convert**, it sets the **result** function to "invalid date". If **the result** is empty immediately after the **convert** command, you can be sure that **convert** has been successful.

This handler shows how to use the **convert** command to simplify date calculations and comparisons:

```
on bouncer
   -- what was the date 18 years ago today?
   put the date into eighteenYearsAgo
   convert eighteenYearsAgo to dateItems
   subtract 18 from item 1 of eighteenYearsAgo -- item 1 is the year
   convert eighteenYearsAgo to seconds
   -- get the user's birthdate
   repeat
```

```
      ask "What's your date of birth?"
      if it is empty then exit bouncer -- user cancelled
      if it is not a date then
         answer "That's not a date!"
      else
         convert it to seconds
         exit repeat
      end if
   end repeat
   -- was the user born less than 18 years ago?
   if it < eighteenYearsAgo then
      answer "Sorry, this program is adult-only."
      doMenu "Quit HyperCard"
   else
      answer "Come on in!"
   end if
end bouncer
```

Seconds are negative for dates before 1/1/04:   The starting point used to compute the seconds is midnight, January 1, 1904. If you convert a date before this to the seconds format, the value returned is the negative number of seconds between your date and 1/1/04.

You can use this to obtain the number of days between any two dates:

```
on findDateDifference startDate, endDate
   convert startDate to seconds
   convert endDate to seconds
   answer "The difference is" && abs(startDate - endDate)/(60*60*24) ¬
   && "days."
end findDateDifference
```

The seconds and dateItems formats can understand any dates between January 1 of the year 1 and December 31, 9999. However, HyperCard cannot convert dates before January 1, 1000 if they are in the other date formats, so if you are dealing with dates earlier than 1/1/1000, be sure you enter them as either seconds or dateItems. (You can convert dates before 1/1/1000 to any format, as long as the *inputDateTime* is in either the dateItems or seconds format.)

A note about convert and the message box: As mentioned above, if you convert a noncontainer, the converted value is placed in the **it** local variable. If you type such a command into the message box rather than executing it from a handler, a ***global*** variable called "it" is created to hold the converted value. This global variable is completely separate from the local variable **it**, and is created only when you use the message box.

Changes to HyperTalk: In versions before 2.2, you can't specify a "from" format; HyperTalk automatically determines what format the input is in, and it's not possible to to force it to interpret a date and time in a specific format.

ALSO SEE

date function; **is a** operator; **it** variable; **result** function; **seconds** function; **time** function

---

copy template command   Introduced in version 2.2

FORMS

```
copy template reportTemplate to stack stackName
copy template "Annual Report" to stack "Personnel"
copy template selectedTemplate to stack (card field "Destination")
```

ACTION

The **copy template** command copies a Print Report template from the current stack to another stack.

COMMENTS

Use the **copy template** command when you want to copy a completed template under script control. You can also copy a report template manually by choosing Print Report, choosing the template, copying it, and pasting it into another stack.

The *reportTemplate* must be the name of a template in the current stack. (You can use the **reportTemplates** property to get a list of template names.) If you try to copy a nonexistent template, **the result** is set to "No such report template". If the destination stack already contains a template with the same name, the new template overwrites it.

Report templates follow the same stack hierarchy as resources: templates in the Home stack or a stack in use are available to the current stack.

ALSO SEE

open report printing command; **reportTemplates** property

---

cos function   Introduced in version 1.0

FORMS

```
[the] cos of angleInRadians
cos (angleInRadians)
the cos of pi -- yields -1
cos(theta)
cos(mu + pi)
```

ACTION

The **cos** function returns the cosine of its argument. Given a right triangle, the cosine of one of its acute angles is defined as the ratio of the length of the adjacent side of the angle to the length of the hypotenuse.

COMMENTS

The argument of the **cos** function must be in radians. One radian is 180/π degrees, or about 57.3 degrees.

The following excessive example draws a pie chart (see Figure III.17):

```
on drawPieChart theData
   -- compute total of values and edges of chart:
   put 250 into pieCenterH
   put 160 into pieCenterV
   put pieCenterH & comma & pieCenterV into pieCenter
   put 150 into pieRadius
   put the number of items in theData into dataCount
   put sum(dataCount) into total
   put pieCenterV - pieRadius into pieTop
   put pieCenterV + pieRadius into pieBottom
   put pieCenterH - pieRadius into pieLeft
   put pieCenterH + pieRadius into pieRight
   -- clear screen and draw bounding circle and first line:
   reset paint
   choose select tool
   doMenu "Select All"
   doMenu "Clear Picture"
   choose oval tool
   set the lineSize to 2
   drag from pieLeft,pieTop to pieRight,pieBottom
   choose line tool
   drag from pieCenter to pieCenterH,pieCenterV - pieRadius
   -- draw a filled wedge for each item in the data
   put zero into angle
```

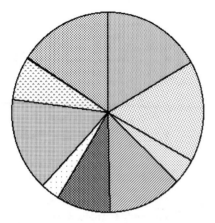

Figure III.17   Pie chart (yours will vary depending on the data you use)

```
   repeat with i = 1 to dataCount
      put pi * item i of theData/total into halfChange
      add halfChange to angle
      put pieCenterH + round((pieRadius - 3) * sin(angle)) into halfH
      put pieCenterV + round((pieRadius - 3) * cos(angle)) into halfV
      add halfChange to angle
      put pieCenterH + round(pieRadius * sin(angle)) into endpointH
      put pieCenterH + round(pieRadius * cos(angle)) into endpointV
      choose line tool
      drag from pieCenter to endpointH,endpointV
      if halfChange > .01 then -- don't try to fill small wedges
         set the pattern to item (i mod 12) + 1 ¬
         of "2,13,11,3,14,6,21,17,31,18,4,32"
         choose bucket tool
         click at halfH,halfV
      end if
   end repeat
   choose browse tool
end drawPieChart
```

HyperTalk has no built-in secant function, but you can write one as follows:

```
function sec angle
   return 1/cos of angle
end sec
```

ALSO SEE
atan function; **sin** function; **tan** function

---

create menu command   Introduced in version 2.0

FORMS
create menu *menuName*
create menu "Utilities"
create menu word 2 of field "Menu Names"

ACTION
The **create menu** command adds a custom menu to the menu bar, to the left of the existing menus. The menu that's created is empty, with no menu items. Use the **put into menu** command to add your custom menu items to the newly created menu.

COMMENTS
The following handler, which belongs in the script of an address stack, creates a menu of names. Choose a name, and the phone number appears in the message box. (This example

creates each menu item with a menu message, rather than handling the custom items in a **doMenu** handler.)

```
on makeCallMenu
   create menu "QuickCall" -- creates empty menu
   put "put line 1 of field" && quote & "Telephone" & quote & "of card" ¬
   into myMessage
   -- now we put items into the menu:
   repeat with thisCard = 1 to the number of cards
     put field "Name" of card thisCard after menu "QuickCall" ¬
     with menuMessage myMessage && thisCard
   end repeat
end makeCallMenu
```

The *menuName* can be up to 201 characters (of course, shorter names are more practical). Menu names can contain spaces (or any other character); however, because a two-word menu looks like two separate menus, menu names in most applications are one word. You should probably stick to this convention to avoid confusing users.

If there is already a menu called *menuName*, HyperCard puts up an error dialog. You can check for the existence of a menu by that name with the **there is** operator:

```
if there is no menu "Utils" then create menu "Utils"
```

Menus you add will remain in the menu bar until you remove them with the **delete menu** command, the **reset menubar** command is executed, or you quit HyperCard.

Peaceful coexistence: Usually, you add custom menus on **openStack** and delete them on **closeStack**. If the user may have other stacks open and switch back and forth from them, you should also make sure to remove your menu on **suspendStack** and re-create it on **resumeStack**. This avoids letting the user see irrelevant menus when in another stack, and helps your stack coexist as a good neighbor with other stacks.

```
on openStack
   makeCallMenu
   pass openStack
end openStack


on suspendStack
   if "QuickCall" is in the menus then delete menu "QuickCall"
   pass suspendStack
end suspendStack


on resumeStack
   if "QuickCall" is not in the menus then makeCallMenu
   pass resumeStack
end resumeStack
```

```
on closeStack
  if "QuickCall" is in the menus then delete menu "QuickCall"
  pass closeStack
end closeStack
```

ALSO SEE

delete menu command; **disable** command; **enable** command; **enabled** property; **menus** function; **put into menu** command; **reset menubar** command

---

create stack command   Introduced in version 2.0

FORMS

```
create stack stackName [with background] [in [a] new window]
create stack "My New Stack"
create stack stackNameVar with this background
create stack (line x of field "Stacks") with background x
create stack "Clients" in a new window
create stack "Preferences" with background "Prefs" in a new window
```

ACTION

The **create stack** command creates a new stack. If you specify a background, the new stack will contain stack a single card of that background; otherwise, the stack contains a single blank card.

If you use the form in a new window, the new stack opens in a new window and the current stack remains open; otherwise, the current stack is closed when the new stack is opened.

COMMENTS

Use the **create stack** command to create a new stack without presenting the dialog that appears when you choose New Stack from the File menu. This command presents no dialog; it just creates the new stack on disk, takes you to it, and sends a **newStack** message to it.

The following handler creates a new stack that contains all the marked cards in the current stack:

```
on extractMarkedCards
  if the number of marked cards is zero then
    answer "There are no marked cards."
    exit extractMarkedCards
  end if
  ask file "Save marked cards in stack:"
  if it is empty then exit extractMarkedCards
  put it into newStackName
  lock screen
  lock messages
```

```
      create stack newStackName
      go back
      repeat with thisCard = 1 to the number of marked cards
         set the cursor to busy
         go to marked card thisCard
         push this card
         doMenu "Copy Card"
         go to last card of stack newStackName
         doMenu "Paste Card"
         pop card
      end repeat
      go to card 1 of stack newStackName
      doMenu "Delete Card" -- get rid of blank card
   end extractMarkedCards
```

The *stackName* must be a valid pathname or filename. If only a filename is given, with no path, the new stack is created in the same folder as the current stack. A Macintosh filename can have up to 31 characters; if you try to create a stack with a name that's too long, **the result** is set to "Couldn't create stack."

The *background* is any valid background descriptor. The *background* must be in the current stack. If you specify a background, the stack is created with a single card that duplicates the objects and scripts of the specified background; otherwise, the stack is created with a single blank card and background. Using the form create stack with this background is equivalent to checking the Copy Current Background checkbox in the New Stack dialog.

The card size of the newly created stack is the same as that of the original stack. To change the card size in the new stack, use the **rectangle** property:

```
   create stack "My New Stack" -- goes to new stack
   set the rect of this card to 0,0,342,512 -- standard Mac size
```

Create stack with background also duplicates stack script and resources: If you specify a background, the stack script, as well as all resources in the original stack's resource fork, are copied to the new stack, in addition to the background script and objects.

Changes to HyperTalk: Versions of HyperTalk earlier than 2.2 allow the *stackName* to start with a period (.), which may cause file system problems; version 2.2 will not create a stack whose name starts with a period.

ALSO SEE
doMenu command/message; **rectangle** property; **save as** command

cursor property

FORMS

```
set [the] cursor [of HyperCard] to {cursorNumber|cursorName}
set the cursor to 4
set the cursor to busy
set the cursor to none
```

ACTION

The **cursor** property reflects the graphic image that appears at the pointer location on the screen.

You cannot get the current value of the **cursor**; this is a write-only property.

COMMENTS

You can use a custom cursor or one of HyperCard's built-in cursors to indicate the current state of the stack. The **cursor** shape can be used to indicate that the stack is busy processing a request or to give the user hints about what a click will do.

The *cursorNumber* is the resource ID of a CURS resource in the current stack, a stack in use, the Home stack, HyperCard itself, or the System file. The *cursorName* is the resource name of a CURS resource. You can create a cursor yourself with ResEdit or a similar tool, or use one of HyperCard's built-in cursors (see Figure III.18).

As a courtesy to users who may panic if they can't get the stack to respond, you should always set the **cursor** to watch, busy, or an appropriate custom cursor if your code is doing something that's going to take more than a couple of seconds. The busy cursor spins 1/8 of a rotation every time you set it within a handler, so it's a good cursor to use when you're carrying out a lengthy repeat loop:

```
on getMaxBalance
   put 0 into maxBalance
   repeat with nextCard = 1 to the number of cards
      set the cursor to busy -- spins each time through the loop
```

Ⅰ	Ibeam	1
+	cross	2
✚	plus	3
⌚	watch	4
✋	hand	
↖	arrow	
●	busy	
	none	

Figure III.18   Cursor Shapes

```
        get field "Balance" of card nextCard
        if it > maxBalance then put it into maxBalance
    end repeat
    answer "Maximum balance is:" && maxBalance
end getMaxBalance
```

Setting the cursor on a Powerbook: A Macintosh Powerbook computer will not sleep if the cursor is set to `watch`, so if you're writing a long procedure for a stack that may run on a Powerbook, you may want to use `set the cursor to watch` to prevent the Mac from sleeping in the middle of your process.

Limitations of the cursor property: At idle time—when all handlers have finished running—HyperCard sets the cursor back to the cursor for the current tool, or to the standard arrow if the pointer is not in the frontmost window. The only way to lock the cursor to a particular shape is to use an XCMD.

There's no way to tell from within your handler whether the cursor has been set to what you asked for. If HyperTalk can't find the requested cursor, it doesn't put up an error dialog or set the **result** function.

Interface guidelines? We don't need no stinking interface guidelines!

Alert and knowledgeable readers will be muttering to themselves that the Macintosh has no cursor, just a pointer and an insertion point. One of the authors of this book begged and pleaded with the language designer (to no avail, obviously) to name this property "the pointer". We apologize for any inconvenience.

Moving the pointer location: Moving the pointer is in flagrant violation of the aforementioned User Interface Guidelines, and tends to be extremely confusing to the user. It's been compared to having the computer reach out from the screen and physically yank your mouse hand around. Nevertheless, for certain situations—for example, to display user actions on screen in a training stack—you may want to do it. The best technique for making the pointer appear to move is to make a button into a fake pointer:

1. Create a custom icon (not cursor) resource with the cursor picture you want to show.

2. Create a transparent button, set its icon to the custom icon you created, and hide it.

3. When you're ready to start your animation, set the cursor to `none` and show the button. You can then move the button around under script control. Since the real cursor is hidden, and the button's icon looks like a cursor, the user has the impression that the moving button is, in fact, the cursor itself.

Changes to HyperTalk: Versions of HyperCard before 1.2 have only the I-beam, cross, plus, and watch cursors, and these must be specified by number, rather than name.

ALSO SEE
mouseLoc function

---

date function

Introduced in version 1.0
Last changed in version 2.2

FORMS

```
the [long|abbr[rev[iated]]|short|English] date
date()
put date() into myDate
if the long date is field "Old Date" then beep
```

ACTION

The **date** function returns the current date, in one of several formats.

COMMENTS

The following example records the last date that any text in the stack was changed:

```
on closeField -- placed in stack script
   put the long date into card field "Last Modified" of card 1
end closeField
```

The forms of **the date** are as follows:

Formats for the *date* Function

| the long date | Thursday, July 7, 1988 |

The fully expanded date, including day of the week, month name, day number, and year.

| the English date | Thursday, July 7, 1988 |

Same as the long date (but see below).

| the abbr{rev{iated}} date | Thu, Jul 7, 1988 |

An abbreviated version of the long date. Abbreviated day names are: Mon, Tue, Wed, Thu, Fri, Sat. Abbreviated month names are: Jan, Feb, Mar, Apr, May, Jun, Jul, Aug, Sep, Oct, Nov, Dec.

| the short date | 7/7/88 |

The month number, day number, and last two digits of the year.

| the date | 7/7/88 |

Same as the short date.

| date() | 7/7/88 |

Same as the short date.

These are the forms **the date** produces when the U.S. system software is running. If you're using a system version that's been localized for another country, or if you have changed the date format with the Date & Time control panel, these date formats may be different. If you rely on, say, the month being the first part of the short date, your stack may run into trouble when running on such systems.

To get around this problem, the form the English date always produces the long date in the format given above, regardless of the current system settings. You can safely assume that the first item of the English date is the day of the week, the second item consists of the month name and the day, and the third item is the year.

If your stacks are being used internationally, store any dates in one of the invariant forms (English date, dateItems, or seconds) and use the **convert** command to change them to the appropriate format:

```
on closeCard
    put the long date into field "Last Seen On:"
    put the English date into field "Hidden Last Seen On:"
    pass closeCard
end closeCard


on openCard
    get field "Hidden Last Seen On:"
    convert it from English date to long date
    put it into field "Last Seen On:"
    pass openCard
end openCard
```

This example adds a date stamp to a Comments field, whenever a user clicks the button to add a new comment:

```
on mouseUp
    show field "Comments"
    put return & the abbrev date & colon & return after field "Comments"
    select after text of field "Comments" -- ready to type in comment
end mouseUp
```

Nuances of the date( ) form: When you use the parentheses form of the **date** function, you can't specify a form. If you do, you'll get a script error. Putting anything into the parentheses will also cause an error.

Changes to HyperTalk: In versions of HyperCard before 2.0, if you specify a form with the **date( )** form of the function, it's ignored instead of causing a script error.

In versions of HyperCard before 2.2, the form the English date is not available.

ALSO SEE
convert command; **time** function

debug command

Introduced in version 1.2
Last changed in version 2.2

FORMS

```
debug {pureQuickDraw {true|false}|sound {on|off}|maxMem|maxWindows|hintBits}
debug hintBits
debug pureQuickDraw true
```

ACTION

The **debug** command lets stack developers access special HyperTalk attributes. Normally, only advanced developers in certain very special circumstances need concern themselves with the **debug** command.

COMMENTS

The **debug pureQuickDraw** form is useful mainly for video system developers. The command debug pureQuickDraw true makes HyperCard use the QuickDraw copyBits call (which all monitors can handle) to draw the screen. Issuing the statement debug pureQuickDraw false makes HyperCard use its own custom routines; these are fast and allow visual effects to work, but they may cause compatibility problems on video cards not produced by Apple.

If you see bizarre symptoms on the screen—for example, instead of seeing a proper card, you see eight little images of the card smeared across the screen—turning on **debug pureQuickDraw** can be useful for diagnosing the problem.

The **debug sound** form turns HyperCard's use of the sound channel on and off.

The **debug maxMem** form purges all purgeable blocks from HyperCard's application heap, leaving the maximum amount of memory free.

The **debug maxWindows** form, new in version 2.2, puts the maximum number of open windows HyperCard will allow into the **it** variable. The base number of windows is 25; for each 200K you add to HyperCard's application memory size in the Get Info dialog, you can open five additional windows. (Remember that HyperCard keeps some windows, such as the tool pallette and the message box, open all the time.)

The **debug hintBits** form adds to the action of the Compact Stack menu item, first bringing up a dialog that lets you change certain internal settings that affect the effectiveness and efficiency of the **find** command. These settings are used during the stack compaction.

Debug hintBits is turned off whenever you switch stacks.

Debug hintBits is mostly for CD-ROM developers

This command was designed to aid CD-ROM developers, so they could fine-tune the parameters in their huge read-only stacks to get the most efficient searching.

HyperCard adjusts the hintBits settings automatically when you compact, so **debug hintBits** is largely redundant for people who aren't making really large stacks (where a change in the hint bits parameters may make a noticeable difference in search speed). Because the hand-tuned values are only used for the current compact, and get lost the next time you compact the stack, this command is essentially useless for stacks that can be recompacted.

How HyperCard uses hint bits in searching: HyperCard creates a hash value for all the text on a given card, and updates this value every time you change any of the text in a field. The hash value is made up of 32-bit numbers (called "longwords"). Certain bits in this 32-bit number are set to give hints about the contents of the text—for example, words that start with H, or that are five characters long. These make up the hint bits after which the command is named. (Precisely how the hash works is a secret, at least for now.)

When you issue a **find** command, HyperCard first does a hash on the text you want to find, creating a set of hint bits for it. HyperCard then begins its search—but it looks at the hint bits, trying to find card hint bits that match the text hint bits, rather than matching the text itself. If the hint bits on a particular card don't match those of the search text, the text you're looking for cannot possibly be in that card, so HyperCard rejects that card and goes on to the next one. If the hint bits do match, then it's possible that this card has text that matches the search text, so HyperCard looks through the text itself to see whether there's a match.

Since hint bits are kept in RAM and are smaller than the text itself, searching hint bits is much faster than searching the text of the card itself. Cards other than the current card are usually on the disk rather than in RAM, and so searching the card text is much slower than searching the hint bits. (Typically, hint bits for hundreds of cards can be taken from the disk in a single read operation.) It's this strategy of using hint bits to eliminate most of the cards from the search, before looking at actual card text, that accounts for HyperCard's speed in searching through stacks.

Because checking a card's hint bits is so much faster than checking its text, the more cards that are rejected during the initial hint-bits search, the fewer cards will have to have their text read, and the faster the search operation will be. The purpose of fine-tuning the hint bits parameters is to decrease the number of cards that match on the first hint-bits search, but don't actually have the search text in them.

Using debug hintBits: If you have issued a **debug hintBits** command, the Compact Stack menu item produces the dialog shown in Figure III.19. This dialog lets you change the parameters HyperCard will use for the hint bits. When you click OK, compacting begins, using the hint bits parameters you specified.

HashCount, hintLongs, and pageSize are internal variables. The numbers immediately below these names indicate the values HyperCard used the last time it created hash values. The numbers in the text boxes are the values HyperCard will use in the newly compacted stack.

The hashCount governs how many hint bints are allowed per card. Increasing the hashCount increases the sensitivity of the search: the higher the hashCount, the more cards are rejected by the initial hint bits comparison, and thus the faster the search. But if you use

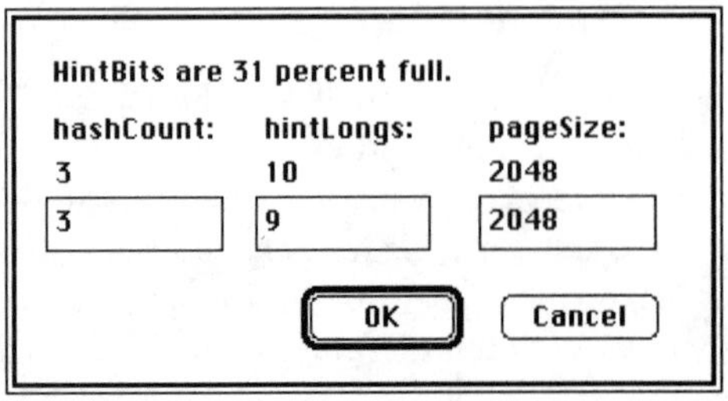

```
+---------------------------------------------+
|                                             |
|   HintBits are 31 percent full.             |
|                                             |
|   hashCount:    hintLongs:    pageSize:      |
|   3             10            2048           |
|   [3        ]   [9        ]   [2048     ]    |
|                                             |
|              ( OK )    ( Cancel )           |
|                                             |
+---------------------------------------------+
```

Figure III.19   HintBits dialog

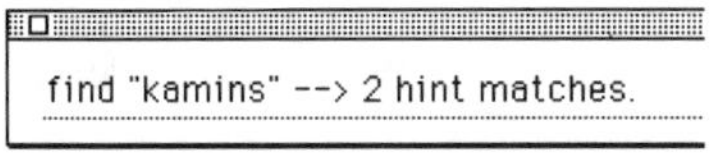

```
find "kamins" --> 2 hint matches.
```

Figure III.20   Matches are shown when you find

too high a number, the hint bits become saturated and the rejection rate declines again. You need to experiment to find the balance point.

The hintLongs variable determines how many longwords are allocated per card for holding hint bits. In especially large stacks, the longwords can quickly become filled up. The cost here is RAM and disk space: the larger hintLongs is, the more disk space and memory is needed.

The pageSize is the number of bytes allocated per page of hint bits. The less available memory you have, the smaller you need to make pageSize.

In Figure III.19, the phrase "HintBits are 31 percent full" means that 31 percent of the bits that can be used for hinting are turned on. This percentage is close to ideal. A much lower number means hintLongs is too high, wasting RAM and disk space; a much higher number indicates that HyperCard isn't rejecting many cards during the hint bits comparison, which means lots of false matches and slows down searching.

Debug hintBits modifies the find command: Each time a **find** command is performed, **debug hintBits** reports the number of matches that occurred during the preliminary hint bits comparison, whether or not the **find** was successful. (See Figure III.20.) This lets you know how well the hint bits are rejecting cards.

At most, only one of the hint matches reflects a card that has what you're looking for; the rest are false matches. The smaller the number of false matches, the less actual text HyperCard has to check, so a smaller number of matches means HyperCard's searches are faster.

The following handler shows the number of matches every time a **find** command is issued:

```
on find
   debug hintBits -- show info on find
   pass find      -- so find will report number of hint matches
end find
```

ALSO SEE

debug checkpoint command; **find** command; **heapSpace** function; **Play** command; **unlock screen** command; **visual effect** command; **windows** function

The joys of redundancy

In prerelease versions, HyperCard made compactions within the original stack. This proved dangerous, because a crash or power failure during the compaction would destroy the stack. HyperCard now compacts the stack to a new stack, then deletes the original and renames the new stack. To the user, it looks like the stack stays the same. You can't lose data even if there's a power failure during compaction; if this happens, HyperCard just reverts to the original stack.

debug checkpoint command

FORMS

```
debug checkpoint
```
debug checkpoint

ACTION

The **debug checkpoint** command sets a debugging checkpoint in a handler. Each time the handler runs, the debugger is invoked at the line where **debug checkpoint** executes.

COMMENTS

You can also set a checkpoint from within the script editor by using the Set Checkpoint item in the Script menu, or by Option-clicking the line at which you want to insert a checkpoint. Checkpoints set this way are temporary and last only until you quit HyperCard. The **debug checkpoint** command, however, sets a permament checkpoint that lasts until you remove the **debug checkpoint** line from the script.

This command is useful for marking incomplete handlers and trapping error conditions during development. For example, the following handler checks a parameter to see whether it's within the proper range. If it's out of bounds, the handler brings up the debugger so you can figure out what's wrong:

```
on mouseUp
   get MyNumber()      -- a function handler that computes a number
   rangeCheck it,0,1   -- was the number within bounds?
   setUp it            -- do something with the number
end mouseUp

on rangeCheck number,lowerBound,upperBound -- a handler for debugging
   if number < lowerBound or number > upperBound ¬
   and the environment is "development" then debug checkpoint
end rangeCheck
```

Once in the debugger, you can check the values of variables, see what messages are being sent, and trace through the offending handler step by step in slow motion.

ALSO SEE

debug command; **debugger** property

debugger property

FORMS

```
set [the] debugger [of HyperCard] to debuggerXCMD
```
set the debugger to "Custom Debugger"
put the debugger into currentDebugName

ACTION

The **debugger** global property is the name of the debugger that appears when you click Debug in a script error dialog, and when a script encounters a checkpoint. By default, the **debugger** property is set to `ScriptEditor`, which is HyperCard's built-in editor and debugger.

COMMENTS

You can set the **debugger** property to use a custom debugger you've written and installed in HyperCard's resource fork (or a stack's resource fork). Debuggers (incuding HyperCard's built-in debugger) are implemented as XCMDs.

If you try to set the **debugger** to an XCMD that's not present, the property is set to the default value of `ScriptEditor`.

In practice, this property is seldom used; most scriptwriters are satisfied with the built-in debugger.

ALSO SEE

debug checkpoint command; **messageWatcher** property; **scriptEditor** property; **variableWatcher** property

---

delete command

Introduced in version 1.0
Last changed in version 2.2

FORMS

```
delete {part|button|field|chunk of container}
delete item 1 of pizzaOrder
delete word 3 to 5 of field "Master List" of card "Lists"
delete last char of the selection
delete the foundChunk
delete card button clickedButton
delete field "Garbage"
delete card part nextPart
```

ACTION

The **delete** command removes the specified text from a container, or removes the specified part (button or field) from the current card.

COMMENTS

The **delete** command can be used either to remove buttons and fields from a card, or to remove text from a container (a field, variable, or the Message Box). This handler removes a line of text from a field:

```
on killName
   ask "Name to remove from the phone book:"
   if it is empty then exit killName -- user cancelled
   if it is not in field "Phone Book" then
     answer "Sorry —" && it && "isn't listed in the book."
```

```
        exit killName
    end if
    find it in field "Phone Book"
    delete the foundLine
end killName
```

(You can add this handler to the auto-dialer script described under the **dial** command to increase that script's usefulness.)

You can delete text described by any chunk expression—characters, items, words, or lines—from a container. You can delete text from any field, including locked fields and shared-text background fields.

If what you are deleting is a part rather than text in a container, the *button* or *field* must be a legal descriptor of a button or field. (See Chapter 7, "Referring to Objects.") The part you delete must be on the current card; if you try to delete a button or field on another card, the **delete** command fails (but no error message appears, and **the result** is not set.)

This example deletes all card objects in the current stack:

```
on mouseUp
  lock messages
  repeat with nextCard = 1 to the number of cards
    go card nextCard
    repeat with theButton = the number of buttons down to 1
      delete button theButton
    end repeat
    repeat with theField = the number of card fields down to 1
      delete card field theField
    end repeat
  end repeat
end mouseUp
```

When you delete a button or field, the **deleteButton** or **deleteField** message is sent to the current card.

Intelligence of delete: The **delete** command is intelligent about returns, spaces, and item delimiters:

- Deleting a word also deletes the space or spaces after it.
- Deleting the last word of a container also deletes the space before it.
- Deleting an item also deletes the item's comma (or other item delimiting character, if you've changed it with the **itemDelimiter** property).
- Deleting the last item also deletes the preceding item delimiter.
- Deleting a line deletes the return after it.
- Deleting the last line deletes the return before it.

A *line* in HyperTalk is defined as a string delimited by return characters. A line in a narrow field may wrap around several times, and look like more than one line on screen, but it is still considered a single line when used in chunk expressions.

Deleting a chunk is different from putting empty into a chunk: A form like

```
delete line 5 of field "List"
```

completely removes line 5 from the field; what was line 6 becomes line 5. On the other hand, the form

```
put empty into line 5 of field "List"
```

removes the text of the line, but leaves the return character that separates it from the next line. The result is that line 5 is now a blank line.

To delete all the text in a container, use the form **put empty into** *container*.

Changes to HyperTalk: In versions of HyperCard before 2.2, you can't use **delete** to remove a button or field. In these versions, use the **select** command to select the undesired part, then use either doMenu "Clear Button" or doMenu "Clear Field" to get rid of it:

```
on deleteButton theNumber
   show button theNumber  -- must be visible to be selected
   select button theNumber -- automatically chooses button tool
   doMenu "Clear Button"
   choose browse tool
end deleteButton
```

There is a bug in version 2.0 and before, in which the forms

```
delete line 0 of container
delete line 0 to number of container
```

delete the first character of the container. Avoid trying to delete line zero in these older versions. (In newer versions, deleting line, character, word, or item zero has no effect.)

ALSO SEE
"Chunk Expressions" in Chapter 8; **deleteButton** message; **deleteField** message; **itemDelimiter** property; **put** command

delete menu command   Introduced in version 2.0

FORMS
```
delete [menuItem {of|from}] menu
delete menu "Companies"
delete menu 7
delete menuItem nextItem from menu "File"
delete last menuItem of menu myMenu
```

ACTION

The **delete menu** command removes the specified menu or menu item from the menu bar.

COMMENTS

Use the **delete menu** command to clean up your custom menus when leaving a stack, or to lock out one or more of HyperCard's standard menus. The following handler prevents users from creating cards, deleting cards, or using any item on the File menu:

```
on lockOutMenus
   set the userLevel to 2
   delete menu "File"
   delete menuItem "Delete Card" from menu "Edit"
   delete menuItem "New Card" from menu "Edit"
   delete menuItem "-2" of menu "Edit" -- get rid of 2nd gray line
end lockOutMenus
```

The *menu* is a descriptor of any menu in the menu bar. A *menuItem* is a descriptor of any item in any menu.

The following example creates a menu called "Parts" containing the names of all buttons and fields on the current card. Choosing a menu item brings up the script of the specified part. Buttons or fields that have no script are shown in italics in the menu (see Figure III.21).

```
on buildPartsMenu
   if "Parts" is in the menus then delete menu "Parts"
   create menu "Parts"
   -- card buttons
   repeat with buttonNumber = 1 to the number of card buttons
      put the name of card button buttonNumber after menu "Parts" ¬
      with menuMessage "edit script of card button" && buttonNumber
   end repeat
   -- card fields
   repeat with fieldNumber = 1 to the number of card fields
      put the name of card field fieldNumber after menu "Parts" ¬
      with menuMessage "edit script of card field" && fieldNumber
   end repeat
   -- background buttons
   repeat with buttonNumber = 1 to the number of background buttons
      put the name of background button buttonNumber after menu "Parts" ¬
      with menuMessage "edit script of background button" && buttonNumber
   end repeat
```

Figure III.21   Parts menu with scriptless objects italicized

```
        -- background fields
        repeat with fieldNumber = 1 to the number of background fields
           put the name of background field fieldNumber after menu "Parts" ¬
           with menuMessage "edit script of background field" && fieldNumber
        end repeat
        -- italicize empty parts
        repeat with itemNumber = 1 to the number of menuItems in menu "Parts"
           if the script of (menuItem itemNumber of menu "Parts") is empty
           then set the textStyle of menuItem itemNumber of menu "Parts" ¬
           to italic
        end repeat
     end buildPartsMenu
```

Can't delete certain menus: You can't delete individual menu items from the Apple, Font, Tools, or Patterns menus (but you can delete the entire menu). Although you can't delete the About HyperCard menu item from the Apple menu, you can rename it with a statement like `set the name of menuItem 1 of menu "Apple" to "About My Standalone"`.

Even if you delete one of HyperCard's standard menus, its items still respond to the **doMenu** command:

```
   delete menu Apple -- menu is removed from the screen...
   doMenu "Key Caps" -- ...but the item is still active
```

In the above example, when Key Caps opens, the Apple icon appears and the entire Apple menu is accessible as long as a desk accessory is the frontmost window. When you close the desk accessory, the Apple icon disappears from the menu bar.

ALSO SEE
put into menu command

deleteBackground message

Introduced in version 1.0

FORMS
```
deleteBackground
```

ACTION
You delete a background by deleting all the cards that belong to it. The **deleteBackground** message is sent to the current card when the card is being deleted, if it's the last remaining card of its background.

If the background's **cantDelete** property is true, the **deleteBackground** message is not sent and the background is not deleted.

COMMENTS

Intercepting the **deleteBackground** message lets you do any necessary cleanup tasks before a background is deleted. However, since **deleteBackground** is only sent once the deletion is in progress, you cannot stop HyperCard from deleting a background by intercepting this message. However, a sly workaround is available:

```
on deleteBackground
   doMenu "Copy Card" -- we make a copy...
   doMenu "Paste Card" -- the original is now deleted
end deleteBackground
```

When a background is deleted, the following messages are sent to the current card:

```
closeCard
closeBackground
deleteCard
deleteBackground
```

Changes to HyperTalk: In versions of HyperCard before 2.0, the message order during deletion is:

```
deleteBackground
deleteCard
```

ALSO SEE

deleteCard message; **deleteField** message; **deleteButton** message; **deleteStack** message; **newBackground** message; **closeBackground** message; **openBackground** message

---

deleteButton message   Introduced in version 1.0

FORMS

```
deleteButton
```

ACTION

The **deleteButton** message is sent to a button when it has been deleted and is about to disappear.

COMMENTS

Since the **deleteButton** message is only sent after the deletion process has actually started, you cannot save the doomed button by trapping this message. However, you can use the following tricky handler to prevent a button from being deleted:

```
on deleteButton
   select empty -- deselects the button
end deleteButton
```

This prevents deletion because a button must be selected for HyperCard to delete it. HyperCard goes through these steps when deleting a button:

1. Receive command to delete a button.

2. Send **deleteButton** message.

3. Delete whatever button is selected.

Since the button's been deselected by the time HyperCard gets to step 3, it becomes confused and cannot delete the button. HyperCard beeps to indicate that there was a problem, and then continues with any handlers that are running.

To prevent the destruction of a particular button, put the above handler in the button's script. If you want to prevent deletion of any buttons in a card, background, or stack, put the handler in the card, background or stack script.

ALSO SEE

deleteBackground message; **deleteCard** message; **deleteField** message; **deleteStack** message; **newButton** message

---

deleteCard message   Introduced in version 1.0

FORMS

```
deleteCard
```

ACTION

The **deleteCard** message is sent to the current card when the card has been deleted and is about to disappear. If the card's **cantDelete** property is true, no **deleteCard** is sent, and the card is not deleted.

COMMENTS

Intercepting the **deleteCard** message lets you perform any necessary cleanup tasks before a card is deleted. The following example removes the deleted card's name from the master list of cards:

```
on deleteCard -- in stack script
   put the short name of this card into deletedName
   get offset(deletedName,field "Master List") -- a sharedText field
   get the number of lines of char 1 to it of field "Master List"
   delete line it from field "Master List"
end deleteCard
```

However, since HyperCard doesn't send **deleteCard** until the deletion is in progress, you can't keep a card from being deleted by intercepting this message (but see the example below for a workaround).

When a card is deleted, the following messages are sent, in order, to the current card:

```
closeCard
closeBackground    (if the next card is of a different background)
deleteCard
deleteBackground (if the deleted card is the last one of its background)
openBackground     (if the next card is of a different background)
openCard
```

The following handler prevents card deletion by copying the card that's about to be deleted, then pasting it back into the stack:

```
on deleteCard
  answer "Are you sure you want to delete this card?" ¬
  with "Delete" or "Undelete"
  if it is "Undelete" then
    doMenu "Copy Card"
    doMenu "Paste Card"
  end if
end deleteCard
```

Changes to HyperTalk: In versions of HyperCard before 2.0, the message order during deletion is:

```
deleteCard
closeCard
```

ALSO SEE

closeCard message; **deleteBackground** message; **deleteButton** message; **deleteField** message; **deleteStack** message; **newCard** message; **openCard** message

---

deleteField message

FORMS

```
deleteField
```

ACTION

The **deleteField** message is sent to a button when it has been deleted and is about to disappear.

COMMENTS

Since the **deleteField** message is only sent after the deletion process has actually started, you cannot save the doomed field by trapping this message. However, you can use sleight of hand to do so:

```
on deleteField
  select empty -- deselects the field
end deleteField
```

This prevents deletion because a field must be selected for HyperCard to delete it. HyperCard goes through these steps when deleting a field:

1. Receive command to delete a field.

2. Send **deleteField** message.

3. Delete whatever field is selected.

Since no field is selected by the time HyperCard gets to step 3, it becomes confused and cannot delete the field. HyperCard beeps to indicate that there was a problem, and then continues with any handlers that are running.

To prevent the destruction of a particular field, put the above handler in the field's script. If you want to prevent deletion of any fields in a card, background, or stack, put the handler in the card, background or stack script.

ALSO SEE

deleteBackground message; **deleteButton** message; **deleteCard** message; **deleteStack** message; **newField** message

---

deleteStack message   Introduced in version 1.0

FORMS

```
deleteStack
```

ACTION

The **deleteStack** message is sent to the current card when the current stack is being deleted and is about to disappear. If the stack's **cantDelete** property is true, you can't delete the stack from within HyperCard, and an attempt to do so does not send **deleteStack**.

You can delete a stack from within HyperCard by using the Delete Stack item in the File menu.

COMMENTS

Since HyperCard doesn't send **deleteStack** until the deletion is in progress, you cannot prevent a stack from being deleted by intercepting this message.

When the stack is deleted, if it was the only open stack HyperCard goes to the first card of the Home stack. Otherwise, it simply closes the stack window.

The following messages are sent, in order, when HyperCard is deleting a stack:

```
closeCard
closeBackground
closeStack
deleteStack
```

Changes to HyperTalk: In versions of HyperCard before 2.0, the message order during deletion is:

```
deleteStack
closeCard
closeBackground
closeStack
```

ALSO SEE

closeStack message; **deleteBackground** message; **deleteButton** message; **deleteCard** message; **deleteField** message; **newStack** message; **openStack** message

---

destination function   Introduced in version 2.2

FORMS

```
the destination
destination()
put the destination into newStackPath
if the destination contains ":Home" then doMenu "Quit HyperCard"
```

ACTION

The **destination** function returns the full pathname of the stack that HyperCard is in the process of going to. If HyperCard is not currently moving between stacks, **the destination** returns the pathname or filename of the current stack.

COMMENTS

The following handler overrides the **go** command, allowing movement within the current stack, but not allowing scripts to go to another stack. (It is also theoretically possible to do this using the **param** function to check what arguments were passed to **go**; unfortunately, **the param** does not operate properly with the **go** command.)

```
on go
  get the long name of this stack
  get the value of word 2 of it    -- the pathname itself
  if it is not the destination then
    return "Can't leave the stack" -- sets the result
  else
    pass go-- allow movement within the stack
  end go
end go
```

The following utility function strips the pathname from the destination, returning only the stack name itself:

```
function shortDestination
  put the itemDelimiter into savedItemDelimiter
```

```
        set the itemDelimiter to colon
        get last item of the destination
        set the itemDelimiter to savedItemDelimiter
        return it
    end shortDestination
```

The **destination** function is also extremely useful in programming a multiple-stack application, since it lets you distinguish between the cases where a user is moving between the application's stacks and leaving the application altogether. For example, many HyperCard applications make changes to the menu bar. To be a good HyperCard citizen, such a stack should undo the changes when the user goes to another stack, so the user doesn't see inappropriate menu items. However, in a multiple-stack application, it is cumbersome and time-consuming to undo your changes when leaving a stack, only to have to redo them immediately because the destination stack is also part of the application.

This example depends upon the existence of a global variable called superStackApp that holds the names of all the stacks in your application:

```
    on closeStack
        cleanUpMenus
        -- other closeStack operations
    end closeStack


    on suspendStack
        cleanUpMenus
        -- other closeStack operations
    end suspendStack


    on cleanUpMenus
        -- this handler uses the shortDestination function above
        global superStackApp,needToUpdateMenus
        if shortDestination() is in superStackApp then
            put true into needToUpdateMenus
        else reset menubar
    end cleanUpMenus


    on resumeStack
        global needToUpdateMenus
        if needToUpdateMenus then updateMenus -- set up custom menus
        put false into needToUpdateMenus
        pass resumeStack
    end resumeStack


    on openStack
        global needToUpdateMenus
        if needToUpdateMenus then updateMenus -- set up custom menus
```

```
      put false into needToUpdateMenus
      pass openStack
   end openStack
```

The above handlers should be in the stack script of each stack in your application. The needToUpdateMenus global tells the stacks in your application whether they need to re-create the custom menus for your application or not.

ALSO SEE

find command; **go** command; **name** property; **pop** command

---

dial command

FORMS

```
dial phoneNumber [with modem [modemCommandString]]
dial "415-555-1212" -- sends touchtones through speaker
dial "415-555-1212" with modem  -- dials on modem connected to Mac
dial field "Phone Number"
dial Tim_Pozar -- the guy who told us the Truth about modems
dial emailNumber with modem "ATZM1E1S0=0"
```

ACTION

The **dial** command produces telephone touch-tones through the Mac's speaker, or (with the with modem option) dials through the modem serial port.

COMMENTS

The **dial** command is intended for automatically dialing the telephone for voice communication. (If you want to do telecom programming in HyperCard, you'll need an XCMD package such as the Serial Toolkit package from APDA; the built-in **dial** command is not robust or sophisticated enough to make telecom programming with it practical.)

The following example dials a long-distance number using a phone credit card:

```
on callLongDistance
   dial "0" & field "Phone Number"
   wait 90 ticks -- until phone company asks for card number
   dial field "Phone Card Number"
end callLongDistance
```

The *phoneNumber* can contain any or all of the following characters:

- The digits 0 through 9
- The characters * and #
- Uppercase A, B, C and D (the extra set that appears on telephone company and ham radio keypads)

- Commas (each comma produces a one-second pause)
- Semicolons (each semicolon produces a ten-second pause)

All other characters are ignored, so you can say

```
dial line 1 of field "Numbers"
```

and even if line 1 of field "Numbers" contains something like "555-1212 Office Number", the **dial** command is smart enough to dial "555-1212".

Beware of unquoted hyphens: If you include a hyphen in your telephone number and don't place quotation marks around the number, HyperCard interprets the hyphen as a minus sign and performs a subtraction:

```
dial 143-5667 -- yields -5524
```

The same thing goes for a slash (/): HyperCard interprets it as a divide sign. It's a good idea to put quotation marks around all numbers that you specify literally. (However, you need not use quotes if you're specifying a container name where the phone number resides.)

The *modemCommandString* is sent to the modem just before the dial string. If you use the form with modem but don't provide a *modemCommandString*, the string "ATS0=0S7=1DT" is sent to the modem. This is a set of standard commands understood by Hayes-compatible modems. (Almost all modern modems are compatible with the Hayes command set.)

Techie alert: The default *modemCommandString* does the following:

- Gets the modem's attention (AT)
- Tells the modem to ignore incoming calls (S0=0)
- Tells the modem to wait 1 second for a carrier before dialing (S7=1)
- Specifies tone dialing rather than pulse (DT)

One second may not be long enough for the dialtone to come up, so you may need to substitute a larger value for the S7 register:

```
dial myNumber with modem "ATS0=0S7=5DT"
```

ALSO SEE
dialingTime property; **dialingVolume** property

---

dialingTime property

Introduced in version 2.1

FORMS
```
set [the] dialingTime [of HyperCard] to numberOfTicks
set the dialingTime to 300 -- 5 seconds
```

An auto-dialing system

The following handlers, when placed in the script of a field, make up a simple phone-dialing system. The field, which holds your personal phone directory, can be copied and pasted into any background; the field's script contains handlers to add names to the phonebook and to dial a number.

Much of the code in these handlers checks for user errors, such as typing in something other than a phone number when one was requested, or trying to call someone who's not listed in the phone directory.

```
on call who -- dials a number
  repeat
    if who is in me then exit repeat
    comment "No entry for" && who && ". Add one?","No","Yes"
    book who
  end repeat
  dial item 2 of matchingLine(who,me) -- with modem
end call


on book who -- makes a new entry in the phone directory
  if who is not empty then get who & ", (111) 111-1111"
  else get "San Francisco Info, (415) 555-1212"
  repeat
    ask "Add to the phonebook:" with it
    if it is empty then exit book
    if the number of items in it is 2 then exit repeat
    comment "A phonebook entry consists of name,number",¬
    "Give Up","Try Again"
  end repeat
  put it into newNumber
  if item 1 of newNumber is in me then
    comment "There's already an entry for" && item 1 of newNumber ¬
    & ". Update it?","No","Yes"
    delete line matchingLine(item 1 of newNumber,me) of me
  end if
  if item 2 of newNumber is in me then
    comment "That number is already in the phone book. Continue" ¬
    && "anyway?","No","Yes"
  end if
  put newNumber & return after me
end book


on comment thePrompt,quitChoice,continueChoice
  if quitChoice is empty then put "Quit" into quitChoice
  if continueChoice is empty then put "Continue" into continueChoice
```

```
      answer thePrompt with quitChoice or continueChoice
      if it is quitChoice then exit to HyperCard
   end comment

   function matchingLine pattern,string
      put offset(pattern,string) into patternLocation
      return the number of lines of (char 1 to patternLocation of string) + 1
   end matchingLine
```

With the above handlers in the field script, you can install the following handler in the script of the background or stack where the Phonebook field resides—or in the Home stack—to make it easy to use the Phonebook:

```
on phone theAction who -- goes in background or stack script
   send theAction && who to field "Phone Book"
end phone
```

You can then type commands like these directly into the message box:

```
phone book          -- to add a number to the phonebook
phone call "Martha"-- to call a number
```

ACTION

HyperCard uses the **dialingTime** global property when dialing with a modem to determine how long to keep the serial connection with the modem open.

The default **dialingTime** is 180 ticks (3 seconds).

COMMENTS

If you are having trouble using HyperCard to dial through the modem, increasing the **dialingTime** may help, particularly if you are using an internal Mac Portable or Powerbook modem. The **dialingTime** doesn't affect how long the telephone line is kept off-hook while dialing; it only determines how long HyperCard waits after sending the **dial** command before closing the Mac's connection to the modem.

A tick is 1/60 of a second. The *numberOfTicks* must be an integer; attempting to use a number that's not an integer causes HyperCard to put up an error dialog. Legal values for the **dialingTime** are between 0 and 32767 ticks (about 9 minutes); if you set this property to a number outside that range, the **dialingTime** is set to 0.

The following example assumes you have a Hayes-compatible modem:

```
on dialIt theNumber
   set the dialingTime to 600 -- allow 10 seconds
   dial theNumber with modem "ATS7=12" -- leave off hook for 12 seconds
end dialIt
```

ALSO SEE

dial command

dialingVolume property

Introduced in version 2.2

FORMS

```
set [the] dialingVolume [of HyperCard] to speakerVolume
set the dialingVolume to 0 -- softest volume
```

ACTION

The **dialingVolume** global property specifies the volume of the touch tones generated by the **dial** command. The default **dialingVolume** is 7.

COMMENTS

Use the **dialingVolume** property to change the volume if the speaker is too loud when you dial the phone.

The *speakerVolume* is an integer between 0 and 7, with 0 the softest and 7 the loudest. A **dialingVolume** of 0, unlike the lowest setting of the Sound control panel, does not silence the speaker. If you provide a *dialingVolume* less than 0, the property is set to 0; if the *dialingVolume* is greater than 7, the property is set to 7.

The **dialingVolume** property applies only when you use the **dial** command to dial through the speaker, and does not affect the operation of dialing with a modem.

ALSO SEE

dial command

disable command

Introduced in version 2.0
Last changed in version 2.2

FORMS

```
disable {button|[menuItem of] menu}
disable card button "Popup"
disable background button myButtonName
disable button ID 7
disable background part "My Button" -- only works for buttons
disable menu "File"
disable the tenth menu
disable the fifth menuItem of menu "Style"
disable the last menuItem of menu 4
disable menuItem "Sounds" of menu myCustomMenu
```

ACTION

The **disable** command disables a menu, menu item, or button. A disabled menu item or button is grayed out and inactive; the normal messages are not sent when you click a disabled button or attempt to choose a disabled menu item.

The command `disable object` is equivalent to `set the enabled of object to false`.

COMMENTS

Use the **disable** command to gray out options that shouldn't be available. For example, the following handler disables menus and menu items if the current user level is too low for them to work:

```
on openStack
   makeUtilitiesMenu -- separate handler that creates a menu
   if the userLevel < 3 then disable menu "Utilities"
   else if the userLevel < 5 then
      disable menuItem "Edit Scripts" of menu "Utilities"
      disable menuItem "Debug" of menu "Utilities"
   end if
   pass openStack
end openStack
```

The *button* is any button in the current stack.

Menus and menu items can be identified by either name or number. Menus are numbered from the left edge of the menu bar, with the Apple menu being first; menu items are numbered from the top of the menu down. You can use ordinal descriptions (for example, `second menuItem of last menu`) as well as menu and menu item numbers.

If you try to disable a button, menu, or menu item that doesn't exist, HyperCard puts up a script error dialog. The following handler, which might be part of a multiple-stack application, disables options that apply to a networked HyperCard server if the server is down or otherwise unavailable. If the server is down when the user first opens the stack, the stack doesn't create the Server menu. Therefore, the handler uses the **there is a** operator to check whether the menu exists before disabling it.

```
on openCard
   if "HyperCard" is not in the programs of "*:Server" then
      -- HyperCard not running on server, so gray out server actions
      disable button "Send Transaction to Central Server"
      disable menuItem "Transactions..." of menu "Preferences"
      -- Server menu might not have been created, so check:
      if there is a menu "Server" then disable menu "Server"
      answer "The server is not available, so you won't be able" ¬
      && "to perform network transactions at this time."
   end if
end openCard
```

Use the **enabled** property to check whether a button, menu, or menu item is disabled or not.

Changing the case of text

This set of handlers (which you should put in the stack script for widest applicability) creates a menu that lets you set any or all of the text in a field to uppercase or lowercase:

```
on openField
  if "Capitalize" is not in the menus then
    -- create the menu, if it doesn't already exist
    create menu "Capitalize"
    put "Words,Sentences,Everything,Nothing" into theItems
    repeat with x = 1 to the number of items of theItems
      put item x of theItems into thisItem
      put thisItem after menu "Capitalize" ¬
      with menuMessage ("capitalize" && theItem)
    end repeat
  end if
  enable menu "Capitalize"
end openField


on idle
  if "field" is not in the selectedChunk
  then disable menu "Capitalize"
end idle


on capitalize toWhat
  -- get the selection if there is one, or else the whole field
  put the selection into originalText
  if originalText is empty then put the value of the selectedField ¬
  into originalText
  put true into sentenceStart
  put true into wordStart
  put empty into changedText
  repeat with nextChar = 1 to the length of originalText
    set the cursor to busy
    get char nextChar of originalText
    if it is space then put true into wordStart
    else if it is "." then put true into sentenceStart
    else if toWhat is "words" then
      if wordStart then
        get uppercase(it)
        put false into wordStart
      else
        get lowercase(it)
      end if
    else if toWhat is "Sentences" then
      if sentenceStart then
        get uppercase(it)
```

```
              put false into sentenceStart
          else
            get lowercase(it)
          end if
        else if toWhat is "Everything" then get uppercase(it)
        else if toWhat is "Nothing" then get lowercase(it)
        put it after changedText
      end repeat
      get the selectedChunk
      if the selection is empty then
        put changedText into the selectedField
      else
        put changedText into the selection
      end if
      select it
    end capitalize


    function uppercase theChar
      put charToNum(theChar) into theASCII
      put charToNum("A") into uppercase_A
      put charToNum("a") into lowercase_a
      put charToNum("z") into lowercase_z
      if lowercase_a < theASCII and theASCII < lowercase_z
      then subtract (lowercase_a - uppercase_A) from theASCII
      return numToChar(theASCII)
    end uppercase


    function lowercase theChar
      put charToNum(theChar) into theASCII
      put charToNum("A") into uppercase_A
      put charToNum("a") into lowercase_a
      put charToNum("Z") into uppercase_Z
      if uppercase_A < theASCII and theASCII < uppercase_Z
      then add (lowercase_a - uppercase_A) to theASCII
      return numToChar(theASCII)
    end lowercase
```

About disabled menu items: Although the user cannot choose a disabled menu item, you can still trigger them from within a handler using the **doMenu** command. Command-key equivalents for disabled menu items do not function as long as the item is disabled, with one exception: Command-Q always quits HyperCard, even if you've disabled the Quit HyperCard menu item.

You can disable any menu—including standard HyperCard menus—but you can't disable any individual menu item in the Apple, Tools, Font, Style, or Patterns menu, or the New Card, Delete Card, and Cut Card items in the Edit menu.

Changes to HyperTalk: In versions of HyperCard before 2.2, the **disable** command cannot be used to disable buttons. Many stack designers, faced with this limitation, use a grayed-out version of the Chicago font to display the button's inactive state:

```
set the textFont of button "Not Now" to "Disabled Chicago"
```

When using this method to disable a button, you can check the current font in the button's script:

```
on mouseUp
   if the textFont of me is "Disabled" then exit mouseUp
   -- do button tasks here
end mouseUp
```

In version 2.1, a bug prevents you from enabling (or disabling) the Tools, Font, and Patterns menus.

ALSO SEE
enable command; **enabled** property

---

diskSpace function

Introduced in version 1.0
Last changed in version 2.2

FORMS
the diskSpace [of disk *diskName*]
diskspace()
```
put the diskSpace of disk "Unknown Magnanimity" into field "Free Space"
if the diskSpace < 10240 then answer "Less than 10K free!"
```

ACTION
The **diskSpace** function returns the amount of free space in bytes remaining on the specified disk.

COMMENTS
The **diskSpace** function is particularly useful in preventing script errors when your handler is about to perform some action that will use disk space. The following example shows how to make sure there's enough room on the disk before writing a text file:

```
on dumpText theText
   ask file "Please name the text file:"
   if it is empty then exit dumpText -- user cancelled
   put it into dumpFile
   set the itemDelimiter to colon
   get item 1 of dumpFile
   if the diskSpace of disk it < the length of theText then
      beep
```

```
        answer "There's not enough disk space to write the text file." ¬
        with "Try Again" or "Cancel"
        if it is "Try Again" then dumpText theText -- recursive call
        exit dumpText
    end if
    open file dumpFile
    write theText to file dumpFile
    close file dumpFile
end dumpText
```

The *diskName* is the name of any volume currently mounted on the desktop. If you don't specify a *diskName*, the **diskSpace** function returns the free space on the disk that contains the current stack.

Changes to HyperTalk: In versions of HyperCard before 2.2, the **diskSpace** function does not have an optional argument; it always returns the amount of free space on the disk containing the current stack, and cannot be used to determine the space remaining on other disks.

ALSO SEE

freeSize property; **heapSpace** property; **size** property; **stackSpace** property; **there is** operator

---

dithering property   Introduced in version 2.0

FORMS

```
set [the] dithering of pictureWindow to {true|false}
set the dithering of window "Staff Snapshot" to true
```

ACTION

The **dithering** property determines how colors in windows created by the **picture** command are displayed. By default, the **dithering** of picture windows is false.

COMMENTS

Each Macintosh monitor is set up to display a specified number of colors or gray scales. However, some pictures you show may contain more colors than the number available on the current screen. If this is the case, your pictures may show a "posterized" effect caused by the system's attempt to display them with too few colors to show all the details of the picture.

Dithering is a process in which colors are mixed together to provide the illusion of more colors than are available on the screen. For example, on a black-and-white screen, you can show a grayscale picture by using different patterns to simulate the gray shades in the picture. On a color screen, the various available colors can be mixed together in patterns to provide a larger effective palette.

Dithering is not available on Macs that have a 68000 processor.

If you're showing pictures deeper than the available color depth—for instance, if you want to display a 24-bit (millions of colors) picture on an 8-bit (256 colors) screen—setting the window's **dithering** property to true will probably give you better results.

ALSO SEE

picture command

---

divide command   Introduced in version 1.0

FORMS

```
divide [chunk of] container by divisor
divide field "Total" by 7
divide thePot by numberOfPlayers
divide totalAllocation by field "Number of Counties"
```

ACTION

The **divide** command divides the number in a container by another number and puts the resulting number in the container. The original number in the container is lost, since the container is overwritten by the final result. However, the value of the expression being divided into the container is unchanged.

COMMENTS

The following handler computes the share of the national debt for each of the fifty states:

```
on debt
   ask "What's the national debt (in trillions of dollars)?"
   divide it by 50
   answer "That's" && it && "trillion per state." with "So Little!"
end debt
```

The **divide** command always puts its result into a container. You cannot divide one number directly by another using **divide** (use the **/** operator instead).

The container must contain a number. If you try to divide a number into a container that contains something other than a number, you will get an error dialog. (You can check a container's contents first with the **is a number** operator.)

You can divide an empty container by a number; **divide** acts as though it contained the number 0. Remember, however, that you must put something into local variables before you can use them; if you have not yet put something—even empty—into the local variable foo, the statement divide foo by 22 will produce an error message, since you have not initialized foo.

If the *container* is a field or the message box, the **numberFormat** property determines the format of the resulting number.

You can divide a container by itself.

INF and NAN: If you divide a number by 0, you'll get a result of INF, which stands for "infinite value" (actually, this indicates a value larger than HyperCard can deal with). A result of NAN means "not a number"; you'll get this if you do something like try to divide 0 by 0.

Techie alert: The **divide** command uses the same code as the / operator. Both use SANE to do floating-point division with up to 19 decimal places of precision.

ALSO SEE

add command; **is a** operator; **multiply** command; **numberFormat** property; **subtract** command

---

do keyword

FORMS

```
do statements [as scriptLanguage]
do line 5 of commandsVariable
do field "Commands"
do "go to card" && line 5 of cardList
do "set clipboard to selection" as AppleScript
```

ACTION

The **do** keyword executes any sequence of HyperTalk statements as though they were contained in a handler. With the *scriptLanguage* parameter, **do** can also be used to execute any script written in an OSA-compliant scripting language, such as AppleScript.

COMMENTS

The following handler uses **do** to send each item in the variable jobList as a message:

```
on doJobs
   put "push card,go to next card,beep 2,pop card" into jobList
   repeat with count = 1 to the number of items in jobList
     do item count of jobList
   end repeat
end doJobs
```

The **do** keyword works by first evaluating the *statements* parameter, then sending that value as a message. **Do** is therefore especially useful when you need to execute a statement which is made up partly of a literal string and partly of a container or the result of a function, because it forces HyperTalk to perform another level of evaluation in such cases. The following handler locates and deletes a line of text by forcing an evaluation of the function **the foundLine**:

```
on findAndDelete theString
   find theString in card field "List"
```

```
    if the result is empty then -- was found
       do "put empty into" && the foundLine
    end if
end findAndDelete
```

The *statements* parameter can be any line or lines of valid code. Multiline statements must be complete: if you include a **repeat** statement, there must be a concluding **end repeat** statement, and **if** structures must be valid and complete. If you use an invalid structure, such as a **repeat** statement without **end repeat**, HyperCard displays an error dialog and halts the handler.

You can also use **do** in the message box, and its ability to execute multiple-line structures can come in handy when you want to execute such a structure without having to create a temporary button to hold it. This example shows how you might use the message box to execute a repeat statement:

```
do "repeat 3 times" & return & "beep" & return & "end repeat"
```

More usefully, the following handler can be placed in a field's script to make it an instant script editor, executing its contents whenever the Enter key is pressed:

```
on enterInField
   do me
end enterInField
```

Other scripting languages: You can use **do** to execute a script in languages other than HyperTalk. The language you want to use is specified in the *scriptLanguage* parameter. It can be AppleScript or any other installed scripting language that implements Apple's Open Scripting Architecture. For example, you might ask the user for a line of AppleScript code, and then execute it, as follows:

```
on mouseUp
   ask "Please enter a line of AppleScript:"
   if it is not empty then do it as AppleScript
end mouseUp
```

The names of the currently available scripting languages appear in the Scripting Language popup in the script editor window. If you specify a *scriptLanguage* that's not currently installed, HyperCard does not alert you to the error or set **the result**. However, you can check whether your desired language is available using the **there is a** operator:

```
if there is a scriptingLanguage "AppleScript"
then do "copy field 1 to clipboard" as AppleScript
```

Send and do are very similar: The keywords **do** and **send** perform nearly the same action in HyperTalk. The only difference is that **do** always sends its message to the object containing the currently running handler (or the current card, if **do** is used from the message box). With **send**, on the other hand, you can specify which object is to receive the message. The statements do *message* and send *message* to me are equivalent.

Changes to HyperTalk: In versions before 2.0, **do** executes only one line. So if you say do field 6, HyperTalk executes line 1 of field 6 and ignores any other lines in the field. (This is true even if that line ends in the line continuation character, ¬.)

In versions before 2.2, you cannot specify a *scriptLanguage*; all statements must be valid HyperTalk.

ALSO SEE

result function; **scriptingLanguage** property; **send** keyword

---

doMenu command/message

Introduced in version 1.0
Last changed in version 2.2

FORMS

```
doMenu menuItem [,menuName] [{with|without} dialog] [with key[,key[,key]]]
doMenu "New Button"
doMenu "Open Stack..." with shiftKey
doMenu "Chooser","Apple"
doMenu "Delete Stack..." without dialog
doMenu myItem,utilsMenuName
if the userLevel < 2 then doMenu "Protect Stack..." with commandKey
```

ACTION

The **doMenu** command simulates choosing an item from one of HyperCard's menus.

COMMENTS

The **doMenu** command executes a menu item, just as though you had chosen the menu item using the mouse. This command lets you use HyperCard menu commands as part of your script.

The following handler opens various desk accessories depending on which Control-key combination the user presses:

```
on controlKey keyNumber
   if keyNumber is 1 then doMenu "Alarm Clock","Apple"     -- 1 is A
   else if keyNumber is 3 then doMenu "Calculator","Apple" -- 3 is C
   else if keyNumber is 16 then doMenu "Puzzle","Apple"    -- 16 is P
   else pass controlKey
end controlKey
```

Choosing a menu item—by choosing it with the mouse, pressing its Command-key combination, or using **doMenu** from a script—sends a **doMenu** message to the current card. The message has two parameters: the name of the menu item and the name of the menu. As with any command/message, you can write a custom handler to override the normal behavior of the menu choices a user makes. This example puts up a confirmation dialog when the user quits:

```
on doMenu theItem
   if theItem is "Quit HyperCard" then
      answer "Are you sure you want to quit?" with "Cancel" or "Quit"
      if it is "Cancel" then exit doMenu -- don't pass, so don't quit
   end if
   pass doMenu -- go ahead and perform the menu action
end doMenu
```

You can use the **param** function to pull out an additional parameter. You can use the **param** function to check the sixth parameter to **doMenu** if you want to find out whether the user was holding down the Shift, Option, and/or Command keys while choosing the menu item. This handler shows how to do it:

```
on doMenu
   get param(6)
   if it is empty then
      answer "No modifier keys were pressed!"
   else
      answer the number of items of it ¬
      && "modifier keys were pressed:" && it
   end if
   pass doMenu
end doMenu
```

The *itemName* is the name of any menu item that is currently available. It must be spelled exactly as it appears in the menu. Items with three dots at the end, such as "Open Stack...", are spelled with three periods, not with the ellipsis generated by Option-semicolon.

The *menuName* is the name of any menu on the menu bar. System 7 has two special menus at the right edge of the menu bar; the names of these menus are "System Help" and "Application". (You can't use **doMenu** to choose an item from the System Help menu.) If WorldScript is installed, there's an additional menu, marked with a flag, in the menu bar; HyperTalk knows this menu as "Keyboard".

Use the *menuName* to resolve the problem that arises when there are two menu items with the same name. For example, you might create a menu called "Utilities" with a special calculator listed in it, but there is also a standard desk accessory called "Calculator". When

---

Make sure to pass doMenu

If you write a **doMenu** handler to trap certain menu items, be sure to include a `pass doMenu` statement. Otherwise, your handler traps *all* menu commands. Including Quit HyperCard. Including Stack Info. Including...well, you get the idea. Failing to include a **pass** statement in a **doMenu** handler can get you into a nasty situation.

If you do find yourself in this pass, try typing Command-Shift-C (to edit the card script), Command-Shift-B (for the background), or Command-Shift-S (for the stack), and edit whatever script the **doMenu** handler is in.

searching from a menu item, HyperCard goes from right to left across the menu bar and from top to bottom of each menu, so the command `doMenu "Calculator"` will always choose the calculator from the Utilities menu. To choose the desk accessory, use the command `doMenu "Calculator","Apple"`.

To skip any confirmation dialog boxes the menu item puts up, use the form **without dialog**. This form skips only confirmation dialogs such as the one that appears when you choose Delete Card; it has no effect on other dialogs, such as the Open and Print dialogs.

The *key* parameters simulate pressing a modifier key while choosing the menu item. This changes the action of some menu items. For example, choosing Print Field while holding down the Shift key brings up the standard Print dialog. The *key* can be any one of `shiftKey`, `optionKey`, or `commandKey`. The following example brings the specified button or field to the front:

```
on bringToFront thePart
   select thePart
   doMenu "Bring Closer" with shiftKey
   choose browse tool
end bringToFront
```

The user level affects available menu items: Lower **userLevel** settings mean fewer menu items are available. If the **userLevel** is below what you need to choose a particular menu item, you can temporarily set it higher:

```
get the userLevel        -- save old level
set the userLevel to 5   -- set to a high enough level
doMenu "New Button"      -- do the operation
choose browse tool
set the userLevel to it -- restore old user level
```

See the **userLevel** property for a list of the menus and menu items available at each user level.

Changing menu item names: The text of some menu items may change, depending on the state HyperCard is in. For example, the Cut menu item can read "Cut Text", "Cut Picture", "Cut Button", and so on, depending on what's selected. You can use the **there is a** operator to determine whether the menu item you want exists before trying to choose it with **doMenu**. Another strategy for dealing with changing menu item names is to use their Command-key equivalents instead. For example, these statements let you choose Cut, Copy, and Paste without worrying about their exact current wording:

```
commandKeyDown "X" -- cuts whatever is selected
commandKeyDown "C" -- copies whatever is selected
commandKeyDown "V" -- pastes whatever is on the clipboard
```

Techie alert: If you don't specify a menu, the **doMenu** command looks for a menu item first in the standard U.S. English HyperCard menus, then in localized menus (if you're using a localized version of HyperCard), and finally in the Apple menu.

Changes to HyperTalk: In versions of HyperCard before 2.2, the *key* parameter is not available, and you can't use the names of the Apple, Application, Keyboard, or Help menus in a **doMenu** command. However, if the menu item has a Command-key equivalent, you can use the **type** command to choose that menu item with a modifier key:

```
on bringToFront thePart
  select thePart
  type "+" with commandKey,shiftKey -- Bring to Front item
  choose browse tool
end bringToFront
```

In versions before 2.0, the *menuName* parameter is not available, and neither is the **without dialog** form.

ALSO SEE

commandKeyDown command/message; **functionKey** command/message; **userLevel** property

---

dontSearch property   Introduced in version 2.0

FORMS

```
set [the] dontSearch of {field|card|background} to {true|false}
set the dontSearch of card part 7 to true -- only works for fields
if "Secret" is in me then set the dontSearch of me to true
if the marked of this card then set the dontSearch of this card to true
```

ACTION

The **dontSearch** property determines whether the **find**, **mark cards by finding**, and **unmark cards by finding** commands skip the specified field, card, or background while searching.

Setting the **dontSearch** property of a card, field, or background is equivalent to setting the Don't Search checkbox in the object's Info dialog. By default, the **dontSearch** is false.

COMMENTS

When a card's **dontSearch** property is true, **find** doesn't look at the contents of any of the card or background fields on that card. When a background's **dontSearch** is true, **find** ignores all the cards in that background. However, setting the **dontSearch** of a background does not affect the **dontSearch** of cards belonging to that background.

The *field*, *card*, or *background* must be in the current stack.

Shared text not searched: Setting the **sharedText** of a background field turns on the Don't Search checkbox in the field's Info dialog. Weirdly, it doesn't set the field's **dontSearch** property to match, even though **find** ignores text in any fields whose **sharedText** is set to true.

Negligible impact on search speed: The **find** command doesn't know whether a card's **dontSearch** property is true until **find** gets to that card. Furthermore, it can't tell what background a card is on until it gets to that card. And if the card's and background's **dontSearch** is false, **find** doesn't know whether a field can be searched until it reaches that field. All this means that setting the **dontSearch** property doesn't have much impact on search speed.

Old HyperCard versions: Versions before 2.0 lack the **dontSearch** property. However, you can use the following handler to make **find** skip any field that has the line

```
-- Don't Search
```

in its script. As a bonus, the handler also prevents searching in hidden fields:

```
on find
  lock screen
  put the ID of this card into startCard
  send the params to HyperCard -- performs the find
  if the result is not empty then exit find -- not found
  put the ID of this card into firstCard
  put the foundChunk into firstField
  repeat while "-- Don't Search" is in the script of the foundField ¬
  or the visible of the foundField is false -- skip hidden fields
    set the cursor to busy
    send the params to HyperCard -- find again
    if the ID of this card is firstCard ¬
    and the foundChunk is firstField then
      go to startCard
      send "find empty" to HyperCard -- deselect find rectangle
      exit find
    end if
  end repeat
end find
```

ALSO SEE
find command; **mark** command; **unmark** command

---

dontWrap property

Introduced in version 2.0

FORMS
```
set [the] dontWrap of field to {true|false}
set the dontWrap of field "Card List" to true
set the dontWrap of part 17 of background 2 to false
```

ACTION

The **dontWrap** property determines whether the lines of a field's text are prevented from wrapping around when they reach the boundary of the field.

Setting the **dontWrap** is equivalent to setting the Don't Wrap checkbox in the Field Info dialog. By default, the **dontWrap** is false, allowing long lines to wrap around.

COMMENTS

Setting the **dontWrap** property is useful when a field contains a list, since each line of the list takes up one screen line and is prevented from wrapping if it's too long to fit in the field. When the **dontWrap** of a field is true, excess text disappears off the edge of the field, but it isn't lost—just hidden. (See Figure III.22.) If you make the field wider or set its **dontWrap** to false, the hidden text becomes visible.

The *field* must be in the current stack.

The following example is useful for editing list fields where each line contains a series of ordered items. For instance, the field might hold an index, with the first item of each line being a name, the second being an address, and so forth; the field is just wide enough for the names. When viewing the index, the **dontWrap** should be set to true, so you can see just the names, without the other items getting in the way. But when you're making changes to the field, you need to be able to see and select all the text that's trailed off the edge of the field, so the **dontWrap** should be set back to false:

```
on openField
   -- set up for editing
   get the selectedChunk
   select empty
   -- Setting a field property loses the selection, thus sending
   -- closeField or exitField, but only after the property is set.
   -- Therefore, we select empty first - this sends exitField - and
   -- only then, when there's no selection, do we set the dontWrap:
   set the dontWrap of me to false
   select it
end openField
```

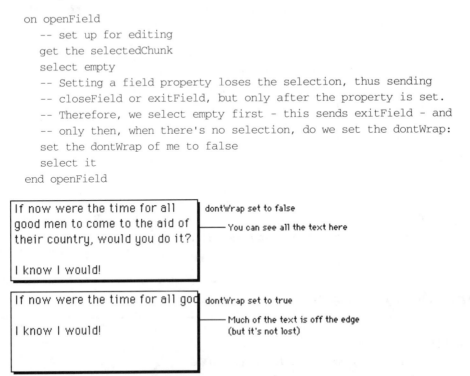

Figure III.22   Same field with dontWrap property set to false (top) and true (bottom)

```
on closeField
  -- set up for viewing
  set the dontWrap of me to true
end closeField


on exitField
  -- set up for viewing
  set the dontWrap of me to true
end exitField
```

Printing respects the dontWrap property: If you use the command `print field` to print a field whose **dontWrap** property is true, only the visible text is printed. However, if you use the form `print (field)`, which uses the **printTextFont** and other default print properties instead of the field's own formatting, the field's **dontWrap** setting is ignored.

ALSO SEE

print command

---

drag command

Introduced in version 1.0

FORMS

```
drag from start to end [with modifierKey1[,modifierKey2[,modifierKey3]]]
drag from 10,10 to 120,350
drag from the clickLoc to the topLeft of button 2
drag from the loc of card button "Clown" to the clickLoc with optionKey
```

ACTION

The **drag** command simulates a user clicking at the starting point and dragging in a straight line to the ending point, optionally "holding down" some combination of the Shift, Command, and Option keys.

The **drag** command is not an exact substitute for clicking and dragging; for instance, you cannot drag a window using this command.

COMMENTS

The **drag** command is most useful with the paint tools, letting you draw shapes and do other painting from a script. You can also use **drag** to move buttons and fields around the stack window at a set speed. (If you just want to move a button or field, it's faster to set its **location** property.)

The following handler draws a small rounded rectangle at the upper-left corner of the current card:

```
on drawSmallRect
   set the pattern to 13      -- get a pattern to fill a shape
   set the filled to true
   choose round rectangle tool
   drag from 10,10 to 75,75   -- draw the shape
end drawSmallRect
```

The *start* and *end* are two points on the card. Each point consists of two integers separated by a comma: the first item is the horizontal distance in pixels from the left edge of the stack window to the point, and the second item is the vertical distance from the top edge to the point.

The *modifierKeys* can be shiftKey, optionKey, or commandKey (or a synonym, cmdKey). To select text in an unlocked field with the **drag** command, you must specify the shiftKey:

```
drag from the selectedLoc to the bottomRight of me with shiftKey
```

(However, unless you want the movement of the dragging to be visible, the **select** command is a simpler and more efficient way to select text.)

The **drag** command automatically clicks at the *start*, so if you're dragging a field or button, you don't need to select it first.

Creating buttons and fields with drag: You can create new buttons and fields by Command-dragging. Doing so in a handler is a convenient way to install a button or field from a script:

```
on makeNewButton
   choose button tool
   drag from 100,100 to 180,120 with commandKey
   -- newly created button is the last one, so...
   set the name of last button to "Dragged"
   set the showName of button "Dragged" to true
   set the style of button "Dragged" to shadow
end makeNewButton
```

Drag and paint tools: The **drag** command drags in a straight line from *start* to *end*. This means that using it with some paint tools has no effect:

- Dragging with the bucket tool is the same as clicking at the start location.
- The **drag** command has no effect when used with the irregular polygon and lasso tools.
- Dragging with the curve tool just produces a straight line.

The **drag** command doesn't change the shape or position of the mouse pointer.

ALSO SEE
click command; **dragSpeed** property; **location** property; **select** command

dragSpeed property

FORMS

```
set [the] dragSpeed [of HyperCard] to pixelsPerSecond
set the dragSpeed to 72 -- an inch per second on a 72dpi monitor
```

ACTION

The **dragSpeed** global property reflects the speed at which the pointer moves in response to the **drag** command. If the **dragSpeed** is zero, the **drag** command moves as fast as possible.

The **dragSpeed** is reset to zero whenever an **idle** message is sent.

COMMENTS

Usually, there is no reason to slow down dragging by setting the **dragSpeed** to anything but zero. However, if you want the user to see the dragging happen—for instance, if you're using **drag** to perform animation—you can use the **dragSpeed** to control the rate of the movement. The following handler assumes there is a small graphic located at the *startPoint*:

```
on slowDrag startPoint,endPoint
   choose select tool
   doMenu "Select" -- lassos the whole card picture
   set the dragSpeed to 60
   drag from startPoint to endPoint
   choose browse tool
end slowDrag
```

The *pixelsPerSecond* must be an integer. If you specify a negative number, the **dragSpeed** is set to zero.

Feature: If you use the **drag** command with the browse tool selected and the **dragSpeed** set to anything but zero, nothing happens; the Macintosh just waits until the **drag** command is completed. ("No, that's actually a feature.")

ALSO SEE

drag command

edit command

FORMS

```
edit [the] script of object
edit the script of this card
edit the script of background button "Fred"
edit the script of field theVariable of card 3
edit the script of background ID 2234
edit the script of card "Whacko"
edit the script of me -- handler edits its own script (bizarre, eh?)
```

ACTION

The **edit** command opens the script of the specified *object* for editing.

COMMENTS

You can use the **edit** command from within a handler or from the message box. The following handler, when placed in the stack or background script, opens the script of the current card when you press the Tab key:

```
on tabKey
   edit script of this card
end tabKey
```

The *object* is a descriptor of any stack—open or not—or of any card, background, field, or button in the current stack.

While the script editor window is open, the execution of the current handler is stopped. After the script window is closed, the handler takes up where it left off. However, if the user clicks the stack window to bring it to the front without closing the script window, the handler is aborted. After editing the script of a card, stack, or background other than the current one, you go back to the card you were on when the **edit** command was issued.

No open or close messages are sent when you edit the script of another card, background, or stack.

The following handler checks the scripts in the message path—the current card, background, and stack scripts, the scripts of any stacks that have been placed in the path with the **start using** command, and the Home stack script—to see who will catch the specified message, and opens the scripts in question in order:

```
on whoGets theMessage
   if the script of this card contains "on" && theMessage
   then edit the script of this card
   if the script of this background contains "on" && theMessage
   then edit the script of this background
   if the script of this stack contains "on" && theMessage
   then edit the script of this stack
   repeat with x = 1 to the number of lines of the stacksInUse
      if the script of stack (line x of the stacksInUse) ¬
```

```
        contains "on" && theMessage
        then edit the script of stack (line x of the stacksInUse)
    end repeat
    if the script of stack "Home" contains "on" && theMessage
    then edit the script of stack "Home"
end whoGets
```

If you want to look through every script in a stack, use `searchScript`, one of the handlers in the Home stack.

Other ways of opening a script: Table III.3 shows more ways to open an object's script.

Table III.3   Script Editing Shortcuts

Script	How to Open It
Any script	Click the script button in the object's Info dialog box
Button	Press Command-Option and click button (browse or field tool selected)
Field	Press Command-Shift-Option and click button (browse or field tool selected)
Stack	Press Command-Option-S
Background	Press Command-Option-B
Card	Press Command-Option-C

Bitter complaints: The **edit** command puts up an error dialog under the following circumstances:

- The **userLevel** is less than 5 (Scripting).
- You're trying to edit the script of HyperCard (which doesn't have a script).
- The *object* doesn't exist.
- There's not enough memory available to use the script editor.

Changes to HyperTalk: In versions of HyperCard before 2.0, when you edit the script of another stack, you end up on the first card of that stack when you close the script editor, instead of where you were when **edit** was executed. However, the **openStack**, **openBackground**, and **openCard** messages are suppressed anyway.

ALSO SEE

"Summoning the Script Editor" in Chapter 2; **debug checkpoint** command; **debugger** property; **script** property; **scriptEditor** property

editBkgnd property

FORMS

```
set [the] editBkgnd [of HyperCard] to {true|false}
set the editBkgnd to true
set the editBkgnd to not (the tool is "browse tool")
```

ACTION

The **editBkgnd** property determines whether painting and creation of fields and buttons takes place in the background layer or the card layer.

Setting the **editBkgnd** property is equivalent to toggling the Background item in the Edit menu. By default, the **editBkgnd** is false, and editing takes place in the card layer.

COMMENTS

The **editBkgnd** is useful when writing handlers to speed up stack development, and for letting the user edit the text of a field whose **sharedText** property is true (such fields can be edited only in background mode).

The following example creates a new background field:

```
on makeBackgroundField fieldName
   get the editBkgnd -- save old setting
   set the editBkgnd to true
   doMenu "New Field" -- creates it in the background
   set the style of last field to rectangle
   set the name of last field to fieldName
   set the editBkgnd to it -- restore original setting
   choose browse tool
end makeBackgroundField
```

When the **editBkgnd** is false, you can select and work with either card or background parts, but you can only paint on the card layer. When the **editBkgnd** is true, only background parts are visible, and you cannot select or edit card parts.

The following handler moves a background button to the card layer:

```
on moveToCard theButton
   set the editBkgnd to false -- make sure we're on the card
   select button theButton -- can select background buttons
   doMenu "Cut Button"
   doMenu "Paste Button" with shiftKey
   -- in versions before 2.2, buttons don't contain text, so you
   -- can use the following line instead:
   --      doMenu "Paste Button"
   choose browse tool
end moveToCard
```

This handler moves a card field plus its text to the background:

```
on moveToBackground theField
   set the editBkgnd to false
   -- For versions before 1.2.2, include this line:
   --    get card field theField -- save text of field
   select card field theField
   doMenu "Cut Field"
   set the editBkgnd to true
   doMenu "Paste Field" with shiftKey
   -- for versions before 2.2, use the following line instead:
   --    type "V" with shiftKey,commandKey
   -- for versions before 1.2.2, use the following lines:
   --    doMenu "Paste Field"
   --    put it into field theField -- restore text of field
   choose browse tool
end moveToBackground
```

Choosing New Background from the Objects menu sets the **editBkgnd** to true.

Changes to HyperTalk: In versions of HyperCard before 2.0, choosing the browse tool or changing cards sets the **editBkgnd** to false.

---

enable command

FORMS

```
enable {button|[menuItem of] menu}
enable button "New Stack…"
enable last button
enable background button ID 7
enable card part 22 -- only works if it's a button
enable menu "File"
enable menuItem "Server" of menu "Preferences"
enable the last menuItem of menu "Style"
enable third menu
```

ACTION

The **enable** command enables a menu, menu item, or button, allowing the user to select it. The command enable *object* is equivalent to set the enabled of *object* to true.

COMMENTS

Use the **enable** and **disable** commands to allow and disallow options, depending on whether you want to make them available to the user. The text of an enabled item, and the outline of an enabled button, is solid black, indicating to the user that it is available; disabled items are drawn in gray.

The *button* is any button in the current stack.

Menus and menu items can be identified by either name or number. Menus are numbered from the left edge of the menu bar, with the Apple menu being first; menu items are numbered from the top of the menu down. You can use ordinal descriptions (for example, `second menuItem of last menu`) as well as menu and menu item numbers.

If you try to enable a button, menu, or menu item that doesn't exist, HyperCard puts up a script error dialog.

Use the **enabled** property to check whether a button, menu, or menu item is currently enabled or not.

Enabling and disabling menus and menu items: When a menu is disabled, all its items are grayed out and cannot be chosen. However, the menu items in a disabled menu still retain their own independent **enabled** property. This means that if you enable a menu item that's in a disabled menu, the item's **enabled** property is set to true, even though right now it's grayed out and can't be chosen. When you enable the menu, its menu items will be enabled or disabled depending on the current setting of their **enabled** property.

The following set of handlers makes sure the Font and Style menus are enabled only when a field is open for editing:

```
on openField
   turnFontMenus on
end openField

on closeField
   turnFontMenus off
end closeField

on exitField
   turnFontMenus off
end exitField

on turnFontMenus toState
   if toState is "off" then   -- turn menus off
      disable menu "Font"
      disable menu "Style"
   else -- turn menus on
      enable menu "Font"
      enable menu "Style"
   end if
end turnFontMenus
```

Changes to HyperTalk: In versions of HyperCard before 2.2, all buttons are enabled: the **enable** command cannot be used to enable buttons.

In version 2.1, a bug prevents you from enabling (or disabling) the Tools, Font, and Patterns menus.

ALSO SEE

disable command; **enabled** property

---

enabled property

Introduced in version 2.0
Last changed in version 2.2

FORMS

```
set [the] enabled of {button|[menuItem of] menu} to {true|false}
set the enabled of card button "Status" to true
if the enabled of menu "Edit" is false then beep
put the enabled of menuItem 1 of menu 1 into field "About Enabled"
```

ACTION

The **enabled** property of buttons, menu items, and menus determines whether the object is enabled—that is, whether it is available to the user and can be selected, or is grayed out.

The command `set the enabled of object to true` does the same thing as `enable object`; `set the enabled of object to false` is equivalent to `disable object`.

The default value of **enabled** for newly created menus, menu items, and buttons is true.

COMMENTS

The following example disables the First or Last menu item in the Go menu when you're already on the first or last card:

```
on openCard -- put this handler in the stack script
   set the enabled of menuItem "First" of menu "Go" ¬
   to (the number of this card is not 1)
   set the enabled of menuItem "Last" of menu "Go" ¬
   to (the number of this card is not the number of cards)
end openCard
```

The *button* is any button in the current stack.

Menus and menu items can be identified by either name or number. Menus are numbered from the left edge of the menu bar, with the Apple menu being first; menu items are numbered from the top of the menu down. You can use ordinal descriptions (for example, `second menuItem of last menu`) as well as button, menu and menu item numbers.

About disabled menu items: Although the user cannot choose a disabled menu item, using the **doMenu** command from a script still works. Command-key equivalents for disabled menu items do not function as long as the item's **enabled** property is set to false, with one exception: Command-Q always quits HyperCard, even if you've disabled the Quit HyperCard menu item.

You can set the **enabled** of any menu to false—including standard HyperCard menus—but you can't disable any individual menu item in the Apple, Tools, Font, Style, or Patterns menu, or the New Card, Delete Card, and Cut Card items in the Edit menu. HyperCard enables and disables certain menu items automatically—for example, Copy Text is only enabled when some text is selected—and you cannot override the **enabled** setting for such items through a script.

To restore all standard HyperCard menu settings, use the **reset menubar** command.

Changes to HyperTalk: In versions of HyperCard before 2.2, **enabled** is not a button property. One way to fake disabled buttons in these versions is to draw a grayed-out picture of the button on the card or background paint layer underneath the button. When the button is visible, the paint cannot be seen; to "disable" the button, simply hide it, and the grayed-out paint version appears in its place.

In version 2.1, a bug prevents you from changing the **enabled** property of the Tools, Font, and Patterns menus.

ALSO SEE
disable command; **enable** command; **reset menubar** command

---

end keyword

FORMS
```
end {handlerName|if|repeat}
end myDefinedFunction
end mouseUp
end repeat
end if
```

ACTION
The **end** keyword is used to start the final line of every multiline structure: **repeat** structures, **if** structures, and function and message handlers.

COMMENTS
The words `end repeat` (plus an optional comment) make up the whole last line of every **repeat** structure.

The words `end if` (plus an optional comment) make up the whole last line of every **if...then** structure, except those that are on one line or end with a one-line **else** statement.

The words `end handlerName` (plus an optional comment) make up the whole last line of every message handler and function handler.

This example shows how **end** is used:

```
on mouseUp
   repeat 3 times
     play "boing"
   end repeat              -- end of repeat structure
   if the shiftKey is down then
```

```
      play "harpsichord"
      flash 2
    end if                      -- end of if...then structure
    play "boing"
  end mouseUp                   -- end of handler structure
```

ALSO SEE

function keyword; **if...then...else** keyword; **on** keyword; **repeat** keyword

---

enterInField command/message   Introduced in version 1.2

FORMS

```
  enterInField
```

ACTION

The **enterInField** message is sent to the field with the current selection when the user presses Enter. As with all messages, it can also be sent explicitly from a handler, and you can write an **enterInField** handler to trap this message if you want to override its behavior.

If the user presses Enter but there is no text selection or insertion point in any field, **enterKey** is sent instead.

If the **enterInField** message reaches HyperCard without being intercepted by a handler in the message-passing path, HyperCard closes the field containing the selection.

COMMENTS

The following example is part of an onscreen form, and ensures that the field whose script contains this handler accepts only "Male" or "Female" as valid entries:

```
on enterInField
  if the first char of me is "M" then put "Male" into me
  else if the first char of me is "F" then put "Female" into me
  else
    beep
    select text of me
  end if
end enterInField
```

ALSO SEE

closeField message; **enterKey** command/message; **returnInField** command/message

enterKey command/message

Introduced in version 1.0

FORMS

```
enterKey
```

ACTION

The **enterKey** message is sent whenever the user presses the Enter key, unless there is a selection or insertion point in a text field. In that case, the **enterInField** message is sent to the field instead.

If the **enterKey** message reaches HyperCard without being intercepted by a handler in the message-passing path, it executes the contents of the message box.

COMMENTS

Use an **enterKey** handler when you want the Enter key to do something other than execute what's in the message box. For example, in a form-entry stack, you might want to make pressing the Enter key a shortcut for going to the next page of the form:

```
on enterKey
  get dataFormatCheck()  -- a custom function
  if it is not "OK" then
    beep
    answer it
    exit enterKey
  end if
  -- create next page of form
  lock screen
  lock messages
  go to last card of next background
  doMenu "New Card"
  unlock screen with visual effect scroll up
end enterKey
```

ALSO SEE

enterInField command/message; **returnKey** command/message

environment property

Introduced in version 2.2

FORMS

```
the environment [of HyperCard]
if the environment is "development" then edit the script of this stack
if the environment is "player" then showFinalAboutBox
```

ACTION

The **environment** global property describes the programming environment that's currently running. It is read-only and cannot be set by a script.

COMMENTS

You can use the **environment** within a handler to determine what capabilities of HyperCard are available to the current stack. The environment is either "development", if the stack is running under HyperCard itself, or "player", if the stack is running either under the HyperCard Player or as a standalone.

This example removes menu items whose function is unavailable when in the Player:

```
on openStack
   if the environment is "player" then
      delete menuItem "Print Field..." from menu "File"
      delete menuItem "Print Stack..." from menu "File"
      delete menuItem "Print Report..." from menu "File"
   end if
end openStack
```

Certain capabilities are available in the HyperCard development environment that are not present if your stack is in a runtime environment. In particular, **the userLevel** is effectively limited to 3 (painting) from the user's point of view; the script editor, message watcher, and variable watcher are not available; and you cannot execute HyperTalk commands (except **find**) from the message box.

ALSO SEE

userLevel property

---

errorDialog message

Introduced in version 2.1

FORMS

```
errorDialog errorMessage
errorDialog "Expected number here."
errorDialog "Can't understand "meep"."
```

ACTION

When there is a script error while the **lockErrorDialogs** property is set to true, HyperCard sends an **errorDialog** message to the current card instead of displaying the usual script error dialog.

COMMENTS

Use the **errorDialog** message when you want to handle script errors yourself, rather than let HyperCard put up its usual error dialog—for example, if you want to avoid confusing users with a script error, or if you want to save the text of script errors in a container.

The following handler logs script errors to a field (it assumes that the **lockErrorDialogs** has been set to true):

```
on errorDialog theMessage
  put theMessage & return after card field "Errors" of card "Dev"
  beep -- to alert you that an error occurred
end errorDialog
```

The *errorMessage* consists of the text that would normally appear in the script error dialog. On encountering a script error, HyperTalk aborts the current handler, regardless of the setting of **lockErrorDialogs**. This message substitutes for the first **idle** message that would be sent in normal mode after HyperTalk cleans up and HyperCard returns to its main event loop.

You can also use an **errorDialog** handler to respond to user input errors. Consider the following example:

```
on mouseUp
  lock error dialogs
  ask "What do you want to add?"
  add it to field "Total"
end mouseUp

on errorDialog theMessage
  beep
  if theMessage contains "expected number"
  then answer "You need to type a number!"
  else answer "There's a problem:" & return & theMessage
end errorDialog
```

Syntax errors and runtime errors are handled differently: If HyperTalk encounters a syntax error (such as a **repeat** statement with no matching **end repeat**) or another problem that causes an error when the handler is compiled rather than when it's run, it displays the error dialog regardless of the setting of **lockErrorDialogs**. In this case, no **errorDialog** message is sent.

Runtime error dialogs have a Debug button, while compile-time error dialogs do not (see Figure III.23).

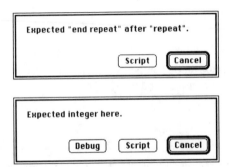

Figure III.23   Syntax (top) and runtime error dialogs

ALSO SEE

HyperTalk Error Messages (Appendix C); **lock error dialogs** command; **lockErrorDialogs**; property; **stackSpace** function; **heapSpace** function

---

exit keyword   Introduced in version 1.0

FORMS

```
exit {handlername|to HyperCard|repeat}
exit myCustomHandler
exit mouseWithin
exit repeat
exit to HyperCard
if total ≠ expectedTotal then exit thisHandler
```

ACTION

The **exit** keyword immediately transfers flow of control out of the current handler or repeat structure. Where the flow of control goes next depends on the structure being executed:

- The `exit handlerName` form transfers control out of the current handler, skipping any remaining statements. *handlerName* must be the name of the current handler.

- The `exit to HyperCard` form stops execution of any pending handlers, throws away any messages currently flowing through the message path, and transfers control back to the user. It also closes any open files.

- The `exit repeat` form transfers control to the line following the next `end repeat`. No further statements in the current repeat structure are executed (but other repeat structures in the handler are unaffected).

COMMENTS

The **exit** keyword is usually used within an **if** construction, to let you stop a handler or repeat structure only under certain conditions (for example, if the input data is in the wrong format, or if the user has cancelled an **ask** or **answer** dialog box).

This example shows how you might use **exit** to bail out of a handler:

```
on openTheDoor
   ask "Who wants the door open?"
   if it is "Dave" then
      answer "I'm sorry, Dave. I'm afraid I can't do that."
      exit openTheDoor  -- leave the handler
   end if
   answer "Come on in." -- gets this far only if Dave ain't knockin'
   go to card "Pod Bay"
end openTheDoor
```

The main difference between `exit` *handlerName* and `exit` `to` `HyperCard` is that the first form only halts the current handler, while the second halts all pending handlers. If the handler was triggered directly by a user action, like a click on a button, this makes no difference, since in that case the current handler is the only one pending. However, if the current handler is running because another handler called it, `exit` *handlerName* returns control to the calling handler (which continues to run), while `exit` `to` `HyperCard` aborts both handlers and returns control to the user.

This two-handler example reads a specified text file into a field and then creates a new, blank card to hold the next file:

```
on mouseUp -- in a button script
   answer file "Which file do you want to read?" of type text
   if it is empty then exit mouseUp -- user cancelled
   fileToField it,"Forms" -- calls handler below
   doMenu "New Card"
end mouseUp


on fileToField theFile,theField -- called by the mouseUp
   open file theFile
   read from file theFile until end
   close file theFile
   if the length of it is 0 then
      answer "There's nothing in file" && theFile & "."
      exit to HyperCard        -- prevents creating the new card
   else if the length of it > 29996 then
      answer "File" && theFile && "is too big to fit in a field."
      exit to HyperCard
   end if
   put it into field theField
end fileToField
```

To exit or to pass...

An `exit` *handlerName* statement prevents the *handlerName* message from going through the rest of the message-passing path, while `pass` *handlerName* halts the current handler, but lets the message go on through the remaining levels of the message path. If *handlerName* is a system message, you'll usually want to make sure the rest of the path gets a crack at the message by using **pass** rather than **exit**.

Using **exit repeat** is the only way to exit a **repeat forever** structure. The **repeat forever** form is especially useful when you want to test whether to continue the loop only after executing the statements (that is, when you want a structure with the test at the bottom of the loop rather than the top).

The following handler, which demonstrates a technique called binary searching, guesses your weight in the most efficient way by zeroing in on it. Each time through the loop, it guesses a value halfway between the highest number that it knows is too low and the lowest number that it knows is too high:

```
on guessYourWeight
   put 0 into tooLow
   put 500 into tooHigh
   put 0 into guessCount
   repeat
     add 1 to guessCount
     put tooLow + ((tooHigh - tooLow) div 2) into guess
     answer "Do you weigh" && guess & "?" ¬
     with "Higher" or "Lower" or "Yes"
     if it is "Yes" then exit repeat
     else if it is "Lower" then put guess into tooHigh
     else if it is "Higher" then put guess into tooLow
   end repeat
   play "boing"
   answer "I got it in only" && guessCount && "guesses!"
end guessYourWeight
```

Exit repeat is extremely useful when you want to guarantee that a user is providing valid information to **ask** requests. The following handler, which might be part of a catalog-ordering stack, makes sure that the item a user wants to order is in the catalog:

```
on orderMerchandise
   repeat
     ask "What item do you want to order?"
     if it is empty then exit orderMerchandise
     find it
     if the result is empty then exit repeat -- it's a valid item
     answer "We don't have that. Want to try again?" ¬
     with "No" or "Yes"
     if it is "No" then exit orderMerchandise
   end repeat
   put it into itemToOrder
   -- now we have a valid item to order, so continue
   answer "How would you like to pay for that?" ¬
   with "Cash" or "Check" or "Charge"
   put it into payMethod
   placeOrder itemToOrder,payMethod -- calls another custom handler
end orderMerchandise
```

The following handler, which is another example of the binary search technique, uses both **exit *handlerName*** and **exit repeat**. It searches a stack whose cards are already sorted by a field to find a card where that field is between a given upper and lower limit. The example finds a value between 25 and 30 in a field called "Retail Price":

```
locate 25, 30, "Retail Price" -- this is how you might call locate

on locate low,high,whichField
   put 1 into tooLowCard
   put the number of cards into tooHighCard
   repeat
     put tooLowCard + ((tooHighCard - tooLowCard) div 2) into guessCard
     get field whichField of card guessCard
     if it ≥ low and it ≤ high then
       go to card guessCard
       select text of field whichField
       exit locate
     end if
     if it < low then
       if guessCard is tooLowCard then exit repeat -- failure
       put guessCard into tooLowCard
     end if
     if it > high then
       if guessCard is tooHighCard then exit repeat -- failure
       put guessCard into tooHighCard
     end if
   end repeat
   answer "Can't find anything between" && low && "and" && high
end locate
```

Techie alert: The **exit to HyperCard** statement is implemented internally the same way as Command-period.

Obscure external/exit to HyperCard bug alert

The **exit to HyperCard** statement works by signalling a quiet error condition—it stops all the pending handlers, without putting up an error dialog. But because of a bug in all versions of HyperTalk through 2.2, an external can't be stopped by a handler that the external has called (or any handler called by that handler). If an external uses the `sendCardMessage` callback to execute a handler, and that handler performs an **exit to HyperCard** statement, all pending handlers are aborted but the calling external is not: when control returns to the external, the error condition is cleared, so the external continues to run.

ALSO SEE

HyperTalk Error Messages (Appendix C); **function** keyword; **on** keyword; **pass** keyword; **repeat** keyword

---

exitField message

FORMS

```
exitField
```

ACTION

The **exitField** message is sent to a field when the selection (or insertion point) is being removed from that field, and the field's text has not changed since the last time it was opened.

COMMENTS

The selection can be removed from the current field by:

- Clicking outside the field
- Tabbing to another field
- Toggling the message box
- Pressing the Enter key
- Switching into background mode
- Going to another card
- Pressing Command-Shift-Z to undo all changes to the field
- Quitting HyperCard

If the selection is being removed from a field and the text has been changed since the last time the field was opened, the **closeField** message is sent instead.

This example, which would be useful for a data-entry screen, outlines the field the insertion point is currently in so the user can easily see which field is active. It assumes there is a button called "Outline" with the style "rectangle", and consists of three handlers (which work whether you put them in the field scripts or in the card, background, or stack script):

```
on openField -- outline the field
   -- set up the rectangle for the outline
   get the rect of the target
   subtract 2 from item 1 of it
   subtract 2 from item 2 of it
   add 2 to item 3 of it
   add 2 to item 4 of it
   set the rect of background button "Outline" to it
   show background button "Outline"
   set the textStyle of the target to bold
end openField
```

```
on closeField
   exitField
end closeField

on exitField -- remove the outline
   hide background button "Outline"
   set the textStyle of the target to plain
end exitField
```

ALSO SEE

closeField message; **openField** message

---

exp function   Introduced in version 1.0

FORMS

[the] **exp** of *number*

exp(*number*)

```
exp(1) -- yields the constant e
the exp of field "Exponential of"
```

ACTION

The **exp** function returns the natural exponential of its argument.

The **exp** function is the mathematical inverse of the **ln** function: for any number x, $\exp(\ln(x)) = \ln(\exp(x)) = x$.

COMMENTS

The exponential of a number is the transcendental constant e raised to the power of the argument: in other words, exp(*number*) = e^{number}. e is approximately 2.718281828459045235. The exponential is most often used in calculations of population growth, radioactive decay, and other statistical phenomena.

The *number* is any positive or negative number.

The following example computes exponential population growth:

```
function newPopulation startingPopulation,growthRate,timeSpan
   put startingPopulation * exp(growthRate * timeSpan) ¬
   into endingPopulation
   return endingPopulation
end newPopulation
```

You might use the above function like this:

```
on mouseUp
   ask "What's the population now?"
```

```
    put it into currentPop
    ask "What's the current yearly rate of increase?"
    put it into rateOfIncrease
    ask "How many years in the future do you want to go?"
    put it into numberOfYears
    --
    put newPopulation(currentPop,rateOfIncrease,numberOfYears) ¬
    into endingPopulation
    --
    get the date
    convert it to dateItems
    put item 1 of it + numberOfYears into targetYear
    answer "The population in" && targetYear && "will be" ¬
    && endingPopulation & "."
  end mouseUp
```

ALSO SEE

exp1 function; **ln** function; **ln1** function

---

exp1 function

Introduced in version 1.0

FORMS

[the] exp1 of *number*
exp1(*number* **)**
```
exp1(10^-5) -- yields 0.00001
the exp of field "Exponential of"
```

ACTION

The **exp1** function returns the natural exponential of its argument minus 1:

$$\exp(number) - 1 = \text{exp1}(number)$$

The **exp1** function is the mathematical inverse of the **ln1** function: for any number x, $\text{exp1}(\text{ln1}(x)) = \text{ln1}(\text{exp1}(x)) = x$.

COMMENTS

The **exp1** function lets you work with very small values of *number* without losing accuracy.

The *number* is any positive or negative number.

The following handler computes a compound interest rate given a simple interest rate. It uses a formula (supplied by Paul Finlayson of Apple Computer) that gives very precise results even when the rate is very small or the frequency of compounding is very large, or both:

```
on mouseUp
  ask "What's the simple interest rate?" with 7
  put it/100 into simpleRate
  ask "Compounded how many times a year?" with 4
  put it into periods
  put exp1(periods * ln1(simpleRate/periods)) into compoundRate
  answer "That's a compound rate of" && compoundRate*100 & "."
end mouseUp
```

ALSO SEE

exp function; **ln** function; **ln1** function

---

exp2 function   Introduced in version 1.0

FORMS

[the] **exp2** of *number*

exp2(*number*)

```
exp2(24) -- yields 16777216, the number of colors with 24-bit video
the exp2 of 8 -- yields 256, the number of colors with 8-bit video
```

ACTION

The **exp2** function returns the value of 2 raised to the *number*. It's equivalent to 2^{number}.

The **exp2** function is the mathematical inverse of the **log2** function: for any number x, `exp2(log2(x))` = `log2(exp2(x))` = `x`.

COMMENTS

The **exp2** function, like several other mathematical functions, is in the language because it's part of SANE (the Standard Apple Numeric Environment), the set of mathematics routines built into the Macintosh system software.

The powers of 2 are particularly useful in computer science, because a bit can take one of two values (0 or 1); therefore, an array of n bits has 2^n possible values. If you start counting with 0, then, the highest value an n-bit array can hold is $2^n - 1$.

The following function produces a terribly useful chart showing the highest possible values for bit arrays of various lengths:

```
function bitValues
  put empty into spaces
  repeat for 10 times
    put space after spaces
  end repeat
  put "Bit Count" && space && "Highest Value" into theChart
  repeat with bits = 1 to 32
    put return && space after theChart
    if the length of bits is 1 then put space after theChart
```

```
      put bits & spaces & exp2(bits) - 1 after theChart
   end repeat
   return theChart
end bitValues
```

You might call this function like this:

```
on printChart
   set the printTextFont to "Courier"
   set the printTextSize to 14
   print bitValues()
end printChart
```

ALSO SEE

log2 function

---

export paint command   Introduced in version 2.0

FORMS

export paint to file *paintFile*
export paint to file "New Paint Document"
export paint to file "Unknown Magnanimity:Book:Screenshots:III-2"
export paint to file pictureName
export paint to file the short name of this card

ACTION

The **export paint** command saves the screen image of the current card to a MacPaint file. The **export paint** command saves the appearance of the entire card window—including buttons and field text, but not including any palettes or other windows—not just the card or background picture.

   This command is equivalent to the Export Paint item in the File menu, except that it does not present a dialog.

COMMENTS

Use the **export paint** command to save an image of the current card for documentation, archiving, or any other purpose. The following example asks the user where to export the current card image:

```
on mouseUp -- in "Export" button script
   ask file "Name the paint file:"
   if it is empty then exit mouseUp -- user cancelled
   choose select tool -- or any paint tool
   export paint to file it
   choose browse tool
end mouseUp
```

The *paintFile* is the name of the file you want to export to. If you provide only a file name without a path, HyperCard creates the file in the current folder. If a file by that name already exists, **export paint** overwrites it without so much as a by-your-leave, so be careful. (You can use the **there is** operator to check whether a file by that name already exists before exporting.)

The following handler exports images of all the cards in the current stack:

```
on dumpPaint
   lock messages
   lock screen
   choose select tool
   repeat with thisCard = 1 to the number of cards
      go to card thisCard
      put "Paint from" && the short name of this card into theName
      export paint to file theName
   end repeat
   go to first card
   choose browse tool
end dumpPaint
```

To use the **export paint** command, you must first choose one of the paint tools (either manually or with the **choose** command). If the current tool is not one of the paint tools, or if **export paint** encounters some other problem, **the result** is set to "Couldn't export paint."

About exported files: The **export paint** command creates a MacPaint file (with file type signature "PNTG") with the specified name. MacPaint-format files are 576 pixels across by 720 pixels down, or the size of an 8.5" by 11" sheet of paper. The stack image appears at the upper-left corner of the MacPaint file. If the stack window is larger, the image is clipped.

The following example is similar to the first one, except that this one exports card images only from the cards that meet a certain condition:

```
on dumpPaintWhere condition
   unmark all cards
   mark cards where condition
   lock messages
   lock screen
   push this card
   repeat with thisCard = 1 to the number of marked cards
      go to marked card thisCard
      put char 1 to 31 of the short name of this card into fileName
      export paint to file ":Images:" & fileName
   end repeat
   pop card
end dumpPaintWhere
```

One application for this handler is a clip-art stack. If the stack has a hidden field called "Keywords", and you want to export images of all the cards that have pictures of dogs, you might call the handler like this:

```
dumpPaintWhere "dog is in field Keywords"
```

Or you could export all the cards that have any card paint by using

```
dumpPaintWhere "there is a card picture"
```

(The condition parameter needs to be quoted or else you'd be passing the value of the parameter instead of the condition itself.)

Other methods of exporting card images: At times—for example, if your card size is larger than a standard MacPaint document—the **export paint** command is too limiting. To copy a full-size image of the current card, choose Copy Card from the Edit menu while holding down the Option key. This places a full-size image of the card on the clipboard, ready to be pasted into another application.

If you don't hold down the Option key while copying the card, the image you paste into the other application is a miniature of the card. This can be useful for developing thumbnails. (If you've copied a card, you can paste the thumbnail directly into HyperCard by holding down the Shift key as you paste.)

ALSO SEE

choose command; **import paint** command; **tool** property

---

family property

FORMS

```
set [the] family of button to familyNumber
set the family of card button "Radio Station KDFC" to 1
set the family of last background button to nextNumber
```

ACTION

The **family** is a property of card and background buttons. Use it when you want to group two or more buttons and coordinate their highlighting. You can also see and change a button's **family** property by using the Button Info dialog.

COMMENTS

The **family** property lets you cluster related buttons in such a way that only one button in the cluster is highlighted at a time. When the user clicks a button that's part of a family, that button is highlighted and the other members of the family are unhighlighted. This property is particularly useful for controlling a radio-button cluster.

A *button* is any button in the current stack.

The *familyNumber* is an integer between 0 and 15. A **family** of 0 means that the button doesn't belong to any family. If you give a number outside this range, HyperCard puts up a script error dialog and halts all running handlers.

You can have up to 15 button families per card or background, and you can assign any number of buttons to a family. However, you cannot put both card and background buttons in the same family. There is no relationship between the buttons in card family *number* and those in background family *number*.

This function handler scans the buttons in the card or background to find out the number of the next available button family:

```
function nextUnusedFamily theLayer
   put empty into theFamilies
   if theLayer is "background" then
      repeat with nextButton = 1 to the number of background buttons
         if the family of background button nextButton is not zero
         then put "Used" into item (the family of background button ¬
         nextButton) of theFamilies
      end repeat
   else -- check card layer
      repeat with nextButton = 1 to the number of card buttons
         if the family of card button nextButton is not zero
         then put "Used" into item (the family of card button ¬
         nextButton) of theFamilies
      end repeat
   end if
   repeat with unusedFamily = 1 to 15
      if item unusedFamily of theFamilies is empty
      then return unusedFamily
   end repeat
   return empty -- no unused families
end nextUnusedFamily
```

Assigning a button to a family automatically sets its **autoHilite** property true.

The following example, which uses the `nextUnusedFamily` function above, takes a list of names and creates a family of radio buttons from them:

```
on makeRadioFamily theList,theLayer
   if theList is empty then return "No list of buttons was provided"
   lock screen
   if theLayer is "Background" then set the editBkgnd to true
   else set the editBkgnd to false
   put nextUnusedFamily(theLayer) into thisFamily
   if thisFamily is empty then return "No more families available"
   repeat with nextButton = 1 to the number of items in theList
      doMenu "New Button"
      put item nextButton of theList into thisButtonName
      if theLayer is "Background" then
         set the name of last background button to thisButtonName
         set the style of background button thisButtonName to radioButton
         set the family of background button thisButtonName to thisFamily
```

```
      else -- set up family in card layer
         set the name of last card button to thisButtonName
         set the style of card button thisButtonName to radioButton
         set the family of card button thisButtonName to thisFamily
      end if
   end repeat
   set the editBkgnd to true
   unlock screen
   answer "A set of radio buttons has been created. You can now" ¬
   && "move the buttons into their correct positions."
end makeRadioFamily
```

You might use the handler like this:

```
makeRadioFamily "Choice 1,Choice 2,Choice 3",card
```

To find out which button in a family is currently selected, use the **selectedButton** function. To make a button in a family the currently selected button, set its **hilite** property to true.

Old HyperCard versions: In versions of HyperCard before 2.2, the **family** property doesn't exist. However, you can use a handler like the following to control a radio cluster. This handler assumes that there's only one radio-button cluster per card. It highlights the button that was clicked and unhighlights the rest of the radio buttons:

```
on mouseDown -- in card, stack, or background script
   if word 2 of the target is "button" then
      if the style of the target is "radioButton" then
         repeat with x = 1 to the number of buttons
            if the style of button x is "radioButton"
            then set the hilite of button x to ¬
            (x = the number of the target)
         end repeat
      end if
   end if
end mouseDown
```

ALSO SEE
autoHilite property; **selectedButton** function; **sharedHilite** property

---

filled property

FORMS
```
set [the] filled [of HyperCard] to {true|false}
set the filled to true
set the filled to not the hilite of card button "Hollow Circles"
```

ACTION

The **filled** global property determines whether shapes you paint are filled with the current pattern or are hollow. By default, the **filled** is false.

Setting the **filled** property is equivalent to toggling the Draw Filled item in the Options menu (visible when a paint tool is chosen).

COMMENTS

Tools affected by the **filled** property are:

rectangle   round rectangle   oval   curve   polygon   regular polygon

The following handler draws five blocks filled with different patterns:

```
on drawFiveBlocks
   set the filled to true
   choose rectangle tool
   put "20,50" into topLeftCorner
   put "50,230" into bottomRightCorner
   repeat 5 times
      set the pattern to random(40)
      drag from topLeftCorner to bottomRightCorner
      add 40 to item 1 of topLeftCorner
      add 40 to item 1 of bottomRightCorner
   end repeat
   choose browse tool
end drawFiveBlocks
```

The next two examples use (respectively) filled regular polygons and filled circles to create designs:

```
on drawPolygons
   put the width of card window div 2 into horizontalCenter
   put the height of card window div 2 into verticalCenter
   set the filled to true
   set the centered to true
   choose regular polygon tool
   repeat until the mouseClick
      set the polySides to any item of "3,4,5,6,8"
      set the pattern to random(40)
      drag from verticalCenter,horizontalCenter to ¬
      verticalCenter + random(100),horizontalCenter + random(100)
   end repeat
   choose browse tool
end drawPolygons

on makeFilledCircles
   set the filled to true
```

```
        choose oval tool
        set the centered to true
        put "200,200" into center
        repeat until the mouseClick
           put center into point
           put 15 into count
           put 10 into size
           add count * size to item 1 of point
           add count * size to item 2 of point
           repeat count times
              subtract size from item 1 of point
              subtract size from item 2 of point
              set the pattern to random(40)
              drag from center to point
           end repeat
        end repeat
        choose browse tool
     end makeFilledCircles
```

ALSO SEE

drag command; **choose** command/message; **reset paint** command

---

find command

Introduced in version 1.0
Last changed in version 2.2

FORMS

```
find [findForm] [international] text [in field] [of marked cards]
find "Wally"
find "space case" in field "Professional Diagnosis"
find myFindString in part 17 -- only works if the part is a field
find words "bell book candle" of marked cards
find string "gular dist" -- finds "angular distribution"
find chars international "Krøner" in field "Monetary Units"
find whole "pushes me through another door" in field "Story"
find comma in card field ID 7
find the selection in field "Text"
```

ACTION

The **find** command searches the fields of the current stack for the text you specify, starting with the current card.

The *findForm* is one of the following:

- [normal]

- chars

- `word[s]`
- `string`
- `whole`

Find only searches text fields; it does not search buttons, scripts, or paint text.

COMMENTS

The **find** command is a versatile and powerful tool that lets you search quickly through the text of a stack for a particular string. You can limit the search to a specific card or background field, or search only the marked cards.

If you don't specify a field to search, the **find** command checks all card and background fields on the current card. If no match is found, it goes to the next card, and so forth. When **find** locates a match, it goes to the matching card and outlines the found text. (If the screen is locked, you won't see the outline.) For forms other than **find string** and **find whole**, HyperCard only outlines the matches for the first word in the *text*.

How **find** operates depends on the form you use:

- **find normal:** This is the default, which **find** uses if you don't specify a form. The **find normal** form searches for each word in the *text* at the start of words. For example, if *text* is "bark", the **find** command finds "<u>bark</u>ing", but not "em<u>bark</u>ed". If the *text* consists of more than one word, **find** looks for a card where there's a match for each of the words. If it finds all the words in *text* on a card, it goes to that card. The words don't need to be together, or even in the same field, but each one must appear at the start of a word somewhere on that card. This is the fastest form of the **find** command.

- **find chars:** This form is like **find normal**, except that it's not restricted to the beginning of words. If the *text* is "bark", **find chars** matches the words "<u>bark</u>ing", "em<u>bark</u>ed", and "birch<u>bark</u>". Like the default form, **find chars** looks for a card that contains each word of the *text*, but the words don't have to be together or in the same field.

- **find words**: This form searches for complete words only. If *text* is "bark", this form does not match "<u>bark</u>ing" or "em<u>bark</u>ed"—only the word "bark" itself is accepted as a match. If *text* is more than one word, this form behaves like previous two, looking for a card that contains all the words in *text* but not necessarily in order or in the same field.

- **find string:** This form searches for a complete string, including spaces. (If the *text* contains no spaces, this form is equivalent to **find chars**.) It only matches cards where *text* appears exactly as given. For example, `find string "ring can be"` would match a card where the string "The st<u>ring can be</u> anywhere" appears, but would not match a card where the words "ring", "can", and "be" appeared separately.

- **find whole:** This form is like **find string**, except that it accepts only entire words. (If the *text* contains no spaces, this form is equivalent to **find word**.)

All forms of the **find** command ignore capitalization; the search is not case-sensitive. The **find** command also ignores text in fields, cards, and backgrounds whose **dontSearch** property is set to true.

If you specify the **international** option, the search recognizes Option-key characters, such as ç, as different from their ASCII equivalents, such as c. (Otherwise, **find** ignores diacritical marks.) This is important in languages in which these characters are distinguished. This option uses the same equivalents as the international form of the **sort** command.

Failed searches and the result: If **find** cannot locate the *text*, the **result** function is set to "not found". If the user level is set lower than 4 (Authoring), HyperCard puts up the dialog in Figure III.24. If the **find** command was executed from the message box, HyperCard also beeps.

Hidden fields searched: Fields that are currently hidden are searched, unless their **dontSearch** property is set to true. However, when a match is found in a hidden field, the field does not become visible, and the box is not drawn at the location of the found text. (If a tree falls in a hidden field, does it make a sound?)

The following example shows the field where the match was found, waits until the user clicks, then hides it again:

```
on findHidden whatEver
   find whatEver
   if the visible of the foundField is false then
      show the foundField
      wait until the mouseClick
      hide the foundField
   end if
end findHidden
```

Speeding up the find command: The hint bits, described in the **debug** command, are only used on words of three characters or more, and only the first three characters of a word are indexed using the hint bits. (The exact algorithm is a secret. Oooh.) Since searches using the hint bits are much faster than searches that must hunt through all the actual text, forms like `find "fre smi"` are much faster than `find "fr sm"`. But using more than three characters per word doesn't speed up the search: `find "fred smith"` isn't any faster than `find "fre smi"`. Furthermore, the more three-letter word beginnings you supply, the faster the search will turn up the desired card: `find "fred smith san francisco"` turns up the card on which all four words appear faster than the two previous examples would.

The **find chars** and **find string** forms can't use the hint bits, since hint bits only work on the start of words, and these forms also search for matches in the middle of a word. So they are considerably slower than the other forms of **find**.

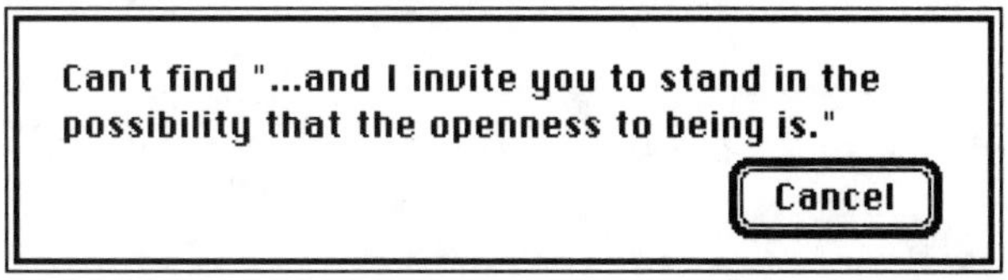

```
Can't find "...and I invite you to stand in the
possibility that the openness to being is."
                              ┌──────────┐
                              │  Cancel  │
                              └──────────┘
```

Figure III.24   Dialog box for Find failures

Some special find handlers

Search and replace: The following handler locates every occurrence of the first parameter and replaces it with the second parameter, in every field of the current stack.
  For example,

```
replace "Republican","Democrat"
```

finds every instance of "Republican" in the card and background fields of the current stack and replaces it with "Democrat". (Two of the authors are not sure this makes any existential difference; the third, more cynical, is certain it does not.)

```
on replace old,new
  repeat
    find string old  -- matches anywhere in word, not just start
    if the result is not empty then exit replace -- not found
    do "put new into" && the foundChunk
  end repeat
end replace
```

Find selected text: This handler finds whatever text the user has selected:

```
on findSelection
  get the selection
  go to next card -- so we won't find the same one
  find it
  put "find" && quote & it & quote into message
  -- so the user can find the next occurrence by pressing return
end findSelection
```

  (Power users can type Command-F and then drag over the text they want to find with the command key to fill in the search string. Try it!)

Search more than one stack: The following handler traps the **find** command so it can override the usual **find** behavior. If the first stack fails to turn up a match, it searches a second stack. (If you're using a version of HyperCard earlier than 1.2.2, substitute the comments for the second and fifth lines.)

```
on find how,what -- in a personal address stack
  send the params to HyperCard -- send "find" && what to HyperCard
  if the result is empty then exit find -- found
  lock screen
  go to stack "Business Address Book"
  send the params to HyperCard -- send "find" && what to HyperCard
  if the result is not empty then go back -- not found there either
end find
```

Little-known find fact: The **visual effect** command works with **find** the same way as with **go**, so if you issue a visual effect command before the **find**, the effect will be performed when **find** goes to the matching card:

```
on findYourself
   global userName -- set in Home stack
   if userName is empty then ask "What's your name?"
   put it into userName
   if userName is empty then exit findYourself
   visual effect dissolve to black -- layered visual effects...
   visual effect dissolve to card
   find userName --...are seen when Find switches cards
end findYourself
```

Problem with special ordinals: The special ordinals middle, last, and any don't work properly in field descriptors used with **find**, so don't use forms like find myString in last field.

Techie alert: The **international** option uses the character equivalence table given in *Inside Macintosh*, vol. I, p 502. The MLCB resource contains flags that can be used to force the international option in **find**.

Changes to HyperTalk: Versions of HyperCard before 2.2 do not have the **find international** form. Versions before 1.2.5 do not support the **find string** or **find whole** forms.

In versions before 2.0, using **find** in a field sometimes produces matches in another field, if the text is not found in the field you specified. Specifically, when you give a background field to search, HyperCard stores the number of that field. If the search progresses to a different background, **find** searches the background field with the same number; if there is no background field with that number, all the fields are searched.

ALSO SEE

debug command; **dontSearch** property; **foundChunk** property; **foundField** property; **foundLine** property; **foundText** property

---

fixedLineHeight property

Introduced in version 2.0

FORMS

```
set [the] fixedLineHeight of field to {true|false}
```
```
set the fixedLineHeight of card field "Help" to true
```

ACTION

The **fixedLineHeight** property determines whether HyperCard adjusts the spacing of each line in a field to fit the size of the text in that line.

field with fixedLineHeight set to true

same field with fixedLineHeight set to false

```
small text
medium text
large text
really large text
We hold these truths to be self-evident, that
all men are created equal, that they are
endowed by their Creator with certain
inalienable Rights, that among these are
Life, Liberty, and the pursuit of Happiness.
That to secure these rights, Governments
are instituted among Men, deriving their just
powers from the consent of the governed.
```

```
small text
medium text
large text
really large text
We hold these truths to be self-evident, that
all men are created equal, that they are
endowed by their Creator with certain
inalienable Rights, that among these are
Life, Liberty, and the pursuit of Happiness.
```

Figure III.25   Effects of fixedLineHeight on the appearance of text

Setting the **fixedLineHeight** of a field is equivalent to setting the Fixed Line Height checkbox in the field's Info dialog.

COMMENTS

Set the **fixedLineHeight** to false if the field will contain widely varying sizes of text. If you need to use a constant line height—for instance, to compute the number of lines that have scrolled off the top—or if you want the lines to have a constant distance from each other for aesthetic reasons, set the **fixedLineHeight** to true.

If all the text in the field is the same font, size, and style, the setting of the **fixedLineHeight** makes no visible difference.

If the **showLines** property of a field is true, its **fixedLineHeight** is automatically set to true, and setting the **fixedLineHeight** to true sets the **showLines** to false.

ALSO SEE

showLines property; **textFont** property; **textHeight** property

---

flash command

Introduced in version 1.0
Last changed in version 2.0

FORMS

```
flash [numberOfTimes]
flash
flash 5
flash field "Number of Flashes"
```

ACTION

The **flash** command (actually an XCMD stored in HyperCard's resource fork) quickly inverts the stack window three times.

COMMENTS

The **flash** command is a flashy (sorry) way of getting the user's attention. The following handler flashes the screen three times when the user makes a wrong guess:

```
on wrongAnswer
  flash 3
  answer "Sorry, but that's not the right answer!"
end wrongAnswer
```

The *numberOfTimes* can be any positive integer from 0 to 32766. (The statement `flash 0` does the same thing as `flash`.)

Beware of runaway flashes: Since **flash** is an XCMD, it doesn't respond to Command-period the way ordinary HyperTalk commands do, so don't use an enormous *numberOfTimes*.
   It's not a good idea to overuse **flash**—such an intrusive effect can get annoying very quickly—but used sparingly, it can add a lot of interest to your stacks.

Changes to HyperTalk: In versions of HyperCard before 2.0, the **flash** command only flashes the screen once, instead of three times.

ALSO SEE

hilite property; **visual effect** command

---

foundChunk function

Introduced in version 1.2

FORMS

```
the foundChunk
foundChunk()
put empty into the foundChunk -- delete what was found
select the foundChunk
```

ACTION

The **foundChunk** function returns a chunk expression giving the starting and ending positions of the text that was located by the most recent **find** command.

COMMENTS

The **foundChunk** function is particularly useful when you want to perform an operation on each occurrence of a string. For example, the following handler searches all the fields in the current stack for each occurrence of a string and replaces it with another string:

```
on findAndReplace toSearchFor,replacement
  put 0 into counter
  repeat
    find string toSearchFor
```

```
        if the result is not empty then exit findAndReplace -- not found
        put replacement into the foundChunk
        add 1 to counter
    end repeat
    if counter is zero then answer "No occurrences were found."
    else answer "Replacement of" && counter && "occurrences complete."
end findAndReplace
```

The **foundChunk** function returns a chunk expression of the form

```
char startChar to endChar of [card|bkgnd] field fieldNumber
```

where *startChar* is the number of the first character in the found string and *endChar* is the number of the last character.

The following function lists all occurrences of a string throughout the current stack:

```
function allOccurrences whatToFind
    push card
    lock screen
    find whole whatToFind
    put the foundChunk into startChunk
    put empty into matchesList
    repeat until the foundChunk is empty
        set the cursor to busy
        put the foundChunk && "of" && the name of this card ¬
        & return after matchesList
        find whole whatToFind
        if the foundChunk is startChunk then exit repeat -- back to beginning
    end repeat
    pop card
    unlock screen
    return matchesList
end allOccurrences
```

You can call the function like this:

```
on mouseUp
    ask "Find all occurrences of:"
    if it is empty then exit mouseUp -- user cancelled
    put it into card field "Phrase"
    put allOccurrences(it) into card field "List"
end mouseUp
```

When the foundChunk is empty: The **foundChunk** function returns empty when the most recent **find** command didn't find anything, or when the user (or a handler) has done any of the following things since the last **find**:

- Moved from one card to another
- Changed tools
- Clicked anywhere on the screen
- Typed anything

The actions that cause the **find** command's outline to disappear from the found word also reset the **foundChunk** to empty. Because **the foundChunk** is so volatile, you'll usually use this function in the same handler as the **find** command.

ALSO SEE

find command; **foundField** function; **foundLine** function; **foundText** function; **selectedChunk** function

---

foundField function   Introduced in version 1.2

FORMS

```
the foundField
foundField()
get the value of the foundField -- entire contents of field
```

ACTION

The **foundField** function identifies the field where the most recent **find** command located text.

The expression `the foundField` is equivalent to `char 6 to 8 of the foundChunk.`

COMMENTS

The **foundField** function is useful when you need to restrict the results of a search to one of several fields, or otherwise make a decision based on the name or contents of the field in which text was found. The following handler extends the **find** command by letting the user find text in any field except the one specified:

```
findExcept theString,theField
  repeat until the foundField is not theField or ¬
  the result is not empty
    find theString
  end repeat
end findExcept
```

The **foundField** function returns an expression of the form

```
[card|bkgnd] field fieldNumber
```

where *fieldNumber* is the number of the field holding the found text.

When the foundField is empty: The **foundField** function returns empty when the most recent **find** command didn't find anything, or when the user (or a handler) has done any of the following things since the last **find**:

- Moved from one card to another
- Changed tools
- Clicked anywhere on the screen
- Typed anything

The actions that cause the **find** command's outline to disappear from the found word also reset the **foundField** to empty. Since ordinary user actions reset **the foundField** so easily, you'll usually use this function in the same handler as the **find** command.

ALSO SEE

dontSearch property; **find** command; **foundChunk** function; **foundLine** function; **foundText** function; **selectedField** function

---

foundLine function   Introduced in version 1.2

FORMS

```
the foundLine
foundLine()
if word 2 of the foundLine is 1 then -- word 2 is the line number
put the foundLine into field "Line" -- descriptor of found line
put the value of the foundLine into field "Text" -- the text itself
```

ACTION

The **foundLine** function returns a chunk expression identifying the line in which the most recent **find** command located text.

COMMENTS

The **foundLine** command is very useful when the data in a particular field is structured by line and you want to limit your search to a particular part of the field. For example, you may have a field called "Mailing Address" that has a different part of the address on each line:

```
on findCity theCity -- find a city in second line of field
  lock screen
  repeat until word 2 of the foundLine is 2
    find theCity in field "Mailing Address"
    if the result is not empty then exit repeat -- not found
  end repeat
  unlock screen
end findCity
```

The **foundLine** function returns the line descriptor in the following form:

```
line lineNumber of [card|bkgnd] field fieldNumber
```

(The field is assumed to be on the current card.)You can use expressions such as `word 2 of the foundLine` to retrieve the line number itself.

To get the actual text of the line, use the **value** function:

```
get the value of the foundLine -- gets actual text
```

A *line* in HyperTalk is defined as a string delimited by return characters. A line in a narrow field may wrap around several times, and look like more than one line on screen, but it is still considered a single line when used in chunk expressions.

The following function returns the text of all the lines in the current stack in which the specified string occurs:

```
function linesContaining theString
  put empty into theLines
  find theString
  put the foundChunk into firstHit
  repeat until the result is not empty
    put the value of the foundLine after theLines
    find theString
    if the foundChunk is firstHit then exit repeat
  end repeat
  return theLines
end linesContaining
```

When the foundLine is empty: The **foundLine** function returns empty when the most recent **find** command didn't find anything, or when the user (or a handler) has done any of the following things since the last **find**:

- Moved from one card to another

- Changed tools

- Clicked anywhere on the screen

- Typed anything

Because the **foundLine** is so easily reset to empty, you'll usually use this function in the same handler as the **find** command.

ALSO SEE

clickLine function; **find** command; **foundChunk** function; **foundField** function; **foundText** function; **selectedLine** function

foundText function

FORMS

```
the foundText
foundText()
put the foundText into actualMatch
```

ACTION

The **foundText** function returns the text located by the most recent **find** command.

COMMENTS

The **foundText** returns the text outlined by the **find** command. Which text is outlined depends on which form of **find** you used: **find normal** outlines the complete word containing the text you searched for, while the other forms outline only the text itself.

The following handler tries to find the exact word you asked for. If it can't, it tries to find your string at the beginning of a word and tells you the difference between what you asked for and what it found. This approach is particularly useful when searching for words that may have variant endings: if you search for "go", this handler will also find "going" and "gone".

```
on findCloseTo whatToFind
   if whatToFind is empty then
      ask "What word do you want to find?"
      if it is empty then exit findCloseTo -- user cancelled
      put it into whatToFind
   end if
   find whole whatToFind -- search for entire word
   if the result is not empty then -- couldn't find as word
      put "Couldn't find" && whatToFind into report
      find whatToFind -- simple find
      if the result is empty then put ¬
      ", only" && the foundText after report
      put "." after report
      answer report
   end if
end findCloseTo
```

When the foundText is empty: The **foundText** function returns empty when the most recent **find** command didn't find anything, or when the user (or a handler) has done any of the following things since the last **find**:

- Moved from one card to another
- Changed tools
- Clicked anywhere on the screen
- Typed anything

The actions that cause the **find** command's outline to disappear from the found word also reset the **foundText** to empty. Because this function is reset to empty so easily, you'll usually use this function in the same handler as the **find** command.

ALSO SEE

clickText function; **find** command; **foundChunk** function; **foundField** function; **foundLine** function; **selectedText** function

---

freeSize property

FORMS

```
the freeSize of stack
get the freeSize of stack "Unknown Magnanimity:Updates:Book"
if the freeSize of this stack ≥ 10000 then doMenu "Compact Stack"
put the freeSize of stack (line x of the stacks) after field "Free"
```

ACTION

The **freeSize** read-only property reports how many unused bytes there are in a stack. This number is the same as the amount or space that appears next to the heading "Free in stack:" in the Stack Info dialog.

COMMENTS

Unused space accumulates within a stack when you delete objects or text from that stack. Unused bytes can slow down your stack's performance as well as wasting space. (Think of them as stack cholesterol.) When you compact a stack, all unused space is reclaimed and the **freeSize** is set to zero.

The following handler checks the stack's **freeSpace** when it closes. If the amount of unused space is more than ten percent of the total, or if it's more than ten percent of the space left on the disk, the handler automatically compacts the stack:

```
on closeStack
  get the freeSize of this stack
  if it > .1 * the size of this stack or it > .1 * the diskSpace then
    answer "This stack has" && it div 1024 & "K of wasted space" ¬
    && "and should be compacted soon. Do it now?" ¬
    with "Not Yet" or "Yes"
    if it is "Yes" then doMenu "Compact Stack"
  end if
  pass closeStack
end closeStack
```

The **freeSize** refers only to the stack's data fork (where information about the stack's objects is stored), not to the resource fork (where resources like XCMDs, sounds, and palettes are stored).

ALSO SEE

diskSpace function; **size** property

---

function keyword   Introduced in version 1.0

FORMS

```
function customFunctionName [parameterList]
function totalThese
function convertToFahrenheit celsiusTemp
function midPoint x1,y1,x2,y2
```

ACTION

The **function** keyword is always the first word of a handler that defines a function. The second word on the line is the name of the function being defined. Any remaining words are parameters passed to the function; parameters are separated from each other by commas.

A function can have up to 50 parameters. The exact number may be larger—it depends upon the amount of memory available—but you can always have at least 50.

The **return** keyword is used to pass the value computed by a function back to the handler that called the function.

COMMENTS

Custom functions use the same message path as system messages. A function handler is one that is designed to compute or process a value, rather than perform an action. Generally speaking, if you want to get the results of a calculation, create a custom function handler; if you want to make HyperCard do something, use a message handler.

Function names and message handler names follow the same rules. Names must begin with a letter or the underscore character (_), and can contain any combination of letters, digits, and underscores. You can't use punctuation or other special characters (*,%,•, etc.) in a function's name. The name can be up to 254 characters long.

This function takes a string and returns a version of the string with spaces between each character:

```
function explode string
  repeat with thisChar = (the length of string - 1) down to 1
    put space after char thisChar of string
  end repeat
  return string -- return the exploded string to the calling handler
end explode
```

The `explode` function might be called like this:

```
put explode("IMPORTANT MESSAGE!") into field "Forms"
```

Parentheses required: As you can see, you can use a custom function such as `explode` the same way you use any built-in HyperTalk function. There is one exception: while some built-in functions have the optional form the *functionName*, custom functions must be called in the form *functionName(parameters)*. (If the function has no parameters, use a pair of empty parentheses.)

Functions and Messages

The reason custom functions need to be written with parentheses, while most built-in functions can be written either with parentheses or in the form the *functionName*, is that when HyperTalk sees a function call with parentheses, it sends a message with that name through the message path, where it can be caught by a function handler. Function calls without parentheses, on the other hand, are sent directly to HyperCard; if the function being called isn't built in, HyperCard won't recognize the function as its own and will complain with an error message.

Another consequence of the way HyperCard sends function calls is that if you call a built-in function in the form the *functionName*, you cannot override it by putting a custom function with the same name in the message path, since a function in this form goes directly to HyperCard without passing through the message path.

Overriding built-in functions: You can change the behavior of a built-in function by creating a function with the same name and placing it at an appropriate point in the message path. Of course, your custom function must be called in the form with parentheses. If you use the *functionName*, the function call skips your custom function and goes directly to the built-in function.

The following example shows how you might override HyperCard's **round** function. If a value is exactly halfway between one number and another, **round** rounds it to the nearest even number. This behavior is useful in statistical and scientific applications, since it avoids sampling bias, but for financial and bookkeeping applications, always rounding such numbers up is preferable:

```
function round theNumber -- overrides built-in round function
   put trunc(theNumber) into integerPart
   if abs(theNumber - integerPart) < .5 then return integerPart
   else return integerPart + 1
end round
```

How parameters are passed: HyperTalk evaluates each parameter in the function call and places the result in the corresponding parameter variable for the function. This means you can pass the contents of any container as a parameter, even if it contains commas or return characters.

The following function removes leading and trailing blank lines from a string, which can be the contents of any container. Like the explode function above, this function returns a modified copy of the string; it doesn't affect the original string.

```
function stripReturns string
  repeat while the first char of string is return
    delete first char of string
  end repeat
  repeat while the last char of string is return
    delete last char of string
  end repeat
  return string
end stripReturns
```

The statement that calls this function might look like this:

```
put stripReturns(field "Dirty File") into field "Clean File"
```

If the function call provides fewer parameters than the function allows, the extra parameters hold empty. For example, if a function whose first line is

```
function myFunction myString,myNumber,myText
```

is called as `get myFunction("string",2)`, then `string` is placed in `myString`, `2` is placed in `myNumber`, and `empty` is placed in `myText`.

On the other hand, if a function is called with more parameters than are named in the function definition, the additional parameters don't get a parameter name, but you can still access them with the **param** function. The following handler puts together one or more strings, with a return after each one, and shows how to use unnamed parameters. For example, the statement

```
get concatenated(field "Name",field "Address",field "Zip Code")
```

returns the contents of the three fields, with a return character between the field contents. The function handler looks like this:

```
function concatenated
  put empty into completeString
  repeat with thisString = 1 to the paramCount
    put param(thisString) & return after completeString
  end repeat
  return completeString
end concatenated
```

Commenting out function handlers: If you comment out the **function** line, the entire handler is effectively commented out. The script editor shows this by removing the indentation for any function handler whose first line is commented out. The lack of indentation indicates that the handler is not a currently active part of the script.

ALSO SEE

"Parameters and Parameter Passing" in Chapter 8; **on** keyword; **param** function; **return** keyword

functionKey command/message

FORMS

```
functionKey keyNumber
functionKey 1 -- does an Undo
functionKey 2 -- does a Cut
functionKey 3 -- does a Copy
functionKey 4 -- does a Paste
```

ACTION

The **functionKey** message is sent to the current card when the user presses one of the function keys on a keyboard that's equipped with them.

COMMENTS

A **functionKey** handler is most often useful as a way of implementing convenient keyboard shortcuts. However, not all Macintosh keyboards have function keys. If you're not sure whether the users of your stack will have extended keyboards, be sure to provide an alternative—such as a menu or floating palette—to using the function keys.

The **functionKey** message, like all system messages, can also be sent explicitly from a handler. If there is no **functionKey** handler in the message path, pressing the first four function keys (F1-F4) corresponds to choosing the first four items on the Edit menu.

Table III.4   Built-In Function Keys

Function Key	Action
F1	Undoes the previous action
F2	Cuts the selected text, paint, or part
F3	Copies the selected text, paint, or part
F4	Pastes whatever is in the clipboard

The following example provides a number of quick shortcuts useful to the stack developer:

```
on functionKey theKey
   if theKey ≤ 4 then pass functionKey -- built-in functions
   else if theKey is 5 then edit script of this card
   else if theKey is 6 then edit script of this background
   else if theKey is 7 then edit script of this stack
   else if theKey is 8 then edit script of home
   else if theKey is 9 then show tool window
   else if theKey is 10 then show pattern window
   else if theKey is 11 then message watcher
   else if theKey is 12 then variable watcher
```

```
        else if theKey is 13 then answer the stacksInUse
        else if theKey is 14 then answer the stacks
        else if theKey is 15 then answer the windows
   end functionKey
```

The *keyNumber* is any integer between 1 and 15, corresponding to the row of 15 function keys. (It's important to realize that function keys are not the same as FKEYs; the latter are the key combinations that are accessed by pressing Command-Shift with a number, and have nothing to do with the extended keyboard's function keys.)

FunctionKey interacts with keyDown: If there is a **keyDown** handler in the message-passing path, and it does not pass **keyDown**, it also traps the **functionKey** message. If you want to use function keys, make certain that any **keyDown** handler contains the line

```
   pass keyDown
```

ALSO SEE
commandKeyDown command/message; **controlKey** message; **keyDown** command/message

---

get command   Introduced in version 1.0

FORMS
```
   get value
   get "Hello"
   get card field "Guido"
   get lotsOfDough
   get the number of chars in the message box
   get the hilite of card button ID 10
```

ACTION
The **get** command puts the value of any source or expression into the **it** variable.
   The statement `get value` is equivalent to `put value into it`.

COMMENTS
The **get** command is considerably faster than putting a value into a variable using **put**, so if your handler doesn't change the value of **it**, the **get** command can be a timesaver:

```
   get field "Name" -- takes about 0.23 ticks on an SE/30
   put field "Name" into theName -- takes about 0.52 ticks
```

If this line is within a **repeat** structure that loops many times, this time difference can add up to one the user can perceive.

When you use **get** from within a script, it puts the value into the local variable **it**; however, using **get** from the message box creates a separate *global* variable, also called **it**.

The following button script uses **get** to dial a phone number:

```
on mouseUp
  lock screen
  get field "Phone Number"
  go to stack "Phone"
  dial it -- dial handler is in "Phone"
  go back
end mouseUp
```

In this example, **get** retrieves the phone number before leaving the current stack; the other stack—from which the field with the number is unavailable—is where the dialing is actually done. (This is how dialing works in the Address stack shipped with HyperCard.)

When you use **get** to get the value of a property, you can omit the word "the":

```
get scriptingLanguage of this stack
```

A historical note

The **get** command is a vestige of the time, before its first release, when HyperTalk had only one variable, **it**. **It** was originally a global variable. Later, when local and global variables came along, **it** was demoted to local variable status, but **get** was still the only way to retrieve the value of properties—you first had to **get** the property's value, then move the value from **it** to some other variable. Eventually, Dan Winkler changed the language so you could use property values directly in any expression. The **get** command is no longer indispensible, but remains in the language for compatibility and convenience.

ALSO SEE

it variable (Chapter 8); **put** command; **set** command

global keyword

Introduced in version 1.0

FORMS

```
global variableList
global theVariable
global this,that,theOther
global customerNames,customerAddresses,customerPhoneNumbers
```

ACTION

The **global** keyword declares the variables whose names follow it as global. (A global variable is one that continues to exist and hold its value until you quit HyperCard, instead of being specific to one handler.) The *variableList* is a comma-separated list of variable names.

If the global variable being declared doesn't already exist, HyperTalk creates it and sets its value to empty. If it already exists, declaring it with the **global** keyword makes it available for use in the current handler.

You must declare a global variable in each handler that uses it. If you use a variable without having declared it as a global in the handler, HyperTalk assumes it is a local variable and does not use the global variable's value.

COMMENTS

The following **openStack** handler sets up three globals to hold user-specific values:

```
on openStack
  global theName,theQuest,theColor
  ask "What is your name?"
  put it into theName
  answer "What is your quest?" ¬
  with "Slay Rabbits" or "Find Grail" or "Run Away"
  put it into theQuest
  answer "What is your favorite color?" ¬
  with "Blue" or "Red" or "Yellow"
  put it into theColor
  pass openStack
end openStack
```

Another handler might use the value of two of the globals as follows:

```
on mouseUp
  global theName,theQuest
  if theQuest is "Run Away" then
    play "Raspberry" -- a sound you've recorded
    answer "I always knew you were a coward," && theName & "!"
  end if
end mouseUp
```

As you can see from this example, setting or changing a global's value in one handler changes it throughout HyperCard. There is only one copy of the global variable, so if you change it anywhere, all other handlers that use that global will use the new value for it:

```
on newGlobal
  global itemCount -- creates itemCount if it didn't already exist
  put 5 into itemCount
  nextHandler -- this handler changes the global
  put itemCount -- puts 8, the NEW value of itemCount
end newGlobal
```

```
on nextHandler
   global itemCount -- at this point, itemCount is 5
   put itemCount -- puts 5 into message box
   add 3 to itemCount -- itemCount is now 8 everywhere, not just here
end nextHandler
```

The value of a global variable is maintained until you quit HyperCard, even if you close the stack and go to another one. It continues to be maintained while HyperCard is in the background under MultiFinder.

But all global variables are lost when you quit HyperCard, or (if you're using System 6.0 and not using MultiFinder) when you use the **open application** command to start up another application. If you want to preserve the value of a global between sessions, put it into a field or write it to a text file in your stack's **closeStack** handler. Then, in the **openStack** handler, you can put the field or text file's contents back into the global.

You can have any number of **global** statements in a handler, and they can appear anywhere in the handler. But you must declare each global before you use it in the handler, or HyperTalk assumes the variable is local. If you try to declare a variable as global after you've already used it, you'll get the error dialog box shown in Figure III.26. The following handler is an example of this error:

```
on initializeOops
   put 5 into oops -- creates oops as a local variable
   global oops     -- this'll never fly - see Figure III.26
end initializeOops
```

As you can see, you cannot use a global and a local variable with the same name in the same handler.

Globals and the message box: Variables created in the message box are always automatically global, and you can only use global variables—not local variables—in statements that you type into the message box. You can use a **global** statement in the message box, but it has no effect.

The problem of pudgy globals: Because global variables hold their value throughout an entire HyperCard session, and because all variables are kept in memory, if you are putting a lot of data into your globals it's a good idea to clear them out when you're done with them (for instance, on **closeStack**), so their memory is freed up for use by HyperCard (an empty global takes up only a few bytes of memory):

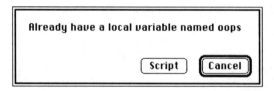

Already have a local variable named oops

Script   Cancel

Figure III.26   What happens when you try to define a local variable as a global

```
on if_I_Were_Prez
  global pershingSites,cruiseSites,mxSites
  put empty into pershingSites
  put empty into cruiseSites
  put empty into mxSites
end if_I_Were_Prez
```

There is no way to destroy a global variable from HyperTalk without quitting the program.

ALSO SEE

"Variables" in Chapter 8

---

globalLoc property   Introduced in version 2.0

FORMS

set [the] globalLoc of *pictureWindow* to {*point|screenDescriptor*}
set the globalLoc of window "My Pict" to 20,20
set the globalLoc of window ID 23498 to the loc of card window

ACTION

The **globalLoc** property determines where the picture window's upper-left corner is on the screen.

This property can only be used with windows created by the **picture** command. It does not apply to any other HyperCard windows.

COMMENTS

Use the **globalLoc** property when you need to know the picture's location relative to the edges of the screen. If you want the picture's position relative to the frontmost stack window, use the **location** property.

The *point* consists of two integers separated by a comma. The first item is the horizontal distance in pixels from the left edge of the main screen to the *point*, and the second item is the vertical distance from the top of the main screen to the *point*. The *point* is located at the upper-left corner of the picture, just below the picture window's title bar (if it has one).

Special descriptors: You can use any of the following special screen descriptors:

- cardScreen—Centers the picture on the screen that contains the frontmost stack window.
- mainScreen—Centers the picture on the screen that contains the menu bar.
- largestScreen—Centers the picture on the largest screen available. (Screen size is measured by the total number of pixels, not the physical size of the screen.)
- deepestScreen—Centers the picture on the screen that has the most colors available. To see how many colors are available on a particular screen, check the Monitors control panel.

You can refer to the individual items of the **globalLoc**:

```
put item 1 of the globalLoc of window thePict into horizLoc
put item 2 of the globalLoc of window thePict into vertLoc
```

The globalLoc and other properties: Changing a window's **globalLoc** also changes its **globalRect**, **location**, and **rectangle** properties.

ALSO SEE

location property; **globalRect** property; **picture** command

---

globalRect property   Introduced in version 2.0

FORMS

set [the] globalRect of *pictureWindow* to { *left, top, right, bottom* | *screenDescriptor* }
```
set the globalRect of window "Icon" to 20,20,100,100
set the globalRect of window 7 to the rect of card window
```

ACTION

The **globalRect** property determines where the corners of the picture window are.

This property can only be used with windows created by the **picture** command. It does not apply to any other HyperCard windows.

COMMENTS

Use the **globalRect** property when you need to know the picture's location relative to the edges of the screen. If you want the picture's position relative to the frontmost stack window, use the **rectangle** property.

The *left*, *top*, *right*, and *bottom* are integers giving, respectively, the distance in pixels between:

- The left edge of the window and the main screen's left edge

- The top of the window and the main screen's top edge

- The right edge of the window and the main screen's left edge

- The bottom of the window and the main screen's top edge

Special descriptors: You can use any of the following special screen descriptors:

- cardScreen—Centers the picture on the screen that contains the frontmost stack window and zooms the window, up to the size of the screen.

- mainScreen—Centers the picture on the screen that contains the menu bar and zooms the window, up to the size of the screen.

- largestScreen—Centers the picture on the largest screen available and zooms the window, up to the size of the screen. (Screen size is measured by the total number of pixels, not the physical size of the screen.)

- deepestScreen—Centers the picture on the screen that has the most colors available and zooms the window, up to the size of the screen. To see how many colors are available on a particular screen, check the Monitors control panel.

You can refer to the individual items of the **globalRect**:

```
put item 1 of the globalRect of window thePict into leftEdge
put item 2 of the globalRect of window thePict into topEdge
put item 3 of the globalRect of window thePict into rightEdge
put item 4 of the globalRect of window thePict into bottomEdge
```

The globalRect and other properties: Changing a window's **globalRect** also changes its **globalLoc**, **location**, and **rectangle** properties.

ALSO SEE
globalLoc property; **location** property; **picture** command

---

go command

Introduced in version 1.0
Last changed in version 2.0

FORMS

```
go [to] {card|background|stack [in [a] new window]} [without dialog]
go [to] {help|home|back}
go [to] {next|prev[ious]|ordinal|any} [card|marked card]
go to card "Artistry"
go background ID 2345
go to stack nextStackName in a new window
go to stack line 3 of the stacksInUse
go to first card of background "Clip Art"
go card ID theID of stack "Disk:Folder:That Stack"
go to last marked card
go marked card 17
go to "Testing, Testing" in new window -- goes to stack "Testing,
Testing"
go first marked card
go last -- same as "go to last card"
```

ACTION

The **go** command changes cards. It is the primary command used for navigation in HyperTalk.

COMMENTS

The following handler hops randomly through the cards of the current stack until the user clicks:

```
on showAny
   repeat until the mouseClick
      visual effect dissolve
      go to any card
   end repeat
end showAny
```

The **go** command lets you go to any card, background, or stack whatsoever.

A *card* is any valid descriptor of a card in any stack. You can specify a card by its name, ID, or number, or by an ordinal number such as `second card of this stack`. If the card is in a stack other than the current one, you must include the stack name in the descriptor of the card: for example, `go to card "Foo" of stack "My Stack"`. You can also specify that the card is in a particular background.

The *background* is any valid descriptor of a background in the current stack or any other stack. Going to a background means going to the next card of that background or, if the background is in another stack, going to its first card. If you're already on a background, going to it has no effect. You can specify the *background* by name, number, ID, or an ordinal number.

The *stack* is the name of any stack, open or not. If you just give the stack's name without specifying a path for it, HyperTalk checks in the locations given on the "Search Paths" card of the Home stack. If the stack isn't located in any of the listed folders, **go** puts up a dialog asking you to locate the stack.

Going to a stack means going to the first card of that stack, even if the stack is already open to another card. (To bring an already-open stack to the front without switching cards, use the **show** command.) The word `stack` is optional; if you don't specify whether the destination is a card, stack, or background, HyperTalk assumes it's a stack.

The following example stores the location of the last card viewed every time you leave the stack. When you re-open the stack, you go straight to that card:

```
on closeStack
   put the ID of this card into card field "Bookmark" of card 1
end closeStack
```

```
on openStack
   get card field "Bookmark" of card 1
   go to card it
   pass openStack
end openStack
```

If the destination is in a stack other than the current one, you can use the `in a new window` form to open the destination in a new window. Otherwise, the current stack is closed as the destination stack is opened.

If the **go** is successful, **the result** is set to empty. If HyperCard can't locate
card or background, it sets **the result** to "No such card." The following exan
baseball statistics, and illustrates how to use the value of **the result** in a hand

```
on showWins teamName,year
  lock screen
  go to card "Wins for" && year
  if the result is not empty then -- no such card
    answer "Sorry, there are no stats for that year."
  else
    answer teamName && "won" && field teamName ¬
    && "games in" && year & "."
  end if
  go back
end showWins
```

If HyperCard can't find the destination stack, it puts up a standard file dialog
to locate it (see Figure III.27). If the user cancels this dialog, **the result** is set

You can prevent the appearance of this dialog by using the `without dialc`
form suppresses the dialog; if HyperCard can't find the destination stack, it se
to "No such stack." Like `in a new window`, this form can be used only if the
in a stack other than the current one.

This handler flips randomly through a sequence of flashcards, and might I
educational stack for drill:

```
on flashCards
  push this card
  mark all cards
  repeat until the number of marked cards is 0
    go to any marked card
    unmark this card
```

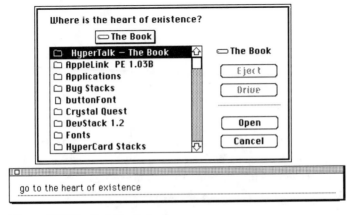

Figure III.27   Spiritual stacks

```
        wait until the mouseClick
     end repeat
     answer "Done!"
     pop card
  end flashCards
```

Anomaly when going to an open stack: If you try to **go** to a nonexistent card in another stack, and the stack is already open, HyperCard sets **the result** to "No such card." But instead of staying on the original card, it brings the destination stack to the front.

Changes to HyperTalk: Versions of HyperCard before 2.0 don't understand the `without dialog` and `in a new window` forms of the **go** command.

ALSO SEE

marked property; **pop** command; **show** command; **visual effect** command

---

grid property

FORMS

```
set [the] grid [of HyperCard] to {true|false}
set the grid to true
```

ACTION

The **grid** global property, when set to true, constrains most paint tools and the movements of paint selections to increments of 8 pixels (about 1/9th of an inch). Setting the **grid** property is equivalent to toggling the Grid menu item in the Options menu. By default, the **grid** is false.

COMMENTS

The **grid** affects the `line`, `rectangle`, `round rectangle`, `oval`, `polygon`, and `regular polygon` tools, as well as determining what increments you can drag selections by.

Because scripts can drag to exact coordinates, **grid** is almost never set from a script, unless you're using a script to set up a painting environment for the user. It's in the language because Winkler and Atkinson decided to make every paint property available to scripts in some way, even if they couldn't think of a good use for some of them at the time. (No, you don't win a toaster if you come up with a good use for **grid**.)

ALSO SEE

drag command; **reset paint** command

hBarLoc property

FORMS

set [the] hBarLoc of window "Variable Watcher" to *number*

```
set the hBarLoc of window "Variable Watcher" to 150
```

ACTION

The **hBarLoc** is a property of the variable watcher window. It determines the position of the vertical split bar in the variable watcher.

Unless a user or script changes it, the **hBarLoc** is 98.

COMMENTS

The Variable Watcher window shows the name and value of each variable in the top pane, with an editing area in the bottom pane. (To edit a variable's value, click its name.) A user can drag the horizontal split bar to change the amount of space allocated to each of these two panes. You can use the **hBarLoc** property to check the location of the split bar, or change it, from a script.

The *number* is the distance in pixels from the top edge of the Variable Watcher window to the split bar. It must be an integer. You can set the **hBarLoc** to any number between -32768 and 32767; practical values depend on how many variables you have, how large the Variable Watcher window is, and how much space you want to allot to the editing area. If you want to set the **hBarLoc** to a value that doesn't leave room for all the variables, you can do so from a script, but not by manual dragging in the window.

The following handler toggles the size of the editing area:

```
on switchVW toMode
   get item 4 of the rect of window "Variable Watcher" ¬
   - item 2 of the rect of window "Variable Watcher" -- height
   if toMode is empty ¬
   and abs(it - the hBarLoc of window "Variable Watcher") < 10
   then put "Edit" into toMode -- already in view mode
   else put "View" into toMode -- already in edit mode
   if toMode is "View" then
     -- make entire window into variable-list area
     set the hBarLoc of window "Variable Watcher" to it
   else -- toMode is "Edit"
     -- make half the window into variable-list, half into editing area
     set the hBarLoc of window "Variable Watcher" to it div 2
   end if
end switchVW
```

You can always set the **hBarLoc** property, whether or not the Variable Watcher is currently visible.

Techie alert: You can use this property with a custom variable watcher XCMD as well as the built-in variable watcher, if the custom XCMD is written to support **hBarLoc**.

ALSO SEE

variableWatcher property; **vBarLoc** property

---

heapSpace function   Introduced in version 1.0

FORMS

```
the heapSpace
heapSpace()
the heapSpace
```

ACTION

The **heapSpace** function returns the amount of free and freeable space in HyperCard's memory allocation, in bytes. This is the total amount of free space that would be available in the heap if all purgeable handles were purged and all relocatable handles were moved to compact the heap.

COMMENTS

This feature was built into the language mainly as an aid in the testing and development of HyperCard itself. However, it can come in handy in certain situations in which you need to know how much memory is available to you, since some operations—like displaying a large color picture with the **picture** command, or using the paint tools—take additional memory and will fail if that memory isn't available. The following example checks to see whether there's enough memory to use the paint tools, avoiding the generic "not enough memory" error dialog:

```
on mouseUp
  if the heapSpace > 120000 then
    beep
    answer "Not enough memory for the Graphing Module."
  else
    drawGraph -- another handler, which uses the paint tools
  end if
end mouseUp
```

The following handler can be used for testing an XCMD. It repeatedly calls the XCMD, checking **the heapSpace** each time through to see whether the XCMD is eating memory and not releasing it when finished:

```
on textXCMD theXCMD,count
  if count is empty then put 100 into count
  put the heapSpace into startSpace
```

```
repeat count times
   do theXCMD
end repeat
put (startSpace - the heapSpace) div 1024 & "K change in heap space."
end testXCMD
```

ALSO SEE

debug command; **stackSpace** function

---

height property

FORMS

```
the height of menubar
set [the] height of {part|button|field|card|window} to integer
set the height of last button to 100
```

ACTION

The **height** property determines the distance in pixels between the top and bottom edges of an element.

COMMENTS

When you change the **height** of an element, that element's center stays where it was, and the upper and lower edges move toward or away from the center. If the new **height** is an odd number, the odd pixel is added to the bottom half of the element.

The following handler sets the height of all buttons on the current card to match the height of the first button:

```
on alignHeights
   repeat with i = 2 to the number of buttons
      set the height of button i to the height of button 1
   end repeat
end alignHeights
```

The *button*, *field*, or *card* is a descriptor of any button, field, or card in the current stack. Setting the **height** of a card changes the height of all cards in the current stack and is equivalent to changing the height in the Resize dialog (accessed from the Stack Info dialog).

The *window* is a descriptor of any open stack window, HyperCard window, or external window. For some windows (such as the tool, scroll, pattern, and message windows), the **height** property is read-only and can't be changed. Heights of windows don't include the title bar or the window borderlines.

The **height** of a stack window and the **height** of a card in that stack may be different if the window has been sized smaller than the card size (for example, using the Scroll command in the Go menu).

The *integer* is the vertical distance in pixels from the top edge to the bottom edge of the element. The minimum **height** of a card window is 64 pixels; if you specify a smaller *integer*, the card's height is set to 64.

The following example by Robin Shank makes a field adjust its own height based on how many lines of text it contains. (This example is suitable for fields such as lists that have a return at the end of each line.) All three handlers should be in the field's script:

```
on closeField
   adjustHeight
end closeField


on returnInField
   put return into the selectedChunk -- do the return
   get the selectedChunk -- store insertion point location
   adjustHeight
   select it              -- restore insertion point
end returnInField


on adjustHeight
   if the number of lines in me > 1 then
     lock screen
     put the topLeft of me into savedTopLeft
     set the height of me to ¬
     the number of lines in me * the textHeight of me + 6
     set the topLeft of me to savedTopLeft
     unlock screen
   end if
end adjustHeight
```

Hiding a part with the height: If you set the height of a button or field to 0 or a negative number, that part disappears from the screen. It won't respond to mouse clicks (since it has no area), but you can send messages to it using **send**. If it's a field, it remains in the tabbing order, and you can type into it and manipulate text selections. An object's **visible** property is unaffected by its **height**.

The width and rectangle properties: The **height** of an element is the difference between item 4 and item 2 of its **rectangle** property. Anything that resizes an element may change its **height** property.

Using the height to set up zones in a button: The following deceptively simple handler, which is based on an idea by Gary Bond, automatically divides a button into a number of vertical zones and computes which zone was clicked. This example shows 26 zones, one for each letter of the alphabet (see Figure III.28):

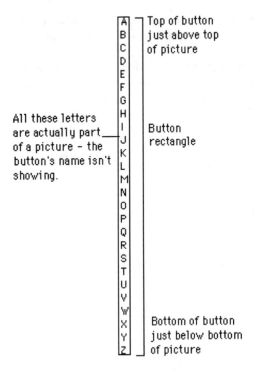

Figure III.28   One button acts like 26 buttons (or as many as you want)

```
on mouseDown
   put 26 into numberOfZones
   put the clickV - the top of me into clickPosition
   put trunc(numberOfZones * clickPosition/the height of me) ¬
   into clickZoneNumber
   put numToChar(charToNum(A) + clickZoneNumber)
end mouseDown
```

Standard button heights: HyperCard creates all new buttons with a height of 22 pixels, regardless of their style. However, you should set standard buttons to a **height** of 20 and default buttons to a **height** of 28 for the standard appearance of these button styles.

Changes to HyperTalk: In versions of HyperCard before 2.2, you cannot describe a button or field with a part descriptor, and you cannot get the **height** of the menu bar.

In versions of HyperCard before 2.0, the size of the card window is fixed and cannot be changed.

ALSO SEE
bottom property; **location** property; **rectangle** property; **top** property; **width** property

help command/message

FORMS

help
help

ACTION

A **help** message is sent to the current card when the user presses the Help key (on an extended keyboard) or chooses Help from the Go menu.

The **help** command is equivalent to choosing Help from the Go menu, and brings you to the first card of the HyperCard Help stack.

COMMENTS

If your stack has its own help system, you can intercept the **help** message and have it take the user to your own help:

```
on help
  -- traps the help message whether it's sent by choosing Help
  -- from the Go menu, pressing the Help key or command-?, or
  -- typing "help" into the message box
  answer "What do you need help with?" ¬
  with "Cancel" or "HyperCard" or "This Stack"
  if it is "Cancel" then exit help
  else if it is "HyperCard" then pass help -- go to HC Help
  else -- use custom help
    push this card
    visual effect dissolve
    go to card "Help"
  end if
end help
```

If you intercept the **help** message, it's a good idea to provide a way for the user to get to the standard HyperCard help stacks, unless your stack is intended for use on an information kiosk or other single-use machine. Another way of providing access to the standard Help system is to place a "HyperCard Help" button on your help card, which goes to the standard help.

Techie alert: The **help** message is not actually handled by HyperCard itself, but by a handler in the Home stack script. To see this handler, type `edit the script of Home` into the message box.

The standard `help` handler lets you specify a topic to go to. For example, typing the line

```
help card
```

into the message box, or using it in a handler, will take you to the "Cards, stacks, and windows" section of the Help stack.

There is also a `hyperTalk` handler in the Home stack script, which takes you straight to the "HyperTalk Reference" stack. If you find that you usually want to go to the HyperTalk reference when you need help, put the following handler into your stack script:

```
on help theTopic
   hyperTalk theTopic
end help
```

ALSO SEE

doMenu command/message

---

hide command

FORMS

hide {*window*|*part*}
hide {*backgroundPicture*|*cardPicture*}
hide {*titlebar*|*menubar*|*groups*}
```
hide card window
hide tool window
hide window "Reports Stack"
hide window "Contents Palette"
hide the message box
hide picture of background 1
hide card picture
hide groups
```

ACTION

The **hide** command hides the specified window, part, or other element.

COMMENTS

Use the **hide** command to hide elements on screen from the user. For example, you may want to hide a button if its function is not currently available, or make detailed data available by showing and hiding fields.

Hidden objects stay hidden even when you close the stack. To make a hidden element visible again, use the **show** command.

The following handler hides a field with a visual effect:

```
on mouseUp
   lock screen
   hide field "Extra Info"
   unlock screen with visual effect dissolve
end mouseUp
```

Another button, to show the field, has the following script:

```
on mouseUp
  lock screen
  show field "Extra Info"
  unlock screen with visual effect dissolve
end mouseUp
```

The **hide** command does not affect the **location** or other properties of hidden elements; it only determines whether they're currently visible or not. You can change the **location**, **style**, and other properties of a hidden element just as you would if it were visible.

Hidden objects don't respond to mouse clicks, even if you know where to click. To send a mouse message to a hidden object, you need to use the **send** keyword.

A *window* is any currently open window. You can refer to windows by name, number, or ID. You can hide (and show) stack windows, HyperCard windows, and windows created by XCMDs or XFCNs. If there is more than one open stack window, and you hide the current stack window, the next one is brought to the front.

A *part* is any button or field in the current stack. The command hide *part* has the same effect as set the visible of *part* to false. If you try to hide a window, button, or field that doesn't exist, HyperCard puts up an error dialog.

This example hides the "Previous" button when you're on the first card, and hides the "Next" button when you're on the last card:

```
on openCard
  if the number of this card is 1 then
    hide background button "Previous"
    show background button "Next"
  else if the number of this card is (the number of cards) then
    show background button "Previous"
    hide background button "Next"
  else
    show background button "Previous"
    show background button "Next"
  end if
end openCard
```

A *backgroundPicture* or *cardPicture* is the picture belonging to the current card or background, or to any card or background in the current stack. The command hide picture of *cardOrBackground* is equivalent to set the showPict of *cardOrBackground* to false.

About hidden fields: You can put text into hidden fields and get text from them, but you cannot select text in a hidden field, and hidden fields are not in the tabbing order. The **find** command searches in hidden fields (unless their **dontSearch** property is set to true), but when it finds text in a hidden field, it doesn't show the field.

About hidden pictures: You can use paint tools from a script on hidden card or

Figure III.29   This dialog appears when you try to paint manually on a hidden card picture

background pictures; the changes are made invisibly, and can be seen when you show the picture again. However, if you try to use a paint tool manually on a hidden picture, HyperCard asks whether you want to show the hidden picture (see Figure III.29). You cannot paint manually on a hidden picture without showing it first.

The command **hide titlebar** hides the title bar across the top of the current stack window. (Before you hide or show a stack window's title bar, that stack must be frontmost.)

The command **hide menubar** makes the menu bar invisible. It is equivalent to `set the visible of menubar to false`.

The command **hide groups** turns off the thick gray underline that designates text whose style is set to "group".

Changes to HyperTalk: In versions of HyperTalk before 2.0, you cannot hide the title bar, and groups do not exist.

In versions before 1.2.5, you cannot hide the card or background picture.

ALSO SEE

show command; **showPict** property; **visible** property

---

hide menubar message   Introduced in version 1.0

FORMS

```
hide menubar
```

ACTION

The **hide menubar** message is sent to the current card when the menu bar is hidden, either with the **hide** command or by pressing Command-space.

COMMENTS

Many stacks are designed to use the entire screen, and must hide the menu bar (at least on smaller screens) so the whole stack window can be seen.

One common problem occurs when you use a stack that hides the menu bar whether it needs to or not. This is often the case for older stacks, whose programmers didn't take large screens into account. The following handler, installed in the Home stack script, eliminates this irritating behavior while still letting stacks hide the menu bar when necessary:

```
on hide theThing -- in Home stack script
   if theThing is not "menubar" then pass hide
   if the commandKey is down then pass hide -- let user command-space
   if the top of card window < 20 then pass hide
   -- go ahead and hide if the menubar is blocking the stack window
end hide
```

ALSO SEE

hide command; **show menubar** message

---

hideIdle property

Introduced in version 2.0

FORMS

```
set [the] hideIdle of window "Message Watcher" to {true|false}
set the hideIdle of window "Message Watcher" to true
```

ACTION

The **hideIdle** is a property of the message watcher window. It determines whether the Hide Idle checkbox in the message watcher window is on or off.

By default, the **hideIdle** property is false.

COMMENTS

The Hide Idle checkbox in the message watcher window tells the Message Watcher whether or not to display **idle** messages along with the other HyperCard messages being sent. You can use the **hideIdle** property to check the setting, or change it, from a script.

You can set the **hideIdle** regardless of whether or not the Message Watcher is currently visible.

Techie alert: You can use this property with a custom message watcher XCMD, as well as the build-in message watcher, if the custom XCMD is written to support **hideIdle**.

ALSO SEE

hideUnused property; **messageWatcher** property

---

hideUnused property

Introduced in version 2.0

FORMS

```
set [the] hideUnused of window "Message Watcher" to {true|false}
set the hideUnused of window "Message Watcher" to true
```

ACTION

The **hideUnused** is a property of the message watcher window. It determines whether the Hide Unused checkbox in the message watcher window is on or off.

By default, the **hideUnused** property is set to true.

COMMENTS

The Hide Unused checkbox in the message watcher window tells the Message Watcher whether or not to display messages that aren't handled by any object in the message-passing path. You can use the **hideUnused** property to check the setting, or change it, from a script.

The **hideUnused** property can be set whether or not the Message Watcher is currently visible.

Techie alert: You can use this property with a custom message watcher XCMD, as well as the build-in message watcher, if the custom XCMD is written to support **hideUnused**.

ALSO SEE

hideIdle property; **messageWatcher** property

---

hilite property   Introduced in version 1.0

FORMS

```
set [the] [hilite|hilight|highlite|highlight] of button to {true|false}
set the hilite of me to true
if the hilite of button "Edit" then select text of field "Name"
```

ACTION

The **hilite** property determines whether the button appears reverse-highlighted (black to white) or not.

By default, the **hilite** of newly created buttons is false.

COMMENTS

The *button* is any button in the current stack.

When the **hilite** of a button changes, any selected text is deselected and the insertion point is removed. This button handler shows how to save and restore the selection so it's not lost 'when the button is highlighted:

```
on mouseDown
   get the selectedChunk -- save it for later
   set the hilite of me to true
   wait 10 ticks -- delay so user can see the hiliting
   set the hilite of me to false
   select it -- restore text selection
end mouseDown
```

The button style affects highlighting: Different button styles are highlighted in different ways (Figure III.30):

- A highlighted radio button has a dot in its center; that is, the **hilite** determines whether the radio choice is selected.

- A highlighted checkbox button has an X in its box; that is, the **hilite** determines whether the checkbox option is selected.

- A transparent or oval button with an icon inverts the name and icon when it highlights.

- The **hilite** property has no effect on popup buttons.

- All other button types, including transparent and oval buttons without an icon, appear in inverse video when highlighted.

Button families and highlighting: When the user clicks a button that's part of a family, that button's **hilite** property is set to true, and the **hilite** of the other members of the family is set to false. This is particularly useful for controlling a radio-button cluster.

Effect of the sharedHilite: If the **sharedHilite** of a background button is true, its **hilite** property has the same value across all cards. If the **sharedHilite** is false, the **hilite** property of a background button can be different on different cards of the background.

ALSO SEE

autoHilite property; **family** property; **selectedButton** function

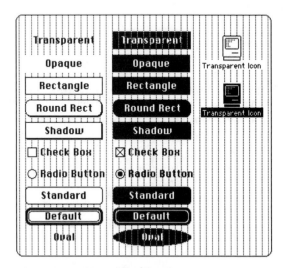

Figure III.30   Unhighlighted and highlighted buttons

hilitedButton property

FORMS

```
set the hilitedButton of window paletteWindow to buttonNumber
set the hilitedButton of window "Contents" to 1
set the hilitedButton of window "Nav Palette" to theNumber
get the hilitedButton of window 1 -- must be a palette
```

ACTION

The **hilitedButton** is a property of the floating palette windows created by the **palette** command. It determines which of the palette's buttons is currently highlighted.

COMMENTS

The Palette Maker lets you choose one of two types of button behavior when you create your palette. If you check the Remain Hilited checkbox, clicking a button highlights it, and the button stays highlighted until you click another button. This kind of palette behaves like HyperCard's tool menu. If you leave Remain Hilited unchecked, buttons only highlight when they're actually being pressed, like the buttons in a dialog box.

All the buttons on a palette have the same behavior.

If the palette is set up with Remain Hilited, the **hilitedButton** is the number of the currently highlighted button. (If there is no highlighted button, the **hilitedButton is** 0.) If the palette has Remain Hilited turned off, the **hilitedButton** is always −1. You can use this fact to determine what kind of buttons a palette has from a handler:

```
if the hilitedButton of window myPalette is -1 then
  put "This palette has transient hiliting."
else
  put "This palette has persistent hiliting."
end if
```

You can set the **hilitedButton** property to track the current state of your stack. The following example belongs to a stack that has a "Table of Contents" palette whose buttons you can click to go to various cards. This handler makes sure the current location is always highlighted on the palette:

```
on openCard
  if there is a window "Stack Contents" then
    set the hilitedButton of window "Stack Contents" ¬
    to the short number of this card
  end if
end openCard
```

If the palette isn't set up with Remain Hilited, setting the **hilitedButton** flashes the specified button three times, instead of changing the highlight permanently.

The following handler highlights each of a palette's buttons and displays the corresponding command:

```
on hilitePaletteButtons thePalette
   put the buttonCount of window thePalette into numberOfButtons
   repeat with thisButton = 1 to numberOfButtons
      set the hilitedButton of window thePalette to thisButton
      put line thisButton of the commands of window thePalette
      wait until the mouseClick --click to continue to next button
   end repeat
   set the hilitedButton of window thePalette to 0 -- unhilite all
end hilitePaletteButtons
```

ALSO SEE

palette command; **buttonCount** property

---

icon property   Introduced in version 1.0

FORMS

```
set [the] icon of button to {iconName|resourceID}
set the icon of me to nextIcon
set the icon of the target to 0 -- no icon
set the icon of button "Fred" to "Ideas"
```

ACTION

The **icon** property describes what icon, if any, is displayed in the button.

You can view the available icons by clicking the Icon button in the Button Info dialog, and edit and create icons using the built-in icon editor.

COMMENTS

The *button* is any button in the current stack.

Icons are stored as resources in the current stack, any other stack in the resource path, or the System file. An icon is a black-and-white graphic that's 32 pixels square.

You can specify the icon to use with either the resource name or the resource ID number. When you retrieve the **icon** of a button, the value reported is the resource ID number; there is no way to get the icon's name from within HyperTalk.

A button has no icon when its **icon** property is set to zero.

Animation using icons: Changing the icon of a button is a simple way to do small animations. The following handler cycles through a series of arrow icons (illustrated in Figure III.31); the effect is to spin the arrow.

```
on spinArrow
   put "Up Arrow,Next Arrow,Down Arrow,Previous Arrow" into theIcons
   repeat until the mouseClick
```

Up Arrow   Next Arrow   Down Arrow   Previous Arrow

Figure III.31   Icons for button animation

```
      repeat with thisIcon = 1 to 4
         set the icon of me to item thisIcon of theIcons
      end repeat
   end repeat
end spinArrow
```

Icons and button style: Checkboxes, radio buttons, and popup buttons don't display an icon, even if one is set for the button. Changing the **icon** of a popup button from a script may change the current popup selection.

Undocumented feature alert: If you set a button's icon to -1, the button looks for a PICT resource with the same name as the button, and displays it instead of an icon. (Since HyperCard's window is black-and-white, color or grayscale PICTs are converted to black-and-white when displayed.)

This feature is not implemented in the version 2.1 HyperCard Player, but it's available in the 2.2 Player, and in all versions of HyperCard except those before 2.0.

ALSO SEE
picture command; **style** property

ID property

Introduced in version 1.0
Last changed in version 2.2

FORMS
```
the [short|abbr[ev[iated]]|long] ID of {object|window|menu|HyperCard}
put the long ID of this card after visitedCardsList
put the short ID of this background into myBackground
if the ID of card part 1 is it then delete card part 1
get the ID of background button "Choose Me"
if the ID of window myPict is savedID then close window myPict
the ID of HyperCard is not "WILD" -- means this is a standalone
```

ACTION
The **ID** read-only property reports the unique identification number of the specified card, button, field, background, window, or menu.

The **ID** property of an object appears in its Info dialog.

COMMENTS

Since an element's **ID** never changes once it's created, and the ID number is guaranteed to be unique, you may want to refer to elements by ID instead of by name if there's a possibility that two elements of the same kind might have the same name. Furthermore, referring to a card by ID is faster than referring to it by name, particularly if the stack contains several hundred or thousand cards. However, it's usually better coding style to refer to objects by name, since it makes your code easier to read. If you do refer to an object by its ID in your scripts, include the name in a comment.

The form `the short ID of` *card* reports the card's ID number by itself:

```
5698
```

The form `the ID of` *card* reports the ID number plus the type of object:

```
card id 5698
```

The form `the abbr[ev[iated]] ID of` *card* reports the same thing as `the ID`.
The form `the long ID of` *card* reports the card's full pathname:

```
card id 5698 of stack "The Book:A HyperTalk - The Book:test"
```

For elements other than cards, all forms of the **ID** property report just the ID number: the IDs look like `the short ID of` *card*.

Changes to HyperTalk: In versions of HyperCard before 2.2, you can't get the **ID** of HyperCard, you can't use a part descriptor to refer to a button or field, and you can't refer to a menu by its resource ID.
In versions before 2.1, you can't refer to a window by ID.

ALSO SEE

name property; **number of object** function; **partNumber** property

---

idle message   Introduced in version 1.0

FORMS

```
idle
```

ACTION

The **idle** message is sent repeatedly to the current card whenever no handler is running and no other message is being sent. HyperCard only sends the **idle** message when the browse tool is the current tool.

COMMENTS

Use the **idle** handler for recurring tasks, like updating a time clock on the current card:

```
on idle
  put the long time into field "Clock"
end idle
```

Typing with an active idle handler: If an **idle** handler uses the **select** or **put** commands, like the one above, it interferes with the user's typing, because these commands remove the insertion point. If your stack contains unlocked fields, you should modify such a handler by saving the insertion point or field selection, then restoring it when your handler is done. This lets the user type normally:

```
on idle
   get the selectedChunk
   put the long time into field "Clock"
   select it -- restore original selection so user can keep typing
end idle
```

When the **idle** message is sent, HyperCard clears any pending visual effects and sets the **numberFormat**, **dragSpeed**, **lockRecent**, **lockMessages**, **lockScreen**, and **itemDelimiter** properties to their default values.

Efficiency impact of idle handler: If your idle handler is complicated, it can noticeably slow down your stack's response to user actions. This makes it especially important to make such handlers efficient. In particular, if you're using the result of an expression that doesn't change, store it in a global variable instead of computing it every time through the **idle** handler.

ALSO SEE
mouseWithin message; **tool** property

---

if...then...else keyword   Introduced in version 1.0

FORMS

```
if condition then statement [else statement]

if condition then statement
[else statement]

if condition
then statement
[else statement]

if condition then
   statementList
else statement
```

```
if condition
then statement
[else
  statementList
end if]

if condition then
  statementList
[else
  statementList]
end if

if condition then          -- this form not preferred - it's hard to read
statement else statement
if condition then statement else -- not preferred - it's hard to read
  statementList
end if
```

ACTION

The **if...then...else** structure lets your handler decide whether to execute statements or skip them, based on whether some condition is true or false.

When *condition* is true, the statements after **then** execute, but any statements after **else** (if there is an **else** in the structure) are skipped. When *condition* is false, on the other hand, the statements after **then** are skipped and any statements after **else** are performed.

COMMENTS

Use an **if...then...else** structure when you want your handler to perform some action, but only under certain conditions. It's also useful when you want to check some value (like which menu item a user chose) and perform a different action for each possible choice.

This handler puts up one of two different responses, depending on what the user does:

```
on guessTheAnimal
   put any item of "dog,bear,cat,mule,lion,goldfish" into theAnimal
   ask "What animal am I thinking of?"
   -- only one of the next two lines is executed:
   if it is theAnimal then answer "Nice going!"
   else answer "No, I was thinking of a" && theAnimal
end guessTheAnimal
```

The *condition* is any expression that evaluates to either true or false. (The *condition* in the above handler is `it is theAnimal`.) A *statement* is any valid HyperTalk command line, and a *statementList* is any group of valid statements, each on a separate line.

Each **if** structure can have only one **else** (but see the section below about emulating case statements).

This example shows how you can use a single handler to perform a separate action for each function key, using the **if...then...else** structure:

```
on functionKey theKey
   if theKey is 1 or theKey is 2 of theKey is 3 or theKey is 4
   then pass functionKey
   if theKey is 5 then doMenu "Card Info..."
   if theKey is 6 then doMenu "Background Info..."
   if theKey is 7 then doMenu "Stack Info..."
end functionKey
```

Nested if structures: You can put **if...then...else** structures inside each other, up to any necessary level:

```
if a = 1 then
   if b = 1 then
      if c = 1 then
         put x
      end if
   end if
end if
```

However, it is often possible to avoid nested **if...then...else** structures (which can be difficult to read and make sense of) by using other features of the language. For example, the above structure is equivalent to this easier-to-understand line:

```
if a = 1 and b = 1 and c = 1 then put c
```

On the other hand, judicious nesting can make your code run faster by reducing the amount of work HyperTalk has to do:

```
if myFunction1() and myFunction2()
-- always computes both functions
if myFunction1() then if myFunction2()
-- only computes both if the first is true
```

Using nesting to emulate a case statement: Although HyperTalk has no case statement (which is a structure in some programming languages that lets you select among several choices), you can use a form of nesting to get the same effect as a case statement. For example, the following handler changes the meanings of the First, Prev, Next, and Last menu choices so they apply to the current background instead of the entire stack:

```
on doMenu theItem
   if theItem is "First" then go to first card of this background
   else if theItem is "Prev" then go to prev card of this background
   else if theItem is "Next" then go to next card of this background
   else if theItem is "Last" then go to last card of this background
   else pass doMenu
end doMenu
```

As you can see, this is a nested **if...then...else** construct, but because each new level of nesting is on a line that begins with the word "else", the script editor does not indent each new level of nesting; this makes it considerably easier to read long nested structures of this kind. The following dice game (such as it is) avoids deep indentation by using a series of **else** clauses:

```
on rollDice
    answer "Click the mouse to get each number."
    put "0 0 0" into rolls
    repeat with roll = 1 to 3
      repeat until the mouseClick
         put random(6) into word roll of rolls
         put rolls
      end repeat
    end repeat
    put 0 into matchCount
    if word 1 of rolls is word 2 of rolls then add 1 to matchCount
    if word 2 of rolls is word 3 of rolls then add 1 to matchCount
    if word 4 of rolls is word 1 of rolls then add 1 to matchCount
    if matchCount is 0 then
       play "boing"
       answer "You lose!" with "Crud."
    else if matchCount is 1 then
       play "harpsichord" c c
       answer "Doubles!" with "Great!"
    else if matchCount is 3 then
       beep 5
       answer "Triples!" with "Wow!"
    end if
end rollDice
```

Choosing the best form: In general, the simpler the form, the easier it is to follow and debug. The first and sixth forms of **if...then...else** listed at the beginning of this section are preferred for reasons of style and readability, but the other forms are also valid HyperTalk and can be used. Here are some rules of thumb:

- If your **if** clause and **else** clause both consist of a single statement, and the entire structure will fit on one line, put it on one line:

  ```
  if theAnswer is 2 then answer "Yes!" else beep
  ```

- If possible, avoid using the line continuation character (¬); it makes reading complex structures more difficult.

- If you have nested **if...then...else** structures, one inside another, HyperCard may become confused about which **else** clause belongs to which **if**. You can see when this is happening because the script editor's indentation will be wrong. If this happens, try putting all the **if...then...else** structures in the first or sixth form.

A guide to ending multiline if forms

If you have a return after the word **then**, the structure must end with either an **end if** or a single-line **else** statement. If you have a return after the word **else**, the structure must be ended with an **end if**.

Changes to HyperTalk: In HyperCard versions before 2.0, the maximum number of nested blocks pending across all handlers is 128. (A nested block is essentially anything that causes a script to indent, so a running handler, an executing **repeat** loop, or an executing **if** structure are all blocks and count toward this total.) However, there are no recorded instances of anyone running out of block space. This limit is removed in version 2.0 and later.

In versions before 2.0, you can't use **if** structures in the message box (not even single-line forms).

ALSO SEE

repeat keyword; **exit** keyword

---

import paint command   Introduced in version 2.0

FORMS

```
import paint from file paintFile
import paint from file "Unknown Magnanimity:Clip Art:Favorites"
import paint from file thePictureName
```

ACTION

The **import paint** command retrieves the contents of a MacPaint file and pastes it into the current card or background picture, replacing the old picture.

This command is equivalent to the Import Paint item in the File menu, except that it does not present a dialog.

COMMENTS

Use the **import paint** command to bring clip art or other paint images into your stack without having to open a paint program.

If background editing mode is on (that is, if the **editBkgnd** property is true), the imported image goes into the background picture. Otherwise, it goes into the card picture. The following example lets the user replace the current background image with another one from a MacPaint file, perhaps a folder full of interesting patterns:

```
on replaceBackgroundImage
   answer file "What image do you want to use?" of type paint
   if it is empty then exit replaceBackgroundImage -- user cancelled
   put the editBkgnd into originalState
```

```
      set the editBkgnd to true
      choose select tool -- or any paint tool
      import paint from file it
      set the editBkgnd to originalState
  end replaceBackgroundImage
```

The *paintFile* is the name of the file you want to import. If you provide only a file name without a path, HyperCard assumes the file is in the current folder.

MacPaint-format files are 576 pixels across by 720 pixels down, roughly the size of an 8.5" by 11" sheet of paper. The upper-left corner of the paint file is placed at the upper left of the card. If the card is smaller than the image in the paint file, the image is clipped to the size of the card (not the current size of the window). If the card is larger than the MacPaint size of 576x720, the part of the current picture outside that boundary remains unchanged. The current size and scroll of the stack window doesn't affect the action of **import paint**.

To use the **import paint** command, you must first choose one of the paint tools, either manually or with the **choose** command. If the current tool is not one of the paint tools, or if there is some other problem that prevents HyperCard from importing the picture, **the result** is set to "Couldn't import paint."

The following example shows a way of using a database of images. The images are located in a MacPaint file in a folder called "Clip Art". The files have names consisting of a size, a color, an animal, and a number—for example, "Large Black Dog 2" or "Small White Fish 5". The list of filenames is stored in a hidden field in the stack. The stack prompts the user for the desired animal, size, and color (any of which may be "anything") and imports all the images in the desired category:

```
on animalBase
   put field "File Names" into fileNames
   --
   ask "What kind of animals do you want?" with "Anything"
   put it into whatKind
   ask "What size animals do you want?" with "Anything"
   put it into whatSize
   ask "What color animals do you want?" with "Anything"
   put it into whatColor
   --
   repeat with thisFile = 1 to the number of lines of fileNames
      get line thisFile of fileNames
      if whatKind is not word 3 of it and whatKind is not "Anything"
      then next repeat
      if whatSize is not word 1 of it and whatSize is not "Anything"
      then next repeat
      if whatColor is not word 2 of it and whatColor is not "Anything"
      then next repeat
      doMenu "New Card"
      import paint from file ":Clip Art:" & it
   end repeat
end animalBase
```

High resolution and color images: To show color or grayscale images in the PICT format, use the **picture** command.

ALSO SEE

choose command; **export paint** command; **picture** command; **read** command; **tool** property

---

is a operator

Introduced in version 2.0
Last changed in version 2.2

FORMS

data is a[n] {number|integer|point|rect[angle]|date|logical}
data is not a[n] {number|integer|point|rect[angle]|date|logical}
field "Date" is a date
the selection is a number
it is a point

ACTION

The **is a** operator evaluates to true if the *data* is of the specified data type and to false if it's not. The forms is a and is an are equivalent.

The **is not a** operator is the logical opposite of **is a**: it evaluates to true if the *data* is not of the specified type, and to false if it is. The forms is not a and is not an are equivalent.

COMMENTS

A point consists of two integers separated by a comma.

A rectangle consists of four integers separated by commas.

A date is any of the date or time formats accepted as valid by the **convert** command.

A logical is one of the HyperTalk constants "true" or "false".

Constructions such as 0/0 and 1/0 which evaluate to NAN (not a number) or INF (infinite) are numbers, but not integers. For example, the expression myVar/0 is a number evaluates to true, but myVar/0 is an integer evaluates to false.

Changes to HyperTalk: In versions of HyperCard before 2.2, the statements empty is a number, empty is an integer, and empty is a date all return true. Also, expressions such as 1/0 which evaluate to INF are considered integers by the **is a** operator.

ALSO SEE

convert command; **there is a** operator

itemDelimiter property

FORMS

```
set [the] itemDelimiter [of HyperCard] to character
set the itemDelimiter to colon
set the itemDelimiter to "$"
set the itemDelimiter to the numToChar of 17
```

ACTION

The **itemDelimiter** global property specifies the character HyperTalk uses to separate items in chunk expressions. By default, the **itemDelimiter** is a comma (,). The **itemDelimiter** is reset to its default at idle, so changes to it are only effective as long as there's a handler running.

COMMENTS

The **itemDelimiter** property is useful when you want to read data that's divided into parts with some character other than the comma. By using the **itemDelimiter**, you can simplify working with such data by using HyperTalk chunk expressions.

The following function gets the path of the folder containing the current stack:

```
function stackFolder
   put the long name of this stack into theStack
   -- of the form        stack "Disk:Folder:Stack Name"
   delete word 1 of theStack
   delete first char of theStack   -- leading quote
   delete last char of theStack    -- trailing quote
   put the itemDelimiter into originalSetting
   set the itemDelimiter to colon
   delete last item of theStack    -- the filename
   set the itemDelimiter to originalSetting
   return theStack
end stackFolder
```

The *character* can be any expression that evaluates to a single character. Attempting to set the **itemDelimiter** to more than one character causes HyperCard to display an error dialog.

The value of the **itemDelimiter** does not affect comma-separated HyperTalk structures such as message parameters, the **location** and **rectangle** properties, date formats, and so forth. These structures are always separated with commas, regardless of what the **itemDelimiter** is currently set to.

In database files, records are often separated by return characters, with the fields within each record separated by tabs. This handler shows how to import such a file, putting each record on a separate card. The handler assumes that you're already on a background with the appropriate number of background fields.

```
on importDBFile
  -- get the data from the file
  answer file "Where is the file to import?" of type text
  if it is empty then exit to HyperCard -- user cancelled
  put it into fileToImport
  open file fileToImport
  read from file fileToImport until end
  -- put one record into each card
  set the itemDelimiter to tab
  repeat for the number of lines of it -- total number of records
    doMenu "New Card"
    put line 1 of it into thisRecord
    repeat with thisField = 1 to the number of items of thisRecord
      put item thisField of thisRecord into field thisField
    end repeat
    delete line 1 of it -- we're done with this line
  end repeat
  -- clean up
  close file fileToImport
  set the itemDelimiter to comma
end importDBFile
```

keyDown command/message

Introduced in version 2.0

FORMS

keyDown *character*
keyDown "A"
keyDown myCharacter
keyDown char 7 of field "Typing Practice"

ACTION

The **keyDown** command simulates typing the specified key.

The **keyDown** message is sent to the field with the selection when the user types any key. If there is no text selection, the message is sent to the current card.

COMMENTS

In practice, the **type** command is more versatile when you want to simulate typing, so **keyDown** is usually used as a message rather than a command.

Since **keyDown** traps keystrokes, if you want your user's typing to appear, you must pass the **keyDown** message at the end of any **keyDown** handlers.

The following handler keeps a log of all keystrokes the user has typed during the current session:

```
on keyDown theKey
  global typingLog
  put theKey after typingLog
  pass keyDown -- let the character appear
end keyDown
```

The *character* parameter is the character typed.

KeyDown interferes with arrowKey and functionKey messages: If there is a **keyDown** handler in the message-passing path, and it does not pass **keyDown**, it also traps the **functionKey** and **arrowKey** messages. If you want to use function or arrow keys, make certain that any **keyDown** handler contains the following line:

```
pass keyDown
```

ALSO SEE

arrowKey command/message; **functionKey** command/message; **type** command

---

language property   Introduced in version 1.0

FORMS

set [the] language [of HyperCard] to {English|*translatorName*}
```
set the language to "French"
set the language of HyperCard to "English"
```

ACTION

The **language** global property is the language in which you read and write scripts.
   By default, the **language** is English.

COMMENTS

To use a language other than English, there must be a translator resource for that language available in the resource fork of the current stack, a stack in use, the Home stack, or the HyperCard application. If you try to set the **language** to a language for which there is no translator available, HyperCard puts up a script error dialog.
   The following handler warns you if the **language** is not English when you edit a script:

```
on edit
  if the language is not "English" then
    answer "The current language is" && the language ¬
    && ". Set it to English?" with the language or "English"
    set the language to it
  end if
  pass edit
end edit
```

Techie alert: Scripts are always stored in the stack in English. The translator translates them when they're displayed by the script editor, and translates them back to English to be stored on the disk again.

Translators are extremely powerful; they can perform any transformation on a script, including turning it into Pascal or BASIC or C and back again.

ALSO SEE

scriptingLanguage property; Translators (Appendix E)

---

left property

Introduced in version 1.2
Last changed in version 2.2

FORMS

```
set [the] left of {part|button|field|window} to integer
the left of {menubar|card}
set the left of message to 25
set the left of pattern window to the left of tool window
set the left of field "List" to the clickH
```

ACTION

The **left** property describes where the left edge of an element is.

COMMENTS

The following handler rapidly increments and decrements the left of the message box, making it shimmy back and forth on the screen until you click the mouse button:

```
on friscoDisco
  get the left of the message box
  show message box
  repeat until the mouseClick
    set the left of the message box to it + 1
    set the left of the message box to it - 1
  end repeat
  set the left of the message box to it
end friscoDisco
```

The *button, field*, or *card* is any button, field, or card in the current stack. (You can get the **left** of a card, but you can't set it.) A *window* is a descriptor of any open stack window, HyperCard window, or external window.

The **left** of a stack window and the **left** of a card in that stack may be different if the window has been sized smaller than the card size (you can do this using the Scroll command in the Go menu).

The *integer* is the horizontal distance in pixels from the left edge—of the screen for stack windows, or of the current stack window for cards, buttons, fields, and other windows—to the element's left edge. If the *integer* is negative, the element's left edge is *integer* pixels to the left of the left edge of the screen or stack window.

The left and other location properties: The **left** of an element is the same as item 1 of its **topLeft** property, and also the same as the first item of the element's **rectangle** property. Changing the **left** of an element moves the element without changing its size, while changing item 1 of the element's **rectangle** changes its size without moving its other three edges.

Changing the left property: Anything that moves or resizes an element may change its **left** property: for example, dragging the element manually or from a script, or changing its **location** or **rectangle** property, or using the **show** command with a new location.

Changes to HyperTalk: In versions of HyperCard before 2.2, you cannot describe a button or field with a part descriptor, and you cannot get the **left** of the menu bar.

ALSO SEE

bottom property; **location** property; **rectangle** property; **right** property; **show** command; **top** property; **topLeft** property

---

length function

FORMS

```
[the] length of string
length(string)
the length of "Hello" -- yields 5
the length of "2^5+3" -- yields 5
length(foo) -- yields the number of chars in the variable "foo"
the length of card field "Movie Name"
```

ACTION

The **length** function returns the number of characters in the value of its argument.

The expression `the length of string` is equivalent to `the number of characters in string`.

COMMENTS

The following handler warns you when a field is nearing the maximum number of characters:

```
on closeField
  if the length of me > 29000 then
    beep
    answer the short name of me && "is almost full."
  end if
end closeField
```

The following example expands tabs to spaces in text, so that the columns line up properly. It assumes the text is going to be displayed in a monospaced font, such as Courier or Monaco:

```
function tabsExpanded theText,columnWidth
  put 1 into charPosition
  put empty into cleanText
  repeat with i = 1 to the number of chars of theText
    set the cursor to busy
    get char i of theText
    if it is tab then -- insert necessary number of spaces
      get space
      repeat
        add 1 to charPosition
        if charPosition mod columnWidth is zero then exit repeat
        put space after it
      end repeat
    else if it is return then -- next line
      put 1 into charPosition
    else
      add 1 to charPosition
    end if
    put it after cleanText
  return cleanText
end tabsExpanded
```

Typically, you'll use the above function when reading text from a file generated by a database or spreadsheet program. You might call it like this:

```
on mouseUp
  open file "Tab-Delimited File"
  read from file "Tab-Delimited File" until end
  close file "Tab-Delimited File"
  put tabsExpanded(it) into card field "Spreadsheet Results"
end mouseUp
```

ALSO SEE
number function

---

lineSize property   Introduced in version 1.0

FORMS
set [the] lineSize [of HyperCard] to *thicknessInPixels*
set the lineSize to 4
set the lineSize to the selectedText of button "Line Size:"

ACTION

The **lineSize** global property determines the thickness of lines and shape borders drawn with the paint tools. Setting the **lineSize** is equivalent to choosing a line thickness from the Line Size dialog in the Options menu, which is visible when a paint tool is chosen. By default, the **lineSize** is 1.

COMMENTS

When you change the **lineSize**, only what you draw subsequently is affected; existing borders don't change.

The *thicknessInPixels* can be 1, 2, 3, 4, 5, or 8. The value you specify must be an integer. If you specify a negative thickness, the **lineSize** is set to 1; if you specify an invalid positive number, the **lineSize** is set to the next lower valid size (so specifying 5 sets the **lineSize** to 4).

This example draws concentric circles with a diminishing **lineSize**. (One of the authors of this book claims the result looks like the ripples from a rock dropped into a pond. Another thinks it looks more like a bullseye. Hmmm…)

```
on ripples
  choose oval tool
  set the centered to true
  put 200,175 into edge
  put edge into center
  repeat with i = 1 to 10
    set the lineSize to 10 - i
    add 10 + the lineSize to item 1 of edge
    add 10 + the lineSize to item 2 of edge
    drag from center to edge
  end repeat
  choose browse tool
end ripples
```

Drawing a borderless shape: You can't set the **lineSize** to zero, but if you hold down the Option key while drawing a filled shape, the border is drawn in the same pattern as the fill, so it's effectively invisible. The following example shows how to do the same thing in a handler:

```
on drawBorderless
  choose rectangle tool
  set the filled to true
  set the pattern to 22 -- gray
  drag from 100,100 to 200,200 with optionKey
  choose browse tool
end drawBorderless
```

ALSO SEE

drag command; **filled** property; **reset paint** command

ln function

FORMS

> **[the] ln of** *number*
> **ln(** *number* **)**
> `ln(1) -- yields 0`
> `the ln of myNumber`

ACTION

The **ln** function returns the natural (base *e*) logarithm of the *number*.

The **ln** function is the mathematical inverse of the **exp** function: for any number x,
`ln(exp(x)) = exp(ln(x)) = x`.

COMMENTS

The *number* can be any positive number.

The following function tells how many digits it will take to write a given number in a given base:

```
function numberLength theNumber,theBase
   return 1 + trunc(ln(theNumber)/ln(theBase))
end numberLength
```

This function can be called like this from another handler:

```
on mouseUp
   ask "What's the number?"
   put it into theNumber
   ask "What base do you want to put the number in?" with "10"
   put it into theBase
   answer "That requires" && numberLength(theNumber,theBase) ¬
   && "digits."
end mouseUp
```

ALSO SEE

exp function; **ln1** function

---

ln1 function

FORMS

> **[the] ln1 of** *number*
> **ln1(** *number* **)**
> `ln1(10^-6)`
> `the ln1 of (myNumber/1000)`

ACTION

The **ln1** function returns the natural logarithm of its argument plus 1:

```
ln1(number) = ln(number + 1)
```

The **ln1** function is the mathematical inverse of the **exp1** function: for any number x,
`ln1(exp1(x)) = exp1(ln1(x)) = x.`

COMMENTS

The **exp1** function lets you work with very small values of *number* without losing accuracy. The *number* is any number greater than -1.

The following handler computes a compound interest rate given a simple interest rate. It uses a formula (supplied by Paul Finlayson of Apple Computer) that gives very precise results even when the rate is very small or the frequency of compounding is very large, or both:

```
on mouseUp
   ask "What's the simple interest rate?" with 7
   put it/100 into simpleRate
   ask "Compounded how many times a year?" with 4
   put it into periods
   put exp1(periods * ln1(simpleRate/periods)) into compoundRate
   answer "That's a compound rate of" && compoundRate*100 & "."
end mouseUp
```

ALSO SEE

exp1 function; **ln** function

---

location property

Introduced in version 1.0
Last changed in version 2.2

FORMS

set [the] loc[ation] of {*part*|*button*|*field*|*card*|*window*} to *point*
set the location of card window to 20,20
set the loc of last card button to the clickLoc

ACTION

The **location** property determines where the specified element is on the card window or screen. The **location** of a window is its upper-left corner; the **location** of other elements is the center point of the element.

COMMENTS

Use the **location** property to move an element without resizing it. The following handler places the card window, tool window, pattern window, and message box at convenient locations for use on a 13" or 14" monitor:

```
on startup
   set the loc of card window to 95,7
   show message box at 19,362
   show tool window at -77,13
   show pattern window at -77,183
end startup
```

The *part, button, field,* or *card* is a descriptor of any button, field, or card in the current stack. A *window* can be any open stack window, HyperCard window, or external window, including windows created by the **palette** and **picture** commands. Movable modal dialogs in HyperCard 2.2, such as Card Info, also have locations:

```
get the loc of window "Card Info"
```

The *point* consists of two integers separated by a comma. For stack windows, the first item of the *point* is the horizontal distance in pixels from the left edge of the screen to the point, and the second item is the vertical distance from the top edge to the point. For other windows and all other elements, the distances are measured from the left and top edges of the frontmost stack window, rather than the edges of the screen. (The top edge of a window is at the bottom of its title bar.)

You can also refer to the individual items of the **location**:

```
put item 1 of the loc of button 1 into horizontalOffset
put item 2 of the loc of button 1 into verticalOffset
```

The location and other properties: Changing an element's **location** may also change its **rectangle, top, bottom, left, right, topLeft,** and **bottomRight**. However, changing the **location** does not change an element's **height** or **width**.

Special locations for picture windows: If the *window* was created by the **picture** command, you can use one of the following special screen descriptors to set its **location**:

- `cardScreen`—Centers the picture on the screen that contains the frontmost stack window.

- `mainScreen`—Centers the picture on the screen that contains the menu bar.

- `largestScreen`—Centers the picture on the largest screen available. (Screen size is measured by the total number of pixels, not the physical size of the screen.)

- `deepestScreen`—Centers the picture on the screen that has the most colors available. To see how many colors are available on a particular screen, check the Monitors control panel.

Techie alert: The location of a stack window is pinned to multiples of 16 pixels horizontally, so it will always be at an even address (a longword boundary) in memory. Additionally, the width of stack windows must be a multiple of 16. These restrictions let HyperCard copy its internal buffer to the screen using a very tight loop that moves whole longwords at a time.

Changes to HyperTalk: In versions of HyperCard before 2.2, you cannot describe a button or field with a part descriptor. Also, the Info dialogs aren't movable modal dialogs, and you can't get or set their locations.

ALSO SEE

bottom property; **left** property; **rectangle** property; **right** property; **top** property

---

lock error dialogs command

Introduced in version 2.1

FORMS

```
lock error dialogs
lock error dialogs
```

ACTION

The **lock error dialogs** command sets the **lockErrorDialogs** property to true, preventing any script error dialogs from appearing.

COMMENTS

The **lock error dialogs** command is particularly appropriate in stacks intended for users who aren't programmers, because it prevents presentation of the standard HyperCard error dialog used by scripters. Nonprogrammers may find this dialog confusing or annoying. The following example shows how to block the standard error dialog and substitute a message that's more appropriate for your users' needs:

```
on mouseUp
   lock error dialogs
   longComplicatedHandler
   -- if there's an error, it will trigger the errorDialog handler
   -- instead of putting up the standard error dialog
end mouseUp


on errorDialog
   global myHomePhone
   answer "Sorry; there was a script error. Please try again," ¬
   && "or call the developer at" && myHomePhone & "." with "Sorry!"
end errorDialog
```

The **lock error dialogs** command is also useful in situations in which a HyperTalk statement is being executed outside a script or with the **do** command. For example, you might use it in a tutorial stack that lets users type a sequence of HyperTalk statements into a field, then click a button to execute them:

```
on mouseUp
  do field "Practice Code"
end mouseUp
```

In this example, because of the way the **do** keyword works, if the user's practice code has an error, the Script and Debug buttons in the standard error dialog open the card script. This is hardly helpful (and may be quite confusing), since the offending code isn't in the card script. You can override the standard dialog in such cases by using the following handlers:

```
on mouseUp
  lock error dialogs -- insert this line to avoid standard dialog
  do field "Practice Code"
end mouseUp


on errorDialog theErrorMessage
  answer theErrorMessage
  -- just presents the message w/o Script and Debug buttons
end errorDialog
```

ALSO SEE

errorDialog message; **lockErrorDialogs** property; **unlock error dialogs** command

---

lock messages command   Introduced in version 2.1

FORMS

lock messages
lock messages

ACTION

The **lock messages** command sets the **lockMessages** property to true, which prevents messages associated with moving between locations from being sent to objects while a script is running.

Specifically, it blocks the following messages:

openCard	openBackground	openStack
closeCard	closeBackground	closeStack
suspendStack	resumeStack	
suspend	resume	

COMMENTS

Use the **lock messages** command when you need to block unwanted system messages from being sent during a handler's execution. For example, the following handler goes to another stack long enough to get some data, then returns. But the other stack's **openStack** handler puts up an **ask** dialog for the user's name. Since we're not staying in that stack, we don't want to make the user log in, so we'll use **lock messages** to avoid triggering the **openStack**:

```
on mouseUp
   lock screen  -- keep user from seeing stacks flashing
   lock messages -- prevent openStack handler from executing
   push this card
   go to card "Data" of stack "Accounts" -- openStack not sent
   put field "Total Payable" into amountOwed
   pop card
   put amountOwed into field "Total Owed"
end mouseUp
```

The **lock messages** command is also useful for speeding up handlers that go to other cards or other stacks. Messages take a certain amount of time to go through the message path, in addition to the time it takes for any open, close, suspend or resume handlers to execute.

Suppose your stack has a custom menu arrangement. In order to be a good HyperCard citizen and interact well with other stacks, such a stack should have a **suspendStack** handler that undoes the menu changes, and a **resumeStack** handler that restores them. (This keeps the user from seeing your custom menu items in other stacks for which they're not appropriate.) However, if one of your stack's handlers goes to another stack and returns immediately, there's no reason to change the menu setup. Using **lock messages** prevents the **suspendStack** and **resumeStack** messages from being sent, so no time is wasted resetting the menu bar and then changing it back.

The **lock messages** command is synonymous with `set the lockMessages to true`.

The **lockMessages** property is automatically set back to false when the **idle** message is sent, so you don't need to **unlock messages** at the end of a top-level handler. However, if your handler is called by another handler that may continue to execute after your handler ends, be sure to set the **lockMessages** property back the way you found it, since the calling handler may depend on it being set to the default of false.

The **lock messages** command only blocks HyperCard from sending automatic messages. If you explicitly send one of the messages from a handler, it will be sent regardless of whether messages are locked:

```
on mouseUp
   lock messages
   go to card "Send OpenCard Here"
   -- the usual automatic openCard message is blocked, but...
   openCard -- ...sent along message path as usual; not blocked
   go to card "No OpenCard Here" -- automatic message blocked
   unlock messages -- not strictly necessary, but included for clarity
end mouseUp
```

ALSO SEE

lock screen command; **lockMessages** property; **unlock messages** command

lock recent command   Introduced in version 2.2

FORMS

```
lock recent
lock recent
```

ACTION

The **lock recent** command sets the **lockRecent** property to true.

COMMENTS

The **lock recent** command is synonymous with `set the lockRecent to true`, and keeps cards you visit from being added to the display shown by the Recent menu item.

This handler shows an animation using the technique of card flipping, without disturbing the Recent cards display:

```
on playMovie
   lock recent -- leave the Recent display as it was
   push this card
   repeat with frameNumber = 1 to 16
     play "Soundtrack" && frameNumber
     go to card frameNumber of background "Movie"
     wait until the sound is done
   end repeat
   pop card
   unlock recent
end playMovie
```

The **lockRecent** property is automatically set to false when the **idle** message is sent.

ALSO SEE

lockRecent property; **lock screen** command; **unlock recent** command

---

lock screen command   Introduced in version 1.2

FORMS

```
lock screen
lock screen
```

ACTION

The **lock screen** command sets the **lockScreen** property to true. This freezes the current image on the screen until an **unlock screen** command is issued, the **lockScreen** is changed to false, or the handler completes and an **idle** message is sent.

COMMENTS

The **lock screen** command lets you make changes to the appearance of the screen—such as changing cards, hiding or showing fields and buttons, or drawing on pictures—without letting the user see them. It's most useful when you go to another card or stack for information and then return immediately, since it lets you do so without confusing the user by flashing another card's image on the screen. Locking the screen also speeds up your handler, since if the screen is locked HyperCard doesn't spend time drawing changes to the screen.

The following handler, when used in a stack with a lot of cards, demonstrates how to use **lock screen** to increase speed:

```
on accountsReceivable
  lock screen
  put 0 into totalBalances
  repeat with i = 1 to the number of cards
    set the cursor to busy
    go to card i
    add field "Balance" to totalBalances
  end repeat
  answer "The total is" && totalBalances
  pop card
  unlock screen
end accountsReceivable
```

At idle time, when all handlers are finished, HyperCard automatically resets the **lockScreen** property to false.

Whether the screen is locked has no effect on the message box or the cursor.

Be kind to users: If your handler takes more than a second or two to run while the screen is locked, be sure to set the **cursor** property to watch or busy so your users know something is happening. It's easy to assume the system has somehow crashed when it seems that nothing is happening—which is the visual impression given by **lock screen**.

Locked screen and recent cards: When you lock the screen, HyperCard automatically sets the **lockRecent** property to true, preventing card images from being added to the Recent display. However, the user can still get back to any cards your handler visited while the screen is locked, by using the Back item in the Go menu.

Locking the screen more than once: HyperTalk keeps count of the times you've used **lock screen** (or the equivalent, set the lockScreen to true). Locking an already locked screen is harmless, but you must balance each **unlock** with a **lock**; if you lock the screen twice and then unlock it once, the screen remains locked. For example, the following pair of handlers draws everything while the display is still locked:

```
on mouseUp
  lock screen    -- first lock
  drawStuff      -- gets locked again and unlocked in drawStuff
```

```
    show card picture
    unlock screen  -- now really unlocked - 2 locks balanced by 2 unlocks
end mouseUp


on drawStuff
    lock screen     -- screen now locked twice
    show card field 2
    unlock screen -- doesn't unlock yet - locked twice, unlocked once
end drawStuff
```

ALSO SEE

find command; **go** command; **lock recent** command; **lockScreen** property; **unlock screen** command

---

lockErrorDialogs property

FORMS

```
set [the] lockErrorDialogs [of HyperCard] to {true|false}
set the lockErrorDialogs to true
if the lockErrorDialogs then do dubiousScript
```

ACTION

The **lockErrorDialogs** global property specifies whether HyperTalk shows a dialog when it encounters a script error. If the **lockErrorDialogs** is true, HyperTalk instead sends an **errorDialog** message to the current card, where a custom handler can deal with the error.

The **lockErrorDialogs** property is reset to its default value of false when **idle** is sent.

COMMENTS

Use the **lockErrorDialogs** property when you want to handle script errors yourself rather than let HyperCard put up its usual error dialog. For example, you may want to avoid confusing users with a script error, or save the text of script errors in a container.

If HyperTalk encounters a script error when the **lockErrorDialogs** is set to true, it sends the **errorDialog** message to the current card, with a parameter consisting of the text of the error message. If **lockErrorDialogs** is false, HyperCard displays the error message in a script error dialog instead.

On encountering a script error, HyperTalk aborts the current handler, regardless of the setting of **lockErrorDialogs**.

The lockErrorDialogs and AppleEvents: When HyperCard receives an AppleEvent and the sending program has specified that no user interaction is allowed, it sets the **lockErrorDialogs** property to true while handling the event.

ALSO SEE

errorDialog message; **heapSpace** function; **lock error dialogs** command; **request** keyword; **send to program** keyword; **stackSpace** function; **unlock error dialogs** command

lockMessages property

FORMS

```
set [the] lockMessages [of HyperCard] to {true|false}
set the lockMessages to true
if the lockMessages then send openCard to this card
```

ACTION

The **lockMessages** global property determines whether or not HyperCard sends suspend, resume, open, and close messages when moving from card to card.

The **lockMessages** property is set to false on **idle**.

COMMENTS

The **lockMessages** property has two uses. First, it takes time for messages to go through the message path, so setting the **lockMessages** to true speeds up handlers that go to another card. Second, if you're only going temporarily to another card—for instance, if you're visiting a stack to fetch some data from one of its fields—you may not want the usual open and close handlers to run.

The following handler sets the **lockMessages** to true to speed up the process of visiting each card in a stack:

```
on countVotes
  set the lockScreen to true
  set the lockMessages to true
  go to stack "Polling Places" -- one precinct per card
  put empty into totals
  repeat for the number of cards
    repeat with i = 1 to the number of fields
      add field i to item i of totals
    end repeat
    go to next card
  end repeat
  put "The winner got" && max(totals) && "votes."
end countVotes
```

You can also use the **lock messages** and **unlock messages** commands to change the value of this property.

The lockMessages only stops automatic messages: You can still send any message with the **send** keyword, even if the **lockMessages** is true and the message is one of those blocked by **lockMessages**. Setting the **lockMessages** to true prevents HyperCard from sending these messages automatically, but it doesn't keep you from sending them yourself in a handler.

ALSO SEE

lock messages command; **lockRecent** property; **lockScreen** property; **unlock messages** command

---

lockRecent property   Introduced in version 1.0

FORMS

```
set [the] lockRecent [of HyperCard] to {true|false}
set the lockMessages to false
if the lockRecent then lock messages
```

ACTION

The **lockRecent** global property determines whether or not HyperCard stores the image of each card visited in the display shown by the Recent menu item.

HyperCard resets the **lockMessages** property to false on **idle**.

COMMENTS

Because adding card images to the Recent display takes a little time, setting the **lockRecent** to true speeds up handlers that move from card to card.

You can also use the **lock recent** and **unlock recent** commands to change the value of this property.

LockRecent and lockScreen: Setting the **lockScreen** property to true effectively sets the **lockRecent** to true, so you'll rarely need to set the **lockRecent** explicitly.

The Recent display is completely independent of both the card list used by the **push** and **pop** commands and the actions of the **go back** and **go forth** commands. The setting of the **lockRecent** property has no effect on these actions.

ALSO SEE

lock recent command; **lockMessages** property; **lockScreen** property; **unlock recent** command

---

lockScreen property   Introduced in version 1.0

FORMS

```
set [the] lockScreen [of HyperCard] to {true|false}
set the lockScreen to false
```

```
set the lockScreen to (the number of this card > 10)
set the lockScreen to it
```

ACTION

The **lockScreen** global property controls whether changes to the display are blocked from being seen on the screen. The screen is updated when the **lockScreen** is set back to false.

HyperCard resets the **lockScreen** property to false on **idle**.

COMMENTS

You can use the **lockScreen** property to control whether the user sees changes that are made during a handler. For example, if your handler visits another card and then returns, setting the **lockScreen** to true prevents the user from seeing (and perhaps being confused by) the card switches. Since drawing screen updates takes time, setting the **lockScreen** to true also speeds up handlers that cause visible changes.

The following handler creates a new card with several default values filled in. It locks the screen while filling in the values so they all appear at once:

```
on fillNewCard
   set the lockScreen to true    -- stops updates
   doMenu "New Card"             -- this doesn't show yet
   repeat with i = 1 to the number of fields
      put the short name of field i into field i
      -- since the screen is locked, user can't see this happening
   end repeat
   set the lockScreen to false  -- now the screen updates
end fillNewcard
```

You can also use the **lock screen** and **unlock screen** commands to set the **lockScreen** property.

Whether the screen is locked has no effect on the message box or the cursor.

Be kind to users: If you're leaving the screen locked for more than a second or two, be sure to set the **cursor** property to `watch` or `busy` so your users know something is happening. It's easy to assume the system has somehow hung when it seems that nothing is happening on the screen—which is the visual impression when the screen is locked.

Locking the screen more than once: HyperTalk keeps count of the times you've set the lockScreen to true. Locking an already-locked screen is harmless, but each lock must be balanced with an unlock; if you lock the screen twice and then unlock it once, the display remains locked.

Setting the **lockScreen** to false forces HyperCard to update the screen.

ALSO SEE

lock screen command; **lockRecent** property; **unlock screen** command

lockText property

FORMS

```
set [the] lockText of field to {true|false}
set the lockText of the target to true
set the lockText of field ID 23 to false
set the lockText of me to not the hilite of button "Edit"
```

ACTION

The **lockText** property determines whether the user can edit text in a field.

Setting the **lockText** is equivalent to setting the Lock Text checkbox in the field's Info dialog. By default, the **lockText** of newly created fields is false.

COMMENTS

The following handler toggles the **lockText** of a field when you Command-click on it:

```
on mouseDown -- in stack, background, or card script
  if word 2 of the name of the target is "field" ¬
  and the commandKey is down then
    set the lockText of the target to not the lockText of the target
  end if
end mouseDown
```

The *field* must be in the current stack.

When a field's **lockText** is false, if the active tool is the browse tool and the **userLevel** is 2 or above, the following things are true:

- The pointer changes to an I-beam when it's over the field.
- Clicking in the field sends the **openField** message and does not send **mouseDown**, **mouseDoubleClick**, **mouseDown**, or **mouseStillDown** messages (unless you hold down the Command key while clicking).
- The field is in the tabbing order.

When the **lockText** is true:

- The pointer doesn't change when it's over the field.
- Clicking on the field sends **mouseDown**, **mouseUp**, **mouseStillDown**, and **mouseDoubleClick** messages.
- You can't edit text in the field (although you can still change it using the **put** command).
- The field is removed from the tabbing order.

Editing, cantModify, and userModify: When the **cantModify** of the current stack is true and the **userModify** is false, you can select text in an unlocked field and copy it, but attempting to change it causes an error dialog. If the **userModify** is true, you can make changes, but they're discarded when HyperCard goes to another card.

ALSO SEE

cantModify property; **mouseDoubleClick** message; **mouseDown** message; **mouseStillDown** message; **mouseUp** message; **send** keyword; **userModify** property

---

log2 function

FORMS

```
[the] log2 of number
log2(number)
log2(1024) -- returns 10: 2^10 = 1024
the log2 of field "Numeric Value"
```

ACTION

The **log2** function returns the base-2 logarithm of the *number*.

COMMENTS

You can use the **log2** function to compute a logarithm on any base. The following handler returns the base-10 log of a value:

```
function log theValue
    return log2(theValue)/log2(10)
end log
```

You call it like this:

```
get log(100) -- returns 2
```

You can write a similar, more general function to produce logarithms on any base:

```
function logX value,base -- thanks to Giovanni Paoletti
    return log2(value)/log2(base)
end logX
```

ALSO SEE

exp2 function; **ln** function

---

longWindowTitles property

FORMS

```
set [the] longWindowTitles [of HyperCard] to {true|false}
set the longWindowTitles to true
```

ACTION

The **longWindowTitles** property determines whether the name that appears in the title bar of stack windows is the stack's full pathname or just its filename.

The default setting for **longWindowTitles** is false, meaning that only the filename appears in the title bar of a stack window.

COMMENTS

Setting the **longWindowTitles** property to true is useful during development, when you may need to know which version of a stack you're working with.

The default setting of this property corresponds to standard Macintosh user interface practice: most Macintosh applications show only the filename in each document's title bar. To follow standard practice, you should leave the **longWindowTitles** set to false.

The setting of the **longWindowTitles** affects the window's **name** property and the **windows** function. This example shows one method of checking whether a stack you're going to is already open:

```
on suspendStack
  lock screen
  set the longWindowTitles to true
  get the windows
  set the longWindowTitles to false
  if the destination is in it then
    answer "Destination stack is already open!"
  else
    answer "Destination stack is now opening!"
  end if
  pass suspendStack
end suspendStack
```

Techie alert: An external window can also be affected by this property, if the XCMD or XFCN that controls it is written to respect the setting of **longWindowTitles**.

Changes to HyperTalk: In versions of HyperCard before 2.0, the **longWindowTitles** property does not exist, and all window titles are in the long form.

ALSO SEE

windows function

---

mark command

Introduced in version 2.0
Last changed in version 2.2

FORMS

```
mark {card|all cards}
mark cards where condition
```

```
mark cards by finding [international] [findForm] findString [in field]
mark this card
mark card "Later List"
mark all cards
mark cards where the hilite of background button "Frequent Flyer" is true
mark cards where field "Breed" contains "Lab"
mark cards by finding "Lab" in field "Breed" -- same as above, but faster
mark cards by finding chars lowerLimit
mark cards by finding word myWord in field theDictionary
mark cards by finding international string "é"
```

ACTION

The **mark** command sets the **marked** property of the specified card or cards to true. It is equivalent to turning on the Card Marked checkbox in the Card Info dialog. It has no effect on cards that are already marked.

You can't mark cards in a locked stack.

COMMENTS

Use the **mark** command to single out specific cards for later action such as printing, display, or further filtering. The following example prints all the recipes in a recipe stack that contain garlic and are low in fat:

```
on greatCuisine
   unmark all cards -- clear results of any previous "mark"
   mark cards where ("Garlic" in field "Ingredients") ¬
   and (the hilite of background button "Low Fat" is true)
   print marked cards
end greatCuisine
```

The **mark** command has the following forms:

- **mark *card***: Marks the card you specify. The *card* must be a valid descriptor of a card in the current stack.

- **mark all cards:** Marks all cards in the current stack.

- **mark cards where *condition***: Marks all cards on which *condition* occurs. The *condition* can be any HyperTalk expression that evaluates to true or false: a mathematical equation, a statement using **contains**, a property or function that evaluates to true or false, etc. The **mark** command ignores cards on which the *condition* can't be tested because a field or button mentioned in the *condition* isn't on that card.

- **mark cards by finding:** Marks all cards found by a search. You can limit the search to a specific field, and specify a *findForm*: **finding normal**, **finding chars**, **finding word**, **finding string**, or **finding whole**. (For a complete explanation of these forms, see the **find** command.) If you don't specify a *findForm*, the **finding normal** form is used.

  To make the search distinguish international (Option-key) characters from their ASCII counterparts, use the **finding international** *findForm* option.

Because the form **mark cards by finding** uses the same hint bits as the **find** command, it's much faster than the equivalent form using **mark cards where**:

```
mark cards by finding "Kamins" in field "Author" -- much faster
mark cards where "Kamins" is in field "Author"    -- slower
```

Combining mark and unmark: The **unmark** command takes the same forms as **mark**, so you can combine **mark** and **unmark** commands to get a filtered set. This example shows how to implement a Boolean search (a search that lets you use "and", "or", or "but not" to specify the set of things you want to find):

```
on findBoolean firstString,boolean,secondString,fieldName
   unmark all cards
   if boolean is "and" then
     if fieldName is empty then
       mark cards by finding firstString && secondString
     else
       mark cards by finding firstString && secondString in field fieldName
     end if
   else if boolean is "or" then
     if fieldName is empty then
       mark cards by finding firstString
       mark cards by finding secondString
     else
       mark cards by finding firstString in field fieldName
       mark cards by finding secondString in field fieldName
     end if
   else if boolean is "but not" then
     if fieldName is empty then
       mark cards by finding firstString
       unmark cards by finding secondString
     else
       mark cards by finding firstString in field fieldName
       unmark cards by finding secondString in field fieldName
     end if
   else
     return "Second parameter must be 'and', 'or', or 'but not'"
   end if
end findBoolean
```

You might call the above handler like this, in a stack containing newspaper clippings:

```
findBoolean "Apple","but not","Computer",field "Article Text"
show marked cards
```

This riffles through all the articles that mention "Apple", but don't contain the word "Computer".

HyperCard historical tidbit: Originally, this feature was to be called "selected cards", but the name was changed to "marked" to avoid confusion with **the selection** and to introduce a pun on "marked cards".

Changes to HyperTalk: In versions before 2.2, you cannot use the **international** option with **mark cards by finding**.

ALSO SEE

debug command; **dontSearch** property; **find** command; **go** command; **marked** property; **number of object** function; **print card** command; **show cards** command; **unmark** command

---

markChar property

Introduced in version 2.0

FORMS

```
set [the] markChar of menuItem of menu to character
set the markChar of menuItem 7 of menu "Bookmarks" to "•"
set the markChar of menuItem "Clipboard" of menu "Edit" to numToChar(19)
set the markChar of menuItem x of menu y to empty -- clears markChar
```

ACTION

The **markChar** property of menu items determines what character (if any) appears to the left of the menu item.

COMMENTS

You can use the **markChar** property to show that some option is currently operating or to set off particular menu items, in accordance with the Apple user interface guidelines.

The *menuItem* is a descriptor of an item in the specified *menu*. Trying to mark a menu item that doesn't exist causes HyperCard to display a script error dialog and abort the rest of the handler.

Special characters available: The Chicago font contains a few useful symbols you can access with the **numToChar** function:

⌘	numToChar(16)
⌘	numToChar(17)
✓	numToChar(18)
◆	numToChar(19)
🍎	numToChar(20)

The **checkMark** property is a special case of the **markChar** property. The statement `set the checkMark of menuItem to true` is equivalent to `set the markChar of menuItem to numToChar(18)`. Setting the **markChar** of a menu item to something other than empty sets its **checkMark** property to true.

Limitations of markChar: The **markChar** of all menu items reverts to false when the menu bar is reset. You can't set a **markChar** property for items in the Apple, Tools, Font, Pattern, Applications, or Help menus. You can set a **markChar** for items in the Style menu, but the setting is ignored and the command has no effect.

ALSO SEE

checkMark property; **reset menubar** command

---

marked property   Introduced in version 2.0

FORMS

`set [the] marked of` *card* `to {true|false}`

`set the marked of last card to true`

`if not the marked of this card then next repeat`

ACTION

The **marked** property describes whether the specified card has been marked for later action.

Setting the **marked** is equivalent to toggling the Card Marked checkbox in the Card Info dialog.

COMMENTS

The **marked** property is usually used to tag a set of cards for future action such as printing, sorting, or further filtering. You can also set a card's **marked** property using the **mark** and **unmark** commands.

The following handler appears to "turn down" the corner of the stack window whenever you go to a marked card. The turned-down corner (which is actually a button with an appropriate icon) serves as a quick reminder to the user that the card has been marked:

```
on openCard
   if the marked of this card then show background button "Dogear"
   else hide background button "Dogear"
end openCard
```

ALSO SEE

go command; **mark** command; **print card** command; **show card** command; **sort** command; **unmark** command

---

max function   Introduced in version 1.0

FORMS

`max(`*numberList*`)`

```
max(3,4,5)
max(it) -- it contains a comma-separated list of numbers
max(item 14 to 24 of scoresList)
max(firstTestRun,secondTestRun,thirdTestRun)
```

ACTION

The **max** function returns the largest number from a comma-separated list of numbers.

COMMENTS

The following function computes the greatest common divisor of two numbers, using Euclid's algorithm:

```
function GCD firstNumber,secondNumber
   -- compute greatest common divisor using Euclid's algorithm
   put max(firstNumber,secondNumber) into upperBound
   put min(firstNumber,secondNumber) into lowerBound
   repeat
      put upperBound mod lowerBound into remainder
      put lowerBound into upperBound
      put remainder into lowerBound
      if remainder is 0 then exit repeat
   end repeat
   return upperBound
end GCD
```

The *numberList* consists of one or more numbers (or containers that contain a number), separated by commas. The numbers can be positive or negative. If any item in the *numberList* is not a number, or if the *numberList* is empty, HyperCard puts up a script error dialog.

You cannot combine single and list values. For example, if the variable theList contains a list of numbers, you can't get the value of max(theList,23,myVariable). Trying to combine lists and numbers this way provokes a script error. This is the way to create a combined list:

```
get max(value(theList & comma & 23 & comma & myVariable))
```

ALSO SEE

average function; **min** function; **sum** function

---

menuMessage property

Introduced in version 2.0

FORMS

```
set [the] {menuMessage|menuMsg} of menuItem to messageName
```

```
set the menuMessage of menuItem "Full Power" of menu "Action" to "meltDown"
set the menuMessage of last menuItem of second menu to answer "No quitting!"
set the menuMessage of item 1 of menu 1 to empty -- clears menu message
```

ACTION

The **menuMessage** property describes what message, if any, HyperCard sends in addition to **doMenu** when you choose the specified menu item.

COMMENTS

The **menuMessage** property makes it simpler and easier to assign handlers to your custom menu items, and to override the usual actions of HyperCard's own menus.

A menu item can have only one menu message assigned to it; assigning another **menuMessage** replaces the first one. Most often, the **menuMessage** is a custom message that triggers a handler.

The following example, which belongs in the script of the Home stack, creates a History menu. You can add any card to the History menu by choosing Add (or pressing Command-A). Thereafter, you can choose that card's name from the History menu to return to it.

```
on makeHistory -- make sure to call this from the startup handler
   create menu "History"
   put "Add This Card,Delete This Card,-" into menu "History"
   set the commandChar of menuItem "Add" of menu "History" to "A"
   set the menuMessage of menuItem "Add" of menu "History" ¬
   to "addToHistory"
   set the commandChar of menuItem "Delete" of menu "History" to "D"
   set the menuMessage of menuItem "Delete" of menu "History" ¬
   to "deleteFromHistory"
end makeHistory


on addToHistory
   if there is no menu "History" then beep
   if the number of menuItems of menu "History" ≥ 64 then
     beep
     answer "The History menu is full." with "Sorry"
     exit addToHistory
   end if
   put the short name of this card after menu "History"
   set the menuMessage of last menuItem of menu "History" ¬
   to "go to" && the long name of this card
end addToHistory


on deleteFromHistory
   if there is no menu "History" then beep
   get the short name of this card
   repeat with x = 4 to the number of menuItems of menu "History"
```

```
      if the name of menuItem x of menu "History" is it then
         delete menuItem x from menu "History"
         exit deleteFromHistory -- done
      end if
   end repeat
   -- if we got this far, the current card isn't in the menu
   beep
   answer "This card is not in the History menu."
end deleteFromHistory
```

You can also assign a **menuMessage** to a menu item at the time you create it, by using the with menuMessage parameter of the **put into menu** command.

The menuMessage, doMenu, and the message path: Whenever you choose a menu item, whether it's a standard HyperCard item or a custom item created with **put into menu**, HyperCard sends a **doMenu** message to the current card. If the **doMenu** message works its way through the whole message path without being trapped by a handler, HyperCard then sends the **menuMessage** (if any) associated with the item to the current card.

If the item is a standard HyperCard menu item, HyperCard performs the normal behavior for the item, if the **doMenu** message isn't trapped and the item has no **menuMessage** assigned to it.

While HyperCard lets you override the normal behavior of standard menu items, doing so can confuse the user. If you want to keep the user from choosing a particular item, it's usually better to disable it by setting the **enabled** property to false.

ALSO SEE
doMenu command/message; **enabled** property; **put into menu** command

---

menus function

Introduced in version 2.0

FORMS
```
the menus
menus()
put the menus into card button "Menus..."
answer the menus
```

ACTION
The **menus** function returns a return-separated list of the menu names currently in the menu bar. The menus are listed from left to right; usually, the first menu is Apple, and the last is Application (if using System 7) or Style (if using System 6).

COMMENTS
Use the **menus** function when you need to check whether a menu already exists, or when you

want to perform some action on each menu in the menu bar.

The following handler checks whether a menu already exists before trying to create it:

```
on makeUtilities
   if "Utilities" is in the menus then exit makeUtilities
   create menu "Utilities"
   makeUtilsItems -- handler creates individual menu items
end makeUtilities2
```

When the menus changes: The menu bar, and consequently the list returned by the **menus** function, changes when you create or delete a menu and when you switch between paint tools and other tools. It may also change when you issue a **reset menubar** command or when you change the **userLevel**.

The following handler implements an extended clipboard which lets you paste the last five text selections that have been cut or copied:

```
on doMenu theItem,theMenu
   global text1,text2,text3,text4,text5 -- last 5 selections cut or copied
   if theMenu is "Paste" then -- custom Paste menu
     if the selectedChunk is empty then answer "Nowhere to paste!"
     else do "put text" & word 2 of theItem && "into the selectedChunk"
     exit doMenu
   else if theItem is "Cut Text" or theItem is "Copy Text" then
     -- update the paste globals to include the text to be cut/copied
     repeat with i = 4 down to 1 -- move over by 1
        do "put text" & it && "into text" & i + 1
     end repeat
     put the selection into text1
     if "Paste" is not in the menus then -- create Paste menu
        create menu "Paste"
        repeat with thisItem = 1 to 5
           put "Text Selection" && thisItem after menu "Paste"
        end repeat
     end if
     repeat with thisItem = 1 to 5
        get value("text" & thisItem)
        if the number of words in it > 1 then get word 1 of it & "..."
        if it is not empty then get "(" & it & ")"
        set the name of menuItem thisItem of menu "Paste" ¬
        to "Paste" && thisItem && it
     end repeat
   end if
   pass doMenu
end doMenu
```

Only HyperCard's menus are returned: The **menus** function returns the names of all HyperCard's menus—including both the standard menus and custom menus you create with **create menu**—but it ignores menus belonging to desk accessories or other ancillary programs.

ALSO SEE

create menu command; **delete menu** command; **id** property; **name** property; **put into menu** command; **reset menubar** command

---

messageWatcher property   Introduced in version 2.0

FORMS

```
set [the] messageWatcher [of HyperCard] to messageWatcherXCMD
set the messageWatcher to "MyMessages"
put the messageWatcher into currentWatcher
```

ACTION

The **messageWatcher** global property is the name of the message watcher window. This window appears when you choose Message Watcher from the Debug menu while in the debugger.

By default, the **messageWatcher** property is set to `MessageWatcher`, which is HyperCard's built-in message watcher window.

COMMENTS

You can set the **messageWatcher** property to use a custom message watcher you've written and installed in HyperCard's resource fork or a stack's resource fork. Message watchers, including the one built in to HyperCard, are implemented as XCMDs.

If you try to set the **messageWatcher** to an XCMD that's not present, HyperCard puts up an error dialog.

In practice, this property is seldom used; most scriptwriters use the built-in message watcher.

ALSO SEE

debug checkpoint command; **debugger** property; **hBarLoc** property; **scriptEditor** property; **variableWatcher** property; **vBarLoc** property

---

min function   Introduced in version 1.0

FORMS

```
min(numberList)
```

```
min(22,17,834)
min(message) -- message box contains a comma-separated list of numbers
min(item 1 to 7 of field "Test Scores")
```

ACTION

The **min** function returns the smallest number from a comma-separated list of numbers.

COMMENTS

The **min** function works only on items. The following example illustrates how to find the minimum line of an expression:

```
function minLine theList
   put line 1 of theList into theResult
   repeat with x = 2 to the number of lines in theList
      put min(line x of theList,theResult) into theResult
   end repeat
   return theResult
end minLine
```

The *numberList* consists of one or more numbers (or containers that contain a number), separated by commas. The numbers can be positive or negative. If any item of the *numberList* is not a number, or if the *numberList* is empty, HyperCard puts up a script error dialog.

You cannot combine single and list values; for example, if the variable `theList` contains a list of numbers, you can't get the value of `min(theList,23,myVariable)`. **Trying to combine lists and numbers this way provokes a script error.** You can use this method to find the minimum of a combined list:

```
get min(value(theList & comma & 23 & comma & myVariable))
```

Using min and max to determine a range: If your stack uses a number that was entered by a user or imported from some other source, your handler should check the number to make sure that it's within the appropriate range. For example, a handler that creates new buttons might ask the user how many buttons to create. The handler should then check the data to make sure that what the user entered is reasonable.

The following example shows how to use the **min** function to make sure a number is between two other numbers. The function returns the upper bound if the number you gave it is too large. It returns the lower bound if the number is too small. Otherwise, it simply returns the number:

```
function constrainedToRange theValue,lowerBound,upperBound
   return min(max(lowerBound,theValue),upperBound)
end constrainedToRange
```

ALSO SEE

average function; **max** function; **sum** function

mouse function

FORMS

```
the mouse
mouse()
repeat until the mouse is down
if the mouse is up then exit to HyperCard
```

ACTION

The **mouse** function returns the state of the mouse button (up or down).

COMMENTS

Use the **mouse** function when you need to check the state of the mouse button from within a handler. If you want to perform a particular action when the user clicks the mouse, use the **mouseUp** and **mouseDown** messages. If you want to know whether the mouse has been clicked but don't care whether the button is up or down, use the **mouseClick** function.

The **mouse** function returns one of the constants down or up, depending on whether the mouse button is being pressed or not.

The following handler repeatedly draws a line from the button holding the handler to wherever the pointer currently is, so if you move the pointer around the card, the handler draws a succession of radial lines. It stops drawing when you release the mouse button:

```
on mouseDown
   reset paint
   choose line tool
   repeat until the mouse is up
      drag from the location of me to the mouseLoc
   end repeat
   choose browse tool
end mouseDown
```

ALSO SEE

mouseClick function; **mouseDown** message; **mouseUp** message

mouseClick function

FORMS

```
the mouseClick
mouseClick()
wait until the mouseClick -- wait for the user to click
```

ACTION

The **mouseClick** function returns either true or false, depending on whether the mouse has been clicked since the last **idle** message.

Calling the **mouseClick** function removes the most recent click from the event buffer.

COMMENTS

Since (unlike the **mouseDown** and **mouseUp** messages) **the mouseClick** can be accessed from within a handler, it's useful when you want to let the user trigger the next action with a click. The following example shows help text and prompts the user to click when finished reading it:

```
on mouseUp
   show card field "Help Text"
   put "Click anywhere to continue..." into message box
   wait until the mouseClick -- same as "...the mouseClick is true"
   hide message box
   hide card field "Help Text"
end mouseUp
```

Clearing the click buffer: The **mouseClick** function returns true if there's a click in the event queue and, as part of its action, it removes the click from the queue. So you can use **mouseClick** to kill inadvertant clicks.

If you have a **mouseDown** or **mouseUp** handler that takes a long time to run, users may click several times in impatience, triggering the handler to run again. To avoid this, place the line

```
wait while the mouseClick
```

near the end of your handler. The above statement clears out any pending mouse clicks.

The following handler uses the same technique to get rid of any clicks that might accumulate as cards are flashing by. Such stray clicks ordinarily pile up while the handler is running; when it stops, the clicks all take effect on the current card. Needless to say, this can lead to unexpected results if the current card happens to have a button in the clicked location. The following handler tells HyperCard to ignore any extra mouse clicks:

```
on showAnimation
   go to next card
   wait for 20 ticks -- user might click during the 20 tick wait
   go to next card
   wait while the mouseClick -- discard any clicks
end showAnimation
```

ALSO SEE

clickLoc function; **mouse** function; **mouseDoubleClick** message; **mouseDown** message; **mouseUp** message

mouseDoubleClick message

FORMS

```
mouseDoubleClick
```

ACTION

The **mouseDoubleClick** message is sent to a button, locked field, or card when the user double-clicks the element.

COMMENTS

Use the **mouseDoubleClick** message to implement the parts of the standard Macintosh interface that requires double clicks, such as double-clicking an icon to open a corresponding file (as in the Finder). Some people, particularly new, young, or physically disabled users, have trouble double-clicking, so you should provide an alternative method for the function when possible. Double-clicking should be a shortcut, not the only way to do something.

HyperCard considers the user to have double-clicked when:

- The time between the downstrokes of the first and second clicks is within the time set in the Mouse control panel

- The second click is within 4 pixels of the first

- Both clicks are on the same element

The double-click action sends all the following messages:

```
mouseDown            (on the first click)
mouseStillDown       (only if the mouse is held down)
mouseUp              (when the mouse is released)
mouseDoubleClick     (when the mouse is clicked again)
```

The second click does not send **mouseDown** or **mouseUp** messages.

If the user clicks quickly several times, every second click triggers a **mouseDoubleClick** message.

Behavior with unlocked fields: When you click in an unlocked field, normally no mouse messages are sent; the insertion point simply appears where you clicked. If you're holding down the Command key, however, the unlocked field receives a **mouseDown** message immediately followed by **mouseUp**, whether or not the user has released the mouse button. If you click again within the time limit, HyperCard also sends **mouseDoubleClick**.

Old HyperCard versions: In versions of HyperCard before 2.2, the **mouseDoubleClick** message doesn't exist. However, you can check for double clicks with a handler like the following:

```
on mouseDown
   wait 20 ticks -- 1/3 second, a good double-click time
```

```
      if the mouseClick then
         -- do double-click action
      else
         -- do single-click action
      end if
   end mouseDown
```

ALSO SEE

click command; **mouse** function; **mouseDown** message; **mouseStillDown** message; **mouseUp** message

---

mouseDown message   Introduced in version 1.0

FORMS

mouseDown

ACTION

The **mouseDown** message is sent to the clicked object (button, field, or card) when the user clicks anywhere in the current stack window.

The **mouseDown** message is not sent to unlocked fields, unless you hold down the Command key while clicking the field.

COMMENTS

For most functional purposes, the **mouseDown** and **mouseUp** messages are interchangeable, particularly in buttons. Handlers that trap either message respond when the user clicks. However, by convention, **mouseUp** handlers (which don't act until the user releases the mouse button) are used if the clicked object is one that highlights automatically. If the object doesn't highlight when clicked, use **mouseDown** instead.

If you click an area of the screen where there is more than one overlapping button or field, the **mouseDown** message is sent to the topmost part directly under the click point. If you click an area where there is no visible button or field, the **mouseDown** message is sent to the current card.

The following example, which belongs in a card, background, or stack script, lets you control all the buttons with a single handler, instead of having to copy the handler into the script of each button. The handler links each card button with a corresponding card field:

```
   on mouseDown
      -- if this handler is in the card script, it affects all
      -- buttons in that card; if it's in the stack script, it
      -- affects all buttons in that stack.
      if word 1 to 2 of the name of the target is "card button" then
         get the short name of the target
         show card field it
```

```
        wait until the mouseClick
        hide card field it
    end if
end mouseDown
```

Behavior with unlocked fields: When you click in an unlocked field, normally no mouse messages are sent; the insertion point simply appears where you clicked. If you click while holding down the Command key, however, the unlocked field receives a **mouseDown** message immediately followed by **mouseUp**, whether or not the user has released the mouse button.

No **mouseDown** message is sent when the user clicks in the scroll bar of a scrolling field.

Using mouseDown to fake autohiliting: Normally, you use the **autoHilite** property to highlight your buttons when they're clicked. However, under some circumstances—when you want to retain the text selection after clicking the button, or when you want to show that the button is active with some method other than the black/white inversion that the **autoHilite** uses—you may want to emulate the action of an **autoHilite** button. The following somewhat complex but useful handler lets you do so:

```
on mouseDown -- in button, card, background or stack script
    put the selectedChunk into theSelection -- preserve selection
    set the hilite of the target to true
    -- you can substitute any other action for the above line - for
    -- example, changing the button style to indicate hilite, or
    -- setting its icon to a hilited version.
    repeat until the mouse is up
        if the mouseLoc is within the rect of the target
        then set the hilite of the target to true -- see above comment
        else set the hilite of the target to false
        -- or change the style, icon, etc to the unhilited state
    end repeat
    if the mouseLoc is within the rect of the target
    then send mouseUp to the target
    set the hilite of the target to false -- see above comments
    select theSelection -- restore original selection
    exit to HyperCard -- see the mouseUp message for why
end mouseDown
```

A button with this handler will highlight when the user clicks it and unhighlight when the mouse button is released. It will also unhighlight if the pointer is dragged off it while the button is still down, and rehighlight if the pointer is dragged back on. If the mouse button is released while the mouse is still over the button, the button's actions are performed; otherwise, no **mouseUp** message is sent. This is exactly the way a standard Macintosh button works, and will improve the feel and consistency of your stacks where you need to keep the text selection alive across button clicks.

Clearing the click buffer: If you have a **mouseDown** or **mouseUp** handler that takes a long time to run, users may click several times in impatience, inadvertantly triggering the handler to run again. To avoid this, place the line

```
wait while the mouseClick
```

near the end of your handler. The above statement clears out any pending mouse clicks.

ALSO SEE

click command; **mouse** function; **mouseDoubleClick** message; **mouseStillDown** message; **mouseUp** message

---

mouseDownInPicture message   Introduced in version 2.0

FORMS

```
mouseDownInPicture windowName,clickLocation
mouseDownInPicture "Hello Kitty","175,70"
```

ACTION

The **mouseDownInPicture** message is sent to the current card when the user clicks inside a window created by the **picture** command.

COMMENTS

The following handler, when placed in the Home stack script, closes any picture window when the user clicks inside it:

```
on mouseDownInPicture thePictureName
   close window thePictureName
end mouseDownInPicture
```

The *windowName* is the name of the picture window.

The *clickLocation* consists of two integers separated by a comma. The first item is the horizontal distance in pixels from the left edge of the window to the clicked point. The second item is the vertical distance from the top edge of the window (that is, just below the window's title bar) to the clicked point.

If the user clicks in the window's title bar or scroll bars (if any), no **mouseDownInPicture** message is sent.

ALSO SEE

location property; **mouseDown** message; **mouseUpInPicture** message; **picture** command

mouseEnter message

Introduced in version 1.0

FORMS

```
mouseEnter
```

ACTION

The **mouseEnter** message is sent to a button or field when the pointer moves into it.

COMMENTS

You can use a **mouseEnter** handler to change the appearance of an element depending on whether the pointer is inside it. This handler changes the cursor when the pointer moves inside a clickable area:

```
on mouseEnter -- in card, background, or stack script
   if word 1 to 2 of the name of the target is "card button" then
      set the cursor to "Clickable" -- an appropriate shape
      repeat while the mouseLoc is within the rect of the target
         if the mouseClick then send mouseDown to the target
      end repeat
   end if
end mouseEnter
```

When you move to another card, if the pointer is located within a button or field on the destination card, **mouseEnter** is sent to that button or field. However, if you're moving from card to card within the same background, HyperCard doesn't send **mouseEnter** to background buttons or fields, even if the mouse happens to be within one of them.

ALSO SEE

mouseLeave message; **mouseWithin** message

---

mouseH function

Introduced in version 1.2

FORMS

```
the mouseH
mouseH()
if the mouseH > the right of me then go to next card
```

ACTION

The **mouseH** function returns the distance in pixels from the pointer to the left edge of the card window.

COMMENTS

The **mouseH** is equal to item 1 of **the mouseLoc**.

This example, which goes in a background or stack script, lets the user move from card to card simply by moving the mouse to the edge of the stack window. It's especially effective in stacks that are meant to be leafed through, like card-flipping animations:

```
on idle
   if the mouseH ≤ 50 then
      visual effect wipe right
      go to previous card
   else if the width of card window - the mouseH ≤ 50 then
      visual effect wipe left
      go to next card
   end if
end idle
```

The following handler returns the location of the mouse in global coordinates. (Global coordinates are measured from the edges of the screen instead of the current stack window.)

```
function globalMouseLoc
   put the mouseH + the left of card window into globalH
   put the mouseV + the top of card window into globalV
   return globalH & "," & globalV
end globalMouseLoc
```

You can use this function to position the card window at the mouse location on a large screen:

```
show card window at globalMouseLoc()
```

ALSO SEE
clickH function; **mouseLoc** function; **mouseV** function

---

mouseLeave message   Introduced in version 1.0

FORMS
mouseLeave

ACTION
The **mouseLeave** message is sent to a button or field when the pointer moves out of it.

COMMENTS
The **mouseLeave** message is usually used in conjunction with **mouseEnter**.

The following example is used in a visual dictionary stack. Each card contains a picture with transparent buttons over each part of the object depicted. When the user moves the pointer to a part of the picture, the name of that part appears in a field:

```
on mouseEnter -- in card, background, or stack script
   if word 1 to 2 of the name of the target is "card button"
   then put the short name of the target into field "Name"
end mouseEnter


on mouseLeave
   put the short name of this card into field "Name" -- object name
end mouseLeave
```

ALSO SEE

mouseEnter message; **mouseWithin** message

mouseLoc function   Introduced in version 1.0

FORMS

```
the mouseLoc
mouseLoc()
if the mouseLoc is within the rect of me then beep
palette "Utilities",the mouseLoc
```

ACTION

The **mouseLoc** function returns the current location of the mouse pointer.

COMMENTS

The mouseLoc returns a point: two integers separated by a comma, where the first number is the horizontal distance in pixels from the left edge of the card window and the second is the vertical distance from the top edge. (The top of the card window is just below the title bar.) The two items of this point are equal to the **mouseH** and **mouseV** functions, respectively.

The following handler tells you continually where the mouse pointer is, and ends when you click:

```
on showMouseLoc
   repeat until the mouseClick
      put "The mouse is at" && the mouseLoc
   end repeat
end showMouseLoc
```

This example reports what parts (fields and buttons) the pointer is currently over:

```
on mouseUp
   repeat until the mouseClick
      get the mouseLoc
      put empty into partsList
```

```
         repeat with i = 1 to the number of card parts
            if it is within the rect of card part i
            then put the name of card part i & comma after partsList
         end repeat
         repeat with i = 1 to the number of background parts
            if it is within the rect of background part i
            then put the name of background part i & comma after partsList
         end repeat
         if partsList is empty then put "No buttons or fields here."
         else
            delete last char of partsList -- the comma
            put partsList
         end if
      end repeat
   end mouseUp
```

The mouseLoc is not necessarily the clickLoc: The location of the last mouse click is not
necessarily the current mouse position, because the user might have moved the mouse since
the last click. To get the position of the most recent mouse click, use the **clickLoc** function.

ALSO SEE
clickLoc function; **mouseH** function; **mouseV** function

---

mouseStillDown message   Introduced in version 1.0

FORMS
```
mouseStillDown
```

ACTION
The **mouseStillDown** message is repeatedly sent to the object the pointer is over—a button,
locked field, or card—while the mouse button is held down.

COMMENTS
If you click an area of the screen where there is more than one overlapping button or field,
the **mouseStillDown** message is sent to the frontmost part directly under the click point. If
you click an area where there is no button or field, **mouseStillDown** is sent to the current card.

The **mouseStillDown** messages are sent continuously to the same object as long as you hold
the mouse button down, even if you move the pointer out of the object that was clicked on.

The **mouseStillDown** message is never sent to an unlocked field, even if you hold down
the Command key while clicking it.

The following example, which belongs in a button handler, scans the cards in the current
background until the mouse button is released:

```
on mouseStillDown
  visual effect scroll left
  go to next card of this background
end mouseStillDown
```

ALSO SEE

click command; **mouse** function; **mouseDoubleClick** message; **mouseDown** message; **mouseUp** message

---

mouseUp message   Introduced in version 1.0

FORMS

mouseUp

ACTION

The **mouseUp** message is sent to the object the pointer is over—a button, locked field, or card—when you release the mouse button.

If the mouse button was pressed while the pointer was outside a button or field, moved inside the object, and then released, no **mouseUp** message is sent.

COMMENTS

Usually, you use a **mouseUp** handler to trigger button actions. For most functional purposes, **mouseDown** and **mouseUp** are interchangeable, particularly in buttons: both messages respond when the user clicks. However, by convention, **mouseUp** handlers (which don't act until the user releases the mouse button) are used when the clicked object highlights automatically. If the object doesn't highlight when clicked, use **mouseDown**.

Moving between cards: If a **mouseDown** handler forces a change to another card (for instance, if the handler contains a **go** command), the corresponding **mouseUp** may follow one of several paths:

- If the user clicked a button or field, and the original card contains a **mouseUp** handler, the **mouseUp** goes first to the part clicked, then to the original card, and on through the message path from there.

- If the target of the **mouseDown** message was a card (rather than a button or field), the **mouseUp** is sent to the destination card.

- If neither the original card, background, nor stack script contains a **mouseUp** handler, the **mouseUp** goes first to the part originally clicked, then to the destination card, and on through the message path.

MouseDown/mouseUp anomaly

Normally, HyperCard sends **mouseUp** only if the pointer is still within the object when the mouse button is released. However, if the object's script contains a **mouseDown** handler that includes a **wait** or **repeat until** statement (such as `wait until the mouse is up`), and you release the mouse button while the handler is executing, the **mouseUp** is sent even if the pointer is outside the object when you release the mouse button.

Clearing the click buffer: If you have a **mouseUp** or **mouseDown** handler that takes a long time to finish, users may click several times in impatience, triggering the handler to run again. To avoid this, place the line

```
wait while the mouseClick
```

near the end of your handler. The above statement clears out any pending mouse clicks.

ALSO SEE

click command; **mouse** function; **mouseDown** message; **mouseDoubleClick** message

---

mouseUpInPicture message

Introduced in version 2.0

FORMS

```
mouseUpInPicture windowName,clickLocation
mouseUpInPicture "Sanrio","400,30"
```

ACTION

The **mouseUpInPicture** message is sent to the current card when the user releases the mouse button after clicking inside a window created by the **picture** command.

COMMENTS

The *windowName* is the name of the picture window.

The *clickLocation* consists of two integers separated by a comma. The first item is the horizontal distance in pixels from the left edge of the window to the clicked point. The second item is the vertical distance from the top edge of the window (that is, just below the window's title bar) to the clicked point.

If the user clicks in the window's title bar or scroll bars (if any), no **mouseUpInPicture** message is sent.

ALSO SEE

location property; **mouseDownInPicture** message; **mouseUp** message; **picture** command

mouseV function

FORMS

```
the mouseV
mouseV()
if the mouseV < the top of me then put true into mouseIsAboveMe
```

ACTION

The **mouseV** function returns the distance in pixels from the pointer to the top edge of the card window, just below the title bar of the window.

COMMENTS

The **mouseV** is equal to item 2 of **the mouseLoc**.

This example shows the menu bar when you move the mouse to the top of the screen, and hides it when you move it away from the top. This is very convenient when your stack window covers the entire screen, but you still want to make the menu bar available:

```
on idle
  if the top of card window + the mouseV ≤ 20 then show menubar
  else hide menubar
end idle
```

The following handler returns the location of the mouse in global coordinates. (Global coordinates are measured from the edges of the current screen instead of the current stack window.)

```
function globalMouseLoc
  put the mouseH + the left of card window into globalH
  put the mouseV + the top of card window into globalV
  return globalH & "," & globalV
end globalMouseLoc
```

ALSO SEE

clickV function; **mouseH** function; **mouseLoc** function

---

mouseWithin message

FORMS

```
mouseWithin
```

ACTION

The **mouseWithin** message is sent repeatedly while the pointer is within the rectangle of a button, field, or card.

COMMENTS

HyperCard interleaves **mouseWithin** messages with **idle** messages. First a **mouseWithin** is sent, then an **idle**, then another **mouseWithin**, and so on, for as long as the pointer remains within the object.

The **mouseWithin** message is not sent while handlers are executing.

ALSO SEE

idle message; **mouseEnter** message; **mouseLeave** message

---

moveWindow message   Introduced in version 2.0

FORMS

```
moveWindow
```

ACTION

The **moveWindow** message is sent to the current card when the frontmost stack window is moved, either manually or from a handler.

COMMENTS

The **moveWindow** message is sent immediately after the window is moved, so you cannot prevent the user from changing the window location by trapping **moveWindow**.

The following example belongs to a museum catalog stack. Each card describes an item in the collection. A color picture of the item (actually a window created by the **picture** command) floats in the left half of the stack window. (See Figure III.32.) The following handler moves the picture window along with the stack window to keep them lined up:

```
on moveWindow -- in stack script
  if there is a window (field "PICT Resource Name") then
    get the topLeft of this window
    add 15 to item 1 of it -- inset 15 pixels from left
    add 25 to item 2 of it -- inset 25 pixels from top
    set the topLeft of window (field "PICT Resource Name") to it
  end
end moveWindow
```

The following actions trigger a **moveWindow** message:

- Dragging the window by its title bar
- Clicking the zoom box (if this changes the window's **location**)
- Changing the window's location by changing its **rectangle** or **location** property;
- Changing the window's location with the scroll palette
- Changing the **rectangle** of a card in the stack

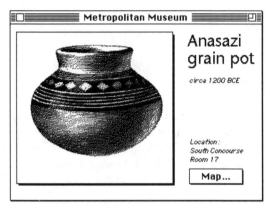

Figure III.32   Catalog with floating picture window

To move a stack window, other than the frontmost one, Command-drag its title bar.

ALSO SEE
height property; **rectangle** property; **sizeWindow** message; **width** property

---

multiple property   Introduced in version 1.0

FORMS
```
set [the] multiple [of HyperCard] to {true|false}
set the multiple to true
if the multiple then set the multiSpace to 10
```

ACTION
The **multiple** property determines whether the line and shape tools produce multiple layered images when the user or a handler draws with them.

Setting the **multiple** property is equivalent to toggling the Draw Multiple item in the Options menu (which can be seen when a paint tool is selected).

COMMENTS
The following tools draw multiple images when the **multiple** is true:

```
line    rectangle    rounded rectangle    oval    regular polygon
```

This example uses the **multiple** to draw concentric rectangles:

```
on drawRectangles
  choose rectangle tool
  set the centered to true
```

```
      set the multiple to true
      set the multiSpace to 5
      set the dragSpeed to 200
      drag from 250,200 to 450,300
      choose browse tool
   end drawRectangles
```

The **multiple** property is false by default, and HyperCard sets it back to false every time you switch from the browse, field, or button tool to a paint tool.

The spacing between successive images is determined by the setting of the **multiSpace** property. If you're using the **drag** command from within a handler instead of drawing manually, you must set the **dragSpeed** property to something other than zero for the **multiple** to have an effect.

ALSO SEE
drag command; **dragSpeed** property; **multiSpace** property

---

multipleLines property   Introduced in version 2.2

FORMS
```
set [the] multipleLines of field to {true|false}
if the multipleLines of field "Hello" then hide field "Hello"
set the multipleLines of card field myField to false
```

ACTION
The **multipleLines** property determines whether a list field—that is, a field with its **autoSelect** property set to true—lets the user select multiple lines by dragging or Shift-clicking.

COMMENTS
The setting of a field's **multipleLines** property has no effect unless its **autoSelect** property is set to true.

ALSO SEE
autoSelect property; **selectedLine** function

---

multiply command   Introduced in version 1.0

FORMS
```
multiply [chunk of] container by divisor
multiply numberOfWeeks by 7
multiply field "Average Assessment" by sagansOfTaxpayers
multiply diameter by pi -- gives circumference of a circle
```

ACTION

The **multiply** command divides the number in a container by another number and puts the resulting product into the container. The original number in the container is lost, since the container is overwritten by the final result. However, the value of the expression being divided into the container is unchanged.

COMMENTS

The following example increases a recipe for a specified number of people:

```
on changeRecipe
   put field "Number of People" into originalNumber
   ask "How many people are you cooking for?"
   if it is empty then exit changeRecipe          -- user cancelled
   if it is originalNumber then exit changeRecipe  -- no change needed
   if it is not an integer then
      beep
      answer it && "is not a legal number!"
      exit changeRecipe
   end if
   put it into field "Number of People"
   divide it by originalNumber
   repeat with thisIngredient = 1 to ¬
   the number of lines of field "Ingredients"
      multiply word 1 of line thisIngredient of field "Ingredients" by it
   end repeat
end changeRecipe
```

The **multiply** command always puts its result into a container. You cannot multiply one number directly by another using **multiply** (use the * operator instead).

The container must contain a number. If you try to multiply a number by a container that contains something other than a number, you will get an error dialog. (You can check a container's contents first with the **is a number** operator.)

You can multiply an empty container by a number; **multiply** acts as though it contained the number zero. Remember, though, that you have to put something into local variables before you can use them. If you have not yet put something—even empty—into the local variable foo, the statement multiply foo by 22 will produce an error message, since you have not initialized foo.

If the *container* is a field or the message box, the **numberFormat** property determines the format of the product.

You can multiply a container by itself.

Techie alert: The **multiply** command uses the same code as the * operator.

HyperTalk uses integer math if both factors are integers whose absolute value is less than 32767; otherwise, it uses SANE to do extended precision multiplication (with up to 19 decimal places of precision).

ALSO SEE

add command; **divide** command; **is a** operator; **numberFormat** property; **sqrt** function; **subtract** command

---

multiSpace property   Introduced in version 1.0

FORMS

```
set [the] multiSpace [of HyperCard] to spaceBetweenShapes
set the multiSpace to 5
set the multiSpace to the width of card window div numberOfShapes
```

ACTION

The **multiSpace** property determines the minimum distance, in pixels, between shapes when drawing with the **multiple** property set to true.

Dragging a paint selection with the Command and Option keys held down duplicates the image continuously as it's being dragged, and the **multiSpace** also determines the distance between these dragged images.

COMMENTS

The **multiSpace** property affects the same tools as the **multiple**:

```
line    rectangle    rounded rectangle    oval    regular polygon
```

The *spaceBetweenShapes* is the minimum number of pixels between the shapes drawn in one drag motion. By default, the **multiSpace** is 1; you can set it to any integer, but values below 1 have the same effect as 1.

Using the **multiple** and various values of the **multiSpace**, you can draw numerous cool designs using a handler. The following example produces the image shown in Figure III.33:

```
on thingee
  reset paint
  choose oval tool
  set the multiple to true
  set the multiSpace to 15
  set the dragSpeed to 100
  put "128,80" into upperLeft
  put "128,272" into lowerLeft
  put "320,80" into upperRight
  put "320,272" into lowerRight
  drag from upperLeft to lowerRight with shiftKey
  drag from lowerRight to upperLeft with shiftKey
  drag from lowerLeft to upperRight with shiftKey
  drag from upperRight to lowerLeft with shiftKey
  choose browse tool
end thingee
```

Figure III.33   MultiSpace at work

Dragging speed affects multiSpace: The **multiSpace** is the minimum distance between successive shapes. If you drag fast enough, the paint tool can skip an image, which makes the spacing greater than the value of the **multiSpace**. The smaller the **multiSpace**, the slower you need to drag to get the minimum spacing with no skipping. This applies to both manual and scripted dragging. To slow down dragging in a handler, set the **dragSpeed** property to a smaller value.

ALSO SEE
dragSpeed property; **multiple** property; **reset paint** command

---

name property

Introduced in version 1.0
Last changed in version 2.2

FORMS
```
set [the] name of element to newName
the [English|short|abbr[ev[iated]]|long] name [of element]
set the name of last card button to "Fred"
set the name of last button to "Button" && the number of last button
if the short name of this card is myCard then exit to HyperCard
get the English name of menu 3
put the long name of HyperCard into myPath
put the long name into myPath -- same as above line
```

ACTION
The **name** property gives the name of the *element*, which can be a card, button, field, background, stack, menu, menu item, or window, or HyperCard itself.

   You can set the name of an object in its Info dialog. By default, buttons created by choosing New Button from the Objects menu are named "New Button"; other objects have no default name.

   If the *element* has no name, HyperCard reports its ID instead.

COMMENTS

You can use an object's **name** in a handler as a source of information. The following handler belongs in the stack script and checks the name of **the target** to make sure it's a button and to see what action to perform. If the button's name starts with "Application", the handler interprets the rest of the name as an application to open; otherwise, it assumes the name is the name of a stack to go to:

```
on mouseUp
    if word 2 of the name of the target is "button" then
      get the short name of the target
      if word 1 of it is "Application" then
        delete word 1 of it
        open it
      else
        go to it
      end if
    end if
end mouseUp
```

A button, field, card, or background must be in the current stack for its name to be accessible.

The form `the English name` reports the English names of standard HyperCard menus and menu items, rather than the translated names they might have in a version of HyperCard that's been localized for another language. (You can use the `English` modifier with the names of other elements, but it doesn't affect the value that's reported.)

The form `the short name` is just the name of the element:

```
Picture Window
Style
My Button
New Field
Address Stack
```

The form `the name` is the element's name (for menus, menu items, and windows) or the element's type plus its short name (for objects):

```
Picture Window
Style
card button "My Button"
bkgnd field "New Field"
stack "Address Stack"
```

The form `the abbr[ev[iated]] name` is the same as `the name`.

The form `the long name` is the element's name (for menus, menu items, and windows) or the element's type, name, and pathname (for objects):

```
Picture Window
Style
```

```
card button "My Button" of card ID 5634 of stack "My Disk:Addresses"
bkgnd field "New Field" of card "Help" of stack "My Disk:Addresses"
stack "My Disk:Addresses"
```

If an object has no name, all forms of the **name** property report the object's ID:

```
card button id 4
bkgnd field id 22
card id 67502
```

The name of HyperCard: The form `the name of HyperCard` reports the word "HyperCard", regardless of whether you're running a standalone or HyperCard itself, or what your copy of the HyperCard application is actually named. However, `the long name of HyperCard` reports the full pathname of the currently running application. You can use the following function to retrieve the name:

```
function runningApp
   put the long name of HyperCard into theApp
   put the itemDelimiter into originalValue
   set the itemDelimiter to colon
   get last item of theApp         -- the filename
   set the itemDelimiter to originalValue
   return it
end runningApp
```

Banner button names: The following handler turns a button's name into a banner that streams across the button:

```
on mouseUp -- based on an idea by XCMD wizard Gary Bond
   set the showName of me to true
   set the textAlign of me to left
   put "              Buy another copy...              " into banner
   repeat with x = 1 to the length of banner
     set the name of me to char x to the length of banner
     wait 5 ticks
   end repeat
   set the showName of me to false
end mouseUp
```

Setting the name of a stack: If you're using MultiFinder and you rename a stack that's in an open folder window, the system takes some time to recognize the name change. If you try to open the stack before the name change appears in the Finder's window, you may experience some anomalous behavior.

Return characters in names: You can include a return character in the names of HyperCard objects other than stacks. However, if you set a button name to a string that includes a return, the return is ignored.

The only way you can include a return in an object's name is with the **set** command. You can't enter such a name manually in the object's Info dialog.

Changes to HyperTalk: In versions of HyperCard before 2.2, you can't use a part descriptor to refer to a button or field.

In versions before 2.1, you can't get the name of HyperCard.

Versions before 2.0 have a bug that affects cards, backgrounds, buttons, and fields whose names are longer than 29 characters. In these versions, HyperCard only sees the first 29 characters of the name, so if you refer to such an object by its name, HyperCard fails to find it.

ALSO SEE

ID property; **number of object** function; **showName** property

---

name of menu property

Introduced in version 2.0
Last changed in version 2.2

FORMS

```
set [the] [English] name of menuItem of menu to newName
the [English] name of menu
set the name of menuItem 1 of menu "Apple" to "About This Stack"
set the name of first menuItem of last menu to "Check Seismograph"
get the English name of menu "Quitar"
```

ACTION

The **name of menu** property describes the names of individual menus and menu items. For menus, this property is read-only and cannot be set by a handler.

COMMENTS

Use the **name of menu** property to identify the menu or item at a specific location, or to change the names of menu items.

The following handler belongs in an address book stack and sets the name of a menu item to either "Business Phone" or "Residence Phone", depending on whether the current card holds a residential or business entry:

```
on openCard
  if there is a menu "Call" then
    if the hilite of button "Residence" then
      set the name of last menuItem of menu "Call" to "Residence Phone"
    else
      set the name of last menuItem of menu "Call" to "Business Phone"
    end if
  end if
end openCard
```

The *menuItem* and *menu* can be any valid descriptors of a menu item and menu name, respectively. If you refer to the name of a nonexistent menu or menu item, HyperCard puts up a script error dialog.

Setting the name of a menu item to the minus sign (-) draws a thin separator line across the menu in place of the name. The first dividing line is named `"-1"`; the second is named `"-2"`; and so on.

Special menu names: The name of the leftmost menu headed by the on is "Apple"; the name of System 7's Help menu is "System Help"; and the rightmost menu in the menu bar under System 7 is "Application". If WorldScript is installed, the name of the keyboard menu is "Keyboard".

The form `the English name of menuItem` is useful when your stack is running under a non-U.S. system. This form reports the English names of standard HyperCard menus and menu items, rather than the translated names they have in a version of HyperCard that's been localized for another language.

Changing the name of a menu: To change the name of a menu, you need to delete the old menu and create a new one with the new name.

You can't retrieve or set the name of any item in the Tools or Patterns menu. You can't set the name of any item on the Apple menu.

A rose by any other name: You can change the names of most standard HyperCard menu items, but renaming them doesn't change what they do.

If the name of a custom menu item is the same as the name of a standard HyperCard menu item, the custom item inherits the behavior of the standard item. For example, if you name a menu item "Home", choosing that menu item goes to the Home stack (unless you've assigned a **menuMessage** with some different behavior to it). However, HyperCard does not automatically take care of checking, unchecking, disabling, and enabling such a menu item, nor does it assign the standard Command-key equivalent.

Changes to HyperTalk: In versions of HyperCard before 2.2, the `English name` form isn't available.

In version 2.0, asking for the **name** of any separator line in a menu produces "-"; the name does not include a number.

ALSO SEE
create menu command; **delete** command; **menus** function; **put into menu** command

---

newBackground message   Introduced in version 1.0

FORMS
`newBackground`

ACTION

The **newBackground** message is sent to the newly created card when the user creates a new background.

COMMENTS

Choosing New Background from the Objects menu creates a new card with a blank background. The **newBackground** message is sent to this card. **NewBackground** is also sent when you paste in a card from another stack, if the card's background isn't shared by any other card in the current stack.

When a new background is created, HyperCard sends the following messages in order:

```
closeCard        -- to previous card
closeBackground  -- to previous card
newBackground
newCard
openBackground
openCard
```

Changes to HyperTalk: In versions of HyperCard before 2.0, messages are sent in the following order when a new background is created:

```
closeCard        -- to previous card
closeBackground  -- to previous card
openBackground
openCard
newBackground
newCard
```

ALSO SEE

closeBackground message; **deleteBackground** message; **doMenu** command/message; **newCard** message; **newStack** message; **openBackground** message

---

newButton message
Introduced in version 1.0

FORMS

```
newButton
```

ACTION

The **newButton** message is sent to a button right after it's created.

COMMENTS

A new button can't catch its own **newButton** handler, since a newly created button doesn't yet have a script, so you usually put **newButton** handlers at the card level or beyond in the message-passing path. However, when you paste a button, HyperCard sends it a **newButton** message, and since a pasted button can contain a script, these buttons may have **newButton** handlers of their own.

The following example belongs in a card, background or stack script. It sets up all new buttons with the properties you specify, automatically:

```
on newButton
    if the short name of the target is not "New Button" then exit newButton
    -- button was pasted from elsewhere, so we won't change it
    set the textFont of the target to Geneva
    set the textSize of the target to 9
    set the textStyle of the target to bold
    set the style of the target to rectangle
    set the autoHilite of the target to true
    doMenu "Button Info..." -- so you can type in the button's name
end newButton
```

Normally, repeatedly choosing New Button from the Objects menu piles all the new buttons on top of each other. This handler puts new buttons at a random spot on the card, avoiding the pile-up effect:

```
on newButton
    set the loc of the target to ¬
    random(the width of card window - 50), ¬
    random(the height of card window - 11)
end newButton
```

ALSO SEE

deleteButton message; **newField** message

---

newCard message

FORMS

`newCard`

ACTION

The **newCard** message is sent to a card right after it's created.

COMMENTS

Use a **newCard** handler when you need to perform certain setup tasks for every newly created card. The following example records the date the card was created and places the insertion point in the first field, so the user can start typing immediately without having to click the field:

```
on newCard -- in background script
  global userName -- created by the Home stack
  put the long date & return & the time into field "Creation Date"
  put userName into field "Created by"
  select text of field "Reference Title" -- ready for typing
end newCard
```

The **newCard** message is usually handled at the background level or above, since a newly created card normally has no script. However, **newCard** is also sent when you paste a card into a stack, and such a card may already contain a script with a **newCard** handler.

When a new card is created, HyperCard sends the following messages, in order:

```
closeCard -- sent to previous card
newCard
openCard
```

Changes to HyperTalk: In versions of HyperCard before 2.0, the message order is:

```
closeCard
openCard
newCard
```

ALSO SEE

closeCard message; **deleteCard** message; **doMenu** command/message; **newBackground** message; **newStack** message; **openCard** message

---

newField message

FORMS

```
newField
```

ACTION

The **newField** message is sent to a field just after it's created.

COMMENTS

A new field can't catch its own **newField** handler, since a newly created field doesn't yet have a script, so you usually put a **newField** handler at the card level or beyond in the message-passing path. However, fields that are copied and pasted also generate a **newField** message, and these fields may contain **newField** handlers of their own.

The following example checks whether a newly-pasted field contains its text, and, if not, offers to re-paste the field with the Shift key down (which pastes the field contents as well as the field itself):

```
on newField
   -- newly created fields have no name, so if the field
   -- isn't nameless, it's being pasted in:
   if the name of me is not the ID of me ¬
   and the text of me is empty then
      answer "Do you want to paste the text also?" with "Yes" or "No"
      if it is "Yes" then
         delete me
         type "v" with shiftKey,commandKey
      end if
   end if
end newField
```

If you put a **newField** handler at the card level or beyond, it's usually because you want to set up defaults for all new fields. The following example immediately brings up the Field Info dialog when a new field is created:

```
on newField
   doMenu "Field Info..." -- field is already selected when created
end newField
```

ALSO SEE

deleteField message; **newButton** message

---

newStack message   Introduced in version 1.0

FORMS

```
newStack
```

ACTION

The **newStack** message is sent when a stack is created (with the **create stack** command or the New Stack menu item), to the first card of the new stack.

COMMENTS

The following example implements an automatic stack backup. When a new stack is created, it asks the user where to put the backup copy. Each time the stack is closed, it saves a copy of itself in the specified location.

```
on newStack
   ask file "Where should the backup copy be kept?" ¬
   with (char 1 to 24 of the short name of this stack) && "Backup"
   put it into backupLocation -- full pathname of stack
   if there is no field "Backup Location" then -- create the field
```

```
      lock screen
      set the editBkgnd to true
      doMenu "New Field"
      set the editBkgnd to false
      set the name of last field to "Backup Location"
      hide field "Backup Location"
      set the sharedText of field "Backup Location" to true
      unlock screen
    end if
    put backupLocation into field "Backup Location"
end newStack


on closeStack -- make a backup
   get field "Backup Location"
   if it is not empty then
      lock screen
      if there is a stack it then
         go to stack it in a new window -- remove old backup
         doMenu "Delete Stack..." without dialog
      end if
      save this stack as it
   end if
end closeStack
```

When a new stack is created, the following messages are sent, in order, to the first card of the new stack:

```
newStack
newBackground
newCard
openStack
openBackground
openCard
```

If the new stack is created with the Copy Current Background box checked (or with a background specified by the **create stack** command), its background or stack script might contain a **newStack** handler. Otherwise, there's no way for the new stack itself to handle this message, since it has no script, but the **newStack** can be passed on in the message path and handled by the Home stack or a stack in use.

Changes to HyperTalk: In versions of HyperCard before 2.0, the message order is:

```
openStack
openBackground
openCard
newStack
```

ALSO SEE

create stack command; **newBackground** message; **newCard** message; **openStack** message

---

next repeat keyword   Introduced in version 1.0

FORMS

```
next repeat
next repeat
if skipFlag is true then next repeat
```

ACTION

The **next repeat** statement stops the current repetition of a **repeat** loop, skipping any remaining statements before **end repeat**, and goes back to the top of the loop.

COMMENTS

Use a **next repeat** statement if you want to skip the rest of the statements and go on to the next pass through the loop. A **next repeat** is usually found inside an **if** statement, as in the following handler:

```
on brainSurgery
   global oops, cutAlongDottedLine
   repeat until cutAlongDottedLine is 0
      subtract 1 from cutAlongDottedLine
      nextIncision
      if oops then next repeat
      send "AddAnotherOne" to card "Billing" -- no charge for errors
   end repeat
end brainSurgery
```

You can put a **next repeat** anywhere within a **repeat** structure. It works with all forms of the **repeat** keyword.

In the following example, you provide two numbers, and the handler tells you all the numbers that are divisible by both of them:

```
on factors num1,num2
   if the message box contains "--"
   then put return into char offset("--",message) of message
   put "--" after message
   repeat with i = max(num1,num2) to num1 * num2
      set the cursor to busy
      if i mod num1 ≠ 0 then next repeat -- not divisible by num1
      if i mod num2 ≠ 0 then next repeat -- not divisible by num2
      put i & space after message
```

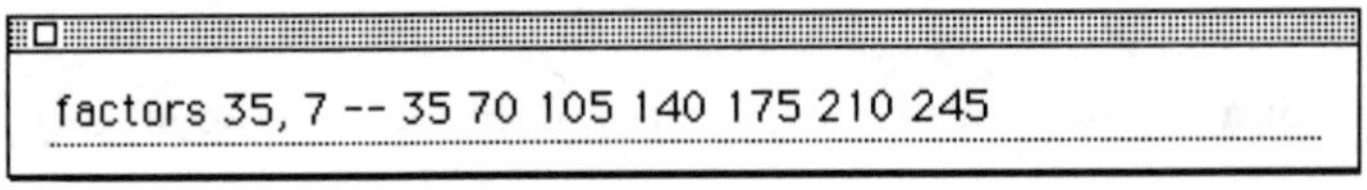

```
factors 35, 7 -- 35 70 105 140 175 210 245
```

Figure III.34   Figuring factors through the message box

```
  end repeat
  beep 2 -- signal that handler is done
end factors
```

If you call this handler from the message box by typing

```
factors 35,7
```

the handler yields the display shown in Figure III.34.

ALSO SEE
>   **repeat** keyword

---

nextLine property   Introduced in version 2.0

FORMS
>   set [the] nextLine of window "Message Watcher" to *text*
>   set the nextLine of window "Message Watcher" to "------" & return

ACTION
The **nextLine** is a property of the message watcher window. It lets you put text directly into the scrolling list of messages.

You cannot **get** the **nextLine**; this property can only be set.

COMMENTS
The **nextLine** property is particularly useful when you want to mark a message for easy visibility. For example, suppose you want to be able to scroll through the Message Watcher and easily see any places where a custom message is sent. You might use the following handler to mark all points where your message appears in the Message Watcher:

```
on myMessage
  set the nextLine of window "Message Watcher" to "••••" & return
end myMessage
```

Techie alert: You can use this property with a custom message watcher XCMD, as well as the built-in message watcher, if the custom XCMD is written to support **nextLine**.

ALSO SEE
hideIdle property; **hideUnused** property; **messageWatcher** property; **text** property

number function

Introduced in version 1.0
Last changed in version 2.2

FORMS

```
[the] number of [card|background] {buttons|fields|parts}
[the] number of backgrounds [{in|of} this stack]
[the] number of cards [{in|of} {background|this stack}]
[the] number of marked cards
[the] number of {characters|words|items|lines} {in|of} string
[the] number of {menus|menuItems {in|of} menu}
[the] number of windows
number([card|background] {buttons|fields|parts})
number(backgrounds [{in|of} this stack])
number(cards [{in|of} {background|this stack}])
number(marked cards)
number({characters|words|items|lines} {in|of} string)
number({menus|menuItems {in|of} menu})
number(windows)
get the number of card parts
put the number of cards of this background into theNumber
repeat for the number of cards
if x > the number of marked cards then next repeat
put the number of words in it into wordCount
repeat with i = 1 to the number of menuItems in menu "Font"
```

ACTION

The **number** function tells you how many there are of a given object or element.

You can substitute the standard abbreviations for the words `card`, `background`, `button`, `field`, and `characters`. (See Chapter 7.)

COMMENTS

The **number** function is especially useful in **repeat** structures when you want to loop through each one of a particular element. The following example changes all the rounded rectangle buttons in the current stack to the standard button style:

```
on changeButtons
  push card
  lock screen
  lock messages
  repeat with nextBackground = 1 to the number of backgrounds
    go background nextBackground
    repeat with nextButton = 1 to the number of background buttons
      if the style of background button nextButton is roundRect
      then set the style of background button nextButton to standard
    end repeat
```

```
        end repeat
        repeat with nextCard = 1 to the number of cards
          go card nextCard
          repeat with nextButton = 1 to the number of card buttons
            if the style of card button nextButton is roundRect
            then set the style of card button nextButton to standard
          end repeat
        end repeat
        pop card
    end changeButtons
```

Chunk expressions: A *line* in HyperTalk is defined as a group of characters delimited by return characters. A line in a narrow field may wrap around several times, and look like more than one line on screen, but it is still considered a single line. Words are delimited by spaces or the beginning or end of a line, or by quotation marks. Any group of characters enclosed in quotes is treated as a single word. Items are delimited by the current **itemDelimiter** character. By default, this is a comma (,).

If you don't specify `card` or `background` for the number of fields, HyperTalk assumes you want the number of background fields. If you don't specify a domain for buttons or parts, you get the number of card buttons or parts.

The following function retrieves the information presented in the Card Info dialog:

```
function cardInfo
    put "Card Name:" && the short name of this card & return ¬
    & "Card Number:" && the number of this card && ¬
    "out of" && the number of cards & return & ¬
    "Card ID:" && the short ID of this card & return into report
    --
    put "Contains" && the number of card fields && "card fields." ¬
    & return after report
    put "Contains" && the number of card buttons && "card buttons." ¬
    & return after report
    --
    put "Card Marked:" && the marked of this card & return ¬
    & "Don't Search Card:" && the dontSearch of this card & return ¬
    & "Can't Delete Card:" && the cantDelete of this card after report
    return report
end cardInfo
```

Checking the position of an element: If you want to know what back-to-front position a window or part is in relative to other elements of the same kind, use the **number** or **partNumber** property.

Changes to HyperTalk: In versions of HyperCard before 2.2, you cannot get the number of parts. However, you can add the number of fields to the number of buttons to get the total number of parts.

In versions before 2.0, you cannot get the number of marked cards, menus, menu items, or windows, since these elements don't exist in earlier versions.

ALSO SEE

itemDelimiter property; **marked** property; **number of object** function; **partNumber** property

---

number of object function

Introduced in version 1.0
Last changed in version 2.2

FORMS

```
the [long|abbr[rev[iated]]|short] number of {field|button|card|background|window}
number(field|button|card|background|window)
the number of this card
the long number of field 2
the number of window "Pict"
the number of card window
the number of part 14 -- number of that field/button, not the partNumber
```

ACTION

The **number** function returns the position number of an element:

- A card's number is the card's position in the stack.

- A part's (button's or field's) number is its back-to-front position on its card or background. Numbers increase as you get closer to the front, so the first part is at the back and the last part is frontmost.

- A background's number is its birth order. The first background created is number 1, the second is number 2, and so forth.

- A window's number is its back-to-front position in the window list. Invisible windows also have a number.

The **number** of an object appears in that object's Info dialog.

COMMENTS

The following handlers show how to make your stack's "go next" and "go previous" buttons hide themselves when you're on the last or first card:

```
on mouseUp -- goes in "go next" button
   lock screen -- lets the openCard handler hide button
   go to next card
end mouseUp
```

```
on openCard -- in stack or background script
   if the number of this card is 1 then
      hide button "Previous" -- not applicable if you're already on 1
   else
      show button "Previous"
   end if
   if the number of this card is the number of cards then
      hide button "Next" -- already on last card
   else
      show button "Next"
   end if
   unlock screen -- matches lock in mouseUp handler above
end openCard
```

Changing the number of an element: You can't change an element's **number** directly. However, when you delete a card, field, or button, or close a window, whose number isn't already highest, all the other elements of that type are renumbered.

You can change the number of a card by cutting it and pasting it somewhere else in the stack. You can change the number of a field or button by selecting it and choosing Bring Closer or Send Farther from the Objects menu. The following handler brings a button to the front:

```
on bringToFront theButton
   select button theButton
   doMenu "Bring Closer" with shiftKey
   choose browse tool
end bringToFront
```

Windows are in two layers: floating palettes (such as the message box) and ordinary windows. All the floating palettes are always in front of the ordinary windows. You can change a window's number by using the **show** command: Showing a window brings it to the front of its layer.

Invisible windows still numbered: If a window has been hidden using the **hide** command, it is still in the window list and still retains its number. Some built-in HyperCard windows, such as the message, scroll, tool, and pattern windows, never go away; clicking their close boxes only hides them.

Changes to HyperTalk: In versions of HyperCard before 2.2, you can't use a part descriptor to specify a button or field.

In versions before 2.1, you can't specify a window by number.

ALSO SEE
ID property; **name** property; **partNumber** property

numberFormat property   Introduced in version 1.0

FORMS

```
set [the] numberFormat [of HyperCard] to formatExpression
set the numberFormat to "0.00"       -- 0.25031 displayed as 0.25
set the numberFormat to "0.000"      -- 0.25031 displayed as 0.250
set the numberFormat to "#.000"      -- 0.25031 displayed as .250
set the numberFormat to "#.###"      -- 0.25031 displayed as .25
set the numberFormat to "0"          -- 0.25031 displayed as 0
set the numberFormat to "#.0000000" -- 0.25031 displayed as 0.2503100
set the numberFormat to "#.000####" -- 0.25031 displayed as 0.25031
```

ACTION

The **numberFormat** global property specifies the precision HyperCard uses when displaying the results of numerical calculations.

HyperCard resets the **numberFormat** to the default value of 0.###### when the **idle**
message is sent.

COMMENTS

Use the **numberFormat** property for greater control over the way numbers are displayed.
The following example shows how to set the **numberFormat** to handle a dollars-and-cents
figure:

```
on bucksPerSucker
   ask "What's the jackpot?"
   put it into jackpot
   ask "How many tickets will you sell?"
   put it into numberOfSuckers
   set the numberFormat to "0.00"
   answer "That's $" & jackpot/numberOfSuckers && "per ticket."
end bucksPerSucker
```

The *formatExpression* consists of any combination of a string of zeroes (0), a decimal
point, and another string of zeroes and pound signs (#). You must enclose the *formatExpression*
in quotation marks; failing to do so, or specifying an otherwise invalid *formatExpression*,
won't cause a script error, but it will cause HyperCard to ignore the command.

The number of zeroes before the decimal point is the minimum number of integer digits
to display. HyperTalk always includes at least enough digits to specify the result of the
calculation. If there are more integer digits in the number than the **numberFormat** calls for,
HyperTalk displays all the digits. If there are fewer digits than the **numberFormat** calls for,
HyperTalk adds leading zeroes to the beginning of the number.

For example, a **numberFormat** with three zeroes before the decimal point indicates that
at least three digits will appear before the decimal point. If the number being displayed has
fewer digits, HyperTalk inserts leading zeroes to pad the number of digits to three:

```
set the numberFormat to "000" -- at least 3 integer digits
put the value of 7        -- yields 007
put the value of 23       -- yields 023
put the value of 475      -- yields 475
put the value of 12986    -- yields 12986
```

Similarly, the number of zeroes after the decimal point is the number of decimal digits to appear in the final display. If the number has more decimal digits, HyperTalk rounds it off. If it has fewer decimal digits, HyperTalk adds as many trailing zeroes as needed:

```
set the numberFormat to ".000" -- exactly three decimal digits
put the value of 1.7      -- yields 1.700
put the value of 1.73     -- yields 1.730
put the value of 1.734    -- yields 1.734
put the value of 1.73461 -- yields 1.735 -- rounded off
```

The number of pound signs after the decimal point is the *maximum* number of decimal digits to appear in the displayed number. If the number has more decimal digits, it's rounded off, but if it has fewer, no trailing zeroes are added:

```
set the numberFormat to ".###" -- at most three decimal digits
put the value of 1.7      -- yields 1.7
put the value of 1.73     -- yields 1.73
put the value of 1.734    -- yields 1.734
put the value of 1.73461   -- yields 1.735 -- rounded off
```

Rounding off:　If a value is exactly halfway between one number and another, the **numberFormat** rounds it to the nearest even number. For example, if the **numberFormat** is 0.#, 99.65 is rounded down to 99.6; but 99.75 is rounded up to 99.8.

The **numberFormat** does not affect HyperCard's internal calculations, which are performed with up to 19 digits of precision. The number is only converted to the precision specified by the **numberFormat** at the time it's put into a field or the message box, or displayed by a dialog.

Furthermore, numbers are not affected by the **numberFormat** unless they have been operated on in some way, by a mathematical operator, the **add**, **subtract**, **multiply**, or **divide** commands, or the **value** function. A displayed literal number does not respect the **numberFormat** property:

```
put pi into message      -- yields 3.14159265358979323846
put pi + 0 into message -- yields 3.141593 with default numberFormat
```

ALSO SEE
　　　　round function; **trunc** function

numToChar function

FORMS

```
[the] numToChar of ASCIIvalue
numToChar(ASCIIvalue)
numToChar(65)            -- A
numToChar(the number of fields)
the numToChar of 103  -- g
the numToChar of fred -- character corresponding to variable fred
```

ACTION

The **numToChar** function returns the character corresponding to the specified ASCII value. (ASCII is a code that lets you translate each character into a number.)

COMMENTS

The **numToChar** function is the inverse of **charToNum**. It's useful in conversions, and when you want to generate a character that HyperCard doesn't let you type directly (such as a control character).

The following handler displays all the characters in a specific font and size in a field called "Font Test":

```
on fontText theFont,theSize
   if theFont is not empty
   then set the textFont of card field "Font Test" to theFont
   if theSize is not empty
   then set the textSize of card field "Font Test" to theSize
   repeat with ASCIIval = 1 to 255
     set the cursor to busy
     if ASCIIval is 13 then -- special case for return character
       put "<return>" into thisChar
     else put numToChar(ASCIIval) into thisChar
     put ASCIIval & colon && thisChar & return ¬
     after card field "Font Test"
   end repeat
   delete last char of card field "Font Test" -- trailing return
   set the scroll of card field "Font Test" to 0
end fontText
```

You might call this handler like this:

```
fontTest "Avant Garde",10
```

The *ASCIIvalue* must be between 1 and 255. If the *ASCIIvalue* is out of this range or is not an integer, HyperCard puts up a script error dialog and aborts the rest of the handler.

The character you get for a given *ASCIIvalue* depends, of course, on the font you use. For example, the numToChar of 92 yields "\" in the New York font, but "∴" in the Symbol font.

HyperTalk doesn't let you use the null character: Zero is a legal value in the ASCII system—its corresponding control character is called the NUL or null character. However, because of the way its strings are stored, HyperTalk cannot handle the null character at all. If you need to use null characters in telecommunications programming or for export to a file, you need to use an XCMD written for that purpose.

Special characters available: The Chicago font contains a few special symbols that can be accessed with the **numToChar** function:

Ú   numToChar(16)
⌘   numToChar(17)
✓   numToChar(18)
◆   numToChar(19)
   numToChar(20)

ALSO SEE
ASCII Chart (Appendix A); **charToNum** function

---

offset function   Introduced in version 1.0

FORMS
offset(*stringToLocate*,*stringToSearch*)
```
offset("pen","appendix") -- returns 3
offset(newCustomer,card field "Customer List")
```

ACTION
The **offset** function returns the character position of the *stringToLocate* in the *stringToSearch*. If the *stringToSearch* doesn't contain the *stringToLocate*, the **offset** function returns 0.

COMMENTS
The extremely handy **offset** function tells you exactly where in a container a string is located, letting you construct a chunk expression with which you can perform any desired operation on the string. The following handler deletes all occurrences of a given string from a global variable by computing the string's starting position, then removing characters from that point through the length of the string to be deleted:

```
on deleteString
   global theContainer
   ask "What string do you want to delete?"
   if it is empty then exit deleteString -- user cancelled
   put it into whatToFind
   put 0 into count
   repeat
```

```
      get offset(whatToFind,theContainer)
      if it is zero then exit repeat -- no occurrences left
      put it into start
      put it + the length of it into finish
      delete char start to finish of theContainer
      add 1 to count
    end repeat
    if count is 0 then
      answer whatToFind && "was not found."
    else
      answer count && "occurrences of" && whatToFind && "deleted."
    end if
end deleteString
```

The **offset** function always returns the first occurrence of the string if it appears more than once:

```
offset("ana","banana") -- returns 2
```

This example function returns the positions of all occurrences of a string:

```
function offsetsList theString,theText
  put empty into theList
  put 0 into charsDeleted
  repeat
    get offset(theString,theText)
    if it is 0 then return theList -- no more occurrences
    else
      put it + charsDeleted ¬
      into item (the number of items of theList + 1) of theList
      delete char 1 to it of theText -- so we can find next occurrence
      add it to charsDeleted
    end if
  end repeat
end offsetsList
```

Both the *stringToLocate* and the *stringToSearch* can be any string of characters. Case is not significant; the **offset** function considers an uppercase letter to be equivalent to its lowercase counterpart. The **offset** function also ignores diacritical marks—for instance, ø and o are treated as the same character. And you may get unexpected results when your *stringToLocate* contains a diphthong: the statement

```
offset("œ","Who's seen Bœrnie?")
```

yields 3, the position of the base letter "o".

The following useful functions extend the concept of the **offset** function. They return the line number, item number, and word number (respectively) where the beginning of the substring occurs:

```
function lineOffset string,where
   if string is not in where then return 0 -- not found
   get offset(string,where)
   return the number of lines of (char 1 to it of where)
end lineOffset


function itemOffset string,where
   if string is not in where then return 0 -- not found
   get offset(string,where)
   return the number of items of (char 1 to it of where)
end itemOffset


function wordOffset string,where
   if string is not in where then return 0 -- not found
   get offset(string,where)
   return the number of words of (char 1 to it of where)
end wordOffset
```

You can use these utility functions for a variety of purposes. For example, the following function returns the text of any line that starts with the specified string:

```
function lineStartingWith theString,theText
   get offset(return & theString,theText)
   if it is 0 then return empty -- not there
   if it is 1 then return line 1 of theText -- starts with theString
   return line lineOffset(return & theString,theText) of theText
end lineStartingWith
```

ALSO SEE
find command

---

on keyword   Introduced in version 1.0

FORMS
on *messageName* [*parameterList*]
on mouseUp
on myCustomHandler
on addTheseUp firstNum,secondNum,thirdNum

ACTION
The **on** keyword is always the first word of a message handler. The second word on the line is the name of the message to which the handler responds. Any remaining words are parameters passed to the handler; parameters are separated from each other by commas.

COMMENTS

When a message that's moving through the message-passing path arrives at an object, HyperTalk checks that object's script to see whether it contains a handler corresponding to the message. If it does, the handler is executed. The message can be one of HyperCard's system messages, such as **mouseDown**, or a command message, or a custom message you've created yourself.

Message names and function names follow the same rules. Names must begin with a letter or the underscore character (_), and can contain any combination of letters, digits, and underscores. You can't use punctuation or other special characters (*,%,•, etc.) in a message name. The name can be up to 254 characters long.

This handler tells you how long it's been since the Mac was last started up:

```
on upTime
   get the ticks
   put (it div 60) mod 60 into theSeconds
   put ((it div 60) div 60) mod 60 into theMinutes
   put ((it div 60) div 60) div 60 into theHours
   answer "The computer has been on for" && theHours && "hours," ¬
   && theMinutes && "minutes," && theSeconds && "seconds."
end upTime
```

Since this is a custom message—one you've made up yourself—once you've defined it, you can use its name as you would any HyperTalk message or command, from a script or in the message box:

```
upTime
```

Overriding built-in commands: Each HyperTalk command you issue goes through the message path before reaching HyperCard. This means that you can change the behavior of a built-in command by creating a custom command with the same name and placing it at an appropriate point in the message path. This example shows how you might override the **hide menubar** command, so the menu bar is only hidden if it blocks part of the card window. You can place it in your Home stack to intercept all unnecessary commands to hide the menu bar:

```
on hide theThing
   if theThing is not "menubar" then pass hide
   if the top of card window < 40 then pass hide
   -- if not passed, the message gets trapped here
end hide
```

How parameters are passed: HyperTalk evaluates each parameter in the message, and then puts the result into the corresponding parameter variable. This means you can pass the contents of any container as a parameter, even if it contains commas or return characters.

The following handler gets two parameters, `amount` and `account`. The `account` holds a customer identifier, which might be the complete record for a particular customer; the first line of `account` is the name of the card that holds the customer's record. The handler performs some simple arithmetic:

```
on debit amount,account
  subtract amount from field "Balance" of card (line 1 of account)
end debit
```

The statement that calls this handler might look like this:

```
debit "20.35",myCurrentCustomer
```

If the message provides fewer parameters than the handler allows, the extra parameters hold empty. If, on the other hand, the message has more parameters than are named in the first line of the handler, the additional parameters don't get a parameter name, but they can still be accessed by using the **param** function. The following handler replaces one word with another in one or more fields, and shows how to mix named and unnamed parameters. For example,

```
replace "Fred","Martha","Forms","Action"
```

would replace the word "Fred" with "Martha" wherever it occurs in the fields "Forms" and "Action". The handler looks like this:

```
on replace oldWord,newWord
  repeat with fieldNum = 3 to the paramCount
    put param(fieldNum) into fieldName -- get unnamed parameter
    get field fieldName
    repeat while it contains oldWord
      put offset(oldWord,it) into startChar
      put startChar + the length of oldWord - 1 into endChar
      put newWord into char startChar to endChar of it
    end repeat
    put it into field fieldName
  end repeat
end replace
```

Commenting out message handlers: If you comment out the **on** line, the entire handler is effectively commented out. The script editor shows this by removing the indentation for any message handler whose first line is commented out. The lack of indentation indicates that the handler is not a currently active part of the script.

ALSO SEE

"Parameters and Parameter Passing", in Chapter 8; **function** keyword; **param** function; **return** keyword

open application command

Introduced in version 1.0
Last changed in version 2.2

FORMS

```
open [document with] application
open "MacWrite"
open "My Spreadsheet" with "Disk:Folder:Excel"
open myDocument with selectedApp
open card field "Document Path" with line 3 of field "Applications"
```

ACTION

The **open application** command launches an application and optionally opens a document within the application. It's the equivalent of double-clicking the application or document in the Finder, or of dropping the document icon onto the application under System 7.

COMMENTS

The following handler asks for the name of a text file, then opens that text file using your preferred application (whose name is stored in a field):

```
on mouseUp
   answer file "What text file do you want to edit?" of type text
   if it is empty then exit mouseUp -- user cancelled
   open it with card field "Text Application"
end mouseUp
```

The *application* must be the name of a Mac application located on your Mac. The *document* must be of a type that the *application* can open (although it doesn't necessarily have to have been created by the *application*). You must spell the names of both *application* and *document* exactly as they appear in the Finder, complete with any special characters such as ©.

You can use **open application** under MultiFinder to open an application that's already running. In this case, the command switches that application to the foreground.

If you don't give the full pathname of the *application* or *document*, HyperCard looks for them in the locations specified in the Applications and Documents global variables, respectively. (These globals are set by the Home stack when HyperCard starts up, and are stored in the appropriate Search Path cards in the Home stack.)

If HyperCard can't find them in any of these locations, it puts up a standard Open dialog and asks you to locate the *application* or *document*. The global variables are updated to include the location you give.

If the user clicks Cancel when HyperCard presents the Open dialog, the **result** function is set to "Cancel".

Works differently under System 6: The details of implementation of the **open application** command are a little different, depending on whether you're using System 6 with or without MultiFinder, or System 7.

If you're using System 6 and MultiFinder is not active, when the application opens, HyperCard sends the **suspend** message to the current card. When you quit the application, instead of returning to the Finder, you return to the card you were on, and HyperCard sends the **resume** message to the current card. (Note carefully: **suspend** and **resume** are *not* the same as **suspendStack** and **resumeStack**. They are completely different messages.) When you return to HyperCard, all global variables are lost, and any commands in the handler after **open application** are ignored.

Under MultiFinder, however, when you launch another application, HyperCard continues to be open in the background. All global variables are maintained, and you can switch back and forth between HyperCard and the other application.

If you're using System 6, whether or not MultiFinder is active, HyperCard uses the operating system routine Launch to open an application or document. If you're using System 7, **open application** works by means of AppleEvents, sending the odoc message to the target application. If the application doesn't handle this AppleEvent, the command fails and the **result** function is set to "Not handled by target application."

Execution continues while HyperCard is suspended: If you launch an application under MultiFinder, HyperCard continues to run while it's in the background, so the rest of the commands in your handler are executed immediately after the application is opened. If you don't want to execute the rest of the handler until the user returns to HyperCard, use the **suspended** property to check whether HyperCard is in the foreground:

```
on mouseUp
   open "My Application"
   -- wait until the application finishes launching...
   wait until "My Application" is in menu "Application"
   -- ...then wait until you're back in HyperCard
   wait while the suspended
   -- other commands here
end mouseUp
```

HyperCard can open itself: With version 2.2, you can use the form

```
open the long name of HyperCard
```

while HyperCard is suspended to switch it to the foreground.

Changes to HyperTalk: In versions of HyperCard before 2.2, you cannot open HyperCard itself to bring it to the front. However, if you're using MultiFinder, you can use the **doMenu** command instead:

```
doMenu "HyperCard"
```

The name you pass to **doMenu** must be the exact name of the HyperCard application. For example, if you've changed the application name to "HyperCard v2.1", the above command won't work.

Also in versions before 2.2, the **open application** command is a asynchronous if you're using MultiFinder. This means that the handler containing the command continues immediately, without waiting for the application to finish launching (this process may take several seconds). In HyperCard 2.2, the handler pauses until the application launch is complete.

ALSO SEE

close application command; **resume** message; **suspend** message; **suspended** property

---

open file command

FORMS

```
open file filePathname
open file "Big Disk:Correspondence:Addresses"
open file myAddressFile
open file (line 12 of field "Address Books")
```

ACTION

The **open file** command prepares or creates a text file for use with the **read** and **write** commands.

COMMENTS

The commands **open file**, **close file**, **read**, and **write** are used for importing and exporting text between HyperCard and text files. Most applications that deal with text data—such as word processors and databases—can export and import text files, so you can use a text file as an intermediate step in moving data to and from other applications.

The following handler exports the text of all the background fields in the stack to a text file:

```
on dumpStackText
   ask file "Where do you want to dump the stack's text?"
   if it is empty then exit dumpStackText -- user cancelled
   put it into dumpFile
   open file dumpFile
   lock screen
   lock messages
   repeat with nextCard = 1 to the number of cards
      go to card nextCard
      repeat with nextField = 1 to the number of fields
         write field nextField & tab to file dumpFile
      end repeat
      write return to file dumpFile -- mark end of card
   end repeat
   close file dumpFile
end dumpStackText
```

The *filePathname* is the full pathname of the file you want to open. If you provide only a filename without a path, the **open file** command assumes the file is in the same folder as the HyperCard application.

If the file does not already exist, HyperCard creates an empty file with the name and location given in *filePathname*. If there is an error creating the file—for example, if the disk is locked or the location is nonexistent—the **result** function is set to "Can't create that file."

If the file exists and is already open from either HyperCard or another application, **the result** is set to "File is already open." If there is some other problem that prevents HyperCard from opening the file, the **open file** command sets **the result** to "Can't open that file."

Three-file limit: HyperCard lets you have up to three text files open at a time. If you try to open a fourth file, **the result** is set to "Can't open any more files."

Warning

HyperTalk does not check the *filePathname* to make sure it's a text file. It opens the data fork of any file you name. You are responsible for making sure you don't inadvertantly open and write to the wrong file. Writing to the data fork of a file that contains something other than text—a stack, for instance—is likely to destroy it.

The new text files created by **open file** are TeachText files. Double-clicking on such a file opens it in TeachText, which every Mac owner has (it comes with the system software). However, since they are text files, you can open them from within almost any word processor.

The following handler is the reverse of the `dumpStackText` handler above: it restores the contents of a stack that was dumped into a text file. (It assumes the current background has the right number of fields.)

```
on restoreStackText
   answer file "Where is the file containing the stack's text?"
   if it is empty then exit restoreStackText -- user cancelled
   put it into restoreFile
   open file restoreFile
   set the itemDelimiter to tab
   repeat
      read from file restoreFile until return
      if it is not empty then
         delete last char of it -- get rid of the return
         doMenu "New Card"
         repeat with nextField = 1 to the number of fields
            put item nextField of it into field nextField
         end repeat
      else -- "it" is empty, reached end of file
         exit repeat
      end if
   end repeat
   close file dumpFile
end restoreStackText
```

Techie alert: The creator signature HyperCard uses to create text files is stored in STR resource ID 128. (As shipped, the creator signature is `ttxt` for TeachText files.) To change the default creator, use ResEdit or a similar program to change this resource to the four-character creator signature you want. The resource is the same in standalone applications as it is in the HyperCard applications, so your standalones can have their own default text file creators.

Changes to HyperTalk: In versions before 2.2, if there's a problem opening the file, HyperCard puts up an error dialog instead of setting **the result**. Also, in these versions, new text files are created as MacWrite documents (with the creator signature MACA).

ALSO SEE

close file command; **read** command; **write** command

---

open printing command

Introduced in version 1.0

FORMS

```
open printing [with dialog]
open printing
open printing with dialog
```

ACTION

The **open printing** command starts the process of printing one or more cards.

COMMENTS

Use the **open printing** command to print a set of cards. The first step is to open the print job with **open printing**. Next, specify what you want to print. Finally, send the job to the printer with the **close printing** command.

Printing cards like this is similar to using the Print Stack command in the File menu, and uses the size, spacing, and header settings from the Print Stack dialog. The only difference is that this scripted method lets you print whatever cards you select, rather than all the cards (or all the marked cards) in the current stack.

The following handler prints five cards—the current card and the four that follow it:

```
on printFive
  open printing
  print five cards
  close printing
end printFive
```

The form **open printing with dialog** brings up the Print Stack dialog, so the user can manually change the print settings. Otherwise, HyperCard assumes you want to use whatever settings are already in the dialog. If the user clicks the Cancel button in the dialog, the **result** function is set to "Cancel". While the Print Stack dialog is on the screen, the handler that displayed it is suspended until the user dismisses it; there is no way to click one of the buttons from a script.

The following profitable handler, used in a stack where button family 1 is a radio cluster with the choice of "Male" or "Female", prints all cards that match the user's preference:

```
on computerDating
   answer "What sex do you prefer?" with "Male" or "Female" or "Either"
   open printing
   repeat for the number of cards
      if it is "Either" ¬
      or the selectedButton of family 1 is background button it
      then print this card
      go to next card
   end repeat
   close printing
   answer "Have a great time! That'll be $195.00, please."
end computerDating
```

Always close print jobs: Always use a **close printing** statement to complete a print job started using **open printing**. If you do not include **close printing**, your pages won't be printed until you either print something else or quit HyperCard.

Only one print job at a time: Each print job must be completed before you print anything else. If you use the **open printing** command and try to print anything else—either manually or from a script—before **close printing** is executed, HyperCard will put up the dialog in Figure III.35 and automatically close your print job before starting the next.

Using the **print document** command while there is an open print job can also reportedly lead to trouble, although theoretically printing from another application should not cause any problems. (Mean people would call this a bug.)

If you want to print the contents of fields from several cards on the same page, use the **open report printing** command.

ALSO SEE
close printing command; **open report printing** command; **print** command

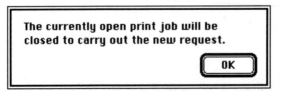

Figure III.35   This dialog appears when you try to open two print jobs at once.

open report printing command Introduced in version 2.0

FORMS

```
open report printing [with {dialog|template templateName}]
open report printing
open report printing with dialog
open report printing with template "Boston"
```

ACTION

The **open report printing** command starts the process of printing data from one or more cards as a report.

COMMENTS

Use the **open report printing** command to print a report consisting of data from a set of cards. The first step is to start the print job with **open report printing**. Next, specify what cards you want to print from. Finally, send the job to the printer with the **close printing** command.

When **open report printing** is active, the **print card** command prints the data from the specified cards as a report, rather than printing an image of the card. Printing reports like this is similar to using the Print Report command in the File menu, except that this scripted method lets you print the data from whatever cards you select, rather than all the cards (or all the marked cards) in the current stack.

This handler assumes you've already used the Print Report dialog to make a template called "Short Reference":

```
on printCommandReference
   open report printing with template "Short Reference"
   repeat with nextCard = 1 to the number of cards of background "Ref"
      if field "Type" of card nextCard of background "Ref" is "Command"
      then print card nextCard of background "Ref"
   end repeat
   close printing
end printCommandReference
```

The *templateName* is the name of any report template that has been saved in the current stack. If you specify a template that doesn't exist, the **result** function is set to "No such report template."

The form **open report printing with dialog** brings up the Print Report dialog so the user can manually change the print settings, select a report template, or create a new template. If the user clicks the Cancel button in the dialog, the **result** function is set to "Cancel". While the dialog is on the screen, the handler that displayed it is suspended until the user dismisses it; there's no way to click one of the buttons from a script.

If you use the **open report printing** form and don't bring up the dialog or specify a template, HyperCard uses the last report template you worked on in the stack. If the stack doesn't have any templates, the **open report printing** command has no effect, and all subsequent **print card** commands print the card image instead of the data.

HyperCard doesn't actually send the data to the printer until **close printing** is issued. So if your script changes the value of a printed field between the **print** and **close printing** commands, the new value is what appears on the printout.

Always close print jobs: Always use a **close printing** statement to complete a print job started using **open report printing**. If you do not include **close printing**, your pages won't be printed until you either print something else or quit HyperCard.

Only one print job at a time: Each print job must be completed before you print anything else. If you use the **open report printing** command and try to print anything else—either manually or from a script—before **close printing** is executed, HyperCard automatically closes your print job before starting the next.

If you want to print selected card images rather than a report, use the **open printing** command.

Using templates in other stacks: A report template must be in the current stack at the time the **open report printing** command is issued. However, you can go to another stack to print cards in the report format. The following handler shows how you might print information from two different stacks in the same report, using a template stored in a third stack:

```
on mouseUp
   lock screen
   lock messages
   push this card
   go to stack "Central Reports"
   open printing with template "Daily Report" -- in "Central Reports"
   go to stack "Cindy's Reports"
   repeat with nextCard = 1 to the number of cards
     go to card nextCard
     if field "Date" is the date then print this card
   end repeat
   go to stack "Joe's Reports"
   repeat with nextCard = 1 to the number of cards
     go to card nextCard
     if field "Date" is the date then print this card
   end repeat
   pop card
end mouseUp
```

ALSO SEE

close printing command; **copy template** command; **open printing** command; **print** command

openBackground message

FORMS

```
openBackground
```

ACTION

When you change backgrounds, the **openBackground** message is sent to the destination card.

COMMENTS

Use an **openBackground** handler when a background requires a particular setup. The following example changes custom menu items to the ones appropriate for the current background:

```
on openBackground
   set the checkMark of menuItem the short name of this background ¬
   of menu "Forms" to true
   if there is no menu "Admission" then create menu "Admission"
   put "Step 1,Step 2,Step 3" into menu "Admission"
end openBackground
```

When moving from one background to another, HyperCard sends the following messages, in order:

```
closeCard          -- to old card
closeBackground    -- to old card
openBackground     -- to new card
openCard           -- to new card
```

This message is not sent as a result of the **show cards** or **print card** command, or when you get information from a card in a different background without going to it. It is also not sent if the **lockMessages** property is true.

ALSO SEE

closeBackground message; **go** command; **newBackground** message; **openCard** message; **openStack** message

openCard message

FORMS

```
openCard
```

ACTION

The **openCard** message is sent to the destination card when you change cards.

COMMENTS

If your stack requires certain actions to be taken whenever the user changes cards, or if a particular card requires a certain setup, use an **openCard** handler.

The following example belongs in the background script, and sets up an icon to show whether or not there's already a note when you go to a new card:

```
on openCard
  if field "Notes" is empty
  then set the icon of background button "Notes" to "New Note"
  else set the icon of background button "Notes" to "Old Note"
end openCard
```

This message is not sent as a result of the **show cards** or **print card** command, or when you get information from another card without going to it first. It is also not sent if the **lockMessages** property is true.

ALSO SEE

closeCard message; **go** command; **newCard** message; **openBackground** message; **openStack** message

---

openField message   Introduced in version 1.0

FORMS

openField

ACTION

The **openField** message is sent to an unlocked field when it's opened for text editing.

COMMENTS

The **openField** message is sent to an unlocked field when:

- The user or a script clicks within the field.
- The user tabs into the field by pressing the Tab key (or by pressing Return, if the previous field's **autoTab** property was set to true).

No **openField** message is sent when you use the **put** command to change a field's text, or when you use the **select** command to select or place an insertion point in a field.

ALSO SEE

closeField message; **exitField** message; **select** command

openPalette message

FORMS

```
openPalette paletteName,windowID
openPalette Navigator,5646788
```

ACTION

The **openPalette** message is sent to the current card when you use the **palette** command to create a floating palette.

COMMENTS

The *paletteName* parameter is the same as the name passed to the **palette** command.

You can store the *windowID* reported in this message for later use. There may be more than one window with the same name, but the window ID is always unique, so you can use it as an unambiguous way to identify a window.

Changes to HyperTalk: In version 2.0, the **openPalette** and **closePalette** messages have the *name* parameter, but not the *windowID* parameter.

ALSO SEE

closePalette message; **openStack** message; **palette** command

---

openPicture message

FORMS

```
openPicture windowName,windowID
openPicture "Dozing Cat",5637788
```

ACTION

The **openPicture** message is sent to the current card when you use the **picture** command to create a picture window.

COMMENTS

The *windowName* parameter is the same as the name passed to the **picture** command.

You can store the *windowID* reported by this message for later use. There may be more than one window with the same name, but the window ID is always unique, so you can use it as an unambiguous way to identify a window.

Changes to HyperTalk: In version 2.0, the **openPicture** and **closePicture** messages have the *name* parameter, but not the *windowID* parameter.

ALSO SEE

closePicture message; **openStack** message; **picture** command

openStack message

FORMS

```
openStack
```

ACTION

When you open a stack, the **openStack** message is sent to the destination card.

COMMENTS

Use the **openStack** handler to set up the environment for your stack, and to do things that should happen when the user first goes to the stack. The following handler displays a splash screen (which might hold the name of the stack, a welcome to the user, stack credits, and so forth) every time its stack opens:

```
on openStack
  picture "Credits",resource,shadow -- displays a PICT resource
  wait until the mouseClick
  close window "Credits"
  pass openStack
end openStack
```

The **openStack** message is sent when:

- HyperCard starts up and opens a stack.
- You open a stack with the **go** command or the Open Stack menu item.
- You create a stack with the **create stack** command or the New Stack menu item.

The message is not sent when you bring an already-open stack's window to the front, however—**resumeStack** is sent instead. HyperCard does not send **openStack** when you get information from another stack without going to it. If the **lockMessages** property is true, HyperCard doesn't send **openStack** at all.

The following messages are sent, in order, when HyperCard is going to another stack:

```
openStack
openBackground
openCard
```

ALSO SEE

closeStack message; **go** command; **newStack** message; **openBackground** message; **openCard** message

optionKey function

FORMS

```
the optionKey
optionKey()
if the optionKey is down then exit mouseUp
put the optionKey into optionState -- store for later use
set the hilite of me to the optionKey is down
```

ACTION

The **optionKey** function returns the state of the Option key (up if the key is being pressed or down if it's not).

COMMENTS

The **optionKey** function is useful when you want to add an alternative function to a button press or menu choice. It's a great way to add useful capabilities for stack development while leaving the main scripts unchanged.

The following example lets you drag a button without switching to the button tool by holding down the Option key:

```
on mouseDown
   if the optionKey is down then
     repeat until the mouse is up
       set the location of the target to the mouseLoc
     end repeat
     exit to HyperCard -- eat the mouseUp message
   else
     play "Tender Is The Night" -- main function of button
   end if
end mouseDown
```

ALSO SEE

commandKey function; **shiftKey** function

owner property

FORMS

```
the [long|short] owner of {window|card}
put the owner of window "My Picture" into pictureXCMDName
if the owner of window "Controls" is "Palette" then beep
get the short owner of card "Server Controls"
put the owner of marked card 17 into field "Card Owner"
```

ACTION

The **owner** property specifies the entity (HyperCard itself or an XCMD) that created a window, or the name of the background a card belongs to.

This property is read-only and cannot be set.

COMMENTS

Use the **owner** property when you need to know how a window was created, or when you want to know what background a card belongs to without going to that card. This handler hides all open windows except the current card window and the windows created by the **picture** built-in XCMD:

```
on mouseUp
  repeat with nextWindow = 1 to the number of windows
    if the owner of window nextWindow is "HyperCard" then
      if the name of window nextWindow ¬
      is not the short name of this stack then
        hide window nextWindow
      end if
    else if the owner of window nextWindow is not "Picture"
    then hide window nextWindow
  end repeat
end mouseUp
```

This example is from a library-management stack that uses a different background for each type of material that can be checked out (books, magazines, tapes, and so on). The following function handler makes a list of overdue materials and their types:

```
function getOverdueList
  unmark all cards
  -- the due date converted to seconds is in hidden field
  mark cards where field "Converted Due Date" < the seconds
  put "Overdue Materials:" into overdueList
  repeat with nextCard = 1 to the number of marked cards
    put return & the short owner of marked card nextCard & "," ¬
    && the name of marked card nextCard after overdueList
  end repeat
  sort lines of overdueList by first item of each
  return overdueList
end function
```

The *window* or *card* can be specified with any valid window or card descriptor. You can use names, numbers, or IDs. For cards, you can also use special descriptors like this card. The card must be in the current stack.

The long owner and short owner of a card yields the long or short name of the card's background. For instance, if a card belongs to a background named "My Background", the various forms of the **owner** property would give the following results:

```
the owner of this card        -- bkgnd "My Background"
the short owner of this card  -- My Background
the long owner of this card
-- bkgnd "My Background" of stack "Unknown Magnanimity:Updates"
```

Using short or long with **the owner of *window*** has no effect.

If the background has no name, **the owner** returns the background's ID.

The ownership of windows is as follows:

- Stack windows and built-in HyperCard windows (such as the message box, scroll window, tool window, pattern window, and FatBits window) are owned by HyperCard; the value of the **owner** property is HyperCard.

- External windows are owned by the XCMD or XFCN that created them; **the owner** is the name of the XCMD or XFCN.

- Under System 6.x without MultiFinder, desk accessory windows that are opened in HyperCard are owned by System.

ALSO SEE

ID property; **name** property; **number of object** function

---

palette command   Introduced in version 2.0

FORMS

palette name[,topLeft]
```
palette "Navigator"
palette thisPalette,"40,40"
palette "My Buttons",myPaletteLoc
```

ACTION

The **palette** command (which is actually an XCMD stored in HyperCard's resource fork) displays a floating palette from the resource fork of any stack in the resource path.

COMMENTS

HyperCard has one built-in, readymade palette called "Navigator". The Navigator palette lets you perform any action available in the Go menu by clicking a button. This handler appends a Navigator item to the Go menu:

```
on startup -- in Home stack script
  put "Navigator" after menu "Go" with menuMessage "toggleNavigator"
  set the commandChar of menuItem "Navigator" of menu "Go" to "G"
  pass startup
end startup
```

```
on toggleNavigator -- handles message sent by the Navigator menu item
   if there is no window "Navigator" then palette "Navigator"
   else if the visible of window "Navigator" then
     hide window "Navigator"
   else show window "Navigator"
end toggleNavigator
```

The *topLeft* is the point at which the palette first appears, relative to the card window. (You can move a palette, like any other window, by dragging its title bar.) The *topLeft* consists of two integers, separated by a comma. The first item is the horizontal distance in pixels from the left edge of the card window to the palette's left edge. The second item is the vertical distance from the top of the card window to the top of the palette.

Making your own palettes: You can create your own palettes by using the Palette Maker card in the Power Tools stack. The Navigator palette is stored in the Home stack; you can store other palettes there, in the current stack, or in any stack in use.

Each button can contain one line of HyperTalk code. This is usually a custom message that triggers a handler in the stack you're using the palette in. When you click one of the buttons in a palette, the button's statement is sent to the current card.

What's in a palette: A palette consists of two resources: a PICT containing the graphic background of the palette, and a PLTE, which contains the information describing the palette's buttons, their location, and their messages. Both of these resources must have the same name and resource ID. The *paletteName* is this resource name.

If you want to add color to your palette, paste the palette's PICT resource into your favorite color paint program, add color, then paste the new picture back into the original PICT resource. (Make sure it's the same size as the original.) Your palette will now appear with the new color PICT.

Techie alert: Here is an MPW Rez description for the PLTE resource:

```
type 'PLTE' {
   integer;                          /* PLTE resource version        */
   integer;                          /* window proc                  */
   integer hilite = -1,button;       /* instantaneous or persistent  */
   integer invert = 0,frame;         /* invert or frame hiliting     */
   integer;                          /* PICT resource ID             */
   point;                            /* origin                       */
   longint;                          /* reserved                     */
   longint;                          /* refCon                       */
   integer = $$CountOf(ButtonArray);
   array ButtonArray {
                   Rect;        /* local to palette       */
                   integer;     /* reserved               */
                   pstring;     /* message sent by button */
                   align word;
                   };
   };
```

You can use the MPW Rez tool to compile this description into a ResEdit template. When the template is installed in ResEdit, it lets you view and edit the various parts of the PLTE resource directly.

ALSO SEE

buttonCount property; **closePalette** message; **commands** property; **hide** command; **hilitedButton** property; **openPalette** message; **show** command

---

param function

Introduced in version 1.0

FORMS

```
[the] param of parameterNumber
param(parameterNumber)
param(0) -- the name of the handler being executed
param(3) -- third parameter passed to the current handler
if param(singh) is "productManager" then ship HyperCard
```

ACTION

The **param** function returns the value of the specified parameter belonging to the current function or message handler.

COMMENTS

The **param** function is particularly useful when you're not sure how many parameters are going to be passed to your handler. The following example computes the product of whatever numbers are passed to it:

```
function product
  put 1 into total
  repeat with nextFactor = 1 to the paramCount
    multiply total by param(nextFactor)
  end repeat
  return total
end product
```

You might call this function like this:

```
get product(3,2,7,9) -- returns 3*2*7*9, or 378
```

A function or message can have up to 50 parameters. The exact number may be larger—it depends upon the amount of memory available—but you can always have at least 50.

The **param** function returns empty if the *parameterNumber* you specify is greater than the number of parameters that were passed. The **param** function always returns empty when you call it from the message box.

Knowledge of parameter passing required: Before you can fully understand this function, you need to know how HyperCard passes parameters. For more information about this topic, see the section "Parameters and Parameter Passing" in Chapter 8.

The param, params, and paramCount functions: These three related functions work together as follows. Suppose you call a message with the line

```
myMessage "foo",1+5
```

When evaluated from within the `myMessage` handler, the three functions return as follows:

```
the paramCount -- returns 2
the params     -- returns myMessage "foo","6"
param(0)       -- returns "myMessage"
param(1)       -- returns "foo"
param(2)       -- returns 6
```

ALSO SEE

"Parameters and Parameter Passing" in Chapter 8; **function** keyword; **on** keyword; **paramCount** function; **params** function

---

paramCount function   Introduced in version 1.0

FORMS

the paramCount
paramCount()
`if the paramCount > stillCount then next repeat`

ACTION

The **paramCount** function returns the number of parameters passed to the current handler. **The paramCount** doesn't count the handler name itself as a parameter.

COMMENTS

You'll usually use **paramCount** in conjunction with the **params** function to loop through all the parameters passed to a custom function or message handler. The following example clears whatever fields you tell it to:

```
on clearFields
  repeat with nextField = 1 to the paramCount
    put empty into field param(nextField)
  end repeat
end clearFields
```

The above handler is called with a series of field names or numbers, like this:

```
clearField "Date","Total","Name" -- as many fields as you want
```

A function or message can have up to 50 parameters. The exact number may be larger—it depends upon the amount of memory available—but you can always have at least 50.

Parameters evaluated before passing: HyperTalk evaluates the expressions in the parameter list before passing them. The number **paramCount** returns is the count of values after evaluation. For example, a message or function call might have the expression `3 * 4 + 5` as one of its parameters; this parameter is passed as the single value 17, rather than as five separate tokens.

The parameter list is a comma-separated list of expressions, so you can think of the **paramCount** as the number of items in the parameter list.

Knowledge of parameter passing required: Before you can fully understand this function, you need to know how HyperCard passes parameters. For more information about this topic, see the section "Parameters and Parameter Passing" in Chapter 8.

ALSO SEE

"Parameters and Parameter Passing" in Chapter 8; **function** keyword; **on** keyword; **param** function; **params** function

---

params function

Introduced in version 1.0

FORMS

```
the params
params()
send the params to this card
answer the params
```

ACTION

The **params** function returns the entire list of parameters that have been passed to the current handler, including the message or function name.

COMMENTS

The **params** function lets you pass a message or function to the next level of the message path, then perform additional statements after the message is passed. The following handler intercepts the **set** command, lets HyperCard reset the user level, and then checks to make sure the user level was set to the requested value:

```
on set theThing
   if theThing is not "userLevel" then pass set
   send the params to HyperCard
```

```
      if the userLevel is not param(3) then
         answer "Failed to set user level!"
      end if
   end set
```

The statement `send the params to HyperCard` is almost the same as `pass` *message*. The only difference is that the **pass** keyword causes HyperTalk to ignore the rest of the handler; the **send** keyword, on the other hand, returns control to the current handler after the message has been sent. Therefore, `send the params to HyperCard` lets you execute more statements after HyperCard has executed the original command.

The first word of the value that **the params** returns is the name of the current handler. After the message or function name come the parameter values. If the current handler is a custom message or function, each parameter is enclosed in quotation marks. For example, suppose you invoke the custom handler "theList" with the following line:

```
   theList pi + 0,32/7,"fred",myNumber,3 + 4 + 5
```

Since HyperCard evaluates parameters before passing them, checking **the params** from within your handler yields the following (supposing the value of the variable "myNumber" is 7):

```
   theList "3.141593","4.571429","fred","7","12"
```

Knowledge of parameter passing required: Before you can fully understand this function, you need to know how HyperCard passes parameters. For more information about this topic, see the section "Parameters and Parameter Passing" in Chapter 8.

Not all commands and functions support the params: You can use the **params** function with all custom messages and functions, but it doesn't work properly with certain built-in commands and functions. (This is Yet Another HyperCard Anomaly, or "YAHA" for short. Unkind people might call this behavior a bug.) The following commands and functions don't work properly with the **params** function:

add	beep	click	commandKeyDown	convert	copy
create	debug	delete	disable	divide	drag
edit	enable	export	functionKey	get	go
import	keyDown	mark	multiply	play	pop
print	push	put	read	reply	request
save	select	sort	subtract	type	unmark
visual	wait	write			
annuity	compound	max	min	number	offset

If you want to check whether **the params** will yield the result you want when used with a particular command, you can use the following test:

```
on commandName
   put the params -- shows you what you're working with
   send the params to HyperCard
end commandName
```

If HyperCard puts up a dialog complaining that it can't understand the parameters, **the params** is not implemented, or is only partially implemented, for that command. However, be careful about writing scripts based on partial implementation, because the way such commands work with the **params** function is guaranteed to change in later versions.

Changes to HyperTalk: In versions of HyperCard before 2.1, the following commands don't support the **params** (in addition to those listed above):

```
start using
stop using
set
```

In versions before 2.0, the following commands don't support the **params** (in addition to those listed above):

```
ask
dial
hide
show
```

ALSO SEE

"Parameters and Parameter Passing" in Chapter 8; **destination** function; **function** keyword; **on** keyword; **paramCount** function; **params** function

---

partNumber property   Introduced in version 2.2

FORMS

```
set [the] partNumber of {part|button|field} to number
set the partNumber of card field "Text" to 1 -- sends to back
if the partNumber of button nextButton ≥ oldButton then beep
set the partNumber of card field "Help" of last card to nextPartNumber
```

ACTION

The **partNumber** property reports the front-to-back position of a button or field within its card or background. Increasing the **partNumber** of a part by 1 is equivalent to choosing Bring Closer from the Objects menu; decreasing it by 1 is equivalent to Send Farther.

COMMENTS

You can compare the **partNumber** property of a field or button with the **partNumber** of other parts on the same card or background to find out whether a part is hidden behind other parts. You can also change the visual layout of your card or background by changing the order of parts.

The following handler changes the **partNumber** of one object to bring it in front of another:

```
on bringInFront frontPart,backPart -- put frontPart in front of backPart
   if the partNumber of frontPart > the partNumber of backPart
   then exit bringToFront -- frontPart is already in front of backPart
   set the partNumber of frontPart to ¬
   the partNumber of backPart + 1
   unlock screen -- force an update
end bringInFront
```

The *button* or *field* is any button or field on any card or background in the current stack. The *number* is any valid part number in the specified card or background; if you give a number greater than the total number of parts, HyperCard puts up an error dialog.

The greater the **partNumber**, the farther forward the object is. If the **partNumber** is equal to **the number of parts**, the object is in front of all other objects on its card or background.

The smaller the **partNumber**, the farther back the object is. If the **partNumber** is 1, the object is behind all other objects on its card or background.

ALSO SEE

number of object function

---

pass keyword

Introduced in version 1.0

FORMS

pass *messageName*
```
pass mouseUp
pass myCustomFunction
pass myHandler
```

ACTION

The **pass** keyword stops execution of the current function or message handler, and passes the message that triggered it to the next step along the message path.

The *messageName* must be the name of the current handler.

COMMENTS

The **pass** keyword, which usually appears in an **if...then...else** construct, is usually used in handlers that override a built-in command or a handler farther along the message path.

This handler captures **doMenu** messages (which are sent whenever a user chooses a menu item), overriding the normal action for the Help item and passing any other items along:

```
on doMenu theItem
   if theItem is "Help" then go to card "Help"
   else pass doMenu
end doMenu
```

If the menu item is Help, the **doMenu** message is intercepted by this handler and goes no farther. If any other menu item was chosen, the handler lets the **doMenu** message pass through it and continue on the message path. If no other handler intercepts it, it eventually gets to HyperCard itself, which performs the usual action for whatever menu item was chosen.

The parameters of *messageName* are sent along unchanged when you pass the message along. Any changes your code has made to the parameters are ignored when you use **pass**, although changes made to nonparameters—the contents of fields, global variables, and so on—remain in effect. If you want to send the message along the path, but with changed parameters, use the **send** keyword instead:

```
on myMessage theVariable -- presumably in a card script
   send "myMessage" && theVariable * 3 to this background
end myMessage
```

Another use for **pass** is to confirm actions before executing a command:

```
on sort
   answer "Are you sure you want to sort this stack?"¬
   with "OK" or "Cancel"
   -- if we don't pass the message, it's blocked and won't execute
   if it is "OK" then pass sort
end sort
```

If another handler named *messageName* is between the passing handler and HyperCard, that handler will catch the message when it's passed on. So the same message can set off a number of same-named handlers at different places along the message path. But **pass** always sends the message to the next level, so **pass** can't make the same handler execute twice.

ALSO SEE

Messages and the Message Order (Chapter 10)**; exit** keyword; **send** keyword

---

pattern property

Introduced in version 1.0

FORMS

```
set [the] pattern [of HyperCard] to patternNumber
set the pattern to 1 -- white
set the pattern to 12 -- black
select line the pattern of card button "Pattern:" -- a popup
```

ACTION

The **pattern** global property specifies the currently selected pattern, used by the paint tools.

Setting the **pattern** is equivalent to choosing a pattern from the Patterns tear-off menu. By default, the **pattern** is 12 (solid black).

Figure III.36   Patterns menu with numeric equivalents

COMMENTS

The *patternNumber* is between 1 and 40, and designates whatever pattern is in the corresponding position in the Patterns menu (see Figure III.36). Patterns are numbered from top to bottom, left to right.

If you use the Edit Patterns item in the Options menu to change a pattern, the new pattern has the same number as the one you edited to create it. (Edited patterns are saved in the stack.)

You can specify any integer as the *patternNumber* without causing a script error. If you specify a number less than one, the **pattern** is unchanged. (Values 65537 through 65576 repeat patterns 1 through 40, but this is an anomaly and may change in future versions.)

The following handler draws 40 circles, each filled with a different pattern (shown in Figure III.37):

```
on balloons
   choose oval tool
   set the filled to true
   set the centered to true
   put 60 into centerH
   put 60 into centerV
   repeat with i = 1 to 40
      set the pattern to i
      drag from centerH,centerV to centerH + 40, centerV + 40
```

Figure III.37   Pattern balloons

```
            add 50 to centerH
            if centerH > 450 then
               put 60 into centerH
               add 50 to centerV
            end if
         end repeat
         choose browse tool
      end balloons
```

ALSO SEE

filled property; **reset paint** command

---

picture command

Introduced in version 2.0
Last changed in version 2.1

FORMS

picture [name[,source[,windowStyle[,visible[,bitDepth[floatingLayer]]]]]]

```
picture-- displays an Open dialog and shows the picture you select
picture "Dog" -- displays the file "Dog"
picture "Dog",clipboard,roundRect
   -- puts clipboard contents in a round rect window titled "Dog"
picture "Dog",resource,dialog,true,8
   -- puts the resource "Dog" into a dialog box window,
   -- with a maximum of 256 colors (8 bits)
```

ACTION

The **picture** command (which is actually an XCMD in HyperCard's resource fork) displays a color or black-and-white PICT or MacPaint image from the clipboard, a file, or a resource in the current stack. You can choose from a variety of window styles for the picture.

COMMENTS

This example displays a status picture to give the user something interesting to look at during a long sort operation:

```
on sortWithPicture
   picture "Sort Screen",file,rect,false
   -- if memory is low, the picture might not be there, so we check:
   put the value of (the result is empty) into pictureWasShown
   if pictureWasShown then set the rect of window ¬
   "Sort Screen" to the rect of card window
   sort by sortKey()
   if pictureWasShown then close window "Sort Screen"
end sortWithPicture
```

The *name* is the name of a MacPaint file, a PICT file, a resource, or a name you choose to give the picture in the clipboard. It is also the name HyperCard will use for the picture window. If you specify a pathname for a file, the window name will be the entire pathname. If you do not specify a name, the **picture** command displays the standard file dialog and asks you to choose a file.

The *source* can be file, resource, or clipboard. The default is file. If you use clipboard and the clipboard does not contain a picture, nothing is displayed and **the result** is set to an error message.

The *windowStyle* can be dialog, plain, document, rect, roundRect, shadow, windoid, zoom, or windoidZoom. (See Figure III.38.) If the *floatingLayer* is not specified, the rect, shadow, windoid, and windoidZoom styles appear on top of the card layer. Card windows can be moved in front of all other window styles. Because the rect, dialog, and shadow styles have no close box, the only way to close them is with the **close window** command.

The *visible* can be true or false, and determines whether the window is visible or not when it's first created. If you want to change some of the window's properties before letting the user see it, create the window invisible, change the necessary properties, then set the window's **visible** property to true.

The *bitDepth* can be any power of 2 from 0 to 32, and sets the number of bits per pixel at which the picture is displayed. For example, if the bit depth is 8, the picture is displayed with a maximum of 256 colors (8 bits). If the bit depth is 0, the picture is drawn directly into the window. A *bitDepth* of 0 lets you display a color PICT in the old (pre-Mac II) QuickDraw format, but it prevents dithering and slows down scrolling.

FloatingLayer can be true or false. If it is set to true, the window appears in the palette layer, in front of card windows. If it's set to false, the window appears in the window layer and palettes appear in front of it. If you don't specify a layer, the *windowStyle* determines what layer the window appears in.

Troubleshooting: If you try to display a picture deeper than 8 pixels on a system that doesn't have 32-bit QuickDraw installed, you will get an empty window. All systems running

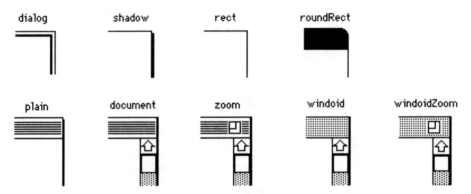

Figure III.38   Picture window styles

System 7.0 or later and all color-capable Macintosh models later than the Mac IIci have 32-bit QuickDraw installed.

The **picture** command sets **the result** to an error message if the picture could not be displayed. The most common problem is lack of sufficient memory. If you are displaying multiple pictures, color pictures, or large pictures, set HyperCard's memory partition to at least 2 megabytes.

Techie alert: Instead of the *windowStyle* names, you can use numbers representing your own window definition functions (WDEFs) and variation codes. The number is:

```
(16 * <WDEF resource ID>) + window variation code
```

For example, to display a PICT named "Apple Logo" using a WDEF whose resource ID is 131, use the command

```
picture "Apple Logo",file,(16 * 131)
```

Using a *bitDepth* of 0 lets you show a simple animation into a picture window: paste each frame of the animation into a PICT document in the order you want the frames to appear, and then save the PICT. When the picture is drawn with bit depth 0, each frame will be drawn in order.

Changes to HyperTalk: In versions of HyperCard before 2.1, there is no *floatingLayer* parameter and the layer of picture windows is determined by their style. The `rect`, `shadow`, `windoid`, and `windoidZoom` styles float, and all other styles are standard windows.

ALSO SEE

closePicture message; **dithering** property; **globalLoc** property; **globalRect** property; **icon** property; **location** property; **mouseDownInPicture** message; **mouseUpInPicture** message; **openPicture** message; **pictureHeight** property; **pictureWidth** property; **rectangle** property; **scale** property; **scroll of window** property; **zoomed** property

---

pictureHeight property

Introduced in version 2.0

FORMS

```
the pictureHeight of pictureWindow
get the pictureHeight of window ID nextID
put the pictureHeight of window "Baby Picture" into field "Height"
```

ACTION

The **pictureHeight** property determines the distance in pixels between the top and bottom edges of a window created by the **picture** command.

This property is read-only and cannot be changed by a handler.

COMMENTS

The **pictureHeight** property reports an integer that's equal to the vertical distance in pixels from the top edge of the picture to its bottom edge.

The pictureHeight and rectangle properties: The **pictureHeight** of a picture window is the difference between item 4 and item 2 of its **rectangle** property. Anything that resizes the window may change its **pictureHeight** property.

ALSO SEE

location property; **rectangle** property; **left** property; **picture** command; **pictureWidth** property; **right** property

---

pictureWidth property   Introduced in version 2.0

FORMS

```
the pictureWidth of pictureWindow
get the pictureWidth of window "Pictures of Lily"
if the pictureWidth of window myPict > 200 then close window myPicture
```

ACTION

The **pictureWidth** property determines the distance in pixels between the left and right edges of a window created by the **picture** command.
  This property is read-only and cannot be changed by a handler.

COMMENTS

The **pictureWidth** property reports an integer that's equal to the horizontal distance in pixels from the left edge oif the picture to its right edge.

The pictureWidth and rectangle properties: The **pictureWidth** of a picture window is the difference between item 3 and item 1 of its **rectangle** property. Anything that resizes the window may change its **pictureWidth** property.

ALSO SEE

location property; **rectangle** property; **left** property; **picture** command; **pictureHeight** property; **right** property

---

play command   Introduced in version 1.0

FORMS

```
play sound {tempo tempo} {notesList}
play stop
play "flute"
```

```
play "Voice Sample" "G3" -- plays the voice in bass register
play mySample tempo 180 C4e C Dq C F Eh
play "boing" myNoteList
play the selectedText of button "Sound:" -- a popup menu button
```

ACTION

The **play** command plays a digitized sound resource located in the current stack, the Home stack, or a stack in use.

The sound volume is set in the Sound control panel.

COMMENTS

You can use the **play** command to play a single digitized sound, or a sequence of notes making up a tune.

The following handler plays the opening notes from a once-popular television series:

```
on bookHimDanno
   play "harpsichord" tempo 200 Ge G Bb D5 Cq. G4h. Ge G F Bbq. Gh.
end bookHimDanno
```

The *sound* is the name of a "snd" resource stored in one of the stacks in the message-passing path. You can think of the *sound* as the characteristic sound of an electronic instrument—the sound you think of when you read the name "piano" or "tuba" or "1957 Chevy". HyperCard comes with three sounds built in: harpsichord, flute, and boing.

The *tempo* is a positive integer specifying the speed at which the sequence of notes plays. The default *tempo* is 120; the higher the tempo, the faster the notes play. If you play a sequence of notes with a fast *tempo* and a long *sound*, the end of each note may be clipped off by the next note.

The *notesList* is a sequence of one or more notes separated by spaces. Each note can have a note name (A-G), an accidental, an octave, and a duration. If you don't specify a *notesList*, the *sound* is played at the pitch it was recorded at, which is designated middle C.

How a note is constructed: Each note must have a note name: A, B, C, D, E, F, or G. (There's no difference between uppercase and lowercase.) The letter R indicates a rest. Accidentals (sharps and flats) are indicated by # and b respectively. For example, D-sharp is written D# and B-flat is written Bb.

A note's octave is expressed as a number. The octave beginning with middle C is octave 4, and 4 is the default. D above middle C is written D or D4; G three octaves above middle C is written G6; F two octaves below middle C is written F2. The octaves range from 1 to 7.

A note can have any duration from whole note to sixty-fourth note. The *duration* is represented by a letter:

w	whole note
h	half note
q	quarter note
e	eighth note
s	sixteenth note
t	thirty-second note
x	sixty-fourth note

Add a period (.) after the duration letter to indicate a dotted note (a note that plays 1.5 times its normal duration); add a 3 after the duration letter to indicate a triplet (a note that plays 2/3 of normal duration). The default *duration* is a quarter note.

You can state the qualities of a note in any order, but if a notes starts with e or b, HyperCard interprets the letter as the note name. Otherwise "e" means "eighth note" and "b" means "flat". To avoid any ambiguity, use the order *name accidental octave duration*.

If you don't state an *octave* or *duration* for a note, it's played in the same octave or with the same duration as the preceding note.

Alternative number notation for notes: You can also use a single number to represent a note's name, accidental, and octave. The numbering is simple: middle C is 60, and a distance of a half step translates to a difference of 1. For example, B below middle C is one half-step down, so its number is 59; D# above middle C is three halt-steps up, so its number is 63.

Six Octaves of Notes by Number

C 3 below Middle C	C 1 below Middle C	C 1 above Middle C
24 C	48 C	72 C
25 ....C#	49 ....C#	73 ....C#
26 ....D	50 ....D	74 ....D
27 ....D#	51 ....D#	75 ....D#
30 ....F	54 ....F	78 ....F
31 ....G	55 ....G	79 ....G
32 ....G	56 ....G#	80 ....G#
33 ....A	57 ....A	81 ....A
34 ....A#	58 ....A#	82 ....A#
35 ....B	59 ....B	83 ....B

C 2 below Middle C	Middle C	C 2 above Middle C
36 C	60 C	84 C
37 ....C#	61 ....C#	85 ....C#
38 ....D	62 ....D	86 ....D
39 ....D#	63 ....D#	87 ....D#
40 ....E	64 ....E	88 ....E
41 ....E#	65 ....E#	89 ....E#
42 ....F	66 ....F	90 ....F
43 ....G	67 ....G	91 ....G
44 ....G	68 ....G#	92 ....G#
45 ....A	69 ....A	93 ....A
46 ....A#	70 ....A#	94 ....A#
47 ....B	71 ....B	95 ....B

The following handler plays the middle C octave:

```
on rubenstein
   repeat with i = 60 to 71
      play harpsichord i
   end repeat
end rubenstein
```

If you have an extended keyboard, you can use the following handler to assign notes to your function keys and pretend to be a big-time rock star. The handler assigns F below middle C to the F1 key, middle C to F8, and G above middle C to F15. Put it into a card script and rock on:

```
on functionKey theKey
   play flute theKey + 52
end functionKey
```

Play is asynchronous: The **play** command, unlike **beep**, is asynchronous, meaning that processing of the current handler continues while the sound is playing. To find out what sound is currently playing, use the **sound** function.

A beep (from either the **beep** command or the system) cancels the playing of any sounds that have been queued up. The sound channel cannot be used for beeps and played sounds at the same time.

The form `play stop` halts whatever sound is playing. This can be useful if the sound is so long that it continues to play after you no longer need it. The following handler plays a sequence of scales (suitable for driving the neighbors crazy, if you hook your Mac's sound port up to a good amplifier):

```
on playScales
   put "CDEFGAB" into theNotes
   repeat with i = 1 to the length of theNotes
      play harpsichord (char i of theNotes)
      repeat with j = the length of theNotes down to i
         if the mouseClick then
            play stop -- shaddup already!
            exit playScales
         end if
         play harpsichord (char j of theNotes)
      end repeat
   end repeat
end playScales
```

Buffering sounds: Sounds take time to load from the disk. To avoid a delay in playing, you can preload the sound at an appropriate time (such as the **openStack** or **openCard** handler) with the following line:

```
play "My Sound" R -- R indicates rest, so sound loads without playing
```

The following handler shows how to use buffering and the **sound** function to coordinate each sound with a corresponding card. The sound samples can be be long—they might be pieces of a digitized song, which must be played one after the other without a pause between pieces.

```
on playMusicVideo
   repeat with x = 1 to the number of cards
      put the short name of card x into nextCard
      play nextCard          -- load sound for next card...
      wait until the sound is nextCard --...wait until it starts...
         go to card nextCard  --...and go to that card as its sound starts
   end repeat
end playMusicVideo
```

Since the amount of memory it takes to play a sound depends on its length (HyperCard requires about 22K of free RAM to play a second of high-quality digitized sound), the above example also illustrates a method of playing very long digitized samples in low memory. Simply use a sound editing program to chop the sample into pieces, and use the double-buffering technique to play them without an audible break between parts.

Things you can't do: You can't change the sound volume from HyperTalk (although there are XCMDs that will do it). You can play only a single voice; you can't play chords with the **play** command. You can't run for President of the United States if you're a naturalized citizen.

If the sound volume is set to 0 in the Sound control panel, an XCMD is using the sound channel, or HyperCard is in the background, **the result** is set to "Sound is off." If **play** can't find the sound you specify, or the **play** command encounters some other problem (such as a memory shortage), it sets **the result** to "Couldn't load sound".

Quotes and the note list: If you don't enclose the *notesList* in quotation marks, HyperCard assumes everything to the end of the line is a note. A statement such as

```
play harpsichord a b c d -- this is a comment
```

can cause some strange things to come out of your speaker, because HyperCard assumes everything after "harpsichord"—including the text of the comment—is part of the note list. When in doubt, enclose the *notesList* in quotes.

A few songs for your listening pleasure...

```
play harpsichord tempo 180 E4 D C D Dh A3h Aq C4 F F Ew
play harpsichord tempo 150 Ae G Gh Be4 C5# D5# E F# G F# E Eh
play harpsichord tempo 180 Fe F F Fq Fe F Gq Fe Fq Fe F F B4bq B4be C5q.
play harpsichord tempo 200 G Bb Bb Bb Abh Gq Bbh..
play harpsichord tempo 180 C C Ch Eq D Ch Eq F Gh D D.
play harpsichord Dq Dq B3e D4q. Ee F#e Ge Aq Ge Eq.
```

Changes to HyperTalk: In versions of HyperCard before 2.2, you are limited to 254 notes in a single **play** command, and **play** doesn't set **the result**, even if there's an error.

The flute sound is not included in versions of HyperCard before 2.0

ALSO SEE

beep command; **sound** function

---

polySides property

Introduced in version 1.0

FORMS

```
set [the] polySides [of HyperCard] to numberOfSides
set the polySides to 5 -- draw pentagons
```

ACTION

The **polySides** property specifies what kind of shape the regular polygon tool draws.

Setting the **polySides** to 3, 4, 5, 6, 8, or 0 is equivalent to choosing (respectively) the triangle, square, pentagon, hexagon, octagon, or circle in the Polygon Sides dialog. By default, the **polySides** is 4.

COMMENTS

The following handler draws lots of different polygons filled with different patterns:

```
on polygonSamples
   choose regular polygon tool
   set the dragSpeed to 300
   put the width of card window div 2 into centerH
   put the height of card window div 2 into centerV
   repeat until the mouseClick
      set the polySides to any item of "3,4,5,6,7,8"
      set the filled to true
      set the pattern to random(40)
      drag from centerH,centerV to random(centerH),random(centerV)
   end repeat
   doMenu "Select All"
   doMenu "Clear Picture"
   choose browse tool
end polygonSamples
```

The *numberOfSides* is an integer between 3 and 50, or 0 for a circle shape. If you specify 1, 2, or a negative number of sides, the **polySides** is set to 3; if you provide a number greater than 50, the **polySides** is set to 50.

The larger the number of sides, the closer the polygon is to a circle.

ALSO SEE

drag command; **reset paint** command; **tool** function

---

pop command   Introduced in version 1.0

FORMS

```
pop card [{before|into|after} [chunk of] container]
pop card -- go to last-pushed card
pop card into myCard -- places ID in myCard variable
pop card after field "Print List" -- adds ID to bottom of list
pop card before line 3 of button "Visited Cards:" -- a popup
```

ACTION

The **pop** command retrieves the location of the most recently pushed card and removes it from the pushed-cards list. If you specify a container, **pop** puts the long ID of the card into the container; otherwise, it goes directly to the card.

COMMENTS

Use the **pop** command, in conjunction with **push**, to return to a previously stored card location. The following handler goes to an address stack to look up a name and address, and uses **push** and **pop** to keep track of the original location and return to it:

```
on lookUp cardCarrier
   lock screen
   push card
   go to stack "ACLU Membership Roster"
   find cardCarrier
   if the result is empty then get field "Street Address"
   else get "not available"
   pop card -- go back to where we were
   put "The address is" && it
   unlock screen
end lookUp
```

If there are no cards in the pushed-cards list, **pop** goes to the first card of the Home stack. When you pop a card into a *container*, the card's long ID is placed in that container; you don't go to the card, however. This lets you check which card is being popped before going to it. This example prevents popping off the end of the pushed-cards list and being sent to the Home stack:

```
on returnToPushed
   pop returnToPushed into theID -- places destination into theID
   if word 5 to 6 of theID is the long name of Home then beep
   else go to theID
end returnToPushed
```

This example shows how to check a card in the pushed-cards list, then put it back into the list:

```
on filterPushed stackName
   -- remove locations in the specified stack from push list
   put empty into pushedCards
   repeat
     -- make list of all pushed cards, leaving out "Updates" cards
     pop card into theCard
     if word 5 to 6 of theCard is the long name of Home then
     -- we've reached the end of the list
       exit repeat
     else if word 5 to 6 of theCard ¬
     is not the long name of stack stackName then
       get the number of lines of pushedCards
       put theCard into line it + 1 of pushedCards
     end if
   end repeat
   -- push the filtered cards back onto the push list
   repeat with x = the number of lines of pushedCards down to 1
     do "push" && line x of pushedCards
   end repeat
end checkPushed
```

The push list is emptied when you quit HyperCard.

Anomaly with messages, pop, and push: When you use **pop** to go to a card, system messages such as **openCard** are sent normally, but any **push** commands in handlers triggered by these messages are ignored.

ALSO SEE
go command; **push** command

---

powerKeys property

FORMS
```
set [the] powerKeys [of HyperCard] to {true|false}
set the powerKeys to true
set the powerKeys to the hilite of button "Hot Paint Keys"
```

ACTION
The **powerKeys** property determines whether you can use keyboard shortcuts when painting.
Setting the **powerKeys** is equivalent to toggling the Power Keys item in the Options menu (visible when a paint tool is chosen). You can also set this property by toggling the Power Keys checkbox on the User Preferences card in the Home stack.

COMMENTS

The **powerKeys** property lets you choose most items from the Paint and Options menus by pressing the first key of the item name.

The initial value of the **powerKeys** property is set according to the Power Keys checkbox on the User Preferences card of Home.

Power keys are not available when the message box is visible or when the browse, field, button, or paint text tool is chosen.

ALSO SEE

blindTyping property; **type** command

---

print command   Introduced in version 2.0

FORMS

```
print {text|container}
print "Hello there!"
print card field 5     -- prints with formatting intact
print (card field 5)  -- prints without formatting
print field "Greeting" of first card
print totalsGlobal
print the selection
print line 1 to 5 of the stacksInUse
print the message box
```

ACTION

The **print** command prints the contents of any field or container, or the value of any expression.

COMMENTS

You can use the **print** command to print any text in HyperCard: the contents of fields, variables, or other containers, or the value of any expression. The following handler prints a text file by reading it into a variable and then printing the variable:

```
on printTextFile
   answer file "Print what file?" of type "TEXT"
   if it is empty then exit printTextFile -- user cancelled
   put it into textToPrint
   open file textToPrint
   read from file textToPrint until end
   close file textToPrint
   print it
end printTextFile
```

The *text* can be any literal text, or any expression that evaluates to text: a variable name, a container such as the message box, a function, or any other expression. Expressions are evaluated before they're printed:

```
print field 3 - 12 -- prints the number in field 3, minus 12
print 12 + 38      -- prints 50
print "John" && "Scribblemonger" -- prints John Scribblemonger
```

The font, size, style, and alignment of the printed text are controlled by the **printTextFont**, **printTextSize**, **printTextStyle**, and **printTextAlign** properties. By default, text from the **print** command is printed in 10-point plain Geneva and is left-aligned.

Printing fields: If you specify a *field* to be printed, everything in it is printed, including any text that's scrolled out of sight on screen. The fonts, sizes, and styles of text in the field are preserved in the printout, and so is the field's word wrapping (the width of the field). If the field's **dontWrap** property is set to true, only the visible width of the field's text is printed; text that runs off the right edge of the field is cut off.

If you want to print the text of the field, but you don't want to retain the field's formatting and width, enclose the field descriptor in parentheses. This forces HyperTalk to treat the field as an expression.

Print command limited to 32K: The **print** command can print only 32K of text (32767 characters) at a time. This is Yet Another TextEdit Limitation. If you're printing a variable that contains more text than this, use a **repeat** loop to print 32K at a time.

Old HyperCard versions: In versions of HyperCard before 2.0, the only way to print the contents of a container is to export it to a text file and use the **print document** command:

```
on printContainer theContainer
   put "Disk:Temp Printing" into fileName
   open file fileName
   write theContainer to fileName
   close file fileName
   print fileName with application "TeachText"
end printContainer
```

ALSO SEE

dontWrap property; **print card** command; **printMargins** property; **printTextAlign** property; **printTextFont** property; **printTextHeight** property; **printTextStyle** property; **printTextSize** property; **reset printing** command

print card command

FORMS

```
print card [from topLeft to rightBottom]
print [number|all] cards [from topLeft to rightBottom]
print marked cards [from topLeft to rightBottom]
print card  -- same as "print this card"
print this card
print next marked card from startPoint to endPoint
print card "Logo" from 0,0 to 100,120
print marked card 3
print 32 cards
print field "Number of Students" cards -- field contains a number
print all cards
print marked cards
```

ACTION

The **print card** command prints a card or cards, using the layout settings from the Print Stack dialog.

The form `print card` is equivalent to choosing Print Card from the File menu.

COMMENTS

Use **print card** to print one or more specific cards, or, with **open printing** and **close printing**, to print a group of cards. The following example prints out only cards where a particular field contains a certain string:

```
on printCardsWith stringToFind,inField
  unmark all cards
  mark cards by finding stringToFind in field inField
  print marked cards
end printCardsWith
```

The **print card** command uses the same settings—header text (if any), card size, spacing, and layout—as the current settings of the Print Stack dialog. There is no way to change these settings from a script, unfortunately. If the users of your stack won't need to use Print Stack manually, you may want to use the **delete menu** command to remove that menu item in order to prevent changes to the Print Stack settings.

The *card* is any card in the current stack. To print a card in another stack, you need to first go to that stack.

The *topLeft* and *rightBottom* are points specifying the portion of the card to be printed. Each point consists of two integers separated by a comma: the first item is the horizontal distance in pixels from the left edge of the card window to the point, and the second item is the vertical distance from the top edge to the point. If you don't specify a *topLeft* and *rightBottom*, the entire card image is printed.

The *number* is an integer specifying how many cards to print. The form `print number cards` prints the specified number of cards from the current stack in sequence, starting with the current card. If the *number* is greater than the number of cards in the stack, the **print card** command prints all the cards in the stack and then starts over with the current card, repeating enough cards so that *number* cards altogether are printed.

Grouping multiple print card commands: All the cards printed as the result of a single **print card** command are printed as a unit, with the appropriate Print Stack settings controlling how many cards make up a page. If you have to use multiple **print card** commands to print the cards you want, but you want them all printed as a single unit, use the **open printing** command before your **print card** commands, and use **close printing** when you're finished.

Print card and messages: HyperCard visits each card as it's printed, returning to the original card when the printing is done, but it doesn't send any system messages such as **openCard** while moving from card to card during printing.

If you don't want the user to see these card changes, set the **lockScreen** property to true before you print. To let the user know something is happening, be sure to set the **cursor** property to `watch` or `busy` while the printing is going on:

```
on printCardsOnList
   global printList -- contains IDs of cards to be printed
   lock screen
   open printing
   repeat with i = 1 to the number of lines of printList
      set the cursor to busy -- spin the beachball cursor
      do "print" && line i of printList
      -- if we just said "print line i of printList", we'd get
      -- the contents of line i rather than the card it names
   end repeat
   close printing
   unlock screen
end printCardsOnList
```

ALSO SEE

close printing command; **marked** property; **open printing** command

---

print document command   Introduced in version 1.0

FORMS

```
print document with application
print "Collected Poems" with "WordMaster 9.5"
print it with myTextApp
```

ACTION

The **print document** command uses an application to print a document. It's equivalent to selecting the document in the Finder and then choosing Print from the File menu.

COMMENTS

Use the **print document** command when you have data in a document that HyperCard can't print directly.

The *application* must be the name of a Mac application located on your Mac. The *application* must support printing.

The *document* must be of a type that the *application* can open (although it doesn't necessarily have to have been created by the *application*). You must spell the names of both *application* and *document* exactly as they appear in the Finder, complete with any special characters such as ®.

If you don't give the full pathname of the *application* or *document*, HyperCard looks for them in the locations specified in the Applications and Documents global variables, respectively. These globals are set by the Home stack handler when HyperCard starts up, taking their values from the Search Path cards in the Home stack. If HyperCard can't find them in any of these locations, it puts up a standard file dialog and asks you to locate the *application* or *document*. The global variables are updated to include the location you give.

If HyperCard presents an Open dialog and the user clicks Cancel, the **result** function is set to "Cancel". If there was a problem launching the application, **the result** is set to "Couldn't open that application."

Works differently under MultiFinder: The details of implementation of the **print document** command are a little different, depending on whether you're using System 6 with or without MultiFinder, or System 7.

If you're using System 6 and MultiFinder is not active, when the application opens, HyperCard sends the **suspend** message to the current card. When you quit the application, instead of returning to the Finder, you return to the card you were on, and HyperCard sends the **resume** message to the current card. (Note carefully: **suspend** and **resume** are *not* the same as **suspendStack** and **resumeStack**.) When you use **print document**, all global variables are lost, and any commands in the handler after **print document** are ignored.

Under MultiFinder, however, when you launch another application, HyperCard continues to be open in the background, and you can switch back and forth between HyperCard and the other application.

If you're using System 7, **print document** works by means of AppleEvents. Specifically, it sends the pdoc message to the target application. If the application doesn't handle this AppleEvent, the command fails and the **result** function is set to "Not handled by target application."

Execution continues while HyperCard is suspended: If you launch an application under MultiFinder, HyperCard continues to run while in the background, so commands in your handler after **open application** are executed immediately after the application is opened. If you don't want to execute the rest of the handler until the user returns to HyperCard, use the **suspended** property to check whether HyperCard is in the foreground:

```
on mouseUp
  open "My Application"
  -- wait until the application finishes launching...
  wait until "My Application" is in menu "Application"
  -- ...then wait until you're back in HyperCard
  wait while the suspended
  -- other commands here
end mouseUp
```

It's not advisable to use the **print document** command if an **open printing** command is pending. While the architecture of the language says you shouldn't have to do this, there are reports that mysterious things happen when you try to mix print jobs.

Techie alert: This command uses the same code as **open application**.

ALSO SEE

open application command; **print** command; **resume** message; **suspend** message

---

printMargins property   Introduced in version 2.0

FORMS

set [the] printMargins [of HyperCard] to *left,top,right,bottom*
set the printMargins to "60,100,60,100"
put item 1 of the printMargins into leftMargin

ACTION

The **printMargins** global property specifies the left, top, right, and bottom margins the **print** command uses.

The default value for **printMargins** is 0,0,0,0, indicating minimum margins.

COMMENTS

HyperCard uses the **printMargins** property when printing an expression with the **print** command. This handler sets a one-inch margin all around, then prints a form letter:

```
on printLetter
  global letterText
  ask "To whom is this letter addressed?"
  if it is empty then exit printLetter   -- user cancelled
  find it in field "Contact Name"
  if the result is not empty then -- not found
    answer it && "isn't in the contacts database."
    exit printLetter
  end if
```

```
        set the printMargins to "72,72,72,72"
        print field "Address" & return & return & the long date ¬
        & return & return & "Dear" && field "Contact Name" & colon ¬
        & return & return & letterText
    end printLetter
```

The width of the margins is given in pixels. (One pixel is about 1/72 of an inch.) The *left, top, right,* and *bottom* must be integers; otherwise, HyperCard presents an error dialog. If you set one of the margins to a negative number, it is treated as though it were zero.

ALSO SEE

print command; **printTextAlign** property; **printTextFont** property; **printTextHeight** property; **printTextSize** property; **printTextStyle** property; **reset printing** command

---

printTextAlign property   Introduced in version 2.0

FORMS

```
set [the] printTextAlign [of HyperCard] to alignment
set the printTextAlign to "left"
```

ACTION

The **printTextAlign** global property sets the alignment of printed text. The possible alignments are `left`, `right`, and `center`.

The default value for **printTextAlign** is `left`.

COMMENTS

HyperCard uses the **printTextAlign** property when printing an expression, and when printing the header of a report. The following handler sets up a number of the print properties and then prints a report:

```
on printMarkedCards
    -- the following three lines set the report header properties
    set the printTextFont to "Helvetica"
    set the printTextStyle to italic
    set the printTextAlign to right
    open report printing
    print marked cards
    close report printing
    reset printing -- put everything back to the defaults
end printMarkedCards
```

In the above example, the page header for the report will appear in italic Helvetica at the upper-right corner of each page.

The *alignment* must be one of `left`, `right`, or `center`. Providing any other value will cause HyperCard to put up an error dialog.

ALSO SEE

print command; **printTextFont** property; **printTextHeight** property; **printTextSize** property; **printTextStyle** property; **reset printing** command

---

printTextFont property

Introduced in version 2.0

FORMS

```
set [the] printTextFont [of HyperCard] to fontName
set the printTextFont to "Avant Garde"
set the printTextFont to menuItem 1 of menu "Font"
```

ACTION

The **printTextFont** global property reflects the font used for printed text.

The default value for **printTextFont** is Geneva.

COMMENTS

HyperCard uses the **printTextFont** property for text printed with the **print** command and in the header of a report. The following example sets the style for a report header and prints the report:

```
on printFullReport
   set the printTextFont to "Palatino"
   set the printTextStyle to bold,italic
   open report printing with template "Full"
   print 5 cards
   close printing
   reset printing -- sets everything back to the default
end printHeadline
```

The *fontName* is any font available to the current stack. The list of available fonts can be seen by checking HyperCard's Font menu, and includes fonts in the following places:

- The System file (or Fonts folder under System 7.1)

- The resource fork of HyperCard

- The resource fork of the Home stack

- The resource fork of any stack that has been placed in the resource path with the **start using** command

- The resource fork of the current stack

The following handler prints out a sample of every available font. It requires that the Font menu be present:

```
on printFontSample theText
   if there is no menu "Font" then
      answer "There is no Font menu. Reset the menubar?" with "Yes" or "No"
      if it is "Yes" then reset menubar
      else exit printFontSample
   end if
   if theText is empty then put ¬
   "How razorback-jumping frogs can level six piqued gymnasts!" ¬
   into theText
   open printing
   repeat with thisFont = 1 to the number of menuItems of menu "Font"
      set the printTextFont to menuItem thisFont of menu "Font"
      print the printTextFont & return & theText & return & return
   end repeat
   close printing
end printFontSample
```

Techie alert: You can set the **printTextFont** by using a FOND family ID instead of a font name:

```
set the printTextFont to 4 -- sets to Monaco
```

FOND ID 0 is reserved for the System font (on systems that use the Roman alphabet, this is Chicago). FOND ID 3 is the current application font (usually Geneva).

ALSO SEE

print command; **printTextAlign** property; **printTextHeight** property; **printTextSize** property; **printTextStyle** property; **reset printing** command

---

printTextHeight property   Introduced in version 2.0

FORMS

set [the] printTextHeight [of HyperCard] to *pixelHeight*
set the printTextHeight to 12

ACTION

The **printTextHeight** global property is the vertical distance in points between printed lines. The default value for **printTextHeight** is 13.

COMMENTS

HyperCard uses the **printTextHeight** property when printing an expression and when printing the header of a report. The following handler sets up a number of the print properties before printing a headline:

```
on printHeadline theText
   set the printTextFont to "Avant Garde"
   set the printTextSize to 24      -- 24-point
   set the printTextHeight to 40  -- lots of space between lines
   print theText
   reset printing -- put everything back to the defaults
end printHeadline
```

The *pixelHeight* must be an integer; otherwise, HyperCard presents an error dialog. The minimum legal **printTextHeight** is the current **printTextSize**. If you try to set it to less than this, HyperCard sets the **printTextHeight** to the current **printTextSize**. The largest possible **printTextHeight** is 1332 points. Trying to set a larger value will set it to the maximum.

When you change the **printTextSize**, the **printTextHeight** is changed automatically to a value compatible with the text size. The formula is:

```
printTextHeight = (printTextSize * 4) div 3
```

Here are a few of the text height values corresponding to various text sizes:

Text Size	Text Height (baseline to baseline)
9-point	12 points
10-point	13 points
12-point	16 points
14-point	18 points
18-point	24 points
24-point	32 points

The following handler takes a point size and sets the **printTextHeight** to double the normal value used with that point size:

```
on doubleSpace thePointSize
   set the printTextSize to thePointSize
   -- printTextHeight is automatically set to the appropriate value for
   -- single-spaced text, so we multiply it by 2 to get double spacing:
   set the printTextHeight to 2 * the printTextHeight
end doubleSpace
```

ALSO SEE

print command; **printTextAlign** property; **printTextFont** property; **printTextSize** property; **printTextStyle** property; **reset printing** command

printTextSize property

FORMS

```
set [the] printTextSize [of HyperCard] to fontSize
set the printTextSize to 14
```

ACTION

The **printTextSize** global property is the font size used when printing. The default value for **printTextSize** is 10.

COMMENTS

HyperCard uses the **printTextSize** property for expressions printed with the **print** command and for printed report headers. This handler prints a message in large type in the center of the page:

```
on printMessage
   ask "What message do you want to print?"
   if it is empty then exit printMessage  -- user cancelled
   set the printTextSize to 48            -- 48-point
   set the printTextAlign to center
   print it
   reset printing -- sets everything back to the default
end printMessage
```

The *fontSize* must be an integer; otherwise, HyperCard presents an error dialog. The smallest legal **printTextSize** is 1 point. If you try to set it to zero or a negative number, the **printTextSize** will be set to 1. The largest legal **printTextSize** is 127 points.

Changing the **printTextSize** automatically sets the **printTextHeight** to (4 * printTextSize) div 3. If you want to set both the **printTextSize** and the **printTextHeight**, change the **printTextSize** first.

ALSO SEE

print command; **printTextAlign** property; **printTextFont** property; **printTextHeight** property; **printTextStyle** property; **reset printing** command

---

printTextStyle property

FORMS

```
set [the] printTextStyle [of HyperCard] to styleList
set the printTextStyle to italic
set the printTextStyle to bold,underline,outline
set the printTextStyle to plain
```

ACTION

The **printTextStyle** global property reflects the style or combination of styles HyperCard uses for printed text.

The default value for **printTextStyle** is `plain`.

COMMENTS

HyperCard uses the **printTextStyle** property for text printed with the **print** command and in the header of a report. The following example sets the style for a report header and prints the report:

```
on printFullReport
   set the printTextFont to "Palatino"
   set the printTextStyle to bold,italic
   open report printing with template "Full"
   print 5 cards
   close printing
   reset printing -- sets everything back to the default
end printHeadline
```

The *styleList* is a set of one or more styles, separated by commas. The available styles are `plain, bold, italic, underline, outline, shadow, condense, extend, group`. `Plain` removes all other styles, but is ignored if you use it in combination with other styles; you must use `plain` by itself or it has no effect.

This handler prints a sample text string in various styles:

```
on printStyleSample theText
   if theText is empty then put ¬
   "The quick brown fox jumped over the lazy dog." into theText
   put "plain,bold,italic,underline,outline,shadow,condense,extend" ¬
   into theStyles
   open printing
   repeat with thisStyle = 1 to the number of items of theStyles
      set the printTextStyle to item thisStyle of theStyles
      print the printTextStyle & return & theText & return & return
   end repeat
   close printing
end printStyleSample
```

ALSO SEE

print command; **printTextAlign** property; **printTextFont** property; **printTextSize** property; **printTextHeight** property; **reset printing** command

programs function

Introduced in version 2.1
Last changed in version 2.2

FORMS

```
the programs [of machine macAddress]
programs()
answer the programs
if "Finder" is in the programs then doMenu "Finder"
put the programs of machine "Corporate:Sally's Mac" into sallyPrograms
```

ACTION

The **programs** function returns a return-separated list of all the System 7-friendly processes running on your Macintosh or on another Mac on the same network.

This function requires System 7. To access the list of programs running on another Mac, the target Mac must have Program Linking turned on in the Sharing Setup control panel.

COMMENTS

The **programs** function is useful in controlling your Mac environment, and in checking whether someone else is running a particular program before attempting to link to it. This handler cycles through every program currently running on your Macintosh:

```
on mouseUp
  repeat with thisProgram = 1 to the number of lines of the programs
    doMenu (line thisProgram of the programs)
    wait for 5 seconds
  end repeat
  if the suspended then doMenu "HyperCard" -- get back
end mouseUp
```

A *macAddress* is the AppleTalk address of another Macintosh running on the same network. It has the form *zoneName:macName*, where the *macName* is set in the Sharing Setup control panel. If you specify a *macAddress* that doesn't exist, **the programs** returns empty.

If the target Mac is in the same zone as yours, or if your network isn't divided into zones, you can use an asterisk (*) for the zone name, or leave it out.

If you do not specify a *macAddress*, the list of programs running on your Mac is returned.

Changes to HyperTalk: In versions of HyperCard before 2.2, you cannot specify the machine whose running processes you want to list; the **programs** function is limited to the current Mac.

ALSO SEE

answer program command; **close** command; **there is a** operator; **send to program** keyword; **systemVersion** function

properties property

FORMS

the properties of *externalWindow*

```
get the properties of window "Message Watcher"
put the properties of window "Palette" into palettePropertyList
if "scroll" is not in the properties of window 7 then beep
```

ACTION

The **properties** is a property of external windows (windows created by an XCMD or XFCN), and reports a comma-separated list of all the HyperTalk properties the window in question supports.

This is a read-only property and can't be changed by a handler.

COMMENTS

Use **properties** when you need to know whether an XCMD's windows support a specific action such as scrolling, or when you're curious about what you can do with a particular external's windows.

HyperCard itself incorporates several XCMDs that create external windows:

```
the properties of window "message watcher"
   -- loc,visible,hideUnused,hideidle,text,nextLine (set only)
the properties of window "variable watcher"
   -- loc,visible,rect,vBarLoc,hBarLoc
the properties of paletteWindow -- created by the palette command
   -- buttonCount,hilitedButton,commands
the properties of pictureWindow -- created by the picture command
   -- visible,loc,globalLoc,rect,globalRect,pictureWidth,
   -- pictureHeight,scroll,zoom,scale,dithering
```

Not all windows have properties: Only windows created by XCMDs or XFCNs support the **properties** property—stack windows and built-in windows such as the message box do not. And not all windows created by an external support **properties**. For example, script windows (which are created by the ScriptEditor XCMD) don't support the **properties** property.

ALSO SEE

messageWatcher property; **palette** command; **picture** command; **variableWatcher** property

push command

FORMS

```
push [card|background|stack]
push card          -- pushes current card
push this card     -- equivalent to line above
push previous card
push recent card
push back           -- previous card in history list
push card "Type List" of stack "Control Center"
push myCard
push next background
push stack ":Projects:Book Updates"
```

ACTION

The **push** command stores the long ID of a card for later retrieval with the **pop** command.

COMMENTS

Use **push** to store the location of a card so you can use **pop** to go back to it later.

The following handler retrieves the top-priority item from a to-do list that's stored in another stack. It uses **push** to store the current location before going to the list, and **pop** to go back there after retrieving the item from the to-do stack:

```
on whatToDo
   lock screen
   lock messages
   push card
   go to stack "To Do"
   get line 1 of field "Hot Items"
   pop card
   put "You'd better work on" && it
   unlock screen
   unlock messages
end whatToDo
```

You can push a card, background, or stack.

A *card* is any valid descriptor of a card in any stack. The form push card pushes the current card.

A *background* is any valid background descriptor. When you return to that background using the **pop** command, you're taken to the first card of that background. The value stored is the long ID of the first card of the *background*.

A *stack* is a descriptor of any stack, including the current stack. When you use **pop** to return to a stack, you go to the first card of the stack. The value stored is the long ID of the first card of the *stack*.

The following **openStack** handler pushes the most recent card so that its "Go Back" button (whose script has the statement `pop card`) will work. It also checks to see what version of HyperCard is running. If it's not recent enough, the stack immediately drops the user back to the most recent card:

```
on openStack
  push recent card
  if the version < 2.0 then
    answer "Please upgrade to version 2.0!"
    pop card
  else
    pass openStack
  end if
end openStack
```

If there are no cards in the Recent display and you issue the command `push recent card`, HyperTalk pushes the ID of the first card in the Home stack.

Techie alert: The **push** list is implemented as a circular (LIFO) stack. When the list is full and you push another card, the first-pushed card is bumped off the list; if you push another, the second-pushed card is bumped; and so on.

ALSO SEE

go command; **pop** command

---

put command

Introduced in version 1.0
Last changed in version 2.2

FORMS

```
put text [{before|into|after} [chunk of] container]
put "Throckmorton Scribblemonger" into card field "Author"
put the sqrt of -1 into notANumber
put return & the long ID of this card after cardIDList
put menu "Font" into background button "Fonts Popup"
put line 4 of field "Print List" into the selection
put comma after word 3 of field "Storytelling"
put it into first line of background button "Storage"
put empty into char 2 to 12 of it
put it into myVariable
put "Hey there..." into message box -- does the same thing as...
put "Hey there..."                 -- ...this line does.
```

ACTION

The **put** command places a copy of the specified text (which may be the result of an expression) into a container.

COMMENTS

The **put** command lets you move text between fields, buttons, variables and the message box, and lets you put the result of any operation into any container. The following example, which is part of a button script, displays a PICT file whose pathname is stored in the button. If there is no pathname, the handler asks you to locate the picture:

```
on mouseUp -- displays a PICT file
   if me is empty then
      ask file "Where is the picture to attach?"
      if it is empty then exit mouseUp -- user cancelled
      put it into me -- "it" is the pathname of the file
   end if
   picture me
end mouseUp
```

The *text* is any literal text, the name of any container (or part of one), the result of a function, or anything else that evaluates to a text string.

The **put into** form replaces the current contents of *container* with *text*. (If a chunk expression is specified, only the current content of that chunk is replaced; the rest of the container is unchanged.) The forms **put before** and **put after** insert the *text* before or after the specified chunk. If you don't give a chunk expression, **put before** inserts the text at the beginning of the *container*, and **put after** inserts it at the end.

You can put text into any legal chunk expression, specifying either entire containers or parts of the container described in terms of lines, words, items, and/or characters. If you want to empty out a container or some chunk of it, use a command like `put empty into word 2 of myVariable`.

If you don't specify a *container*, **put** places the *text* in the message box. If the message box was hidden, putting something into it shows it.

The following especially tricky handler gives you a miniature mail merge function. Each card in the Mail Merge stack lists a different customer name and address, along with the name of the item the customer last purchased (see Figure III.39):

```
function mailMerge formLetter
   repeat until "$" is not in formLetter
      put offset("$",formLetter) into startChar -- start of substitution
      delete char startChar of formLetter        -- first $
      put offset("$",formLetter) into endChar    -- end of substitution
      -- get the name of the item you're substituting...
      put char startChar to (endChar - 1) of formLetter into whichField
      -- ...and substitute the field contents for the name
      put field whichField into char startChar to endChar of formLetter
   end repeat
   return formLetter
end mailMerge
```

The above function might be called from another handler like this:

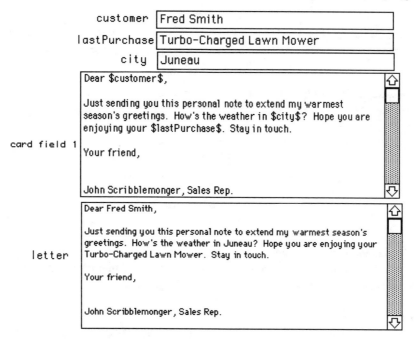

Figure III.39   Mail merge function at work

```
put mailMerge(card field "Greeting" of card "Templates") ¬
into field "Letter"
```

Put and variables: If the *container* is a variable name that you haven't yet used in the current handler, using **put** creates it as a local variable.

If you use **put** from the message box, and the *container* is a variable name, HyperCard assumes it's a global variable and creates it, if no global by that name already exists.

Put, fields, and buttons: If you put text into a background field that has the **sharedText** property turned on, the text appears on all cards on which that field appears. Text you put into a popup button makes up the menu items of the popup; text in other button styles can be used for whatever you want. Background buttons behave like fields that have **sharedText** set to true, so you can't put different text on each card into a background button.

If the *container* is a field, **put** doesn't send **openField**, **closeField**, or **exitField** messages to it.

Changes to HyperTalk: In versions of HyperCard before 2.2, buttons aren't containers; you can't put anything into them.

ALSO SEE

blindTyping property; **delete** command; **get** command; **put into menu** command; **select** command; **set** command; **value** function; **write** command

put into menu command

FORMS

```
put itemList [into|before|after] {menuItem of} menu  ¬
{with menuMessage[s] messageList}
put "Card" into menu "Scripts"
put thisItem after menu 3 -- third menu from left
put "Goodbye" after menu "Additions" with menuMessage "go home"
put word 2 of the short name of button 4 before menuItem 2 of menu "Book"
put "Fred,Julia,Martha" into menu "People"  ¬
    with menuMsgs "go card Fred,go card Julia,go card Martha"
```

ACTION

The **put into menu** command adds menu items to standard or custom menus.

If you include a menuMessage parameter, the new menu item's **menuMessage** property is set to that value, and the item sends that message to the current card when the user chooses it.

COMMENTS

New menus made with the **create menu** command are initially blank: they appear in the menu bar, but have no menu items. Use the **put into menu** command to construct custom menus for your stacks and to add new menu items to HyperCard's standard menus.

The following handler, which belongs in an Addresses stack script, creates the menu "Emergency" and adds three items to it (see Figure III.40):

```
on openStack
  -- create Emergency menu
  create menu "Emergency"
  -- and put in its menu items:
  put "Police" into menu "Emergency" with menuMsg "find Police"
  put "Fire" after menu "Emergency" with menuMsg "find Fire"
  put "Pizza" after menu "Emergency" with menuMsg "find Pizza"
  pass openStack
end openStack
```

The *itemList* consists of the names of one or more new menu items. To add more than one menu item at once, separate the names with commas or returns.

To add a dividing line across a menu, add a menu item named "-" (the minus sign):

```
put "-" after menu "Utilities"
```

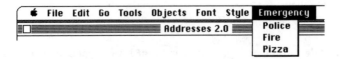

Figure III.40   New Addresses menu

A *menuItem* is any existing menu item. (Menu item descriptors are of the form `menuItem` *itemName*, `menuItem` *itemNumber*, or *ordinalNumber* `menuItem`.) Use `before` to insert the *itemList* above the specified item; use `after` to insert the new menu items below the specified item; and use `into` to replace the specified menu item with the new item.

A *menu* is a descriptor of an existing menu. (Menu descriptors are of the form `menu` *menuName*, `menu` *menuNumber*, or *ordinalNumber* `menu`.) You can put menu items into a custom menu, or into any of HyperCard's menus except the Apple, Font, Tools, and Patterns menus. The form `put` *itemList* `after` *menu* appends the new item or items to the end of the menu; the form `put` *itemList* `before` *menu* inserts the *itemList* at the top of the menu; and the form `put` *itemList* `into` *menu* replaces any existing menu items with the *itemList*.

The *messageList* is an optional list of menu messages that are assigned to the respective menu items. The messages can be separated with commas or return characters. The number of messages must be equal to the number of items in *itemList*; if it's not, HyperCard puts up an error dialog. If you want to assign a message to some items but not others, use an empty item:

```
put "foo,No Message,bar" into menu "New" ¬
with menuMessage "doIt,,doSomethingElse"
```

Each menu can have up to 64 menu items.

The following example creates the same menu as the previous example, but adds the menu items as a list instead of one by one:

```
on openStack
    -- create Emergency menu
    create menu "Emergency"
    -- and put in its menu items:
    put "Police,Fire,Pizza" into menu "Emergency" ¬
    with menuMsg "find Police,find Fire,find Pizza"
    pass openStack
end openStack
```

Menu messages: When the user chooses a menu item, it sends a **doMenu** message to the current card. If you have specified a custom message for the menu item, either in the **put into menu** command that created it or by setting its **menuMessage** property after it was created, that custom message is also sent to the current card.

Changing menu items: Menus and menu items you've created remain until you quit HyperCard, issue a **reset menubar** command, or otherwise change or delete them. You can make several other changes to the menu bar:

- To remove an individual menu or menu item, use the **delete menu** command.
- To rename a menu item, set its **name** property to the new name.
- To change the message a menu item sends, set its **menuMessage** property.
- To change the text style of a menu item, set its **textStyle** property.
- To put a check or other special character next to a menu item, set its **checkMark** or **markChar** property.

- To assign a Command-key equivalent to a menu item, set its **commandChar** property.
- To enable or disable a menu item, set its **enabled** property (or use the equivalent **enable** and **disable** commands).

New menu items with standard names: When you create a menu item with the same name as a standard HyperCard menu item, it inherits the behavior of the standard item.

The following set of handlers creates a menu that lets you move the current card to any position in the current stack:

```
on makeCardMenu
   create menu "Move"
   put "To First Card,To Last Card,To..." into menu "Card" ¬
   with menuMessages "moveCardTo 1,moveCardTo last,moveCardTo"
end makeCardMenu


on moveCardTo theNewPosition
   if theNewPosition is "last" then
      put the number of cards of this stack into theNewPosition
   else if theNewPosition is empty then
      ask "New number of this card:"
      if it is empty then exit moveCardTo -- user cancelled
      put it into theNewPosition
   end if
   put max(theNewPosition,1) into theNewPosition
   put min(theNewPosition,the number of cards) into theNewPosition
   if theNewPosition is the number of this card then exit moveCardTo
   lock messages -- prevent any open/close messages
   lock screen
   doMenu "Cut Card"
   if theNewPosition is 1 then -- must handle first card specially
      go to first card
      doMenu "Paste Card" -- the card is now card 2
      go to first card
      doMenu "Cut Card"    -- original card is now first
      doMenu "Paste Card" -- moves old card 1 to second place
      go to card 1         -- the original card
   else
      go to card theNewPosition - 1
      doMenu "Paste Card"
   end if
end moveCardTo
```

Identifying menus and menu items: To get the number of menus in the menu bar, or the number of menu items in a menu, use the **number** function. To find the name of a specific menu item or menu when you know its number, check its **name of menu** property. To get a list of the names of all menus in the menu bar, use the **menus** function.

Cleaning up after yourself: In most cases, when you use a custom menu or change HyperCard's menus, you should undo your changes when you leave the current stack. Use **reset menubar** to change all the menus back to the standard HyperCard menus, or use the **delete menu** command to delete your custom menus and menu items.

ALSO SEE

create menu command; **delete menu** command; **doMenu** command/message; **reset menubar** command

---

quit message   Introduced in version 1.0

FORMS

quit

ACTION

The **quit** message is sent to the current card when Quit HyperCard has been chosen from the File menu and HyperCard is about to quit.

COMMENTS

HyperCard doesn't send the **quit** message until the process of quitting is already underway, so you can't keep users from quitting your stack by trapping this message.

When HyperCard is quitting, it sends the following messages to the current card of the frontmost stack, in order:

```
closeCard
closeBackground
closeStack
-- the frontmost stack then closes, and any other stacks also get
-- the above three messages before closing.
quit
```

Because of the way **quit** works, the **quit** message is sent to the current card of the last stack to be closed, not to the current card of the stack that was frontmost when the user chose Quit HyperCard, as you might expect.

ALSO SEE

resume message; **startup** message; **suspend** message

random function

FORMS

[the] `random of` *upperLimit*
`random(`*upperLimit*`)`
```
random(52) -- pick a card, any card
random(the width of card window)
the random of the number of cards
```

ACTION

The **random** function returns a random number between 1 and *upperLimit*.

COMMENTS

The **random** function is particularly useful in graphics, where you may want to seed a drawing algorithm with a random value, and in programming games of chance. The following handler rolls virtual dice and is useful for role-playing games:

```
on rollDice numberOfDice,sidesPerDie
   if sidesPerDie is empty then put 6 into sidesPerDie
   put empty into results
   repeat with die = 1 to numberOfDice
      put random(sidesPerDie) into item die of results
   end repeat
   put "You rolled" && results && "for a total of" && sum(results)
end rollDice
```

The *upperLimit* is an integer between 1 and 2,147,483,648 (which is equal to 2^31). If you specify a number that isn't an integer, **random** uses the integer part of the *upperLimit*. If you specify a number less than 1, the returned value is always 1. If you specify a number greater than 32767, **random** acts as though you had specified 2147483648.

The following example draws a bar chart with random data. For even greater amusement value, it tears off the pattern window so you can see the handler switching from pattern to pattern:

```
on mouseUp
   put empty into randomData
   repeat with i = 1 to 5 + random(30) -- from 5 to 35 bars
      put random(100) into item i of randomData
   end repeat
   show pattern window at the topLeft of card window
   makeBarChart randomData
   hide pattern window
end mouseUp
```

```
on makeBarChart theData
   put 10 into topEdge
   put 10 into leftEdge
   put the height of this card - 10 into bottomEdge
   put the width of this card - 10 into rightEdge
   -- clear screen and set up tools
   reset paint
   choose select tool
   doMenu "Select All"
   doMenu "Clear Picture"
   choose rectangle tool
   set the filled to true
   -- draw the chart
   put leftEdge into currentBar
   put max(theData) into maxValue
   put the number of items in theData into dataCount
   put round((rightEdge - leftEdge)/dataCount) into horizStep
   put round(horizStep * 3/4) into barWidth
   repeat with nextBar = 1 to dataCount
      put round((bottomEdge - topEdge) ¬
      * item nextBar of theData / maxValue) into barHeight
      set the pattern to random(40)
      drag from currentBar,(bottomEdge - barHeight) ¬
      to (currentBar + barWidth),bottomEdge
      add horizStep to currentBar
   end repeat
   choose browse tool
end makeBarChart
```

Changes to HyperTalk: In versions of HyperCard before 2.0, using a negative number or a number that's not an integer causes a script error, and **random** can handle only numbers less than 32767 (which is equal to 2^15 - 1).

ALSO SEE
numberFormat property

---

read command

Introduced in version 1.0
Last changed in version 2.2

FORMS

read from file *filePathname* **[at** *start***]** **{until** **{***char***|end|eof}|for** *numberOfChars***}**
read from file "My Disk:Stuff Folder:Addresses" for 120
read from file thisFile until return
read from file "Local Hero" until "Jim" -- stops at J

```
read from file myFile until field "Customer Name"
read from file (line 12 of field "Text Files") for maximumChars
read from file "My Disk:Stuff Folder:Addresses" at 120 for 120
read from file whatever until end
read from file it at -240 until end -- reads last 240 characters
```

ACTION

The **read** command gets data from a text file that has been opened using the **open file** command, and puts the data it reads into the **it** variable.

COMMENTS

The commands **open file**, **close file**, **read**, and **write** are used for importing and exporting text between HyperCard and text files. Most applications that deal with text data, such as word processors and databases, can export text files, so you can use a text file as an intermediate step in moving data from other applications into a stack.

The following function fetches the contents of a text file:

```
function readFile theFilepath
   if theFilepath is empty then
      answer file "What file do you want to read?" of type text
      if it is empty then return empty -- user cancelled
      else put it into theFilepath
   end if
   open file theFilepath
   read from file theFilepath until end
   close file theFilepath
   return it
end readFile
```

The *filePathname* is the full pathname of the file you want to read from. If you provide only a filename without a path, the **read** command assumes the file is in the same folder as the HyperCard application.

The *start* is an integer that specifies where you want to start reading. If *start* is positive, the **read** command begins at the *start*h character of the file. If *start* is negative, HyperCard begins reading at the *start*h character before the end of the file.

If you don't specify a *start*, **read** begins right after the last character that was read. If this is the first time you've read from the file since you opened it, **read** starts at the beginning of the file.

The following handler is an implementation of the UNIX command "tail". It displays the last 200 characters of a file:

```
on tail theFile
   open file theFile
   read from file theFile at -200 to end
   close file theFile
   answer it
end tail
```

You must specify either the number of characters to read or where you want the read operation to stop.

The **read for *numberOfChars*** form lets you specify any positive integer as the number of characters to read. If you don't specify a *start* character, the next **read** takes up where the previous one left off.

If you use the **read until** form, you can specify either the character you want to stop on, or one of the constants `eof` or `end`. These constants are synonymous: they indicate the end of the file. If you specify a character, **read** stops after reading the first occurrence of that character, so it becomes the last character in the **it** variable. You can specify more than one character for **read until**, but all characters except the first are ignored.

Null characters: The null character (ASCII 0) cannot be handled by HyperTalk. You cannot specify null as the *char* you want to **read until**; if **read** encounters a null in the file, it's converted to a space.

The following handler is a simple spelling checker and is located in a dictionary stack. It reads each word in a file that you specify, and returns a list of words that aren't in the dictionary:

```
function misspelledWords theFilePath
   put empty into spellingErrors
   open file theFilePath
   repeat
      read from file theFilePath until return -- get one line
      if it is empty then exit repeat
      repeat with nextWord = 1 to the number of words in it
         find word nextWord of it in field "Word"
         if the result is not empty then -- not in dictionary
            if word nextWord of it is not in spellingErrors
            then put word nextWord of it & return after spellingErrors
         end if
      end repeat
   end repeat
   close file theFilePath
   if last char of spellingErrors is return
   then delete last char of spellingErrors
   return spellingErrors
end misspelledWords
```

The **read** command is case-sensitive: an uppercase letter is treated as distinct from its lowercase counterpart.

If you have already read past the end of the file, further **read** commands put empty into the **it** variable. Since each **read** replaces the contents of **it**, you need to move **it** to another container before doing another **read**.

The amount of text you can read is limited only by available memory. If there isn't enough memory for the text to fit, the **result** function is set to "Not enough memory to read from file." Since fields can hold only about 30,000 characters, if you're importing the contents of a long file into a field, you should use a handler structured like the following example to avoid overflowing the field:

```
on importFile theFilePath,destinationField
  open file theFilePath
  repeat
    read from file theFilePath for 29000
    if it is not empty then
      doMenu "New Card"
      put it into field destinationField
    else exit repeat -- done reading file
  end repeat
  close file theFilePath
end importFile
```

The following function checks whether a file is empty:

```
function isEmpty theFile
  open file theFile
  read from file theFile for 1
  close file theFile
  if it is empty then return true    -- file is empty
  else return false                  -- file has at least 1 character
end isEmpty
```

Techie alert: Every Macintosh file consists of two parts: a data fork and a resource fork. (For some files, one of the forks may be empty.) The resource fork contains data that's handled by the Resource Manager, such as sounds, icons, windows, menus, code, fonts, and so on. The data fork holds an unstructured sequence of bytes, and is used by different programs for different things.

While you can put resources into a stack's resource fork with impunity, HyperCard (along with many other programs) uses the data fork in its own mysterious way. The moral: While you *can* use the file commands to mess around with a stack's data fork, it is a Very Bad Idea to do so. Use these commands only on text files.

Changes to HyperTalk: In versions of HyperCard before 2.2, the form **read from file** *filePath* **until** *char* can only read 16K (16384 characters) at a time, and in versions before 2.1, the length of all forms of **read** is limited to 16K. To work around this limitation and read an entire file, use a **repeat** structure:

```
open file filePath
put empty into holderVariable
repeat
  read from file filePath for 16384 -- maximum read
  if it is empty then exit repeat    -- reached end of file
  else put it after holderVariable
end repeat
close file filePath
```

In versions before 2.2, you cannot read at a negative number.

In versions before 2.0, you cannot specify where you want to start reading, and the **end** and **eof** constants don't exist. To read until the end of the file in these versions, use the **repeat** structure above.

ALSO SEE

close file command; **open file** command; **write** command

---

rectangle property

Introduced in version 1.0
Last changed in version 2.2

FORMS

```
set the rect[angle] of {part|button|field|card|cardwindow} to left,top,right,bottom
the rect[angle] of {window|menubar}
set the rectangle of button 1 to 100,100,200,200
set the rect of card window to the clickLoc & comma & the mouseLoc
if the mouseLoc is within the rect of card part 3 then beep
```

ACTION

The **rectangle** property describes the location of the corners of any HyperCard field, button, card, or window.

COMMENTS

The *button*, *field*, or *card* must be in the current stack.

The *window* can be any open stack window, HyperCard window, or external window (including windows created by the **palette** and **picture** commands).

The **top** of a stack window and the **top** of a card in that stack may be different if the window has been sized smaller than the card size (for example, using the Scroll command in the Go menu).

The *left*, *top*, *right*, and *bottom* are integers giving, respectively, the distance in pixels between:

- The left edge of the frontmost card window and the element's left edge

- The top of the frontmost card window and the element's top edge

- The left edge of the card window and the element's right edge

- The top of the card window and the element's bottom edge

(For stack windows, the distances are measured from the left and top edges of the screen, rather than the edges of the card window.) The top edge of a window is at the bottom of its title bar.

The following handler, given a set of local coordinates (such as `the rect of part`, which is measured relative to the frontmost stack window), returns the equivalent global coordinates (which are measured relative to the screen):

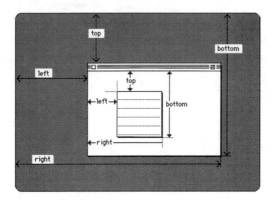

Figure III.41   The rectangle and derived properties of a stack window and field

```
function localToGlobal theRect
  return ¬
  the left of card window + item 1 of theRect & comma & ¬
  the top of card window + item 2 of theRect & comma & ¬
  the left of card window + item 3 of theRect & comma & ¬
  the top of card window + item 4 of theRect
end localToGlobal
```

This handler does the reverse, transforming global coordinates into coordinates relative to the frontmost stack window:

```
function globalToLocal theRect
  return ¬
  item 1 of theRect - the left of card window & comma & ¬
  item 2 of theRect - the top of card window & comma & ¬
  item 3 of theRect - the left of card window & comma & ¬
  item 4 of theRect - the top of card window
end globalToLocal
```

The rectangle and other properties: The four items making up the **rectangle** are the same (respectively) as the **left**, **top**, **right**, and **bottom** properties of the element. The **topLeft** is the first two items of the **rectangle**; the **bottomRight** is the last two items. The **width** is item 3 minus item 1. The **height** is item 4 minus item 2. Changing any of these properties, or changing the **location**, changes the **rectangle** of the affected element.

If you want to change the position of one edge of an element without moving the other edges, use the **left**, **top**, **right**, and **bottom** properties. To change the element's size without changing its location, use **width** or **height**.

The following handlers show what field or button (if any) the mouse is currently over:

```
on mouseUp
  repeat until the mouseClick
    put whatIsUnder(the mouseLoc)
```

```
      end repeat
   end mouseUp


   function whatIsUnder thePoint
      repeat with x = 1 to the number of card parts
         if thePoint is within the rect of card part x
         then return the name of card part x
      end repeat
      repeat with x = 1 to the number of background parts
         if thePoint is within the rect of background part x
         then return the name of background part x
      end repeat
      return "No button or field."
   end whatIsUnder
```

Special rectangles for picture windows: If the *window* was created by the **picture** command, you can use one of the following special screen descriptors to set its **rectangle**:

- cardScreen—Centers the picture on the screen that contains the frontmost stack window and zooms the window, up to the size of the screen.

- mainScreen—Centers the picture on the screen that contains the menu bar and zooms the window, up to the size of the screen.

- largestScreen—Centers the picture on the largest screen available and zooms the window, up to the size of the screen. (Screen size is measured by the total number of pixels, not the physical size of the screen.)

- deepestScreen—Centers the picture on the screen that has the most colors available and zooms the window, up to the size of the screen. To see how many colors are available on a particular screen, check the Monitors control panel.

Changes to HyperTalk: In versions of HyperCard before 2.2, you can't refer to buttons or fields with a part descriptor, and you can't get the **rectangle** of the menu bar.

ALSO SEE
bottom property; **bottomRight** property; **height** property; **left** property; **location** property; **right** property; **top** property; **topLeft** property; **width** property

---

repeat keyword   Introduced in version 1.0

FORMS
```
repeat repeatForm
   statementList
end repeat
```

Forms of repeat

repeat forever: With this form, the *statementList* is repeated as long as HyperCard has breath in its body, until an **exit, pass,** or **return** statement executes (or the user loses patience and presses Command-Period):

```
repeat
  beep
  if the mouseClick then exit repeat -- shut up already!
end repeat
```

repeat for *number* times: HyperCard executes the set of statements inside the loop for the specified number of times. (Of course, *number* must evaluate to an integer; otherwise you get an error dialog.)

```
repeat for the number of cards
  go to next card    -- visits each card in this stack
  wait for 2 seconds -- pauses at each
end repeat
```

repeat until *condition*:   HyperCard checks the status of the *condition* each time through the loop. When *condition* evaluates to true, the loop ends and control goes to the next statement after `end repeat`:

```
repeat until the sound is done
  set the hilite of button "Flash" to (not the hilite of button "Flash")
end repeat
```

repeat while *condition*:   HyperCard checks the status of the *condition* at the start of each repetition of the loop. When *condition* evaluates to false, the loop ends:

```
repeat while the mouse is down
  put the mouseLoc into message box
  -- keeps updating until you release the mouse button
end repeat
```

The statement `repeat until` *someCondition* is exactly equivalent to `repeat while not` *someCondition*.

repeat with *countVariable* = *start* [to | down to] *finish*:   When the **repeat** statement begins, HyperTalk sets the *countVariable* to *start*. Each time the loop goes back to the top for another repetition, *countVariable* is increased by 1 (or, if you're using the **down to** form, decreased by 1). When *countVariable*'s value exceeds the value in *finish*, the loop ends and control goes to the statement after `end repeat`. The repetition where *countValue* = *finish* is the last one.

```
    repeat with thisField = 1 to the number of fields
        put empty into field thisField
    end repeat


    repeat with countdown = 10 down to 1
        put "Liftoff in" && countdown && "seconds!" into message box
    end repeat
```

HyperTalk compares the value of *countVariable* to the value of *finish* at the top of the loop, so **repeat** structures with contradictory forms (such as `repeat with loopCounter = 1 to 0` or `repeat with loopCounter = 15 down to 16`) don't execute even once; the whole **repeat** structure is bypassed.

Which *repeatForm* you should use depends upon your situation and what you need to test for. If you want to run through a specified list of items, you'll usually want to use either **repeat with** *countVariable* (if a statement inside the loop needs to know which repetition the loop is currently on) or **repeat for** *number* **times**. If you want the loop to keep going until a certain condition is met, use **repeat until** or **repeat while**.

The `repeatForm` is one of the following:

- `[forever]`
- `for` *number* `[times]`
- `until` *condition*
- `while` *condition*
- `with` *countVariable* `=` *start* `{to|down to}` *finish*

ACTION

The **repeat** structure executes the HyperTalk commands in *statementList*, then loops back to the beginning of *statementList* and performs them again, repeating this process until some condition is met or an **exit**, **pass**, or **return** statement is executed. How many times the loop runs depends on the *repeatForm* you use.

The *statementList* consists of any number of valid HyperTalk statements, separated by returns.

COMMENTS

You can use the **repeat** structure to run through a list of the items in a string, the cards in a stack, the fields on a card, and so on. This example checks each character of a string to make sure the string contains only numbers:

```
function justDigits theString
    repeat with thisChar = 1 to the length of theString
        if thisChar is not a number then return false
    end repeat
```

```
            return true
      end justDigits
```

When the **repeat** loop concludes, control passes to the statement following `end repeat`.

To terminate the current pass through the repeat loop and start again at the top of the loop, use the **next repeat** statement.

To leave the repeat loop entirely and go to the statement following `end repeat`, use the **exit repeat** statement.

Testing at the top versus testing at the bottom: All the **repeat** structures check the condition under which the loop will keep going at the top of the loop; that is, first the condition is checked, then, if necessary, the loop's *statementList* is executed. This means that if the condition is false when the loop is encountered, the statements in it won't execute even once:

```
repeat until the shiftKey is down
   -- if it was up, this statement never gets executed:
   beep
end repeat
```

If you want to test the condition at the bottom of the loop, after the statements are executed, use the **repeat forever** form, and use **exit repeat** to terminate the loop if the condition is met:

```
repeat
   -- this always gets executed at least once, since we haven't
   -- checked the shift key state yet:
   beep
   if the shiftKey is down then exit repeat
end if
```

Repeat to delete:　If you use the **repeat with** *countVariable* form, avoid changing the value of *final* inside your loop; it can lead to unpredictable results that you may have to work around. For example, consider the following handler, which is intended to delete all the buttons on a card:

```
on mouseDown
   repeat with thisButton = 1 to the number of card buttons
      -- the number of card buttons decreases each time through
      -- the loop, because you're deleting them:
      delete card button thisButton
   end repeat
end mouseDown
```

To see why this handler doesn't do what it's supposed to, suppose there are three card buttons. The first time through the loop, *thisButton* is 1, and the number of card buttons is 3; card button 1 is deleted. So far, so good. The second time, *thisButton* is 2, and the number of card buttons is 2. However, the third time through, *thisButton* is 3, but the number of card buttons is now 1, so the *statementList* does not execute and the third button is not deleted.

To avoid this problem, use the **down to** form instead:

```
on mouseDown
   repeat with thisButton = the number of card buttons down to 1
      -- 1 does not change, so we're OK.
      delete card button thisButton
   end repeat
end mouseDown
```

Using nested repeats: You can put a repeat inside another repeat structure, nesting up to 32 levels deep. This example handler takes input text and word-wraps it to the desired length, which is a very handy capability when you're doing telecommunications with a remote system that requires a return at the end of each line on the screen:

```
function wordWrap theText,lineLength
   repeat with thisLine = 1 to the number of lines in theText
      -- work through each line of input text
      get line thisLine of theText
      if the number of chars in it > lineLength then
         repeat with checkForSpace = lineLength - 1 down to 1
            -- if the line's too long, find a word break to wrap it at
            if char checkForSpace of it is space then
               put return into char checkForSpace of line thisLine of theText
               exit repeat
         end repeat
         if checkForSpace is 1 then -- no spaces in this line
            put return before char (lineLength - 1) of it
         end if
      end if
      add 1 to thisLine
   end repeat
   return theText
end wordWrap
```

Changes to HyperTalk: In versions of HyperCard before 2.0, the total number of *all* running repeats—including nested repeats and calls to other handlers that might contain **repeat** structures of their own—is 32. Also, in these versions, the form **repeat with** *countVariable* **is** *start* **to** *finish* is a legal synonym for **repeat with** *countVariable = start* **to** *finish*.

ALSO SEE

exit keyword; **next repeat** keyword; **pass** keyword

reply command

FORMS

```
reply replyString [with keyword replyKeyword]
reply error replyString
reply "Response from" && the address
reply error myCustomErrorString
reply card field "Respond" with keyword "----"
```

ACTION

The **reply** command, when used in a handler to which AppleEvents are being sent, sets the **result** function on the sending copy of HyperCard to a response string.

To use the **reply** command, both your Mac and the sending Mac must be running System 7.

COMMENTS

Use the **reply** command to respond to another copy of HyperCard that's sent an AppleEvent (with the **send to program** keyword or the **request** command). When a sending Mac sends an AppleEvent to a target, a message handler in the target stack can use **reply** to send a response back to the sender. This response is stored in **the result** function on the sender.

The **reply** command for HyperCard-to-HyperCard communications is analogous to the **return** keyword for communication between message handlers.

This example shows how to confirm that a target stack is receiving your events:

```
on mouseUp -- this handler is on sending machine
   global targetProgram
   answer program "Choose a copy of HyperCard running on the network:"
   if it is empty then exit mouseUp
   put it into targetProgram
   send confirmCheck to program targetProgram
   if the result is not empty then answer the result
   else answer "Problem communicating with target program."
end mouseUp


on confirmCheck -- this handler is on target machine
   reply "Target Mac is receiving messages."
end confirmCheck
```

When a program responds to an AppleEvent, it returns several different pieces of information. Each piece corresponds to a keyword. The **reply with keyword** form of this command lets you specify these pieces, and is most useful if the AppleEvent came from an application other than HyperCard.

The statement reply *string* with keyword "----" is equivalent to reply *string*. The statement reply *string* with keyword "errs" is equivalent to reply error *string*.

If you specify the keyword errn, the number you provide is returned to the sender:

```
reply "100" with keyword "errn" -- on target Mac
```

The sending Mac puts up the message "Got error 100 when sending Apple™ event."

When the AppleEvent you're responding to results from a **request** command, you must use the **reply error** form of this command or the equivalent **reply with keyword "errs"**. The other form has no effect on the sending copy of HyperCard. This is because **request** is used to get information from another program—it's analogous to a function call—and functions do not normally set **the result** except to report an error.

The **reply** command sets **the result** to "No current Apple™ event." if it is executed when there is no AppleEvent pending.

ALSO SEE

appleEvent message; **request** command; **result** function; **return** keyword; **send to program** keyword

---

reportTemplates property

FORMS

the reportTemplates of *stack*
```
answer the reportTemplates of this stack
get the reportTemplates of stack "Publication"
put the reportTemplates of stack (line 1 of the stacksInUse) into temp
```

ACTION

The **reportTemplates** property produces a return-separated list of the report templates saved in the specified stack. This property is read-only and cannot be changed by a handler.

COMMENTS

This handler lets the user set up a custom report template, which can then be used in printing from a script:

```
on mouseUp
  put the reportTemplates of this stack into oldTemplates
  answer "Please set up a template to be used in printing reports."
  doMenu "Print Report..."
  put the reportTemplates of this stack into newTemplates
  if oldTemplates is newTemplates then
    answer "No new template was created."
  else
    answer "The template" && quote & last line of newTemplates ¬
    & quote && "has been stored in the stack."
    put last line of newTemplates into card field "Custom Template"
  end if
end mouseUp
```

You can store up to 16 report templates in each stack. The following function tells you how many template slots you have remaining:

```
function templateSlots
   return (the number of lines of the reportTemplates of this stack) - 16
end templateSlots
```

ALSO SEE

copy template command; **open report printing** command

---

request command

Introduced in version 2.1
Last changed in version 2.2

FORMS

```
request evaluation {of|from} programAddress
request "myFunction()" from program "Twilight Zone:Sandy's Mac:HyperCard"
request "the short name of this stack" of program remoteHyperCard
request "{Home}" from program "MPW Shell"
```

ACTION

The **request** command asks another program, which may be running on another Mac on the network, for information. The resulting value is placed in the sending HyperCard's **it** variable.

To use the **request** command, both your Mac and the target Mac must be running System 7, and the target Mac must have Program Linking turned on in the Sharing Setup control panel.

COMMENTS

You can use the **request** command to get information from any copy of HyperCard on the network, or from any other program that accepts evaluation requests via AppleEvents. This example queries another Mac to find out how long it's been since it was last restarted:

```
function uptime theMacAddress
   if theMacAddress is empty then
      answer program "Please locate a copy of HyperCard:"
      if it is empty then exit to HyperCard
      put it into theMacAddress
   end if
   request "the ticks" from program theMacAddress
   if the result is not empty then return "Error:" && the result
   -- compute the number of minutes, hours and seconds
   put it div 60 into theSeconds -- "it" is the value from the request
   put theSeconds div 60 into theMinutes
   subtract theMinutes * 60 from theSeconds
```

```
      put theMinutes div 60 into theHours
      subtract theHours * 60 from theMinutes
      -- set up the uptime as a string
      put theSeconds && "seconds." into timeString
      if theMinutes > 0 then put theMinutes && "minutes, " ¬
      before timeString
      if theHours > 0 then put theHours && "hours, " before timeString
      -- get the Mac name
      set the itemDelimiter to colon
      delete last item of theMacAddress
      get last item of theMacAddress
      return it && "has been up for" && timeString
   end upTime
```

Another handler might call the above function like this:

```
on mouseUp
   answer upTime("My Zone:Server Mac:HyperCard")
end mouseUp
```

The *evaluation* parameter must be an expression in a form that the target application understands. If the target application is HyperCard, *evaluation* can be any legal HyperTalk expression: a built-in function, a custom function defined in the target stack's inheritance path, a container in the target stack, or anything else HyperTalk can evaluate. The **request** command is the program-to-program analog of the **value** function, and operates in much the same way.

The *programAddress* is the full AppleTalk address of the application you are getting information from. An AppleTalk address consists of three parts, separated by colons (:):

- The zone the target Macintosh is in

- The name of the target Macintosh (you can set this in the Sharing Setup control panel)

- The name of the target program

For example, if a Mac is named "Rod Serling" and resides in the zone "Twilight Zone", the *programAddress* of a copy of HyperCard running on that Mac is written as follows:

```
"Twilight Zone:Rod Serling:HyperCard"
```

The AppleTalk address is similar to a file pathname, as you can see. Each successive part of the address is nested one level deeper, down to the application itself.

If the target Mac is in the same zone as the sender (or the network consists of only one zone), you can omit the zone from the *programAddress*:

```
"Rod Serling:HyperCard"
```

If the source and target applications are on the same Macintosh, you can omit both zone and Mac name, and simply use the name or ID of the target application. (A program's ID is its four-character creator signature; for example, HyperCard's ID is WILD.) You can also use the form `this program` to refer to the current foreground application.

If the application you're requesting data from is a copy of HyperCard, the evaluation is done just as though you had typed `value(evaluation)` into the message box on the target Mac. For example, function calls use the inheritance path of the current stack on the target Mac, and container references are interpreted as applying to the target stack.

The **result** function is set when the **request** command encounters an error. These are the errors, other than script execution problems, that **request** may encounter:

- User cancelled the login dialog: **the result** is set to "Cancel".
- The target program couldn't handle the "evaluate expression" AppleEvent: **the result** is set to "Not handled by target program."
- The target program timed out: **the result** is set to "Timeout".
- The AppleEvent Manager or the target program returned an error number: **the result** is set to "Got error *errorNumber* when sending Apple™ event."

Techie alert: The **request** command sends the `eval` AppleEvent to the target program. This event is part of the `misc` suite and is not a required AppleEvent, so a program can be considered System 7-friendly even if it fails to handle this AppleEvent.

Changes to HyperTalk: In versions of HyperCard before 2.2, you cannot specify a program by ID—only by name.

ALSO SEE

appleEvent message; **reply** command; **request appleEvent** command; **send to program** keyword; **systemVersion** function; **value** function

---

request appleEvent command

Introduced in version 2.1

FORMS

```
request {ae|appleEvent} {class|ID|sender|returnID|data [{of|with}keyword AEkeyword]}
request appleEvent sender
request ae class
request appleEvent data
request appleEvent data with keyword "trans" -- gets transaction ID
```

ACTION

The **request appleEvent** command gets data about an AppleEvent that's currently being processed, and places the data in the **it** variable.

You must be running System 7 to use the **request appleEvent** command.

COMMENTS

You can use the **request appleEvent** command any time HyperCard has received an AppleEvent. (It exists to let you get information about the current AppleEvent, so it doesn't make sense to use it unless there's an AppleEvent being handled.) The **request appleEvent** command should be used from within a handler that's involved in processing the AppleEvent. This might be an **appleEvent** handler, or any handler that's triggered when another program sends you an AppleEvent with the **request** or **send to program** commands.

The following mildly fascistic example intercepts all incoming AppleEvents and checks who sent them, making sure that only authorized people can send AppleEvents to your copy of HyperCard:

```
on appleEvent
   global authorizedMacs -- contains list of Mac names
   request appleEvent sender
   put it into sendingAddress
   set the itemDelimiter to colon
   if item 2 of sendingAddress is not in authorizedMacs then
      -- this line goes back to the sender:
      reply "You are not authorized to access that Mac!"
      -- these lines warn you about the access attempt:
      play "Dragnet Theme"
      answer "Unauthorized access was attempted by" && sendingAddress
      -- these lines log the attempt on a central security server:
      put sendingAddress && "tried to access" && the address ¬
      && "at" && the long time && the date into stringToSend
      send "put" && stringToSend to program ¬
      "Corporate Zone:Security:HyperCard"
   else pass appleEvent -- allow authorized access
end appleEvent
```

The form **request appleEvent data with *AEKeyword*** lets you get any parameter or attribute of the current AppleEvent by using its *AEKeyword*. (For more information about AppleEvent parameter and attributes and their keywords, see *Inside Macintosh*, vol. VI.) For example, to get the timeout value of an incoming AppleEvent, use the `timo` keyword:

```
request appleEvent data with keyword "timo"
```

The syntax of the **request appleEvent** command also has synonyms for the four most-used *AEKeyword*s:

- **request appleEvent class:** This is equivalent to `request appleEvent data with keyword "evcl"`. It gets the four-character class of the AppleEvent (for example, `misc` or `aevt`).

- **request appleEvent ID:** This is equivalent to `request appleEvent data with keyword "evid"`. It gets the four-character name of the specific AppleEvent being handled (for example, `dosc` or `eval`).

- **request appleEvent sender:** This is equivalent to `request appleEvent data with keyword "addr"`. It gets the network address of the program that sent the AppleEvent to you (see below).

- **request appleEvent return ID:**   This form is equivalent to `request appleEvent data with keyword "rtid"`. It gets the AppleEvent's return ID number.

The form **request appleEvent data**, when used without a specific *AEKeyword*, gets the contents of the AppleEvent. For example, if the AppleEvent was triggered by another copy of HyperCard using the **send to program** keyword to send you a command, the data part of the AppleEvent consists of the command that was sent.

The following example shows how to override any **answer** commands that another program tries to send you. It lets local **answer** commands operate normally, but puts the text from remote **answer** commands into a field instead of displaying the dialog:

```
on answer -- place in stack script
   request appleEvent data
   put it into theEvent
   if the result is not empty then
     -- no AppleEvent, so this was sent from within a local stack
     pass answer
   else
     request appleEvent sender
     put "Sent by:" && it & return & param(3) of theEvent & return ¬
     into card field "Remote Messages" of card "Network"
   end if
end answer
```

The network address retrieved by `request appleEvent sender` is the full AppleTalk address of the program that sent the AppleEvent to you. The address consists of three parts separated by colons:

- The zone the sending Macintosh is in

- The name of the sending Macintosh (you can set this in the Sharing Setup control panel)

- The name of the program that sent the AppleEvent

If your network doesn't have separate zones, the zone part of the address is "*".

If you issue a **request appleEvent** command but no AppleEvent is currently being handled, the **result** function is set to "No current Apple™ event." If you use the form **request appleEvent data with** *AEKeyword*, and there is no such parameter or attribute, **the result** is set to "Not found"; if the parameter or attribute exists but can't be displayed as text, **the result** is set to "Unknown type".

Techie alert: For more information about the internal workings of AppleEvents, check *Inside Macintosh*, vol. VI.

ALSO SEE

appleEvent message; **request** command; **send to program** keyword; **systemVersion** function

reset menubar command Introduced in version 2.0

FORMS

```
reset menubar
```
reset menubar

ACTION

The **reset menubar** command restores HyperCard's standard menus and menu items, undoing any changes made with the **create menu**, **put into menu**, or **delete menu** commands.

HyperCard has several different standard menu bars, depending on the currently chosen tool and the user level. The **reset menubar** command restores the standard menu bar that's appropriate for the current settings.

COMMENTS

If you've installed custom menus or menu items that are specific to your stack, be sure to reset the menu bar when leaving the stack, so that users don't find themselves choosing your custom menus in another stack that can't handle those items.

The following handlers show how to clean up after your stack:

```
on openStack
   setUpMenus -- another handler
   pass openStack
end openStack


on suspendStack
   reset menubar
   pass suspendStack
end suspendStack


on resumeStack
   setUpMenus -- another handler
   pass resumeStack
end resumeStack


on closeStack
   reset menubar
   pass closeStack
end closeStack
```

The standard menu bar is restored, and custom menus are deleted, automatically when you quit HyperCard.

ALSO SEE

create menu command; **delete menu** command; **put into menu** command; **userLevel** property

---

reset paint command   Introduced in version 1.0

FORMS

```
reset paint
```
reset paint

ACTION

The **reset paint** command restores all paint properties to their default values.

COMMENTS

Use **reset paint** to set all the paint properties back to a known state before drawing. This lets you avoid unpleasant surprises if a previous handler has set a paint property to some unusual value.

Table III.5   Paint Property Defaults

Property	Default Value
brush	8
centered	false
filled	false
grid	false
lineSize	1
multiple	false
multiSpace	1
pattern	12 (black)
polySides	4
textAlign	left
textFont	Geneva (or the application font)
textHeight	16 (or 4 * textSize div 3)
textSize	12
textStyle	plain

The following handler sets all the paint properties back to their defaults before drawing a picture:

```
on mouseUp
   reset paint
```

```
      choose brush tool
      drag from 210,130 to 250,105
      drag from 250,105 to 250,300
      drag from 200,300 to 300,300
      choose browse tool
   end mouseUp
```

The **reset paint** command sets the properties listed in Table III.5 to their defaults. All paint properties are set to their defaults automatically when you quit HyperCard.

ALSO SEE
set command

---

reset printing command

FORMS
reset printing
reset printing

ACTION
The **reset printing** command restores the various properties that are used with the **print** command to their default values.

COMMENTS
The **reset printing** command sets the print properties, which are listed in Table III.6, to their defaults.

Table III.6   Print Property Defaults

Property	Default Value
printTextSize	10
printTextHeight	13
printTextFont	Geneva
printTextAlign	left
printTextStyle	plain
printMargins	0,0,0,0

All printing properties are set to their defaults automatically when you quit HyperCard.

ALSO SEE
set command

result function

Introduced in version 1.0
Last changed in version 2.2

FORMS

```
the result
result()
answer "There was a problem:" && the result
if the result is not empty then beep
```

ACTION

The **result** function returns the status of the last command executed.

If the last command was one of those listed below, **the result** returns the appropriate error message if the command failed, or empty if it succeeded. All other commands set **the result** to empty.

A custom message handler can also set **the result** by using the **return** keyword.

COMMENTS

You can check the **result** function in a handler to deal with certain kinds of command errors. The commands listed in Table III.7 set **the result** to something other than empty if they fail. (The specific strings used by **the result** may change in future HyperTalk versions, so it's safest to simply check whether **the result** is empty. If it's not, the command failed.)

Table III.7   Result Values and Their Causes

Command	Values of the result
answer file	Cancel—The user clicked the Cancel button instead of choosing a file.
answer program	Cancel—The user clicked Cancel instead of choosing a program.
	Not supported by this version of the system.—The system version is earlier than 7.0.
ask	Cancel—The user clicked the Cancel button in the dialog.
ask file	Cancel—The user clicked the Cancel button in the dialog.
close application	No such application—The specified System 7-friendly process isn't currently running.
	Not supported by this version of the system.—The system version is earlier than 7.0.
close file	File not open— The specified file isn't currently open.
convert	invalid date—The input isn't in a date or time format HyperCard recognizes.
create stack	Couldn't create stack.—The pathname is invalid or there's already a file by that name.

(continued)

Table III.7   Result Values and Their Causes   *(continued)*

Command	Values of the result
export paint	`Couldn't export paint.`—The current tool is not a paint tool, or the pathname is invalid.
find	`not found`—HyperCard couldn't find the specified string.
go	`No such card.`—The specified card or background doesn't exist.
	`Cancel`—The user clicked Cancel in the "Where is stack?" dialog.
	`No such stack.`—The specified stack doesn't exist (seen when using the `without dialog` option).
import paint	`Couldn't export paint.`—The current tool is not a paint tool, or the specified file doesn't exist.
open application	`Not handled by target application.`—Under System 7, the target application doesn't handle the `odoc` AppleEvent.
	`Cancel`—User clicked cancel in the "Where is application?" dialog.
	`Couldn't open that application.`—Another problem, such as insufficient memory, prevented HyperCard from launching the application.
open file	`Can't create that file.`—Usually means the file name is invalid.
	`File is already open.`—The file exists, but HyperCard or another application has already opened it.
	`Can't open any more files.`—HyperCard already has three text files (the maximum) open.
	`Can't open that file.`—Some other problem prevented opening the file.
open printing	`Cancel`—The user clicked Cancel in the Print Stack dialog.
open report printing	`Cancel`—The user clicked Cancel in the Print Report dialog.
	`No such report template`—You specified a non-existent template.
picture	`Couldn't display picture.`—This generic error message is followed by a sentence giving the specific reason, such as "Resource not found."
play	`Sound is off`—The sound volume is set to 0 in the control panel, or an XCMD or other application is using the sound channel.
	`Couldn't load sound`—The sound resource couldn't be found or there's not enough memory.

(continued)

Table III.7   Result Values and Their Causes   *(continued)*

Command	Values of the result
print document	`Cancel`—The user clicked Cancel in the "Where is file?" dialog.
	`Couldn't open that application.`—There was a problem (such as insufficient memory) launching the document's application.
read	`Not enough memory to read from file.`—You tried to read too large a piece of the file to fit in memory.
	`No open file named` *fileName*.—You haven't yet used the **open file** command to open the file.
reply	`No current Apple`™ `event.`—No AppleEvent has been received by HyperCard.
	`Not supported by this version of the system.`—The system version is earlier than 7.0.
request	`Cancel`—The user cancelled the login dialog.
	`Not handled by target program.`—The target program can't handle the `eval` AppleEvent.
	`Timeout`—The target program timed out.
	`Got error` *number* `when sending Apple`™ `event.`—The Apple Event Manager returned the specified error.
	`Not supported by this version of the system.`—The system version is earlier than 7.0.
request appleEvent	`No current Apple`™ `event.`—HyperCard hasn't received an AppleEvent.
	`Not found`—You requested a nonexistent parameter or attribute of the AppleEvent.
	`Unknown type`—The parameter exists but can't be coerced to text format.
	`Not supported by this version of the system.`—The system version is earlier than 7.0.
save stack as	`Can't duplicate stack.`—A file by that name already exists.
	`Couldn't create that file.`—You specified an invalid filename.
	`No such stack.`—The stack you're trying to copy doesn't exist.
set	`Can't find that icon.`—Tried to set the icon property of a button to a nonexistent icon.
write	`File is open read-only.`—The file is on a locked or read-only AppleShare volume.
	`No open file named` *fileName*.—You haven't yet used the **open file** command to open the file.

This example checks whether the **find** command was successful:

```
on findAddress theName
  lock screen
  lock messages
  push this card
  go to stack "Address Book"
  find theName in field "Names"
  if the result is empty then -- succeeded
    get field "Mailing Address"
    pop card
    put it into field "Address To"
  else -- result was not empty, so find failed
    pop card
    answer "There's no address for" && theName && "on file."
  end if
  unlock screen
  unlock messages
end findAddress
```

Each command resets the result: HyperCard resets the **result** function when each command is executed, so if you're going to use the function's value, you need to check it immediately after the command you're interested in. Otherwise, the next command will reset **the result**. You can store the value of **the result** in a variable if you need to use it later in the handler.

Most of the time, commands fail because of syntax or runtime errors, and such errors put up a script error dialog instead of setting **the result**. A script error dialog aborts the running handler. This is why you can't use **the result** to construct an "on error" handler.

Commands from the message box don't set the result: If you execute one of the above commands (except for **play** and **picture**) from the message box, and the command fails, it puts up a dialog instead of setting **the result**. The text in the dialog is the same as the result text.

Changes to HyperTalk: In versions of HyperCard before 2.2, the **play** command does not set **the result**.

In versions before 2.0, the **ask** command does not return a result; there's no way to tell whether the user cancelled or simply didn't type anything into the text box.

Other changes to **the result** have been made over the course of time, and the exact strings returned are very likely to change further in future versions.

ALSO SEE

errorDialog message; **return** keyword

resume message

FORMS

```
resume
```

ACTION

The **resume** message is sent to the current card when the user returns from another application that was launched with the **open application** or **print document** command.

If MultiFinder is running, HyperCard doesn't send the **resume** message. Since MultiFinder is always on when you're using System 7, this means **resume** is never sent under System 7.

COMMENTS

When MultiFinder is not running and HyperCard launches another application with **open application** or **print document**, it puts itself away until the user quits the other application. Because HyperCard is not running during this time, all global variables are lost, and any parts of handlers that have not yet executed do not run.

The following example shows how to reload global variables after returning from the other application. It assumes that a **suspend** handler (see **suspend** for an example) has already run when the **open application** command executed:

```
on resume
   global accountNumber,currentName,lastOrder
   put line 1 of card field "Saved Globals" into accountNumber
   put line 2 of card field "Saved Globals" into currentName
   put line 3 of card field "Saved Globals" into lastOrder
   put empty into card field "Saved Globals"
end resume
```

Important: The **resume** message is never sent if you're using MultiFinder or System 7. Under MultiFinder, you can check the **suspended** property to see whether HyperCard is in the background.

When HyperCard resumes running, the following messages are sent to the current card:

```
resume
openStack
openBackground
openCard
```

Changes to HyperTalk: In versions of HyperCard before 2.0, the message order when resuming is:

```
openStack
openBackground
openCard
resume
```

ALSO SEE

open application command; **print document** command; **resumeStack** message; **suspend** message

---

resumeStack message

FORMS

```
resumeStack
```

ACTION

The **resumeStack** message is sent when you bring a stack's window to the front. The message is sent to the current card of the destination stack.

COMMENTS

Usually, you use **resumeStack** in conjunction with a **suspendStack** to save and restore changes to the environment that are specific to your stack, such as custom menus, global properties, or windoid arrangements.

The **resumeStack** message is sent to the current card in the destination stack when any of these things happen:

- The user clicks in the stack's window to bring it to the front.

- The current stack is closed and another stack becomes the frontmost stack.

- A script issues a **go** or **show** command that brings the stack to the front.

ALSO SEE

resume message; **show** command; **suspendStack** message; **suspended** property

---

return keyword

FORMS

```
return value
return "Handler error"
return myTotal
return calculationResult - correctionTerms
```

ACTION

The **return** keyword has two actions, depending on what kind of handler you use it in. If it appears in a function handler, it assigns a value to the function that's being defined. If it appears in a message handler, it sets **the result** to the *value* you specify.

After execution of a **return** statement, control leaves the current handler and returns to the calling handler. This is true even if the **return** statement is not the last line in its handler. Any remaining commands in that handler are ignored.

COMMENTS

The **return** keyword is most commonly used in function handlers. This function converts temperatures between Fahrenheit and Celsius. (Every computer programming book is required to contain a Fahrenheit-to-Celsius conversion program. It's traditional.)

```
function change temperature, fromScale
  if first char of fromScale is "f" then
    return (temperature - 32) * 5/9 -- Does this and ends...
  else if first char of fromScale is "c" then
    return (9/5 * temperature) + 32 -- ...or does this and ends...
  end if
  -- if it's gotten this far, we know the scale isn't right
  answer "I don't know how to convert that scale!"
  exit to HyperCard -- halt all handlers, since we had an error
end change
```

When you use **return** in a message handler, it's usually to pass error messages and ancillary information back to the calling handler. The following example shows how you can use **return** in a message handler to set **the result**:

```
on mouseUp
  compactStack -- calls the handler below
  answer the result && "bytes recovered."
end mouseUp


on compactStack
  get the size of this stack
  doMenu "Compact Stack"
  return (it - the size of this stack) -- placed in the result
end compactStack
```

Normally, every custom function handler contains at least one **return** statement. The value returned can be any HyperTalk expression. The following handler returns true if its argument is odd and false otherwise:

```
function isOdd theInteger
  return theInteger mod 2 ≠ 0
end isOdd
```

The following function, which uses the isOdd function defined above, finds the corners of a rectangle given its center, width, and height:

```
function centerToRect center,width,height
   put item 1 of center - (width div 2) into item 1 of theRect
   put item 2 of center - (height div 2) into item 2 of theRect
   put item 1 of center + (width div 2) into item 3 of theRect
   put item 2 of center + (height div 2) into item 4 of theRect
   if isOdd(width) then add 1 to item 3 of theRect
   if isOdd(height) then add 1 to item 4 of theRect
   return theRect
end centerToRect
```

The return keyword in message handlers: Using **return** in a message handler sets the **result** function, and since many built-in HyperTalk commands (such as **find** and **go**) set **the result** to indicate that an error occurred, the most typical use of **return** in message handlers is to return error messages:

```
on atm
   ask "How much money would you like?"
   withdraw it -- calls withdraw handler below
   if the result is not empty then
      answer "I'm sorry, but" && the result & "."
   else
      answer "Here's your money."
   end if
end atm
```

```
on withdraw theAmount -- "theAmount" gets value of "it" passed above
   global cashOnHand
   if theAmount > field "Balance"
   then return "your balance is only" && field "Balance"
   if theAmount > cashOnHand
   then return "this branch can't cover this withdrawal"
   subtract theAmount from field "Balance"
   subtract theAmount from cashOnHand
end withdraw
```

You can also use **return** to pass extra information other than error messages back to the calling handler. The following handlers belong to a library stack. Each card describes a book in the library. This example uses **return** to pass messages to the library patron:

```
on mouseUp
   ask "What book do you want to check out?"
   if it is empty then exit mouseUp
   checkOut it
   answer the result
end mouseUp
```

```
on checkOut theBook
   find theBook in field "Title"
   if the result it not empty then
      return "The library doesn't have that book."
   else if the hilite of background button "Reserved" is true then
      return "That book is on reserve." -- checkbox button
   else if field "Copies On Hand" ≤ 0 then
      return "That book is checked out."
   else -- successful checkout
      subtract 1 from field "Copies On Hand"
      if the hilite of background button "New Book" is true then
         return "Please return this book in two weeks."
      else return "Please return this book in four weeks."
   end if
end checkOut
```

ALSO SEE

function keyword; **on** keyword

---

returnInField command/message   Introduced in version 1.2

FORMS

`returnInField`

ACTION

When the user presses the Return key, the **returnInField** message is sent to whatever field holds the current selection.

If there is no text selection or insertion point in any field, pressing Return causes the **returnKey** message to be sent to the current card instead. No **returnInField** message is sent.

As with all messages, you can use **returnInField** as a command. Write a **returnInField** handler to trap this message if you want to override its behavior.

COMMENTS

If the **returnInField** message reaches HyperCard without being intercepted by a handler, HyperCard adds a return character to the current field, if it is unlocked. If the selection is in a locked field, **returnInField** deselects the selection without making any changes to the field's contents.

Autotabbing fields: If the current field's **autoTab** property is true and the selection is on the last visible line of the field, **returnInField** sends a **tabKey** message. This makes **returnInField** behave the same way as if the user had pressed the Return key.

An automated menu

The following set of handlers turns a nonscrolling locked field into a menu. You make a choice by clicking a line in the field; you move to the next line by pressing the Return key. Pressing the Enter key executes the currently selected choice. (See Figure III.42.)

```
on mouseDown
  select the clickLine
end mouseDown


on returnInField
  moveSelectedLine 1
end returnInField


on moveSelectedLine amount
  get the selectedLine
  add amount to word 2 of it -- the line number
  if word 2 of it > the number of lines in value(the selectedField)
  then put 1 into word 2 of it -- go back to the top
  if word 2 of it < 1
  then put the number of lines in value(the selectedField) ¬
  into word 2 of it
  select it
end moveSelectedLine


on enterInField
  answer "You chose" && the selection
  -- or do whatever you want with the selection, depending on
  -- what the menu is for.
  select empty
end enterInField


on arrowKey theKey -- in card script or higher
  if the selectedField is empty then pass arrowKey
  if the script of the selectedField contains "moveSelectedLine" then
    if theKey is "down" then
      send "moveSelectedLine 1" to the selectedField
    else if theKey is "up" then
      send "moveSelectedLine -1" to the selectedField
    else pass arrowKey
  else pass arrowKey
end arrowKey
```

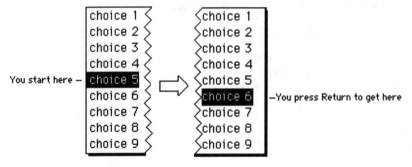

Figure III.42   Menu choices

ALSO SEE

enterInField command/message; **returnKey** command/message; **type** command

---

returnKey command/message   Introduced in version 1.0

FORMS

```
returnKey
```

ACTION

When the user presses the Return key, the **returnKey** message is sent to the current card.

If there is a selection or insertion point in a field, **returnKey** is not sent. Instead, a **returnInField** message is sent to that field instead.

If the **returnKey** command is not trapped before it reaches HyperCard, it simulates pressing Return. If there is a text selection in a field, it inserts a return character. Otherwise, it executes the contents of the message box.

COMMENTS

In standard Macintosh dialog boxes, pressing the Return key is equivalent to clicking the default button. However, HyperCard's default button style does not automatically behave this way. This example, which belongs in a card, background, or stack script, implements the default-button behavior:

```
on returnKey
   repeat with x = the number of background buttons
      if the style of background button x is default then
         click at the location of background button x
         exit repeat
      end if
   end repeat
end returnKey
```

```
on returnInField -- in case some text is selected
   returnKey -- do same thing
end returnInField


on enterKey -- enter key also should select the default button
   returnKey
end returnKey


on enterInField
   returnKey
end enterInField
```

If not trapped by a handler, **returnKey** and **enterKey** both do exactly the same thing: execute the message box's contents.

Historical note: In prerelease versions of HyperCard 1.0, pressing Return did a **find** of the contents of the message box. Pressing Enter executed its contents. The following handler recreates that behavior:

```
on returnKey
   find message
end returnKey
```

ALSO SEE
enterKey command/message; **returnInField** message

---

right property

Introduced in version 1.2
Last changed in version 2.2

FORMS
set [the] right of {*part*|*button*|*field*|*window*} to *integer*
the right of {menubar|*card*}
```
set the right of last card field to 22
set the right of window "Message" to the left of field "Login"
set the left of button "Follow Me" to item 1 of the mouseLoc
```

ACTION
The **right** property describes where the right edge of an element is.

COMMENTS
The following handler moves a button across the screen and back by adjusting its **right** property:

```
on travelingButton -- with yet another thanks to Gary "XCMD" Bond
   repeat 50 times
      lock screen -- gets rid of distracting screen flicker
      set the right of me to the right of me + 5
      unlock screen
   end repeat
   repeat 50 times
      lock screen
      set the right of me to the right of me - 5
      unlock screen
   end repeat
end travelingButton
```

The *button, field,* or *card* must be in the current stack. (You can read the **right** of a card, but you can't set it). A *window* is any open stack window, HyperCard window, or external window.

The **right** of a stack window and the **right** of a card in that stack may be different if the window has been set to a size that's smaller than the card size (for example, using the Scroll command in the Go menu).

The *integer* is the horizontal distance in pixels from the left edge—of the screen for stack windows, or of the current stack window for cards, buttons, fields, and other windows—to the element's right edge. If the *integer* is negative, the element's right edge is *integer* pixels to the left of the left edge of the screen or stack window.

The right and other location properties: The **right** of an element is the same as item 1 of its **bottomRight** property. It's also the same as the third item of the element's **rectangle** property.

Changing the right property: Anything that moves or resizes an element may change its **right** property. For example, dragging the element manually or from a script, changing its **location** or **rectangle** property, and using the **show** command with a new location can all change the **right** of the element.

Changing the **right** of an element moves the element without changing its size. Changing item 3 of the element's **rectangle** changes its size without moving its other three edges.

Changes to HyperTalk: In versions of HyperCard before 2.2, you cannot describe a button or field with a part descriptor, and you cannot get the **right** of the menu bar.

ALSO SEE
bottom property; **bottomRight** property; **left** property; **location** property; **rectangle** property; **show** command; **top** property

round function

FORMS

```
[the] round of number
round(number)
round(3.5) -- yields 4
round(4.5) -- yields 4
the round of card field "Stellar Age"
round(total/1.2)
```

ACTION

The **round** function returns the *number*, rounded off to the nearest integer. For a *number* ending in .5, if the integer part is odd, the number is rounded up; if the integer part is even, the number is rounded down.

COMMENTS

If the *number* is exactly halfway between one number and another, **round** rounds it to the nearest even number. This behavior is useful in statistical and scientific applications, since it avoids a sampling bias, but for financial and bookkeeping applications, it's better to always round such numbers up. The following example shows how you might replace HyperCard's **round** function with one that's better suited for a banking application:

```
function round theNumber -- overrides built-in round function
   if theNumber < 0 then return trunc(theNumber - .5)
   else return trunc(theNumber + .5)
end round
```

The *number* is any number between -2147483648 and 2147483648.

Difference between trunc and round: The **trunc** function simply throws away any part of the number it's given that falls after the decimal point. For instance, the truncated value of 6, 6.2, or 6.7 is simply 6. The **round** function, on the other hand, rounds to the nearest integer, so it looks at the part after the decimal point to see whether it should round up or down. The rounded value of 6.2, like the truncated value, is 6, but the rounded value of 6.7 is 7, since 7 is closer to the original number than 6.

Techie alert: This function calls the SANE routine Num2LongInt with rounding set to ToNearest. Because a Macintosh longint is 32 bits, with one bit reserved for the sign, the highest value this routine can be used with is $31^2 - 1$; that is, 2147483647.

Trekkie alert: Mr. Spock is half-human.

ALSO SEE

numberFormat property; **trunc** function

run message

FORMS

```
run
run -- goes through the message-passing path
send run to card "AppleScript Example"
send run to background part nextPart
```

ACTION

The **run** message, when sent to an object whose **scriptingLanguage** is something other than HyperTalk, executes the script of that object.

COMMENTS

Use the **run** message to run scripts written in languages that don't handle messages like **mouseUp**.

When an object receives the **run** message, HyperCard examines the object's script and executes any part of the script that's not inside a message handler. If there is nothing to execute, the **run** message is passed on to the next object in the message-passing path.

If you send **run** without specifying an object to receive it, it travels through the message-passing path in the usual way until it reaches an object that has statements outside any handler.

The **run** message has no effect when received by an object whose script is written in HyperTalk.

Techie alert: The **run** message is implemented internally as a command.

ALSO SEE

"Using Other Scripting Languages" in Chapter 5; **do** keyword; **send** keyword

---

save stack as command

FORMS

```
save stack as stackCopyName
save this stack as "Backup"
save stack "Original" as theBackupPath
save stack nextStack as "Unknown Magnanimity:Book:Updates"
```

ACTION

The **save stack as** command saves a copy of a stack under a new name. It is equivalent to going to the stack and choosing the Save a Copy item from the File menu, except that it doesn't present a dialog.

COMMENTS

The following handler saves a backup copy of the current stack in a folder called "Backups":

```
on mouseUp
  put "Copy of" && char 1 to 24 of the short name of this stack ¬
  into backupName
  save this stack as ":Backups:" & backupName
end mouseUp
```

The *stack* can be any stack, including the current one.
The following example adds a Save As item to the File menu:

```
on startup -- belongs in Home or stack script
  put "Save As..." after menuItem "Save a Copy..." ¬
  of menu "File" with menuMsg "userSaveAs"
end startup
```

```
on userSaveAs -- triggered when you choose Save As
  ask file "Save stack as:" with the short name of this stack
  if it is empty then exit userSaveAs -- user cancelled
  save this stack as it
  if the result is empty then
    go to it
  else -- stack already exists, so delete old copy
    lock screen
    go to stack it
    doMenu "Delete Stack" without dialog
    save this stack as it
  end if
end userSaveAs
```

The **save stack as** command sets the **result** function to "Couldn't duplicate stack." if it encounters a problem such as the stack already existing.

ALSO SEE

doMenu command/message

---

scale property   Introduced in version 2.0

FORMS

set [the] scale of *pictureWindow* to *integer*

```
set the scale of window "Staff Snapshot" to 0 -- actual size
set the scale of window myPicture to 2          -- 4x actual size
set the scale of window ID 89345 to -1          -- 1/2 actual size
```

ACTION

The **scale** property determines the scale at which a picture created by the **picture** command is shown. By default, the **scale** of picture windows is zero (actual size).

COMMENTS

You can use the **scale** property to blow up or shrink a picture window, to see details or to fit all of a large picture in a small space. The **scale** property is particularly useful for maps.

The *integer* is a number between -5 and 5. The picture is displayed at *integer*^{2}:

Scale	Displays at
-5	1/32 actual size
-4	1/16 actual size
-3	1/8 actual size
-2	1/4 actual size
-1	1/2 actual size
0	actual size
1	2 times actual size
2	4 times actual size
3	8 times actual size
4	16 times actual size
5	32 times actual size

ALSO SEE

picture command; **zoom** property

screenRect function

Introduced in version 1.2

FORMS

```
the screenRect
screenRect()
if the rect of this card is not the screenRect then show scroll window
put item 3 of the screenRect - item 1 of the screenRect into screenWidth
put item 4 of the screenRect - item 2 of the screenRect into screenHeight
```

ACTION

The **screenRect** function returns a rectangle that specifies the borders of the screen.

If there is more than one screen, the **screenRect** returns the rectangle of the screen that contains the larger portion of the frontmost stack window.

COMMENTS

Use this function to determine where to place windows that you open as you use HyperCard. For instance, if you know you have room, you can arrange palette windows around the stack window instead of on top of it:

```
on startup
    if item 4 of the screenRect - item 4 of the rect of card window ¬
    ≥ 70 then
        show message window at 0,the height of card window + 12
        show tool window at -69,0
        show pattern window at -69,100
    end if
end startup
```

The screenRect is a rectangle, consisting of four integers—the left, top, right, and bottom of the rectangle—separated by commas. If there is one screen, the first and second items are always zero, the third item is the screen width, and the fourth item is the screen height. If there is more than one screen, **the screenRect** reports the left, top, bottom, and right edges of the current screen, relative to the top left of the main screen. (The main screen is the one that contains the menu bar.)

The following handler hides the tool, pattern, and message windows, if the screen is the same size as the stack window:

```
on hideWindows
    if the rect of card window is the screenRect then
        hide tool window
        hide pattern window
        hide message window
    end if
end hideWindows
```

ALSO SEE

rectangle property

---

script property

Introduced in version 1.0

FORMS

set [the] script of *object* to *scriptText*
```
get the script of stack "Home"
if the script of part nextPart contains "--edit" then beep
set the script of this background to myNewScript
set the script of card ID 23655 to card field "New Script"
set the script of the target to field "AppleScript Code"
```

ACTION

The **script** property determines the contents of a specified object's script.

COMMENTS

Usually you'll use the script editor to make changes to scripts. However, the **script** property lets you check, change, or replace any script from within a handler.

The *object* is any stack, any card or background in the current stack, or any button or field on the current card.

You can retrieve all of a script or only a chunk expression:

```
put line 3 to 5 of the script of this card into field "Script"
put the script of button "Click Me" into myScript
```

But the **script** is a property, not a container. You can't set a chunk expression in a script: setting the **script** property replaces the entire script. The following handler appends the given text (which might consist of one or more handlers) to the bottom of a script:

```
on appendToScript theText,theObject
   -- theObject is the name of the object whose script you
   -- want to modify
   get the script of theObject
   set the script of theObject to it & return & return & theText
end appendToScript
```

You might call this handler like this:

```
appendToScript card field 1,"card button 1"
-- use quotes so the object's name is passed, not the contents
```

With clever use of the **script** property, you can create objects that are self-modifying. The following button script installs the button that contains it in the Home stack, then deletes the installation code:

```
on mouseUp  -- the first mouseUp message is executed
   lock messages
   select me
   doMenu "Copy Button"
   go home
   doMenu "Paste Button"
   -- change the pasted copy's script
   get the script of me
   delete char 1 to offset("***",it) of it -- this handler
   delete line 1 of it -- the line beginning ***
   put "Drag the button where you want it and press command-Tab..."
end mouseUp
```

```
*** real script begins here ***
on mouseUp
  go to stack "Card Tricks" -- the stack that installed this button
end mouseUp
```

If you change the script of an object that already has a handler running, HyperCard doesn't replace the script until all the running handlers complete. For instance, if a handler contains the line `set the script of me to newScript`, HyperTalk lets the handler finish before changing the script.

Script size limit: The script of an object can have up to 30,000 characters. HyperCard complains if you try to make a script longer, either manually or with **set**. If you reach this limit, move some of your handlers to a level further in the message-passing path. If a button script is full, you can move some of its handlers to the card or background script; if the stack script is full, you can use **start using** to place another stack into the message path, and put excess handlers into that stack's script.

In versions before 2.0, which don't have the **start using** command, you can put ancillary handlers into another object (such as a hidden button) and send messages to it as required:

```
send myRemoteHandler to background button "Handler Library"
```

The script editor removes leading spaces from handlers when it stores a script and re-indents when you get or display the script. It leaves Option-spaces alone, however. The following handler belongs in the script of a field used for editing (perhaps in a HyperTalk tutorial stack), and takes advantage of the script editor's ability to indent:

```
on enterInField
  set the script of button "Hidden" to me
  -- when the script comes back, it's indented
  put the script of button "Hidden" into me
end enterInField
```

ALSO SEE
edit command; **scriptEditor** property; **start using** command

---

scriptEditor property   Introduced in version 2.0

FORMS
```
set [the] scriptEditor [of HyperCard] to scriptXCMD
set the scriptEditor to customEditor
set the scriptEditor to "ScriptEditor"
```

ACTION
The script editor in HyperCard is implemented as an XCMD. (XCMDs are usually written

by Pascal, C, and assembly-language programmers and are, therefore, not discussed in polite company.) The **scriptEditor** global property determines which XCMD is used when you edit scripts.

The built-in script editor XCMD is named `ScriptEditor`. HyperCard resets the **scriptEditor** to this default value every time you quit.

COMMENTS

HyperCard uses the **scriptEditor** whenever you open a script. If you want to write a custom script editor, use this property to make your custom editor the default.

The script editor XCMD must reside in the resource fork of the current stack, any stack in use, the home stack, or HyperCard itself. Specifying a script editor that doesn't exist causes HyperCard to put up a script error dialog and abort the rest of the handler.

ALSO SEE

debugger property; **edit** command; **messageWatcher** property; **variableWatcher** property

---

scriptingLanguage property   Introduced in version 2.2

FORMS

```
set [the] scriptingLanguage [of object] to scriptingLanguage
set the scriptingLanguage to AppleScript -- sets globally
set the scriptingLanguage of card "Test" to myTestLanguage
```

ACTION

The **scriptingLanguage** is a property of all objects—stacks, backgrounds, cards, fields, and buttons—as well as a global property of HyperCard itself.

This property determines whether the object's script is written in HyperTalk, AppleScript, or some other script language. The **scriptingLanguage** of HyperCard determines the language accepted by the message box.

COMMENTS

You can set the **scriptingLanguage** of an object manually by opening its script and choosing from the popup menu at the top of the script window.

If the *scriptingLanguage* you specify is not installed, HyperCard ignores the command to set the **scriptingLanguage** property. The exception is AppleScript: if the software to use scripting is installed but AppleScript itself is not, you can set the **scriptingLanguage** to AppleScript.

The following example searches for all buttons that contain AppleScript code and copies them to another stack:

```
on mouseUp
   lock screen
   lock messages
```

```
      set the cursor to busy
      create stack "AppleScript Library" in a new window
      go back
      repeat with nextBackground = 1 to the number of backgrounds
        go background nextBackground
        repeat with nextButton = 1 to the number of background buttons
          set the cursor to busy
          if the scriptingLanguage of background button nextButton ¬
          is "AppleScript" then
            select background button nextButton
            doMenu "Copy Button"
            push this card
            go to last card of stack "AppleScript Library"
            doMenu "Paste Button"
            doMenu "New Card" -- for next button
            pop card -- back to source stack
          end if
        end repeat
      end repeat
      repeat with nextCard = 1 to the number of cards
        go card nextCard
        repeat with nextButton = 1 to the number of buttons
          set the cursor to busy
          if the scriptingLanguage of button nextButton is "AppleScript" then
            select button nextButton
            doMenu "Copy Button"
            push this card
            go to last card of stack "AppleScript Library"
            doMenu "Paste Button"
            doMenu "New Card" -- for next button
            pop card -- back to source stack
          end if
        end repeat
      end repeat
      push card
      go to last card of stack "AppleScript Library"
      if the number of buttons is zero
      then doMenu "Delete Card" without dialog
      pop card
    end mouseUp
```

ALSO SEE

    there is a operator

scriptTextFont property   Introduced in version 2.0

FORMS

set [the] scriptTextFont [of HyperCard] to *fontName*
set the scriptTextFont to "Courier"

ACTION

The **scriptTextFont** property specifies the font used by the script editor.
The default **scriptTextFont** is Monaco.

COMMENTS

You can use this and other script properties to set up your own custom scripting environment in accordance with your preferences. The following handler assumes you have created a card in your Home stack to store your scripting preferences:

```
on startup
  lock screen
  lock messages
  go to card "Script Prefs" of stack "Home" -- custom prefs card
  set the scriptTextFont to card field "Font"
  set the scriptTextSize to card field "Size"
  set the visible of window "Message Watcher" ¬
  to the hilite of button "Show Message Watcher"
  set the visible of window "Variable Watcher" ¬
  to the hilite of button "Show Variable Watcher"
  pass startup
end startup
```

The *fontName* is the name of a currently installed font. If you try to set the **scriptTextFont** to a nonexistent font, it is set, instead, to Geneva. If the font's name has more than one word, it must be enclosed in quotation marks.

ALSO SEE

edit script command; **scriptEditor** property; **scriptTextSize** property

---

scriptTextSize property   Introduced in version 2.0

FORMS

set [the] scriptTextSize [of HyperCard] to *pointSize*
set the scriptTextSize to 12

ACTION

The **scriptTextSize** property specifies the font size used by the script editor. The default **scriptTextSize** is 9.

COMMENTS

The *pointSize* must be an integer between 1 and 127.

This example uses a large point size to display a script to an audience:

```
on toggleScriptFont -- in a checkbox button's script
  if the scriptTextSize ≤ 9 then
    set the scriptTextSize to 36 -- for display to a class
  else
    set the scriptTextSize to 9  -- for normal script editing
  end if
end toggleScriptFont
```

ALSO SEE

edit script command; **scriptEditor** property; **scriptTextFont** property

---

scroll property

Introduced in version 1.0

FORMS

set [the] scroll of *scrollingField* to *integer*

```
set the scroll of field "Comments" to zero -- top of field
set the scroll of me to savedScroll
```

ACTION

The **scroll** of a scrolling field is the number of pixels that have scrolled off its top. You can also change a field's **scroll** manually using its scroll bar. Setting the **scroll** moves the field's scrollbar thumb.

When you quit, HyperCard automatically sets the **scroll** of all fields to zero.

COMMENTS

The *field* must be in the current stack. Its **style** must be scrolling; if you try to get or set the **scroll** of a nonscrolling field, HyperCard puts up an error dialog.

The maximum scroll is 32767 pixels. (This is a limit imposed by the TextEdit routines HyperCard uses to draw text on the screen.) You can force a field to scroll to the bottom of its text with the command `set the scroll of` *field* `to 32767`.

If your field has short lines or the field's **textHeight** is large, you may hit the scroll limit of 32767 pixels before you reach the maximum amount of text that can be put in a field. If this happens, you can still use HyperTalk commands to access and change the field's contents, but its scroll bar may behave strangely.

The following example computes how many lines have scrolled off the top of a particular field:

```
on linesOffTop
  return trunc(the scroll of the target/the textHeight of the target)
end linesOffTop
```

```
on getCommentsScroll
  send linesOffTop to field "Comments"
  put the result
end getCommentsScroll
```

This handler scrolls a field smoothly through its length:

```
on scrollField theField -- Thanks again, Gary Bond!
  set the scroll of theField to 0
  put the height of theField div the textHeight of theField ¬
  into visibleLinesInField -- works only if fixedLineHeight is true
  put the textHeight of theField + 1 - linesPerField ¬
  into totalPixels -- height in pixels of all the data
  repeat with theScroll = 1 to totalPixels
    set the scroll of theField to theScroll
    wait 2 ticks -- slow things down a bit
  end repeat
end scrollField
```

You might call the above handler like this:

```
scrollField "card field 1"
```

ALSO SEE

fixedLineHeight property; **select** command; **textHeight** property

---

scroll of window property   Introduced in version 2.0

FORMS

set [the] scroll of *window* to *horizOffset,vertOffset*
```
set the scroll of card window to 23,23
set the scroll of window "My Picture" to thePoint
set the scroll of window ID theWindow to 0,0 -- no scroll
```

ACTION

The **scroll** property of a window describes the number of horizontal and vertical pixels the window has been scrolled by.

You can scroll card windows manually by using the Scroll item in the Edit menu.

COMMENTS

Usually, you'll want to let users scroll manually. However, setting the **scroll** property of a window lets you control what portion of the stack or picture the user sees. The following handler shows a color picture of a landscape and pans slowly over it:

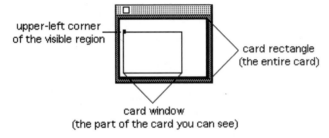

upper-left corner
of the visible region

card rectangle
(the entire card)

card window
(the part of the card you can see)

Figure III.43   Scroll palette, showing the card and the visible region

```
on showPanorama
  picture "Panorama",resource,rectangle,false -- invisible
  set the rect of window "Panorama" to 100,100,400,300
  -- the picture is actually 200 pixels tall by 900 wide
  play "Desert Theme" -- a long musical piece
  show window "Panorama"
  repeat with hScroll = 1 to 600
    set the scroll of window "Panorama" to hScroll,0
  end repeat
  wait until the sound is done
  close window "Panorama"
end showPanorama
```

The *window* can be the current stack window or a window created with the **picture** command. Some external windows also support the **scroll** property.

The *horizOffset* is the number of pixels that are scrolled off the left edge of the window. The *vertOffset* is the number of pixels scrolled off the top. You can also think of the offset parameters as the horizontal and vertical coordinates of the upper left corner of the card's visible region (see Figure III.43).

Changing the **scroll** of a stack window that's already at full size has no effect. To shrink the stack window, set its **rectangle**, **width**, or **height** properties. You can then set the window's **scroll** to the desired value. You can also shrink a card window manually, either by dragging a corner or side of the card image in the scroll window or by pressing Command-Shift-E to get a size box (Figure III.44).

ALSO SEE

rectangle property; **scroll** property

Figure III.44   Size box revealed when you press Command-Shift-E

seconds function

FORMS

```
the sec[ond]s
sec[ond]s()
the seconds
secs()
seconds()
the secs
```

ACTION

The **seconds** function returns the number of seconds since 12:00:00 AM, January 1, 1904. The **seconds** function assumes that the time set in the Control Panel is the current time.

COMMENTS

Because it's a number-only way of expressing a date and time, **the seconds** doesn't depend on any particular language or national conventions for writing dates and times. You can use the **seconds** as a neutral format in which to store a date and/or time if your stack may be used in different countries. Use the **convert** command, which checks the date and time formats set in the system software, to change the stored value to the appropriate form when you want to display it.

You can also use **the seconds** to measure the elapsed time between two events. This example implements a stopwatch:

```
on stopwatch theButton
   get the ticks
   global secondsCount
   if theButton is "start" then
     put it into secondsCount
   else
     subtract secondsCount from it
     put it && "seconds elapsed"
     put empty into secondsCount
   end if
end stopwatch
```

You can call the `stopwatch` handler like this:

```
on mouseDown
   global secondsCount
   if secondsCount is empty then stopwatch start
   else stopwatch stop
end mouseDown
```

If you want to measure elapsed time in intervals smaller than a second, use the **ticks** function.

Why January 1, 1904?

The original Macintosh development team (circa 1983) determined that January 1, 1904, would be The Day That Time Began. That date was chosen for several reasons:

- A longword seemed like an adequate amount of memory to allocate to date-keeping; its 32 bits can produce an unsigned number high enough to represent just over 130 years worth of seconds.

- The team wanted to include the birthdays of most Macintosh users, so a date somewhere around the turn of the century looked like a great target.

- Projecting from the beginning of this century forward for 130 years brought the date to 2030, which meant that clocks in Macs would work for 46 years before Time would run out (and reset to 1/1/04). Nobody wanted to speculate on the life of the Mac (or of the current operating system) beyond that point.

- For calculation purposes, it was arithmetically convenient to have time start on a leap year (which 1900 wasn't, being a century year not divisible by 4).

The philosophical implications of these facts are dizzying. The authors are therefore taking a short nap.

ALSO SEE

convert command; **ticks** function; **time** function

select command

Introduced in version 1.2
Last changed in version 2.2

FORMS

```
select [before|after] {text|chunk} of {field|message}
select part
select line of popupButton
select empty
select text of field "Address" -- selects text inside field
select field "Address"        -- selects field itself with field tool
select word 1 of message box
select after text of field "Notes"
select before line nextRef of card field "References"
select line 2 of field "List" of card "Contents"
select char 5 to 4 of msg -- places insertion point between 4 and 5
select empty -- deselects everything
select the clickLine
select button "Move Me"
select line 12 of background button "Font Popup"
```

ACTION

The **select** command selects the designated text or object, or makes a choice from a popup button.

The **select** command cannot be used to select paint graphics.

COMMENTS

The following example belongs in a stack where the user usually changes the text of the "Latest Impression" field on opening a card. As a convenience, it selects the text in that field for the user:

```
on openCard
   select text of field "Latest Impression"
end openCard
```

The *chunk* is any valid chunk expression. If you select a line that doesn't exist in a field—for example, if you try to select line 10 of a field that only contains 5 lines—the **select** command adds extra lines to fill to the line you selected. However, **select** doesn't pad characters, words, items, or ranges of text. If you say `select word 7 of field "My Field"` but "My Field" has fewer than 7 words, the command just places the insertion point after the last word.

The *field* must be on the current card, unless it's a list field that has its **autoSelect** property set to true; you can select a line of a list field on any card in the current stack. You cannot select text in a field whose **visible** property is false—again, unless it's a list field—but you can select text and type into a field even if the field is hidden behind another object, or if its **width** or **height** is set to zero.

The *message* is any legal descriptor of the message box. If the message box is hidden, selecting text in it causes it to become visible.

A *part* is any descriptor of a button or field on the current card. Selecting a button or field chooses the button or field tool first, so to use this form of **select**, the **userLevel** must be set to 4 (Authoring) or 5 (Scripting).

The form `select empty` deselects anything—text, button, or field—that is currently selected, removing any text insertion point. However, it does not alter the selected line of an **autoSelect** field, or the current choice in a popup button.

Selecting a line of a popup button has the effect of choosing the menu item on that line.

Using select in a locked field: You can use the **select** command to select text that's in a locked field. You can then manipulate the selected text with commands like this:

```
put someThing into the selectedChunk
get the selectedText
doMenu "Copy Text"
```

Using select to set an insertion point: The **select** command can set the text insertion point, as well as selecting one or more characters (the insertion point is a selection of zero length). The form `select before text of container` places the insertion point at the beginning of the container. `select after text of container` places it at the end. Similarly, you can select before or after a chunk expression to place the insertion point at the designated location in the container.

The chunk expression `char x to x-1` designates the space between the xth character and the previous character, so the form `select char 3 to 2 of` *container* places an insertion point between character 2 and character 3. It is equivalent to `select before char 3 of` *container* or `select after char 2 of` *container*.

Dragging and selecting: If the field or button tool is already chosen, you don't need to select a field or button before dragging it:

```
on moveTheButton thisButton
   choose button tool
   set the dragSpeed to 72
   -- don't need to select button thisButton
   drag from the loc of button thisButton to 150,200
   choose browse tool
end moveButton
```

Special find handlers

The following handler simulates the action of the Find menu item:

```
on myFind
   put "find" && quote & quote
   select before last char of the message box
end myFind
```

This slightly more complicated version also specifies the form of the **find** command (char, word, normal, string, or whole). You call it with a form such as `myFind string`:

```
on myFind theForm
   if theForm is empty then put "normal" into theForm
   put "find" && theForm && quote & quote
   select before last char of the message box
end myFind
```

The following handler finds text the way a word processor does: it selects the found text so you can type over it.

```
on findAndSelect searchString
   find searchString
   if the result is empty then select the foundChunk
end findAndSelect
```

Selecting graphics: Instead of **select**, use **drag** to select card or background paint:

```
choose select tool
drag from 10,10 to 250,300 -- or whatever points contain the image
```

And by the way: The correct form is `select text of field "Foo"`, not `select the text of field "Foo"`, even though any right-thinking person would assume the latter form would work. "Anomaly, thy name is HyperTalk."

Changes to HyperTalk: In versions of HyperCard before 2.2, there are no popup buttons, so you can't select a line of a popup button.

In versions of HyperCard before 1.2.2, selecting text that's scrolled out of sight in a scrolling field causes the selected text to scroll into view. But HyperCard doesn't update the scrollbar thumb's position or the value of the field's **scroll** property.

In versions of HyperCard before 2.1, if the line of text you select consists of a button or field descriptor—for example, if you `select line 3 of field 5` and that line happens to read "card button 2"—HyperCard selects the described part rather than the text of the line. To work around this problem, enclose the described part in quotation marks:

```
select "line 3 of field 5"
```

ALSO SEE

choose command; **clickText** function; **drag** command; **scroll** property; **selectedButton** function; **selectedChunk** function; **selectedField** function; **selectedLine** function; **selectedLoc** function; **selectedText** function

---

selectedButton function   Introduced in version 2.2

FORMS

```
the selectedButton of [card|background] family number
put the short name of the selectedButton of family 3 into myChoice
if the selectedButton of card family 2 is oldButton then exit mouseUp
```

ACTION

The **selectedButton** function returns the currently selected button in a button family. The returned identifier is of the form `[card|background] button number`. It has the same form as a button's **number** function.

COMMENTS

Use the **selectedButton** function to tell which member of a family is the one currently highlighted. The following handler prints several different types of reports. The report format depends on which radio button of a family is selected:

```
on printReport
   -- the buttons in background family 1 are named for all the
   -- report templates in the stack
   get the short name of the selectedButton of background family 1
   open report printing with template it
   print marked cards
   close printing
end printReport
```

The *number* is the number of a button family. This is a number between 1 and 15. You can specify either a card or background family; if you don't, HyperTalk assumes you're asking for the **selectedButton** of a card family.

The **selectedButton** function returns a button number. You can substitute this value in any statement where you can use a button number. For example, the following function returns the name of the selected button in a card family you specify:

```
function chosenButtonName theFamily
   get the selectedButton of family theFamily
   return the short name of it
end chosenButtonName
```

If none of the buttons in the family is highlighted, the **selectedButton** function returns empty.

Don't use a family that has no buttons: If you specify the *number* of a family that doesn't exist—that is, a family that doesn't have any buttons belonging to it—HyperCard presents a script error dialog. To avoid this, you can use the following function handler to find out where the family exists before you try to get its **selectedButton**:

```
function familyExists theNumber,where
   if where is "background" then
      repeat with x = 1 to the number of card buttons
         if the family of card button x is theNumber then return true
      end repeat
   else -- check the card buttons
      repeat with x = 1 to the number of background buttons
         if the family of background button x is theNumber then return true
      end repeat
   end if
   return false -- family not found
end familyExists
```

To determine whether there are any buttons in background family 3, you'd call the above function like this:

```
if familyExists(background,3)
then get the selectedButton of background family 3
```

To change the **selectedButton** to another button in the same family, set the button's **hilite** property to true.

ALSO SEE

family property; **hilite** property

---

selectedChunk function

FORMS

```
the selectedChunk
selectedChunk()
put the selectedChunk into savedSelection
if the selectedChunk is empty then answer "Select some text first."
```

ACTION

The **selectedChunk** function returns a chunk expression giving the starting and ending positions of the current text selection. If no text is currently selected, **the selectedChunk** returns empty.

COMMENTS

The **selectedChunk** function is particularly useful when you want to get the selection's location so you can restore it after doing something that deselects text. The following example restores the text selection (if any) after updating a clock field:

```
on idle -- belongs in a card script
  get the selectedChunk
  put the long time into card field "Clock"
  select it -- the previously stored selectedChunk
end idle
```

The **selectedChunk** function returns a chunk expression of the form

char *startChar* to *endChar* of {[card|bkgnd] field *fieldNumber*|message box}

where *startChar* is the number of the first character in the selection and *endChar* is the number of the last character. If there is a blinking insertion point and no text is selected, **the selectedChunk** returns an expression of the form

char *number* + 1 to *number* of {[card|bkgnd] field *fieldNumber*|message box}

where the insertion point is after character *number*. (It's useful to think of an insertion point as a selection of zero length.) The following function returns the type of selection (text selection, insertion point, or no selection at all):

```
function whatIsSelected
   if the selectedChunk is empty then return "nothing"
   -- if we get this far, we know the selectedChunk is not empty
   if the selectedText is empty then return "insertion point"
   return "selection"
end whatIsSelected
```

HyperCard loses the current text selection whenever one of the following things happens:

- A **find** or **sort** command executes.

- The **cantModify** or **lockScreen** property, the current tool, or the current card changes.

- A button is highlighted (for example, when the user clicks a button whose **autoHilite** is set to true).

- The user clicks anywhere on the screen or presses any key.

If you are going to use **the selectedChunk** in a handler, be sure to get its value before your handler does anything that deselects the current selection.

This example belongs in a field's script. It lists the number of characters, words, and lines in the field each time you press Return while typing in that field:

```
on returnInField
   get the selectedChunk
   set the name of card button 1 to ¬
   the number of characters in me && "characters," ¬
   && the number of words in me && "words," ¬
   && the number of lines in me && "lines."
   select it
   pass returnInField -- to add the return character to the field
end returnInField
```

ALSO SEE

clickChunk function; **foundChunk** function; **select** command; **selectedField** function; **selectedLine** function; **selectedText** function;

---

selectedField function

Introduced in version 1.2

FORMS

the selectedField
selectedField()
get the value of the selectedField -- entire contents of field

ACTION

The **selectedField** function identifies the field (or the message box) that holds the current text selection or insertion point. If there is no selection, **the selectedField** returns empty.

COMMENTS

The following example implements a Select All function that works in fields and in the message box. Whenever you press the Enter key, this handler selects all the text in whatever container the selection or insertion point is in:

```
on enterKey
   if the selectedField is not empty
   then select text of the selectedField
end enterKey


on enterInField
   select text of the selectedField
end enterInField
```

The **selectedField** function returns an expression of the form

```
{[card|bkgnd] field fieldNumber}|message box
```

where *fieldNumber* is the number of the field (if any) that holds the current selection. If there is no selection, **the selectedField** returns empty.

HyperCard deselects the current selection whenever one of the following events happens:

- A **find** or **sort** command executes.
- The **cantModify** or **lockScreen** property, the current tool, or the current card changes.
- A button is highlighted (for example, when the user clicks a button whose **autoHilite** is set to true).
- The user clicks anywhere on the screen or presses any key.

If you're going to use **the selectedField** in a handler, be sure to get its value before your handler does anything that will deselect text.

ALSO SEE

selectedText function; **select** command; **selectedChunk** function; **selectedText** function

---

selectedLine function

Introduced in version 1.2
Last changed in version 2.2

FORMS

the selectedLine[s] [of {*popupButton*|*field*}]
selectedLine({[*popupButton*|*field*]})
put word 2 of the selectedLine into lineNumber
put the selectedLine of background button "User Level:" into currentChoice
get the selectedLines of field "List"

ACTION

The **selectedLine** function returns one of three things, depending on its argument:

- The line and container that holds the current text selection or insertion point.
- The choice currently selected from the specified popup button.
- The currently hilited line in the specified **autoSelect** field.

COMMENTS

If you use the form **the selectedLine**, without specifying a button or field, the function returns a value of the form

```
line lineNumber of {message box|[card|bkgnd] field fieldNumber}
```

If there is no insertion point, **the selectedLine** returns `empty`.

This example selects whatever line of the field the insertion point is currently in whenever you press Shift-Enter:

```
on enterInField
   if the shiftKey is up then pass enterInField
   get the selectedLine
   if the value of it is the selectedText then -- already selected
     -- select next line instead
     add 1 to word 2 of it -- the line number
     if word 2 of it > the number of lines in text of the selectedField
     then put 1 into word 2 of it
   end if
   select it
end enterInField
```

A *line* in HyperTalk is defined as a string that's delimited by return characters. A line in a narrow field may wrap around several times, and look like more than one line on screen, but it is still considered a single line.

HyperCard deselects the current selection whenever one of the following happens:

- A **find** or **sort** command executes.
- The **cantModify** or **lockScreen** property, the current tool, or the current card changes.
- A button is highlighted (for example, when the user clicks a button whose **autoHilite** is set to true).
- The user clicks anywhere on the screen or presses any key.

If you use **the selectedLine** in a handler, be sure to get its value before your handler does anything that causes the selection to be lost.

The selected menu choice in a popup button: The form **the selectedLine of *button*** returns an expression of the form:

```
line menuItemNumber of [card|bkgnd] button buttonNumber
```

If no choice has been selected, or if the button's style is something other than popup, the function returns empty.

The following handlers, in the script of a popup button, send the message "menuChanged" if the user changes the setting of the popup.

```
on mouseDown -- tell whether there was a change
  global lastItem
  put the selectedLine of me into lastItem
end mouseDown


on mouseUp
  global lastItem
  if the selectedLine of me is not lastItem
  then menuChanged the name of me,lastItem,the selectedLine of me
  put empty into lastItem
end mouseUp
```

The highlighted line of an autoSelect field: The form **the selectedLine of** *field* returns an expression of the form

```
line startNumber to endNumber of [card|bkgnd] field number
```

If no lines are selected, or if the field's **autoSelect** property is not set to true, the function returns empty. (To get the line of the current editing text selection, use the form **the selectedLine** without specifying a field.)

If the field's **multipleLines** property is set to false, *startNumber* and *endNumber* are the same.

To get the text of the currently selected line, use the **value** function.

Changes to HyperTalk: In versions of HyperCard before 2.2, there are no popup buttons, so you can't use the **selectedLine** function to get the currently selected line in a popup.

ALSO SEE

autoSelect property; **clickLine** function; **select** command; **selectedChunk** function; **selectedField** function; **selectedText** function

---

selectedLoc function   Introduced in version 2.0

FORMS

the selectedLoc
selectedLoc()
put the selectedLoc into storedLoc

ACTION

The **selectedLoc** function returns the screen location of the current insertion point or the beginning of the current selection. If no field text is selected, **the selectedLoc** returns empty.

COMMENTS

The **selectedLoc** function returns the physical location of the current selection—that is, the point where it can be found on screen.

The point consists of two items separated by a comma. The first item is the horizontal distance in pixels from the left edge of the stack window. The second item is the vertical distance from the top edge. For example, if the selection point is 30 pixels in from the left edge and 112 pixels down from the top edge, **the selectedLoc** is 30,112.

The following handler continuously displays the mouse location and the location of the selection:

```
on idle -- place in card, background or stack script
   get the selectedChunk -- save the current selection
   put "Selection:" && the selectedLoc && "Mouse:" && the mouseLoc
   select it -- restore the selection after the put
   pass idle
end idle
```

If the selection is not visible on screen because it's scrolled out of the visible portion of a scrolling field, the second item of **the selectedLoc** is adjusted by the amount of scroll.

The following handler assumes that the field "Text" is a rectangle field, and changes it to a scrolling field if the text overflows the field boundaries:

```
on idle
   if the style of me is not "rectangle" then pass idle
   get the selectedChunk -- save the selection while typing
   if the selectedLoc is not within the rect of me
   then set the style of me to "scrolling"
   select it              -- restore the selection
   pass idle
end idle
```

Techie alert: The **selectedLoc** function returns the same value as the TEGetPoint routine.

ALSO SEE

location property; **select** command; **selectedChunk** function

selectedText function

Introduced in version 1.2
Last changed in version 2.2

FORMS

```
the selectedText [of {popupButton|field}]
selectedText({[popupButton|field]})
put the selectedText into stuffToFind
set the userLevel to the selectedText of background button "User Level:"
do the selectedText of field "AppleScript Commands" as AppleScript
```

ACTION

The **selectedText** function returns one of three things, depending on its argument:

- The field or message box text that is currently selected

- The name of the choice currently selected from the specified popup button

- The text of the currently highlighted line in the specified **autoSelect** field

COMMENTS

If you use the form **the selectedText**, without specifying a button or field, the function returns the text that is currently selected. If there is no text selection, **the selectedText** returns empty.

This example appends any currently selected text to a global variable when you press Enter:

```
on enterInField
   global collectedNotes
   if the selectedText is not empty
   then put return & the selectedText after collectedNotes
end enterInField
```

The above handler can be used with a button that puts the collected notes into a field:

```
on mouseUp
   global collectedNotes
   put collectedNotes into card field "Notes"
   put empty into collectedNotes
end mouseUp
```

The current text is deselected whenever one of the following things happens:

- A **find** or **sort** command executes.

- The **cantModify** or **lockScreen** property, the current tool, or the current card changes.

- A button is highlighted (for example, when the user clicks a button whose **autoHilite** is set to true).

- The user clicks anywhere on the screen or presses any key.

If you use **the selectedText** in a handler, be sure to get its value before your handler does anything that deselects text.

The selected menu choice in a popup button: The form **the selectedText of** *button* returns the current choice showing in the popup button. If no choice has been selected yet, or if the button's style is something other than popup, the function returns empty.

The highlighted line of a field: The form **the selectedText of** *field* returns the contents of the currently selected line (or lines, if the field's **multipleLines** property is set to true). If no lines are selected, or if the field's **autoSelect** property is not set to true, the function returns empty. (To get the current edit-text selection, use the form **the selectedText** without specifying a field.)

Changes to HyperTalk: In versions of HyperCard before 2.2, there are no popup buttons, so you can't use the **selectedText** function to get the contents of the currently selected line in a popup.

ALSO SEE
"The Selection" in Chapter 8; **autoSelect** property; **clickLine** function; **select** command; **selectedChunk** function; **selectedField** function; **selectedLine** function

---

send keyword

Introduced in version 1.0
Last changed in version 2.0

FORMS
```
send message [parameterList] [to {object|externalWindow}]
send "initializeColumn 5" to card "Spreadsheet"
send variableHoldingMessage to this card
send field "Do This" -- same as "send to me"
send random(5) to HyperCard
send "customXCMDMessage" to window "My XCMD"
```

ACTION
The **send** keyword sends the specified message directly to the specified object, along with any parameters you supply, without going through HyperTalk's normal message path. If the destination object doesn't handle the message, the message continues along the message path from that point.

If you don't specify a destination object, HyperTalk sends the message to the object that contains the currently running handler.

You can also use **send** to pass custom messages to an external window displayed by an XCMD or XFCN. In this case, the external must be written to handle the xSentEvt event and do whatever is appropriate on receiving the message in question. Otherwise, the **send** is ignored. Check your external's documentation or source code to see whether it can receive events from **send**.

COMMENTS
The **send** keyword is useful when you want to reroute a message from the normal message path to some other object. This example handler makes pressing the right and left arrow keys equivalent to clicking the "Previous" and "Next" buttons you've placed on the background:

```
on arrowKey theKey -- in background script
   if the commandKey is down then pass arrowKey
   if theKey is "right" then
      send "mouseUp" to background button "Next"
   else if theKey is "left" then
      send "mouseUp" to background button "Previous"
   else pass arrowKey
end arrowKey
```

If the scripts of the "Next" and "Previous" buttons do anything other than go to the next and previous cards, this example lets you duplicate their function with the arrow keys without having to duplicate the code.

The *object* is any object descriptor (including **me** and **the target**) that evaluates to one of the following:

- Any button, field, card, or background in the current stack
- Any stack
- HyperCard itself

The *message* can be any valid HyperCard message, either built-in or defined with an **on** handler. If the message has parameters, you must enclose the message and its *parameterList* in quotation marks.

If you want to skip any handlers that override a built-in command, use a statement of the form send *builtInCommand* to HyperCard. The following line skips over any **set** handlers in the message path, letting you set the **userLevel** without interference:

```
send "set the userLevel to 5" to HyperCard
```

When you send a message to a specific object, the object you send it to becomes **the target**.

If you send a message to another card, background, or stack, HyperCard does not actually go there, so no open or close message for those objects are issued.

The message path and send: Since **send** delivers its message directly to the specified object, no handler can intercept it before it gets to that object. However, if the specified object's script doesn't have a handler for the message, the message continues normally from that point on through the message path.

Using send for debugging: You can use **send** from the message box, so it's an excellent way to test specific handlers. For instance, you might want to check the **mouseDown** handler of a button that's currently hidden, or test in isolation a handler that normally is only called by other handlers, or see how one of your handlers deals with an unusual set of parameters.

The following handler sends a **mouseUp** message to every button on the current card. This is a useful way to find syntax errors in button scripts, or to entertain yourself late at night:

```
on tryAllButtons
   repeat with thisCardButton = 1 to the number of card buttons
      push this card -- in case button does a "go"
      send "mouseUp" to card button thisCardButton
```

```
      pop card -- come back in case etc.
    end repeat
    repeat with thisBackgroundButton = 1 to the number of card buttons
      push this card -- in case button does a "go"
      send "mouseUp" to background button thisBackgroundButton
      pop card -- come back in case etc.
    end repeat
  end tryAllButtons
```

Send and do are very similar: The keywords **send** and **do** perform nearly the same action. The only difference is that, unlike **do**, **send** lets you specify which object is to receive the message. The statements *message*, do *message*, and send *message* to me are equivalent, except that **do** and **send** evaluate their parameters before sending the message:

```
fred      -- sends a message called "fred"
send fred -- sends the message that the variable "fred" contains
do fred   -- same as "send fred"
```

Send and custom functions

Although you can't use **send** to call a function handler, you can create a message handler that calls the function. Then you can use **send** to call the message handler. This lets you make the function available to any script by using **send** with the function-calling message. This pair of handlers shows how to set this up:

```
function gradeOf theStudent -- the original function
  get field "Score" of card theStudent
  if it ≥ 90 then return "A"
  else it it ≥ 80 then return "B"
  else if it ≥ 65 then return "C"
  else if it ≥ 50 then return "D"
  else return "F"
end gradeOf

on getGrade theStudent -- calls the above gradeOf function
  return gradeOf(theStudent) -- sets the result to the grade
end getGrade
```

The getGrade handler must be before gradeOf in the message path, or at the same level, so the function call can find the appropriate function handler. You can call the function indirectly from any handler, like this:

```
send "getGrade Kamins" to card button "Compute Grade" of card "Kamins"
put the result into myGrade -- was set by getGrade to the grade
```

Changes to HyperTalk: In versions of HyperCard before 2.0, externals cannot create windows, so you can't send a message to a window.

ALSO SEE

do keyword; **messages; pass** keyword; **send to program** keyword

---

send to program keyword

Introduced in version 2.1
Last changed in version 2.2

FORMS

```
send message [parameterList] to program programAddress [{with|without} reply]
send "choose bucket tool" to program "MyZone:Mike's Mac:HyperCard"
send theMessage to program theRemoteProgram without reply
send "go to stack" && myStack to program "Unexpected Grace:HyperCard"
send "customFunction(14)" to program mikesHyperCardAddress
```

ACTION

The **send to program** keyword sends the specified message to another program. The target program can be one that's running on your Mac or on another Macintosh on the AppleTalk network.

You can only use **send to program** if both your Mac and the target Mac are using System 7, and the target Mac has Program Linking turned on in the Sharing Setup control panel.

COMMENTS

The **send to program** keyword lets you send messages to any application that accepts the AppleEvent command to run a script. One of its more useful applications is to control one or more copies of HyperCard running on other Macs on the network. This example displays an answer dialog on the screen of the target Macintosh:

```
on warnAboutShutdown
   send "answer" && quote & "The library catalog system is about" && ¬
   "to shut down for the evening. Please complete your checkout now." ¬
   & quote to "LibraryZone:Card Catalog:HyperCard" without reply
end warnAboutShutdown
```

If you are sending to another copy of HyperCard, the *message* and its *parameterList* can be any legal HyperTalk message—a built-in command or system message, or a message that triggers a custom **on** or **function** handler. As usual, any parameters to the message are separated by commas, and the entire message with its parameters must be enclosed in quotation marks if it is more than one word long. The message itself is sent to the current card on the target Mac and follows the normal message path from there, just as though you were sitting at the target Mac and typed it into the message box.

The *programAddress* is the full AppleTalk address of the application you are sending the message to. An AppleTalk address consists of three parts, separated by colons (:):

- The zone the target Macintosh is in
- The name of the target Macintosh (you can set this in the Sharing Setup control panel)
- The name of the target program

For example, if a Mac is named "Bug Central" and resides in the zone "Software QA Zone", the *programAddress* of a copy of MPW running on that Mac is written as follows:

```
"Software QA Zone:Bug Central:MPW"
```

The AppleTalk address is similar to a file pathname, as you can see. Each successive part of the address is nested one level deeper, down to the program itself.

If the target Mac is in the same zone as the sender (or the network consists of only one zone), you can omit the zone from the *programAddress*:

```
"Bug Central:MPW"
```

If the source and target applications are on the same Macintosh, you can omit both zone and Mac name, and simply use the name or ID of the target application. (A program's ID is its four-character creator signature; for example, HyperCard's ID is WILD.) You can also use the form `this program` to refer to the current foreground application.

By default, HyperCard waits for the target application to finish running the script before continuing. If you use the `without reply` form, the sending handler continues immediately after the **send to program**, without waiting for a response from the target application.

If you don't specify `without reply`, **the result** is set to whatever response the target program sends back. If the target application is HyperCard, it returns either its value of **the result** (if you sent a message) or the returned value (if you sent a function).

This example searches for a word in a target stack, then either replaces it or alerts the sending Mac's user to a problem, depending on whether the word was found:

```
on findRemote theWord,theMac
   global currentZone
   put currentZone & ":" & theMac & ":HyperCard" into theAddress
   send "find" && theWord to program theAddress
   -- if the target Mac couldn't find the word, it sets the result to
   -- "not found"; that result gets returned to the sending Mac and
   -- stored in the sender's result function:
   if the result is not empty then
      answer "Couldn't find" && theWord && "on" && theMac & "."
      exit to HyperCard
   else
      send "replaceFoundWord" to program theAddress without reply
   end if
end findRemote
```

A note about security: The **send to program** keyword relies on System 7's program linking mechanism, so it can only be used if the target Macintosh has Program Linking turned on. The first time HyperCard establishes a link with the target program, it presents a login dialog, asking for the user's name and password. If the target Mac does not allow guest logins, the user and password must be registered through the Users & Groups control panel on the target Mac. See your Macintosh manual for more details about making your Mac's programs available for linking over the network.

Like **do**, the **send to program** keyword can execute multiline messages, as long as they make up a valid HyperTalk structure. This example causes a dialog to pop up on the target Mac's screen, and sends back the user's reply:

```
on bother user,message
   if user is empty then -- put up dialog to locate user
      answer program "Please locate the user you want to bother:"
      if it is empty then exit bother     -- user cancelled
      put it into theAddress
      set the itemDelimiter to colon
      put item 2 of theAddress into user  -- the Mac's name
      set the itemDelimiter to comma
   else
      put user & ":" & "HyperCard" into theAddress -- assume same zone
   end if
   if message is empty then
      ask "What message do you want to bother" && user & "with?"
      if it is empty then exit bother     -- user cancelled
      put it into message
   end if
   put "ask" && quote & message & quote & return & "return it" ¬
   into theMessage -- two lines, so we can get what user typed in
   send theMessage to program theAddress
   answer user && "says:" & return & the result
end bother
```

The **result** function is set when the **send to program** keyword encounters an error. While the target HyperCard is executing the message you sent it, its **lockErrorDialogs** property is temporarily set to true. If the target Mac encounters an error that would normally cause an error dialog, it sends back the text of the error, which ends up in **the result**.

These are the errors, other than script execution problems, that **send to program** may encounter:

- User cancelled the login dialog: **the result** is set to "Cancel".
- The target program couldn't handle the "do script" AppleEvent: **the result** is set to "Not handled by target program."
- The target program timed out: **the result** is set to "Timeout".
- The AppleEvent Manager or the target program returned an error number: **the result** is set to "Got error *errorNumber* when sending Apple™ event."

Techie alert: The **send to program** keyword sends the `dosc` AppleEvent to the target application.

Changes to HyperTalk: In versions of HyperCard before 2.2, you cannot specify a program by ID—only by name.

ALSO SEE

address function; **appleEvent** message; **reply** command; **request** command; **result** function; **send** keyword; **systemVersion** function

---

set command

FORMS

```
set [the] property [of object] to value
set the userLevel to 5
set the hilite of card button "Click Me" to true
set the dragSpeed to userSpeedLevel
set the script of background button "Executive Decisions" to empty
```

ACTION

The **set** command changes the value of a property.

COMMENTS

The following example belongs in a button script. It changes the button's **location** property to make it follow the mouse around the card:

```
on mouseStillDown
   set the loc of me to the mouseLoc
end mouseStillDown
```

The *property* can be any settable HyperCard property. If you try to set a read-only property, HyperCard puts up an error dialog and aborts the rest of the handler.

The *object* is any valid descriptor of the element (field, button, card, background, stack, window, or HyperCard itself) to which the property applies. If the *object* is HyperCard (that is, if the property is a global one), you can omit the *object*.

The *value* must be a legal value for the *property*.

The following handler, which you can put in a card, background, or stack script, changes a number of default properties for newly created fields:

```
on newField
   set the name of the target to "New Field"
   set the style of the target to transparent
   set the textFont of the target to Helvetica
   set the textSize of the target to 10
   set the showLines of the target to true
   set the autoTab of the target to true
   set the scriptingLanguage of the target to "AppleScript"
end newField
```

A sliding gauge

This pair of button scripts operates a sliding gauge. The gauge is made up of two buttons: a highlighted (black) button named "Gauge" in front of a rectangle button named "Gauge Background". The scripts work by adjusting the right edge of the Gauge button to make the black area larger or smaller (see Figure III.45).

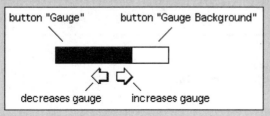

Figure III.45   Sliding gauge

```
on mouseStillDown -- goes in right arrow button; increases gauge
  get the rect of button "Gauge"
  add 10 to item 3 of it -- right edge
  if item 3 of it ≥ the right of button "Gauge Background"
  then put (the right of button "Gauge Background" - 1) ¬
  into item 3 of it
  set the rect of button "Gauge" to it
end mouseStillDown


on mouseStillDown -- goes in left arrow button; decreases gauge
  get the rect of button "Gauge"
  subtract 10 from item 3 of it -- right edge
  if item 3 of it ≤ the left of button "Gauge Background"
  then put (the left of button "Gauge Background" + 1) ¬
  into item 3 of it
  set the rect of button "Gauge" to it
end mouseStillDown
```

ALSO SEE

> **get** command

sharedHilite property

FORMS

`set [the] sharedHilite of` *backgroundButton* `to {true|false}`

`set the sharedHilite of background button "Choice" to true`

ACTION

The **sharedHilite** property determines whether a background button's highlighting is the same on all cards of that background or whether the highlighting can be different on each card.

Setting the **sharedHilite** is equivalent to setting the Shared Hilite checkbox in the button's Info dialog. By default, the **sharedHilite** of a newly created button is true.

COMMENTS

The **sharedHilite** property is most useful with checkboxes and radio buttons. Typically, such buttons are used to store a state on a form.

For instance, a stack that stores personnel records—one person per card—might have a checkbox labelled "Has Children". The record for childless Fred Ferfee would be unchecked (that is, the button's **hilite** would be set to false), while Mary Scribblemonger, mother of 16, would check this box, setting the **hilite** to true. Setting the **sharedHilite** of the checkbox to false lets each card store its own value of the **hilite** for the button.

ALSO SEE

autoHilite property; **family** property; **hilite** property

---

sharedText property

FORMS

`set [the] sharedText of` *backgroundField* `to {true|false}`

`set the sharedText of field "Show Everywhere" to true`

ACTION

The **sharedText** property determines whether a background field displays the same text on every card.

Setting the **sharedText** is the same as setting the Shared Text checkbox in the field's Info dialog. By default, the **sharedText** of newly created background fields is false.

COMMENTS

Use the **sharedText** property when you want the contents of a particular field—such as a section title—to contain the same text on all cards of the background. When you're using **sharedText** for this purpose, you'll usually set the value at the time you first create the field:

```
on makeTitleField
   ask "What text should the field have?"
   if the result is "Cancel" then exit makeTitleField
   put it into fieldText
   set the editBkgnd to true
   doMenu "New Field"
   set the sharedText of last background field to true
   put fieldText into last background field
   set the name of last background field to "Title"
   set the style of last background field to "Shadow"
   set the rect of last background field to 10,10,502,20
   set the textAlign of last background field to center
   set the editBkgnd to false
   choose browse tool
end makeTitleField
```

The *backgroundField* is any field in the current background.

Editing shared text: You can use the **put** command to change the shared text in a field regardless of whether you're in background mode. However, you can manually edit shared text only when in background mode. While the **editBkgnd** is false, the field acts as though its **lockText** property were true. The following handlers belong in the script of a shared text field, and let you edit the text of the field by clicking it:

```
on mouseDown
   set the editBkgnd to true -- go into background so you can edit
   click at the clickLoc -- put the insertion point where you want
end mouseDown

on closeField
   set the editBkgnd to false
end closeField

on exitField
   set the editBkgnd to false
end exitField
```

Shared and unshared text can coexist: Each background field can have both shared text, which is common to all cards, and card-specific text. Which one is visible in the field depends on the setting of its **sharedText** property. When the **sharedText** is false, the card-specific text is displayed. When you set **sharedText** to true, the shared text is displayed instead. While **sharedText** is true, the card-specific text is invisible and cannot be edited or accessed, but it's still there.

The following handler makes a popup field that doesn't need a separate button. The field has two states. One looks like a small button (its shared text is the button name); the other is expanded and displays the card-specific text. (See Figure III.46.)

"button" field with shared text visible

same field, expanded and with card text visible

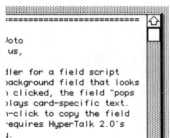

Figure III.46 "Button" field

```
on mouseDown
   lock screen
   if the sharedText of me is true then
      -- the field isn't popped up, so show as field
      -- line 1 of the shared text is the button name, line 2
      -- is the popped-up rect
      put line 2 of me into fieldRectangle
      put the rect of me into buttonRectangle
      set the sharedText of me to false
      set the rect of me to fieldRectangle
      set the scroll of me to 0
      set the textAlign of me to left
   else
      -- the field *is* popped up, so show as button
      set the sharedText of me to true
      set the rect of me to buttonRectangle
      set the textAlign of me to center
   end if
   unlock screen with visual effect dissolve fast
end mouseDown
```

ALSO SEE

dontSearch property; **find** command

shiftKey function

Introduced in version 1.0

FORMS

`the shiftKey`
`shiftKey()`
`if the shiftKey is up then choose browse tool`

ACTION

The **shiftKey** function returns the state of the Shift key (up if the key is being pressed or down if it's not).

COMMENTS

The following handler displays the number of words in the field you're currently editing when you press Shift-Enter:

```
on enterInField -- can go in field, card, background or stack script
   if the shiftKey is down then
      get the selectedChunk
      put the number of words in the target && "words."
      select it
   else
      pass enterInField
   end if
end enterInField
```

ALSO SEE

commandKey function; **optionKey** function

---

show command

Introduced in version 1.0
Last changed in version 2.0

FORMS

```
show {window|part} [at location]
show [backgroundPicture|cardPicture]
show [titlebar|menubar|groups]
show window "My Stack"
show window (line 1 of the stacks) at 0,0
show card window at myLocation
show the message box at 0,40
show tool window at the clickLoc
show picture of card "Reference"
show background picture
show menubar
```

ACTION

The **show** command shows the specified window, object, or other element.

COMMENTS

Use the **show** command to display previously hidden elements and, for objects and windows, to change their location. (If you don't give a location, the button, field or window appears at its most recent location on the screen.)

If you specify a *location*, the window appears with its top-left corner at the location given. For stack windows, the *location* is the distance from the top-left corner of the main screen. For other elements, the *location* is the distance from the top-left corner of the frontmost stack window.

A *location* consists of two integers separated by a comma. The first item is the horizontal distance in pixels to the horizontal location of the element. The second item is the vertical distance to the vertical location of the element.

A *window* is any currently open window. You can refer to windows by name, number, or ID. You can show (and hide) stack windows, HyperCard windows, and windows created by XCMDs or XFCNs. The **show** command brings the specified window to the front.

Moving a window using **show** sends the **moveWindow** message to the current card.

If you show a window that's already visible, it moves to the front.

The following example keeps the tool window in the same location relative to the card window, no matter where you move the card window. It assumes that the user's preferred location for the tool window is stored in the field "Tool Location":

```
on openStack
   global theToolLoc
   put card field "Tool Location" of first card into theToolLoc
   pass openStack
end openStack

on idle
   global theToolLoc
   if theToolLoc is not empty then show tool window at theToolLoc
   pass idle
end idle
```

A *part* is any button or field in the current stack. The command `show part` has the same effect as `set the visible of part to true`. If you try to show a window, button, or field that doesn't exist, HyperCard puts up an error dialog.

A *backgroundPicture* or *cardPicture* is the paint layer belonging to the current card or background, or to any card or background in the current stack. The command `show picture of cardOrBackground` is equivalent to `set the showPict of cardOrBackground to true`.

The command **show titlebar** shows the title bar of the current stack window. To show or hide a stack window's title bar, that stack must be frontmost.

The command **show menubar** makes the menu bar visible. It is equivalent to **set the visible of menubar to true**.

The command **show groups** displays a thick gray underline beneath all text whose style is set to "group".

When show doesn't show anything: If you issue a command such as `show field 1`, and field 1 is covered up by another object or a window, you still won't be able to see it. If this happens, you can move the mouse pointer to some convenient bare spot on the card and enter this command into the message box:

```
show field 1 at the mouseLoc
```

If you use **show** to move a part outside the card window, it will not be visible on the screen until you move it back within the window's boundaries.

ALSO SEE

hide command; **location** property; **show card** command; **showPict** property; **visible** property

---

show cards command

FORMS

```
show [numberOfCards|marked|all] cards
show cards
show 23 cards
show marked cards
show thisMany cards
show all cards
```

ACTION

The **show cards** command flips through a series of cards, starting with the current card.

COMMENTS

The following handler shows a five-page flipbook animation repeatedly until the user holds down the mouse:

```
on flipBook
  repeat until the mouse is down
    go to card "Flip Book Start"
    show 5 cards
  end repeat
end flipBook
```

Clicking the mouse halts the **show cards** command on the current card.

The *numberOfCards* is a positive integer. If you specify a *numberOfCards*, **show cards** flips through that number of cards, starting from the current one, and then stops. You end up *numberOfCards* cards from where you started.

The form `show all cards` flips through every card in the current stack, ending on the card you started with. The form `show cards` continues looping through every card in the current stack until you click the mouse.

Show cards doesn't send messages: HyperCard doesn't send any system messages (such as **openCard** or **closeCard**) when the **show cards** command is running, and the displayed cards aren't added to the Recent display (except the first and last card). Visual effects aren't displayed either. To show visual effects while flipping through cards, use a handler like this one:

```
on showCards numberOfCards
   lock messages
   lock recent
   repeat for numberOfCards
      visual effect dissolve to black
      visual effect dissolve to card
      go next
      if the mouseClick then exit showCards
   end repeat
end showCards
```

Whenever HyperCard shows a card, it retains the card's image in memory until it needs the memory for something else. The following handler makes HyperCard cache as many of the cards in the current stack as it has memory for. This "prewarming" makes the cards more quickly accessible for animation sequences:

```
on prewarmCards
   lock screen
   show all cards
end prewarmCards
```

At **idle** time, HyperCard automatically prewarms the card after the current one, because it knows you're very likely to go there next.

Techie alert: The form show cards isn't really an infinite loop, although it might as well be. Actually, it shows 4,294,967,295 cards—the maximum value of a 32-bit number—which is, according to calculations performed by one of the authors, enough to keep a Macintosh II busy for at least ten years.

Changes to HyperTalk: You can't show marked cards in versions of HyperCard before 2.0.

ALSO SEE
go command; **openCard** message

---

show menuBar message   Introduced in version 1.0

FORMS
```
show menubar
```

ACTION
The **show menubar** message is sent to the current card when the menu bar is shown, either with the **show** command or by pressing Command-Space.

COMMENTS

The following handler prevents the user from showing the menu bar:

```
on show theThing
    if theThing is not "menubar" then pass show
    if the commandKey is up then pass show -- let script show menubar
end show
```

Important: The menu bar is an important part of the Macintosh interface, and you should not hide it except in particular circumstances. For example, if your stack is designed to run on an information kiosk where it's the only application, or if it's a full-screen animation, it is permissible to hide the menu bar. In most applications, however, hiding the menu bar is confusing and annoying for the user, so think carefully before designing a stack that does so.

ALSO SEE

hide menubar message; **show** command

---

showLines property   Introduced in version 1.0

FORMS

```
set [the] showLines of field to {true|false}
set the showLines of field ID 32 to false
set the showLines of field "Editing" to true
```

ACTION

The **showLines** property determines whether HyperCard shows the text baselines of a field as dotted lines.

Setting the **showLines** property is equivalent to setting the Show Lines checkbox in the field's Info dialog. By default, the **showLines** is false.

COMMENTS

The **showLines** has no functional effect on field operations; it is purely aesthetic. Setting the **showLines** to true may be useful for editable fields, since it shows the user where each line of text will appear.

This property has no effect on scrolling fields. The lines don't appear regardless of the setting of **showLines**.

ALSO SEE

fixedLineHeight property

showName property

FORMS

```
set [the] showName of button to {true|false}
set the showName of background button "Icon" to true
set the showName of me to false
```

ACTION

The **showName** property determines whether a button's name appears inside the button.

Setting the **showName** of a button is equivalent to setting the Show Name checkbox in the button's Info dialog. By default, the **showName** is true for buttons created with the New Button menu item and false for buttons created by Command-dragging with the button tool.

COMMENTS

Like many object properties, the **showName** of a button is usually set in the handler that creates the button.

The following example toggles the **showName** property, which causes the button's name to flash and catch the user's attention:

```
on openCard
  repeat until the mouseClick
    set the showName of button "Big Sale Today!" ¬
    to not the showName of button "Big Sale Today!"
    wait 10 ticks
  end repeat
end openCard
```

The *button* is any button in the current stack.

Where the name appears: If the button has an icon, its name appears in 9-point Geneva beneath the icon. Otherwise:

- If the button is a radio button or checkbox, its name appears to the right of the button.

- If the button is a popup, its name appears to the left of the popup button.

- For all other button styles, the name appears inside the button's rectangle, and is centered (the default), right-aligned, or left-aligned, depending on the button's **textAlign** property.

ALSO SEE

style property; **textAlign** property; **textFont** property; **textSize** property; **textStyle** property; **titleWidth** property

showPict property

FORMS

```
set [the] showPict of {card|background} to {true|false}
set the showPict to false
set the showPict of this card to not the showPict of this background
```

ACTION

The **showPict** property determines whether the specified card or background picture is visible.

By default, the **showPict** of all cards and backgrounds is true.

COMMENTS

The picture of a card or background consists of all the paint on that card or background. The **showPict** property does not affect fields or buttons. When you hide a card or background picture, it remains hidden until it is shown again, even after you quit HyperCard.

You can also use the **show** and **hide** commands to set the **showPict** property.

The *card* or *background* must be in the current stack.

About hidden pictures: You can use paint tools from a script on hidden card or background pictures. The changes are made invisibly, and can be seen when you show the picture again. However, if you try to use a paint tool manually on a hidden picture, HyperCard asks whether you want to show the hidden picture. You cannot paint manually on a hidden picture without showing it first.

ALSO SEE

hide command; **show** command; **there is** operator; **visible** property

sin function

FORMS

```
[the] sin of angleInRadians
sin(angleInRadians)
the sin of pi -- yields 0
sin(lambda)
cos(omega + pi)
```

ACTION

The **sin** function returns the sine of its argument.

Given a right triangle, the sine of one of its acute angles is defined as the ratio of the length of the opposite side from the angle to the length of the hypotenuse.

COMMENTS

The argument of the **sin** function must be in radians. One radian is 180/π degrees, or about 57.3 degrees.

You can use the **sin** function to create "spirographs" with the paint tools (see Figure III.47):

```
on drawSpiro
   reset paint
   choose regular polygon tool
   put 200,150 into theCenter
   put 100 into startX
   put 100 into startY
   put 300 into endX
   put 180 into maxHeight
   put startX into xCoord
   repeat 30 times
      add 5 to xCoord
      put maxHeight * sin((xCoord-startX)/(endX-startX) * pi) ¬
      into height
      drag from theCenter to xCoord,round(startY + height)
   end repeat
   choose browse tool
end drawSpiro
```

ALSO SEE

atan function; **cos** function; **tan** function

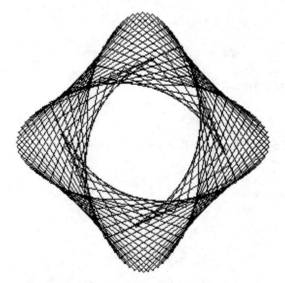

Figure III.47   Design created with sin

size property

FORMS

the size of *stack*

```
if the size of this stack > 785408 then answer "Too big for floppy!"
```

ACTION

The **size** property reports the number of bytes a stack takes on the disk. This property is read-only and can't be set by a handler.

COMMENTS

The **size** property is particularly useful when you need to move stacks around, or keep track of the total size for a stack that will be shipped on floppy disks or other limited-space media. The following handler saves a backup copy of the current stack, first checking whether the target disk has enough space:

```
on makeBackup
   ask file "Save backup as:" with ¬
   char 1 to 24 of the short name of this stack && "Backup"
   if it is empty then exit makeBackup -- user cancelled
   put it into backupPath
   -- get the disk name
   get the itemDelimiter -- save old delimiter
   set the itemDelimiter to colon
   put item 1 of backupPath into backupDisk
   set the itemDelimiter to it
   -- check disk space
   if the diskSpace of backupDisk < the size of this stack then
      beep
      answer "There's not enough space on the disk to back up."
   else
      save this stack as backupPath
   end if
end makeBackup
```

The minimum stack size is 4096 bytes. The upper limit on stack size is 512M.

ALSO SEE

diskSpace function; **freeSpace** property

sizeWindow message

FORMS

```
sizeWindow
```

ACTION

The **sizeWindow** message is sent to the current card when the size of the frontmost stack window is changed, either manually or from a script.

COMMENTS

The **sizeWindow** message is sent right after the window is resized, so you cannot keep the user from changing the window size by trapping **sizeWindow**. Window properties such as the **rectangle** reflect the new values pertaining to the resized window.

The following example moves a button when the stack window is resized, to keep the button centered within the visible area of the window:

```
on sizeWindow
   set the location of background button "Control Panel" to ¬
   the width of card window div 2, the height of card window div 2
end sizeWindow
```

The following actions trigger a **sizeWindow** message:

- Clicking the zoom box (if it changes the window's size)
- Resizing the window with the Scroll palette
- Changing the window's size by changing its **rectangle** or **location** property.

The frontmost stack window is the only one whose size you can change. To change the size of another stack window, you must first bring it to the front.

ALSO SEE

height property; **moveWindow** message; **rectangle** property; **width** property

---

sort command

FORMS

```
sort [[marked] cards of] {[this] stack|background}] [direction] [sortType] by sortKey
sort by the short name of this card
sort cards of this stack ascending by field "Last Name"
sort stack descending by word 1 of field "Job Titles"
sort marked cards numeric by field "Salary"
sort this background descending dateTime by last line of field "Absences"
sort cards of background "Sales" by the length of field "Territory"
```

```
sort marked cards of background 2 by mySortKey() -- custom function
sort numeric by random(the number of cards)
```

ACTION

The **sort** command sorts all the cards of the current stack, the marked cards only, or the cards of a specified background, by whatever criterion you specify.

To be sorted, a stack must be unlocked.

COMMENTS

You can use the **sort** command to change the ordering of all the cards in the stack, or of a specific set of cards you select, with a single command. Sorting cards is most useful when you have one record on each card—for instance, in an address stack that has an address on each card, or a sales stack where each card is used for a different customer—and you want to shuffle the cards into a new order for viewing or printing.

You can specify that you want to sort all the cards of the current stack, the marked cards, or the cards of any background in the current stack. If you don't specify what part of the stack to sort, the **sort** command works on all the cards in the stack.

The *direction* is either `ascending` or `descending`—that is, normal order or reverse order. If you don't specify a direction, the sort is ascending, with the lowest values first.

There are four options for the *sortType*:

- **sort text:**   Sorts by the ASCII value of each character. This form is used if you don't specify a *sortType*.

- **sort numeric:**   Sorts in numeric order. Use this *sortType* if your sort key consists of numbers.

- **sort dateTime:**   Sorts in date order. Use this form if what you want to sort by is a date and/or time in one of the formats that HyperCard understands. (See the **convert** command for more information about date and time formats.)

- **sort international:**   Like the **sort text** form, except that this form makes sure the ordering of international (Option-key) characters is correct.

The *sortKey* can be any valid HyperTalk expression: the contents of a container, a property, a built-in or custom function, or any combination. References to "this card" in the *sortKey* are interpreted as references to each card being sorted. For example, to sort cards by their card ID, you would use

```
sort numeric by the short ID of this card
```

If the *sortKey* doesn't have a value on a card, that card is treated as though the value for it were empty. Since empty is the lowest possible value, these cards are shuffled to the beginning of the stack (or, if the *direction* is `descending`, to the end).

You can do very complex sorts by writing your own function and using the value of that function as the *sortKey*. This example takes the quality ratings for a movie review stack and converts them into a single letter for sorting:

```
function movieRating
```

```
      get field "Rating"
      if it is "See At All Costs!!!" then return "A"
      if it contains "Excellent" then return "B"
      if it contains "Good" then return "C"
      if it is "Wait Until It Comes Out On Video" then return "D"
      if it contains "Ugh" then return "E"
      if it is "Sign That The World Will End Soon" then return "Z"
   end movieRating
```

You can sort by this function with the command

```
   sort by movieRating()
```

Sorting by more than one criterion: HyperCard's sort is stable: if two cards have the same sort key, **sort** doesn't change their order in the stack. This means you can do two or more successive sorts to get subcategories. The following example produces a stack that is sorted by state, and within each state, by city:

```
on mouseUp
   sort by field "City"    -- subcategory
   sort by field "State"  -- main category
end mouseUp
```

Sort by the subcategory first, then by the main category. During the second sort, because it is stable, cards with the same state stay in the same order after the sort, and so they are still ordered by city name after being sorted by state.

Compact after sorting: HyperCard keeps an internal list of the order of cards in a stack. The **sort** command updates this list, but it doesn't physically move the cards around. Compacting the stack writes the card data in the new order, to match the internal list, and so moving from card to card is faster after you compact the stack.

Changes to HyperTalk: In versions of HyperCard before 2.0, you cannot sort marked cards or the cards of a specific background; all sorts work on the whole stack.

Techie alert: The only time the **sort** command is actually sorting is when the beachball is spinning. The rest of the time is spent gathering sort keys and writing out the newly sorted card list.

   The **sort international** form uses the character ordering table given in *Inside Macintosh*, vol. I, page 502.

ALSO SEE

ASCII Chart (Appendix A); **date** function; **sort container** command; **random** function; **time** function

sort container command

Introduced in version 2.0
Last changed in version 2.2

FORMS

```
sort [{lines|items} of] container [direction] [sortType] [by sortKey]
sort field "Card List"
sort lines of card field 3 descending
sort items of myVariable ascending by last character of each
sort lines of field nextField numeric by item 2 of each
sort items of nameList descending international by word 2 to 3 of each
sort lines of field "List" by the number of card field each
```

ACTION

The **sort container** command shuffles the lines or items in a container into a new order.

COMMENTS

You can sort either the lines or items of a container. If you don't specify one or the other, **sort container** sorts the lines.

The *container* can be any field on the current card, a variable, or the message box. Unlike **sort**, the **sort container** command can be used on the fields of a locked stack. However, if the stack is locked, the changes to the field will be lost when you leave the current card.

The *direction* is either ascending or descending—that is, normal order or reverse order. If you don't specify a direction, the sort is ascending, with the lowest values first.

There are four options for the *sortType*:

- **sort text:** Sorts by the ASCII value of each character. This form is used if you don't specify a *sortType*.

- **sort numeric:** Sorts in numeric order. Use this *sortType* if your sort key consists of numbers.

- **sort dateTime:** Sorts in date order. Use this form if what you want to sort by is a date and/or time in one of the formats that HyperCard understands. (See the **convert** command for more information about date and time formats.)

- **sort international:** Like the **sort text** form, except that this form makes sure the ordering of international (Option-key) characters is correct.

The *sortKey* specifies what part of each line or item is used as the sort key. References to "each" in the *sortKey* are interpreted as references to each line or item being sorted. If you don't specify a *sortKey*, **sort** uses the whole line or item as the sort key. See the **sort** command for information about how to specify complex sorts with a custom function.

Changes to HyperTalk: In versions of HyperCard before 2.2, you cannot specify a *sortKey*; the entire line or item is always used as the sort key.

Techie alert: The **sort international** form uses the character ordering table given in *Inside Macintosh*, vol. I, page 502.

ALSO SEE
  itemDelimiter property; **sort** command

---

sound function   Introduced in version 1.0

FORMS
```
the sound
sound()
put the sound into currentSound
wait until the sound is done
```

ACTION
  The **sound** function returns the name of the sound the **play** command is currently playing.
  If no sound is playing, **the sound** returns "done".

COMMENTS
  The **play** command reads a sound resource into memory, starts playing it, and returns control to
  the current handler while the sound continues. If you're working with long sounds or with a tune
  made up of several notes, the **sound** function lets you check whether the sound is still playing.
      The following example uses icon animation to show a pair of hands clapping. It continues
  as long as the applause sound-effect does:

```
on applaud
   play "Applause"
   show button "Clapping Hands"
   repeat until the sound is done
      set the icon of button "Clapping Hands" to "Open Hands"
      set the icon of button "Clapping Hands" to "Closed Hands"
   end repeat
   hide button "Clapping Hands"
end applaud
```

  The following handler plays a song that has been divided into several sound resources.
  (You can split up a long song like this if the whole thing is too big to fit in memory.) This
  handler keeps two sounds in the queue at all times, and fetches another sound into the queue
  as soon as the first one is finished. This technique plays the sounds without any audible pause
  between them:

```
on smoothSound playList
   play item 1 of playList
   repeat with soundNumber = 2 to the number of items in playList
      play item soundNumber of playList
      wait until the sound is item soundNumber of playList
   end repeat
end smoothSound
```

ALSO SEE

play command

---

sqrt function   Introduced in version 1.0

FORMS

[the] **sqrt** of *number*
sqrt(*number***)**
the sqrt of 4 -- yields 2
sqrt(2) -- yields 1.414214

ACTION

The **sqrt** function returns the square root of the *number*.

The expression sqrt(*number*) is equivalent to *number*^(1/2).

COMMENTS

The following handler uses the Pythagorean theorem to compute the length of the hypotenuse of a right triangle, given the two other sides. (We knew you'd want this one.)

```
on getHypotenuse
    ask "How long is side 1?"
    put it into side1
    ask "How long is side 2?"
    put it into side2
    put sqrt(side1^2 + side2^2) into hypotenuse
    answer "The triangle's hypotenuse measures" && hypotenuse & "."
end getHypotenuse
```

The *number* must be non-negative. If you pass **sqrt** a negative number, it returns the error value NAN(001). (NAN means "Not A Number".)

The following handler, whose basic formula comes from Paul Finlayson of Apple Computer, calculates the distance between you and the horizon. It assumes you're standing at sea level, and there are no mountains, buildings, or computers in the way:

```
function horizonDistance yourHeight
    put 5280 into feetPerMile
    put 7926.41 into earthDiameter
    put earthDiameter * feetPerMile into diameterInFeet
    return sqrt(yourHeight * (diameterInFeet + yourHeight))/feetPerMile
end horizonDistance
```

You can call the above function from another handler:

```
on mouseUp
   ask "How many feet tall are you?" with "5.5"
   if it is empty then exit mouseUp
   set the numberFormat to 0.#
   answer "The horizon is" && horizonDistance(it) ¬
   && "miles away for you."
end mouseUp
```

---

stacks function   Introduced in version 2.0

FORMS

the stacks
stacks()
```
put line 2 of the stacks into backgroundStack
if myPath is not in the stacks then go to stack myPath in a new window
```

ACTION

The **stacks** function returns a list of the full pathnames of all the open stacks, separated by return characters.

COMMENTS

The **stacks** function is useful when you need to check on which stacks are currently open. This function returns the number of stack windows currently open:

```
function numberOfStacks
   return the number of lines in the stacks
end numberOfStacks
```

The **stacks** function differs from the **windows** function in two ways. First, **the windows** returns the names of all open windows, including external windows and built-in HyperCard windows like the message box as well as stack windows. Second, **the stacks** returns full pathnames instead of window names.

The following example flips through each open stack window in turn, stopping when you click the mouse button:

```
on showStacks
   put the stacks into stackList
   put the number of lines of stackList into numberOfStacks
   if the longWindowTitles is false then -- strip pathnames
      set the itemDelimiter to colon
      repeat with thisStack = 1 to numberOfStacks
         put last item of line thisStack of stackList ¬
         into line thisStack of stackList
      end repeat
```

```
      set the itemDelimiter to comma
    end if
  put 1 into stackShowing
  repeat until the mouseClick
    set the cursor to busy
    put stackShowing mod numberOfStacks + 1 into stackShowing
    show window (line stackShowing of stackList)
    wait 1 second
  end repeat
end showStacks
```

The above handler works something like the **show cards** command, except for stack windows. It's particularly useful on a small screen, where you can only see one standard-sized stack at a time.

ALSO SEE
windows function

---

stacksInUse property   Introduced in version 2.0

FORMS
the stacksInUse [of HyperCard]
```
get the stacksInUse
repeat with x = 1 to the number of lines of the stacksInUse
answer the stacksInUse
```

ACTION
The **stacksInUse** global property reflects what stacks (if any) have been added to the message-passing path by the **start using** command.

The **stacksInUse** is a read-only property. You can change what stacks are in use with the **start using** and **stop using** commands. HyperCard resets the **stacksInUse** to the default value of empty whenever you quit.

COMMENTS
Use the **stacksInUse** to check whether a particular stack is in use, or to get a complete list of stacks that have been inserted into the message path. This example, which serves as a quick debugging aid, puts the list of stacks in use into a global variable whenever the Variable Watcher is visible:

```
on idle
  global inUseList
  if the visible of the variable watcher then
    put the stacksInUse into inUseList
  else
```

```
      put empty into inUseList
   end if
end idle
```

The **stacksInUse** reports a return-separated list of stack pathnames. The stacks are listed in the order they receive messages. The last stack in the **stacksInUse** comes just before the Home stack in the message-passing path. When you **start using** a stack, its pathname becomes the first line of the **stacksInUse**.

Compacting a stack in use: HyperCard doesn't let you compact a stack that's currently in use. The following handler intercepts the Compact Stack menu choice and, if the stack to be compacted is in use, takes it out of use temporarily while compacting:

```
on doMenu theItem
   if theItem is "Compact Stack" ¬
   and the value of word 2 of the long name of this stack ¬
   is in the stacksInUse then
      stop using this stack
      send "doMenu Compact Stack" to HyperCard
      start using this stack
   else pass doMenu
end doMenu
```

The **stacksInUse** is cleared when you quit HyperCard. To clear the stacks in use and reset the message-passing path without quitting (thus setting the **stacksInUse** to empty), use the following handler:

```
on clearPath
   repeat for the number of lines in the stacksInUse
      stop using stack (line 1 of the stacksInUse)
   end repeat
end clearPath
```

ALSO SEE
stacks function; **start using** command; **stop using** command

---

stackSpace function

Introduced in version 1.0

FORMS
```
the stackSpace
stackSpace()
the stackSpace
```

ACTION

The **stackSpace** function returns the amount of space left on the system memory stack, in bytes.

(Note: this refers to the system data structure known as a "stack", not to a HyperCard stack.)

COMMENTS

This feature was built into the language mainly as an aid in the testing and development of HyperCard itself. However, it can come in handy in certain situations in which you need to know how much system stack space is available to you.

For instance, recursion (the technique in which a handler calls itself) requires a certain amount of stack space for each iteration. If you have too many levels of recursion, HyperCard puts up an error dialog. The following example displays stack space decreasing as a handler recurses:

```
on testRecursion
  global numberOfLevels
  add 1 to numberOfLevels
  put numberOfLevels && space && the stackSpace div 1024 & "K left"
  wait for 10 ticks
  if the stackSpace > 10000 then
    testRecursion -- recursion
  else
    put "levels of recursion." into word 2 to 3 of message
    put 0 into numberOfLevels
  end if
end testRecursion
```

If you want to see the levels of recursion stacking up, show the Message Watcher window before calling this handler:

```
show window "Message Watcher"
testRecursion
```

ALSO SEE

stackSpace function

---

start using command   Introduced in version 2.0

FORMS

```
start using stackToUse
start using stack "The Latest Stuff"
start using stack libraryStack
start using this stack
start using (line 3 of field "Long Stack Names")
```

ACTION

The **start using** command adds the specified stack's script to the message-passing path. You can add up to 16 stacks to the message-passing path with **start using**.

COMMENTS

The **start using** command gives the current stack access to all handlers in the stack scripts of the stacks in use, as well as all resources in their resource forks. A stack in use acts like a shared code library of handlers and resources. This is very useful when designing a multiple-stack application. If you put all the common handlers in one stack, and **start using** it, all the other stacks can use those handlers too, with no need to put a separate copy in each stack.

Once you **starting using** a stack, that stack remains in the message-passing path until you either quit HyperCard or remove it from the path with the **stop using** command. The following simple example shows how to start using a stack and how to clean up by removing it from the message path when it's no longer needed:

```
on openStack
   start using stack "Shared Handlers"
   pass openStack -- in case "Shared Handlers" has an openStack handler
end openStack


on closeStack
   stop using stack "Shared Handlers"
   pass closeStack
end closeStack
```

The *stackToUse* is a valid descriptor of any stack, including the current stack. If HyperCard cannot find the stack you specify, it puts up a standard file dialog and asks you to locate the stack.

How the message path is extended: When you **start using** a stack, HyperTalk inserts it into the message path just before the Home stack. If you add more than one stack to the path, the last-added stack comes first in the message path, right after the current stack.

If you **start using** a stack that's already in use, HyperTalk removes it from its current position in the message-passing path and puts it after the current stack.

Compacting a stack in use: HyperCard doesn't let you compact a stack that's currently in use. The following handler intercepts the Compact Stack menu choice and, if the stack you're compacting is in use, takes it out of use temporarily:

```
on doMenu theItem
   if theItem is "Compact Stack" ¬
   and the value of word 2 of the long name of this stack ¬
   is in the stacksInUse then
      stop using this stack
      send "doMenu Compact Stack" to HyperCard
      start using this stack
   else pass doMenu
end doMenu
```

Avoiding duplicate name errors: Suppose one stack contains a handler that has the same name as, but does something different than, a handler in another stack. If both stacks are in the message-passing path, and the handler is called, the stack that's earlier in the path will be the one to execute the handler. This may cause unexpected results if the other stack's handler is the one that should be called.

To avoid this problem:

- Use unique handler names whenever possible. Avoid names that are too generic.

- Don't add a stack to the path until you need it, and remove it from the path with the **stop using** command as soon as you're done with it.

Techie alert: When you add a stack to the message-passing path, HyperCard caches information about that stack's handlers in RAM. Each time a message goes through the path, HyperCard checks the cached information to see whether that message has any handlers in the stacks in use. Because the handler information is in memory, putting stacks in use has little impact on the time it takes for messages to traverse the message path, so it seldom causes a degradation in performance.

Changes to HyperTalk: In versions of HyperCard before 2.2, you can use only 10 stacks at a time with **start using**.

In versions before 2.1, the **params** function does not work properly from within a **start using** handler.

In versions before 2.0, the **start using** command doesn't exist. However, you can redirect messages to an auxilliary stack by placing stubs for each of them in the Home stack script:

```
on messageName
    send the params to stack "Handler Library"
end messageName
```

This lets you work around the 30K character limit on script length.

ALSO SEE

Messages and the Message Order (Chapter 10); **stacksInUse** property; **stop using** command

---

startup message   Introduced in version 1.0

FORMS

```
startup
```

ACTION

When HyperCard or a standalone application first starts up, the **startup** message is sent to the first card of the first stack opened.

COMMENTS

One use for a **startup** handler is to set up your development environment to your liking. On startup, you can position and show the message box and other tool palettes, set the Message Watcher and Variable Watcher properties, and so forth. Usually you'll install such routines in the Home stack's **startup** handler, so they will be executed no matter which stack is opened first.

If you want to do something specific to one stack, like installing a custom menu, put the code into the stack's **openStack** handler rather than its **startup** handler. That way, it's executed whenever you open that stack instead of only when you double-click the stack to start HyperCard.

In HyperCard 2.x, the **startup** message is sent before the stack window appears, so you can go to a card other than the first one, show and hide objects, and so on before the user sees the stack window by handling **startup** in your stack:

```
on startup
   go to card "Table of Contents"
   show card field "Greeting"
   pass startup
end startup
```

Important: The Home stack's **startup** handler sets up the user level and other properties whose setting is stored in the Home stack. Unless your stack is a standalone, be sure to include the line `pass startup` in any **startup** handler in your stack, or these properties won't be set properly.

Changes to HyperTalk: In versions of HyperCard before 2.0, the **startup** message is sent after the **openStack** message. This causes a problem if you want your stack to set a property (such as the **userLevel**) that's also set by the Home stack's **startup** handler. First your stack receives **openStack** and sets the user level, but immediately after, the **startup** message is sent and the Home stack's **startup** handler resets the user level—possibly to a different value.

To avoid this problem, put the following handlers into your stack script:

```
on openStack
   send "startup" to stack "Home"
   -- do your setting here
end openStack
```

```
on startup
   -- trap the startup message
end startup
```

The first of these handlers lets the Home stack do all its setup; then you can set the environment up for your stack. Since Home has already received the **startup** message and initialized all the necessary variables and properties when you sent it from **openStack**, you can block the real **startup** message at the stack level without causing any problems.

ALSO SEE

openStack message; **quit** message

---

stop using command   Introduced in version 2.0

FORMS

```
stop using stackToRemove
stop using stack "Unknown Magnanimity:Latest Stuff"
stop using this stack
stop using stack (last line of the stacksInUse)
```

ACTION

The **stop using** command removes a stack from the message-passing path. (The stack must previously have been added to the message path with the **start using** command.)

COMMENTS

The following example changes the list of stacks in use to a list of stacks you specify:

```
on setStacksInUse stacksToUse
   -- the stacksInUse is a read-only property. This handler shows
   -- how to change it:
   repeat with x = 1 to the number of lines in stacksToUse
     start using stack (line x of stacksToUse)
   end repeat
   repeat with x = the number of lines of the stacksInUse down to 1
      if line x of the stacksInUse is not in stacksToUse
      then stop using stack (line x of the stacksInUse)
   end repeat
end setStacksInUse
```

The *stackToUse* is a valid descriptor of any stack that's in use. If the stack isn't in use, HyperTalk puts up an error dialog.

The **stop using** command only affects the extensions to the message path made by **start using**. You can't use **stop using** to prevent messages from getting to stacks that are in the normal static and dynamic paths.

All stacks in use are cleared when you quit HyperCard. To clear the stacks in use and reset the message-passing path without quitting, use the following handler:

```
on clearPath
   repeat for the number of lines in the stacksInUse
     stop using stack (line 1 of the stacksInUse)
   end repeat
end clearPath
```

Changes to HyperTalk: In versions of HyperCard before 2.1, the **param** function does not work properly from within a **stop using** handler.

ALSO SEE

Messages and the Message Order (Chapter 10); **stacksInUse** property; **start using** command

---

style property

Introduced in version 1.0
Last changed in version 2.2

FORMS

```
set [the] style of part to style
set the style of card button "Help" to rectangle
set the style of last background button to popup
set the style of field 1 to scrolling
set the style of card part nextPart to transparent
```

ACTION

The **style** property of a button or field determines its appearance. You can also see and set the style in the Field Info or Button Info dialog.

COMMENTS

You can change the style of a button or field to give a different look to your cards. For example, you might want to change a field style from rectangle to transparent when printing a card, and change it back when finished printing. Some button styles—popup, radioButton, and checkBox—also behave in special ways.

The *button*, *field*, or *part* can be any button or field in the current stack. For a button, these styles are available (Figure III.48):

opaque	rectangle	roundRect	shadow
checkbox	radioButton	standard	default
transparent	oval	popup	

For a field, you can choose from the following styles (Figure III.49):

transparent	opaque	rectangle	shadow	scrolling

The Macintosh interface guidelines say there should be only one default button in a window. That button is automatically clicked when the user presses Return or Enter. HyperCard does not automatically click the default button for you, so if you want your default buttons to act in the standard way, you'll need to write **enterKey** and **returnKey** handlers for your stack.

The following handler, which can be placed in a stack script and called from the message box, cycles through each available style for a button or field, letting you see what the different styles look like. Each time through, it advances the part to the next style. Call it repeatedly until you find the style that works best:

button styles as they appear

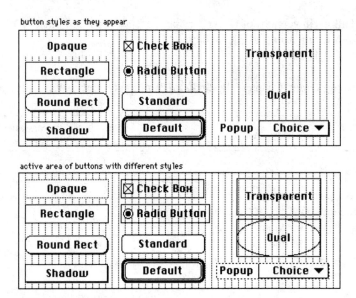

active area of buttons with different styles

Figure III.48   Button styles

```
on cycleStyles thePart
   if thePart is a field then
      put "transparent,opaque,rectangle,shadow,scrolling" into styleList
   else
      put "transparent,opaque,rectangle,shadow,roundRect,checkbox," ¬
      & "radioButton,standard,default,oval,popup" into styleList
   end if
   get the style of thePart
   repeat with nextStyle = 1 to the number of items in styleList
      if item nextStyle of styleList is it then exit repeat
   end repeat
   add 1 to nextStyle
   if nextStyle > the number of items in styleList
   then put 1 into nextStyle
   set the style of thePart to item nextStyle of styleList
end cycleStyles
```

This is some text in a **transparent** field.   This is some text in an **opaque** field.   This is some text in a **rectangle** field.

This is some text in a **shadow** field.   This is some text in a **scrolling** field.

Figure III.49   Field styles

Call the `cycleStyles` handler like this:

```
cycleStyles "card field 1"
```

Default styles: The default style of newly created fields is `transparent`. For buttons, the default style is either `roundRect` (if you created the button by choosing New Button from the Objects menu) or `transparent` (if you created the button by Command-dragging with the button tool chosen).

   The following handler, when placed in the Home stack script, changes the default style of all newly created fields to `scrolling`:

```
on newField
   set the style of the target to scrolling
end newField
```

   The following handlers, inspired by a script written by Gary Bond, can be put in the Home stack script. They change a field's style so it has a scrollbar only if it needs one:

```
on returnInField
   if the style of the target is scrolling then
      if the scroll of the target > 0 then pass returnInField
   end if
   get the selectedChunk -- save the selection while typing
   lock screen
   select after text of the target
   if the selectedLoc is not within the rect of the target
   then set the style of the target to "scrolling"
   else set the style of the target to "rectangle"
   unlock screen
   select it               -- restore the selection
   pass returnInField
end returnInField


on closeField
   get the selectedChunk
   lock messages
   lock screen
   select after text of the target
   if the selectedLoc is not within the rect of the target
   then set the style of the target to "scrolling"
   else set the style of the target to "rectangle"
   unlock screen
   select it               -- restore the selection
   pass closeField
end closeField
```

Button style gotcha: If you change the **style** of a button that has an icon to popup, the icon will be lost. Similarly, if a popup button's style is changed to something else, it forgets which of its lines was selected. If for some reason you need to switch back and forth between styles, be sure to save the button's **icon** or **selectedLine** in a container, so you can restore it later.

Changes to HyperTalk: In versions of HyperCard before 2.2, you cannot use the word part to refer to a field or button.

ALSO SEE

icon property; **selectedLine** function; **titleWidth** property

---

subtract command   Introduced in version 1.0

FORMS

```
subtract number from [chunk of] container
subtract 17 from it
subtract refund from field "Total"
subtract newWithdrawal from line 2 of field "Account Status"
subtract sum(line 2 of field "Deductions") from grossIncome
```

ACTION

The **subtract** command subtracts a numeric value from the number in a container and places the resulting number in the container. The original number in the container is lost, since the container is overwritten by the final result. However, the value of the expression being subtracted from the container is unchanged.

COMMENTS

The following handler displays a countdown in a field:

```
on countDown
   put "T minus 10 and counting..." into field "Counter"
   repeat until field "Counter" is 0
     wait one second
     subtract 1 from word 3 of field "Counter"
   end repeat
   put "Liftoff!" into field "Counter"
   play "Blastoff"
end countDown
```

The **subtract** command always puts its result into a container. You cannot subtract one number directly from another using **subtract** (use the - operator instead).

The container must contain a number. If you try to subtract a number from a container that contains something other than a number, you will get an error dialog. You can check a container's contents with the **is a number** operator before subtracting something from it.

You can subtract a number from an empty container; **subtract** acts as though it contained the number 0. Remember, though, that you have to put something into local variables before you can use them. If you have not yet put something—even "empty"—into the local variable `foo`, the statement `subtract 22 from foo` causes an error message, since you have not initialized `foo`.

If the *container* is a field or the message box, the **numberFormat** property determines the format of the resulting number.

You can subtract a container from itself.

Techie alert: If both values are integers, and if both have absolute values less than 1,073,741,823 (the greatest value possible for a 30-bit number), HyperCard uses integer math to do the subtration. Otherwise, it uses SANE floating-point math.

The **subtract** command uses the same code as the - (minus sign) operator.

ALSO SEE

add command; **divide** command; **is a** operator; **multiply** command; **numberFormat** property

---

sum function   Introduced in version 2.2

FORMS

```
sum(numberList)
sum(1,-3,6.5,3)
sum(item 1 to 6 of field "Elements")
sum(savingsBalance,checkingBalance,cdBalance)
sum(cumulativeList)
```

ACTION

The **sum** function returns the total of a comma-separated list of numbers.

COMMENTS

The *numberList* consists of one or more numbers (or containers that contain a number), separated by commas. The numbers can be positive or negative.

If any item of the *numberList* is not a number, or if the *numberList* is empty, HyperCard puts up a script error dialog.

Old HyperCard versions: The **sum** function does not exist in versions of HyperCard before 2.2. However, you can create your own replacement:

```
function sum
  put 0 into total
  repeat with nextItem = 1 to the paramCount
    add param(nextItem) to total
```

```
      end repeat
      return total
   end sum
```

ALSO SEE

add command

---

suspend message   Introduced in version 1.0

FORMS

suspend

ACTION

The **suspend** message is sent to the current card when you launch another application using the **open application** or **print document** command.

If MultiFinder is running, HyperCard doesn't send the **suspend** message. Since MultiFinder is always on when you're using System 7, this means **suspend** is never sent under System 7.

COMMENTS

When MultiFinder is not running and HyperCard launches another application with **open application** or **print document**, it puts itself away until the user quits the other application. Because HyperCard is not running during this time, all global variables are lost, and any parts of handlers that had not yet executed do not run.

The following example shows how to save global variables before launching another application. It assumes that a **resume** handler (like the one in the section on **resume**) will run later to restore the globals.

```
on suspend
  global accountNumber,currentName,lastOrder
  put accountNumber into line 1 of card field "Saved Globals"
  put currentName into line 2 of card field "Saved Globals"
  put lastOrder into line 3 of card field "Saved Globals"
end suspend
```

Important: The **suspend** message is never sent if you're using MultiFinder or System 7. Under MultiFinder, you can check the **suspended** property to see whether HyperCard is in the background.

When HyperCard is about to suspend, the following messages are sent, in order, to the current card:

```
closeCard
closeBackground
closeStack
suspend
```

ALSO SEE

open application command; **print document** command; **resume** message; **suspendStack** message

---

suspended property

FORMS

```
the suspended [of HyperCard]
get the suspended
if the suspended of HyperCard then hide card window
```

ACTION

The **suspended** global property is set to true if HyperCard is in the background under MultiFinder, and false if HyperCard is the frontmost application.

This property is read-only and cannot be set by a handler. The **suspended** is meaningless if MultiFinder isn't turned on.

COMMENTS

Since HyperCard keeps sending messages and running handlers even when it's in the background, you may want to suppress visual effects, sounds, and other distracting manifestations when some other application is frontmost. Such effects distract the user, and one assumes that if the user wanted to be distracted, HyperCard would be in the foreground. The following utility handlers block sounds, visual effects, and **wait** states unless HyperCard is frontmost:

```
on play
   if not the suspended then pass play
end play

on beep
   if not the suspended then pass beep
end beep

on visual
   if not the suspended then pass visual
end visual

on wait
   if not the suspended then pass wait
end wait
```

Sometimes it's convenient to have HyperCard send a message when the user switches HyperCard into and out of the foreground. Unfortunately, HyperCard doesn't send special messages at these times, but you can use the handler below to send them yourself:

```
on idle
  global isSuspended
  if the suspended is not isSuspended then -- state has changed
    if the suspended is true then
      send suspendHC to this card -- custom message
    else
      send resumeHC to this card -- custom message
    end if
    put the suspended into isSuspended
  end if
  pass idle
end idle
```

HyperCard and MultiFinder: When HyperCard is in the foreground, it gives time to the system for other processes:

- While the cursor is spinning during sorts, compaction, and printing
- Periodically while executing **show cards** and **wait**
- After each statement in a handler

When HyperCard is in the background, if it needs you to respond (to a dialog box, for instance), it uses the standard notification methods. The speaker beeps once, the HyperCard icon flashes at the end of the menu bar, and a diamond appears next to HyperCard's name in the Apple menu (System 6) or the Applications menu (System 7).

ALSO SEE

open application command; **programs** function; **resumeStack** message; **suspendStack** message

---

suspendStack message

Introduced in version 2.0

FORMS

```
suspendStack
```

ACTION

The **suspendStack** message is sent to the current card when you bring another stack's window to the front.

COMMENTS

Handling the **suspendStack** message lets you clean up changes made by your stack before the user brings another one to the front:

```
on suspendStack
   delete menu "Custom" -- belongs to this stack
   hide window "My Palette" -- windoid created by palette command
end suspendStack
```

HyperCard sends the **suspendStack** message when:

- You create or open a stack in a new window

- You click in another stack's window to bring it to the front

- A script issues a **go** or **show** command that brings another stack to the front

ALSO SEE

destination function; **go** command; **resumeStack** message; **show** command; **suspend** message; **suspended** property

---

systemVersion function

Introduced in version 2.1

FORMS

the systemVersion
systemVersion()
```
put the systemVersion into thisSystem
if the systemVersion < 7.1 then answer "This stack needs a later system."
```

ACTION

The **systemVersion** function returns the system software version that's currently running.

COMMENTS

Your handlers should check the **systemVersion** function before using commands that require specific versions of system software. The following example shows how to make sure the system version is compatible with your stack:

```
on openStack
   if the systemVersion < 7.0 then
      answer "Sorry, but this stack requires System 7."
      doMenu "Quit HyperCard"
   else
      pass openStack
   end if
end openStack
```

The **systemVersion** function returns the version number as a decimal string, so you can use it with comparison operators such as <. For instance, if you're currently running under System 7.0.1, **the systemVersion** returns 7.01.

Even if your stack can be used with any system version, specific features may require a particular version. In general, you should take the least restrictive approach to compatibility. If some features don't work on earlier systems, but the stack can still be used without those features, you should block access to the features but still let the user open the stack.

This example disables a program-linking feature that requires System 7 if the system version is too early:

```
on openCard
   if the systemVersion < 7.0 then
      disable button "Link..."
      hide card field "Linked Spreadsheet"
      answer "You can use the graphing capabilities on this" && ¬
      "card, but your system version is too early for you " && ...
      "to link with other programs on the network."
   end if
   pass openCard
end openCard
```

ALSO SEE

address property; **answer program** command; **programs** function; **reply** command; **request** command; **send to program** keyword; **version** property

---

tabKey command/message   Introduced in version 1.0

FORMS

```
tabKey
```

ACTION

The **tabKey** message is sent whenever the user presses the Tab key. If a field is currently open for editing, the message is sent to that field; otherwise, it's sent to the current card.

If the **tabKey** message reaches HyperCard without being intercepted by a handler, it moves the text selection to the next field.

COMMENTS

Trapping the **tabKey** message lets you modify the normal field-to-field tabbing behavior. (For more on the tabbing order, see the **autoTab** property.) Tabbing into a field normally selects any existing text in the field. The following handler modifies this behavior to place the insertion point after the field's text:

```
on tabKey -- in card, background, or stack script
   send tabKey to HyperCard -- moves to next field
   select after text of the selectedField
end tabKey
```

The statements `tabKey` and `type tab` are equivalent in a handler. Both send a **tabKey** message to the appropriate field or card, just as though you had manually pressed the tab key. If the Shift key is being held down when **tabKey** is sent, the selection moves backward through the fields in the tabbing order. To tab backward from a handler, use the form `type tab` with `shiftKey`.

If the current field's **autoTab** property is true, pressing the Return key to auto-tab sends the **tabKey** message.

This example lets the user tab through the fields on a card in the normal way, but tabbing out of the last field goes to the first field on the next card:

```
on tabKey
   if word 1 to 2 of the name of the target is "bkgnd field" then
      if the shiftKey is down and ¬
      the short number of the target is 1 then
         -- first field on this card; back to to previous card
         go previous card
         select text of last background field
      else if the short number of the target ¬
      is the number of fields then
         -- last field on this card; go forward to next card
         go next card
         select text of first background field
      else pass tabKey
   else pass tabKey
end tabKey
```

ALSO SEE

autoTab property; **enterKey** command/message; **returnKey** command/message; **type** command

---

tan function

Introduced in version 1.0

FORMS

[the] tan of *angleInRadians*
tan(*angleInRadians*)
the tan of pi -- yields 0
tan(alpha)
tan(beta + pi)

ACTION

The **tan** function returns the tangent of its argument.

Given a right triangle, the tangent of one of its acute angles is defined as the ratio of the length of the opposite side to the length of the adjacent side. This can also be written as the formula tan(*x*) = sin(*x*)/cos(*x*).

The **tan** function is the mathematical inverse of the **atan** function: for any x, `tan(atan(x))` = x, and for $\pi/2 < x < \pi/2$, `atan(tan(x))` = x.

COMMENTS

The argument of the **tan** function must be in radians. One radian is $180/\pi$ degrees, or about 57.3 degrees.

The following example calculates the height of a structure, given the angle at which you have to tilt your head to see the top and your distance to the foot of the structure. (You need a sextant to measure the angle accurately, but that's better than crawling up the outside of a skyscraper with a measuring tape.)

```
on triangulate
   ask "Distance to the structure in feet?"
   put it into distance
   ask "Angle to the top in degrees?"
   put pi * it/180 into angle -- convert to radians
   answer "That structure is" && distance * tan(angle) ¬
   && "feet tall."
end triangulate
```

Yet Another HyperTalk Anomaly: The tangent of pi/2 is an infinite number, since tan(x) = sin(x)/cos(x) and cos(x) = 0. However, HyperTalk does not return `INF` (infinity) when you try to take the value of `tan(pi/2)`, as you might expect. Instead, it returns a very large number. This anomaly occurs because HyperTalk cannot compute the value of pi with infinite precision.

ALSO SEE

atan function; **cos** function; **sin** function

---

target function

Introduced in version 1.2
Last changed in version 2.2

FORMS

```
the [short|abbr[ev[iated]]|long] target
target
put the long target into fieldName
put target into fieldContents
if word 1 to 2 of the target is "card button" then exit mouseUp
put the hilite of the target into isTurnedOn
put target into buttonContents
```

ACTION

The **target** function returns the name of the object that first received the current message, whether the message was sent by HyperCard or with the **send** keyword.

If **the target** is a field or button, the special form **target** returns the contents of the field or button.

COMMENTS

The **target** function is particularly handy when you need to determine whether the current object is the first to receive the message, or whether it's been passed on from another level of the message-passing path. For instance, if you click on a button that has no script, the **mouseUp** message is first received by that button, and so the button is **the target**—even if the **mouseUp** message is handled by some other object, such as the current card.

The following "hot key" handler illustrates this concept. This handler belongs in the card, background, or stack script; when the user presses a key, the handler checks whether **the target** is a field. If so, the typing is done normally. Otherwise, pressing one of the keys A-G plays the corresponding note:

```
on keyDown theKey
   if word 2 of the target is "field" then
      pass keyDown
   else
      if theKey is in "abcdefg" then play harpsichord theKey
   end if
end keyDown
```

The short, abbreviated, and long forms correspond to the short name, abbreviated name, and long name of the target object, respectively. (For more information about these forms, see the **name of object** function.) If the object has no name, **the target** returns the object's ID.

Using the **pass** keyword to pass the current message along the message path does not change **the target**; it's still the same object.

The me descriptor and the target function: The **me** descriptor and the **target** function serve similar purposes. **The target** is the object that originally received the message, and **me** is the object that's currently handling it. If the current handler is in the script of the object that first got the message—for example, if a **mouseDown** handler in a button script is currently executing—**the name of me** is the same as **the target**.

Changes to HyperTalk: In versions of HyperCard before 2.2, buttons aren't containers, so you can't use the form **target** to specify their contents.

In versions before 2.0, you can also use the form **target( )**. However, because of a bug, the form **target( )** causes an error message when the target is a field.

ALSO SEE

name property

text property   Introduced in version 2.0

FORMS

```
set [the] text of window "Message Watcher" to text
put the text of window "Message Watcher" after field "Saved Messages"
```

ACTION

The **text** is a property of the Message Watcher window. It determines the text that is currently shown in the Message Watcher's scrolling list.

COMMENTS

This example displays the number of times a particular message appears in the Message Watcher. It's useful when you want to track the actions the user takes:

```
on showMessages theMessage
   if theMessage is empty then put "mouseUp" into theMessage
   put 0 into numberOfTimes
   get the text of window "Message Watcher"
   repeat while it contains theMessage
      add 1 to numberOfTimes
      delete char offset(theMessage,it) of it
   end repeat
   answer theMessage && "appears" && numberOfTimes && "times."
end showMessages
```

The following handler clears the Message Watcher:

```
on clearMessages
   set the text of window "Message Watcher" to empty
end clearMessages
```

The **text** property can be set whether or not the Message Watcher is currently visible.

Techie alert: You can use this property with a custom message watcher XCMD, as well as the built-in message watcher, if the custom XCMD is written to support **text**.

ALSO SEE

hideIdle property; **hideUnused** property; **messageWatcher** property; **nextLine** property

---

textAlign property   Introduced in version 1.0

FORMS

```
set [the] textAlign [of HyperCard|of {part|button|field}] to alignment
set the textAlign to "left" -- sets paint text alignment
```

```
set the textAlign of field "Title" to center
set the textAlign of background button nextButton to right
```

ACTION

The **textAlign** property sets the alignment of text in a field or button, or of text painted with the text tool. The possible alignments are `left`, `right`, and `center`.

The default value for the **textAlign** of fields and paint text is `left`. For buttons, the default **textAlign** is `center`.

COMMENTS

The *alignment* must be one of `left`, `right`, or `center`. Providing any other value causes HyperCard to put up an error dialog.

The form `the textAlign [of HyperCard]` sets the paint text's alignment.

Checkbox, popup, and radio buttons: These button styles are always left-aligned, regardless of the setting of their **textAlign** property.

Once text is painted, you can't retrieve or change its **textAlign** setting. However, you can check the current setting of the **textAlign**, which will affect all subsequently painted text, as follows:

```
get the textAlign
```

ALSO SEE

printTextAlign property; **reset paint** command; **showName** property; **textFont** property; **textHeight** property; **textSize** property; **textStyle** property

---

textArrows property

Introduced in version 1.1

FORMS

```
set [the] textArrows [of HyperCard] to {true|false}
set the textArrows to true
set the textArrows to the hilite of card button "Text Arrows"
```

ACTION

The **textArrows** property determines whether the arrow keys move the insertion point or move from card to card.

The User Preferences card in the Home stack sets the **textArrows** every time HyperCard starts up. By default, the **textArrows** is false.

COMMENTS

If **textArrows** is true and there is a selection or insertion point in a field or the message box, pressing the arrow keys moves the insertion point:

Left	Moves back one character
Right	Moves forward one character
Up	Moves up one line
Down	Moves down one line

If **textArrows** is false, or if it's true but there's no selection, pressing the arrow keys moves you to another card:

Left	Previous card in the stack
Right	Next card in the stack
Up	Card viewed immediately after this one
Down	Card viewed immediately before this one

The best of both worlds: When the **textArrows** is true, pressing Option-arrow moves to another card even if there's an insertion point.

Changes to HyperTalk: In versions of HyperCard before 1.2.1, when the **textArrows** is true and there is no selection, pressing the arrow keys does nothing. To change this and implement the behavior described above, place the following handler in the Home stack script:

```
on arrowKey
   set the textArrows to (the selectedChunk is not empty)
   pass arrowKey
end arrowKey
```

ALSO SEE
arrowKey command/message

---

textFont property

Introduced in version 1.0
Last changed in version 2.0

FORMS
set [the] textFont [of HyperCard|of *message*|of *button*|of {*chunk* of} *field*] to *fontName*
```
set the textFont to "Avant Garde" -- sets paint text
set the textFont of button "Hello" to menuItem 1 of menu "Font"
set the textFont of card field nextField to nextFont
set the textFont of line 3 of field ID 44 to "Geneva"
set the textFont of the selectedChunk to "Helvetica"
set the textFont of the message box to Zapf Dingbats -- uhh....
```

ACTION

The **textFont** property determines the font of the text in a field, of the name of a button, or of text painted with the text tool.

Setting the **textFont** is equivalent to selecting the object (or the paint text tool) and choosing a font, either from the Style menu or in the Text Style dialog.

The default value for the **textFont** of fields and paint text and the message box is `Geneva`. For buttons, the default **textFont** is `Chicago`.

COMMENTS

The form `the textFont [of HyperCard]` sets the paint text's font.

Once text is painted, you can't retrieve or change its **textFont** setting. However, you can check the current setting of the **textFont** used for painting like this:

```
get the textFont
```

The *fontName* is any font available to the current stack. You can see all the available fonts can be seen in HyperCard's Font menu. You can use any fonts located in the following places:

- The System file (or Fonts folder under System 7.1)
- The resource fork of HyperCard
- The resource fork of the Home stack
- The resource fork of any stack that has been placed in the resource path with the **start using** command
- The resource fork of the current stack

If you specify a font that doesn't exist, HyperCard substitutes the default application font (Geneva).

The *message* is any descriptor of the message box.

Multiple fonts in a field: The **textFont** of a field is the default font for that field. You can change the font of any characters in the field, either by using the Font menu or from a handler. If you change the **textFont** of a field, only the text that's in the field's default font is affected. For example:

```
set the textFont of field 3 to "Geneva" -- sets all text to Geneva
set the textFont of word 1 of field 3 to "Chicago" -- just that word
set the textFont of field 3 to "Monaco" -- word 1 still Chicago
```

If the characters in a chunk expression are in different fonts, the **textFont** of that chunk yields "mixed".

When you cut and paste text from field to field, the text retains its formatting (font, size, and style). However, when you move text with the **put** command, the text takes on the attributes of the field into which it's moved.

The textFont of icon buttons: If a button has an icon, its name always appears in 9-point Geneva, regardless of the setting of its **textFont** property.

Techie alert: You can set the **textFont** by using a FOND family ID instead of a font name:

```
set the printTextFont to 4 -- sets to Monaco
```

FOND ID 0 is reserved for the System font (on systems that use the Roman alphabet, this is Chicago). FOND ID 3 is the current application font (usually Geneva). If you set the **textFont** to an ID that's not available, the object appears in Geneva, but its **textFont** is set to the ID you specified:

```
set the textFont of field 1 to 5 -- Venice (but it isn't installed)
put the textFont of field 1 -- yields 5
```

Changes to HyperTalk: In versions of HyperCard before 2.2, you cannot get or change the **textFont** of the message box.

In versions before 2.0, you cannot set the **textFont** of a chunk expression; all text in a field has the same font.

ALSO SEE

printTextFont property; **reset paint** command; **scriptTextFont** property; **showName** property; **textAlign** property; **textHeight** property; **textSize** property; **textStyle** property

---

textHeight property   Introduced in version 1.0

FORMS

set [the] textHeight [of HyperCard|of *field*|of *button*] to *pixelHeight*
```
set the textHeight to 12 -- sets height for paint text
set the textHeight of field "Announcements" to myHeight + 3
```

ACTION

The **textHeight** global property is the vertical distance in points allowed for each lines of text. You can also change the **textHeight** of fields and paint text in the Text Style dialog.

COMMENTS

Although HyperTalk lets you change the **textHeight** of a button, doing so has no effect.

The *pixelHeight* must be an integer; otherwise, HyperCard presents an error dialog. The smallest legal **textHeight** is the current **textSize**. If you try to set the **textHeight** to less than the minimum, the **textHeight** will be set to the current value of the **textSize**.

When you change the **textSize**, the **textHeight** is changed automatically to a value compatible with the text size, using this formula:

```
textHeight = (textSize * 4) div 3
```

The form `the textHeight [of HyperCard]` sets the paint text's line height. Once text is painted, you can't retrieve or change its **textHeight** setting. You can check the current setting of the paint **textHeight**, which will affect all subsequently painted text, as follows:

```
get the textHeight
```

ALSO SEE

fixedLineHeight property; **printTextHeight** property; **reset paint** command; **textAlign** property; **textFont** property; **textSize** property; **textStyle** property

---

textSize property   Introduced in version 1.0

FORMS

set [the] textSize [of HyperCard|of *message*|of *button*|of {*chunk* of} *field*] to *fontSize*

```
set the textSize to 14
set the textSize of card button "Popup" to nextSize
set the textSize of line 4 of card field 3 to 22
set the textSize of message window to 10
```

ACTION

The **textSize** property is the font size of paint text, text in a field, or the name of a button.

Setting the **textSize** is equivalent to selecting the object (or the paint text tool) and choosing a size, either from the Style menu or in the Text Style dialog. The default value for **textSize** is 12.

COMMENTS

The form `the textSize [of HyperCard]` sets the paint text's size. The current setting of the **textSize** affects all subsequently painted text. However, once you've painted text, you can't retrieve or change its **textSize** setting.

The *fontSize* must be an integer; otherwise, HyperCard presents an error dialog. The smallest legal **textSize** is 1 point; if you try to set it to zero or a negative number, the **textSize** will be set to 1. The largest legal **textSize** is 127 points.

If you choose a *fontSize* that isn't available, HyperCard uses the closest existing smaller size and spaces the characters appropriately for the size you requested.

The *message* is any descriptor of the message box. Reducing the message box's **textSize** lets you fit more text into it.

Changing the **textSize** of a field automatically sets its **textHeight** to an appropriate value, using the formula:

```
textHeight = (4 * textSize) div 3
```

If you want a different **textHeight**, be sure to set it *after* changing the **textSize**.

Multiple sizes in a field: The **textSize** of a field is the default size for that field. If you change the **textSize** of a field, only the text that's in the field's default size is affected. For example:

```
set the textSize of field 3 to 9 -- sets all text to 9-point
set the textSize of word 1 of field 3 to 24 -- just that word
set the textSize of field 3 to 12 -- word 1 still 24-point
```

If the characters in a chunk expression are in different sizes, the **textSize** of that chunk yields "mixed".

When you cut and paste text from field to field, the text retains its formatting (font, size, and style). However, when you move text with the **put** command, the text takes on the attributes of the field into which it's moved.

Changes to HyperTalk: In versions of HyperCard before 2.2, you cannot get or change the **textSize** of the message box.

In versions before 2.0, you cannot set the **textSize** of a chunk expression; all text in a field has the same size.

ALSO SEE

printTextFont property; **reset paint** command; **scriptTextFont** property; **showName** property; **textAlign** property; **textHeight** property; **textFont** property; **textStyle** property

---

textStyle property   Introduced in version 1.0

FORMS

set [the] textStyle [of HyperCard|of *message*|of *button*|of {*chunk* of} *field* to *styleList*

set [the] textStyle of *menuItem* to *styleList*

```
set the textStyle to bold
set the textStyle of card button "Popup" to myStyle
set the textStyle of line 4 of card field 3 to group,italic
set the textStyle of msg to shadow -- why? why on earth?
set the textStyle of menuItem "Card" of menu "Scripts" to underline
set the textStyle of last menuItem of menu 3 to plain
```

ACTION

The **textStyle** property reflects the style or combination of styles used for text.

Setting the **textStyle** is equivalent to selecting the object (or the paint text tool) and choosing one or more styles from the Style menu, or choosing Text Style from the Edit menu and changing the style. The default value for **textStyle** is plain.

COMMENTS

The form `the textStyle [of HyperCard]` sets the paint text's alignment. The current setting of the **textSize** affects all subsequently painted text. Once text is painted, you can't retrieve or change its **textSize** setting.

The *styleList* is a set of one or more styles, separated by commas. The available styles are: plain, bold, italic, underline, outline, shadow, condense, extend, group (the group style can only be used with field text). `Plain` removes all other styles, but is ignored if you use it in combination with other styles; you must use `plain` by itself in order for it to have an effect.

The *message* is any descriptor of the message box.

Multiple styles in a field: The **textStyle** of a field is the default style for that field. You can change the style of any characters in the field, either by using the Style menu or from a handler. If you change the **textStyle** of a field, only the text that's in the field's default style is affected.

If the characters in a chunk expression are in different styles, the **textStyle** of that chunk is reported as "mixed".

When you cut and paste text from field to field, the text retains its formatting (font, size, and style). However, when you move text with the **put** command, the text takes on the attributes of the field into which it's moved.

About the group style: The `group` style lets you stick together any contiguous run of characters in a field. Grouped text is handled specially by the **clickChunk**, **clickText**, and **clickLine** functions. Setting the style of text to `group` paints a heavy gray underline under it, if you've used the command `show groups`; if not, grouped text appears the same as any other text.

Changes to HyperTalk: In versions of HyperCard before 2.2, you cannot get or set the **textStyle** of the message box.

In versions before 2.0, you cannot set the **textStyle** of a chunk expression; all text in a field has the same style. The `group` style does not exist in these versions, and you cannot set the **textStyle** of a menu item.

ALSO SEE

hide command; **printTextFont** property; **reset paint** command; **scriptTextFont** property; **show** command; **show groups** command; **showName** property; **textAlign** property; **textFont** property; **textHeight** property; **textSize** property

---

there is a operator

Introduced in version 2.0
Last changed in version 2.2

FORMS

```
there is [a[n]|not a[n]|no] elementType elementDescriptor
there is a menu "Utilities"
there is no menuItem "Tabs" in menu "Formatting"
there is a card part 1
there is not a window ID mySavedID
if there is a card picture then doMenu "Select"
if there is a file it then open file it else beep
```

ACTION

The **there is a** operator evaluates to true if the specified element exists and to false if it does not. The forms `there is a` and `there is an` are equivalent.

The **there is no** operator is the logical opposite of **there is a**: it evaluates to true if there is no such element, and to false if the element exists. The forms `there is no`, `there is not a`, and `there is not an` are equivalent.

COMMENTS

The most common use for this operator is to test for the existence of an object before doing some operation on it, thus avoiding error messages. For instance, before making any changes to a menu, you should make sure the menu already exists, since HyperCard puts up an error dialog when you try to change a nonexistent menu:

```
if there is a menu myMenu then put it into menu myMenu
```

The possible *elementTypes* whose existence can be tested by this operator are as follows:

- `there is a [card|background] button` *buttonDescriptor*—The *buttonDescriptor* is the **name**, **number**, or **ID** of any button in the current card or background. If you don't specify the layer, the button is assumed to be on the card.

- `there is a [card|background] field` *fieldDescriptor*—The *fieldDescriptor* is the **name**, **number**, or **ID** of any field in the current card or background. If you don't specify the layer, the field is assumed to be in the background.

- `there is a [card|background] part` *partDescriptor*—The *partDescriptor* is the **name**, **number**, or **ID** of any part (button or field) in the current card or background. If you don't specify a card or background, the part is assumed to be on the card.

- `there is a card` *cardDescriptor*—The *cardDescriptor* is the **name**, **number**, or **ID** of a card in the current stack.

- `there is a background` *backgroundDescriptor*—The *backgroundDescriptor* is the **name**, **number**, or **ID** of any background in the current stack.

- `there is a stack` *stackName*—If you specify a stack's filename without giving its pathname, the **there is a** operator looks first in HyperCard's folder, then in the folder containing the current stack, and then in the locations listed in the Stack Search Paths card of the Home stack. (This list is also kept in the Stacks global variable).

- `there is a {card|background} picture`—This form evaluates to true if there's any image in the card or background paint layer, and false if there is no image. If there is any opaque (white) paint in the card layer, `there is a card picture` evaluates to true even if there's no black paint.

- `there is a window` *windowDescriptor*—The *windowDescriptor* is the **name**, **number,** or **ID** of any open window. If a window is invisible, it still exists. HyperCard never closes some built-in windows, so expressions like

    ```
    there is a window "message"
    ```

    always evaluate to true.

- `there is a program {`*name*`|ID` *signature*`}`—The *signature* is the program's four-character type signature. (For instance, the *signature* of HyperCard is WILD.) This form returns true if there is a System 7-friendly process with the specified name or signature currently running, and false otherwise. System 7-friendly processes are those that appear in the **answer program** dialog. This form of the **there is a** operator is only useful under System 7.

- `there is a scriptingLanguage` *languageName*—This form of the **there is a** operator returns true if the specified script language is installed and available.

- `there is a disk` *diskName*—This form returns true if the image of a disk named *diskName* is on the desktop and false otherwise. The disk need not be currently inserted into the Mac.

- `there is a folder` *folderPath*—This form returns true if the specified folder exists. The *folderPath* must end with a colon (:).

- `there is an application` *appName*—The *appName* can be either the full path or just the filename of the application. If you don't specify a pathname, HyperTalk looks in in the locations listed in the Application Search Paths card of the Home stack (this list is also kept in the Applications global variable).

- `there is a document` *docName*—The *docName* can be either the full path or just the name of the file. If you don't specify a pathname, HyperTalk looks in the locations listed in the Document Search Paths card of the Home stack (this list is also kept in the Documents global variable).

- `there is a file` *fileName*—The *fileName* is either the full path or just the name of the file. If you don't specify a pathname, HyperTalk looks for the file in the folder containing the current stack. Unlike the form `there is a document`, this form does not use the paths in the Documents global variable to locate the file. If the file isn't in the current directory, the expression evaluates to false.

- `there is a menu` *menuDescriptor*—The *menuDescriptor* is the **name**, **number** or resource ID of the menu in question. All HyperCard's built-in menus still exist even if they're not visible, so an expression like

```
there is a menu "Options"
```

always evaluates to true, even if none of the paint tools is selected.

- `there is a menuItem` *itemDescriptor* `{of|in} menu` *menuDescriptor* —The *itemDescriptor* is the **name** or **number** of any menu item in the specified menu.

Changes to HyperTalk: In versions of HyperCard before 2.2, the **there is a** operator can't be used to check for the existence of card and background pictures, applications, disks, scripting languages, and documents. This handler shows a technique that lets you check for the existence of a picture:

```
function hasPicture
    -- returns true if the current card has a picture, else false
    -- this function is from "Cooking With HyperTalk 2.0",
    -- by Dan Winkler and Scott Knaster
```

```
      put the tool into savedTool
      put the lockScreen into savedLockScreen
      lock screen
      choose select tool
      doMenu "Select All"
      doMenu "Select"
      -- if there's any paint, HyperCard chooses the lasso tool;
      -- otherwise the tool remains the select tool. This trick
      -- discovered by Robin Shank.
      get (the tool is "lasso tool")
      choose savedTool
      set the lockScreen to savedLockScreen
      return it
   end hasPicture
```

In versions before 2.1, **there is a** can't check for the existence of a program or folder.

In versions of HyperCard before 2.0, which lack the **there is a** operator, you can check for a card's existence with the following function:

```
function cardExists theCard
   set the lockScreen to true
   push this card
   go to card theCard
   get (the result is empty)
   -- the result is empty if the card exists
   pop card
   set the lockScreen to false
   return it
end cardExists
```

ALSO SEE

ID property; **is a** operator; **name** property; **number of object** function; **result** function

---

ticks function

FORMS

the ticks
ticks()
the ticks

ACTION

The **ticks** function returns the amount of time since the Macintosh was last started up, in ticks. A tick is 1/60 of a second.

COMMENTS

One use for the **ticks** function is to check how long your Mac has been up. For example, if you back up every time you shut down, you may want to check how long it's been since you did backups.

```
on showTimeSinceRestart
    get the ticks
    get it div (60 * 60 * 60) -- get the number of hours
    put it div 24 into theDays
    subtract 24 * theDays from it
    if theDays is 0 then
        if it is 0 then put "less than an hour" into timeFromRestart
        else put theHours && "hours" into timeFromRestart
    else
        put theDays && "days and" && theHours && "hours" into timeFromRestart
    end if
    answer "It has been" && timeFromRestart && "since startup."
end showTimeSinceRestart
```

A more common use for **the ticks** is to compare the value at two different events to get the elapsed time between them. This example shows a word and measures how quickly the user can click after seeing the word:

```
on elapsedTime theWord
    put theWord into field "Display"
    get the ticks -- start clock
    wait until the mouseClick
    put the ticks into totalTicks
    subtract it from totalTicks
    set the numberFormat to 0.##
    answer "It took you" && totalTicks && "ticks (" ¬
    & totalTicks/60 && "seconds) to click after seeing the word."
end elapsedTime
```

A third use for the **ticks** function is to benchmark your code, measuring how long a particular statement or handler takes to run. The following handler is a generic benchmarker. You pass it the name of the message or function handler whose speed you want to check, and the number of test runs to do:

```
on benchMark handlerType,commandLine,numberOfRuns
    -- "handlerType" is either "function" or "message"
    -- "commandLine" is the full name with parameters: for example,
    --     "myHandler 25,17"
    --     "customFunction()"
    if numberOfRuns is empty then put 100 into numberOfRuns
    put the ticks into startTicks
    if handlerType is "function" then put "get" & space before commandLine
    repeat for numberOfRuns times
```

```
      do commandLine
   end repeat
   put the ticks - startTicks into elapsedTicks
   set the numberFormat to 0.##
   answer numberOfRuns && "calls took" && elapsedTicks ¬
   && "ticks (" & elapsedTicks/60 && "seconds)." & return ¬
   & elapsedTicks/numberOfRuns && "ticks per call."
end benchMark
```

You might call the benchmarking handler like this, from the message box:

```
benchMark function,"the ticks",1000
```

(You need to enclose "the ticks" in quotation marks to prevent HyperCard from evaluating the function and passing the current tick count, instead of the function name.) The greater the *numberOfRuns* in this handler, the more accurate the result—but of course more runs take more time.

You might want to compare the speed of two operations—for instance, you may want to know whether going to another stack takes longer than going to another card in the same stack. Here's a benchmarking handler similar to the one above:

```
on mouseUp
   lock screen
   lock messages
   --
   put the ticks into startTicks
   repeat for 10 times
     go next card
     go previous card
   end repeat
   put the ticks - startTicks into cardTicks
   --
   put the ticks into startTicks
   repeat for 10 times
     go stack "Home"
     go back
   end repeat
   put the ticks - startTicks into stackTicks
   --
   set the numberFormat to 0.##
   answer "It takes" && cardTicks/20 && "ticks to change cards." ¬
   & return & "It takes" && stackTicks/20 && "ticks to change stacks." ¬
   & return & return & "A card change takes" ¬
   && 100 * cardTicks/stackTicks & "% the time of a stack change."
end mouseUp
```

ALSO SEE

seconds function; **time** function

time function

Introduced in version 1.0
Last changed in version 2.2

FORMS

```
the [long|abbr[ev[iated]]|short|English] time
time()
put time() into currentTime
if last word of the time is "AM" then answer "Good morning!"
```

ACTION

The **time** function returns the current time in one of several formats.

COMMENTS

You can use **time** for a number of things: recording a time stamp in your stack, for instance. The following example displays the current time in two different time zone:

```
on idle -- placed in card script
  put the time into card field "Time Here"
  convert (the seconds + card field "Zone Number" * 60 * 60) to time
  put it into card field "Time There"
  pass idle
end idle
```

The forms of **the time** are as follows:

Formats for the time function

```
    the long time                4:01:11 PM (or 16:01:11)
```
The time in colon-separated form with seconds. Whether 12-hour or 24-hour clock format is used depends on which is set in the Control Panel.

```
    the English time             4:01:11 PM
```
The long time, in 12-hour U.S. format (see below).

```
    the abbr{rev{iated}} time    4:01 PM (or 16:01)
```
The time in colon-separated form without seconds.

```
    the short time               4:01 PM (or 16:01)
```
Same as the abbreviated time.

```
    the time                     4:01 PM (or 16:01)
```
Same as the abbreviated time.

```
    time()                       4:01 PM (or 16:01)
```
Same as the abbreviated time.

The above forms are the ones **the time** produces under the standard U.S. system software. If you're using a version of the system that's been localized for another country, or if you have changed the time format with the Date & Time control panel under System 7.1, you cannot rely on **the time** producing exactly these formats.

To get around this problem, the form `the English time` always produces the long time in the format given above, regardless of the current system settings. You can safely assume that the the hours, minutes, and seconds of `the English time` are separated by colons, and that it's in 12-hour format.

If your stacks are being used internationally, store any times in one of the invariant forms (the `English time`, `dateItems`, or `seconds`) and use the **convert** command to change them to the appropriate format.

Nuances of the time( ) form: When you use the parentheses form of the **time** function, the only date form available is the default long time. If you try to specify a form—even the long form—you'll get a script error. If you put anything into the parentheses, you'll get an error also.

Changes to HyperTalk: In versions of HyperCard before 2.0, if you specify a form with the **time( )** form of the function, it's ignored instead of causing a script error.

In versions of HyperCard before 2.2, the `English time` form is not available.

ALSO SEE
convert command; **date** function

---

titleWidth property   Introduced in version 2.2

FORMS
set [the] titleWidth of *popupButton* **to** *pixelWidth*
```
set the titleWidth of button "My Popup Menu" to 30
set the titleWidth of last card button to standardTitleWidth
set the titleWidth of myButton to (field "Button Width")
```

ACTION
The **titleWidth** button property determines how much space is allowed for the title of a popup button. If the button's style is something other than "popup", the setting of this property has no effect.

COMMENTS
Use the **titleWidth** property to adjust how much of a popup menu's total width is taken by its title. A popup button's title appears to the left of the menu outline. (See Figure III.50.)

Changing a popup's **titleWidth** property is equivalent to typing a new value for the title width into the Button Info dialog, or adjusting the title width manually by dragging the bar between the title and the menu. This example creates a new Font popup:

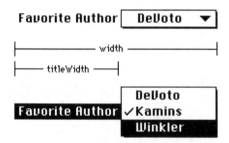

Figure III.50   Width and titleWidth properties of a popup button

```
on makeFontPopup where
   lock screen
   set the cursor to watch
   doMenu "New Button"
   set the name of last button to "Font"
   set the style of button "Font" to "Popup"
   set the loc of button "Font" to where
   set the width of button "Font" to 175
   set the titleWidth of button "Font" to 40
   put menu "Font" into button "Font"
   unlock screen
end makeFontMenu
```

The *popupButton* is a descriptor of any button in the current stack. You can refer to buttons by name, number, or ID. You can set and get the **titleWidth** of buttons that are not popup menus, but the **titleWidth** property has no effect on such buttons.

The *pixelWidth* must be a positive integer. If you provide a negative integer, the **titleWidth** is set to 0. Using a non-integer causes a script error dialog.

Changing the **titleWidth** does not change the button's **width** property; it simply increases the portion taken up by the title, and decreases the portion available for the popup itself. You can set the **titleWidth** of a popup to be greater than the button's **width**, but doing so has little practical use.

ALSO SEE
   style property; **width** property

---

tool function   Introduced in version 1.0

FORMS
```
the tool
tool()
if the tool is not "browse tool" then choose browse tool
if word 1 of the tool is in "browse button field" then beep
```

ACTION

The **tool** function returns the name of the currently selected tool.

COMMENTS

The following example shows how to save the current tool before choosing a new one so you can restore it later:

```
on import
  -- the import paint command requires a paint tool be chosen;
  -- this handler intercepts the command and makes sure one is.
  if the tool is "browse tool" ¬
  or the tool is "button tool" ¬
  or the tool is "field tool" then
    put the tool into savedTool
    choose select tool -- or any paint tool
    send the params to HyperCard -- go ahead and do the import
    choose savedTool
  else pass import
end import
```

The **tool** function returns one of the following values:

browse tool	button tool	field tool
select tool	lasso tool	pencil tool
brush tool	eraser tool	line tool
spray tool	rectangle tool	roundRect tool
bucket tool	oval tool	curve tool
text tool	regular polygon tool	polygon tool

ALSO SEE

choose command/message

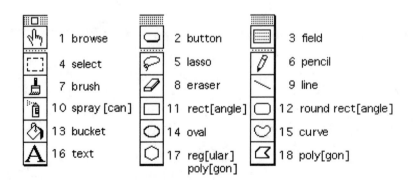

Figure III.51   Tool names and numbers

top property

FORMS

```
set [the] top of {part|button|field|window} to integer
the top of {menubar|card}
set the top of last button to 100
set the top of message window to the bottom of card window
```

ACTION

The **top** property describes where the top edge of an element is.

COMMENTS

The *button*, *field*, or *card* can be any button, field, or card in the current stack.

A *window* is a descriptor of any open stack window, HyperCard window, or external window. The top of a window is at the bottom of its title bar.

The **top** of a stack window and the **top** of a card in that stack may be different if the window has been sized smaller than the card size (for example, using the Scroll command in the Go menu).

The *integer* is the vertical distance in pixels from the top edge—of the screen for stack windows, or of the current stack window for cards, buttons, fields, and other windows—to the element's top edge. If the *integer* is negative, the element's top edge is *integer* pixels *above* the top edge of the screen or stack window.

The top and other location properties: The **top** of an element is the same as item 2 of its **topLeft** property, and also the same as the second item of the element's **rectangle** property.

Changing the **top** of an element moves the element without changing its size, but changing item 4 of the element's **rectangle** changes its size without moving its other three edges.

Changing the top property: Anything that moves or resizes an element may change its **top** property—for instance, dragging the element manually or from a script, or changing its **location** or **rectangle** property, or using the **show** command with a new location.

Changes to HyperTalk: In versions of HyperCard before 2.2, you cannot describe a button or field with a part descriptor, and you cannot get the **height** of the menu bar.

ALSO SEE

bottom property; **left** property; **location** property; **rectangle** property; **right** property; **show** command; **topLeft** property

topLeft property

FORMS

```
set [the] topLeft of {part|button|field|window} to location
the topLeft of {menubar|card}
set the topLeft of window "Scroll" to "20,20"
set the topLeft of button "Clip Art" to the clickLoc
if the topLeft of field 1 is within the rect of button 1 then hide field 1
```

ACTION

The **topLeft** property describes the location of an element's upper-left corner.

COMMENTS

The *button*, *field*, or *card* can be any button, field, or card in the current stack. A *window* can be any open stack window, HyperCard window, or external window.

The **topLeft** of a stack window and the **topLeft** of a card in that stack may be different if the window has been sized smaller than the card size (for example, using the Scroll command in the Go menu).

The *location* is a point on the screen, consisting of two integers separated by a comma. The first item is the horizontal distance in pixels from the left edge of the frontmost card window to the point. The second item is the vertical distance from the top edge to the point. (For stack windows, the *location* is measured from the edges of the screen rather than the card window.) The top edge of the card window is at the bottom (not the top) of its title bar.

The name of this property is backward: Although the name is **topLeft**, the coordinates appear in the order *left*, *top*.

The topLeft and other location properties: Since the two coordinates of **topLeft** are separated by a comma, you can refer to them independently as two separate items:

```
put item 1 of the topLeft of field 6 into theHorizontal
```

In fact, item 1 of the **topLeft** is the **left** of the element, and item 2 is the **right** property. The value of the **topLeft** is the same as the first two items of the element's **rectangle** property.

Changing the topLeft property: Anything that moves or resizes an element changes its **topLeft** property—for instance, dragging the element manually or from a script, or changing its **location** or **rectangle** property, or using the **show** command with a new location.

Changes to HyperTalk: In versions of HyperCard before 2.2, you cannot describe a button or field with a part descriptor, and you cannot get the **topLeft** of the menu bar.

ALSO SEE

bottomRight property; **left** property; **location** property; **rectangle** property; **show** command; **top** property

traceDelay property

FORMS

```
set [the] traceDelay [of HyperCard] to delayTicks
set the traceDelay to 60
```

ACTION

The **traceDelay** property determines how long the HyperCard debugger pauses between statements when tracing a handler. The default **traceDelay** is 0.

COMMENTS

You can also set the trace delay using the Trace Delay item in the Debugger menu. This property is useful mainly when you want to set up a delay automatically (for instance, in a **startup** handler), as part of your scripting environment.

The *delayTicks* is the number of ticks between each statement. (A tick is 1/60 of a second). The *delayTicks* must be an integer, or you'll get an error message. You can set the **traceDelay** to any number between 0 and 32767 (approximately 9 minutes). A **traceDelay** of 0 causes traces to run with no pause between statements.

ALSO SEE

scriptEditor property

trunc function

FORMS

```
[the] trunc of number
trunc(number)
the trunc of 2 -- yields 2
trunc(43.567)  -- yields 43
trunc(-223.75) -- yields 223
```

ACTION

The **trunc** function returns the integer part of its argument, throwing away any fraction.

COMMENTS

The **trunc** function is useful when you want to make certain the value you're passing to a function, command, or property is an integer. For example, the following handler shrinks the text in a field every time it's clicked:

```
on shrinkText theField
   get the textSize of field theField/1.5
   if it < 6 then beep -- can't shrink below 6 point
```

```
        else set the textSize of field theField to trunc(it)
        -- can't set the point size to a fraction
    end shrinkText
```

The *number* can be any number between -2147483648 and 2147483647.

Difference between trunc and round: The **trunc** function simply throws away any part of the number it's given that falls after the decimal point. The truncated value of 6, 6.2, or 6.7 is simply 6. The **round** function, on the other hand, rounds to the nearest integer, so it looks at the part after the decimal point to see whether it should round up or down. The rounded value of 6.2, like the truncated value, is 6. But the rounded value of 6.7 is 7, since 7 is closer to the original number than 6.

Techie alert: This function calls the SANE routine `Num2LongInt` with rounding set to `TowardZero`. Because a Macintosh longint is 32 bits, with one bit reserved for the sign, the highest value this routine can be used with is $31^2 - 1$; that is, 2,147,483,647.

ALSO SEE
numberFormat property; **round** function

---

type command   Introduced in version 1.0

FORMS
type *characters* [**with** *modifierKey1* [*, modifierKey2* [*, modifierKey3*]]]
```
type "B" with commandKey    -- toggle background mode
type field "Original"       -- types contents of field at insertion point
type foo with shiftKey,optionKey
```

ACTION
The **type** command simulates the user typing one or more characters.

If there is an insertion point or selection, **type** places the *characters* there. If the text paint tool is chosen and you've clicked to place an insertion point, **type** creates paint text characters at the insertion point. If any other tool is chosen, or if there is no insertion point, **type** places the typed characters in the message box.

COMMENTS
Use the **type** command when you need to simulate actual typing: for instance, to type paint text. You can also use the **type** command to put text into the message box without making it appear. See the **blindTyping** property for more details.

The following example puts a friendly greeting in the paint layer:

```
on mouseUp
   choose text tool
   set the textSize to 36
   click at 50,200
   type "Welcome to HyperCard!"
   choose browse tool
end mouseUp
```

The *characters* can consist of any string of characters. This string is case-sensitive.

The *modifierKeys* can be `shiftKey`, `optionKey`, or `commandKey` (or a synonym, `cmdKey`).

Not an exact simulation of typing: The **type** command is not an exact substitute for typing, since some actions done with modifier keys require that the physical keys be down. For instance,

```
type "1" with commandKey,shiftKey
```

does not eject the floppy disk in drive 1, even though the same action performed manually would do so. Typing lowercase letters `with shiftKey` does not create uppercase letters. However, you can use `type` *character* `with commandKey` to choose any menu command that has a Command-key equivalent.

Using the **type** command does not send a **keyDown** message.

Getting creative with type: This handler takes advantage of the fact that **type** places its characters one at a time:

```
on flashMe
   set the textAlign of card field "Display" to center
   set the textStyle of card field "Display" to bold, outline
   set the lockText of card field "Display" to false
   put "(Click the mouse to stop)" into line 3 of card field "Display"
   set the textStyle of line 3 of card field "Display" to plain
   repeat until the mouseClick
      select line 1 of card field "Display"
      type "Am I being artistic yet?"
      wait for 1 second
      put empty into line 1 of card field "Display"
   end repeat
   delete text of card field "Display"
end flashMe
```

ALSO SEE

click command; **keyDown** command/message

unlock error dialogs command

FORMS

```
unlock error dialogs
unlock error dialogs
```

ACTION

The **unlock error dialogs** command sets the **lockErrorDialogs** property to false.

COMMENTS

The **unlock error dialogs** command is synonymous with `set the lockErrorDialogs to false`, and prevents HyperCard from displaying an error dialog in case of a script error. If HyperCard encounters a script error while error dialogs are locked out, it sends the **errorDialog** message to the current card.

   HyperCard sets **lockErrorDialogs** is set to false at **idle**, so **unlock error dialogs** has no effect unless it's used within a handler.

ALSO SEE

errorDialog message; **lock error dialogs** command; **lockErrorDialogs** property

---

unlock messages command

FORMS

```
unlock messages
unlock messages
```

ACTION

The **unlock messages** command sets the **lockMessages** property to false.

COMMENTS

The **unlock messages** command is synonymous with `set the lockMessages to false`, and allows close, open, suspend and resume messages to be sent to objects automatically when moving between cards or stacks.

   HyperCard sets **lockMessages** to false at **idle**, so **unlock messages** is only effective when you use it within a handler.

ALSO SEE

lockMessages property; **unlock messages** command

unlock recent command

Introduced in version 2.2

FORMS

```
unlock recent
unlock recent
```

ACTION

The **unlock recent** command sets the **lockRecent** property to false.

COMMENTS

The **unlock recent** command is synonymous with `set the lockRecent to false`, and prevents cards from being added to the display shown by the Recent menu item.

HyperCard sets the **lockRecent** property to false at **idle**, so **unlock recent** is only effective if you use it within a handler.

ALSO SEE

lock recent command; **lockRecent** property

unlock screen command

Introduced in version 1.2
Last changed in version 2.2

FORMS

```
unlock screen [with visual [effect] effectName [speed] [to destinationImage]]
unlock screen
unlock screen with visual effect dissolve
unlock screen with visual barn door open slowly
unlock screen with visual effect zoom open
```

ACTION

The **unlock screen** command sets the **lockScreen** global property to false. This updates the screen with any changes that have been made since the screen was locked.

COMMENTS

Use the **unlock screen** command with **lock screen** to make changes to the appearance of the screen—such as changing cards, hiding or showing fields and buttons, or drawing on pictures—and then show them all at once.

Locking the screen while making multiple changes has two benefits. It's less jarring to the user to see all the changes at once than to see them happening one at a time, and it's faster for HyperCard to make changes "behind the scenes" with the screen locked than to have to redraw the screen at each step. This example shows how you might use **lock screen** and **unlock screen** to hide these actions:

```
on clearCard
  lock screen
  repeat with nextField = 1 to the number of fields
    put empty into field nextField
  end repeat
  hide background button "Subcategory"
  unlock screen
end clearCard
```

At **idle** time, when all handlers are finished, HyperCard automatically resets the **lockScreen** property to false.

Using **unlock screen** when the screen isn't locked has no effect.

Visual effects without changing cards: You can use **unlock screen with visual effect** to show visual effects without having to move to another card:

```
on mouseUp -- hides a Comment field
  lock screen
  if the visible of field "Comments" then hide field "Comments"
  else show field "Comments"
  unlock screen with visual effect dissolve -- dissolves field in/out
end mouseUp
```

If you use a visual effect, HyperCard adds the specified transition between the previous image and the newly updated screen image. The *effectName* is one of the following:

```
cut|plain
dissolve
wipe [left|right|up|down]
barn door [open|close]
scroll [left|right|up|down]
push [left|right|up|down]
iris [open|close]
zoom [open|close|out|in]
shrink to [top|center|centre|bottom]
stretch from [top|center|centre|bottom]
venetian blinds
checkerboard
```

For more information about the different effects and advice about when to use them, see the **visual effect** command.

The *speed* is one of the following:

```
very fast   fast   normal   slow (or slowly)   very slow (or very slowly)
```

If you don't specify a speed, the **visual effect** command uses normal. If you use very fast, the **visual effect** is executed as quickly as the current Mac can display it, so the very fast *speed* varies between different models of Macintosh.

The *destinationImage* is one of the following:

```
card       inverse      gray (or grey)     black      white
```

If you don't specify a *destinationImage*, `card` is used. Otherwise, the visual effect makes the transition from the previous image to the *destinationImage*—a black, white, or gray screen, or the inverse of the destination card—and then cuts to the final unlocked image.

Unlike the **visual effect** command, **unlock screen with visual effect** does not let you stack effects: you are limited to a single visual effect. Because of this, you usually will not want to specify a *destinationImage*, since this option is most useful with stacked effects.

Locking the screen more than once: HyperTalk keeps count of the times you've used **lock screen** (or the equivalent, `set the lockScreen to true`). Locking an already-locked screen is harmless, but you must use an **unlock** for each **lock**. If you lock the screen twice and then unlock it once, the screen remains locked. For example, the following pair of handlers draws everything while the display is still locked:

```
on mouseUp
   lock screen -- first lock
   drawStuff  -- gets locked again and unlocked
   show card picture
   unlock screen -- now really unlocked - 2 locks balanced by 2 unlocks
end mouseUp


on drawStuff
   lock screen -- screen now locked twice
   show card field 2
   unlock screen -- doesn't unlock yet - locked twice, unlocked once
end drawStuff
```

Changes to HyperTalk: In versions of HyperCard before 2.2, you can't use the **push** visual effect. The **shrink** and **stretch** visual effects are not available in versions before 2.0.

If you're using a version of HyperCard before 2.2, visual effects cannot be seen if the monitor is set to 16-bit (thousands of colors) or 24-bit (millions of colors). In versions before 2.0, visual effects cannot be seen if the number of monitor colors is set to anything other than 2-bit (black-and-white). To change the color setting, use the Monitors control panel.

ALSO SEE

find command; **go** command; **lock screen** command; **lockscreen** property; **visual effect** command

unmark command

FORMS

```
unmark {card|all cards}
unmark cards where condition
unmark cards by finding [international] [findForm] findString [in field]
unmark recent card
unmark card ID 17
unmark all cards
unmark cards where the short number of this card > 300
unmark cards by finding chars lowerLimit
unmark cards by finding word myWord in field theDictionary
unmark cards by finding international word "Sørensen"
```

ACTION

The **unmark** command sets the **marked** property of the specified card or cards to false. It's equivalent to turning off the Card Marked checkbox in the Card Info dialog. This command has no effect on cards that are already unmarked.

You can't unmark cards in a locked stack.

COMMENTS

Use the **unmark** command to clear the marked property of all cards before doing a **mark** operation, or to selectively unmark previously marked cards to further filter them.

The following example shows how to cull duplicates from a database using **unmark**. It belongs in a stack where each card is the record of a song on CD, and includes fields for the name of the song, artist's name, a list of topics, and so on. The handler lists all artists who have performed a song about a particular topic:

```
on findArtistsByTopic
   ask "What topic are you interested in?"
   if it is empty then exit findArtistsByTopic -- user cancelled
   unmark all cards -- clear all existing marks
   mark cards by finding it in field "Topic"
   put empty into artistList
   push this card
   repeat until the number of marked cards is zero
      go to next marked card
      put field "Artist" into line ¬
      (the number of lines of artistList + 1) of artistList
      unmark cards by finding field "Artist" in field "Artist"
   end repeat
   pop card
   put artistList into card field "List of Artists"
end findArtistsByTopic
```

The **unmark** command has the following forms:

- **unmark** *card*: Unmarks the card you specify. The *card* must be a valid descriptor of a card in the current stack.

- **unmark all cards:** Unmarks all cards in the current stack.

- **unmark cards where** *condition*: Unmarks all cards on which *condition* occurs. The *condition* can be any HyperTalk expression that evaluates to true or false—a mathematical equation, a statement using **contains**, a property or function that evaluates to true or false, etc. The **unmark** command ignores cards where the *condition* can't be tested because a field or button mentioned in the *condition* isn't on that card.

- **unmark cards by finding:** Unmarks all cards found by a search. You can limit the search to a specific field, and specify a *findForm*: **finding normal**, **finding chars**, **finding word**, **finding string**, or **finding whole**. (For a complete explanation of these forms, see the **find** command.) If you don't specify a *findForm*, the **finding normal** form is used.

  To make the search distinguish international (Option-key) characters from their ASCII counterparts, use the **finding international** *findForm* option.

Because the form **unmark cards by finding** uses the same hint bits as the **find** command, it's much faster than the equivalent form of **unmark cards where**:

```
unmark cards by finding "Winkler" in field "Author"   -- much faster
unmark cards where "Winkler" is in field "Author"     -- slower
```

Combining mark and unmark: The **mark** command takes the same forms as **unmark**, so you can combine **mark** and **unmark** commands to get a filtered set.

Changes to HyperTalk: In versions before 2.2, you can't use the **international** option with **unmark cards by finding**.

ALSO SEE

debug command; **dontSearch** property; **find** command; **go** command; **mark** command; **marked** property; **number of object** function; **print card** command; **show cards** command

---

userLevel property

Introduced in version 1.0

FORMS

```
set [the] userLevel [of HyperCard] to levelNumber
set the userLevel to 4
set the userLevel to word 2 of the selectedLine of button "Level"
set the userLevel to savedUserLevel
if the userLevel < 3 then beep
```

ACTION

The **userLevel** property determines the current user level, which defines what powers the user has when working with a stack.

The **userLevel** is set by the User Preferences card in the Home stack when HyperCard starts up. By default, the **userLevel** is 2 (Typing).

COMMENTS

You may want to set the **userLevel** to something lower than 5 (Scripting) for a variety of reasons, such as to protect your stack from young users, to prevent changes to the stack, or to ensure simplicity. If the user has specified a level lower than 5, you may also need to set the **userLevel** to a higher value so that your handlers can run—for instance, the **userLevel** must be 3 or above to use the paint tools. If you change the **userLevel**, be sure to save the old setting and restore it after you're done.

Table III.8 lists the available levels:

Table III.8   User Levels and Their Powers

Level	Name	Powers
1	browsing	Can use browse tool, Go menu, shortened File menu, and shortened Edit menu
2	typing	Can also edit text in unlocked fields
3	painting	Can also use paint tools and menus, full File and Edit menus
4	authoring	Can also create objects and use Objects menu
5	scripting	All HyperCard and HyperTalk capabilities. HyperGodhood.

The *levelNumber* is an integer between 1 and 5. If you specify a *levelNumber* less than 1, the **userLevel** is set to 1; if you specify a number greater than 5, it's set to 5.

Warning: If you specify a *levelNumber* that isn't an integer, HyperCard puts up a script error dialog and aborts the rest of the handler, but it also sets the **userLevel** to 1 in its confusion.

Protect Stack and the userLevel: The Protect Stack dialog box lets you set a limit on the **userLevel** for a particular stack. If you're in a protected stack, you can't set the **userLevel** to a value above the stack's limit.

By the way, the shortened File menu available when the **userLevel** is 1 or 2 doesn't include the Protect Stack menu item. But don't panic—holding down the Command key while you pull down the menu always displays the full File menu, regardless of the current user level.

The following "wrapper" handler sets the **userLevel** as appropriate before running another handler. If the stack doesn't allow access to the needed user level, the handler puts up a dialog to warn the user:

```
on doHandler theHandler,theLevel
   if theLevel is empty then put 5 into theLevel -- the default
   put the userLevel into savedUserLevel
   if the userLevel is not theLevel then
     set the userLevel to theLevel
     if the userLevel is not theLevel then -- stack is protected
        answer "This stack limits the user level."
        exit doHandler
     end if
   end if
   doHandler
   set the userLevel to savedUserLevel -- restore original level
end doHandler
```

You might call the above handler like this:

```
doHandler "makeButton",4   -- you need level 4 to make buttons
doHandler "drawStuff",3    -- you need level 3 to paint
doHandler "showScripts"    -- you need level 5 to script
```

ALSO SEE

choose command/message; **doMenu** command/message; **export paint** command; **import paint** command

---

userModify property

FORMS

```
set [the] userModify [of HyperCard] to {true|false}
set the userModify to true
if the userModify then choose pencil tool
```

ACTION

The **userModify** global property determines whether you can make temporary changes to a stack whose **cantModify** is set to true, or which is otherwise write-protected.

Whenever you switch stacks, HyperCard resets the **userModify** to its default value of false.

COMMENTS

A stack is write-protected if any of the following things is true:

- The stack's **cantModify** is set to true.
- The Locked checkbox in its Get Info dialog in the Finder is checked.
- The stack is on a locked disk.
- The stack is in a read-only folder on a server.

Ordinarily, the user can't make any changes to a write-protected stack and is limited to browsing.

If the **userModify** property is true, however, the user can make changes to such a stack, type in text, use the paint tools, and so on. (However, you can't change the scripts in a write-protected stack, regardless of the setting of **userModify**.)

All such changes are discarded when the user leaves the current card or when the **cantModify** setting changes. You can use a handler like the following to save the changes:

```
on closeCard
  select text of field "Edit Me"
  doMenu "Copy Text"    -- save the changes before they disappear
  set the cantModify of this stack to false
  select text of field "Edit Me"
  doMenu "Paste Text" -- restore the changed text
  set the cantModify of this stack to true
end closeCard
```

The following handler, which can be placed in a card, background, or stack script, lets the user make changes to a field if you've put the string `--editable` into the field's script:

```
on openField
  set the userModify to ¬
  (the script of the target contains "--editable")
end openField
```

If the current stack is not write-protected, the setting of **userModify** makes no difference.

ALSO SEE

cantModify property; **userLevel** property

---

value function   Introduced in version 1.0

FORMS

[the] value of *factor*
value(*expression*)
```
the value of "This text string"
value(the selectedField)
the value of "Hello there" -- returns Hello there without quotes
the value of the message box
```

ACTION

The **value** function evaluates any HyperTalk expression and returns the result.

COMMENTS

Use the **value** function when you need to force HyperTalk to evaluate an expression rather than taking it literally. The following handler finds the requested text and returns the entire line it was found in, even though only a single word was matched:

```
on putFoundInfo
   find "nauseated" in field "Election Year"
   answer the value of the foundLine
end putFoundInfo
```

This handler calculates the value of any arithmetic expression passed to it:

```
on pocketCalculator
   ask "What do you want to compute?"
   answer "The value is" && value(it) & "."
end pocketCalculator
```

The following example looks for a card that meets any conditions you specify:

```
on findCardWhere theCondition
   lock screen
   push this card
   repeat for the number of cards times
     set the cursor to busy
     if the value of theCondition then exit findCard -- found!
     go to next card
   end repeat
   pop card
   answer "Can't find any cards where" && theCondition
end findCardWhere
```

You might call this handler like this:

```
findCardWhere "field 1 is empty and the length of field 2 > 10"
```

Changes to HyperTalk: In versions of HyperCard before 2.2, the **value** of a quoted text string only takes its first token into account. For example, `the value of "Hello world"` is `Hello`, and `the value of "this,that,the other"` is `this`.

In versions before 2.2, expressions are limited to 255 characters.

ALSO SEE

request command

The value of the value

Most HyperTalk references treat **the value** as a mere shortcut for computing arithmetic expressions. But it's much more than that. The **value** function can evaluate any HyperTalk expression at all. It can resolve geometric operations, chunk expressions, booleans, and a great deal more. Much of the power of HyperTalk is accessible through clever use of **the value** to force HyperTalk into evaluating an expression.

For example, the **clickLine** function returns a chunk expression that describes a line. But what if you want the actual text of the line, instead of the line number? You could do this manually, by typing commands into the message box to get **the clickLine** and then substituting that number into another command:

```
put the clickLine -- this might yield "line 3 of card field 5"
put line 3 of card field 5 -- you'd have to substitute by hand
```

But you can use **the value** to force HyperTalk to do the same thing automatically, with the following statement:

```
get the value of the clickLine
```

This statement tells HyperTalk, "Get **the clickLine**. Then, instead of returning the chunk expression, feed it back into the language to get the text it refers to."

This powerful function is also handy when you need to concatenate two strings together to form the name of a container. For example, suppose you have a set of variables named `var1`, `var2`, `var3`, and so on. If you want to put each variable into the corresponding card field, you can include a line for each variable:

```
put var1 into card field "Variable 1"
put var2 into card field "Variable 2"
put var3 into card field "Variable 3"
```

and so on, for whatever number of variables you have. However, this solution is far from ideal. For one thing, if you have a lot of these variables, these lines consume a lot of space in your code. For another, the solution won't work at all if you don't know exactly how many variables the handler will use. However, you can use the power of **the value** to condense these statements into a single **repeat** structure:

```
repeat with thisVar = 1 to numberOfVars
  put value("var" & thisVar) into card field ("Variable" && thisVar)
end repeat
```

The wise scripter will contemplate the power of **the value** whenever a handler seems to call for parsing an expression in an unorthodox way.

variableWatcher property

FORMS

```
set [the] variableWatcher [of HyperCard] to variableWatcherXCMD
set the variableWatcher to "MyVarWindow"
put the variableWatcher into currentWatcher
```

ACTION

The **variableWatcher** global property is the name of the Variable Watcher window. This window appears when you choose Variable Watcher from the Debug menu while in the debugger.

By default, the **variableWatcher** property is set to `VariableWatcher`, which is HyperCard's built-in variable watcher window.

COMMENTS

Variable watchers, incuding the one built in to HyperCard, are implemented as XCMDs. You can set the **variableWatcher** property to use a custom variable watcher you've written and installed in HyperCard's resource fork or your stack's resource fork.

If you try to set the **variableWatcher** to an XCMD that's not present, HyperCard puts up an error dialog.

In practice, this property is seldom used. Most scriptwriters are satisfied with the built-in variable watcher.

ALSO SEE

debug checkpoint command; **debugger** property; **hBarLoc** property; **messageWatcher** property; **scriptEditor** property; **vBarLoc** property

vBarLoc property

FORMS

```
set [the] vBarLoc of window "Variable Watcher" to number
set the vBarLoc of window "Variable Watcher" to 100
```

ACTION

The **vBarLoc** is a property of the Variable Watcher window. It determines the position of the vertical split bar in the Variable Watcher.

Unless a user or script changes it, the **vBarLoc** is 99.

COMMENTS

The Variable Watcher shows the names of variables in the left pane, and their values in the right pane. A user can drag the vertical split bar to change the width of these two panes. You can use the **vBarLoc** property to check the location of the split bar, or change it, from a handler.

The *number* is the distance in pixels from the left edge of the Variable Watcher window to the split bar. It must be an integer. You can set the **vBarLoc** to any number between -32768 and 32767; the practical values are between 50 and 500, depending on how large you want to make the window.

The following handler checks the properties of the Variable Watcher window and stores them in a field for later use (for instance, by a **startup** handler):

```
on mouseUp
    put "set the visible of window" && quote & "Variable Watcher" ¬
    & quote && "to" && the visible of window "Variable Watcher" ¬
    into line 2 of card field "Variable Watcher Properties"
    --
    put "set the vBarLoc of window" && quote & "Variable Watcher" ¬
    & quote && "to" && the vBarLoc of window "Variable Watcher" ¬
    into line 2 of card field "Variable Watcher Properties"
    --
    put "set the hBarLoc of window" && quote & "Variable Watcher" ¬
    & quote && "to" && the hBarLoc of window "Variable Watcher" ¬
    into line 2 of card field "Variable Watcher Properties"
    --
    put "set the loc of window" && quote & "Variable Watcher" ¬
    & quote && "to" && the loc of window "Variable Watcher" ¬
    into line 2 of card field "Variable Watcher Properties"
    --
    put "set the rect of window" && quote & "Variable Watcher" ¬
    & quote && "to" && the rect of window "Variable Watcher" ¬
    into line 2 of card field "Variable Watcher Properties"
end mouseUp
```

The **vBarLoc** property can be set whether or not the Variable Watcher is currently visible.

Techie alert: You can use this property with a custom variable watcher XCMD, as well as the built-in variable watcher, if the custom XCMD is written to support **vBarLoc**.

ALSO SEE
hBarLoc property; **variableWatcher** property

version property

Introduced in version 1.0
Last changed in version 1.2

FORMS

```
the [short|abbr[ev[iated]]|long] version [of {HyperCard|stack}]
if the version < 2.2 then getNewVersion atOnce
get item 2 of the version of this stack
if char 5 of the long version of HyperCard is not 8 then beep
```

ACTION

The **version** property supplies information about the version of HyperCard, or about the versions of HyperCard used to create and modify the current stack.

The **version** property is read-only and cannot be set in a handler.

COMMENTS

The most common use of the **version** property is to make certain the user's version of HyperCard will work with your stack. For example, if your stack uses the AppleEvent commands and functions introduced in HyperCard 2.1, you might include the following handler in its script:

```
on openStack
   if the version < 2.1 then -- user's HyperCard is too early
      answer "Sorry, but this stack requires HyperCard 2.1 or later."
      if the number of lines in the stacks is 1
      then doMenu "Quit HyperCard"
      else doMenu "Close Stack"
   end if
   pass openStack
end openStack
```

The form `the version` is the same as `the version of HyperCard`, and reports the version family of the HyperCard application that's currently running. For instance, version 1.2.5 and 1.2.2 both have a **version** of 1.2. The `short version` and `abbreviated version` report the same number as `the version`.

The form `the long version` reports an eight-digit hexadecimal number representing the full version number. (See Figure III.52.)

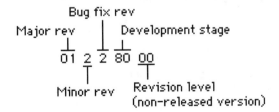

Figure III.52   The long version of HyperCard

The development stage is development (20), alpha (40), beta (60), or shipping (80). So 01236006 is version 1.2.3b6, and 02208000 is the shipping version of 2.2.

All versions of HyperCard before 1.2 are designated by `00000000`.

The following function converts a version number into a more readable form:

```
function readable theVersion
   if theVersion is 0 then return "1.#" -- could be anything before 1.0
   -- strip leading zero, if present
   put the value of char 1 to 2 of theVersion into majorRev
   put char 3 of theVersion into minorRev
   put char 4 of theVersion into bugFixRev
   put char 5 to 6 of theVersion into devStage
   put char 7 to 8 of theVersion into devRelease
   -- build version number:
   put majorRev & "." & minorRev into versionString
   if bugFixRev is not 0 then put "." & bugFixRev after versionString
   if devStage is not 80 then
      if devStage is 20 then put "d" & devRelease after versionString
      if devStage is 40 then put "a" & devRelease after versionString
      if devStage is 60 then put "b" & devRelease after versionString
   end if
   return versionString
end readable
```

The form `version of` *stack* reports a list of five numbers, separated by commas. The first four numbers are in the format of Figure III.52, and specify:

- The version of HyperCard that created the stack
- The version that last compacted the stack
- The oldest version that's modified the stack since the last compaction
- The version that last modified the stack

The last number is the time and date, in seconds format, of the last time the stack was saved to disk. You can use the **convert** command to get the date and time:

```
convert last item of the version of this stack to date and time
put it
```

The following handler displays a stack's version in a more readable form:

```
on showStackVersion
   put the version of this stack into theVersion
   convert last item of theVersion to time and date
   answer "Created by:" && readable(item 1 of theVersion) & return ¬
   & "Compacted by:" && readable(item 2 of theVersion) & return ¬
   & "Oldest:" && readable(item 3 of theVersion) & return ¬
   & "Latest:" && readable(item 4 of theVersion) & return ¬
   & "Modified:" && item 5 of theVersion
end showStackVersion
```

Techie alert: The eight-digit format used for reporting versions is the same as the format of the first eight digits of the standard Macintosh `vers` resource.

Changes to HyperTalk: In versions of HyperCard before 1.2.5, the `long version` and `version of` *stack* forms don't exist; you can only get the version family of the currently running copy of HyperCard.

ALSO SEE
convert command

---

visible property

FORMS

```
set [the] visible of {part|button|field|window|menubar} to {true|false}
if the visible of card button "Beep" is true then beep
put the visible of window "Tools" into line 3 of field "Prefs"
set the visible of menubar to (not the visible of menubar)
```

ACTION

The **visible** property of an element determines whether or not it can be seen on the screen.

The command `set the visible of` *object* `to true` has the same effect as `show` *object*; the command `set the visible of` *object* `to false` is equivalent to `hide` *object*.

COMMENTS

Use the **visible** property to determine whether a window or part has been hidden or whether the menu bar is visible, and to hide and show them.

This example handler belongs in the script of a "Notes" button that brings up a text field for the user's notes:

```
on mouseUp
   if the visible of field "Notes" then
     -- already showing, so put it away
     hide field "Notes"
   else
     -- hidden, so show it
     show field "Notes"
     select after text of field "Notes" -- put insertion point at end
   end if
end mouseUp
```

The *button* or *field* is a descriptor of any field or button in the current stack.

The *window* is any currently open window—a built-in HyperCard window, a stack window, or a window created by an XCMD or XFCN.

You can move an invisible element, and get and change any of its properties, just as though it were visible. However, the changes will not appear until you make the element visible again.

Visible doesn't always mean visible: Because an element's **visible** property is set to true doesn't necessarily mean you can see that element. Some things that can make an object invisible even though its **visible** property is true are:

- The **height** or **width** of a button, field, or window has been set to a negative number.
- The **location**, **rect**, or other location-related properties have been set so that a window is off the screen, or a part is outside the card's boundaries.
- A field or button is covered by other fields or buttons, or by opaque white paint.

Changes to HyperTalk: In versions of HyperCard before 2.2, you cannot get the **visible** of the menu bar, although you can hide and show it.

ALSO SEE

hide command; **show** command; **showPict** property

---

visual effect command

Introduced in version 1.0
Last changed in version 2.2

FORMS

```
visual [effect] effectName [speed] [to destinationImage]
visual effect dissolve
visual wipe up fast
visual stretch to black
visual effect barn door close very slowly to inverse
visual effect push down
```

ACTION

The **visual effect** command stores a transition special effect for display the next time the current handler changes cards.

COMMENTS

You can use the **visual effect** command to make your stacks more attention-getting and polished, and to give a hint to the user about what is happening during navigation from card to card. This example uses a visual effect in a Next button to indicate the direction the user is moving:

```
on mouseUp
  visual effect wipe left -- gets executed when you "go"
  go to next card
end mouseUp
```

The *effectName* is one of the following:

cut|plain—cuts from the previous image directly to the destination image, with no intervening effect. Using **cut** or **plain** by itself is the same as not using the **visual effect** command at all, but can be useful in setting up stacked visual effects (see below).

dissolve—fades from the previous image to the destination image.

wipe [left|right|up|down]—rolls the destination image out over the previous image, like rolling out a sheet of canvas, in the indicated direction.

barn door [open|close]—wipes from the center of the screen out to the left and right edges (for barn door open), or vice versa.

scroll [left|right|up|down]—slides the destination image over the previous image, like sliding a playing card over the top of the deck.

push [left|right|up|down]—slides the destination image onto the screen from one edge while the previous image is pushed out of the way off the opposite edge.

iris [open|close]—shows a rectangle in the center of the card through which you can see the destination image, gradually growing larger until it reaches the edges of the card window and replaces the previous image.

zoom [open|close|out|in]—draws a series of expanding (zoom open) or contracting (zoom close) rectangles on the current screen image, then cuts to the destination image. The zoom open effect expands from the last point clicked; zoom close contracts to the center of the window. The zoom effect is similar to the Finder's "zooming rectangles" when opening an application. zoom out is the same as zoom open, and zoom in is the same as zoom close.

shrink to [top|center|centre|bottom]—squeezes the previous image toward the top or bottom of the window, or from top and bottom to the center of the card window, revealing the destination image underneath.

stretch from [top|center|centre|bottom]—pulls the destination image from the top, bottom, or in both directions from the center, as if it were made of taffy.

venetian blinds—divides the card window into horizontal stripes and wipes each stripe at once, from top to bottom.

checkerboard—divides the card window into a grid of squares and replaces the part of the image, first in the odd squares, then in the even squares.

Which effect you should choose depends partly on what message you want to convey to the user, and partly on the differences between the previous and destination images. Some effects, such as **dissolve** and **wipe**, are most appropriate when portions of the two images are identical—for instance, when the two images share a graphic frame, and only what's inside the frame differs from card to card. Other effects, such as **iris**, **venetian blinds**, and **checkerboard**, are most effective when the previous and destination images are very different.

The *speed* is one of the following: `very fast`, `fast`, `normal`, `slow` (or `slowly`), `very slow` (or `very slowly`). If you don't specify a speed, the **visual effect** command uses `normal`. If you use `very fast`, the **visual effect** is executed as quickly as the current Mac can display it, so the `very fast` *speed* varies between different models of Macintosh.

The *destinationImage* is one of the following: `card`, `inverse`, `gray` (or `grey`), `black`, `white`. If you don't specify a *destinationImage*, `card` is used. Otherwise, the visual effect makes the transition from the previous card to the *destinationImage*—a black, white, or gray screen, or the inverse of the destination card—and then cuts to the destination card.

Stacking visual effects: If you want to create a more complex visual effect, you can stack up to ten effects. They are all saved up and executed the next time HyperTalk moves to another card. For example, this combination imitates an old-fashioned slide projector:

```
on showSlides
   repeat for the number of cards
      visual effect scroll left to black
      visual effect scroll right to card
      go to next card
   end repeat
end showSlides
```

Another very effective combination is a dissolve through `black`, `white`, or `gray`:

```
on mouseUp
   visual effect dissolve fast to black
   visual effect dissolve fast to card
   go to card "Master List"
end mouseUp
```

You can also combine the stretch and shrink effects for an interesting combination:

```
on goToContentsPage
   visual effect shrink to bottom to gray
   visual effect stretch from bottom to card
   go to card "Contents Page"
end goToContentsPage
```

Whether to use a simple effect or a combination depends on your stack. In general, a combination effect gives the user the impression of having moved a greater distance than a single effect, and so you may prefer to reserve combinations for moving between major divisions of your stack.

Visual effect gotchas: There are a few things to be aware of if your visual effect doesn't seem to be working. First of all, visual effects are not shown if the **lockscreen** property is set to true while the stack is moving from one card to the other. You may need to check your **closeCard** handlers to make sure they're not locking the screen.

Since HyperCard clears the list of pending visual effects at **idle** time, any visual effects that haven't yet been seen are lost when HyperTalk stops executing and control returns to the user. (However, the **visual effect** command and the card switch that triggers it don't necessarily have to be in the same handler; one handler could call another that sets up a visual effect, and a third that goes to another card.)

In general, if the stack window is straddling more than one monitor, the **visual effect** command won't work.

Visual effects work with find: If a **find** command causes HyperCard to move to another card, any pending visual effects are executed. The following handler traps any **find** commands, adds a visual effect, then sends the **find** on along the message path to be executed:

```
on find
   visual effect dissolve
   pass find
end find
```

If you use a visual effect during **find**, however, **find** does not draw its usual rectangle around the found text.

Changes to HyperTalk: In versions of HyperCard before 2.2, you can't use the **push** visual effect. The **shrink** and **stretch** visual effects are not available in versions before 2.0.

If you're using a version of HyperCard before 2.2, visual effects cannot be seen if the monitor is set to 16-bit (thousands of colors) or 24-bit (millions of colors). In versions before 2.0, visual effects cannot be seen if the number of monitor colors is set to anything other than 2-bit (black-and-white). To change the color setting, use the Monitors control panel.

There is a bug in versions before 2.2 that sometimes causes a crash on Macs with a 68030 processor and black-and-white monitor; if you try to do a visual effect when the card window is partly offscreen, the Mac may crash.

ALSO SEE

find command; **go** command; **lockscreen** property; **pop** command; **unlock screen** command

---

wait command   Introduced in version 1.0

FORMS

```
wait [for] time [tick[s]|second[s]]
wait {while|until} condition
wait for 30 -- waits 30 ticks
wait stallTime seconds
wait until the mouse is down
wait while the mouseCliok
```

ACTION

The **wait** command makes HyperCard pause before executing the rest of the statements in the current handler.

COMMENTS

The **wait** command is useful when you want to display something and give the user enough time to look at it before continuing, or to let a process (such as the playing of a sound) complete before you do anything else. The following handler shows a sequence of cards, pausing for a fifth of a second after each card. This technique is useful when doing "card-flipping" animation:

```
on slowShow howManyCards
   repeat howManyCards times
      go to next card
      wait for 12 ticks
   end repeat
end slowShow
```

The *time* is a positive integer that gives the number of ticks or seconds to wait. One tick is a 60th of a second. If you don't specify which unit of time to use, **wait** assumes you're giving a number of ticks.

A *condition* is any expression that evaluates to either true or false.

HyperCard stops while waiting: While HyperCard is waiting, the user cannot perform any actions such as typing, drawing, or choosing menu items. However, you can click another application's window to bring it to the front during a **wait**.

The following handler prevents HyperCard from leaving the current card until all sounds have finished playing:

```
on closeCard
   wait until the sound is done
end closeCard
```

ALSO SEE

sound function

---

wideMargins property

Introduced in version 1.0

FORMS

set [the] wideMargins of *field* to {true|false}

```
set the wideMargins of field ID 234 to true
set the wideMargins of part nextPart to false -- only works for fields
if the wideMargins of me then add 6 to fieldHeight
```

ACTION

The **wideMargins** property reflects whether there's extra blank space at the edges of the specified field.

Setting the **wideMargins** is equivalent to toggling the Wide Margins checkbox in the Field Info dialog.

COMMENTS

HyperCard ordinarily leaves a border five pixels wide around the top and side edges of a field that uses 12-point Geneva. If the field's **wideMargins** is true, the margin is increased to nine pixels. You may want to use this property when creating a field with a handler:

```
on makeNewNote
   lock screen
   doMenu "New Field"
   set the name of last card field ¬
   to "Note:" && the short name of this card
   set the loc of last card field to the clickLoc
   set the style of last card field to shadow
   set the wideMargins of last card field to true
   unlock screen with visual effect iris open
   select text of last card field
end makeNewNote
```

The **wideMargins** property does not affect the mechanics of entering text into a field; its effect is purely aesthetic.

---

width property

Introduced in version 1.2
Last changed in version 2.2

FORMS

```
set [the] width of {part|button|field|card|window} to integer
the width of menubar
set the width of last card field to 22
set the width of card window to the width of message box
```

ACTION

The **width** property determines the distance in pixels between the left and right edges of an element.

COMMENTS

When you change the **width** of an element, that element's center stays where it was, and the left and right edges move toward or away from the center. If the new **width** is an odd number, the odd pixel is added to the right half of the element.

The *button*, *field*, or *card* is a descriptor of any button, field, or card in the current stack. Setting the **width** of a card changes the width of all cards in the current stack and is equivalent to changing the width in the Resize dialog (accessed from the Stack Info dialog).

A *window* can be a descriptor of any open stack window, HyperCard window, or external window. For some windows (such as the tool, scroll, pattern, and message windows), the **width** property is read-only and can't be changed.

The **width** of a stack window and the **width** of a card in that stack may be different if the window has been sized smaller than the card size (for example, using the Scroll command in the Go menu).

The *integer* is the horizontal distance in pixels from the left edge to the right edge of the element. The minimum **width** of a stack window is 64 pixels; if you specify a smaller *integer*, the card's width is set to 64. The **width** of stack windows must be a multiple of 32; if you specify an *integer* that's not a multiple of 32, the **width** is set to the next smallest multiple.

Hiding a part with the width: If you set the width of a button or field to zero or a negative number, that part disappears from the screen. It won't respond to mouse clicks, since it has no clickable area, but you can send messages to it using **send**. If it's a field, it remains in the tabbing order, and you can type into it and manipulate text selections. An object's **visible** property is unaffected by its **width**.

The width and rectangle properties: The **width** of an element is the difference between item 3 and item 1 of its **rectangle** property. Anything that resizes an element may change its **width** property.

Changes to HyperTalk: In versions of HyperCard before 2.2, you cannot describe a button or field with a part descriptor, and you cannot get the **width** of the menu bar.

In versions of HyperCard before 2.0, the size of the card window is fixed and cannot be changed.

ALSO SEE

location property; **rectangle** property; **left** property; **right** property; **titleWidth** property

---

windows function   Introduced in version 2.0

FORMS

```
the windows
windows()
answer the windows
if the short name of myStack is in the windows then beep
```

ACTION

The **windows** function returns a return-separated list of all open HyperCard windows, including hidden windows.

COMMENTS

You can use the **windows** function to determine whether a window is already open or not.

This is often important; for example, the **picture** command lets you open the same picture multiple times, so if a picture window is hidden you may not realize it already exists. The following example checks whether a picture is already open, and makes it visible (and brings it to the front) if it is:

```
on mouseUp
   put field "Picture Name" into thisPicture
   if thisPicture is in the windows then show thisPicture
   else picture thisPicture, file, document
end mouseUp
```

The list returned by **the windows** always includes the following windows. They may be hidden, but they are always open as long as HyperCard is running:

```
Message
Variable Watcher
Message Watcher
Scroll
FatBits
Patterns
Tools
```

The windows are listed in order from front to back, and, of course, floating palettes are listed before standard windows.

ALSO SEE
longWindowTitles property

---

write command

Introduced in version 1.0
Last changed in version 2.2

FORMS
write *text* **to file** *filePathname* **[at {***start***|end|eof}]**
write "Hello" to file "Hard Disk:Projects:New File"
write card field "Address" to file "Address Book"
write return & the long date to file thisFile at end
write infoChunk to file (line 3 of field "File Paths") at 220
write replacementVar to file theFile at -theLocation

ACTION
The **write** command puts data into a text file that was previously opened with the **open file** command.

COMMENTS
Use the commands **open file**, **close file**, **read**, and **write** when you want to import and export text between HyperCard and text files. Most applications that deal with text data—such as

word processors and databases—can export text files, so you can use a text file as an intermediate step in moving data from a stack into another application or vice versa.

The following handler writes the contents of every background field in the current card to a text file:

```
on writeThisCard toFilePath
  open file toFilePath
  repeat with nextField = 1 to the number of fields
    write field nextField to file toFilePath
  end repeat
  close file toFilePath
end writeThisCard
```

The *filePathname* is the full pathname of the file you want to write to. If you provide only a filename without a path, the **write** command assumes the file is in the same folder as the HyperCard application.

The *start* is an integer that specifies where in the file you want to start writing. If *start* is positive, the **write** command begins at the *start*h character of the file. If *start* is negative, HyperCard begins writing at the *start*h character before the end of the file. You can also use one of the constants `eof` or `end`. These constants are synonymous: they indicate the end of the file.

If you don't specify a *start*, **write** begins at the last character you read or wrote, or, if this is the first time you've written to the file since you opened it, at the beginning of the file.

Warning: If you write to any location other than the end of an existing file, **write** overwrites whatever is at the location you write to. If you open an existing file and then write to it immediately, **write** replaces the contents of the file.

Null characters: The null character (ASCII 0) cannot be handled by HyperTalk. If you want to write a null to a file, you'll need to use an XCMD written for this purpose.

Read-only files: If you try to write to a file that's read-only—for instance, a file on a locked disk—HyperTalk sets the **result** function to "File is open read-only."

Techie alert: Every Macintosh file consists of two parts: a data fork and a resource fork. (For some files, one of the forks may be empty.) The resource fork contains data of various types—sounds, icons, windows, menus, code, fonts, and so on—that is handled by the Resource Manager. The data fork holds an unstructured sequence of bytes, and is used by different programs for different things. While you can put resources into a stack's resource fork with impunity, HyperCard (along with many other programs) uses the data fork in its own mysterious way. The moral: While you can use the file commands to mess around with a stack's data fork, it is a Very Bad Idea to do so. For your safety and that of your data, use these commands *only* on text files.

Changes to HyperTalk: In versions before 2.2, you cannot start writing at a negative number—that is, you can't specify how far from the end of the file you want to start.

In versions before 2.0, you cannot specify where you want to start writing, and the end and eof constants don't exist. To write at the end of the file in these versions, read in the entire file. The file pointer is then set to the end of the file, and the next **write** command will place the new text at the end of the file:

```
on appendToBottom theText,theFilePath
  open file theFilePath
  repeat until it is empty
    read from file theFilePath for 16384 -- limitation in 1.x
  end repeat
  write theText to file theFilePath
  close file theFilePath
end appendToBottom
```

ALSO SEE

close file command; **open file** command; **write** command

---

zoom property

Introduced in version 2.0

FORMS

```
set [the] zoom of pictureWindow to {in|out}
set the zoom of window "Staff Snapshot" to out
```

ACTION

The **zoom** property determines whether a picture window is zoomed out or not. Setting the **zoom** to out centers the window on the current screen and expands it to its full size (or the size of the screen, whichever is smaller).

Changing the **zoom** property is equivalent to clicking the window's zoom box.

COMMENTS

The **zoom** of picture windows that don't have a zoom box, such as windows created with the rectangle or dialog styles, is empty. Setting the **zoom** of such windows doesn't cause an error, but it has no effect.

ALSO SEE

picture command; **rectangle** property; **zoomed** property

---

zoomed property

Introduced in version 2.2

FORMS

```
set [the] zoomed of card window to {true|false}
the zoomed of window
```

```
set the zoomed of card window to true -- zoom card window
get the zoomed of window "Another Stack"
```

ACTION

The **zoomed** property determines whether a window is zoomed out or not. When **zoomed** is true, a card window is at its full size and in the center of the screen.

Toggling the **zoomed** property is equivalent to clicking the window's zoom box.

COMMENTS

You can set the **zoomed** property only for the frontmost stack window; trying to set the **zoomed** of other stack windows doesn't cause a script error, but the command has no effect.

The **zoomed** of built-in windows that don't have a zoom box, such as the tool window, is always false.

ALSO SEE

zoomWindow message; **zoom** property

Part IV

Appendixes

Appendix A

ASCII Chart

The following chart shows the complete Macintosh character set for characters 0 through 255. The first half of the set, characters 0–127, comprise the standard set of ASCII characters. Characters 128–255 are Apple's extensions to the ASCII standard.

To produce all the characters in a given font (other than control characters, most of which aren't printable), use the following handler. We used this handler to produce the chart for this appendix:

```
fontTest "Courier",12 -- We used these parameters to get this chart

on fontTest fontName,fontSize
   put empty into card field "Font Test"
   set the textFont of card field "Font Test" to fontName
   if fontSize is not empty
   then set the textSize of card field "Font Test" to fontSize
   repeat with charNum = 32 to 255
     set cursor to busy
     put numToChar(charNum) into thisChar
     put charNum & ":" && thisChar & return after card field "Font Test"
   end repeat
   set the scroll of card field "Font Test" to zero
end fontTest
```

0	NULL	46	.	92	\
1	SOH	47	/	93	]
2	STX	48	0	94	^
3	ETX	49	1	95	_
4	EOT	50	2	96	`
5	ENQ	51	3	97	a
6	ACK	52	4	98	b
7	bell	53	5	99	c
8	backspace	54	6	100	d
9	horizontal tab	55	7	101	e
10	linefeed	56	8	102	f
11	vertical tab	57	9	103	g
12	formfeed	58	:	104	h
13	return	59	;	105	i
14	shift out	60	<	106	j
15	shift in	61	=	107	k
16	DLE	62	>	108	l
17	DC1	63	?	109	m
18	DC2	64	@	110	n
19	DC3	65	A	111	o
20	DC4	66	B	112	p
21	NAK	67	C	113	q
22	SYN	68	D	114	r
23	ETB	69	E	115	s
24	CAN	70	F	116	t
25	EM	71	G	117	u
26	SUB	72	H	118	v
27	escape	73	I	119	w
28	FS	74	J	120	x
29	GS	75	K	121	y
30	RS	76	L	122	z
31	US	77	M	123	{
32	space	78	N	124		
33	!	79	O	125	}
34	"	80	P	126	~
35	#	81	Q	127	delete
36	$	82	R	128	Ä
37	%	83	S	129	Å
38	&	84	T	130	Ç
39	'	85	U	131	É
40	(	86	V	132	Ñ
41	)	87	W	133	Ö
42	*	88	X	134	Ü
43	+	89	Y	135	á
44	,	90	Z	136	à
45	-	91	[	137	â

138	ä		178	≤		218	/
139	ã		179	≥		219	¤
140	å		180	¥		220	‹
141	ç		181	µ		221	›
142	é		182	∂		222	fi
143	è		183	Σ		223	fl
144	ê		184	Π		224	‡
145	ë		185	π		225	·
146	í		186	∫		226	,
147	ì		187	ª		227	„
148	î		188	º		228	‰
149	ï		189	Ω		229	Â
150	ñ		190	æ		230	Ê
151	ó		191	ø		231	Á
152	ò		192	¿		232	Ë
153	ô		193	¡		233	È
154	ö		194	¬		234	Í
155	õ		195	√		235	Î
156	ú		196	ƒ		236	Ï
157	ù		197	≈		237	Ì
158	û		198	Δ		238	Ó
159	ü		199	«		239	Ô
160	†		200	»		240	
161	°		201	…		241	Ò
162	¢		202	option-space		242	Ú
163	£		203	À		243	Û
164	§		204	Ã		244	Ù
165	•		205	Õ		245	ı
166	¶		206	Œ		246	ˆ
167	ß		207	œ		247	˜
168	®		208	–		248	¯
169	©		209	—		249	˘
170	™		210	"		250	˙
171	´		211	"		251	˚
172	¨		212	'		252	¸
173	≠		213	'		253	˝
174	Æ		214	÷		254	˛
175	Ø		215	◊		255	ˇ
176	∞		216	ÿ			
177	±		217	Ÿ			

Appendix B

Boundaries and Limits

This appendix lists HyperTalk's various boundary conditions and size limitations.

Maximum stack size: **512 megabytes**
   (A bug in versions before 1.2.5 causes stacks above 8 megabytes to become corrupted.)
Minimum stack size: **4,096 bytes**
Maximum number of cards, background, and bitmaps (total) per stack: **16,777,216**
Maximum stack name length: **31 characters**
Maximum total number of resources in a single stack: **2727**

Minimum window/card size: **64 × 64 pixels**
Maximum window/card size: **1280 × 1280 pixels**
Maximum number of open stacks: **16**

Maximum possible card picture size (for a 512 × 342 card): **44K**
Maximum possible background picture size (for a 512 × 342 card): **22K**
Maximum number of buttons & fields per card or background: **32,767**
   (A bug in versions before 1.2.2 allows only 127 fields per card.)
Maximum field length: **29,996 characters**
Maximum card, background, field or button name length: **255 characters**
   (A bug in versions through 1.2.2 allows only 29 characters to be used in object references.)
Minimum overhead for each card and background: **64 bytes**
Minimum overhead for each button and field: **30 bytes**
Note: The current card and background must fit into available memory for a card to be displayed.

Maximum script length: **30,000 characters**
Maximum length of a command line: **254 characters**
Maximum number of nested repeats: **32**

Maximum number of variables: **unlimited**
Maximum variable value size: **limited only by available memory**
Maximum variable name length: **31 characters**
Maximum handler name length: **254 characters**

Appendix C

HyperTalk Error Messages

HyperTalk version 2.2 has over 140 error dialogs. This appendix lists each error message.
Where the reason for the error is not obvious, an explanation is also given. HyperTalk uses
*the error strings listed below as parameters to the **errorDialog** system message.*

Compile-Time Errors and Runtime Errors

A compile-time error is a script problem that prevents HyperCard from compiling the script—for example, a **repeat** statement with no matching **end repeat**. Compilation error dialogs have two buttons (see Figure C.1).

A runtime error is a script problem that doesn't prevent HyperCard from compiling the script, but prevents it from running—for example, a reference to a nonexistent object. Runtime error dialogs have an additional Debug button which lets you enter the debugger at the error point (see Figure C.2).

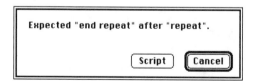

Figure C.1   Compile-time error dialog

Figure C-2   Runtime error dialog

Error Strings

"On" can appear only once per handler.

"*fileName*" is not an application.

> You used the **open** or **print** command with a file that is not an application.

number is not a valid family number.

> You specified a family number that's not between 1 and 15.

sortExpr was not a valid expression for any card.

> You tried to sort by an expression that didn't make sense for any card in the stack. You probably mistyped a field name or made some other simple error.

Already have a local variable named *variableName*.

> HyperCard has encountered a variable named *variableName* in a global statement that has already been used as a local variable in the same handler. The code that produces this error might look like this:
>
> ```
> put 22 into foo
> global foo
> ```

Already have a menu named *menuName*.

> You tried to create a menu with the same name as one that's already in the menu bar. (HyperCard's paint menus are there even when the current tool isn't a paint tool, so you can't create a menu named Paint, Options, or Patterns unless you use the **delete menu** command to get rid of the built-in one first.)

Can have "else" only after "then".

> See the **if...then...else** keyword.

Can have "then" only after "if".

> See the **if...then...else** keyword.

Can't access fields or buttons in other stacks. Use "go".

Can't close that window.

Can't create that file.

> There was a problem with the **create stack**, **export paint**, or **open file** command that prevented file creation. One common cause is that the name is invalid. Macintosh filenames can have up to 31 characters, cannot contain any colons (:), and (for files you create in HyperCard) cannot start with a period(.).

Can't DIV by zero.

Can't duplicate stack.

Can't edit script of HyperCard.

Can't find *object*.

Can't find a translator for that language.

> To set the **language** property to anything other than English, you need to have a translator resource located in the resource fork of HyperCard, the Home stack, the current stack, or a stack in use. See the **language** property and Appendix E, "The Translator Interface."

Can't find icon named *iconName*.

> You tried to set a button's icon to one that's not in the current resource path.

Can't find menu item "*itemName*".

Can't find that icon.

> You tried to set a button's icon to one that's not in the current resource path.

Can't get scroll of that window.

Can't get that property.

Can't have "end" here.

Can't have more than 16 parameters for an external command.

Can't load that external.

> HyperCard couldn't find an XCMD or XFCN you called for. Externals must reside in the resource fork of the current stack, a stack in use, the Home stack, HyperCard itself, or the System file.

Can't load that translator.

> HyperCard couldn't find a translator resource you called for by setting the **language** property. Translators must reside in the resource fork of the current stack, a stack in use, the Home stack, HyperCard itself, or the System file.

Can't MOD by zero.

Can't modify that menu.

> HyperCard doesn't let you make changes to the Apple, Tools, Patterns, or Font menu, although you can delete any of these menus from the menu bar.

Can't modify this stack.

> The stack's **cantModify** property is set to true.

Can't open any more files.

> HyperCard limits you to three open text files at one time.

Can't open stack

Can't open stack's resource fork.

`Can't open the Message Watcher named` *XCMDName*.

HyperCard couldn't find an alternative message watcher resource you called for by setting the **messageWatcher** property. Message watchers must reside in the resource fork of the current stack, a stack in use, the Home stack, HyperCard itself, or the System file.

`Can't open the Variable Watcher named` *XCMDName*.

HyperCard couldn't find an alternative variable watcher resource you called for by setting the **variableWatcher** property. Variable watchers must reside in the resource fork of the current stack, a stack in use, the Home stack, HyperCard itself, or the System file.

`Can't set properties of that object.`

`Can't set rectangle of that window.`

`Can't set scroll of that window.`

The window is a nonscrolling one (for example, the message box).

`Can't set that property.`

`Can't set that` *object* `property.`

`Can't start using home.`

The Home stack is always in the message-passing path, so you can't use **start using** to put it in the path.

`Can't start using that stack.`

`Can't take the value of that expression.`

`Can't understand "`*commandName*`".`

You used a custom message (that is, a message that's not built in to HyperTalk as a command or function), and no handler trapped it before it reached HyperCard on the message-passing path.

`Can't understand arguments of "`*statement*`".`

`Can't understand arguments to this function.`

`Can't understand arguments to this keyword.`

`Can't understand that message.`

`Can't understand this.`

`Can't use null characters in names.`

HyperTalk cannot use the null character, ASCII 0.

`Couldn't create stack.`

`Couldn't edit script of that object.`

`Couldn't export paint.`

Couldn't import paint.

Couldn't load external command.

Couldn't open that application.

Couldn't send to that window.

Couldn't set that field.

Destination does not contain a number.

>The **add**, **subtract**, **multiply**, and **divide** commands require that their second parameter, which is a container, contain a number.

Don't know how to tell if something is a *dataType*.

>You specified an invalid data type with the **is a** operator.

Error writing to file "*fileName*".

Expected ")" but found "*somethingElse*".

Expected ")".

Expected "end if" after "else".
Expected "end if" after "if".
Expected "end if" after "then".

>See the **if...then...else** keyword.

Expected "end repeat" after "repeat".

Expected "end *keyword*"

Expected "end" after "on".

Expected "of" after this function.

Expected "true" or "false" here but found *somethingElse*.

Expected a button here but found a field.

Expected a button or field here.

Expected a field here but found a button.

Expected a number between 1 and 255 here.

>The **numToChar** function requires a number in the range of Apple's extended ASCII. See Appendix A, "ASCII Chart."

Expected a point but found *somethingElse*.

>A point consists of two integers separated by a comma.

Expected a rectangle but found *somethingElse*.

>A rectangle consists of four items separated by commas.

Expected a single character here.

Expected a variable name but found *somethingElse*

Expected end of line after "end if".

Expected end of line after "end repeat".

Expected stack here.

Expression too complicated.

Extra statements after end of handler.

Failed to sort this stack.

Fields and buttons can't hold more than 30000 characters.

File "*fileName*" is already open.

> You tried to use **open file** to open a file that was already open.

File not open.

> You tried to use **read** or **write** to on a file that hasn't been opened with the **open file** command.

Found "exit repeat" outside a repeat loop.

Found "next repeat" outside a repeat loop.

Got error *errorNumber* while trying to open file "*fileName*".

Got file system error *errorNumber*.

Handler too long.

Invalid date.

> You passed the **convert** command a date in a format it doesn't recognize.

Invalid expression.

Menus don't have that property.

No current Apple® event.

> You used the **reply** or **request appleEvent** command when HyperCard didn't have an AppleEvent pending.

No such bkgnd.

No such button or field.

No such card or bkgnd.

No such card.

No such menu item.

No such menu.

No such program.

No such stack.

No such window.

Not a scrolling field.

>   You cannot set the **scroll** of a field unless its style is scrolling.

Not enough memory to read from file.

Not enough memory to sort this stack.

Not handled by target program.

>   You sent an AppleEvent to a program that can't handle that event. See the **send to program** keyword.

Not supported by this version of the system.

>   You're running System 6.x, and you tried to use a language element (like an element that deals with AppleEvents) that requires System 7.

Number of menu messages must be equal to number of menu items.

>   You used the **put into menu** command to add menu items along with their messages, but you sopecified more (or fewer) messages than items.

Old translator failed on quit.

>   The previously installed translator didn't return a successful result code when you replaced it with another. (See the **language** property and Appendix E.)

Only cards and backgrounds have pictures.

Only fields, buttons, cards, and backgrounds have numbers.

Only start and stop using can change the stacksInUse.

>   You tried to change the **stacksInUse** property, which is read-only.

Out of memory.

Script too silly to execute.

>   HyperTalk looked at a script and decided it couldn't in good conscience execute this code.

Sort by what?

>   You issued a **sort** command that didn't include a sort key.

Stack not in use.

>   You tried to **stop using** a stack that wasn't in use. (See the **stacksInUse** property.)

String too long.

That button or field has been deleted.

That *element* name is too long.

The translator failed to translate that script into English.

> The installed translator didn't return a successful result code when called. (See the **language** property and Appendix E.)

There is no card family *familyNumber*.

There is no background family *familyNumber*.

There is no card *object* id *idNumber*.

There is no background *object* id *idNumber*.

There is no card *object* named *name*.

There is no background *object* named *name*.

There is no card *object* number *number*.

There is no background *object* number *number*.

There isn't any selection.

> You referred to the selection when no text was selected.

Too many "exit repeat"s.

Too many menus with messages.

Too many nested blocks.

Too many nested repeats.

Too many pending messages.

Too many responses.

Too many stacks in use.

> You can put up to 16 stacks in use.

Too many types.

Too many windows open.

Too much recursion.

> There are too many handler calls pending and they will soon overflow HyperCard's memory stack.

Translator failed to indent.

> The installed translator is capable of indenting scripts, but when HyperCard asked it to indent it didn't return a successful result code. (See the **language** property and Appendix E.)

`Translator failed to initialize itself.`

The installed translator didn't return a successful result code when called. (See the **language** property and Appendix E.)

`Translator failed to translate indent strings.`

The installed translator didn't return a successful result code. (See the **language** property and Appendix E.)

`Translator failed to translate the message box into English.`

The installed translator didn't return a successful result code. (See the **language** property and Appendix E.)

`User level is too low to edit scripts.`

The **userLevel** must be at least 5 to use the **edit** command.

Appendix D

Formal Syntax Description

This appendix presents the syntax of HyperTalk for version 2.2 and version 1.2.5. You'll find this appendix especially valuable if you're an advanced scripter who wants a more formal and precise presentation of the syntax than appears within the context of individual vocabulary words, or if you're an experienced programmer who likes BNF formats.

Don't be alarmed

This appendix presents in a formal way the complete and precise syntax of every vocabulary word. It is valuable both in its own right and as the ultimate resource for settling bets at cocktail parties.

It isn't necessary to totally grasp, or even read, all the information in this appendix to use HyperTalk well. It is, however, the Final Word.

Syntax Symbols

The following is a list of syntactic symbols and terms you must know for the rest of this appendix to make sense.

SPECIAL SYMBOLS

< > Angle brackets enclose a general term (as in <card>). This ***nonterminal*** (as the general term is formally called) is replaced by a specific instance of that term. For example, in the syntactic statement go <card>, you can replace <card> with any valid form of a card reference—go card 7, go back, and so on. The next section, "Syntactic Terms," is a complete list of all the non-obvious terms that might appear within angle brackets.

651

| A vertical bar separates mutually exclusive options. For example, the syntactic statement go { help | home | back } means that it's legal to say go help or go home or go back (but you can't say go help home or go home back).

[ ] Square brackets enclose optional elements that you can use or ignore. For example, the syntactic statement go [to] <card> means that legal forms for the **go** command include go <card> and go to <card>.

{ } Curly braces enclose a group of related terms. Curly braces are often used to indicate precedence of consideration. For example, part of the syntax for backgrounds is background {id <unsigned> | <endLine> | <expr> | <token>}. The braces indicate that HyperCard first looks for the word ID (to indicate an ID number); if it can't find one, it looks to see if the next character after the word background is an end-of-line marker; and so it goes.

@ The At sign (used only in the formal syntax definition of HyperTalk 1.2) means that the syntax treats expressions as expandable—an expression that yields text in the proper syntactical form is as acceptable as text that already appears in the proper syntactical form. (An expression is any value or any group of values, sources of value, and operators meant to be taken as a single whole.)

For example, the formal syntax for the **click** command is

```
click at {<integer>, <integer>}@
```

The following statement already appears in the proper syntactical form:

```
click at 100, 300
```

The statement

```
click at field 1
```

also works if field 1 contains a value that matches the required syntax for **click**—a pair of integers separated by a comma.

If @ appears before the phrase, HyperTalk tries to evaluate the phrase as an expression before it tries to evaluate the phrase as a literal (that is, a group of characters to be taken for their actual face value). This process applies only to stacks. If @ appears after the phrase (as it does in the example), HyperTalk tries to evaluate the phrase as a literal before it tries to evaluate the phrase as an expression.

SYNTACTIC TERMS

<bkgnd> is any valid background reference.

<button> is any valid button reference.

<card> is any valid card reference.

<empty> is the null string.

<endLine> is the end of line character (which is ASCII 13).

<expr> is any expression—value, source of value, or group of values—meant to be resolved and taken as a single value. Expressions are covered in detail in Chapter 9.

<factor> is the first fully resolvable portion of an expression. Factors are covered in detail in Chapter 9.

<field> is any valid field reference.

<line> is everything remaining in a line up to the end of the line or a comment.

<numericFactor> is a factor that can be converted to a number.

<object> is any object.

<ordinal> is one of the ordinal numbers first through tenth, plus the special ordinals last, middle (or mid), and any. (If the something that middle is in has an even number of units, then middle moves toward the high end. So the middle of 6 is 4.)

<return> is the return character, entered by pressing the Return key or appended within a script by the vocabulary word **return** or the expression numToChar(13).

<stack> is any valid stack reference.

<token> is a single word without quotation marks meant to be taken literally.

<unsigned> is any expression that can be converted to an integer whose value is zero or greater.

The adjectives this, prev, and next refer only to cards and backgrounds in the current stack.

All words that are not within angle brackets must appear in a reference exactly as they appear in the given syntax examples. So in the phrase <ordinal> card the word ordinal is replaced with one of the ordinal numbers (first, second, third...), but the word card (or its legal synonym cd) must appear as in the example.

SYNONYMS

Here's a list of legal synonyms for objects, tools, and containers:

bg	bkgnd	background
bgs	bkgnds	backgrounds
button	btn	
buttons	btns	
card	cd	
cards	cds	
char	character	
chars	characters	
commandChar	cmdChar	
fields	flds	
fld	field	

```
gray                    grey
menuMessage             menuMsg
msg                     message
pict                    picture
poly                    polygon
prev                    previous
reg                     regular
```

So, for example, wherever you see syntax that uses the word "bg", you could also use either "background" or "bkgnd" and get the same results.

Formal Syntax of HyperTalk version 1.2.5

This section describes the One True Syntax for the HyperTalk scripting language on the Macintosh, HyperCard versions through 1.2.5. It shows precisely what's allowed in every construct. It uses the syntax symbols listed in the first section of this appendix.

SCRIPTS

```
<script> = <script> <handler> | <handler>

<handler> =
   on <messageKey> <return>
      <stmntList>
   end <messageKey> <return>

<stmntList> = <stmnt> | <stmntList> <stmnt>

<stmnt> = {<messageSend> | <keywordStmnt> | <empty>} <return>

<keywordStmnt> =
   do <expr> |
   exit repeat | exit <messageKey> | exit to HyperCard |
   global <identList> |
   next repeat |
   pass <messageKey> |
   return <expr> |
   send {<expr> | <token>} [ to <object> ] |
   <ifBlock> | <repeatBlock>

<ifBlock> =
   if <logical> [ <return> ] then {<singleThen> | <return> <multiThen>}

<singleThen> = <stmnt> [ [<return>] <elseBlock> ]

<multiThen> = <stmntList> { end if | <elseBlock>}
```

```
<elseBlock> = else {<stmnt> | <return> <stmntList> end if}

<repeatBlock> =
   repeat [forever | <duration> | <count> | with <identifier> = <range>] <return>
      <stmntList>
   end repeat

<duration> = until <logical> | while <logical>
<count> = [ for ] <unsigned> [ times ]
<range> = <integer> [ down ] to <integer>
```

EXPRESSIONS

```
<expr> = <source> | - <factor> | not <factor> | <expr> <op> <expr> |
   (<expr>) | <chunk> <factor>

<op> =
   + | - | * | / | & | && | ^ | = | < | > | <> | ≠ |
   <= | >= | ≤ | ≥ | and | or | contains | div | mod |
   is | is not | is in | is not in | is within | is not within

<source> =
   <literal> | <constant> | <simpleContainer> |
   [ <adjective> ] <function> |
   [ <adjective> ] <property> of {<object> | <window>}

<literal> = "quoted string"

<constant> =
   down | empty | false | formFeed | lineFeed |
   pi | quote | space | tab | true | up   |
   zero | one | two | three | four | five |
   six | seven | eight | nine | ten

<adjective> = long | short | abbrev | abbr | abbreviated

<function> = the <theFunc> | [ the ] <theFunc> of <oneFuncArg> |
   <identifier> ( <funcArgs> )

<theFunc> =
   abs | annuity | atan | average | charToNum | clickH | clickLoc |
   clickV | commandKey | cmdKey | compound | cos | date | diskSpace |
   exp | exp1 | exp2 | foundChunk | foundField | foundLine |
```

```
foundText | heapSpace | length | ln | ln1 | log2 | mouse |
mouseClick | mouseH | mouseLoc | mouseV | number |
numToChar | offset | optionKey | param | paramCount | params |
random | result | round | screenRect | seconds |
selectedChunk | selectedField | selectedLine | selectedText |
shiftKey | sin | sound | sqrt | stackspace | tan | target |
ticks | time | tool | trunc | value
```

Syntax for each individual function appears in the "Functions" section.

```
<property> =
    autoHilite | autoTab | blindTyping | botRight | bottom |
    bottomRight | brush | cantDelete | cantModify | centered |
    cursor | dragSpeed | editBkgnd | filled | freeSize | grid |
    height | highlight | highlite | hilight | hilite | icon |
    id | language | left | lineSize | loc | location |
    lockMessages | lockRecent | lockScreen | lockText |
    multiple | multiSpace | name | numberFormat | pattern |
    polySides | powerKeys | rect | rectangle | right |
    script | scroll | showLines | showName | showPict |
    size | style | textAlign | textArrows | textFont |
    textHeight | textSize | textStyle | top | topLeft |
    userLevel | userModify | version | visible | wideMargins | width
```

Syntax for each individual property appears at the end of the "Commands" section, in the notes about the **set** command.

OBJECTS

```
<object> =
    {HyperCard | me | [ the ] target | <button> | <field> |
    <card> | <bkgnd>}@ | <stack>
```

Note: "card field 1" is a field and "card (field 1)" is a card.

```
<button> =
    {button id <unsignedFactor> | button {<factor> | <token>} |
    <ordinal> button} [ of <card> ]
```

```
<field> =
    {field id <unsignedFactor> | field {<factor> | <token>} |
    <ordinal> field} [ of <card> ]
```

```
<part> = <button> | <field>
```

```
<ordinal> =
   last | mid | middle | any |
   first | second | third | fourth | fifth |
   sixth | seventh | eigth | ninth | tenth

<card> =
   recent card | back | forth |
   {card id <unsigned> | card {<expr> | <token>} |
   card <endLine> | <ordinal> card | <position> card} [ of <bkgnd> ]

<position> = this | prev | next


<bkgnd> =
   bkgnd id <unsigned> | bkgnd {<expr> | <token>} | bkgnd <endLine> |
   <ordinal> bkgnd | <position> bkgnd

<stack> = {this stack | stack {<expr> | <line>} | stack <endLine>}@ |
   {@{<expr> | <line>}}
```

CONTAINERS

```
<simpleContainer> = <variable> | <field> | <messageBox> | [ the ] selection

<container> = <chunk> <simpleContainer> | <simpleContainer>

<messageBox> = [ the ] msg [ box | window ]


<chunk> =
   [{<ordinal> char | char <expr> [ to <expr> ]} of]
   [{<ordinal> word | word <expr> [ to <expr> ]} of]
   [{<ordinal> item | item <expr> [ to <expr> ]} of]
   [{<ordinal> line | line <expr> [ to <expr> ]} of]
```

COMMANDS

Command Nonterminals

These nonterminals appear in the command syntax that follows.

```
<dateItems> =
   <unsigned>,<unsigned>,<unsigned>,<unsigned>,<unsigned>,<unsigned>,
   <unsigned>
```

```
<date> =
   <unsigned> | <dateItems>
   <humanDate> [ <humanTime> ] |
   <humanTime> [ <humanDate> ]

<dateFormat> = [ <adjective> ] {seconds | dateItems | date | time}

<dayOfWeek> =
   Sunday | Sun | Monday | Mon | Tuesday | Tue | Wednesday |
   Wed | Thursday | Thu | Friday | Fri | Saturday | Sat

<dest> =
   {{<card> | <bkgnd>} [ of <stack> ]}@ | <stack>

<duration> = until <logical> | while <logical>

<humanDate> =
   [ <dayOfWeek> , ] <month> <unsigned> , <unsigned> |
   <unsignedFactor> {/ | -} <unsignedFactor> {/ | -} <unsignedFactor>

<humanTime> =
   <unsigned> : <unsigned> [ : <unsigned> ] [ am | pm ]

<month> =
   January | Jan | February | Feb | March | Mar |
   April | Apr | May | June | Jun | July | Jul |
   August | Aug | September | Sep | October | Oct |
   November | Nov | December | Dec

<point> = {<integer> , <integer>}@

<preposition> = before | after | into

<rect> = {<integer> , <integer> , integer> , <integer>}@

<springKeys> = <springKeys> , <springKey> | <springKey>

<springKey> = shiftKey | optionKey | commandKey

<style> =
   {transparent | opaque | rectangle | roundrect |
   shadow | checkBox | radioButton | scrolling}@

<textAlign> = {right | left | center}@

<textStyleList> = <textStyleList> <textStyle> | <textStyle>
```

```
<textStyle> =
   {plain | bold | italic | underline | outline |
   shadow |condense | extend}@

<visEffect> = <visKind> [ [ very ] {slow | slowly | fast} ] [ to <visSrc> ]

<visKind> =
   barn door {open | close} |
   cut | plain | dissolve | venetian blinds | checkerboard |
   iris {open | close} |
   scroll {left | right | up | down} |
   wipe {left | right | up | down} |
   zoom {open | out | close | in }

<visSrc> = card | black | white | gray | inverse

<window> = {card | pattern | tool} window | <messageBox>
```

Commands

```
add
   <arith> to <container>
answer
   {<expr> | <token>} [with {<factor> | <token>} [or {<factor> |
   <token>} [or {<factor> | <token>} ]]]
arrowkey
   left | right | up | down
ask
   [ password ] {<expr> | <token>} [ with {<expr> | <line>} ]
beep
   [<unsigned>]
choose
   {tool <unsigned>}@ |
   {browse | button | field | select | lasso | pencil |
   brush | eraser | line | spray [ can ] | rect |
   round rect | bucket | oval | curve | text |
   reg poly | poly} tool}@
click
   at <point> [ with <springKeys> ]
close
   file {<expr> | <line>} | printing
controlkey
   <unsigned>
convert
   {<container> | <date>} to <dateFormat> [ and <dateFormat> ]
```

```
debug
   {<expr> | <line>}
delete
   {<chunk> <simpleContainer>}@
dial
   <expr> [ with modem | with [ modem ] <expr> ]
divide
   <container> by <float>
domenu
   <expr> | <line>
drag
   from <point> to <point> [ with <springKeys> ]
edit
   [ the ] script of <object>
enterInField
enterkey
find
   [ whole | string | words | word | chars | normal ]
   {<expr> | <token>} [ in <field> ]
functionkey
   <unsigned>
get
   <expr> | [ the ] <property> [ of <object> ]
go
   [ to ] {{<ordinal> | <position>} <endLine> | <dest>}
help
hide
   menuBar | picture of {<object>}@ |
   { card | bkgnd } picture | <window> | {<part>}@
lock
   screen
multiply
   <container> by <arith>
open
   printing [ with dialog ] |
   file {<expr> | <line>} |
   {<expr> | <token>} [ with {<expr> | <line>} ] |
   <expr> | <line>
play
   stop | {<expr> | <token>} [ [ tempo <unsigned> ] {<expr> | <line>} ]
pop
   card [ <preposition> <container> ]
print
   {<expr> | <token>} with {<expr> | <line>} |
   <unsigned> cards | all cards | <card>
push
   <dest>
```

```
put
   {<expr> | <token>} [ <preposition> <container> ]
read
   from file {<expr> | <token>} {until {<expr> | <token>} | for <unsigned>}
reset
   paint
returnInField
returnkey
select
   {[ before | after ] {{text of | <chunk> } { <field> | <message>}@}@} |
   {<part>}@ | <emptyExpr>
set
   [ the ] <property> [ of {<window> | <object>} ] to <propVal>
```
(See notes on **set**, below.)
```
show
   menuBar | picture of {<object>}@ |
   { card | bkgnd } picture |
   {<window> | {<part>}@} [ at <point> ] |
   [ all | <unsigned> ] cards
sort
   [ ascending | descending ]
   [ text | numeric | international | dateTime ]
     by <expr>
subtract
   <arith> from <container>
tabkey
type
   <expr> [ with <springKeys> ]
unlock
   screen [ with {[ visual [ effect ]] <visEffect>}@ ]
visual
   [ effect ] <visEffect>
wait
   <duration> | <count> [ ticks | tick | seconds | second | sec ]
write
   <expr> to file {<expr> | <line>}
```

The following syntax refers only to the **set** command. The general syntax for **set** is:

```
   [ the ] <property> [ of {<window> | <object>} ] to <propVal>

<propVal> =
   {<expr> | <line>} | <integer> | <unsigned> | <logical> |
   <point> | <rect> | <style> | <textAlign> | <textStyleList>
```

Set has a different syntax for different groups of properties. The following list shows which nonterminals apply to which properties:

```
{<expr> | <line>}
   name,textFont,icon,script,language,cursor,numberFormat
<integer>
   top,bottom,left,right,width,height
<unsigned>
   textHeight,textSize,lineSize,pattern,brush,polySides,
   multiSpace,userLevel,dragSpeed,scroll
<logical>
   freeSize,showName,lockText,showLines,wideMargins,visible,
   powerKeys,grid,filled,centered,multiple,editBkgnd,hilite,
   lockScreen,lockRecent,autoHilite,blindTyping,lockMessages,
   textArrows,showPict,cantDelete,cantModify,autoTab,userModify
<point>
   loc,topLeft,botRight
<rect>
   rect
<style>
   style
<textAlign>
   textAlign
<textStyleList>
   textStyle
```

FUNCTIONS

Note that `<funcArith>`, `<funcFloat>`, `<funcExpr>`, and `<funcUnsigned>` all take expressions when they're called with parentheses, but they all take factors when they're called with "of".

```
abs
   <funcArith>
annuity
   <float> , <float>
atan
   <funcFloat>
average
   {<arithList>}@
chartonum
   <funcExpr>
clickh
clickloc
clickv
commandkey
```

```
compound
   <float> , <float>
cos
   <funcFloat>
date
diskspace
exp
   <funcFloat>
exp1
   <funcFloat>
exp2
   <funcFloat>
foundChunk
foundField
foundLine
foundText
heapspace
length
   <funcExpr>
ln
   <funcFloat>
ln1
   <funcFloat>
log2
   <funcFloat>
max
   {<arithList>}@
min
   {<arithList>}@
mouse
mouseclick
mouseh
mouseloc
mousev
number
   cards [ in <bkgnd> ] |  bkgnds |
   [ card | bkgnd ] {buttons | fields} |
   {chars | words | items | lines} in <funcExpr> |
   <object>
numtochar
   <funcUnsigned>
offset
   <string> , <string>
optionkey
param
   <funcUnsigned>
paramcount
```

```
params
random
   <funcUnsigned>
result
round
   <funcFloat>
screenrect
seconds
selectedChunk
selectedField
selectedLine
selectedText
shiftkey
sin
   <funcFloat>
sound
sqrt
   <funcFloat>
stackspace
tan
   <funcFloat>
target
ticks
time
tool
trunc
   <funcFloat>
value
   <funcExpr>
```

Formal Syntax of HyperTalk Version 2.2

This section describes the One True Syntax for the HyperTalk scripting language on the Macintosh, HyperCard version 2.2. It shows precisely what's allowed in every construct. It uses the syntax symbols listed in the first section of this appendix.

HyperTalk 2.x syntax is much simpler than the syntax of earlier versions, making it closer to natural language. It allows automatic expansion (designated in the 1.x syntax by the @ sign) throughout the language: HyperTalk 2.x accepts an expression in place of any nonterminal or any sublist (items enclosed in square brackets or curly braces). It allows unquoted tokens everywhere, and the use of the ancillary "the" is allowed in more cases.

These new freedoms have a minor cost. In previous versions of HyperTalk, "in" and "of" were lexically equivalent. In HyperTalk 2.x, there are two places where they're not:

- When you use `find` *expr* `in field` (indicated by the nonterminal `<inOnly>`)

- When you refer to properties—for example, `the name of card 1` (indicated by the nonterminal `<ofOnly>`)

This restriction does not hold in versions before 2.0 because they are fully interpreted, and thus have information not available to a compiler that lets them handle these cases properly.

SCRIPTS

```
<script> = <script> <handler> | <handler>

<handler> =
   on <messageKey> <return>
      <stmntList>
   end <messageKey> <return>

<stmntList> = <stmnt> | <stmntList> <stmnt>

<stmnt> = {<messageSend> | <keywordStmnt> | <empty>} <return>

<keywordStmnt> =
   do <expr> |
   exit repeat | exit <messageKey> | exit to HyperCard |
   global <identList> |
   next repeat |
   pass <messageKey> |
   return <expr> |
   send <expr> [ to {<object> | window <expr>} | program <expr>] |
   <ifBlock> | <repeatBlock>

<ifBlock> =
   if <logical> [ <return> ] then {<singleThen> | <return> <multiThen>}

<singleThen> = <stmnt> [ [<return>] <elseBlock> ]

<multiThen> = <stmntList> { end if | <elseBlock>}

<elseBlock> = else {<stmnt> | <return> <stmntList> end if}

<repeatBlock> =
   repeat [ forever | <duration> | <count> | with <identifier> = <range> ] <return>
      <stmntList>
   end repeat

<duration> = until <logical> | while <logical>
<count> = [ for ] <unsigned> [ times ]
<range> = <integer> [ down ] to <integer>
```

EXPRESSIONS

```
<expr> = <source> | - <expr> | not <expr> | <expr> <op> <expr> |
   ( <expr> ) | <chunk> <expr> | there is { a | an | no } <expr>

<op> =
   + | - | * | / | & | && | ^ | = | < | > | <> | ≠ |
   <= | >= | ≤ | ≥ | and | or | contains | div | mod |
   is | is not | is in | is not in | is within | is not within |
   is a[n] | is not a[n]

<source> =
   <literal> | <constant> | <simpleContainer> |
   [ <adjective> ] <function> |
   [ <adjective> ] <property> of {<object> | <window> |
   <menuItem> of <menu> | <chunk> <field> }

<literal> = "quoted string" | unquotedToken

<constant> =
   down | empty | false | formFeed | lineFeed |
   pi | quote | space | tab | true | up   |
   zero | one | two | three | four | five |
   six | seven | eight | nine | ten

<adjective> = long | short | abbrev | abbr | abbreviated

<window> = [the] {card | pattern | tool | scroll } window | <messageBox>

<menuItem> = <ordinal> menuItem | menuItem <expr>
<menu> = <ordinal> menu | menu <expr>

<function> = the <theFunc> | [ the ] <theFunc> of <oneFuncArg> |
<identifier> ( <funcArgs> )

<theFunc> =
   abs | annuity | atan | average | charToNum | clickChunk | clickH |
   clickLine | clickLoc | clickText | clickV | cmdKey | commandKey |
   compound | cos | date | destination | diskSpace | exp | exp1 | exp2 | foundChunk |
   foundField | foundLine | foundText | heapSpace | length | ln | ln1 |
   log2 | max | menus | min | mouse | mouseClick | mouseH | mouseLoc |
   mouseV | number | numToChar | offset | optionKey | param |
   paramCount | params | programs | random | result | round |
   screenRect | seconds | selectedButton | selectedChunk |
   selectedField | selectedLine | selectedLoc | selectedText |
   shiftKey | sin | sound | sqrt | stacks | stackSpace | sum |
```

```
systemVersion | tan | target | ticks | time | tool | trunc |
value | windows
```

Syntax for each individual function appears later in the "Functions" section.

```
<property> =
    address | autoHilite | autoSelect | autoTab | blindTyping |
    botRight | bottom | bottomRight | brush | cantAbort |
    cantDelete | cantModify | cantPeek | centered | checkMark |
    cmdChar | commandChar | cursor | debugger | dialingTime |
    dialingVolume | dontSearch | dontWrap | dragSpeed | editBkgnd |
    enabled | environment | family | filled | fixedLineHeight |
    freeSize | grid | height | highlight | highlite | hilight |
    hilite | icon | id | itemDelimiter | language | left |
    lineSize | loc | location | lockErrorDialogs | lockMessages |
    lockRecent | lockScreen | lockText | longWindowTitles |
    markChar | marked | menuMessage | menuMsg | messageWatcher |
    multiple | multipleLines | multiSpace | name | numberFormat |
    owner | partNumber | pattern | polySides | powerKeys |
    printMargins | printTextAlign | printTextFont |
    printTextHeight | printTextSize | printTextStyle | rect |
    rectangle | reportTemplates | right | script | scriptEditor |
    scriptingLanguage | scriptTextFont | scriptTextSize | scroll |
    sharedHilite | sharedText | showLines | showName | showPict |
    size | stacksInUse | style | suspended | textAlign |
    textArrows | textFont | textHeight | textSize | textStyle |
    titleWidth | top | topLeft | traceDelay | userLevel |
    userModify | variableWatcher | version | visible | wideMargins |
    width | zoomed
```

Syntax for each individual property appears at the end of the "Commands" section, in the notes about the **set** command.

ORDINALS AND POSITIONS

```
<ordinal> = [ the ]
    { last | mid | middle | any |
    first | second | third | fourth | fifth |
    sixth | seventh | eigth | ninth | tenth }

<position> = this | [ the ] prev | [ the ] next
```

CHUNKS AND CONTAINERS

```
<simpleContainer> = <variable> | <part> | <menu> | <messageBox> | [ the ] selection
```

```
<container> = <chunk> <simpleContainer> | <simpleContainer>

<messageBox> = [ the ] msg [ box | window ]

<chunk> =
    [{<ordinal> char | char <expr> [ to <expr> ]} of]
    [{<ordinal> word | word <expr> [ to <expr> ]} of]
    [{<ordinal> item | item <expr> [ to <expr> ]} of]
    [{<ordinal> line | line <expr> [ to <expr> ]} of]
```

OBJECTS

```
<object> =
    HyperCard | me | [ the ] target | <button> | <field> | <card> | <bkgnd> | <stack>
```

Note: "card field 1" is a field and "card (field 1)" is a card.

```
<button> =
    {button id <unsignedFactor> | button <factor> | <ordinal> button} [ of <card> ]

<field> =
    {field id <unsignedFactor> | field <factor> | <ordinal> field} [ of <card> ]

<part> = <button> | <field> | {part id <unsignedFactor> |
    part <factor> | <ordinal> part} [ of <card> ]

<card> =
    recent card | back | forth |
    {card id <unsigned> | card <expr> | card <endLine> | <ordinal> card |
    <position> card} [ of <bkgnd> ] |
    <ordinal> marked card | <position> marked card | marked card <expr>

<bkgnd> =
    bkgnd id <unsigned> | bkgnd <expr> | bkgnd <endLine> |
    <ordinal> bkgnd | <position> bkgnd

<stack> = this stack | stack <expr> | stack <endLine>
```

COMMANDS

Command Nonterminals

These nonterminals appear in the command syntax that follows.

```
<dateItems> =
    <unsigned>,<unsigned>,<unsigned>,<unsigned>,<unsigned>,<unsigned>,
    <unsigned>

<date> =
    <unsigned> | <dateItems>
    <humanDate> [ <humanTime> ] |
    <humanTime> [ <humanDate> ]

<dateFormat> = [ <adjective> ] {seconds | dateItems | date | time}

<dayOfWeek> =
    Sunday | Sun | Monday | Mon | Tuesday | Tue | Wednesday |
    Wed | Thursday | Thu | Friday | Fri | Saturday | Sat

<dest> =
    { <card> | <bkgnd> } [ of <stack> ] | <stack> |
    { <card> | <bkgnd> } of [ <stack> ] <exprOrLine>

<duration> = until <logical> | while <logical>

<humanDate> =
    [ <dayOfWeek> , ] <month> <unsigned> , <unsigned> |
    <unsignedFactor> {/ | -} <unsignedFactor> {/ | -} <unsignedFactor>

<humanTime> =
    <unsigned> : <unsigned> [ : <unsigned> ] [ am | pm ]

<month> =
    January | Jan | February | Feb | March | Mar |
    April | Apr | May | June | Jun | July | Jul |
    August | Aug | September | Sep | October | Oct |
    November | Nov | December | Dec

<point> = {<integer> , <integer>}

<preposition> = before | after | into

<rect> = {<integer> , <integer> , integer> , <integer>}

<springKeys> = <springKeys> , <springKey> | <springKey>
```

```
<springKey> = shiftKey | optionKey | commandKey

<style> =
    transparent | opaque | rectangle | roundrect |
    shadow | checkBox | radioButton | scrolling | oval | popup

<textAlign> = right | left | center

<textStyleList> = <textStyleList> <textStyle> | <textStyle>

<textStyle> =
    plain | bold | italic | underline | outline |
    shadow |condense | extend | group

<visEffect> = <visKind> [ [ very ] {slow | slowly | fast} ] [ to
<visSrc> ]

<visKind> =
    barn door {open | close} |
    cut | plain | dissolve | venetian blinds | checkerboard |
    iris {open | close} |
    scroll {left | right | up | down} |
    wipe {left | right | up | down} |
    zoom {open | out | close | in } |
    shrink to {top | bottom | center } |
    stretch from {top | bottom | center } |
    push {left | right | up | down}

<visSrc> = card | black | white | gray | inverse

<window> = {card | pattern | tool | scroll | fatBits} window | <messageBox>
```

Commands

```
add
    <arith> to <container>
answer
    <expr> [with <factor> [or <factor> [or <factor>]]] |
    file <expr> [ of type <factor> [or <factor> [or <factor>]]] |
    program <expr> of type <factor>
arrowkey
    left | right | up | down
ask
    { password [clear]| file } <expr> [ with <expr> | <line> ]
beep
    [<unsigned>]
```

```
choose
   tool <unsigned> |
   { browse | button | field | select | lasso | pencil |
   brush | eraser | line | spray [ can ] | rect |
   round rect | bucket | oval | curve | text |
   reg poly | poly } tool
click
   at <point> [ with <springKeys> ]
close
   file <exprOrLine> | printing | application <exprOrLine> | <window>
commandKeyDown
   <expr>
controlkey
   <unsigned>
convert
   { <container> | <date>} [from <dateFormat> [and <dateFormat> ] ]
   to <dateFormat> [ and <dateFormat> ]
copy
   template <expr> to <stack>
create
   stack <expr> [ with <bkgnd> ] [ in [a] new window ]
   | menu <expr> ]
debug
   hintBits | pureQuickDraw { true | false } | checkPoint |
   maxmem | sound { on | off }
delete
   <chunk> <simpleContainer> | [<menuItemExpr> { of | from }] <menuExpr>
   <part>
dial
   <expr> [ with modem | with [ modem ] <expr> ]
disable
   [ <menuItem> of ] <menu> | <button>
divide
   <container> by <float>
domenu
   <exprOrLine> | <expr> [ , <expr> ] [ without dialog ]
drag
   from <point> to <point> [ with <springKeys> ]
edit
   [ the ] script of <object>
enable
   [ <menuItem> of ] <menu> | <button>
enterInField
enterKey
export
   paint to file <expr>
```

```
find
   [ whole | string | words | word | chars | normal ]
   [ international ] <expr> [ in <field> ] [ <ofOnly> marked cards ]
functionkey
   <unsigned>
get
   <expr> |
   [ the ] <property>
   [ of { <window> | <object> | [ <menuItem> of ] <menu> |
   <chunk> <field> }]
go
   [ to ] {{<ordinal> | <position>} <endLine> |
   <dest>} [ in [ a ] new window ] [ without dialog ]
help
hide
   menuBar | picture of <object> |
   { card | bkgnd } picture | <window> | <part>
import
   paint from file <expr>
keyDown
   <expr>
lock
   screen | messages | error dialogs | recent
mark
   all cards | <card> | cards where <expr>
   | cards by finding [ whole | string | words | word | chars | normal ]
   [ international ] <expr> [ in <field> ]
multiply
   <container> by <arith>
open
   [report] printing [ with dialog ] |
   file <exprOrLine> |
   <expr> [ with <exprOrLine> ] |
   <exprOrLine>
play
   stop | <expr> [ [ tempo <unsigned> ] <exprOrLine> ]
pop
   card [ <preposition> <container> ]
print
   <expr> with <exprOrLine> |
   <unsigned> cards | all cards | marked cards | <card> |
   <field> | <expr>
push
   <dest>
put
   <expr> [ <preposition> [<container> | [ <menuItem> of ]
```

```
  <menu> [with menuMessage[s] <expr> ]]
read
  from file <expr> {until <expr> | for <unsigned>}
reply
  <expr> [ with keyword <expr> ]
  error <expr>
request
  <expr> { of | from } <expr>
  { ae | appleEvent } { class | ID | sender | returnID
  | data [ { of | with } keyword <expr> ] }
reset
  paint | menubar | printing
returnInField
returnkey
save
  { [ this ] stack | stack <expr> } as [ stack ] <expr>
select
  [ before | after ] {text of | <chunk> } { <field> | <message>} |
  <part> | <emptyExpr>
set
  [ the ] <property> [ <ofOnly> {<window> | <object> |
  <menuItem> of <menu> | <chunk> <field>} ] to <propVal>
```
(See Notes on set below.)
```
show
  menuBar | picture of <object> |
  { card | bkgnd } picture |
  {<window> | <part>} [ at <point> ] |
  [ all | marked | <unsigned> ] cards
sort
  [ [cards of ] { this stack | <bkgnd> } | marked cards }
  [ ascending | descending ]
  [ text | numeric | international | dateTime ]
  by <expr>
  [ { lines | items } of ] <container> by <expr>
start
  using <stack>
stop
  using <stack>
subtract
  <arith> from <container>
tabKey
type
  <expr> [ with <springKeys> ]
unlock
  screen [ with [ visual [ effect ]] <visEffect> ]|
  error dialogs | recent | messages
```

```
unmark
   all cards | <card> | cards where <expr>
   | cards by finding [ whole | string | words | word | chars | normal ]
   [ international ] <expr> [ in <field> ]
visual
   [ effect ] <visEffect>
wait
   <duration> | <count> [ ticks | tick | seconds | second | sec ]
write
   <expr> to file <exprOrLine>
```

Notes on set

The following syntax refers only to the **set** command.

```
<style> =
   transparent | opaque | rectangle | roundrect |
   shadow | checkBox | radioButton | scrolling | oval | popup


<textAlign> = right | left | center


<textStyleList> = <textStyleList> <textStyle> | <textStyle>


<textStyle> =
   plain | bold | italic | underline | outline |
   shadow | condense | extend | group


<propVal> =
   <exprOrLine> | <integer> | <unsigned> | <logical> | <point> | <rect> |
   <style> | <textAlign> | <textStyleList>
```

exprOrLine:
   commandChar, cursor, debugger, environment, itemDelimiter, language,
   markChar, menuMessage, messageWatcher, name, numberFormat, owner,
   printTextFont, reportTemplates, script, scriptEditor,
   scriptingLanguage, scriptTextFont, stacksInUse, textFont,
   variableWatcher, version

integer:top, bottom, left, right, width, height

unsigned:
   brush, dialingTime, dialingVolume, dragSpeed, family, freeSize, icon,
   ID, lineSize, multiSpace, partNumber, pattern, polySides,
   printTextHeight, printTextSize, scriptTextSize, scroll, size,
   textHeight, textSize, titleWidth, traceDelay, userLevel

logical:

    autoHilite, autoSelect, autoTab, blindTyping, cantAbort, cantDelete,
    cantModify, cantPeek, centered, checkMark, dontSearch, dontWrap,
    editBkgnd, enabled, filled, fixedLineHeight, grid, hilite,
    lockErrorDialogs, lockMessages, lockRecent, lockScreen, lockText,
    longWindowTitles, marked, multiple, multipleLines, powerKeys,
    sharedHilite, sharedText, showLines, showName, showPict, suspended,
    textArrows, userModify, visible, wideMargins, zoomed

point: loc, topLeft, botRight, bottomRight, scroll (of window)

rect: rect, printMargins

style: style

textAlign: textAlign, printTextAlign

textStyleList: printTextStyle,textStyle

FUNCTIONS

Note: `<funcArth>`, `<funcFloat>`, `<funcExpr>`, and `<funcUnsigned>` all take expressions where they're called with parentheses, but factors otherwise.

abs
    `<funcArith>`
annuity
    `<float>` , `<float>`
atan
    `<funcFloat>`
average
    `<arithList>`
charToNum
    `<funcExpr>`
clickChunk
clickH
clickLine
clickLoc
clickText
clickV
cmdKey
commandKey
compound
    `<float>` , `<float>`
cos
    `<funcFloat>`

```
date
destination
diskSpace
exp
   <funcFloat>
exp1
   <funcFloat>
exp2
   <funcFloat>
foundChunk
foundField
foundLine
foundText
heapSpace
length
   <funcExpr>
ln
   <funcFloat>
ln1
   <funcFloat>
log2
   <funcFloat>
max
   <arithList>
menus
min
   <arithList>
mouse
mouseClick
mouseH
mouseLoc
mouseV
number
   cards [ in <bkgnd> ] |  bkgnds |
   [ card | bkgnd ] {buttons | fields | parts} |
   {chars | words | items | lines} in <funcExpr> |
   <object> |
   menus | menuItems {in | of } <menu> | marked cards | windows
numToChar
   <funcUnsigned>
offset
   <string> , <string>
optionKey
param
   <funcUnsigned>
paramCount
```

```
params
programs
   {machine <funcExp>}
random
   <funcUnsigned>
result
round
   <funcFloat>
screenRect
seconds
selectedButton
   [card | bkgnd] family <funcUnsigned>
selectedChunk
selectedField
selectedLine
selectedLoc
selectedText
shiftKey
sin
   <funcFloat>
sound
sqrt
   <funcFloat>
stacks
stackSpace
sum
   <arithList>
systemVersion
tan
   <funcFloat>
target
ticks
time
tool
trunc
   <funcFloat>
value
   <funcExpr>
windows
```

Appendix E

The Translator Interface

The little-known translator interface is very similar to the interface used for writing XCMDs and XFCNs, with added provisions for static data. The translator interface lets you write translators that convert what the user sees in the script editor to whatever form you want.

Typically, the translator interface is used to translate HyperCard's English language scripts into other languages. But you can use the translator to do much more than substitute one set of words for another. This appendix shows you how.

The language in which scripts are displayed in the HyperCard script editor window is controlled by the **language** property. By default, **language** is set to English. You can change the value of the **language** property by using the **set** command:

```
set the language to French
```

For this command to work (and not cause an error message), the named script translator must exist as a Macintosh resource of type WTRN (case significant) in the HyperCard application, the current stack, a stack in use, or the Home stack. WTRN stands for "WildTalk Translator". (WildTalk was the code name for HyperTalk during development, and would have been the released name for the language if some company besides Apple hadn't already owned the name.)

How a Translator Works

A WTRN resource is a code segment with no header bytes, like an XCMD or XFCN. It's written in a Macintosh development language such as Pascal, C, or 68000 assembly language. You attach it to the HyperCard application or a stack file using a resource editor such as ResEdit.

All scripts are always stored on disk in English and executed in English. When the **language** property is set to a value other than English, HyperCard invokes the appropriate translator whenever it displays or saves a script. So the user sees and edits the script in the language that's specific to the current translator, but the translator translates the script back to English before putting it away. If the user edits the script again, the translator translates it again into the current language (that is, the one that the **language** property calls for) before displaying it in the script editor window.

So HyperCard can execute any script, regardless of the language in which it was created, and regardless of the language translators available at execution time.

Figure E.1 shows the position of the script translator in the script editing process.

When you use the **set** command to change the **language** property to a non-English value, HyperCard looks for a WTRN resource named the same as the requested value. Virtually any number of WTRN script translator resources can exist in a resource file, but only one language can be current at a time. (The default language, English, requires no translator resource.)

As long as their names are unique, there can be different translators for the same base language, although each constitutes a different "dialect" of HyperTalk and has its own **language** property value. For example, you could have a French1 WTRN that would do simple word substitution, plus a French2 WTRN that would also transpose adjectives to appear after, rather than before, modified words. A user who wants to write scripts in a French dialect of HyperTalk can choose either French1 or French2.

WHEN A TRANSLATOR IS INVOKED

HyperCard invokes a script translator at the following times:

- When the **language** property is set (using the **set** command) to a value other than English, HyperCard calls the appropriate script translator which might in turn initialize itself, set up translation tables in RAM, and so on.

- When the **language** property is reset from non-English HyperTalk to English, HyperCard calls for the departing script translator to deallocate static memory.

- When the current language isn't English and the script editor is opened, HyperCard calls the script translator to translate the script from English to the current language before displaying it.

- When the current language isn't English and a script is saved from the script editor, HyperCard calls the script translator to translate the displayed script into English before writing it to the disk file of the stack.

- When the current language isn't English and the user sends a message from the Message box, HyperCard calls the translator to translate the message into English before trying to interpret it.

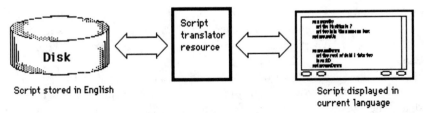

Script stored in English

Script displayed in current language

Figure E.1   Position of script translator in script editing process

- When the current language isn't English and the user formats a script in the script editor window by pressing the Tab or Return key, HyperCard can call the script translator to indent the displayed script, rather than doing it itself. (At initialization time, the translator specifies whether or not it will do its own indenting.)

Interface Details

Script translators communicate with HyperCard through the translator data block in the same way that external commands and functions communicate with HyperCard through the XCMD data block. The translator data block and its request and result codes have the following forms, expressed here in MPW Pascal:

```
UNIT HyperTrans;

INTERFACE

CONST

    { request codes }
    transInit   = 0;      { init the translator's static data }
    transQuit   = 1;      { deallocate static data before quit }
    transToEng  = 2;      { translate to English }
    transFromEng = 3;     { translate from English }
    transIndent = 4;      { indent }
    { result codes }
    succTrans   = 0;      { success }
    failTrans   = 1;      { failure }
    cantTrans   = 2;      { not implemented }
    { flag masks }
    indentMask  = 1;      { BOR this onto flags to allow custom indenting }

TYPE

    TransPtr = ^TransBlock;
    TransBlock =
      RECORD
        request:   INTEGER; { uses request codes defined above }
        result:    INTEGER; { uses result codes defined above }
        srcHandle: Handle;  { zero terminated text to translate }
        dstHandle: Handle;  { zero terminated translation }
        selLoc:    INTEGER; { location of insertion point }
        flags:     LongInt; { bit 0 = indentFlag, others reserved }
        reserved:  LongInt; { reserved for future use }
        userData:  ARRAY[1..16] OF LongInt; { for translator's static data }

      END;

END;
```

DATA FIELDS

When HyperCard invokes a script translator, it passes only one parameter to the translator: a pointer to the translator data block. HyperCard then executes a jump-to-subroutine instruction to the translator's entry point, and the translator code segment begins executing. Next, the translator examines the request field of the translator data block to see what HyperCard wants it to do. The fields of the translator data block are described in the following sections.

REQUEST CODES

HyperCard puts one of the request codes (listed above among the constants) into this field to be examined by the translator. The request code `transInit` is made when the user executes a **set** command for the language specific to the translator. Typically, the translator initializes itself at this time, setting up tables of non-English words to substitute for English words, and so on. You can allocate these tables in the heap as static data that remains between invocations of the translator.

The ability to maintain static data, plus the fact that HyperCard calls WTRN resources automatically, differentiates WTRN resources from XCMD and XFCN resources. When you set the language again, HyperCard puts `transQuit` into the request field. At this time, the translator should deallocate the static data.

HyperCard puts the request `transToEng` into the request field when the user saves a script after editing in a non-English language or sends a non-English message from the Message box.

HyperCard puts the request `transFromEng` into the request field when the user invokes the script editor to view any script (and the language is not English).

If `indentFlag` is set in the flags field, HyperCard puts the request `transIndent` into the request field whenever the user presses the Tab or Return key or opens a script.

RESULT CODES

The translator places one of the result codes (listed above among the constants) into the result field when it returns control to HyperCard after executing a request. If, for example, the translator passes `failTrans` after HyperCard requests `transInit`, HyperCard displays the error message "Translator failed to initialize itself", and the **language** reverts to English.

SRCHANDLE

When HyperCard calls the translator to translate a script, either to or from English, it places into this field a handle to the zero-terminated string where the untranslated script currently resides in memory. So, for example, if the value of request is `transToEng` the srcHandle field contains a handle to a non-English string.

DSTHANDLE

When the translator finishes translating a script, either to or from English, it writes the translated script to dstHandle (already allocated by HyperCard).

SELLOC

When an error occurs in English HyperTalk and you click the script button on the error dialog, HyperCard places the insertion point as close to the error as it can when it opens the script editor. It uses the selLoc field to pass an integer that represents the location of the insertion point.

HyperCard places the insertion point at the location in the English version of the script, always the executing version. It's the translator's responsibility to replace this value with one representing the appropriate point in the translated version of the script that HyperCard then displays.

The value of `selLoc` is an integer representing the number of characters from the beginning of the translated script to the cursor location. If `selLoc` is 1, then the cursor is after the first character.

FLAGS

If the translator sets bit 0 to 1 (by OR'ing the `indentMask` onto the flags field), HyperCard doesn't try to indent the translated script when it displays it: rather, the translator should indent the translated script by inserting space characters after each return character, and HyperCard displays the string exactly as received. If the flag isn't set to `1`, HyperCard attempts to indent the translated script by finding non-English keywords that correlate to the English HyperTalk keywords at the beginning of each line.

The remainder of the flags field is reserved for future use.

RESERVED

This field is reserved for future use.

USERDATA

This array comprises 16 long integer values that the translator can use to maintain data between invocations of the translator.

For example, the French translator example included in a later section of this document uses three elements of this array. The first two long integers hold handles: the first to the string resource containing HyperTalk keywords and their French equivalents, the second to the hash table the translator builds in memory from the strings so that it can do fast translations. The third long integer is interpreted by the translator as two integers representing the number of entries in the hash table and its size.

The translator must dispose of its static data when HyperCard calls it with a `transQuit` request; otherwise the memory allocated by the translator is tied up until the user quits HyperCard.

Placement of WTRN Resources

HyperCard uses the standard HyperCard resource hierarchy when it looks for a script translator. So your WTRN translator resource can be in the current stack, a stack that's been placed in the message path with the **start using** command, the Home stack, or the HyperCard application. (The WTRN could also be in the System file, but putting it there is pointless because no application other than HyperCard can use it.)

Place WTRNs highly

In versions of HyperCard through 2.0 (at least), placing the WTRN in a stack other than Home causes HyperCard to crash if you perform the following steps:

1. Set the language to the non-English value of a WTRN in the current stack.

2. Go to another stack (so that the WTRN is no longer present)

3. Try to edit a script.

Blooie.

Thus the prudent programmer will attach all translators to the Home stack or to HyperCard itself.

The French Script Translator

The following listing illustrates a language translator created in MPW Pascal with a hash function written in 68000 assembly language. This translator also requires a STR# resource, named French, containing strings of English HyperTalk and French HyperTalk vocabulary words in alternating sequence. The translator uses the string resource to build its hash table at initialization time, so the strings can be modified independent of the WTRN code.

```
{$R-}
{$D+}
{
French -- a HyperCard language translator.
To compile and link this file using Macintosh Programmer's Workshop,
        pascal French.p
asm TransUtil.a
link -o French -sn Main=French -sn STDIO=French ∂
    French.p.o TransUtil.a.o ∂
    -sn INTENV=French -rt WTRN=0 ∂
    reno:mpw:libraries:interface.o

    then paste the resulting WTRN into HyperCard or a HyperCard stack.
```

```
}

UNIT DummyUnit;

INTERFACE

USES MemTypes, QuickDraw, OsIntf, ToolIntf, HyperTrans;

IMPLEMENTATION

CONST return = 13;

TYPE WordPtr = ^INTEGER;

PROCEDURE FrenchTrans(arg: TransPtr);                FORWARD;
FUNCTION  TransHash(hashStart: WordPtr; modulo: INTEGER; str: Str255):
WordPtr;  EXTERNAL;

PROCEDURE EntryPoint(arg: TransPtr);
{ entry point cannot have local procs, but forward routines can }
BEGIN
   FrenchTrans(arg);
END;

PROCEDURE FrenchTrans(arg: TransPtr);
TYPE
   Str255Ptr = ^Str255;
   { private interpretation of the block that HyperCard passes in }
   FrenchPtr = ^FrenchBlock;
   FrenchBlock =
     RECORD
        { fields used by HyperCard }
        request:   INTEGER; { uses request codes defined above }
        result:    INTEGER; { uses result codes defined above }
        srcHndl:   Handle;  { zero terminated text to translate }
        dstHndl:   Handle;  { zero terminated translation }
        selLoc:    INTEGER; { location of insertion point }
        flags:     LongInt; { bit 0 = indentFlag, others reserved }
        reserved:  LongInt; { reserved for future use }

        { fields for use by this translator only }
        strings:   Handle;
        hashTab:   Handle;
        hashCount: INTEGER;
        hashSize:  INTEGER;
     END;
```

```
CONST
   dstGrowSize = 2048;{ grow dest handle in chunks of this size }
   maxLineLen = 1024;

VAR
   blockPtr: FrenchPtr;
   selFixed: BOOLEAN;

   PROCEDURE Fail;
   BEGIN
      blockPtr^.result := failTrans;
      EXIT(FrenchTrans);
   END;


   PROCEDURE QuitTranslator;
   BEGIN
      WITH blockPtr^ DO
         BEGIN
         HPurge(strings);
         DisposHandle(hashTab);
         END;
   END;


   PROCEDURE InitTranslator;
   { read in strings and build hash table }
   VAR strNum,strCount,offset,i: INTEGER;
       strPtr,transPtr,basePtr: Ptr;
       hashEnd,hashStart,entryPtr: WordPtr;

      PROCEDURE AddHashEntry(strPtr: Ptr);
      VAR str: Str255;
          i,stepSize: INTEGER;
      BEGIN
        BlockMove(strPtr,@str,strPtr^+1);
        FOR i := 1 TO Length(str) DO IF str[i] = ' ' THEN Fail;
        UprString(str,FALSE);
        entryPtr := TransHash(hashStart,blockPtr^.hashCount,str);
        stepSize := BSL(strPtr^,1);  { cheap double hash }
        WHILE entryPtr^ <> 0 DO
        BEGIN
           entryPtr := Pointer(ORD(entryPtr)+stepSize);
           IF ORD(entryPtr) >= ORD(hashEnd)
           THEN entryPtr := Pointer(ORD(entryPtr)-blockPtr^.hashSize);
        END;
        entryPtr^ := offset;
      END;
```

```
BEGIN
     WITH blockPtr^ DO
        BEGIN
        strings := GetNamedResource('STR#','French');
        IF strings = NIL THEN Fail;

        strCount := WordPtr(strings^)^;  { english and french strings are interleaved }

        IF strCount > 1000 THEN Fail; { can't handle that many strings }

        { pick a prime hash table size based on the number of strings }
        hashCount := 1361;
        IF strCount < 900 THEN hashCount := 1201;
        IF strCount < 800 THEN hashCount := 1069;
        IF strCount < 700 THEN hashCount := 937;
        IF strCount < 600 THEN hashCount := 809;
        IF strCount < 500 THEN hashCount := 673;
        IF strCount < 400 THEN hashCount := 541;
        IF strCount < 300 THEN hashCount := 401;
        IF strCount < 200 THEN hashCount := 269;
        IF strCount < 100 THEN hashCount := 137;

        hashSize := hashCount*2;       { two bytes per entry }
        hashTab := NewHandle(hashSize);
        IF hashTab = NIL THEN Fail;       { couldn't get enough RAM for hash table }

        hashStart := Pointer(hashTab^);
        entryPtr := hashStart;
        FOR i := 1 TO hashCount DO      { zero out the hash table }
           BEGIN
              entryPtr^ := 0;
              entryPtr := Pointer(ORD(entryPtr)+2);
           END;
        hashEnd := entryPtr;

        basePtr := strings^;  { offsets are from this base }
        strPtr := Ptr(ORD(strings^)+2); { skip count }
        transPtr := Pointer(ORD(strPtr)+strPtr^+1);
        FOR strNum := 1 TO strCount DIV 2 DO
           BEGIN
              offset := ORD(strPtr)-ORD(basePtr);
              AddHashEntry(strPtr);
              AddHashEntry(transPtr);
              strPtr := Pointer(ORD(transPtr)+transPtr^+1);
              transPtr := Pointer(ORD(strPtr)+strPtr^+1);
           END;
```

```
        END;
END;


PROCEDURE Translate;
VAR srcPtr,dstPtr: Ptr;
    srcOffset,dstOffset: INTEGER;
    size: LongInt;

  PROCEDURE CopyByte;
  BEGIN
    dstPtr^ := srcPtr^;
    dstPtr := Pointer(ORD(dstPtr)+1);
    srcPtr := Pointer(ORD(srcPtr)+1);
  END;


  FUNCTION IdentChar(ch: INTEGER): BOOLEAN;
  BEGIN
    ch := BAND($FF,ch);
    IdentChar := FALSE;
    IF (ch < ORD('A')) AND (ch <> ORD('''')) THEN EXIT(IdentChar);
    IF (ch >= ORD('[')) AND (ch <= ORD('^')) THEN EXIT(IdentChar);
    IF ch = ORD('≠') THEN EXIT(IdentChar);
    IF ch = $7F THEN EXIT(IdentChar); { rubout char }
    IdentChar := TRUE;
  END;


  PROCEDURE CopyToIdent;
  { copy whitespace, literals, punctuation, numbers, and comments }
  VAR ch: INTEGER;
  BEGIN
    WHILE (srcPtr^ <> return) AND (srcPtr^ <> 0) DO
    BEGIN
      ch := srcPtr^;
      IF IdentChar(ch) THEN EXIT(CopyToIdent); { found start of ident }
      CopyByte;
      IF ch = ORD('"') THEN { copy literal }
        BEGIN
          WHILE (srcPtr^ <> 0) AND (srcPtr^ <> return) AND
                     (srcPtr^ <> ORD('"')) DO CopyByte;
          IF srcPtr^ = ORD('"') THEN CopyByte;
        END
      ELSE IF (ch = ORD('-')) AND (srcPtr^ = ORD('-')) THEN { copy comment }
        BEGIN
          CopyByte; { copy second "-" }
          WHILE (srcPtr^ <> 0) AND (srcPtr^ <> return)
                     DO CopyByte; { copy till end of line }
```

```
            END;
      END;
END;


PROCEDURE HashLookup(identPtr,transPtr: Ptr);
VAR entryPtr,hashStart,hashEnd: WordPtr;
   matchPtr,subsPtr,swapPtr,basePtr: Ptr;
    stepSize: INTEGER;
BEGIN
   basePtr := Pointer(blockPtr^.strings^);
   hashStart := Pointer(blockPtr^.hashTab^);
   hashEnd := Pointer(ORD(hashStart)+blockPtr^.hashSize);
   entryPtr := TransHash(hashStart,blockPtr^.hashCount,Str255Ptr(identPtr)^);
   stepSize := BSL(identPtr^,1);   { cheap double hash }
   WHILE entryPtr^ <> 0 DO
   BEGIN
      matchPtr := Pointer(ORD(basePtr)+entryPtr^);
      subsPtr := Pointer(ORD(matchPtr)+matchPtr^+1);
      IF blockPtr^.request = transToEng THEN
         BEGIN
            swapPtr := matchPtr;
            matchPtr := subsPtr;
            subsPtr := swapPtr;
         END;
      IF EqualString(Str255Ptr(identPtr)^,Str255Ptr(matchPtr)^,
                       FALSE,FALSE) THEN { found it }
         BEGIN
            BlockMove(subsPtr,transPtr,subsPtr^+1);
            EXIT(HashLookup);
         END;
      entryPtr := Pointer(ORD(entryPtr)+stepSize);
      IF ORD(entryPtr) >= ORD(hashEnd)
      THEN entryPtr := Pointer(ORD(entryPtr)-blockPtr^.hashSize);
   END;
END;


PROCEDURE TranslateIdent;
VAR len: INTEGER;
   ident,translation: Str255;
BEGIN
   len := 0;
   WHILE IdentChar(srcPtr^) DO
   BEGIN
      len := len + 1;
      ident[len] := CHR(srcPtr^);
      srcPtr := Pointer(ORD(srcPtr)+1);
```

```
      END;
      IF len = 0 THEN EXIT(TranslateIdent);
      ident[0] := CHR(len);
      BlockMove(@ident,@translation,len+1); { default translation is original ident }
      UprString(ident,FALSE);
      HashLookup(@ident,@translation);
      BlockMove(Pointer(ORD(@translation)+1),dstPtr,Length(translation));
      dstPtr := Pointer(ORD(dstPtr)+Length(translation));
   END;


PROCEDURE CheckSel;
VAR srcOffset,dstOffset: INTEGER;
BEGIN
   WITH blockPtr^ DO
      BEGIN
         srcOffset := ORD(srcPtr) - ORD(srcHndl^);
      IF srcOffset >= selLoc THEN
         BEGIN
            dstOffset := ORD(dstPtr) - ORD(dstHndl^);
            selLoc := selLoc + dstOffset - srcOffset;
            selFixed := TRUE;
         END;
   END;
END;


PROCEDURE TranslateLine;
BEGIN
   WHILE (srcPtr^ <> 0) AND (srcPtr^ <> return) DO
   BEGIN
      CopyToIdent;
      IF NOT selFixed THEN CheckSel;
      TranslateIdent;
   END;
   dstPtr^ := srcPtr^; { copy the 0 or return }
   IF srcPtr^ <> 0 THEN
      BEGIN
      srcPtr := Pointer(ORD(srcPtr)+1);
         dstPtr := Pointer(ORD(dstPtr)+1);
      END;
   END;


BEGIN
   WITH blockPtr^ DO
      BEGIN
      SetHandleSize(dstHndl,dstGrowSize);
      dstPtr := dstHndl^;
```

```
            srcPtr := srcHndl^;
            selFixed := FALSE;
            WHILE srcPtr^ <> 0 DO
              BEGIN
                TranslateLine;
                dstOffset := ORD(dstPtr) - ORD(dstHndl^);
                size := GetHandleSize(dstHndl);
                IF size - dstOffset < maxLineLen THEN
                  BEGIN
                  srcOffset := ORD(srcPtr) - ORD(srcHndl^);
                  SetHandleSize(dstHndl,size+dstGrowSize);
                  dstPtr := Pointer(ORD(dstHndl^)+dstOffset);
                  srcPtr := Pointer(ORD(srcHndl^)+srcOffset);
                  END;
              END;
            dstPtr^ := 0;
            END;
      END;

BEGIN
  blockPtr := Pointer(arg); { cast to type FrenchPtr }
  CASE blockPtr^.request OF
    transInit: InitTranslator;
    transQuit: QuitTranslator;
    transToEng,transFromEng: Translate;
    OTHERWISE
      blockPtr^.result := cantTrans; { this translator can't satisfy that request }
  END;
END;

END.
```

The following listing is the hash function, written in 68000 assembly language, which is used by the foregoing translator to build its translate table.

```
;
;
; TransUtil.a, assembly language for translators
;
;
        SEG   'Main'

        BLANKS ON
        STRING ASIS

TransHash FUNC EXPORT
```

```
; -----------------------------------------------------------
;
;  FUNCTION  TransHash(hashStart: WordPtr;
;            modulo:        INTEGER;
;            str:           Str255): WordPtr;
;
            MOVE.L        (SP)+,A0              ;POP RETURN ADDR
            MOVE.L        (SP)+,A1              ;GET STR
            MOVEQ         #0,D0                 ;get ready for bytes
            MOVEQ         #0,D2                 ;init hash
            MOVE.B        (A1)+,D2              ;to string length
            MOVE          D2,D1                 ;copy string length
            LSL.W         #7,D2                 ;start length in hi byte
            BRA.S         START                 ;go to loop start
NEXTCHAR    ROL.W         #1,D2                 ;rotate hash left
            MOVE.B        (A1)+,D0              ;get character
            EOR.B         D0,D2                 ;xor into hash
START       DBRA          D1,NEXTCHAR           ;loop all chars in string
            DIVU          (SP)+,D2              ;DIVIDE BY MODULO
            CLR.W         D2                    ;DISCARD QUOTIENT
            SWAP          D2                    ;GET REMAINDER
            ADD           D2,D2                 ;TIMES 2 FOR EACH ENTRY
            ADD.L         (SP)+,D2              ;ADD HASH START
            MOVE.L        D2,(SP)               ;UPDATE FCN RESULT
            JMP           (A0)                  ;AND RETURN

            END
```

Secondary Translator Uses

As you saw in the first section of this chapter, the translator was designed to provide a mechanism by which HyperCard scripts can be displayed and created in dialects of HyperTalk other than English. Most commonly the translator takes text on its way to the script editor, "translates" it into some appropriate language from English, and then translate it back to English before the script information is sent to the disk.

But the translator interface can transform the information in other ways. To understand how, think of the translator as a filter that stands between the disk and the script editor. Information gets sent from the disk to the translator, the information is somehow massaged, and finally the information (presumably in some new form) gets sent to the script editor. But how that information is massaged is entirely up to the translator.

BLOCK COMMENTS "TRANSLATOR"

The following fully functional sample shows how to use the translator to do something besides translate from one language to another: It lets you write Pascal-style block comments in a script. You call it with the following statement:

```
set the language to "BlockComments"
```

Here's how you might write and see a script with the blockComments translator active. Pascal-style comment delimiters comment out the repeat loop:

```
on mouseUp
   get 1
   get 2
   {
   repeat 5
     beep 10
   end repeat
   }
   get 4
   if true then
     get 5
   end if
   play "boing"
end mouseUp
```

And here's how the same script would look with the language property set to English, the version of the script that's actually stored to disk:

```
on mouseUp
   get 1
   get 2
   --! {
   --!   repeat 5
   --!      beep 10
   --!   end repeat
   --!   }
   get 4
   if true then
     get 5
   end if
   play "boing"
end mouseUp
```

And here's the Pascal code to make it happen:

```
{$R-}
{$D+}
(*
         BlockComments --
            a HyperCard language translator to implement
            Pascal-style block comments.
```

To compile and link this file using Macintosh Programmer's Workshop,

```
        directory "reno:reference book:translators:"
        pascal BlockComments.p
        link -o TestStack -sn Main=BlockComments ∂
                BlockComments.p.o -rt WTRN=5 {libraries}interface.o
```

then paste the resulting WTRN into HyperCard or a HyperCard stack.

```
*)

UNIT DummyUnit;

INTERFACE

USES MemTypes, Memory, OSUtils, HyperTrans;

IMPLEMENTATION

PROCEDURE BlockComments(arg: TransPtr);

FORWARD;

PROCEDURE EntryPoint(arg: TransPtr);
{ entry point cannot have local procs, but forward routines can }
BEGIN
  BlockComments(arg);
END;

PROCEDURE BlockComments(arg: TransPtr);
CONST growSlop = 1024;
VAR srcPtr,dstPtr: Ptr;
    freeBytes: LongInt;
    commentStr: Str31;
    commentDone: BOOLEAN;

  PROCEDURE Fail;
  BEGIN
    arg^.result := failTrans;
    arg^.dstHndl^^ := 0; { return empty string }
    EXIT(BlockComments);
  END;

  PROCEDURE SetUp;
  BEGIN
    SetHandleSize(arg^.dstHndl,growSlop);
    IF MemError <> 0 THEN Fail;
```

```
    freeBytes := growSlop;
    srcPtr := arg^.srcHndl^;
    dstPtr := arg^.dstHndl^;
    commentStr := '--! ';
END;


PROCEDURE MakeRoom(count: INTEGER);
VAR srcOffset,dstOffset: LongInt;
BEGIN
  IF count <= freeBytes THEN EXIT(MakeRoom);
  srcOffset := ORD(srcPtr) - ORD(arg^.srcHndl^);
  dstOffset := ORD(dstPtr) - ORD(arg^.dstHndl^);
  SetHandleSize(arg^.dstHndl,GetHandleSize(arg^.dstHndl)+count+growSlop);
  IF MemError <> 0 THEN Fail;
  freeBytes := freeBytes + count + growSlop;
  srcPtr := Pointer(ORD(arg^.srcHndl^)+srcOffset);
  dstPtr := Pointer(ORD(arg^.dstHndl^)+dstOffset);
END;


PROCEDURE Finish;
BEGIN
  MakeRoom(1);
  dstPtr^ := 0; { zero terminate }
END;


PROCEDURE OutBytes(fromPtr: Ptr; count: INTEGER);
BEGIN
  MakeRoom(count);
  BlockMove(fromPtr,dstPtr,count);
  dstPtr := Pointer(ORD(dstPtr)+count);
END;


PROCEDURE EchoBytes(count: INTEGER);
BEGIN
  MakeRoom(count);
  BlockMove(srcPtr,dstPtr,count);
  srcPtr := Pointer(ORD(srcPtr)+count);
  dstPtr := Pointer(ORD(dstPtr)+count);
END;


PROCEDURE EchoLine;
VAR endPtr: Ptr;
BEGIN
  endPtr := srcPtr;
  WHILE (endPtr^ <> 0) AND (endPtr^ <> 13) DO
    BEGIN
```

```
            IF endPtr^ = ORD('}') THEN commentDone := TRUE;
            endPtr := Pointer(ORD(endPtr)+1);
        END;
    IF endPtr^ = 13 THEN endPtr := Pointer(ORD(endPtr)+1);
    EchoBytes(ORD(endPtr)-ORD(srcPtr));
END;


PROCEDURE BlocksOut;
VAR commentPtr: Ptr;
BEGIN
    SetUp;
    REPEAT
        { find the start of the next comment }
        commentPtr := srcPtr;
        WHILE (commentPtr^ <> ORD('{')) AND (commentPtr^ <> 0)
        DO commentPtr := Pointer(ORD(commentPtr)+1);

        { copy up to the comment }
        EchoBytes(ORD(commentPtr)-ORD(srcPtr));

        IF srcPtr^ = ORD('{') THEN
            BEGIN
                { copy the comment, inserting commentStr }
                commentDone := FALSE;
                REPEAT
                    OutBytes(Pointer(ORD(@commentStr)+1),Length(commentStr));
                    EchoLine;
                UNTIL commentDone OR (srcPtr^ = 0);
            END;
    UNTIL srcPtr^ = 0;
    Finish;
END;


PROCEDURE BlocksIn;
VAR commentPtr: Ptr;

    FUNCTION VerifyMatch: BOOLEAN;
    VAR i: INTEGER;
    BEGIN
        VerifyMatch := TRUE;
        FOR i := 1 TO Length(commentStr) DO
        IF ORD(commentStr[i]) <> Ptr(ORD(commentPtr)+i-1)^ THEN
            BEGIN
                VerifyMatch := FALSE;
                EXIT(VerifyMatch);
            END;
```

```
          END;

     BEGIN
        SetUp;
        REPEAT
           { find next commentStr }
           commentPtr := srcPtr;
           WHILE (commentPtr^ <> 0) & NOT ((commentPtr^ = ORD('-')) & VerifyMatch)
           DO commentPtr := Pointer(ORD(commentPtr)+1);

           { copy up to commentStr }
           EchoBytes(ORD(commentPtr)-ORD(srcPtr));

           { jump over commentStr }
           IF srcPtr^ <> 0 THEN srcPtr := Pointer(ORD(srcPtr)+Length(commentStr));

        UNTIL srcPtr^ = 0;
        Finish;
     END;

  BEGIN
     CASE arg^.request OF
        transInit,transQuit: { do nothing } ;
        transToEng: BlocksOut;
        transFromEng: BlocksIn;
        OTHERWISE arg^.result := cantTrans; { can't satisfy that request }
     END;
  END;


  END.
```

Glossary

This glossary provides a summary definition of every HyperTalk vocabulary word except commands, functions, keywords, properties, and messages (which are defined in Part III, "The Elements of HyperTalk"). Definitions of HyperTalk conceptual terms are also included.

&   is the concatenation operator; it joins two strings into one.

&&   is the word-concatenation operator; it joins two strings into one with a space between them.

*   is the multiplication operator.

+   is the addition operator.

-   is the subtraction operator.

/   is the division operator.

<   is the relational operator for "less than."

<=   is the relational operator for "less than or equal to."

<>   is the relational operator for "less than or greater than."

=   is the relational operator for "equal to."

>   is the relational operator for "greater than."

>=   is the relational operator for "greater than or equal to."

^   is the exponentiation operator. It raises one number to the power of another.

≠   is the relational operator for "not equal to." It's equivalent to <>.

≤   is the relational operator for "less than or equal to." It's equivalent to <=.

≥   is the relational operator for "greater than or equal to." It's equivalent to >=.

¬   is the line-continuation character, which lets you split a line of HyperTalk code for better readability.

Abbreviated (or **abbr** or **abbrev**) is an adjective that affects the way certain commands, functions and properties—**convert**, **date**, **time**, **ID**, **name**, **number**, **target**, and **version**—report their values.

After is a preposition used with the **put** and **put into menu** commands to insert text at a specific point, to position the insertion point in the message box or a field, or to place a menu item in a specific location in a menu.

Ampersand see **&**

And operator combines two logical values to produce a logical result. If both operands are true, the result is true; otherwise the result is false.

Anomaly is an unusual deviation from some otherwise-consistent way of behaving. It's HyperTalk's way of providing you with an opportunity for growth through adversity. ("We're only doing this for you.")

Argument is a value upon which a function operates.

Arrow is one of the values for the **cursor** property.

Ascending is one of two orders (the other being **descending**) for sorting.

ASCII is an acronym for American Standard Code for Information Interchange, a system that represents each text character or special code by a specific number. For a list of these codes, see Appendix A.

Back, usually used with the **go** and **push** commands, refers to the card before the current card in HyperCard's Recent list.

Background (also **bkgnd** and **bg**) as a noun designates one of HyperTalk's objects. As an adjective, it designates the domain of a button or field. See also **card**.

Barn door is one of the special effects used with the **visual effect** and **unlock screen** commands.

Before is a preposition used with the **put** and **put into menu** commands to insert text at a specific point, to position the insertion point in the message box or a field, or to place a menu item in a specific location in a menu.

Bg see **background**

Bkgnd see **background**

Black is one of the optional destination images used with the **visual effect** and **unlock screen** commands.

Bold is one of the possible styles for a menu item or the text in a field or button.

Box see **Message**

Browse is the name of the default tool, chosen with the **choose** command or returned by the **tool** function. The browse tool is indicated by a hand cursor.

Brush is the name of one of the paint tools, chosen with the **choose** command or returned by the **tool** function. It's also a property that reflects the current shape of the brush tool.

Btn see **Button**

Bucket is the name of one of the paint tools, chosen with the **choose** command or returned by the **tool** function.

Bug is a programming or scripting error. The HyperTalk scripting language has no bugs. (It does, however, have a number of "anomalies" and "heretofore undocumented features.")

Busy is one of the values for the **cursor** property. Its shape is a spinning beachball.

Button designates one of HyperCard's objects. It 's also the name of the tool you use to work with buttons, which can be chosen with the **choose** command or returned by the **tool** function.

Caller is that which summons. For example, if Handler A sends the message doSomething (causing the doSomething handler to execute), then Handler A is the caller of the doSomething handler.

Card (or **cd**) as a noun designates one of HyperTalk's objects. As an adjective it designates the domain of a button or field. It's also one of the optional destination images used with the **visual effect** and **unlock screen** commands.

Center (or **centre**) is one of the values for the alignment of text in a field or a button. It's also an option for some of the special effects used with the **visual effect** and **unlock screen** commands.

Character (or **char**) is the smallest element of a chunk expression: a single character.

Chars (or **char**) is a modifier used with the **find** command, allowing a match for the search string anywhere in a word.

Checkbox is one of the values for the **style** of a button.

Checkerboard is one of the special effects used with the **visual effect** and **unlock screen** commands.

Chunk is any portion of the text of any source of value. A chunk of any container is itself a container.

Colon is the constant for the character ":".

Comma is the constant for the character ",".

Command is an instruction to HyperCard to do something.

Command message is a message that makes HyperCard do something if it gets all the way through the message-passing path.

Comment is any information between a double dash (--) and the end of a line within any handler, or any text in a script that's not part of a handler. HyperTalk ignores comments; they're strictly for the use of the scripter.

Concatenation is the joining together of two strings.

Condense is one of the possible styles for a menu item or the text in a field or button.

Constant is a value that doesn't change; a symbolic name representing a value (such as `pi`).

Container is something that holds information supplied either by a scripter or an end-user. HyperTalk's containers are fields, buttons, menus, variables, the selection, the message box, and chunks of any of these containers.

Contains is the relational operator testing whether the string to its left contains the string to its right.

Control structure is a set of keywords in a statement list that define the order of execution of statements within that list. HyperTalk control structures include **if...then...else** and **repeat** loops.

Cross is one of the values for the **cursor** property.

Curve is the name of one of the paint tools, chosen with the **choose** command or returned by the **tool** function.

Custom message is any message whose handler you create, as opposed to one native to HyperCard.

Cut is one of the special effects used with the **visual effect** and **unlock screen** commands.

DateItems is one of the formats used with the **convert** command.

DateTime is a modifier used with the **sort** command.

Descending is one of two orders (the other being **ascending**) for sorting.

Deselect is to unhighlight the selected text, or remove the insertion point from the message box or a field.

Dialog (also **dialog box**) is any box (other than the message box) on the display that asks for and/or presents information; so called because the user must respond to the box (that is, complete a dialog) before anything else can happen.

Dissolve is one of the special effects used with the **visual effect** and **unlock screen** commands.

Div operator divides the operand to its right into the operand to its left and returns an integer result.

Domain is a sphere of influence. For example. all the cards belonging to a given background are said to be in that background's domain.

Down is a constant, as in `if the shiftKey is down`.

Dynamic path is the extended message-passing path that a message traverses if a handler has changed cards.

Eight is the constant for the value 8.

Eighth is a HyperTalk ordinal.

Empty is the constant for the null string.

Empty script is a script with no code in it.

English is a modifier used with the **name** property, **convert** command, and **date** and **time** functions to return the date and/or time in the standard U.S. format, regardless of whether the current operating system has been localized to another country.

Eraser is the name of one of the paint tools, chosen with the **choose** command or returned by the **tool** function.

Error dialog is a dialog from HyperCard indicating a scripting error.

Evaluate is to determine the value of; to compute.

Execute is to activate. To execute a handler is to send all the messages in that handler, in order, or in the order that the control structures within that handler dictate.

Expression is any value or any group of values, sources of value, and operators meant to be taken as a single whole.

Extend is one of the possible styles for a menu item or the text in a field or button.

External is a vocabulary word not native to HyperTalk but added as a resource through the HyperCard external interface. HyperCard allows external commands (XCMDs) and external functions (XFCNs).

Factor is the first fully resolvable portion of an expression.

False is a constant, as in `set property to false`.

Fast is a speed at which a visual effect occurs.

Feature is everything this book talks about (except in bug boxes). Also, a bug that the language designer decides not to fix.

Field designates a HyperTalk object. It's also the name of the tool you use to work with fields, which can be chosen with the **choose** command or returned by the **tool** function.

Fifth is a HyperTalk ordinal.

File is a named collection of information that resides on a disk. On the Macintosh, each file appears as an icon in the Finder.

First is a HyperTalk ordinal.

Five is the constant for the value 5.

Formatting is the way that text appears in a script or that numbers appear in a visible container.

Formfeed is the constant for the formfeed character (ASCII 12).

Forth, when used with the **go** and **push** commands, refers to the card that comes after the current one in HyperCard's Recent list.

Four is the constant for the value 4.

Fourth is a HyperTalk ordinal.

Function call is the use of a function to get a value.

Function handler is a user-defined function.

Function is a HyperTalk vocabulary word that calculates and returns a value.

Geometric is a type of operator that determines whether a point is within the area of a rectangle: the operators **is within** and **is not within**.

Global coordinates are coordinates measured relative to the screen (as opposed to local coordinates, which are relative to the current stack window).

Global variable is a variable whose value is available throughout HyperCard until you quit the program (as opposed to a local variable, which is available only in the handler that created it).

Gray (or **grey**) is one of the optional destination images used with the **visual effect** and **unlock screen** commands.

Group is a style for a chunk of text in a field, letting the **clickText** and **clickChunk** functions treat any contiguous run of characters as a single unit.

Hand is one of the values for the **cursor** property.

Handler is a named group of HyperTalk statements beginning with an **on** or **function** statement and ending with an **end** statement. The handler is the basic HyperTalk structure.

HyperTalk is the object-oriented scripting language that automates HyperCard.

Ibeam is one of the values for the **cursor** property.

In see **geometric**

Inheritance path see **message-passing path**

Initialize is to create a variable; to give a variable its first value.

Integer is a positive or negative whole number; a number with no fractional part.

International is a modifier used with the **sort** and **find** commands to make them use the full international alphabet, including diacritical marks.

Into is a preposition used with the **put** and **put into menu** commands to replace text in a container or to place a menu item in a specific location in a menu.

Inverse is one of the optional images used with the **visual effect** and **unlock screen** commands.

Iris is one of the special effects used with the **visual effect** and **unlock screen** commands.

It is the special local variable created by **get, answer, ask, read,** and (sometimes) **convert**.

Italic is one of the possible styles for a menu item or the text in a field or button.

Item is a chunk of a source of value separated by commas (or by another character set with the **itemDelimiter** property).

Iteration is a single execution of all the statements in a loop; one repetition.

Keyword is a vocabulary word interpreted directly by HyperTalk. Keywords don't traverse the message-passing path.

Lasso is the name of one of the paint tools, chosen with the **choose** command or returned by the **tool** function.

Last is a HyperTalk ordinal.

Layer is the position of a field or button among all buttons and fields on its background or card, reflected by its **partNumber**. Also, the position of a part or picture on either the card or background (the card layer; the background layer).

Line is the chunk of a source of value terminated by a return character. It's also the name of one of the paint tools, chosen with the **choose** command or returned by the **tool** function.

Line continuation character is the character produced by pressing Option-L. In a script, this character lets you break a single long line into an arbitrary number of shorter segments.

Linefeed is the constant for the linefeed character (ASCII 10).

Literal is anything taken at face value; a group of characters to be taken for their actual, as opposed to symbolic, value.

Local coordinates are coordinates measured relative to the current stack window (as opposed to global coordinates, which are relative to the screen).

Local variable is a variable whose existence ceases when the current handler finishes execution (as opposed to a global variable, whose value is available throughout HyperCard until you quit HyperCard).

Logical is a kind of operation resulting in the value "true" or "false"; also a kind of operator (**and, or, not**) used to produce a logical result.

Long is an adjective that affects the way certain commands, functions and properties—**convert, date, time, ID, name, number, target**, and **version**—report their values.

Me is the object containing the currently-running handler.

Message (also called **the message box**) is a single-line HyperTalk windoid which can be used to send messages to the current card.

Message handler is a handler whose statements execute when it catches a message with the same name.

Message-passing path is the order in which objects are given the opportunity to respond to a message. A message-passing path can be static or dynamic.

Middle (or **mid**) is a HyperTalk ordinal referring to the middle element of a series.

Mixed is a special descriptor indicating that a chunk of text includes more than one font, style, or size.

Mod is an arithmetic operator that returns the remainder after dividing its first operand by its second.

Msg see **Message**

Native vocabulary word is a HyperTalk word; a word that HyperCard understands.

Navigator is the name of a built-in palette you can use with the **palette** command.

Next (or **next card**) refers to the next card in the current stack.

Next background refers to the next background in the current stack.

Nine is the constant for the value 9.

Ninth is a HyperTalk ordinal.

Non-whitespace character is any printable character except the space character (ASCII 32, created by pressing the space bar), return character, or tab character.

None is one of the values for the **cursor** property.

Normal is a modifier used with the **find** command. It restricts the search to the start of words.

Not is the unary negation operator; it negates the factor following it.

Null string is the string with no characters; the value of the expression ""; empty.

Numeric is a modifier used with the **sort** command to sort in numeric order. The word also means a value composed entirely of digits and an optional decimal point and minus sign.

Object is a HyperCard unit capable of sending and receiving messages. HyperCard objects are buttons, fields, cards, backgrounds, stacks, and the HyperCard application itself.

Object-oriented is a type of computer language in which programming modules are associated with individual objects, which respond to messages that execute those modules. In other computer languages, all modules are part of a single linear program list.

One is the constant for the value 1.

Opaque is one of the values for the **style** of a button or field.

Operand is an expression upon which an operator performs some action.

Operator is a symbol or word that either changes the value of a single operand or combines operands to produce a single result.

Or operator combines two logical values. If either operand is true, the result is true; otherwise the result is false.

Ordinal is one of the positional constants `first` through `tenth`, or one of the special words `any`, `middle` (or `mid`), or `last`.

Outline is one of the possible styles for a menu item or the text in a field or button.

Oval is the name of one of the paint tools, chosen with the **choose** command or returned by the **tool** function. It is also the name of a button **style**.

Parameter variable is a local variable in a handler that receives the value of a passed parameter. It has the same name as the parameter.

Parameter is a value that's passed to a command or function.

Part is a synonym for a field or button.

Pass is to transfer a value or parameter from one handler to another, or to put a message back on the message-passing path.

Pathname is the full name and location of a file, beginning with the name of the disk and including the names of all folders in nesting order, down to the filename itself. Each item is separated from its neighbors by a colon (:).

Pencil is the name of one of the paint tools, chosen with the **choose** command or returned by the **tool** function.

Pi is the constant for the value 3.14159265358979323846.

Plain is one of the possible styles for a menu item or the text in a field or button. It indicates the absence of all other text styles. It's also one of the special effects used with the **visual effect** and **unlock screen** commands.

Plus is one of the values for the **cursor** property.

Polygon is the name of one of the paint tools, chosen with the **choose** command or returned by the **tool** function.

Popup is the name of a button **style**. A popup button acts like a popup menu when clicked.

Positional number is an object's position in its domain.

Precedence is the order of execution. Operations with higher precedence are executed before operations with lower precedence.

Prev see **previous**

Previous (or **previous card**) refers to the previous card in the current stack.

Previous background refers to the previous background in the current stack.

Property is an attribute of an object, menu, or window.

Push is one of the special effects used by the **visual effect** and **unlock screen** commands.

Quote is the constant for the double-quote character (ASCII 34).

Quoted literal is a string that appears in a HyperTalk statement between pairs of double quotation marks (").

RadioButton is one of the values for the **style** of a button.

Recent card, usually used with the **go** and **push** commands, refers to the last card you were on before going to the current one.

Recursion is a condition in which a handler calls itself.

Region is a geometric area expressed in pixels that defines the space of an object.

Regular polygon is the name of one of the paint tools, chosen with the **choose** command or returned by the **tool** function.

Relational is a kind of operation in which two values are compared, resulting in the value "true" or "false"; also, a kind of operator ($>, <, \geq, \leq, =, \neq, <>$) used to compare two values.

Resource fork is one of two forks that make up every Macintosh file. (The other fork is called the **data fork**.) All externals, fonts, sounds, and icons reside in a stack's resource fork.

Return is the constant for the return character (ASCII 13). It's also the name of the keyword that halts the current handler and returns control to the handler that called it.

Right is one of the values for the alignment of text in a field or a button. It's also a property.

Round rectangle is the name of one of the paint tools, chosen with the **choose** command or returned by the **tool** function.

RoundRect is one of the values for the **style** of a button.

SANE is an acronym for Standard Apple Numerics Environment, a set of mathematical routines common to all Macintosh computers that guarantee the accuracy of computations.

Script is the collection of handlers and comments associated with a particular object.

Script editor is the text editor that allows you to construct and modify HyperTalk scripts.

Scroll is a special effect used with the **visual effect** and **unlock screen** commands. It's also a property of scrolling fields.

Scrolling is one of the values for the **style** of a field.

Second is a HyperTalk ordinal.

Select is the name of one of the paint tools, chosen with the **choose** command or returned by the **tool** function. It's also a command.

Selection is the HyperTalk container defined as the currently selected text or the insertion point.

Sending order is the order in which HyperCard sends system messages, when it sends more than one in response to a single action.

Seven is the constant for the value 7.

Seventh is a HyperTalk ordinal.

Shadow is one of the values for the **style** of a button or field. It's also one of the possible styles for a menu item or the text in a field or button.

Short is an adjective that affects the way certain commands, functions and properties—**convert**, **date**, **time**, **ID**, **name**, **number**, **target**, and **version**—report their values.

Shrink is one of the special effects used with the **visual effect** and **unlock screen** commands.

Six is the constant for the value 6.

Sixth is a HyperTalk ordinal.

Slow (or **slowly**) is a speed at which a visual effect occurs.

Space is the constant for the space character (ASCII 32), created when you press the space bar.

Spray can is the name of one of the paint tools, chosen with the **choose** command or returned by the **tool** function.

Stack designates one of HyperTalk's objects; a HyperCard file.

Standard file dialog is the dialog from which you choose a file. Standard file dialogs usually list only files that are appropriate for a given operation. (For example, the standard file dialog that appears when you choose Open Stack from the File menu contains just names of stacks.)

Statement is any single valid line of HyperTalk code consisting of a message name and any accompanying parameters.

Statement list is a group of statements separated by return characters within the same handler. Statements outside of control structures (**if...then...else** or **repeat**) are meant to execute in the order listed. The execution of statements within a control structure depend on the nature of the structure.

Static path is the message-passing path if the currently executing handler hasn't changed cards.

Stretch is one of the special effects used with the **visual effect** and **unlock screen** commands.

String is a modifier used with the **find** command. It restricts the search to a contiguous group of characters, including embedded spaces. **String** is also used generally to mean any collection of characters.

System message is a message sent by HyperCard to announce that some event has occurred or is about to occur.

Tab is the constant for the tab character (ASCII 9).

Ten is the constant for the value 10.

Tenth is a HyperTalk ordinal.

Text is a modifier used with the **sort** command to sort by ASCII ordering. It's also the name of one of the paint tools, chosen with the **choose** command or returned by the **tool** function.

The is an article which may optionally appear before any of the following: `target`, `selection`, `message` (or `msg`), the name of any property (as in `the size`), and references to any function that uses the "of" form (as in `the number of cards in this stack`). It's required before argumentless functions (for example, `the time` or `the date`) when you don't follow the function name with parentheses. These comprise the only legal uses of **the** in all versions through 1.2.5. Version 2.0 and later also allow **the** when using ordinal numbers to refer to an object, window, or menu (for example, `go to the first card`).

There is a is the existence operator. It reports whether its operand exists or not.

Third is a HyperTalk ordinal.

This is an adjective used to refer to the current card, background, or stack.

Three is the constant for the value 3.

To is the preposition used to define the limits of a range in a chunk expression, as in word 2 **to** 5; as a preface to the image word in visual effects, as in dissolve slowly **to** black; before the destination object with **send,** as in send myMessage **to** button 5; and optionally after **go** for a more natural sounding syntax, as in go **to** card 5.

Translator is a filter through which a script is passed before and after it's displayed. It was originally designed to let non-English speaking scripters edit scripts in their native language, but clever hackers are finding new ways to use this feature. (See Appendix E.)

Transparent is one of the values for the **style** of a button or field.

True is a constant, as in set *property* to true.

Two is the constant for the value 2.

Underline is one of the possible styles for a menu item or the text in a field or button.

Unquoted literal is any string of characters meant to be interpreted literally that doesn't appear between pairs of double quotation marks ("").

Up is a constant, as in the shiftkey is up.

Variable is a user-created invisible container that resides in memory, and whose existence ends when a handler stops running (local variable) or when you quit HyperCard (global variable).

Venetian blinds is one of the special effects used with the **visual effect** and **unlock screen** commands.

Very fast is a speed at which a visual effect occurs.

Very slow (or **very slowly**) is a speed at which a visual effect occurs.

Watch is one of the values for the **cursor** property.

White is one of the optional destination images used with the **visual effect** and **unlock screen** commands.

Whole is a modifier used with the **find** command. It restricts the search to a complete word or phrase, including embedded spaces.

Windoid is a term for pseudo-windows from off-planet: the message box, the tool or pattern windows after they've been torn off the menu bar, or any floating palette.

Wipe is one of the special effects used with the **visual effect** and **unlock screen** commands.

Within see **is within**

Word is a chunk of text that's delimited by spaces.

Words (or **word**) is a modifier used with the **find** command. It restricts the search to a perfect match for each of the words in the search string, although their order is not considered.

WYSIWIG is the acronym for "What you see is what you get," meaning that what you see on the screen is what you get on paper when you print a document.

XCMD is the resource type for, and popular name given to, an external command.

XFCN is the resource type for, and popular name given to, an external function.

Zero is the constant for the value 0.

Zoom is one of the special effects used with the **visual effect** and **unlock screen** commands.

Index of Handlers

This index lists the most useful example handlers from Chapters 1-10 and Part III of this book. Handlers that only illustrate a concept or HyperTalk element, without performing some useful function, are not listed in this index.

Cards

Compacting

Cursor

Data Conversion

Data Validation

Date (see Time and Date)

Development Tools

Dialing

Encryption (see Security)

Fields

Files

Financial Applications

Fonts

Geometry

Highlighting

Hypertext

Icons

Messages

Mouse

Multiple-Stack Applications

Navigation

Networked Applications

Obsolete Version Workarounds

Overriding Standard Functions and Commands

Painting

Palettes

Pictures

Printing

Screen Appearance

Scripting

Scrolling Fields

Searching

System Messages

Text Entry

Text Processing

Time and Date

Index